Readings in

CANADIAN

Foreign Policy

Readings in
CANADIAN
Foreign Policy

Classic Debates and New Ideas

Edited by

DUANE BRATT AND CHRISTOPHER J. KUKUCHA

OXFORD
UNIVERSITY PRESS

OXFORD

UNIVERSITY PRESS

70 Wynford Drive, Don Mills, Ontario M3C 1J9
www.oup.com/ca

Oxford University Press is a department of the University of Oxford.
It furthers the University's objective of excellence in research, scholarship,
and education by publishing worldwide in

Oxford New York

Auckland   Cape Town   Dar es Salaam   Hong Kong   Karachi
Kuala Lumpur   Madrid   Melbourne   Mexico City   Nairobi
New Delhi   Shanghai   Taipei   Toronto

With offices in

Argentina   Austria   Brazil   Chile   Czech Republic   France   Greece
Guatemala   Hungary   Italy   Japan   Poland   Portugal   Singapore
South Korea   Switzerland   Thailand   Turkey   Ukraine   Vietnam

Oxford is a trade mark of Oxford University Press
in the UK and in certain other countries

Published in Canada
by Oxford University Press

Library and Archives Canada Cataloguing in Publication
Readings in Canadian foreign policy: classic debates and new ideas/
edited by Duane Bratt, Christopher J. Kukucha

Includes bibliographical references.

ISBN-13: 978-0-19-542369-3
ISBN-10: 0-19-542369-0

1. Canada—Foreign relations—Textbooks.   I. Bratt, Duane, 1967–
II. Kukucha, Christopher John

2 3 4 - 10 09 08 07

This book is printed on permanent (acid-free) paper ∞.
Printed in Canada

Contents

Preface

This project originated in February 2004 over drinks in a Calgary pub. After the usual discussion of family and friends, the conversation shifted to our careers at Mount Royal College and the University of Lethbridge, and the lack of an appropriate collection of readings for our courses in Canadian foreign policy. Although we both shared MA and PhD supervisors—Terry Keenleyside at Windsor and Tom Keating at Alberta—we frequently disagreed on most academic questions. On this issue, however, we had a number of similar ideas. Full of courage, ambition, and beer, we decided it was time to put together our own edited volume.

Our proposal found a home at Oxford University Press. We began to compile a wish list of potential new contributors and, to our surprise, the response was overwhelmingly positive. Not only did virtually everyone say yes, but the commissioned chapters were of exceptional quality, which made the timely completion of the volume possible. It should be noted that a conscious decision was made to not approach individuals with previously published articles already selected for the collection. While this appeared to be a wise decision at the time, it meant that some important contributors were not included in the final volume due to inevitable, and extremely difficult, decisions regarding length.

Acknowledgements

There are obviously numerous people to acknowledge regarding the completion of this text. First, we are fortunate to participate in a community of scholars that are exceptional academics and people. The individuals who study Canadian foreign policy are a diverse and collegial group. They approach issues from both 'traditional' and 'critical' perspectives and do so in a way that promotes important dialogue. At conferences there is also the guarantee of good company, food, and drink. Hopefully, some of this collegiality is captured in the following chapters.

We also owe a debt of gratitude to Christine Cozens, Lise Mills, and Michael J. Young at Pearson Education Canada who not only supported the initial idea but also made sure it safely arrived at Oxford. Our experience at Oxford University Press was extremely positive and professional. As first-time collaborators we were well looked after by Senior Acquisitions Editor Laura Macleod, Developmental Editors Paula Druzga and Rachael Cayley, and Assistant Editor Jessica Coffey. Finally, we are indebted to the anonymous reviewers who provided excellent suggestions for improvement. By our count this volume was subject to a total of six different peer reviews, making it perhaps one of the most reviewed projects in Canadian history. Although these critiques were anonymous we are especially grateful to Heather Smith for suggesting the idea of combining new and 'classic' articles.

Finally, both of us are fortunate to be surrounded by people who provide the required support and inspiration for a project such as this.

CHRIS KUKUCHA

First, I want to thank my colleagues in the Department of Political Science at the University of Lethbridge for their commitment to a respectful and collegial university environment. To Duane—thanks for making this a wonderful collaborative experience. This is proof our friendship is far more than just shared history and hockey. I also want to extend my love and appreciation to my wife Renee and my son James, who tolerated all the evenings and weekends that went into this project. Together with my family and friends in Vancouver you are a constant reminder of what is truly important in life. Finally, I want to dedicate this volume to the memory of Leslie Aaron Brown, who passed away unexpectedly in March 2005. Les and I shared good times and bad over three decades of remarkable friendship.

DUANE BRATT

First, I want to thank my colleagues in the Department of Policy Studies at Mount Royal College. Several of them have gone through the process of editing a reader for classroom usage and I tested their experience through frequent questions. I would also like to recognize the students in 'Foreign Policy of the Major Powers' in the Winter 2006 semester. These students were the first to be exposed to many of the chapters contained in this volume and constituted my focus group. My collaboration with Chris could not have gone smoother. The only disagreements occurred when the Canucks and the Flames met in the playoffs. Although my wife Teresa and my children Chris and Dorothy played no role in the editing of this book, they did hear an awful lot about the twists and turns of the project's development for two years. I know they are glad that the project is now complete.

PERMISSIONS

Don Barry, 'Managing Canada–U.S. Relations in the Post-9/11 Era: Do We Need a Big Idea?'. Originally published as *Managing Canada–U.S. Relations in the Post-9/11 Era: Do We Need a Big Idea?* CSIS Policy Papers on the Americas (November 2003), by the Center for Strategic and International Studies, Washington, DC. © 2003 by the Center for Strategic and International Studies. All rights reserved.

Stephen Clarkson, 'Conclusion', *An Independent Foreign Policy for Canada? University League for Social Reform* (Toronto: McClelland and Stewart, 1968). Reprinted by permission of the author.

Ann Denholm Crosby, 'Myths of Canada's Human Security Pursuits: Tales of Tool Boxes, and Tickle Trunks', pp. 90–107 in Claire Turenne Sjolander, Heather A. Smith, and Deborah Stienstra, eds, *Feminist Perspectives on Canadian Foreign Policy*. Copyright © 2003 Oxford University Press. Reprinted by permission of the publisher.

David B. Dewitt and John Kirton, *Canada as a Principal Power: A Study in Foreign Policy and International Relations* (Toronto: John Wiley and Sons, 1983), 13–20, 36–46. Reprinted by permission of the authors.

Elizabeth Riddell-Dixon, 'Canada at the United Nations in the New Millennium', pp. 256–86 in David Carment, Fen Osler Hampson, and Norman Hillmer, eds, *Canada Among Nations 2003: Coping with the American Colossus*. Copyright © 2003 Oxford University Press. Reprinted by permission of the publisher.

John English, 'The Member of Parliament and Foreign Policy', pp. 69–80 in Fen Osler Hampson and Maureen Molot, eds, *Canada Among Nations 1998: Leadership and Dialogue*. Copyright © 1998 Oxford University Press. Reprinted by permission of the publisher.

John Holmes, 'Most Safely in the Middle', *International Journal* 39, 2 (Spring 1984): 366–88. Reprinted by permission of the Canadian Institute of International Affairs.

Douglas MacDonald and Heather A. Smith, 'Promises Made, Promises Broken: Questioning Canada's Commitments to Climate Change', *International Journal* 55, 1 (Winter 1999–2000): 107–24. Reprinted by permission of the Canadian Institute of International Affairs.

Maureen Appel Molot, 'Where Do We, Should We, Or Can We Sit? A Review of Canadian Foreign Policy Literature', *International Journal of Canadian Studies* 1, 2 (Spring–Fall 1990): 77–96. Reprinted by permission of the author.

Mark Neufeld, 'Hegemony and Foreign Policy Analysis: The Case of Canada as a Middle Power', *Studies in Political Economy* 48 (1995): 7–29. Reprinted by permission of the author and *Studies in Political Economy*.

Kim Richard Nossal, 'Analyzing Domestic Sources of Canadian Foreign Policy', *International Journal* 39, 1 (Winter 1983–4): 1–22. Reprinted by permission of the Canadian Institute of International Affairs.

Cranford Pratt, 'Competing Rationales for Canadian Development Assistance', *International Journal* 54, 2 (Spring 1999): 306–23. Reprinted by permission of the Canadian Institute of International Affairs.

Cranford Pratt, 'Dominant Class Theory and Canadian Foreign Policy: The Case of the Counter-Consensus', *International Journal* 39, 1 (Winter 1983–4): 99–135. Reprinted by permission of the Canadian Institute of International Affairs.

Christopher Sands, 'Fading Power or Rising Power: 11 September and Lessons from the Section 110 Experience', pp. 49–73 in Norman Hillmer and Maureen Appel Molot, eds, *Canada Among Nations 2002: A Fading Power*. Copyright © 2002 Oxford University Press. Reprinted by permission of the publisher.

Claire Turenne Sjolander, 'Of Playing Fields, Competitiveness, and the Will to Win: Representations of Gender and Globalization', pp. 55–73 in Claire Turenne Sjolander, Heather A. Smith, and Deborah Stienstra, eds, *Feminist Perspectives on Canadian Foreign Policy*. Copyright © 2003 Oxford University Press. Reprinted by permission of the publisher.

Brian W. Tomlin, 'Leaving the Past Behind: The Free Trade Initiative Assessed'. Reprinted with permission of the Publisher from *Diplomatic Departures: The Conservative Era in Canadian Foreign Policy, 1984–93* by Nelson Michaud and Kim R. Nossal © University of British Columbia Press 2001. All rights reserved by the Publisher.

Contributors

Don Barry is a Professor in the Department of Political Science at the University of Calgary.

David Black is an Associate Professor in Political Science and a member of the Centre for Foreign Policy Studies at Dalhousie University.

Duane Bratt is a Political Science instructor, with a speciality in International Relations, in the Department of Policy Studies at Mount Royal College.

Stephen Clarkson is a Professor Emeritus in the Department of Political Science at the University of Toronto.

Ann Denholm Crosby is an Associate Professor and Graduate Program Director in the Department of Political Science at York University.

David B. Dewitt is the Associate Vice-President Research, Social Sciences & Humanities, at York University.

John English is a Professor of History at the University of Waterloo.

Paul Gecelovsky is an Assistant Professor in the Department of Political Science at the University of Lethbridge.

John Holmes (1910–88) served in the Department of External Affairs in the late 1940s and the 1950s and was later the head of the Canadian Institute of International Affairs.

Tom Keating is a Professor in the Department of Political Science at the University of Alberta.

John Kirton is an Associate Professor of Political Science and Director of the G8 Research Group at the University of Toronto.

Chris Kukucha is an Assistant Professor in the Department of Political Science at the University of Lethbridge.

Douglas MacDonald is Director of the Environmental Studies Program at Innis College, University of Toronto.

Nelson Michaud is a Professor of International Relations and Associate Director of the Groupe d'études, de recherche et de formation internationales at *L'École Nationale d'Administration Publique* in Québec City.

Maureen Appel Molot is a Professor and Director of The Norman Paterson School of International Affairs at Carleton University.

Mark Neufeld is an Associate Professor in the Department of Political Studies at Trent University.

Kim Richard Nossal is a Professor and Head of the Department of Political Studies at Queen's University.

Cranford Pratt is a Professor Emeritus in the Department of Political Science at the University of Toronto.

Elizabeth Riddell-Dixon is a Professor of International Relations in the Department of Political Science at the University of Western Ontario.

Christopher Sands is a Fellow and Director of the Canada Project at the Center for Security and International Studies, Washington, DC.

Claire Turenne Sjolander is an Associate Professor in the Department of Political Science and Associate Dean (Academic) of the Faculty of Social Sciences at the University of Ottawa.

Heather Smith is an Associate Professor of International Studies at the University of Northern British Columbia.

Elizabeth Smythe is an Associate Professor of Political Science at Concordia University College of Alberta.

Brian W. Tomlin is a Professor of International Affairs and Director of the Centre for Negotiation and Dispute Resolution at Carleton University.

Studying Canadian Foreign Policy: Various Approaches

What is Canadian Foreign Policy?

Historically, Canada has attempted to define its foreign policy in both explicit and implicit terms. *Canada in the World*, the 1995 government white paper on foreign policy, for example, stated that 'domestic policy is foreign policy. Foreign policy is domestic policy.'[1] Lester Pearson, on the other hand famously suggested that 'foreign policy is domestic policy, but with your hat on.' Ottawa's 2003 *Dialogue on Foreign Policy*, however, clearly articulated three main 'pillars': ensuring global security and the security of Canadians, promoting the prosperity of Canadians and global prosperity, and projecting Canada's values and culture.[2] These three pillars were reinforced in the 2005 International Policy Statement, released by Paul Martin's Liberal government, which stated that its foreign policy would rest on 'three core priorities—prosperity, security, and responsibility'.[3] This volume will examine the relevance of these statements in the context of security, trade, and social issues. This text will also argue that most studies of Canadian foreign policy tend to focus on one aspect of a state's external relations, such as international developments, the domestic policy process, or the role of individuals. In the Canadian case, therefore, there is a need to adopt a more holistic framework in evaluating foreign policy. As Kim Nossal has made clear 'foreign policy is forged in the nexus of three political environments—international, domestic, and governmental. It is within these three spheres that the sources, or the determinants, of a state's foreign policy are to be found.'[4]

In addition to accepting that Canadian foreign policy is a nexus, it is also essential to consider issues of system, process, and change. In terms of systemic issues there is the obvious understanding that international developments have an impact on Canada's global relations, and that these external variables can take many forms. For most western developed states, including Canada, foreign policy is guided by certain ideational assumptions regarding the international system, namely realist and neo-liberal institutionalist perspectives. These perspectives accept the reality of a state-centric competitive anarchic international system in terms of both political and economic relationships. At the same time, however, co-operation is still possible at the international level in the form of regimes and other institutions, which allows for an evaluation of both absolute and relative gains. It is important to note, however, that this does not restrict Canada's ability to pursue issues related to its own self-interest. Neo-liberal institutionalism is based on the understanding that sovereignty and economic protectionism are real-ities, and Canada has demonstrated repeatedly that these options will be embraced in the formulation of Canadian foreign trade policy. Neo-idealism also accepts liberal efforts to engage civil society and promote greater democratization.

Non-state actors are also influenced by many of the same realist and neo-lib-eral systemic considerations, especially corporate and sectoral interests. At the same time, however, many also have very different 'structural' assumptions that are instead guided by gender, class, or ethnicity. These 'critical' approaches chal-lenge the basic core organizing principles of the modern state system, and repre-sent alternative international structural interpretations. It is important to under-stand that these considerations can also shape the foreign policy of states, namely in the form of non-traditional factors not usually accounted for in realist or neo-liberal frameworks.

In addition, Canadian foreign policy is also influenced by 'process' issues, which can include domestic institutional factors such as constitutional and judi-cial realities, the role of the prime minister, provincial premiers, cabinets and executives at both levels of government, federal and provincial legislatures, bureaucratic interests, and intergovernmental relations linked to international affairs. At the same time, however, process factors must also examine non-institu-tional inputs. Sectoral actors, for example, consist of industry associations, spe-cific corporations, individual executives, advisory groups, and consultative links with federal government departments or officials. In addition, societal interests— which are typically treated as secondary considerations in studies of Canadian for-eign policy—incorporate organized labour, environmental groups, First Nations, civil society, and a wide range of other non-governmental actors. Finally, ideational issues focus on how 'dominant ideas' are transferred, or entrenched, at both levels of analysis, contributing to exploitive relationships related—but not limited—to ideology, class, gender, ethnicity, and culture.

To fully understand 'process' related issues, however, causal relationships must also be explored, especially in terms of state autonomy. Specifically, there is a need to evaluate the international and domestic activities of institutional, sectoral, societal, and ideational actors. Additionally, these observations must also account for the transnational activity *between* states that contributes to policy convergence. Finally, international pressures related to treaties, financial markets, and global capital can also lead to limitations of domestic autonomy, although this will vary greatly from sector to sector.[5] What is also missing, however, is the acknowledgement that domes-tic actors can have a direct impact on the international system. The institutional poli-cies of central and non-central governments, for example, are often transferred between levels of analysis as states consult, negotiate, and implement agreements.

Finally, any discussion of foreign policy must incorporate a review of 'change' that moves beyond traditional discussions of state autonomy. In other words, 'change' must identify developments that represent a pattern of relations that are significantly different from previous relationships. This could include shifts in power-based capabilities, re-interpretations of regime-based norms and standards, and/or membership in international institutions. In order to fully evaluate outcomes, however, it is useful to also engage critical interpretations of foreign policy. In fact, tangible benefits can be gained by including these issues in rational, realist, or neo-liberal approaches. In terms of trade policy, for example, issues of class are relevant to the role of organized labour and civil society's backlash to neo-liberalism within the state, while also being relevant to the obvious economic disparities between the developed and developing world. Gender-based NGO's and social movements also place pressure on states at both the international and domestic levels, although liberal feminists would take a much different view of the neo-liberal patriarchy than would a socialist or more critical perspectives. Ethnic and cultural issues present further challenges in terms of neo-liberalism's insensitivity to non-western-oriented economic considerations and issues of collective rights. All of these social issues are relevant to questions involving state autonomy and the level of analysis problem, in terms of structure, process, and change.

How is Canadian Foreign Policy Studied?

TRADITIONAL FRAMEWORKS

The first three chapters of Part I outline the traditional frameworks for analyzing Canadian foreign policy. Maureen Appel Molot, in a seminal article reprinted in Chapter 4, points out that the vast majority of the thinking about Canadian foreign policy has been preoccupied with Canada's place in the world—its role, status, position, influence, and power. There are three different images that have prevailed: Canada as a middle power, a principal power, or a satellite power. The dominant image is of Canada as a middle power. Historically, middle powers were perceived as situated below the great powers of the United States, Russia, the United Kingdom, France, China, Germany, and Japan. The middle power perspective assumes that Canada has an important role to play both in multilateral and bilateral regimes and in institutions because of its wealth, geographic location, and human capacity. Initially, Canada's functional role in strong multilateral regimes was viewed as a way of constraining the *realpolitik* of great power rivalry by providing an alternative rules-based mechanism for ensuring world order.

Several authors have adopted this approach when examining the evolution of Canadian foreign policy. The most prominent observer of Canada as a middle power was John Holmes.[6] His 'classic' discussion of being 'safely in the middle' in Chapter 1 touches on a number of traditional themes. Tom Keating's brief update, however, focuses more on the principle of multilateralism and reflects the increasing tendency of some scholars to question the utility of categorizing states as middle powers due to the ambiguity of this standing in the contemporary international system. Specifically, Keating argues that Canadian policy-makers have repeatedly relied on both economic and security regimes to fulfill a wide range of foreign policy objectives. Keating, however, also suggests that Canadian support for international regimes is not unconditional. In response to both international and domestic pressures Ottawa has pursued unilateral and selected bilateral arrangements in its external relations. At the same time, what becomes apparent over time 'is that these alternatives are deviations from the norm, are short-lived, and are frequently combined with complimentary multilateral activities'.[7] Kim Nossal and Andrew Cooper have also addressed Canada's traditional role as a middle power.[8]

An alternative image is that of Canada as a principal power. Canada has many capabilities—abundant natural resources, high levels of technology, well-educated people, a high standard of living, and membership in exclusive groups like the G7/8—that rank it far ahead of other middle powers. Principal power theorists argue that Canada is able to pursue its own policies in the international system with relatively little interference. The first to acknowledge this position was James Eayrs, who wrote in 1975 that the rising importance of oil producing states, the increasing significance of natural resources in the global political economy and the declining economic status of the United States, all increased Canadian power.[9] Norman Hillmer and Garth Stevenson also adopted this approach in 1977 when they suggested that Canada was not a 'modest power'.[10] It was David Dewitt and John Kirton, as noted in Chapter 2, who argued most strongly in favour of Canada being labelled a 'principal power' because of the decline in status of the United States. Although they were writing almost a decade after Eayrs they also cited a decrease in American hegemony that portrayed Canada as an 'ascending power' whose 'star was on the rise'[11] in comparison. Kirton provides an update to this thesis with an examination of Canada's role in the G8, in Chapter 18, arguing that Ottawa played a 'principal' role regarding a wide range of issues including institutional reform, terrorism, the G20 forum, and the New Plan for African Development (NEPAD). Although the popularity of the principal power approach has declined in recent years it still serves as a core foundation for studying Canadian foreign policy.

Another alternative image, and the opposite of the principal power approach, is that Canada is a peripheral-dependent/satellite country. In this conception, Canada moved seamlessly from existing as a British colonial dependency to being pulled into the orbit of the American empire. The origins of the satellite model date back to the 1920s when Archibald MacMechan complained that Canada was becoming nothing more than a 'Vassal State' of the United States.[12] A.R.M. Lower also echoed this sentiment in the 1940s when he described Canada as a 'subordinate state' or 'satellite' to its American neighbour.[13] The satellite approach gained increasing momentum during the 1960s when several observers argued that Canada was adopting policy decisions that were deferential to the United States, especially in terms of military and security issues. Although George Grant touched on many of these themes in *Lament for a Nation*,[14] the most prominent 'voice' of the satellite movement in terms of Canadian foreign policy came from Stephen Clarkson. For Clarkson the problem was largely one of leadership; senior officials were not willing to distance themselves from American influence.[15] The answer, as described in Chapter 3, was to aggressively protect Canadian sovereignty by promoting greater government intervention in the economy through the establishment of mechanisms such as the Foreign Investment Review Agency (FIRA) and the National Energy Program (NEP). More recent contributors sympathetic to this argument include Stephen McBride, John Helliwell, and Alex Michalos.[16] Stephen Clarkson has recently re-entered the debate by suggesting that institutions such as the North American Free Trade Agreement (NAFTA) and the World Trade Organization (WTO) have imposed a 'supraconstitution' that constrains 'authority that was once the exclusive preserve of domestically elected legislatures'.[17] Clarkson presents a brief retrospective of *An Independent Foreign Policy* as an addendum to Chapter 3.

As previously mentioned, Maureen Appel Molot argues in Chapter 4 that the traditional approaches to the study of Canadian foreign policy—especially the middle, principal, and satellite models discussed in the preceding three chapters—are no longer adequate for a number of reasons. Not only do the traditional methods fail to evaluate the complexity of Canadian foreign policy in terms of a holistic analysis of system, process, and outcome, but they also suffer from the following weaknesses:

a) They are atheoretical, with only implicit ties to IR theory.
b) The approaches fail to focus on domestic politics and/or international/domestic linkages (the level of analysis problem).
c) Problems and opportunities related to Canadian foreign policy are largely scrutinized through the lens of state autonomy. Other more 'critical' approaches are required.
d) There is no real discussion of economic issues (trade and finance).

In addition, non-institutional actors, both sectoral and societal, are usually ignored. For these and other reasons, David Black and Heather Smith have called for the application of non-traditional models in the study of Canadian foreign policy. In particular, they argue, there is a need for models that explore 'the interaction between state, society, and global levels of analysis'.[18]

Non-Traditional Models

One of the main non-traditional models is feminist analysis. Feminist analysis explores, in the words of Deborah Stienstra, 'how gender relations are shaped and how they, in turn, shape Canadian foreign policy'.[19] Stienstra's article, which is only a decade old, was particularly critical of the fact that, despite an increase in the application of gender-based analysis in the study of international relations, it has not been extended to examining Canadian foreign policy. This was a groundbreaking study that added to the voice of a group of scholars led by Sandra Whitworth, Heather Smith, Edna Keeble, and Claire Sjolander that critiqued Canada's international role from a feminist perspective.[20] Specifically, it is argued that 'women and gender issues have been excluded from the study of Canadian foreign policy' because the 'feminine is devalued in the way that people think'.[21]

In Chapter 5, Claire Turenne Sjolander uses feminist analysis to offer a different perspective on Canada's international economic relations. In fact, her contribution takes issue with statements by Canadian officials that female entrepreneurs drive small and medium sized businesses. Instead, the argument is presented that Canadian foreign trade policy has been 'constructed' by 'analogies' related to the 'jungle' of competitive sports. Therefore, Ottawa defends the need for multilateral and regional trade rules to 'tame the jungle' in which there are clear winners and losers. Sjolander's critique is that power-based discussions define these concerns in 'masculine' terms, which has direct implications for Canadian policy-makers. Ultimately, globalization and interdependence relate to a 'gendered' policy process that prohibits federal and provincial governments from fully understanding ideational or ideological considerations because of their role in the 'construction' of this reality. In other words, a broader perspective is required to counteract vague and patriarchal interpretations of Canada's response to globalization.

A second critical perspective is Gramscian structural analysis and 'dominant-class' theory,[22] which is reviewed by Mark Neufeld in Chapter 6. Antonio Gramsci (1891–1937) was an Italian socialist, activist, and political theorist. His prison notebooks, not published until the 1950s, were filled with critical commentary about socialism, capitalism, communism, and fascism. Robert Cox and Stephen Gill have applied many of Gramsci's ideas to the study of world politics.[23] Of particular importance is the Gramscian notion of hegemony whereby the institution and maintenance of a world order serves the interests of the dominant social class in a wide range of states. Gramscian hegemony, then, is not based on coercive force, but on consent gained through intellectual and moral leadership. Neufeld uses the Gramscian approach to explain Canada's middle power policies through its 'material context' and its 'politico-normative content' based on 'creative social agents'.

Plan of the Book

This book is structured with three primary goals. The first goal is to illustrate that the setting of Canadian foreign policy exists at the intersection of the international, state, and societal levels of analysis. The second goal is a thorough examination of the stated purpose of Canadian foreign policy, namely physical security, economic prosperity, and the promotion of Canadian values. The third goal aims to draw attention to some of the weaknesses in the Canadian foreign policy literature and to offer a critical, or more holistic, approach to studying Canada's global relations.

Part I develops the various mainstream and critical approaches to the study of Canadian foreign policy identified in this introduction. Part II examines the constraints and opportunities facing Canada in the international environment through an examination of Canada–United States relations and the United Nations. Part III begins with a 'classic' debate between Kim Nossal and Cranford

Pratt on the domestic sources of Canadian foreign policy. This is followed by chapters on the role of the prime minister, parliament, and the provinces. Part IV, the first of three issue-specific sections, examines Canada's pursuit of physical security by discussing Canadian peace support policies, the security of the Canada–American border, and an evaluation of human security. Part V examines Canada's pursuit of economic prosperity through the historic Canada–United States Free Trade Agreement (FTA), Canada's economic policy coordination with the other large industrialized economies in the G7/G8, and investment. Part VI begins with Nelson Michaud's examination of culture as a variable in Canadian foreign policy. Selections that analyze Canada's efforts to promote its values abroad in the areas of environmental protection, foreign aid, and African development complete the section.

Notes

1. Canada, *Canada in the World: Government Statement* (Ottawa: Canada Communications Group, 1995), 4.
2. Department of Foreign Affairs and International Trade, *A Dialogue on Foreign Policy: Report to Canadians* (Ottawa: Communications Services Division, 2003).
3. Canada, *Canada's International Policy Statement, A Role of Pride and Influence in the World* (Ottawa: Government of Canada, 2005), 5.
4. Kim Richard Nossal, *The Politics of Canadian Foreign Policy*, 3rd ed. (Scarborough, ON: Prentice-Hall, 1997), 7.
5. George Hoberg, Keith G. Banting, and Richard Simeon, 'The Scope for Domestic Choice: Policy Autonomy in a Globalizing World', in Hoberg, ed., *Capacity for Choice: Canada in a New North America* (Toronto: University of Toronto Press, 2002), 252–99.
6. John W. Holmes, *Canada: A Middle-Aged Power* (Toronto: McClelland and Stewart, 1976); John W. Holmes, *The Shaping of Peace: Canada and the Search for World Order, 1943–1957* (Toronto: University of Toronto Press, 1979).
7. Tom Keating, *Canada and World Order: The Multilateralist Tradition in Canadian Foreign Policy*, 2nd ed. (Don Mills, ON: Oxford University Press, 2002), 23.
8. Nossal, *The Politics of Canadian Foreign Policy*; Andrew F. Cooper, *Canadian Foreign Policy: Old Habits and New Directions* (Scarborough, ON: Prentice-Hall, 1997); Andrew F. Cooper, Richard A. Higgott, and Kim Richard Nossal, *Relocating Middle Powers: Australia and Canada in a Changing World Order* (Vancouver: UBC Press, 1993).
9. James Eayrs, 'Defining a New Place for Canada in the Hierarchy of World Powers', *International Perspectives* (May–June 1975): 15–24.
10. Norman Hillmer and Garth Stevenson, eds, *A Foremost Nation, Canadian Foreign Policy in a Changing World* (Toronto: McClelland and Stewart, 1977).
11. David B. Dewitt and John Kirton, *Canada as a Principal Power: A Study in Foreign Policy and International Relations* (Toronto: John Wiley and Sons, 1983), 38.
12. Archibald MacMechan, as cited in Nossal, *The Politics of Canadian Foreign Policy,* 61.
13. A.R.M. Lower, as quoted in Phillip Resnick, 'Canadian Defence Policy and the American Empire', in Ian Lumsden, ed., *Close the 49th Parallel Etc: The Americanizaiton of Canada* (Toronto: University of Toronto Press, 1970), 99.

14. George Grant, *Lament for a Nation: The Defeat of Canadian Nationalism* (Toronto: McClelland and Stewart, 1965).

15. Stephen Clarkson, ed., *An Independent Foreign Policy for Canada?* (Toronto: McClelland and Stewart, 1968).

16. Stephen McBride, *Paradigm Shift: Globalization and the Canadian State* (Halifax: Fernwood, 2001); John Helliwell, *Globalization and Well-Being* (Vancouver: UBC Press, 2002); Alex C. Michalos, *Good Taxes: The Case for Taxing Foreign Currency Exchange and Other Financial Transactions* (Toronto: Dundurn, 1997); Alex C. Michalos, 'Combining Social, Economic and Environmental Indicators to Measure Sustainable Human Well-Being', *Social Indicators Research* 40 (1997): 221–58.

17. Stephen Clarkson, *Uncle Sam and US: Globalization, Neoconservatism, and the Canadian State* (Toronto: University of Toronto Press, 2002).

18. David R. Black and Heather A. Smith, 'Notable Exceptions? New and Arrested Directions in Canadian Foreign Policy Literature', *Canadian Journal of Political Science* 26, 4 (December 1993): 745–75.

19. Deborah Steinstra, 'Can the Silence be Broken? Gender and Canadian Foreign Policy', *International Journal* 50, 1 (Winter 1994–5): 126–7.

20. For other examples of gender analysis in Canadian foreign policy see Claire Turenne Sjolander, Heather A. Smith, and Deborah Stienstra, eds, *Feminist Perspectives on Canadian Foreign Policy* (Don Mills, ON: Oxford University Press, 2003) and Edna Keeble and Heather A. Smith, *(Re)Defining Traditions: Gender and Canadian Foreign Policy* (Halifax: Fernwood, 1999).

21. Keeble and Smith, *(Re)defining Traditions*, 20.

22. Cranford Pratt, 'Dominant Class Theory and Canadian Foreign Policy: The Case of the Counter-Consensus', *International Journal* 39 (Winter 1983–4): 99–135.

23. Robert W. Cox, 'Gramsci, Hegemony and International Relations: An Essay in Method', *Millennium, Journal of International Studies* 12, 2 (Summer 1983): 162–75; Stephen Gill, *American Hegemony and the Trilateral Commission* (Cambridge: Cambridge University Press, 1990); Stephen Gill, ed., *Gramsci, Historical Materialism, and International Relations* (Cambridge: Cambridge University Press, 1993).

1
Most Safely in the Middle

John W. Holmes

Medio tutissimus ibis.
—*Ovid*

It seemed like sound advice for Canada when we were launched after the Second World War into the giddy world of international diplomacy: 'You will go most safely in the middle.' There was enough of Mackenzie King in it to carry the cabinet and enough of forward motion for an impatient body of foreign service officers and a public that seemed more anxious than Mr King to accept rather than avoid commitments. He probably sensed all along, however, a Canadian disinclination to pay much for status or to maintain the requisite armed forces for an aspiring major power. Mr King did not much like the classification 'middle' power. As far as status was concerned, he regarded it as somewhat demeaning to be ranked with, say, Mexico, but he had little zeal for the entangling responsibilities, as, for example, membership in a United Nations commission to seek the peaceful reunification of Korea. In any case the idea that Canada was a middle power did gain wide acceptance. What we had considered ourselves before is hard to say, our preference for smallness when contributions were in order conflicting with the sense of bigness that came from

being the second largest country in the world. The ambiguity has persisted.

Whatever has become of the middle power and its role in the past twenty-five years? At the end of the fifties we seemed to have got it neatly defined. It had been conceived in the first place as a way of explaining to the world that Canadians were of greater consequence than the Panamanians but could not take on the obligations of the Americans, or even the French. It was useful in encouraging a wallflower people to get responsibly involved in keeping the peace and unleashing the world economy while warning them at the same time that they should not expect to wield the influence of a 'great' power. Canada's early forays into international diplomacy encouraged confidence that we were needed and, if we did not set our sights too high, that we could impinge. Mackenzie King's conviction that we should keep our noses out of distant problems because we had no distant interests was turned upside down. That became our qualification for intermediary therapy in the United Nations and elsewhere. So 'middle' power took on an unexpected meaning. Altogether it fitted very well a country which was recognizing that it could best work through combinations, through international institutions, and there were three major (the United Nations, the Commonwealth, and the North Atlantic Treaty Organization) and many minor associations that fitted our needs aptly. The variety, furthermore, made us more confident of the freedom of movement we had come to cherish in a long history of groping for our own place in the sun.

The high point had come in 1955 and 1956 when our accomplished leaders, Paul Martin, Sr and Lester Pearson, with wide if not universal international acclaim, led the lesser powers in the General Assembly in revolt against great power arrogance over the issues of new members and Suez. The replacement, shortly afterwards, of this skilled team by the inexperienced Conservatives slowed us down but did not substantially alter the concept. The satisfactions, however, diminished, and as new issues—the rise of the Third World, nuclear escalation, continental economics, provincial claims in foreign policy—began to press us harder, one could see that middlepowermanship, while still a valid concept, did not tell us much about how to handle 90 per cent of the agenda that crowds the day of a foreign service officer.

It was really only after the so-called golden decade of the middle power had passed that we began to grow self-conscious about it. Having been as guilty as any in analyzing and defining this mystic role, I became worried by the mid-sixties over the glorification and formalization of a kind of diplomacy that was really just common-sensical and not as unique as we were hinting. At a conference in Banff in 1965 I asked: 'Is there a future for middlepowermanship?' For a generation who knew Stephen Potter, the irony would, I thought, be grasped. The term 'brinkmanship' had been coined by James Reston to deflate John Foster Dulles, but it was then incorporated into the language as if Dulles had said it himself. I should have listened to Charles Lamb: 'Clap an extinguisher on your irony, if you are unhappily blessed with a vein of it.' The mood in the land was earnest. A new breed of scholars was now adding greatly to our sophistication about foreign policy but seeking somewhat too arduously to define the indefinable. The word 'middlepowermanship' began to buzz. Editors and politicians needed something to cling to, and in a time of increasing uncertainty the illusion gained ground that the multifarious range of international involvements could be subsumed in a succinctly definable 'foreign policy'.

There was already an anxiety to cling to what seemed fleeting glories. More regrettable was the consuming interest in what one might, if one still dared, call rolemanship. For scholars it was less seductive than for politicians. There was nothing wrong in the efforts, scientific or intuitive, to draw a bead on Canada in world politics and economics, provided the abstractions were restrained and not pressed too far. Middlepowermanship got boring, however, and by the end of the sixties a new prime minister proclaimed a revolt. He questioned whether the national interest had been adequately served in all the strenuous 'helpful fixing'—another term that was drafted ironically but interpreted solemnly—that went with middlepowermanship. Pierre Trudeau's grasp of foreign policy and diplomacy was dubious, but he was posing a question being widely asked by an 'attentive public' disenchanted with formulae too oft repeated. The 'role of a middle power' was under critical review. The idea had become increasingly associated with 'peace-keeping', and attitudes to that proud Canadian function were soured by the expulsion of the United Nations Emergency Force (UNEF) from Egypt in 1967 and the embarrassment and frustrations of trying as a member of three international supervisory commissions to control the peace in Indochina at war.

It was certainly time for a review, but it is unfortunate that the role of the middle power had become confused with 'do-goodism', constantly misconstrued in a debate over 'nationalism' and 'internationalism.' The idea gained ground that somehow the national interest of Canada, particularly its economic interests vis-à-vis the United States, had been sacrificed because Lester Pearson was off at the United Nations for a few days a year. A much greater number of public servants and cabinet ministers, among them the redoubtable C.D. Howe, had been guarding our trade and commerce than those few engaged in the high profile acts in New York or Geneva. Canada had been drawn into accepting responsibilities for world order because it was wanted. Canadians had not gone looking for distinguished service, although in general they welcomed the challenge. If there was any soliciting of such assignments it was tentative. The determination to play as effective a role as was possible for a middle power was based on a very hardheaded calculation of national interest at the end of a war in which too many Canadians had been killed following a depression in which too many Canadians had starved. It was a firm rejection of the prewar assumption that Canada could escape disaster by dancing on the periphery. It was taken for granted that there was no national interest greater than the preservation of a world in which Canadians could survive and prosper. Collective defence and collective law as the best means of serving and protecting Canada itself were better understood by those who had passed through the thirties and forties than by later generations who, nurtured on the new 'victimization' school of Canadian history, took a more claustrophobic view of the national interest. It was of course always arguable ad hoc that some national interest had been ill defended, but it was intellectually slipshod to see this in either/or terms. The same simple thinking was evident in the simultaneous debate over the efficacy of 'quiet diplomacy', associated persistently with feckless middlepowermanship. That quiet diplomacy had quite often failed to move other powers, especially the United States, was easy to prove, but it did not follow that loud shouting would have moved a mountain either. It was still not widely recognized that there are no sure ways and means for a middle power to get its way at all, that abstractions are to be handled with care, and that a more discriminating look at specifics is a better way to further the national interest and avoid despair.

The attack on classical middlepowerism came from two directions. There were those on the right who thought all Canada's energies should be directed to selling apples and reactors. The more articulate critics on the left did want Canada to play a grand peace-inducing role in the world but thought that we were hindered by our alignment. They saw 'uncommitment' as a means to a worthy end. Then almost inevitably 'independence' came to be seen as an end in itself. In particular that meant independence of the United States, partly, it was thought, because we could not be regarded as objective actors in world diplomacy if we were allied to one of the superpowers, and partly because the close economic tie was believed to be intimidating us from foreign policies that would serve specifically Canadian ends and help to keep the world in balance. The independentist school of thought strayed from the Canadian tradition of regarding independence functionally. We had pursued self-government but not independence from Britain for the simple reason that our national interests seemed better served that way. We needed Britain as counterweight and the prestigious Foreign Office to conduct Canadian diplomacy on the cheap. Independence was a Yankee word that even Mackenzie King rejected. In practice we acted independently when we wanted to and joined a team when that was more useful. The new nationalism was based on a persistent misreading of the postwar period, popularized regrettably by a great Canadian historian, Donald Creighton. The assumption that the Canadian government had embraced 'continentalism' with enthusiasm when they had broken with the shackles of the British is an anti-American version of our history based ironically on the tenets and mythologies of certain American scholars. It is essentially anti-Canadian also because it assumes Canadian incompetence. Since our historians have been able to delve into postwar Canadian as well as American files, the record has been very considerably revised, but 'Canada as victim' lingers in textbooks to which students are still subjected. It suffuses also much masochistic comment on our foreign policy, which does not accord us even middle power status.

In all this clamour the pursuit of the national interest got derailed, and the role of this middle power confused. That Mr Trudeau has worked his way eventually to his predecessor's concept of the basic national interest would seem to have been proved latterly by his dedication to reconciliation between North and South and the restoration of the dialogue between East and West. He was, nevertheless, responsible initially for setting Canadians off on a few false scents and for leaving the impression that there did occur in the early seventies a profound change in Canadian foreign policy. The Pearson-Martin years of the sixties were written off as more of the same old middlepowermanship, although with less spectacular results. The extent to which change has been attributable in fact more to the turning earth than to policy planning in Ottawa has been ignored. Already during the Diefenbaker regime it was clear that the configuration of power in which this middle state had flourished was becoming unhinged.

The world has changed and we along with it. The intensification of economic competition in the world at large, the price of oil, nuclear escalation, the banking crises, the relative decline of both the United States and Canada in the world economy, and the rigidifying of East–West as well as North–South relations have profoundly affected the states of North America. They have altered our predicaments and challenged the rules and habits by which we have played. If we seek the causes for patterns of change in Canada–United States relations, for example, I suggest that we are more likely to find them in these alterations than in the philosophical stance and the Weltanschauung of Mr Trudeau. Because Pierre Trudeau is one of the few statesmen around with a sophisticated philosophy and a reasonably consistent prospect of the world, Canadians, and other peoples as well, tend to see him as causal rather than influential. That is even more true of his critics than his admirers. When I say that he is reasonably consistent, I am aware of perceived contradictions in his attitudes to nuclear weapons

or economic protectionism, but his philosophy does embrace paradox. He must be a politician as well as a philosopher, and he is constrained by the will of cabinet colleagues and the Liberal caucus. His Weltanschauung of 1983 is not that of 1968, and he is probably more willing then most prime ministers (male or especially female) to admit that he has changed his mind—although not much. That his views, his beliefs, and his prejudices have considerably influenced Canadian foreign policy is undeniable. He has certainly changed the style.

My main point, however, is that Canadian policies in recent years have been determined more by what has happened in Washington or Houston, Brussels, or Tegucigalpa, than by what has been decided or sought in Ottawa. I suggest, although without total conviction, that Canadian policies would not have been very different if there had been another Liberal leader or a longer Conservative government during these years. The range of Canadian foreign policies is considerably more restricted by basic geopolitical, economic, and cultural factors than critics and opposition spokesmen assume, and the room for radical change is circumscribed. I am not hereby proclaiming, as do our archaic Marxists, that Canada is a bound victim of American imperialism. We have considerably more room for manoeuvre than most middle powers, but even superpowers have a limited range of choice in these intervulnerable times.

The reason for the undue attention to Trudeauism is probably to be found in the prime minister's stance on foreign policy when he came to office. Foreign policy was not his major preoccupation, and at least until recently it has not been. His views on the subject were highly academic, reflecting those widely held by many other professors at that time. His exposure to the contradictions of actual policy-making was limited. In fact he revealed a certain lack of understanding of what foreign policy, diplomacy, and the foreign service were all about. He was impatient of the diplomats because they had to obtrude certain inescapable facts of international life on his visions. He mistakenly thought embassies abroad were engaged simply in reporting on the world scene and could be replaced by more subscriptions to *Le Monde* or the *New York Times*. Among his many misjudgments was his insistence that Canadian policy had been too reactive. In his innocence he failed to see that, however energetic and imaginative Canada could be in the world, it could not hope to shape in advance the circumstances to which it would have to respond.

For these reasons Mr Trudeau wanted a brand new foreign policy for Canadians. We and our allies were led to expect radical change. Attracting most attention were his questioning of Canada's commitment to NATO and its failure to establish relations with the Beijing government. He set in motion a review that culminated in the white paper, *Foreign Policy for Canadians*—in fact many-hued brochures on various aspects of foreign policy in which loyal civil servants sought to distil what they thought the prime minister would want, tempered by the advice given during the review by 'the people' (mostly politicians and professors). It was time for a thorough review of post-war policies in a changing world, and the effort was worthwhile. The white paper suffered, as it was bound to suffer, from the fact that no government can discuss its relations with other countries in entire candour, as one might in a post-graduate thesis. Beneath the inevitable circumlocutions were pockets of sound advice. It was a learning experience for the PM and all concerned; but the booklets are primarily of interest now as indicators of the philosophical base from which Mr Trudeau set out to learn about foreign policy.

To his credit he did listen and learn to a greater extent than his critics have allowed. Within a year he had accepted the argument that NATO was a good thing and that Canada should withdraw not all but only half its forces from the European theatre. He found out soon that events in faraway Africa would require him to play the mediatory role expected of Canada in the Commonwealth, whether he sought to save the world or leave it to others to patch up. He proved to be a good diplomat and decided that the Commonwealth was also a good thing. He learned too that his favourite project of recognizing the People's Republic of China was more complex than just standing up to the Department of External Affairs and the Yankees; it would involve extended and fancy diplomatic negotiation by his best professionals before a satisfactory formula could be reached. The professionals were not opposed to recognizing Beijing, but they did not want their prime minister to fall on his face. They had to make sure at an uncertain time that Canadian recognition would not be rejected by the Chinese. The satisfactory result was attributable not only to his policy and the eventual acceptance by Beijing of a clever formula covering the Taiwan problem, but also to the coincidence of a shift of Chinese policy towards more normal international relations. Washington was less upset because of the new China policy being conceived by Henry Kissinger. Mr Trudeau deserves credit for making a commitment about China before an election and sticking to it, but recognizing Beijing was not a new policy. Canadian governments since 1949 had stated that intention but had always been stalled by some temporary obstacle. There was more in the way of a new will and new circumstances than new policy.

It is not surprising, however, that the impression was left that we were being ushered into a revolutionary change in direction. When the world proved intractable and perversely went its own course, policy did not look all that new. So there was a tendency, not so much by Mr Trudeau as by his devotees, to offer a some-what re-arranged version of what had gone on before in order to simulate contrast. Previous leaders, as mentioned earlier, were portrayed as having been too intent on international high jinks to protect the store. Those in Washington and elsewhere who had actually faced the formidable C.D. Howe in his defence of Canada's industrial programme or Lester Pearson's polite but really quite resonant diplomacy were puzzled, but no matter. The conviction of a new national stubbornness was an essential element of Trudeaumania—even if it was not really a part of Trudeau's own philosophy.

A man by profound conviction anti-nationalist, concerned with broader issues than transborder bargaining, was made to seem like a red-hot nationalist when nationalism was in the wind. Canada's so-called 'economic nationalism' of the seventies, whether wise or unwise, was in fact attributable not to the PM's philosophy but to the threat of American 'economic nationalism' as perceived in the import surcharge and the domestic international sales corporations (DISC) legislation of 1971. It was a reactive policy. The misinterpretation has persisted, particularly in the United States, and it is little wonder that American business circles, rallied by the *Wall Street Journal,* have of late ascribed the disease they call Canadian economic nationalism to the anti-American vagaries of this exotic Canadian leader. In this confusion they are, of course, stoked by their admirers in Calgary now that anti-nationalism has become trendy. Mr Trudeau is a nationalist in the sense that he wants to strengthen the Canadian fabric. He wants Canada to be influential abroad as a model of internal internationalism, of peaceful living together. He has said many times that a failure of Canadians to maintain our kind of federation would be viewed with dismay throughout the world because most countries now have to consolidate more than one language and tribe. He emphatically rejects the kind of nationalism that is simple anti-Americanism. He is more inclined to take Canada's independence for granted than to make a false goal of it—and that is healthy. As Harald von Riekhoff has pointed out, 'Trudeau's reasoning is . . . most firmly linked to the global society paradigm and has less of the traditional state-centric orientation.'[1] The middle power is seen as the model power.

There was detectable a new will, or a new stubbornness, in certain aspects of foreign policy. Or was it renewed will? In 1945 it had been largely an alteration of will rather than a whole new philosophy of foreign policy that led Canada into its new era of world diplomacy. A new impulse was perhaps required. Lester Pearson had reluctantly agreed in the early sixties to accept nuclear weapons because we had promised our allies to do so. His stated intention was, however, to negotiate decently with NATO to get out of that role. That process was delayed and Mr Trudeau pressed it to a conclusion. Lester Pearson had hoped to transfer at least some of the forces in Europe to Canada, which, he had always insisted, was part of the NATO front. Mr Trudeau showed a stronger will to defy criticism and act, but he scaled down his original intentions regarding NATO very considerably and emphatically accepted the importance of the treaty as an element of detente, and of Canadian participation in it. Mr Pearson had always wanted to recognize Beijing but never had adequate support in cabinet or the country to act boldly. Mr Trudeau made his pledge before the election and had to go through with it.

A clearer example of this new will of the seventies, frequently cited, was the Arctic Waters Pollution Prevention Act of 1970 in which the government, responding to a chauvinistic hullabaloo over the northern voyage of the American tanker *Manhattan,* proclaimed unilaterally a hundred-mile zone which the coastal state would police and defied the International Court of Justice to intervene. It was said that this bold act differed from the previous habit of Canadian governments to go for a compromise. There is some truth in this. The act may have been attributable in part to the easier confidence of a man who had been less exposed to the corrosive game of international compromise, but it was also in the spirit of traditional functional middlepowermanship. It was in fact a compromise with the domestic demand for the claiming of Arctic sovereignty *tout court.* It claimed precisely what was needed for practical purposes without grandiloquence. It asserted the right of a lesser power not only to challenge but also to push along international law when the great powers were intransigent—reminiscent somewhat of Paul Martin's defiance over new members of the United Nations in 1955. It was certainly successful, for the Americans and others were soon proclaiming an analogous principle in the 200-mile economic zone favoured at the United Nations Conference on the Law of the Sea. It launched the Trudeau administration on its most effective and laudable international enterprise, a leading and highly constructive role in the most important contribution to world order since San Francisco. It was the culmination of efforts, which had actually begun during the Diefenbaker regime in 1958–60, to adapt the historic maritime laws to a new age. It was 'helpful fixing' of the highest order, a worthy contribution to international structure in which, furthermore, the Canadian national interest has been somewhat more than decently advanced.

The rejection of the grand enterprise by the Reagan administration was a disastrous blow, but instead of submission in Ottawa there has been firm resistance accompanied by quiet diplomacy. In the classical tradition of Canada's United Nations activities there have been persistent efforts, not by hortatory rhetoric but by unobtrusive collaboration with other middle powers, to seek out the compromises that might enable the Reaganites to return to the fold. The helpful fixers—our old associates, the Scandinavians, the Australians, etc.—have been labelled, even by the Americans, 'the good Samaritans'.[2] Plus, *peut-être, c'est la même chose*. It has not yet achieved the desired goal, but the strategy is long range. The constructive leadership and brilliant diplomacy of the Canadians in the whole evolution of the United Nations law of the sea has enabled survivors like me to insist that their fixing is as helpful as it was in the golden decade; it is just that now it is performed in exhausting nocturnal negotiations beyond the television cameras. They serve alike the national and the international interest, mindful of the wise admonition of an eighteenth-century essayist, William Shenstone: 'Laws are generally found to be nets of such a texture as the little creep through, the great break through, and the middle-sized are alone entangled in.'

So where does all this leave the role of a middle power in the eighties? Those who think foreign policy is simple proclaim confusion and inconsistency, and, of course, decline. Those who realize the complexities might more charitably detect a learning experience not only for the prime minister but for all the citizenry. We have been aided by an expanding crop of political scientists and historians, cutting through the mythologies and, of course, occasionally creating new ones. In accordance with the times, the debate became excessively ideological in the late sixties and early seventies. The ideologies were usually imported and hard to fit to the real facts of a middle power that had been pretty successfully defying a great capitalist power for a couple of centuries, and which had also been an imperialist power of sorts in its own right. The political scientists and historians are by no means untinged by ideology, but the more clinical approaches are bearing fruit, as we rise for snatches of air above the fog of clichés. There has been unhappily a new fog of unintelligibility that keeps the masses unconverted, but one must in this case believe in the trickle-down theory.

There is abroad in the land a new pragmatism, often mistakenly identified as conservatism because it rejects the simplicities of the left as well as those of the far right, and too often obscured from editors and speechifiers by their dedication to partisan combat. The persistent effort to identify the major parties with certain foreign policies is perverse. The extent to which foreign policy is determined more by the changing scene than by changing ministers is shown in the fact that in 1984 the Conservatives are seeking election on the grounds that the Liberals have messed up Canada's relations with the United States. That is one of the grounds on which the Liberals ousted the Conservatives in 1963. Is it perhaps also of some significance that the leaders of all three political parties say that they are cleaving to the middle ground in the Ovidian tradition even though they are tempted to please variant audiences with immoderate pitches.

It may be counted as progress that the role of a middle power is now seen in a more discriminating way. History has provided the scholars with many more case studies than they had when our world was new. There is a groping for different terms. James Eayrs sees Canada as a 'foremost power', and John Kirton and David Dewitt call it a 'principal power'. Those terms are in themselves interesting because they challenge the more popular assumption that Canada has sunk in the international pecking order. Our power is, of course, infinitely broader and stronger than it was in the golden decade, but there is more competition. The concept of power is regarded more searchingly. The nuclear power of the super players is increasingly seen as inapplicable, deluding them into assumptions about the extent to which they can manage the world. Distinctions are being made between military, economic, and diplomatic influence. Canada's claim to be an effective middle power in security questions was made in the forties on the strength of its major contribution to the allied forces during the war. After we had demobilized, however, we were ourselves reluctant to sustain the military strength required to maintain that kind of clout in the United Nations or NATO. The stark contradictions became apparent with the call to support the United Nations cause in Korea in the summer of 1950. When we had to match our high-flown rhetoric about the United Nations and collective security with deeds, the Canadian public realized that the barracks were bare. Our medium rare reputation in the United Nations now depended on the skills of our diplomacy rather than the might of our arms. We were propelled for a short time into high-level company because we had been one of the three atom powers of 1945, but we soon realized that when you are not a major contributor to the problem you can't make very convincing offers to deal with it. In any case the influence we had in arms control circles rested less on our own nuclear capacity than on the diplomatic prowess and reputation of two generals turned ambassadors, McNaughton and Burns.

It was in any case Canada's economic capacity that first gave it recognition as an important actor and which has proved much more enduring. The military capacity which we could offer was for peace-keeping rather than peace-enforcing, and it was important not for its quantity but for its quality, especially technological. Our particular kinds of middling power have had to be assessed in terms of their applicability. We have our wheat and our diplomacy and certain skilled and bilingual soldiers to offer, but military power in the abstract has really mattered little to our role as a middle power. It can be argued, in the abstract of course, that our influence in NATO would be increased from fair to middling if our military contribution was increased, but when one gets down to concrete decisions it is harder to see that there would be much difference. It is true, of course, that if we had no armed forces and were non-aligned, we would almost certainly get shorter shrift from all our allies. Whether that immaculate position would give us greater moral strength in world affairs is the subject of persistent debate, with the skeptics still dominant in Ottawa.

From the beginning Canada's approach to the role of a middle power was functional. We had demanded our due place in allied decisions on *matériel*, where we counted, during the war and made our first pitch for appropriate representation in postwar bodies over the United Nations Relief and Rehabilitation Administration on the grounds that we would be a major supplier. The issue was distorted by our ill-advised campaign to get a special place on the Security Council, not as a great power but as a middle power deserving attention for military merit. God knows what would have happened when the cabinet had grasped the financial and manpower implications of maintaining that heady status. After the Korean enterprise, when the Security Council tacitly abandoned its pretensions to maintain a workable system of universal collective security and devoted itself to 'helpful fixing', the irrelevance of military force to a special status in its deliberations or to sustain across-the-board middle power became obvious. It had nothing to do with the strength of Canada's voice in the International Monetary Fund, the General Agreement on Tariffs and Trade (GATT), or the International Wheat Agreement where we mattered a good deal more.

Judging our power by its applicability ad hoc should save us from delusions. It might enlighten (without entirely discouraging) those who see foreign policy largely as a simple matter of taking resonant stances on wickedness in a naughty world. We have too much debate about stances and too little about method. It is the cynics rather than the do-gooders who profit from that situation. Economic sanctions, whether against the Soviet Union or South Africa, are considered as moral gestures, but they ought to be carefully calculated as means to some definable end. Otherwise we risk the kind of reverse suffered over the pretentious sanctions against the USSR over Afghanistan. A successful foreign policy requires concentrated attention. Denouncing villains is sloppy diplomacy. In most issues the problem is not identifying the villain but coping with the predicament. Some of the time we are all more or less guilty.

When Prime Minister Trudeau initiated his peace campaign in the autumn of 1983 he was wise to furnish himself with specific proposals worked out by the professionals with long direct experience of the realities of arms control negotiations. The early successes of Canada as a middle power were attributable to our skill in producing sound ideas for the general rather than just the Canadian interest. That is the way to be listened to. In various international institutions our representatives, whether they are our scientists in the World Meteorological Organization or the United Nations Environment Programme or our engineers or our diplomats, are still being constructive without getting headlines. That is how the international infrastructure is laid. The Canadians agree or disagree with the Americans and balance the national and international interest ad hoc. What they do is sensational only in the long haul and largely ignored by the media for regrettable

but understandable reasons; so the perpetual disparagers hold sway. The more dogged nationalists repeat their irrelevant slogans about Canadian foreign policy being an echo of Washington's, revealing thereby their essential anti-Canadianism and their ignorance of the substance of a modern foreign policy. The anti-nationalists on the right display, as they did in imperial days, their lack of confidence in the intelligence and capacity of their own people, by advocating simple docility to a greater power. But in real foreign policy there is such a long agenda, so many ways of succeeding or failing, and these generalizations are almost always wide of the mark. Pleading the rights of a middle power as such is one of the generalizations that will rarely get us far. Applying pressures surgically has got us a good deal. The public has to think functionally, and in this it is now getting some good leadership from a new crop of scholar analysts—at least when it can get the gist of what they are saying.

How useful is it then to talk still of the role of a middle power? The hierarchies, such as they were, are breaking down and the categorization of states shifts. Countries are what they are for all kinds of historical, geographical, and other reasons. Each is unique, and all bilateral relationships are special. Cuba or Israel often act like great powers, and South Africa is treated as one by its enemies. Aside from the somewhat anachronistic categorization of five great powers in the Security Council, there is no fixed classification of states in the United Nations. Countries pay their dues in accordance with individual assessments based largely on economic factors. Membership in the so-called 'Western European and Others' group assures Canada of a reasonable chance for election to the Security Council or other bodies. We still have the advantage of not being tied too tightly to any bloc in multilateral diplomacy, an attribute traditionally associated with our kind of middlepowerism. Loyalty to collective NATO agreements and perceptions of basic common interests properly limit our freedom of action somewhat. So does a sense of respect for the feelings of Commonwealth or francophone associates and the large neighbour. Our greater need for an open world economy restricts our instinct for protection. There is, however, much more flexibility in our situation than is usually assumed. No country has an 'independent foreign policy'.

In the beginning Canada had regarded blocs as obstacles to sound decision-making, and we have always rejected the idea of a conformist NATO or Commonwealth voting bloc, as distinct from a consultative group. As the number of members of United Nations bodies has increased we have come to realize the importance of blocs in overcoming the anarchy of multilateral negotiation. They work best, however, if the membership shifts in accordance with the subject, as has been the case pre-eminently in the United Nations Conference on the Law of the Sea. As one of the coastal states we often opposed our major allies while paying due respect to their concern for certain strategies on which we too depend. On other issues we worked with other partners. We accept the validity of the Group of 77 as a voting and bargaining instrument while protesting against the kind of across-the-board voting on political issues that is a major cause of stalemate in the General Assembly. On the Law of the Sea we are a major power because of our fish and nickel and enormous seacoast, and we can confidently act as such. In nuclear matters our endeavours are better conceived as lateral rather than frontal, except in the matter of the proliferation of uranium or reactors. Although we could hardly expect to settle, for example, the Soviet–Chinese border dispute, in other conflicts there is quite often something we can do in good company if we retain a due sense of proportion.

Ours is not a divine mission to mediate, and the less that far too specific verb is used the better. It is the mission of all countries and in particular all statesmen and diplomats, with the probable exception of Albanians, to be intermediaries or to seek out compromises in the interests of peace. Our hand is strengthened by acknowledged success, but it is weakened if planting the

maple leaf becomes the priority. Whether or not the role of a middle power is now an exhausted concept (or just a boring one), the fact is that the world still needs a good deal of the kind of therapy we thought of as 'middlepowermanship'.

Our idea of the role of great powers is just as much in need of review. It is doubtful if the great, and especially the super, powers ever had as much sway in the managing of the globe as is implied in current theory. In the early postwar years the United States had the economic and military wherewithal and the residual authority that went with it to act almost as a surrogate United Nations while some kind of world order was being established. This was done with widespread if not universal and certainly not formal assent from the world community. It did not 'run' the United Nations, however. It could influence the voting and often, though not always, block by rough or smooth means what it did not like. It was never able to 'control' the votes of a majority because to get support it had to make concessions. It is well not to exaggerate the erstwhile power of the United States now that we are concerned with diluting it. The world must cope with an American administration that wants to revive the past. Aside from Mr Reagan and friends there seems to be wide agreement that the United States cannot count any more on the kind of authority it once had. By the same token the United States cannot be counted upon for that kind of management or for the residual resources. It was never the ideal arrangement, but what is now to be feared is that there will be no management at all.

The obvious alternative to unilateralism is multilateralism, but the latter is, as the painful lessons of over forty years make clear, extraordinarily difficult to achieve. Hence the fears that beset us all as a familiar framework of power crumbles. In inveighing against the abuses of power, great, middle, or small, we tend to forget the responsibility that goes with each gradation of power. The transition from superpower dominance to a healthier distribution is not going to be accomplished simply by demanding that the supers surrender. What, if anything, the Russians are doing about it in their bloc heaven only knows. The Americans, on our side, tend too simply to see this as letting their allies supply more funds and troops while they go on making the decisions as demanded by their system of government. The rest of us want first of all to share in the decision-making but have to struggle with the paradoxes between something like cantonal democracy and the veto. Middle powers and the lesser greats have to show leadership in accepting wider responsibilities even when that means risking American displeasure. That kind of foreign policy requires positive thinking. There is everything to be said for persuading the superpowers and their proxies to withdraw from Central America, the Middle East, and all of Africa, but that is only a beginning. Something still must be done about the endemic problems of El Salvador, Lebanon, Afghanistan, Grenada, or Chad. We have been arguing that these problems may be ascribed to domestic causes rather than to foreign conspiracies and that means they will not be solved simply by American or Soviet or Cuban withdrawal. They threaten the security of Canadians or New Zealanders as much as they do that of Texans or Ukrainians.

If there is still a point in Canadians seeing ourselves as a middle power in the eighties, it may be to discipline ourselves. When we found a mission as intermediary mediums we began to get some grip on our Canadian capabilities. When a definition that was analytical and descriptive came to be seen as prescriptive we got a little frenetic. However we still need guidelines to cling to and knowing one's strength remains a sound principle. If we are now more discriminating and calculating in our estimates of our own as well as others' powers, so much the better. Skepticism about spreading our good offices too wide may have induced a sense of proportion about the number of rescue missions, crusades, or moral interventions a country of twenty-five million can conduct at one time. We have to contend with the persistent feeling of other countries that we are

smug, self-righteous, and officious. Our moral majority may want the government to pass judgment on every misbehaviour in the world, and no doubt they will feel better if we do so, but it is the surest way to undermine the beneficent role of a middle power. It is furthermore a kind of cop-out by some well-intentioned people whose attention might better be directed to the baffling contradictions we face over policies that hit closer to home. If one were to judge from questions in the House of Commons one might conclude that Canadian foreign policy was largely a matter of deciding what to do over El Salvador and South Africa.

The middle power that is a major power in the world economy is caught in dilemmas not unlike those of a major military power, and they require hard thinking. It is not only a question of deliberately using power. There is the inescapable question of withholding it. Canada cannot help, for example, being a food power of decisive proportions and a producer of a wide array of mineral resources. It is not difficult to reject as immoral the idea of using food as a weapon to gain political ends, but if food is so scarce that it has to be rationed, on what bases do we make it available and to whom? That is the kind of issue we face in a rudimentary way with our none too plentiful energy supplies in the International Energy Agency. How much greater our problems will be if, with our broad territory and small population, we have to feed the new billions of Asians and Latin Americans. The experience of economic sanctions over Rhodesia and Afghanistan has led us to the too simple conclusion that they don't work and that's that. But the concept of sanctions is inseparable from the trading and aiding that are recognized as high priorities of Canadian foreign policy. We will grapple with these issues more safely in the middle of international institutions. The United Nations system remains of central importance because we of all countries need international disciplines, but where our vote really matters now is not in the Assembly or Security Council but in GATT or the International Monetary Fund or the World Bank, which are at least as important parts of the United Nations as is the General Assembly. Those are the places where, for example, we register our differences with the United States over Nicaragua or Grenada in Votes on loans that count. Our positions on the increase of financing for the Fund or the International Development Association are not decisive but they can be marginally so.

The distinguished British scholar, Denis Brogan, told Canadians thirty years ago: 'The very fact that Canada is now one of the treasure houses of the world makes the naive isolationship of the inter-war years . . . impossible. A uranium producing country cannot be neutral.'³ That means not privilege but responsibility for a middle power. One thing that has changed is that the role of a middle power costs more, not just financially but politically. Helpful fixing in the postwar period impinged much less on the priorities of the electorate. When the big international issues now are resources and coastal waters, defence spending, Asian imports, and non-tariff barriers, the things on which our future depends, the ridings will be less quiescent. Our idea of foreign policy has been stretched, and it is no longer true to say that it is not a major issue in elections. Public awareness of the long-range view for a middle power is more essential than ever.

It was in the setting of the wide international community that Canada first saw itself as a 'middle' power. Like all other countries Canada was adapting itself to the shift of power from Europe to the United States. There was never a question, as legend has it, of a conscious decision to transfer allegiance from the British to the American protector. Canadian governments worked hard to restore the triangular balance in which we had felt comfortable, to bring Europe and America together in alliance, and to create the international institutions in which we could be ourselves. It was a giant step out of the colonial mentality. Although American power was more nearly omnipotent then than it is now, we had not become so much obsessed by it. Increasingly one feels that Canadians see their foreign policy only

in the context of American foreign policy. The fact that it would be seen in better perspective if we compared it with those of other countries our size, with our European allies, with Australia, or with Mexico, is ignored in the single-minded concentration on what Reagan or Shultz, Mrs Kirkpatrick or Dan Rather, are up to. It is not a matter of being pro- or anti-American; the obsession is common to both.

If the Americans have come to dominate our foreign policy, it is not, as nationalists have thought, by arm-twisting and threatening sanctions. We have let the American media capture us for their debate. The danger is not that we support their policies; we associate ourselves just as often with the critics. It is rather that our minds are on what the United States is or should be doing, not how we, with our very different kind of role to play in the world, should be acting. It is irresponsible. Statements by politicians and others often imply that our foreign policy consists simply of approving or disapproving American action. When we criticize the Russians for shooting down airliners or take action against them over Afghanistan, this is persistently described as supporting or not supporting the Americans, as if we were helping them out in their private struggle with the Russians and not pursuing our own quarrel with aggressors in the broad company of the United Nations and NATO. By treating NATO as a United States-dominated organization, we and the Europeans have only helped to make it so and dimmed in the process the moral strength of the alliance. Surely the lesson of Canadian experience of middlepowermanship is that we can be a stronger world citizen and a stronger ally if we act in accordance with our own wisdom. The colonial tradition dies hard. It was reported (incorrectly, I hope) that one of our major political parties had been unable to reach a position over Grenada because it did not know whether to follow Mr Reagan or Mrs Thatcher. That is a kind of 'middle' policy that I thought we had long since abandoned. As Norman Snider wrote recently in the *Globe and Mail*, 'Canadians would be better advised to suppress all those neo-colonial urges to jump up and salute at the most powerful English-speaking nation around and continue to do their own thinking.'[4]

It is unfortunate that the excesses of the nationalists of a few years ago helped to discredit the kind of healthy, self-respecting nationalism that Canada needs to combat the cringing anti-nationalism, the idolatry of foreign gods, from which we suffer at present. Surely there is a middle way here that is more sensible and safer and in our own best tradition. Is it so demeaning in a churning world to maintain our peculiar reputation for good sense, moderation, a will to see all sides of a question, and an instinct for compromise? Must we call that mediocrity?

Notes

1. 'The Impact of Prime Minister Trudeau on Foreign Policy', *International Journal* 33, 2 (Spring 1978): 268.
2. Leigh S. Ratiner, 'The Law of the Sea: A Crossroads for American Foreign Policy', *Foreign Affairs* 60 (Summer 1982): 1015.
3. 'An Outsider Looking In', Canada's Tomorrow Conference, Quebec City, 13–14 November 1953.
4. 'Rethinking our Allegiance', *Globe and Mail*, 3 December 1983, L9.

Update
Canada and the New Multilateralism

Tom Keating

We seek nothing less than a new multilateralism, in which the real and pressing needs of people are addressed. Canada has always contributed to and benefited from multilateralism. We believe strongly in finding cooperative solutions. But we also recognize that we must be ready to change with the times and lead where we can, especially where multilateral institutions are acting too slowly or are not up to the task.

—Rt Hon. Paul Martin,
Prime Minister of Canada, May 2005

Introduction

The American government's decision to abandon efforts for a compromise at the United Nations (UN) in the Spring of 2003 and to invade Iraq with a 'coalition of the willing', set off, yet again, commentaries on the condition of the UN, on the idea and practice of multilateralism, and on the value of both as cornerstones of Canadian foreign policy. Multilateralism has been maligned in Canada and more extensively in the wider international community.[1] Within Canada, multilateralism has been criticized for failing to support Canadian interests and for a preoccupation with form over substance. The Canadian government has also been criticized during the past 10–15 years for failing to support its rhetorical commitment to multilateralism with tangible resources.[2] Despite this, the Canadian government continues to provide a considerable amount of support for multilateralism and for the principal institutional forum for multilateralism, the UN. In the late summer of 2005, the government committed its unwavering support to the United Nations and the extensive reform measures proposed by the UN Secretary General Kofi Annan. More specifically, the Canadian government strongly promoted the doctrine of Responsibility to Protect and a UN Peacebuilding Commission. Both of these proposals would legitimate extensive UN involvement in the domestic affairs of member governments. As such they were representative of what Prime Minister Martin referred to as the 'new multilateralism' in his foreword to Canada's 2005 foreign policy statement. The 'new multilateralism' identified by the Prime Minister is not completely new, as there have been comparable murmurings within Canadian policy circles since the early 1990s. As discussed by the Prime Minister, the 'new multilateralism' suggests both a more interventionist set of international institutions as well as the possibility of moving beyond these institutions to intervene, if and when, the institutions fail to act. From this vantage point, the 'new multilateralism' challenges both past practice on the part of foreign policy makers in Canada and longstanding principles of international order.

Canadian support for a multilateralist foreign policy can be traced back many years. Most significantly it emerged as a cornerstone of Canadian foreign policy during and in the immediate aftermath of the Second World War. At the time multilateralism was the lesser evil of the only apparent bilateral options, under the colonial wing of a fading British Empire or as part of the emergent American superpower's sphere of influence. In certain respects, the latter was unavoidable, but multilateral institutions would help restrain the embrace. Multilateralism was, however, more than a way of securing a degree of Canadian independence in a world dominated by more powerful players. Multilateralism was also favoured as a desirable way of organizing international politics. It was an approach to global politics that not only allowed a space for lesser powers to have some input, but also sought to insure

that political principles and practices at the global level would be developed in a manner that would support peace, order, and good governance while protecting the sovereignty and interests of lesser powers. Multilateralism was, as a result, viewed as a foreign policy orientation that would acknowledge and support the sovereign equality (roughly considered) of member states, guaranteeing them both a voice (commensurate with some notion of contribution) and protection from absorption by more powerful states. The multilateral system was in essence a statist one.

Canadian support for multilateralism rested on several important assumptions. Perhaps foremost among these was an assumption that multilateralism was not only compatible with Canadian sovereignty and independence, but would actually reinforce these, pressed as they were by the power and proximity of the United States. It is misleading to argue, as some have done, that the government's support for multilateralism necessarily entailed an abnegation of interests as if this was some sort of altruistic gesture on the part of the Canadian government for the good of the international community. Indeed it was the ability of multilateral initiatives and processes to serve Canadian interest in such an effective manner that enabled multilateralism to achieve such prominence in the discourse and practice of Canadian foreign policy. On the other hand it is wrong to conclude that the support for multilateralism has been nothing more than the blind pursuit of narrowly defined national interests under a façade of community spiritedness. It is apparent that over time and across issues Canada's multilateralist foreign policy has also made a constructive contribution to world order. One of the principle strengths of multilateralism, both as a foreign policy orientation and as a guide for managing world order, is its ability to promote the involvement of a multiplicity of players in a process that provides good opportunities for interests to be pursued and secured in a manner that is widely accepted as legitimate by the participating states.

If this is true, as I would argue it is, then it could be argued, alongside John Holmes that countries such as Canada who have such extensive multilateral connections and commitments, have 'a greater responsibility for making the system work'. Over the past five decades Canadian foreign policy has often been dedicated to doing just that. Starting from the recognition that the country's interests required a stable international system in which Canadians had both opportunities and the necessary capabilities to inject their own views, policy makers favoured institutions that would guarantee Canada a voice. The support of successive Canadian governments for an institutionalized world order based on principles such as state sovereignty, liberal trading practices, and regional security arrangements reflects what Hedley Bull once described as a Grotian view of the world.[3] This is a view that privileges order above other values, in part because order served Canadian interests, but also because order allowed for the pursuit of more substantive goals. These efforts may in part be seen as a sacrifice of principle and a commitment to process over end results. Yet in an environment where the failure of process can also generate a failure to achieve the desired results a concern for process is not inappropriate. This approach, in my view, was based on a belief that the process was not independent of the outcome in two critically important ways. First, that the process of global governance was instrumental in shaping the outcome and certain processes would tend to favour outcomes more likely to meet Canadian objectives than were others. Second, that the process itself was a critically important part of global politics and that to encourage particular processes encouraged a particular form of global politics. It was not so much a matter of form replacing substance as much as a view that form was substance. What has been generally true of Canadian foreign policy is perhaps indicative of the place of lesser powers in an anarchic system dominated by great powers. As Holmes wrote: 'foreign policies of middle powers are inevitably directed not only at the substance

of an issue but also at the means by which they can affect the resolution of that issue. The machinery of world politics is their special concern.'[4] Since the early 1940s Canadian officials have devoted a considerable amount of skill and effort to keep the multilateral machinery working.

For a country of Canada's stature, size, and demography, multilateralism continues to make good sense. It seems at some level obvious that the Canadian government should seek out and support a multilateral framework of international institutions and rules that would provide a degree of order in an otherwise anarchic system, especially an order that is so much in accord with Canadian values and interests. Yet what at one level seems so obvious becomes less clear as one considers both the changing character of that multilateral framework and rules, attitudes, and practices of the country's closest and most important foreign policy partner, the United States.

One of the most significant developments affecting multilateralism has been the clear and at times explicitly vehement opposition to multilateral processes and agreements displayed by the United States government. This is not to deny the fact that the United States government has been under some pressure (both at home and abroad) to try or to be seen to be trying to seek multilateral support for its policy preferences and to seek to bring multilateral agreements in line with American interests.[5] One of the distinguishing features of the immediate post-Second World War environment was the strong US government support given to international institutions. This support has declined dramatically. The reasons are not unimportant but cannot be fully elaborated here. Part of the explanation lies in the unique circumstances that shaped American foreign policy in the 1940s. Other reasons can be found in changing political coalitions in the United States, shifting perceptions and realities of American power, and the growth of ever more intrusive international institutions. The effect has been to make the US government increasingly skeptical of the value of international institutions and less committed to using them or making them more effective. While George W. Bush's current administration is particularly critical of these institutions, it is misleading to see this as simply a reflection of the whims of those presently in power in Washington, for the attitudes are more widespread and deeply seeded in the United States.

This creates a particular difficulty for Canada. For many years working in support of multilateral institutions was fully consistent with maintaining good relations with the United States. Recently, Canadian and American interests have frequently clashed in international institutions over issues such as environmental agreements, the International Criminal Court, and the UN's role in Iraq. International institutions need the support of dominant powers such as the United States and countries such as Canada need institutions that are able to have some influence on the United States. This was one of the primary motivations of Canadian foreign policy in the 1940s. There is no compelling evidence to suggest that this motivation should be any different today. Though the task itself may require a different strategy. In the short term, gaining American support will likely mean changing multilateral institutions more than changing American foreign policy. It will mean insuring that multilateral institutions are not used to isolate the United States and that sincere and constructive efforts be made to reconcile American interests with the work of these institutions.

Other developments in the global arena and in the conduct of Canadian foreign policy have had an effect on the practice of multilateralism and responsibilities of international institutions. There has been a substantial increase in the number of multilateral agreements, institutions, and jurisdictional reach. But these developments are not restricted to trade and are not simply a function of the process of economic globalization. There has also been a proliferation of agreements in other areas such as the environment that act as a constraint on national policies as they seek to impose globally determined standards and prac-

tices. It has been estimated that the number of international treaties has more than tripled since the early 1970s and that the number of institutions has increased by two thirds since 1985. This development poses strains for many governments, but especially for a committed participant such as Canada, whose government has sought to maintain the country's internationalist credentials, not only by signing on to these agreements, but by encouraging many of them.

This is in part a reflection of the changed character of global politics and the increased demands for more substantive forms of governance at the regional and international levels. These developments are best reflected in the expanding agendas of international trade and financial institutions. These developments also reflect a more substantive view of the global order, one that goes beyond the procedural norms of earlier periods and demands more substantive policy changes by states in areas that previously fell within their domestic jurisdictions. Finally, it also reflects an attempt on the part of states to address significant social and economic problems with international level agreements. An examination of the sources of these developments lies beyond the scope of this discussion paper, though it is worth noting that while some lie beyond the Canadian government's ability to control, others have been supported or encouraged by the government. Additionally some fall directly within the control of the government and result from explicit government policies. On their own, and especially in combination, these developments have created a new set of circumstances that affect the role of multilateral processes and institutions in global politics and in the conduct of Canadian foreign policy.

There has been a tendency for much of multilateral activity in recent years to challenge the sovereignty and capacity of states as the principal political agents. One of the most important areas of activity for Canadian foreign policy makers has been in advancing a rules based system governing relations among states. Over time these rules have evolved from procedural rules into more substantive ones that challenge the sovereignty and capacity of states as they seek to regulate relations within states, between governments and their citizens. For some observers, this continues a growing tendency within many quarters to challenge the legitimacy and capacity of states. 'Indeed, in the 1980s and in the early 1990s, scholars began a full-fledged assault on state-centered international politics based on sovereignty. Since that time, new rationales for intervention and expanded conditionalities have been opened up, the increased participation of nongovernmental organizations (NGOs) has been encouraged, and concepts of "global civil society" have been developed. There has been a tendency, in other words, to move away from state-centered views of international relations and toward a more global approach.'[6] Concerns about the implications of challenges to states and about the lack of legitimacy accorded to such challenges have been raised in different quarters. In a commentary on the nature of internationalism in the foreign policies of different countries, including Canada's, Peter Lawler argues '[a]dditionally, the now commonplace concern that a commitment to internationalism necessarily serves to naturalize what are in fact contingent and contestable values rightly recommends a critical posture towards much contemporary internationalist practice, but it also risks the erasure of internationalism as a critical standpoint against the excesses of a neoliberal globalization process and Western neo-imperial pretensions.'[7]

In addition, under emerging practices of global governance, international and regional institutions are assuming increased responsibility for the security and welfare of individuals in various parts of the world. This alters the context in which states must operate. It limits, or at the least questions, their legitimacy at the same time that states have been encouraged to adopt more democratic forms of domestic government. These practices are also expanding the responsibility of the institutions through which global governance is being conducted. It often appears, however, that the aspirations for these institutions to act are

not in line with the political will and the concomitant resource contributions of member governments. To date both internationa governmental organizations (IGOs) and NGOs have repeatedly demonstrated that they lack the capacity to provide welfare and security to people in need. Not only do they lack the necessary resources to make a difference but also often lack the interest, the political will, the legitimacy, and the long-term commitment. Thus, what is problematic, in much of the advocacy and activity surrounding new approaches to global governance, is the tendency to assume that institutions do indeed possess the capacity and will to act. Yet the capacity of institutions is at best, a limited one, influenced by competing interests, and the commitment of supporters. Even the best IGOs and NGOs encounter donor fatigue and a flagging of volunteer spirit. To raise expectations beyond what one is prepared or able to deliver might create a 'false sense of security' and thereby prevent the pursuit or acceptance of a less severe alternative. It might also severely undermine the long-term support for not only specific institutions, but also the very process of multilateralism.

As one embarks on a campaign for global governance one must be sensitive to the limits of both ends and means. For a country such as Canada that has relied extensively on multilateralism and international institutions, these developments carry special significance. Perhaps foremost among these factors is the importance of considering the role that states are to play in securing global order. Governance issues are arguably the most important issue facing the global commons. They also remain critically important at the national level. In the absence of effective governance at the global level and given the pressing demands that encumber states as a result of globalization, emergent international norms, transnational threats, and democratic pressures from within, states throughout the globe are facing significant challenges to their sovereignty.

While the new multilateralism in Canadian foreign policy has done much to further these trends, there are also indications that the government recognizes the necessity to secure a broader base of support for multilateral cooperation and the institutions that sustain it. For example, Prime Minister Martin promoted the idea of a League of Twenty (L20), based on the Group of 20 (G20) Finance Ministers that includes states such as China, India, Brazil, and Indonesia, among others. The L20 proposal reflected a concern for the lack of representation in the Group of 8 (G8) and other international financial institutions. The 'breadth of membership is crucial', Martin stated 'for we have learned a fundamental truth about policies to promote development: they will work only if the developing countries and emerging markets help shape them, because inclusiveness lies at the heart of legitimacy and effectiveness.'[8] The same can be said for other arenas of global governance, and for a country, such as Canada, that sees value in the process as well as the content of multilateralism, it will be important to keep this in mind.

Notes

1. See for example, Frank Harvey, 'Addicted to Security: Globalized Terrorism and the Inevitability of American Unilateralism', *International Journal* 59, 1 (Winter 2003–4): 27.
2. See for example, Michael Ignatieff, 'Canada in the Age of Terror: Multilateralism Meets a Moment of Truth', *Policy Options* (February 2003): 14–18.
3. Hedley Bull, *The Anarchical Society* (Toronto: Macmillan, 1977).
4. John Holmes, *The Better Part of Valour* (Toronto: McClelland and Stewart, 1970), viii.
5. Even Richard Haas, a former State Department official in the Bush administration, has been advocating for a more multilateralist foreign policy for the United States. See *The Opportunity: America's Moment to Alter History's Course* (New York: Public Affairs, 2005).
6. Ngaire Woods, 'Good Governance in International Organizations', *Global Governance* 5, 1 (January–March 1999): 39–62.
7. Peter Lawler, 'The Good State: In Praise of "Classical" Internationalism', *Review of International Studies* 31 (2005): 440.
8. Paul Martin, 'Notes for an Address by the Honourable Paul Martin to the Royal Institute of International Affairs', London, 24 January 2001, (Ottawa: Department of Finance Canada, 2001). Available at http://www.fin.gc.ca/news01/01-009e.html.

2
Three Theoretical Perspectives

David B. Dewitt and John J. Kirton

Despite their differences over themes, interpretations, and values, scholars of Canadian foreign policy share an implicit interest in a single set of fundamental questions about Canada's behaviour in international affairs. These questions have been developed through public debate concerning Canada's role abroad.

The first debate centred on whether Canada should use its new formal freedom from the United Kingdom, attained in the 1931 Statute of Westminster, to sustain the League of Nations, enhance Canada's position as a North American nation, or support Britain in maintaining a broader global balance of power.[1] Although support for this last alternative was reflected in Prime Minister W.L. Mackenzie King's September 1939 decision to enter the Second World War and in Canada's substantial contribution to the Allied cause, the end of the war saw a new debate between those preferring a retreat to quasi-isolationism and those urging active international participation commensurate with Canada's new material strength.[2] The victory of the latter group gave Canada two decades under Prime Ministers Louis St Laurent, John Diefenbaker, and Lester Pearson during which the precepts of liberal internationalism evolved. The 1968 election of

Prime Minister Pierre Trudeau's Liberal government began a new debate about whether Canada was reverting to the isolationist and continental instincts of the interwar era, modifying its internationalist traditions to reflect new circumstances, or defining a new approach to Canadian behaviour abroad.[3]

Out of this debate has emerged the need for a more explicit, rigorous, and comprehensive analytical framework for the study of Canadian foreign policy. By drawing upon the literature of Canadian foreign policy, general foreign policy analysis, and international relations, it is possible to identify the most fundamental questions about Canada's international behaviour.[4]

Based on the thesis that a country's external activities and international presence are related to its size and capabilities—population, resources, and specialized skills and knowledge—a central question for students of international affairs and foreign policy has been to determine the relationship between these attributes and international behaviour. In the Canadian context, a postwar issue has been whether Canada's attributes are sufficient to propel it from its former status as a minor actor through small- and middle-power ranking to a more prominent place in the community of nation-states. In the shadow first of the United Kingdom and more recently of the United States, Canada has been perceived as a regional power without a region, and recognized as a middle-range partner in the Western coalition. One set of questions relating to this issue concerns Canada's historic position, or *rank*, in the hierarchy of the international system; the next questions provide the explanatory focus for Canada's *activity*, *association*, and *approach to world order*, examining the relative significance of *external*, *societal*, and *governmental* determinants.

The Central Questions of Foreign Policy Analysis

INTERNATIONAL PRESENCE
Rank

Virtually all students of foreign policy begin their explorations with a perception of a state's historical experience. Formulated into models that may try to account for the past, these evolutionary myths are partly the inherited results of exposure to particular historical traditions, partly ideological or philosophic orientations conditioning one's interpretations of evidence, and partly crude summations of easily measurable attributes. Yet in most cases, they are grounded in an underlying conception of whether the state's capacity to pursue its national interests—most basically, self-help in a competitive international system—is being diminished, maintained, or expanded over time.[5]

What is Canada's place in the international system relative to that of other states? The concern with defining Canada's position was heightened by its leading international stature at the end of Second World War, when a newly emerging world order was being shaped out of the ruins of global conflict. Canada's ability to influence these efforts was seen as linked directly to its ascribed status. In the study of international relations, this focus on a state's rank has been sustained by mounting evidence of the salience of national capabilities in determining foreign policy behaviour.[6]

The question of rank includes the state's relative capability, as measured by a standard set of objective attributes such as population size and distribution, indigenous fuel supplies, and size of standing armed forces. It is also concerned with the position that it ascribes to itself and that it asserts internationally, and with the acknowledged status ascribed to it by other international actors.[7] It includes the consistency of these elements across varying international systemic configurations, geographic regions, substantive issue areas, and critical power resources.[8] And it is based on the state's maintenance of minimum levels of performance in meeting the basic requisites of statehood—notably security, sovereignty, and legitimacy.[9]

INTERNATIONAL BEHAVIOUR
Activity

The importance of a state's international ranking—both ascribed and achieved—is based upon the hypothesized relationship between rank and externally oriented behaviour.[10] The primary aspect of a state's behaviour is the activity it directs towards other actors in the international realm. Concern here centres on the *degree* of a state's activity, or the simple volume of interaction it has with its 'targets' abroad; the *variety* of this activity, or the similarity across time, issues, and targets in the volume and intensity of action; and the *diffusion* of this activity among targets abroad.[11]

Association

Association is the intersection of one state's external activities with those of another, and includes the question of *initiative*—the extent to which the state maintains its membership in an existing group, participates in forming a new or altered group, or acts without direct reference to any group. It embraces a country's *commitment*—the time, resources, and effort expended to produce similarity between the country's own position and the group position. And it contains the element of *focus*, or the extent to which the central target of the country's activity lies within or outside existing or emerging groups.[12] Characterized by degrees of conflict and co-operation, association can be measured by the extent to which a country's activity is similar in time, content, and target to that of other states.

Approach to world order

Also relevant is a state's attempt to foster a global order in which relationships are organized into regimes and institutions that promote a particular distribution of political power and economic resources.[13] The first aspect is the *degree* to which the state considers that order should be registered in a comprehensive, well-developed, interrelated, and autonomous network of international organization and law. A subsequent aspect is that of scope, that is, the extent to which a state seeks to ensure that international order, at all levels of institutionalization, has the full, active participation of all members of the state system, and embraces a broad range of subjects. A third aspect is *transformation,* the extent to which a state supports moderate, specific alternatives or more permanent alterations in the structure of existing and emerging regimes and organizations.

DETERMINANTS OF INTERNATIONAL BEHAVIOUR
External determinants

To explain a country's particular pattern of activity, association, and quest for order, most scholars focus on the stimuli that a country receives from states and organizations abroad, whether or not these are directed at it. Their initial interest centres on the *relative salience* of this external environment—the extent of variation in a state's foreign policy behaviour caused by these states and organizations as compared to the variations explained by forces at home.[14] A further concern is the *scope* of relevant external determinants—the number and range of states and international organizations with a direct impact on a state's foreign policy behaviour. A third issue deals with a state's *sensitivity* to external stimuli—the immediacy, directness, and specificity with which exter-

nal events and conditions affect the decisions of leaders and the behaviour they authorize.[15] Finally, interest centres on *actor relevance*—the identity of those particular major powers, groupings of middle and smaller powers, and leading international organizations that have the most salient, wide-ranging, and immediate impact on a state's foreign policy behaviour.

Societal determinants

A similar set of questions arises in regard to domestic influences on a state's international behaviour.[16] The *relative salience* of domestic organizations is of fundamental concern, as is the issue of the *scope* of societal actors—the extent of differentiated, specialized, and autonomous nongovernmental institutions that have a direct impact on foreign policy behaviour.[17] Further aspects are the *sensitivity* of the government to these organizations and the *relevance* of particular actors, notably Parliament, political parties, interest groups, labour, media, business communities, and provincial governments. Also of importance is the country's profile of population, resources, and technology and the impact of these critical factors on the structure and activity of societal actors.

Governmental determinants

The final set of questions addresses the influence of the executive branch of a state's central government on foreign policy making and ensuing behaviour.[18] The central questions remain the relative overall *salience* of governmental factors, the *scope* of institutional differentiation and autonomy, the state's *sensitivity* to its foreign policy process, and the *relevance* of specific governmental actors.[19] Attention is directed at the relevance of the prime minister and his closest associates, the government's foreign office, and especially the domestically oriented departments and agencies responsible for critical changes in the state's pattern of growth in population, resources, and technology.[20] The complexity of the modern state requires that attention be given to the central foreign policy co-ordinative structures and processes in attempts to define autonomously and implement overarching conceptions of the national interest.[21]

Table 2.1 provides a schematic overview of the seven basic foreign policy questions and the predictions of each of the three theoretical perspectives.

The Complex Neo-Realist Perspective

Preoccupied with the powerful challenge that peripheral dependence presents to liberal internationalism, students of Canadian foreign policy have devoted relatively little attention to the possible relevance of a third interpretive perspective, one derived from the realist theory that has dominated the study of international relations as a whole. As expressed in the major work of its most popular proponent, Hans Morgenthau, classic realism highlights the ceaseless interplay among great powers preoccupied with maximizing their military security by manipulating the balance of power to secure a fragile stability within an international system characterized by anarchy.[22] It portrays this central theme of the history of international relations as a cyclical pattern in which the short-term stability produced by a balance of power is followed by a breakdown of this equilibrium, leading to war and the creation of a new transitory balance. It focuses almost exclusively on the small set of great powers involved in arranging the balance, the military security interests that motivate their activity, the conflictual quest for advantage relieved only by temporary military alliances, and the structure of the resulting balance of power as the only form of order that a context of anarchy allows.

Given the fundamental fact of anarchy, states are portrayed as giving predominant weight to external determinants, as each is preoccupied with monitoring and adjusting to shifts in the balance abroad. Neither societal nor governmental processes are given significance as determinants, since they are forced by the requirements of the security dilemma to be aggregated in advance, within the impermeable shell of the sovereign state, as 'factors of national power' and 'quality of leadership', respectively.

This standard realist portrait has had little appeal to students of Canadian foreign policy, for several reasons. Generally, it seemed intuitively irrelevant to the dilemmas of a newer country, beset internally by regional and ethnic cleavages and foreign penetration, preoccupied by a full array of nation-building imperatives, and confronted externally with the necessities of managing interdependencies in collaboration with like-minded but vastly more powerful neighbours. More precisely, preoccupation with security dilemmas, military interests, and the instruments of force appeared secondary to practitioner and scholar alike. For both, armed conflict had been an intermittent, somewhat discretionary concern, always conducted in association with larger external powers, and aimed centrally at sustaining the systems of deterrence within which the primary tasks of foreign policy were pursued.

Realist precepts seemed to be further contradicted by the fundamental features of Canada's historic emergence as a nation. Until well after the First World War, Canada's external *vision* had been affected by a profound and practical attachment to a stable and benign British imperial system.[23] During the interwar period, in a deliberate effort to distinguish themselves from the United Kingdom and the central European system, Canadian leaders eagerly embraced a North American identity defined by the very absence of power politics and by the invention of a uniquely co-operative and peaceful form of international relations.[24] And after Second World War, the very tenacity with which American leaders adopted realism as a justification for their policy of global containment engendered skepticism on the part of Canadian leaders, armed with the legacy of distinctive visions and experienced in detaching themselves from the doctrines and accompanying demands of their imperial leaders abroad.

Table 2.1   Theoretical Perspectives on Canadians Foreign Policy: Predictions Based on Ideal Types

Foreign Policy Questions	Liberal Internationalism	Peripheral Dependence	Complex Neo-Realism
International Presence			
1. Rank	Middle power	Small, penetrated power	Principal power
International Behaviour			
2. Activity			
Degree	Active participation	Low interaction	Global involvement
Variety	Responsible Participation	Undifferentiated Interactive	Interest-based Involvement
Diffusion	Multiple participation	Imperial-focused Interaction	Autonomous bilateral involvement
3. Association			
Initiative	combination	adherence	unilateralism
Commitment	consensus	acquiescence	divergence
Focus	constraint	support	diversification
4. Approach to World Order			
Degree	moderate institutionalization	existing institutionalization	revised institutionalization
Scope	multilateralization	hegemony and marginal universalism	concert
Transformation	reformation	marginal redistribution	modification
Determinants of International Behaviour			
5. External Determinants			
Relative Salience	moderate	high	low
Scope	moderate	low	high
Sensitivity	moderate	low	high
Actor Relevance			
United Kingdom	moderate	high	low
United States	moderate	high	low
USSR	moderate	low	high
China	moderate	low	high
Large European States and Japan	moderate	low	high
Non-European Middle Powers	high	low	moderate
Small European States	high	low	moderate
Other Small States	high	low	moderate
NATO	moderate	low	high
United Nations	high	Low	moderate

. . . continued

Table 2.1   *Continued*

Foreign Policy Questions	Liberal Internationalism	Peripheral Dependence	Complex Neo-Realism
6. Societal Determinants			
Relative Salience	moderate	low	high
Scope			
Institutional Differentiation	moderate	low	high
Institutional Autonomy	moderate	low	high
Sensitivity	moderate	low	high
Actor Relevance			
Parliament	high	low	moderate
Parties	high	low	moderate
Associational Interest Groups	moderate	low	high
Labour	moderate	low	high
Media	low	moderate	high
Business Community	low	moderate	high
Provincial Governments	low	high	moderate
Critical Capabilities	resources and technology	resources	population, resources, and technology
7. Governmental Determinants			
Relative Salience	moderate	low	high
Scope			
Institutional Differentiation	moderate	low	high
Institutional Autonomy	moderate	low	high
Sensitivity	moderate	low	high
Actor Relevance			
Prime Ministerial Group	moderate	low	high
Department of External Affairs	high	low	moderate
Foreign Service Departments	low	moderate	high
Other Domestic Departments	low	moderate	high
Agencies and Crown Corporations	low	moderate	high
Central Foreign Policy			
Co-ordinative Structures	moderate	low	high

To the attitudes of heritage was added an accident of history. It was the fate of the modern phase in the study of Canadian foreign policy to emerge at a time when the dominant actor in the international system, the United States, was itself moving beyond the immediate demands of the security dilemma, and when the precepts of realism were beginning to lose their intellectual appeal.[25] At the outset of the 1960s, the emergence of an apparent bipolar stability, confirmed by the outcome of the Berlin and Cuban crises, provided American scholars and their Canadian counterparts with the vision of a system in which security was assured in the short term, rendered permanent by the new nuclear balance, and superseded by the tasks of enhancing abroad a range of values formerly perceived as subordinate.[26] In such a mood, there was little incentive to continue debates about Canada's precise role in North American defence and nuclear deterrence or general concerns about its place in a North Atlantic alliance.[27] Realism seemed to have little to offer the student of Canadian foreign policy.

As America's global dominance faced new challenges in the late 1960s, so too did the precepts of standard realism. The emerging dynamics of global politics provided an empirical foundation for a renewed interest in a realist theory considerably more complex, as were the dilemmas it addressed.[28]

The 'complex neo-realist' perspective begins by accepting the fundamental premise of standard realism: the primacy of politics. It sees separate states pursuing distinctive interests in an international milieu in which no natural harmony of interests exists. Its new contribution is the emphasis it places on the prevalence of international order—tentatively defined by the convergence of the interests of principal actors leading to an emerging stable global system, but still grounded in the values of an internationally predominant power.[29] Most importantly, it highlights the complex constellation of interests and values that states and nonstate actors in such an ascendant, system-defining position are able to pursue.[30]

Complex neo-realism thus focuses on the role of hegemonic powers in ensuring, defining, and extending international order in a system in which universal values remain secondary, in which a common security calculus and interest in balance provide no substitute, and in which leadership is required to transform convergent interests into stable order.[31] It sees the history of international relations characterized by the rise to positions of international primacy of a succession of hegemonic powers, with periods of balance among roughly equal powers as relatively rare, temporary, and particular to periods in which one state has lost its hegemony before another has emerged.[32] And in the critical transition from balance to hegemony, it highlights the way in which order may be defined by a concert of principal powers.

Collectively substituting for states exercising individual hegemony, such 'principal powers' are not merely the familiar great powers of realist theory.[33] Rather they are principal states in three senses. First, they are the states in the international hierarchy that stand at the top of the international status ranking, collectively possessing decisive capability and differentiated from lower-ranking powers by both objective and subjective criteria. Secondly, they act as principals in their international activities and associations, rather than as agents for other states or groupings or as mediators between principals. And thirdly, they have a principal role in establishing, specifying, and enforcing international order.

At the heart of a state's position as a principal power is its possession of surplus capability: a margin of strength in a broad array of sectors well beyond that required to meet the basic requisites of statehood and the minimal performance expected of modern states.[34] Surplus capability relieves principal powers from the tyranny of responding to short-term security dilemmas and provides them with the luxury of basing their international behaviour on the outcomes of political debates within their societies and on the definitions provided by their state apparatus. Surplus capability thus provides such states the discretion to act autonomously, on the basis of internal choices, on a global stage. Such choices derive not from an exclusive or predominant concern with security but from a multiplicity of values in which priority is given to those political interests that integrate, assign weights to, and provide coherence to specific concerns of military, economic, social, and cultural spheres.[35] This configuration of internal values is embedded in a historically evolved and distinctive array of specialized capabilities, which channels the external activity of a principal power and renders it competitive with those of its counterpart.[36] Surplus and specialized capability together enable principal powers to define the characteristics of international order in a way that disproportionately reflects their distinctive values and to extend that order, and hence their values, into member states throughout the international system.[37]

Traditionally, scholars of Canadian foreign policy have not conceived of their country as having the capabilities or performing the functions of a principal power. Yet, led by key individuals within the state apparatus, they have begun in the past two decades to develop from themes that move in that direction.[38] The first such theme, developed from 1960 to 1968, was a thrust towards globalism, especially significant because of the intent to employ aid as an instrument to advance specifically Canadian interests worldwide, on a bilateral basis, Canada extended its formal diplomatic presence to all regions and major capitals in the world, dealt with quite distinctive cultural groupings, and supplemented conventional diplomacy by the deliberate use of such new techniques as cultural relations and development assistance.[39]

The most dramatic manifestation was the programmatic and geographic expansion of Canada's development assistance. Constituting the major division between the distributive thrust of liberal internationalism and the globalist thrust of complex neo-realism, this transition was initiated in the 1960s when significant Canadian aid began to be deployed in specific francophone countries for the domestic political purpose of meeting the challenges to Canadian foreign policy from Quebec and France.

A second major theme, which emerged from 1968 to 1971, advocated an interest-based initiation of external behaviour. Rejecting the reactiveness that they thought characterized Canadian foreign policy in the Pearsonian approach, dissatisfied domestic critics and officials of the new Trudeau government sought to ensure that the Canadian government would be capable of discerning future trends at home and abroad, identifying their impact on Canadian interests, and formulating policies in advance, enabling Canada to withstand the impact of forces from abroad and thereby maximize its self-determined interests. This emphasis presumed both a direct focus on national interests as the basis for policy calculation and the initiation of policies and programs having little direct dependence on the international situation at the time.[40] In its initial form, this theme of internationally projected values offered the image of a 'new' Canada whose policies—concerned with such values as bilingualism, ethnic relations, federalism, techniques of parliamentary government, income redistribution, and environmental protection—provided an example for other states to emulate and a foundation for Canadian behaviour abroad. And after 1973 it was enriched by an emphasis on a third major theme: the way in which unique Canadian assets—deriving from its small, diverse, skilled population, extensive resource base, and developed technology—gave Canada a more active role in defining a new international order based on these values.[41]

The emergence of these major themes of principal-power capability and behaviour are logically based on a series of premises and precepts that address the seven central questions of foreign policy analysis from the perspective of complex neo-realism. In application to Canada's post-Second

World War foreign policy experience, this begins with a view, similar to the other perspectives, of an international system characterized by the disappearance, over the years 1945 to 1957, of the United Kingdom's hegemonic legacy and its replacement by an American hegemony. However, in contrast to liberal internationalism and peripheral dependence, complex neo-realism sees the key factor as the erosion of the hegemonic position of the US from 1968 onward.[42] Canada's international experience is seen as one of secular, sustained development, reflected most profoundly in its steadily increasing ability to define, advance, secure, and legitimize distinctive national interests and values in a competitive process with adversaries and associates.[43]

In response to the question of international rank, the complex neo-realist perspective portrays Canada, particularly since 1968, as an ascending principal power in an increasingly diffuse, nonhegemonic international system.[44] Placed in the context of the most prevalent global configuration—a top tier of eight powers, with an average of seven involved in the central, European-based system, and nine on a global basis if the central and peripheral systems are combined—Canada is argued to be part of the classically defined 'top tier' group.[45]

In addition to a location in this configuration, principal powers have three specific characteristics. The first is a rank roughly comparable to other states in the top range, unexcelled by states outside it, and closer to those within than to outside states immediately below.[46] The second is a set of organizations and instruments sufficient to help deter significant direct assaults on its homeland and to provide a strategic presence abroad. The third consists of special rights in determining and preserving international order in political, military, and economic spheres, together with distinctive values and sufficiently strong influence to attract the attention of other principals and to help define the orientation of some lesser states.

With these criteria, the complex neo-realist argument asserts that Canada's objective capability—grounded in the relative size, breadth, and diversity of its natural resources, advanced technology, and skilled population and in other standard calculations of national power—places it predominantly within the top tier of the system.[47] Canada's designated rank is reinforced by its involvement in groupings composed of members drawn exclusively or predominantly from this top tier.[48] While acknowledging Canada's lack of independent nuclear and conventional military deterrence, complex neo-realism recognizes that Canada's military capability at home and abroad directly contributes to strategic stability in several critical regions. Moreover, it assigns Canada a prominent position within the top tier in defining and managing global regimes in major issue areas, and leadership within a distinctive grouping or network of lesser states on such questions.[49]

The degree, variety, and diffusion of Canada's external activities provide the initial indication of aspects of its international behaviour that characterizes it as an emerging principal power. The degree of Canadian activity is expressed by the maintenance of permanent political involvement in virtually all regions, sectors, and forums of world politics. Such global involvement is registered in the consistently high volume of interactions that Canada exchanges with a large number of actors abroad. Grounded in a need to manage continuously a state's immediate, direct, durable interests, global involvement arises when several relatively stringent conditions are met: the existence of societal actors sufficiently powerful to influence behaviour and critical security interests or commitments; the presence of a full range of concerns and values that give the international behaviour additional significance; the recognition that behaviour be based at least partly on state-specific interests, vulnerabilities, and values, rather than universal doctrines; and the desire of partner countries to maintain the involvement.

From these conditions, the variety of activity

is defined as one of interest-based involvement predicated on the distinctively national interests and values previously identified as the touchstone of Canadian participation. Canadian policy and behaviour are likely to exhibit some inconsistency over time and across issues as officials also seek to make their contributions in the context of past efforts while maintaining congruence with the accumulated expectations and interests of others. Such activity may appear as a large number of highly complex patterns quite distinct from one another, irregular and seemingly unpredictable as a variety of interests and decision strategies compete.

As a further consequence of Canada's global behaviour, the diffusion of activity is seen as a tendency towards autonomous bilateral involvement. Reflecting the need to develop and maintain direct ties worldwide, distinctive effort is made on specific state-to-state relations while relatively less involvement occurs with international organizations having universal membership. In this mode, new and multiple membership, concern with balance across affiliations, and stress on fluidity assume lesser prominence. Priority is given to employing the state's resources in servicing the particular interest of each specific bilateral relationship. In practice, this suggests a more full and equal association with a larger number of non-universal organizations and, more importantly, the development of direct bilateral relations with groups and actors beyond the Anglo-American sphere. More specifically, in this thrust bilateral diplomatic representation on a resident basis is given and received with most actors, posts acquire a 'multiprogram' character, regular visits by heads of government increase, and joint organizations are formed with regional bodies and individual countries.

From the complex neo-realist perspective, this tendency towards global, interest-based, bilateral activity is supplemented by associative behaviour characterized by a set of competitive orientations: a predisposition towards unilateral initiatives, a divergence in policy commitment, and a diversi-

fication of focus away from any associated imperial state. Emphasizing unilateral initiatives, Canada's diplomatic behaviour does not necessarily concentrate on inducing other states to act, does not require their active co-operation, passive support, or subsequent imitation for success, and is therefore not heavily dependent on calculations of their likely behaviour for its initiation. In short, this diplomatic behaviour is not a heavily context-dependent attempt to preserve or engender co-operative arrangements, but a self-motivated effort to operate within the confines of the existing system to national advantage. A desire to act primarily with equivalent states, on the one hand, and to maintain relatively exclusive spheres of influence, on the other, reinforces this emphasis on selective involvement of other actors as dictated by each issue.

The second competitive tendency, divergence, is reflected in actions in which relatively little effort is made to ensure consistency with the actions of other states and in which dissimilar actions often result. Positions may be taken at variance with those of members in existing groups, and sometimes this exercise of leadership will initiate a new grouping. Little emphasis is given to offsetting the weight of given bloc or eroding bloc cleavages. As a result, Canada often adopts positions on major issues discrepant with those of traditionally associated states.

The third and most significant competitive tendency is that of diversification, manifested in active efforts to concentrate behaviour on actors other than an associated imperial power or its groups, with the aim of obtaining alternative sources of resources such as information, markets, investment, and general political support. In particular, it involves a deliberate attempt to forge relations and assume compatible positions with other states that are roughly equivalent in status or even more powerful and thus capable of serving as a substitute for, or rival to, the traditional imperial power. Diversification rests on the belief that in the absence of such action, existing behavioural domination by the prevailing imperial power would continue, that this is not in Canada's interest, that Canada has the power to force a more acceptable balance by itself, and that this effort can be sustained even in the face of active opposition from the imperial power.

In overseas relations, the rivalry induced by diversification is constrained somewhat by the fundamental responsibility of all major powers to preserve a general balance of power and reduce the likelihood of war. However, these tasks are performed by individual as well as collective actions, rest on negotiated settlements among equals more than on compromises forwarded or facilitated by other parties, and provide only an overarching framework in which major power interests are pursued in a competitive fashion. Within this framework, diversification engenders the establishment of co-operative relationships with other major or emerging powers as an alternative to its affiliation with an associated imperial power. At that point the process may extend into an intensive and increasingly competitive relationship in which Canada becomes involved in the internal political processes of its new partner, incompatible interests become apparent, and diplomatic conflict results. Alternatively, the continuation and reinforcement of a close, co-operative relationship may result in an effort at counterweight, in which the new partner is deliberately invoked as an ally directly against the preferences of the previous imperial power.

Canada's pursuit of diversification within North America breeds an emphasis on arm's-length diplomacy. Bilateral relations with the United States resemble those between any two sovereign states, with unified governments, formally equal while differing in objective, formulating national positions in advance, guarding information, and seeking to outmanoeuvre adversaries, link issues, and dominate policy implementation. Within Canada itself, the corresponding value of an autonomous society prompts a reliance on strategies that prohibit outright further American penetration and actively reduce the existing America presence.

In an emerging principal power, in the complex neo-realist view, the defence of national interests and the promotion of distinctive values engender a strong incentive to follow and promote a detailed conception of world order compatible with its purposes. The first manifestation of this incentive is an active effort to revise the existing patterns of international institutionalization. Believing that such frameworks preserve old values and inhibit emergent powers from securing equality with their established counterparts, these states reduce their verbal and material support for the standard set of international institutions, seek to forge alternative organizations or informal groupings, and forge alliances with new states that have attained success within the existing order. Moreover, efforts to promote a well-developed, highly autonomous, and fully consistent structure of international law are reduced, on the grounds that such constructions introduce rigidities that impede the process of revision.

A second component of a complex neo-realist approach to world order is the promotion of principal-power concerts through the creation of groupings in which effective participation is restricted to states within the top tier, and more particularly to states with a rank equal to or greater than one's own. Premised on the recognition of Canada's principal-power rank and claims, this tendency is directed at strengthening the distinction between groups made up exclusively of principal powers and mixed groups of principal and lesser powers, and increasingly transferring important questions from the latter into the former, in the interests of a more rapid and realistic revision and more effective management of the international order.

Modification of the existing international order in keeping with its distinctive interests and values is the third criterion of a principal power's approach to world order. Accepting the basic legitimacy of those structures that allowed it to ascend to principal-power status, Canada devotes few resources to conducting direct, comprehensive assaults on the formal framework of existing institutions. Yet, in an attempt to rein-force its new position, it seeks to forge alliances with those who have manipulated the existing system successfully, and who are likely candi-dates for major-power status in the near future. And in an effort to register the particular contri-bution it can make to the management of the global system and to secure the support of emerging powers who sustain its position, it for-wards distinctive conceptions of what a new international order should be.

Implicit in complex neo-realist writing is the assumption that these action tendencies and doc-trines are sustained by an external environment rather more open and less concentrated than in the classical formulation. This configuration, when combined with Canada's principal-power status, reduces to a low level the overall salience of the external environment, disperses its influ-ence across a wide number of states, and endows a multitude of states with a noticeable, if minor, impact on Canadian behaviour. Thus complex neo-realism assigns the 'imperial' actors—the United Kingdom and the United States—a significantly reduced role in providing a stimu-lus, framework, and referent for Canadian behav-iour. At the same time it allows the major European powers and Japan, the Soviet Union, and China a relatively high impact, not only by providing a broader affiliation to balance Canada's relations with the United States but also in serving as comparable, autonomous actors in their own right.

The significant weight attached to the posi-tions and initiatives of these major states reduce to a moderate level the significance of the smaller European and overseas middle powers as associ-ates of Canada in international diplomacy and as a factor when Canada undertakes autonomous action. Within this sphere, attention shifts from states with a historical relationship with Canada to those with similar sociocultural attributes or convergent population, resource, and technology characteristics and to those emerging into the major-power realm. Finally the United Nations,

as the institutional codification of an increasingly obsolete pattern of international relations, declines to a moderate position as an influence on Canadian behaviour, while the North Atlantic Treaty Organization (NATO), a more restricted body with a direct role in security and in defining systems, experiences an offsetting increase.[50] Moreover, a much greater influence is enjoyed by such new, restricted-membership, task-specific bodies as la Francophonie, the Namibia Contact Group within the Security Council, the Organization for Economic Co-operation and Development, the International Energy Agency, the London Suppliers Group on nuclear materi-als, and the Western Economic Summits held since 1975.

A complex neo-realist orientation perceives the domestic environment as being marked by the emergence of highly salient, ongoing disputes over foreign policy issues, grounded in the inter-est of autonomous major organizations through-out the national society. The high importance of domestic organizations rests in the first instance on the likelihood that the country's possession of a surplus margin of capability allows for and prompts an effective debate within society about the purposes for which that power should be employed. Furthermore, the existence of routine global involvements by societal organizations increases the number of actors whose primary interests are affected by foreign affairs, who pos-sess direct, specialized international expertise, and who thus have legitimate, divergent perspec-tives about the best course to pursue. Moreover, the stress on national interest and initiative emphasizes the desirability of considering domes-tic sources and taking the time for domestic actors to mobilize, organize, and debate. Together these factors produce a domestic process that, in conformity with a pluralist conception of politics, contains a highly developed set of differentiated institutions, each autonomously defining and pursuing specific interests among societal com-petitors and organizations in the external and governmental realm. Thus, Canada's international behaviour becomes highly sensitive to such societal factors.

The depth and durability of these societal interests give the overtly political and directly accessible institutions—Parliament and the party system—only a moderate role in influencing government behaviour. In contrast, associational interest groups, labour, the media, and the business community all enjoy a high degree of influence, in keeping with the precepts of interest-group theory. Finally, provincial governments possess a moderate degree of influence. The result is a highly dispersed and evenly balanced process, in which all types of institutions and those organizations whose strength is based on population, resource, or technological capabilities have substantial impact.

Within the executive branch of the federal government, complex neo-realism predicts the existence of a decision-making process resembling bureaucratic politics, but one in which strong central co-ordinative mechanisms operate to produce overall order. The decision-making process of government is viewed as highly salient in foreign policy behaviour, resulting from the vigorous debate taking place among a well-developed constellation of organizational subunits capable of registering their missions with considerable specificity. Within this constellation, a rel-

atively moderate influence is assigned to the Department of External Affairs and its career foreign service officer corps, and a high degree of influence, in contrast, is assigned to other foreign service departments and domestic departments. Exercising dominant influence are those within the prime ministerial group and in the central foreign policy co-ordinative structures closest to it, given their role in defining overarching values and the overall national interest. Indeed, great emphasis is placed on the emergence of a large, highly specialized, and tightly controlled set of such co-ordinative structures as a means for integrating and transcending the multitude of powerful competing missions within the government and competing interests within domestic society. Therefore, Canadian foreign policy behaviour is argued to be, in the context of complex neo-realism, highly sensitive to key governmental actors but durable, interrelated, and comprehensive nonetheless.

These three theoretical perspectives on Canadian foreign policy provide our entry into the study of Canada's postwar international behaviour. Determinations about the usefulness, accuracy, and validity of each one must be made in the context of the empirical record, not on an *a priori* basis.

Notes

1. R.A. MacKay and E.B. Rogers, *Canada Looks Abroad* (Don Mills, ON: Oxford University Press, 1938). See also Robert Bothwell and Norman Hillmer, eds, *The In-Between Time: Canadian External Policy in the 1930s* (Toronto: Copp Clark, 1975). The most authoritative history of this period is contained in C.P. Stacey, *Canada and the Age of Conflict, Vol. 1, 1867–1921* (Toronto: Macmillan, 1977), and *Vol. 2, 1921–1948* (Toronto: University of Toronto Press, 1981).

2. John W. Holmes, *The Shaping of Peace: Canada and the Search for World Order, 1943–1957*, 2 vols (Toronto: University of Toronto Press, 1979, 1982).

On the move towards the war and its legacy, see James Eayrs, *In Defence of Canada*, 4 vols (Toronto: University of Toronto Press, 1964, 1965, 1972, 1980).

3. See Dale Thomson and Roger Swanson, *Canadian Foreign Policy: Options and Perspectives* (Toronto: McGraw-Hill Ryerson, 1971); Peter Dobell, *Canada's Search For New Roles: Foreign Policy in the Trudeau Era* (Don Mills, ON: Oxford University Press, 1972); Peyton V. Lyon, 'A Review of the Review', *Journal of Canadian Studies* 5 (May 1970): 34–47; Lyon, 'The Trudeau Doctrine', *International Journal* 26, 1 (Winter 1970–1): 19–43; James

Hyndman, 'National Interest and the New Look', *International Journal* 26 (Winter 1970–1): 5–8; and Kal Holsti, *Proceedings of the Standing Committee on External Affairs and National Defence*, Statement no. 7, 19 July 1971.

4. The most influential framework provided by students of general foreign policy analysis is presented in James N. Rosenau, 'Pre-theories and Theories of Foreign Policy', in R.B. Farrell, ed., *Approaches to Comparative and International Politics* (Evanston, IL: Northwestern University Press, 1966), 27–92. For a view of the development and application of this framework, see Patrick McGowan and Howard Shapiro, *The Comparative Study of Foreign Policy: A Survey of Scientific Findings* (Beverly Hills, CA: Sage Publications, 1973); and James N. Rosenau, ed., *Comparing Foreign Policies: Theories, Findings and Methods* (Toronto: John Wiley & Sons, 1974).

5. The prevalence of such myths and models in the social sciences is noted, by specific example, in Larry Ward et al., 'World Modelling: Some Critical Foundations', *Behavioral Sciences* 23 (May 1978): 135–47. The major traditions in Canadian historical writing are discussed in Carl Berger, ed., *Approaches to Canadian History* (Toronto: University of Toronto Press, 1967); and Berger, *The Writing of Canadian History: Aspects of English-Canadian Historical Writing: 1900 to 1970* (Don Mills, ON: Oxford University Press, 1976). A brief portrait of the implicit models on the writing on Canadian foreign policy is offered in John W. Holmes, 'After 25 Years', *International Journal* 26, 1 (Winter 1970–1): 1–4.

6. Kal Holsti, *International Politics: A Framework for Analysis*, 3rd ed. (Englewood Cliffs, NJ: Prentice-Hall, 1977), 390; Maurice East and Charles Hermann, 'Do Nation-Types Account for Foreign Policy Behaviour?' in Rosenau, ed., *Comparing Foreign Policies*, 269–303.

7. The best treatment of the classic formulations of relative capability, position, and status is provided in Martin Wight, *Power Politics* (Harmondsworth, England: Penguin, 1979). For modern extensions and applications, see Klaus Knorr, 'Notes on the Analysis of National Capabilities', in James N.

Rosenau et al., eds, *The Analysis of International Relations* (New York: Free Press, 1972); Knorr, *The Power of Nations: The Political Economy of International Relations* (New York: Basic Books, 1975); and Ray Cline, *World Power Trends and US Foreign Policy for the 1980s* (Boulder, CO: Westview Press, 1980). Recent applications to individual states include Ezra Vogel, *Japan as Number One: Lessons for America* (Cambridge, MA: Harvard University Press, 1979); and Wolfram Hanrieder, 'Germany as Number Two? The Foreign and Economic Policy of the Federal Republic', *International Studies Quarterly* 26 (March 1982): 57–86. Yet to appear is a piece in this tradition arguing the case for 'Canada as Number Seven'.

8. See K.N. Waltz, *Theory of International Politics* (Reading, MA: Addison-Wesley, 1979); Charles Pentland, 'The Regionalization of World Politics: Concepts and Evidence', *International Journal* 30, 4 (Autumn 1975): 599–630; William Zimmerman, 'Issue Area and Foreign Policy Process: A Research Note in Search of a General Theory', *American Political Science Review* 67 (December 1973): 1204–12; William C. Porter, 'Issue Area and Foreign Policy Analysis', *International Organization* 34 (Summer 1980): 405–28; A.F.K. Organski, *World Politics,* 2nd ed. (New York: Knopf, 1968); and W.W. Rostow, *The World Economy* (Austin: University of Texas Press, 1978).

9. Following the treatment in Joseph Frankel, *International Relations in a Changing World* (Don Mills, ON: Oxford University Press, 1979), 8–27, security is defined as the possession of defined, externally recognized boundaries unlikely to be changed in the short term by outside force. Sovereignty is defined as the capacity of the central government to enforce its jurisdiction and preserve the identity of its major societal institutions, and legitimacy as its ability to attract regularly high degrees of voluntary compliance from its citizenry.

10. The three basic categories of externally oriented behaviour are formed by viewing state behaviour at progressively higher levels of analysis: activity (acting state), association (state in interaction with other states), and order (system of interacting

states). Each of these categories is divided in turn by the three stages of behaviour offered in events data analysis: emission, transmission, and reception or impact. See J. David Singer, 'The Level of Analysis Problem in International Relations', in Klaus Knorr and Sidney Verba, eds, *The International System: Theoretical Essays* (Princeton, NJ: Princeton University Press, 1961), 77–92; and Charles Hermann, 'What Is a Foreign Policy Event?' in Wolfram Hanrieder, ed., *Comparative Foreign Policy: Theoretical Essays* (New York: David McKay, 1971), 295–321.

11. Diffusion is defined more specifically as the number of, balance among, and intensity of relations with the targets of Canadian action abroad. Analytically, the impact of Canadian behaviour on a target transforms Canadian 'activity' into 'relations'. It thus leads to the next level of analysis—association—in which attention is directed at the internal character of a pattern of relations (or a 'relationship').

12. Analytically, because the overall focus of Canadian behaviour is directed at the distribution of power in the international system and can affect that distribution, it gives rise to the subsequent concern with order, or the structure of the international system that a given distribution of power yields.

13. The basic concept of world order is discussed in Hedley Bull, *The Anarchical Society: A Study of Order in World Politics* (New York: Columbia University Press, 1979). See also Robert Tucker, *The Inequality of Nations* (New York: Basic Books, 1977). For a current debate on regimes, see *International Organization* 36 (Spring 1982), entire issue.

14. The importance of systemic attributes, such as the actions of individual states on a state's international activity, is argued in James Harf et al., 'Systemic and External Attributes in Foreign Policy Analysis', in Rosenau, ed., *Comparing Foreign Policies*, 235–50. Evidence that the relative status and salience of external actors has a particular impact on Canadian foreign policy behaviour is contained in Don Munton, 'Lesser Powers and the Influence of Relational Attributes: The Case of Canadian Foreign Policy Behaviour', *Études Internationales* 10

(September 1979): 471–502. Salience includes the concept of vulnerability, which refers to 'the relative availability and costliness of the alternatives that the actors face'. It is defined as 'an actor's liability to suffer costs imposed by external events even after policies have been altered' and is measured by 'the costliness of making effective adjustments to a changed environment over a period of time'. Robert O. Keohane and Joseph S. Nye, Jr, *Power and Interdependence: World Politics in Transition* (Boston: Little, Brown, 1977), 13.

15. Compare the concept of sensitivity as degree and speed of costly impacts from, and responsiveness to, outside events, including social, political, and economic contagion effects, 'before policies are altered to try to change the situation'. Keohane and Nye, *Power and Interdependence*, 12–13.

16. For an introduction to the literature on domestic sources of foreign policy, see Henry Kissinger, 'Domestic Structure and Foreign Policy', *Daedalus* 95 (Spring 1966): 503–29; James N. Rosenau, ed., *Domestic Sources of Foreign Policy* (New York: The Free Press, 1967); McGowan and Shapiro, *Comparative Study*, 107–32; and Peter J. Katzenstein, ed., 'Between Power and Plenty: Foreign Economic Policies of Advanced Industrialized States', *International Organization* 31 (Autumn 1977).

17. For societal determinants, a further breakdown of scope includes the concepts of institutional differentiation and autonomy derived from Samuel Huntington, *Political Order in Changing Societies* (New Haven: Yale University Press, 1968), and the discussion of penetrated political societies in Rosenau, 'Pre-theories and Theories'. On the dual nature of the influence relationship between domestic and governmental actors in the Canadian case, see Denis Stairs, 'Publics and Policy Makers: The Domestic Environment of the Foreign Policy Community', *International Journal* 26, 1 (Winter 1970–1): 221–48; and Stairs, 'Public Opinion and External Affairs: Reflections on the Domestication of Canadian Foreign Policy', *International Journal* 33, 1 (Winter 1977–8): 128–49.

18. See Richard Snyder, H.W. Bruck, and B.M. Sapin, eds, *Foreign Policy Decision Making* (New York: Free

Press, 1962); Graham Allison, *Essence of Decision: Explaining the Cuban Missile Crisis* (Boston: Little, Brown, 1971); McGowan and Shapiro, *Comparative Study*, 65–106; and, most usefully, Stephen D. Krasner, *Defending the National Interest: Raw Material Investments and US Foreign Policy* (Princeton, NJ: Princeton University Press, 1978); Alfred Stepan, *The State and Society: Peru in Comparative Perspective* (Princeton, NJ: Princeton University Press, 1978); and Eric A. Nordlinger, *On the Autonomy of the Democratic State* (Cambridge, MA: Harvard University Press, 1981).

19. 'A principal task of research is to determine the extent to which any particular state (a) is procedurally neutral and allows an autonomous and competitive process of interest aggregation to present binding demands on the state, (b) is a class instrument in which the full range of its coercive, administrative and legal powers is used to dominate some class fractions and protect others, or (c) achieves some degree of autonomy from civil society and thus contributes its own weight to civil society.' Stepan, *State and Society*, xii–xiii.

20. These three groups emerge from most empirical analyses of a state's foreign policy apparatus; for example, I.M. Destler, *President, Bureaucrats and Foreign Policy: The Policy of Organizational Reform* (Princeton, NJ: Princeton University Press, 1972).

21. These co-ordinative structures and processes are staffed by what Stepan terms the 'strategic elite' and depend for their efficacy on the 'ideological and organizational unity of that elite'. Stepan, *State and Society*, xiii.

22. Hans Morgenthau's classic work is *Politics Among Nations: The Struggle for Power and Peace* (New York: Knopf, 1948). Other classic works in the realist tradition, broadly conceived, are E.H. Carr, *The Twenty Years' Crisis, 1919–1939: An Introduction to the Study of International Relations* (New York: St. Martin's Press, 1939); Raymond Aron, *Peace and War: A Theory of International Relations* (New York: Praeger, 1967); and Bull, *Anarchical Society*.

23. Carl Berger, *The Sense of Power: Studies in the Idea of Canadian Imperialism, 1867–1914* (Toronto: University of Toronto Press, 1970).

24. Don Page, 'Canada as the Exponent of North American Idealism', *The American Review of Canadian Studies* 3 (Autumn 1973): 30–46.

25. John H. Herz, 'Rise and Demise of the Territorial State', *World Politics* 9 (July 1957): 473ff; and Herz, *International Politics in the Atomic Age* (New York: Columbia University Press, 1959). See also the criticisms summarized in Stanley Hoffman, *The State of War: Essays on the Theory and Practice of International Relations* (New York: Praeger, 1965).

26. This broadening of the concepts of security and national interest and the introduction of a more prominent role for values and moral considerations were led by Arnold Wolfers, *Discord and Collaboration* (Baltimore: Johns Hopkins University Press, 1962).

27. For example, R.J. Sutherland, 'Canada's Long-Term Strategic Situation', *International Journal* 17 (Summer 1962): 199–233; James Eayrs, 'Sharing a Continent: the Hard Issues', in J.S. Dickey, ed., *The United States and Canada* (Englewood Cliffs: Prentice-Hall, 1967), 55–94; Klaus Knorr, 'Canada and Western Defence', *International Journal* 18 (Winter 1962–3): 1–16; and Melvin Conant, *The Long Polar Watch: Canada and the Defence of North America* (New York: Harper and Row, 1962). From an earlier period, see the great classics, J.B. Brebner, *North Atlantic Triangle: The Interplay of Canada, the United States and Great Britain* (Toronto: Ryerson, 1945); 'A Changing North Atlantic Triangle', *International Journal* 3 (Autumn 1948): 309–19; and Harold Innis, *Great Britain, the United Nations and Canada* (Nottingham, England: University of Nottingham Press, 1948).

28. For the best summaries, see Keohane and Nye, *Power and Interdependence*; and Stanley Hoffman, *Primacy or World Order: American Foreign Policy Since the Cold War* (New York: McGraw-Hill, 1978).

29. Wight, *Power Politics*, 30–40; and Jeffrey Hart, 'Dominance in International Politics', *International Organization* 30 (Spring 1976).

30. Hans Morgenthau, *The Purpose of American Politics* (New York: Knopf, 1960); Arnold Wolfers, 'Statesmanship and Moral Choice', *World Politics* 1 (January 1949): 175–95; and Wolfers, *Discord and*

Collaboration. While this broader conception of interests and values follows many of the recent extensions of realist thinking, it does *not* embrace the globally derived, universally common, or inherent 'cosmopolitan values', argued in John H. Herz, 'Political Realism Revisited', *International Studies Quarterly* 25 (June 1981): 182–97, and suggested in Stanley Hoffman, *Duties Beyond Borders: On the Limits and Possibilities of Ethical International Politics* (Syracuse, NY: Syracuse University Press, 1981). Essentially, our argument asserts that balance-of-power dynamics do not usually prevent a state from acquiring a position of hegemony, that such states have 'milieu' goals, and that such goals are partially determined by a historically engendered conception of national values.

31. The major works that provide the basis in the general literature for our complex neo-realist model are George Liska, *Imperial America: The International Politics of Primacy* (Baltimore: Johns Hopkins University Press, 1967); Raymond Aron, *The Imperial Republic* (Englewood Cliffs, NJ: Prentice Hall, 1974); and David Calleo, *The Imperious Economy* (Cambridge, MA: Harvard University Press, 1982). Equally important is a stream of literature focusing on the dynamics within and between states, which give rise to processes of hegemony. See, in particular, Nazli Choucri and Robert C. North, *Nations in Conflict: National Growth and International Violence* (San Francisco: W.H. Freeman, 1975).

32. See A.F.K. Organski, *World Politics*, 364–7; and Wight, *Power Politics*, 30–40.

33. On great powers, see Wight, *Power Politics*, 41–53.

34. The concept of surplus capability is drawn from Charles Kindleberger, 'Dominance and Leadership in the International Economy', *International Studies Quarterly* 25 (June 1981): 245. In our formulation, it is not only an absolute criterion based on internal capability but also a criterion relative to domestic demands, external security threats, and ultimately the demands for creating international order that different external distributions of power breed.

35. Collectively, a particular configuration of interests and values is termed 'the national interest'. The traditional, security-focused concept of national interest has met with considerable skepticism from scholars of international politics, for reasons well summarized in James N. Rosenau, 'National Interest', in David L. Sills, ed., *International Encyclopedia of the Social Sciences, Vol. II* (New York: Crowell, Collier, and Macmillan, 1968), 34–40. Our concept derives from subsequent efforts to defend and refine the concept, such as Joseph Frankel, 'National Interest: A Vindication', *International Journal* 24 (Autumn 1969): 717–25; Donald Neuchterlein, *National Interests and Presidential Leadership: The Setting of Priorities* (Boulder, CO: Westview Press, 1978); and, especially, Krasner, *Defending the National Interest*. In our conception, the national interest is a set of premises, perceptions, and policy-relevant priorities that is durable (extending for a minimum of, say, five years), comprehensive (in embracing interests from several issue areas or sectors of society), interrelated (in specifying the relationships among interests), internally prioritized (in providing a particular scale of order or weighting to components), and general (in relating directly overarching values that structure the scale of priorities). In process terms, 'the national interest' is seen in broad foreign policy declarations, doctrines, or the calculus underlying seminal decisions when these endure beyond the electoral cycle, actively involve a number and range of government departments, require extensive interdepartmental interaction, engender interdepartmental conflict or major efforts at harmonization, and stimulate more than formal authorization, monitoring, or servicing activities from the chief executive group or central co-ordinative structures. Thus 'the national interest' embraces both 'interests', which are specific to societal sectors and government departments and affected by decision in a direct and immediate way, and 'values', which are general to society and the state and produced by the chief executive group and central co-ordinative structures. Because society lacks unified control and central co-ordinative structures, interests are primarily the preserve of society, while values reside primarily in the state.

36. The concept of specialized capabilities is drawn from Choucri and North, *Nations in Conflict*, 14–43.

37. In short, they present the possibility of leadership, as conceived in Kindleberger, 'Dominance and Leadership'.

38. In addition to the works cited in the Introduction, our presentation of complex neo-realism draws on the following literature in the Canadian foreign policy field: Hyndman, 'National Interest and the New Look'; Ivan Head, 'The Foreign Policy of the New Canada', *Foreign Affairs* 50 (January 1972): 237–52; 'Dossier Canada', *Politique Internationale* 12 (Summer 1981): 181–302; A.E. Gotlieb, 'The Western Economic Summits', Notes for Remarks to the Canadian Institute for International Affairs, 9 April 1981, Winnipeg; and Charles Doran, 'Politics of Dependency Reversal: Canada', Paper prepared for the International Studies Association Annual Meeting, 21–24 March 1979, Toronto.

39. Note the co-existence of the two themes in the prescriptions of Reid in 'Canadian Foreign Policy, 1967–1977'. Distinctive cultural groups included, most notably, the francophone countries and the People's Republic of China.

40. See Clarkson, ed., *Independent Foreign Policy*, 253–69; and Hyndman, 'National Interest and the New Look'.

41. See Head, 'Foreign Policy of the New Canada'; and James Eayrs, 'Defining a New Place for Canada in the Hierarchy of World Powers', *International Perspectives* (May/June 1975): 15–24.

42. More particularly, we see the United States acquiring hegemony from 1945 to 1960 and exercising stable, virtually unchallenged 'high' hegemony from about 1960 through 1967.

43. Robert Bothwell, Ian Drummond, and John English, *Canada Since 1945: Power, Politics and Provincialism* (Toronto: University of Toronto Press, 1981).

44. 'Canada is a large power; to call us a "middle power" is inaccurate. . . . As an immigrant country, with a barely developed national resource base to our economy, and a rapidly adapting capability in technology and processing, we are to some extent only now beginning to reach our true potential.' A.E. Gotlieb, 'Canada–US Relations: The Rules of the Game', Christian A. Herter Lecture Series, The Johns Hopkins School of Advanced International Studies, 1 April 1982, Washington DC, 4, 10. The term 'principal power' is used by Marc Lalonde, 'Le Canada et l'indépendance énergétique du monde libre', *Politique Internationale* 12 (Summer 1981): 206.

45. A.F.K. Organski and Jacek Kugler, *The War Ledger* (Chicago: University of Chicago Press, 1980), 43.

46. For an illustration of this calculation, see Gotlieb, 'Western Economic Summits'.

47. For an example of a national capabilities presentation, see Peyton V. Lyon and Brian W. Tomlin, *Canada as an International Actor* (Toronto: Macmillan, 1979), 56–76.

48. Such groupings include the Western Economic Summit, the Namibia Contact Group, and, less clearly, the four-power Caribbean Consultative Group, the 1970 uranium cartel group, the initial London Suppliers Group on nuclear materials, the executive directors of the International Monetary Fund, and historically, the United Nations Atomic Energy Commission.

49. These groupings include states in the Commonwealth and francophonie, particularly those from the Caribbean and Africa and, less clearly, small and middle powers from the North Atlantic region. One very stringent measure of such states are those that Canada has represented at one time as an executive director on the International Monetary Fund: Norway, Iceland, Ireland, Jamaica, Guyana, Barbados, and the Bahamas. From this perspective, the standard observation of Canada—as a 'regional power without a region' because of the dominating presence of the United States—overlooks the three major poles of Canada's regional sphere: as a transcontinental and trans-Atlantic power, beginning with Confederation in 1867 and culminating in the admission of Newfoundland into the Dominion in 1949; as a northern power, symbolized by the Arctic Waters Pollution Prevention Act of 1970 and conceptualized in Franklyn Griffiths, *A Northern Foreign Policy* (Toronto: Canadian Institute of International Affairs, 1979); and as a

Caribbean power, based on this historic Canada–West Indies trade and currently registered in Canada's leading role in development assistance in the region.

50. More precisely, within the United Nations, greater emphasis is given to the Security Council and to the new generation of organizations and special conference groupings created in the 1970s to deal with new 'global' issues.

3
The Choice to be Made

Stephen Clarkson

In most cases disagreements over Canadian foreign policy appear to revolve round matters of fact. Von Riekhoff believes that our membership in NATO increases our political influence, while McNaught rejects the link between the Atlantic alliance and Canada's international effectiveness. Yet only part of the dispute is really concerned with 'hard facts'. The major points at issue are questions of evaluation and interpretation. We can establish as facts what amounts of money and manpower we devote to our NATO commitments, but this does not *prove* von Riekhoff right in his contention that our contribution of guns and troops increases Canada's power in West Europe or Washington. Nor does it *prove* McNaught's contrary thesis that the influence we may have is not worth the cost that would better be devoted to peace-keeping through an international police force. In both cases the authors are really invoking the support of conflicting assumptions to which they make tacit appeal: that political influence through collective action is desirable in von Riekhoff's view (insignificant in McNaught's), that the communist threat is serious (or unreal), that the Atlantic area is more (or less) important to Canada than the under-developed world, and so on. The authors of all the chapters bring to their discussions a group of assumptions and beliefs that they do not have the space to develop fully.

Two Alternatives

Once we recognize this, we can see that the key to the often confusing debate on what Canadian foreign policy should be can be found in the underlying clash between two opposing foreign policy theories. Each theory contains a complete, if implicit, explanation of the world situation and of Canada's role in it, including a view of the American relationship and a statement of objectives for Canadian diplomacy. Let's follow current fashion and call the contending theories 'quiet' and 'independent'. By the 'quiet' foreign policy approach I mean the official policy as expressed in statements, the government's practice as seen over the last five years and the image projected by our diplomats in their execution of this policy. Although what has been referred to throughout this book as an 'independent' foreign policy has not been systematically articulated as a coherent doctrine, I shall present briefly what appear to me to be the major positions of each theory in order to crystallize their differences and so make possible a choice between these opposing approaches to Canada's foreign policy.

THE INTERNATIONAL SITUATION
Quiet approach

As in the late 1940s and 1950s, the world is still polarized along ideological lines between the forces of Communism and the West. Despite the splits in the Marxist-Leninist bloc, the defence of the free world is still the major priority. Revolution is a continuing threat to world stability, especially in the under-developed continents of Asia, Africa, and Latin America. This makes it all the more important to contain Communism in Vietnam and Cuba lest the whole 'third world' fall to the Reds like a row of dominoes. The United States is the only power able to pursue a containment policy on a world-wide basis. Its allies must support this effort.

Independent approach

The stabilization of Soviet and European communism has reduced the former Communist military threat to the West, turning the Cold War into a cold peace. The major world problem is no longer the East–West ideological confrontation but the North–South economic division of the world into rich and poor. Revolution is less a Red menace than an aspect of achieving the urgently needed socio-economic transformations in the under-developed world; in any case it is no direct threat to our society. Naive American impulses to save the world from Communism are misguided, out of date, and a menace to world peace. The breakdown of the monolithic unity of both the Communist and Western blocs gives middle powers like Canada greater margins for independent manoeuvre.

CANADA'S NATIONAL INTERESTS
Quiet approach

As a Western, democratic, and industrial country, Canada's national interests are essentially similar to those of our continental neighbour and friend, the USA, which is still the arsenal and defender of the free world. Worrying about national unity is of far less importance than pulling our weight in the Atlantic Alliance. Collective security is the only defence against new Hitlers or Stalins; we must not forget the lessons of 1939 and 1948.

Independent approach

A less ideologically but more socially concerned view of the world shows that Canada's national interests coincide more with general progress than with the maintenance of the USA's super-power status. Our external economic and political interest in trade with Communist countries diverges from American restrictions against 'trading with the enemy'. Canada's internal political divisions and our national identity crisis create another urgent national task for our policy: reinforce Canada's sense of bicultural personality.

INDEPENDENCE
Quiet approach

Foreign policy independence is an illusion in the present-day world unless it is defined as head-in-the-sand isolation. We might just as well try to cut Canada off from North America and float out into the Atlantic. Independence must also mean a narrow and harmful anti-Americanism.

Independent approach

Far from being illusory, independence—being able to control one's own socio-economic environment—is an essential condition for the healthy development of the nation-state. Independence means neither isolation nor anti-Americanism, unless making up our own minds on the merits of individual foreign policies is considered un-American.

INTERDEPENDENCE
Quiet approach

Relations of interdependence are the situations within which middle powers must normally operate. Alliances and supranational organizations provide Canada with the best way to exercise influence and be useful in day-to-day international affairs. Ties of interdependence also guarantee weaker powers against arbitrary action by the strong, both by binding the super-powers to listen and by giving the small a forum within which to unite their forces.

Independent approach

Obligations freely undertaken in co-operation with other countries are perfectly legitimate if they improve both the national and the world situation, e.g. IMF or GATT. Interdependence can create new opportunities that can be exploited to further the national interest commercially and increase our influence diplomatically. Fulfilling our many international commitments is the staple of our diplomatic activity and the means of building our influence. But we must be ready to use this credit when initiatives are needed. Too much interdependence can become glorified dependence.

INTERNATIONAL OBJECTIVES

Quiet approach

In the light of this analysis of the international situation and our national interests, we should strive to defend the status quo, nurturing our influence in Washington and helping maintain the solidarity of the Western alliance as the expression of our commitment to internationalism and the defence of democracy. Our order of priorities should be the American relationship first, then the Atlantic Alliance, finally the developing countries. All our actions should keep in mind the central importance of collective actions as the appropriate activity of a middle power.

Independent approach

Given the more relaxed international environment and our internal need for a more distinctive foreign activity, Canadian objectives should outgrow our anti-communism to embrace the aims of international equality and socio-economic modernization. This may entail more economic sacrifice and more tolerance of revolutionary change, but an enlightened nationalism requires re-evaluating our aims in terms of the most pressing needs of the whole world and will refuse to hide behind any alliance apron strings. Accordingly the 'third world' should now come first in our priorities as the affairs of the Atlantic community can more easily take care of themselves. Our American relationship should not prejudice these international priorities.

OVERALL FOREIGN POLICY STRATEGY

Quiet approach

Our general strategy should be affiliation, or close alignment and cooperation with our superpower neighbour to achieve maximum diplomatic power by our influence on the Western bloc leader. We can only enjoy this influence by accepting the American foreign policy framework and restraining our urge to criticize the Americans. This then gives us access to the inner corridors of US power.

Independent approach

Canada is too unimportant in Washington's worldview for us to have significant direct influence on American foreign policy. Our strategy should be to act directly in a given situation after making an independent evaluation of the problem. Except for continental matters of direct Canadian–American concern, influence on Washington would normally be a secondary objective. Even then our power to affect Washington's policy will depend on our international effectiveness, not our allegedly 'special' relationship.

TACTICS TO IMPLEMENT THE STRATEGY

Quiet approach

'Quiet diplomacy' describes the foreign policy method most appropriate to implement an affiliation strategy. It puts special emphasis on confidential, friendly contacts with our allies, primarily the Americans, so that any differences that may arise are ironed out before they can reach crisis proportions and come out in the open. American views should be anticipated and taken into consideration as part of our own policy-making. Publicity is to be avoided as are public declarations of criticism by our leader. Rather, our role should be to seek common ground between those in disagreement.

Independent approach

Communications between our diplomats and those of other countries are by definition quiet. Carrying on our routine diplomatic business will therefore be unobtrusive. But there is no reason to make quietness a cardinal feature of our foreign policy, for this is to renounce in advance one of the most effective of a small power's bargaining tools, the use of exposure and public pressure to strengthen our position against a big power. If we have something to say and want to be heard, we must speak up. In dealing with the State Department that has dozens of importunate allies to cope with, not to mention its enemies, the demure may earn some gratitude from harried American diplomats. It does not follow that the 'smooth' diplomat will get more response than his 'raucous' rival.

FOREIGN POLICY STYLE
Quiet approach
Our international style for quiet diplomacy should be that of the discreet professionals who operate outside the glare of the TV lights and the prying eye of the press in close harmony with the diplomats of our allies, unobtrusively husbanding our stock of goodwill and influence. This would maintain our credit as a responsible friend in Washington, preserve our special access to inside information and so maximize our ability to affect American policy-making when we do disagree privately with it.

Independent approach
A hush-puppy style may be proper for our diplomats but is not the manner that our political leaders should adopt if they want to reinforce the Canadian identity. Without having to bang their shoes on the United Nations podium they could adopt a more assertive stance that makes clear Canada's existence as a bicultural nation with a unique set of policies. It is unrealistic not to be concerned with the 'public relations' aspect of our foreign policy, since the way we present ourselves in the world—our international image—has a direct bearing on our international effectiveness. To this extent it is true that the posture of independence is a vital part of the policy.

THE AMERICAN RELATIONSHIP
Quiet approach
As it is this relationship that gives Canada special influence through our geographical, political, and psychological proximity, nurturing the American relationship should have highest priority. We should not question the ultimate goals of the United States that has, after all, world-wide responsibilites for the defence of the free world. In addition we must realize that Canada cannot survive economically without the goodwill of the Americans upon whom we depend for our high standard of living. It would be 'counter-productive' to try to influence American policies by publicly opposing them. This would only reinforce the extremist elements advocating the policies we opposed.

Independent approach
Our relations with the USA are 'special' because of the disparity of our power and the degree to which we depend on American trade and capital inflows. We should for this reason devote careful attention to our relations, especially if we are planning international moves of which they do not approve. The huge military and political power of the USA should make us particularly critical of American policies however well-intentioned the Average American may be. Our well-being is not a product of bounteous concessions made by the US but of economic development considered to be to both countries' advantage. Our relationship should be governed by this awareness of mutual benefit. There is no evidence that independent actions strengthen extremism in the USA. If we really wish to influence American public opinion, we have to make it clear what policy we advocate. There is no better way than actually pursuing it.

RETALIATION
Quiet approach
We are so dependent on the American economy that we cannot afford to do anything that might annoy them such as taking some foreign policy initiative that displeases Congress or the Admin-

istration. The price of independence would be a 25 per cent drop in our standard of living, according to Mr Pearson. We are, after all, the little pig that must be eternally vigilant lest the big pig roll over, in Mr Plumptre's phrase. We cannot increase this risk by provoking it to roll deliberately. In such areas as the Defence Production Sharing Agreements we gain enormously from being able to bid on American defence contracts. The share of the US market we have won pays for our own purchases of American war material at prices cheaper than we could produce it ourselves. We cannot afford the luxury of independence, whatever our conscience might say, since independent actions might jeopardize these arrangements.

Independent approach
The possibility of retaliation is present in all international relationships. It is true that we are more vulnerable to American than the US is to Canadian retaliation, but we must not forget that retaliation is a reaction of last resort showing that all milder negotiation has failed. By being willing to use the whole armory of diplomatic weapons—bilateral and multilateral, informal and public—we could reduce the dangers of retaliation conjured up by the all-or-nothing approach of Quiet Diplomacy. We must realize that as the little power, we have important advantages. We can concentrate our whole attention on defending our interests in the continental relationship, which, from the American point of view, is but one of dozens of issues of greater importance. We have important hostages in Canada, the very subsidiaries that are the instruments of US political and economic pressure. We can also use the threat of mobilizing public opinion to strengthen our hand against possible intimidation and economic blackmail. Our goodwill and our favourable image in the US as a long-standing friend is a further asset we should not ignore.

INTERNAL IMPACT OF FOREIGN POLICY
Quiet approach
The internal implications of our diplomacy are negligible and should remain so. Foreign policy should be practised to achieve specific external goals and not to boost the national ego. If Canadians have an identity problem, they should cure it themselves, not resort to artificial stimulation. Similarly we should not let our concern for internal problems of biculturalism distort our foreign policy. External affairs and internal politics should be kept in their proper places. Quebec should not drag foreign policy into her federal arguments with Ottawa.

Independent approach
It is impossible to dissociate external from internal policies if only because external relations are carried out by all branches of government—Finance, Commerce, Defence, and Citizenship are involved and even the provinces, quite apart from External Affairs. Foreign policy must in any case be seen as only one aspect of the government's total network of policies. We cannot afford *not* to exploit the nation-building potential of our foreign policies, since the way others perceive us—dynamic and bicultural, or ineffectual and divided—can, strengthen, or undermine, our own national identity. Similarly, if we accept French-Canadian desires for cultural equality and Quebec's demands for greater self-control, our foreign policy should reflect and reinforce Canada's new binational politics.

The 'quiet' approach to our foreign policy is not an extremist absurdity, however unlike most nations' foreign policy doctrines it may appear. It is the rationale of Canadian diplomacy. The overriding concern for kid glove relations with our American neighbours was articulated in 1965 by the Merchant-Heeney Report with all the hallmarks of official policy. The feeling of economic dependence is not an Opposition charge but a situation acknowledged by the Prime Minister himself.[1] The surprisingly unsophisticated cold warrior analysis complete with Domino Theory of Asian Communism is heard time after time from our diplomats, both senior officers and newly inducted recruits. In our discussions with these foreign service officers during our ULSR seminars, we found them cut off from the Canadian public whose views they take to be adequately expressed by *Globe and Mail* editorials or questions posed in the House of Commons. More disconcerting is the professionals' scorn for the amateur which colours their attitude towards the value of the public's opinion. Far from being a straw man set up for easy refutation, Quiet Diplomacy is enshrined as the conventional wisdom of our federal political establishment.

Independence Yes, Quiet Diplomacy No

However accepted this doctrine may be, I would submit that it is no longer suitable for Canadian foreign policy in the late sixties. It is inappropriate, first of all for the reasons stated in the 'independent' replies to the 'quiet' positions summarized above: its view of the world is ten years out of date; its understanding of Canada's international needs and capabilities is hopelessly circumscribed.

'Quiet' foreign policy is also unacceptable in a mass democracy. If to be effective, our quiet foreign policy must be carried on in complete secrecy so that even its successes should not be known lest they compromise further success, as Peyton Lyon argues, how is the voter ever to know whether the policy is justified? Is he simply to accept the protestations of diligence and sincerity by the Minister of External Affairs or the Prime Minister and the assurances of our diplomats, all claiming to plead impartially in their own cause? Until all the files are open, Peyton Lyon writes, we cannot know for sure. But even then how would proof be certain? To be sure that the quiet approach had been the more effective it would be necessary to show what results the independent approach would have produced in exactly the same circumstances—an obviously impossible condition. We cannot wait fifty years for the files to be open, even if they did promise final proof. Quiet diplomacy has been practised long enough for the onus to be on its defenders to

demonstrate their case. The record does not lend them very strong support. Such a diplomatic success as Pearson's constructive role in the 1956 Suez crisis is an example of independent initiative, well conceived at an appropriate time, as both Hanly and Cox Point out.

Nor is it good enough for the Merchant-Heeney Report to admonish Canadians to

> have confidence that the practice of quiet diplomacy is not only neighbourly and convenient to the United States but that it is in fact more effective than the alternative of raising a row and being unpleasant in public.

One can readily agree that it is more 'convenient' for the United States that Canada be quiet, but it is less convincing that Canadian foreign policy will be more 'effective' as a result. The only alternative envisaged by this defence of quietness is 'raising a row and being unpleasant in public'. Either accept American policy or protest, we are told; don't consider acting independently. This paints a disconcertingly small picture of the possible role Canada can play. Surely Canada can aspire to a more significant international activity than just having some influence in Washington, as if we were one more state in the Union with two Senators and a dozen Representatives all clamouring bilingually in Congress for patronage and action on Vietnam!

When the defenders of quiet diplomacy expound on our influence in Washington, their argument raises more doubts. To start with they are hard put to provide empirical evidence of Canada's power to make Washington act in the way we want. They go on to insist that this putative special influence in Washington is the basis for Canada's power in other countries who take us seriously because they assume we have a unique path to American waiting chambers. But they then warn that we should not actually try to use this influence for this would undermine this special position and so our international status. Strange logic, a sophisticated rationalization for inaction. Influence is like credit: it has to be used to exist. The quiet diplomatists manage to underrate Canada's real power to act by exaggerating our potential influence.

The alternative to quiet diplomacy is not 'raising a row'; it is developing an independent foreign policy. Independence means above all striving for maximum effectiveness. Those times when Canada has been most clearly effective she has acted directly, achieving negotiations in Korea or the exclusion of South Africa from the Commonwealth. This means neither that she acted alone nor against a big power. Kicking Uncle Sam in the shins or twisting the Lion's tail has no necessary part in any of Canada's more independent actions. Canadians are not even aware that our enlightened aid programme towards Tanzania was pushed forward despite Dar-es-Salaam's rupture of relations with Britain. Such acts are satisfactory because they are effective. They are effective because the Canadian initiative itself contributed directly to achieve the particular goal. They achieved this goal because in these situations the Canadian government acted flexibly; not out of deference or automatic loyalty to another power. To act flexibly means to make up one's own mind—to be independent.

To make independence the standard for our foreign policy is not to opt out of the many undramatic areas of collective diplomacy in which Canada makes a continuing major contribution at a supranational level. Nor does independence imply anti-Americanism, however much the bogey of 'making a row' is raised. Deciding policies on their own merits may well lead to disagreement with American policy. Still there is no reason to inflate such policy disagreements to disastrous proportions unless the defendants of quiet diplomacy really believe the Americans to be the most vindictive politicians on earth. According to Stairs' study we have followed a line directly counter to American policy on a problem of the highest sensitivity, Cuba, and still not suffered retaliation. The point is that if we diverge it is not for the sake of a quarrel but to

practise what we feel to be the correct policy, after due consideration of the Americans' reasons. It is hard to believe that a more assertive Canadian foreign policy would be countered in Washington by a concerted anti-Canadian policy. The more truculent General de Gaulle has become, the gentler has been the Americans' treatment of France. With so much direct investment in Canada, it is unlikely that the Americans, in Baldwin's phrase, would want to get rid of a blemish on the finger by amputating the arm.

Independence also requires realism in our conception of the American relationship. Our interactions with the USA are so intense and multitudinous at all levels of political, economic, cultural, and personal contact that we should make a fundamental distinction between our foreign policies on one hand and our American policies on the other. While pursuing what we consider to be the best policy abroad, it is in our interest to place the strongest emphasis on the maintenance of good neighbourly relations with the USA. In all matters of mutual concern, whether financial investment, tariff policy, resource development or cultural interchange, the policies of both countries toward each other must continue to be formulated in close consultation. We clearly have an essential unity of self-interests with the Americans in our continental partnership. But partnership requires equality, and equality implies independence.

That the obsession with the Americans should not stifle our foreign activity is the first message of the independent approach; that our fascination with American power should not blind us to the extent of our own influence on American policy is the second. Canada has a comparatively strong bargaining position it can use *if it wants to* in dealing with the United States. The continentalists point out the many relations of dependence exposing Canada to American pressure and retaliation. But it is elementary political science to recognize that dependence is a two-way street. Every aspect of our relationship—our resources (our highly coveted supplies of fresh water very much included), the American branch plants, our debts, our trade deficit, our goodwill as a reliable ally— can be used by a determined leadership *if necessary* to achieve its objectives. 'If necessary', for most bargaining weapons are more effective as a threat than in use—as the continentalists' terror of US retaliation shows.

An independent foreign policy is an ethically just policy. Peyton Lyon attacks the critics of quiet diplomacy for being 'ostentatiously on the side of virtue, regardless of practical consequences'. One can heartily agree that a 'tub-thumping moralistic approach' is distasteful and that a disregard for practical consequences is irresponsible. Yet an argument for independence is not *moralistic* for raising *moral* problems. As Hanly argues, an independent approach is necessarily more ethical for it requires an autonomous calculation for every policy of the probable consequences both for Canada and for those our policy will affect. It is the defenders of quiet diplomacy who are open to the charge of moralism if they cling dogmatically to a moral judgment of American policy made twenty years ago.

An independent foreign policy also presupposes responsibility. As only a free man is considered responsible for his actions, only a nation which makes its own decisions can be considered in charge of its destiny and can expect its citizenry to believe in its integrity. And like the youth who can only develop maturely if he liberates himself from parental controls, the nation-state can only achieve full expression if it is master in its own house, able to act in the community of nations as a fully responsible entity.

The Problem of Reform

If independence is more desirable as an overall guideline for our foreign policy, why is quietness still the guiding light of Canadian diplomacy? Not from American pressure. Nor for lack of international scope, particularly in the underdeveloped world. The conclusion must be that the problem is here at home. Yet we can hardly blame public opinion. The opinion polls, for all their inaccuracies, indicate that the general public's views have been consistently more nationalist on foreign policy issues like Vietnam, the Dominican Republic and China than the Government.[2] All the major parties have, at the very least, strong wings in favour of a more independent diplomacy. Predominant editorial opinion, church statements, students groups, and academic protests complete the general picture of a public opinion that increasingly rejects quietness.

While the University League for Social Reform is particularly oriented towards making reform proposals, it would be superficial to conclude with facile exhortations to the leadership to change its policy. The conditions are so favourable for an independent foreign policy that the persistence of a quiet approach indicates more fundamental problems are involved. If we are to make some proposals for reform we must assess the underlying reasons for this anomalous state of affairs. These are threefold and interconnected: a decision-making structure that isolates the Government from public participation and control, an elitist ideology for the civil service that legitimizes this insulation, and a leadership that perpetuates this situation.

As Griffiths shows in his discussion of our political institutions, the foreign policy making process is almost completely sealed off from the normal give and take between public and government. Even Members of Parliament have no significant access to this 'closed circuit'. In a recent article surveying the problems of the Department of External Affairs, the Under-Secretary of State for External Affairs, Marcel Cadieux, deals quite extensively with his relationship with the Minister. Yet, with the exception of consulting university specialists, he makes no mention of the contribution that members of the public, Parliamentarians included, can make to the formation of the nation's foreign policy. 'Without public understanding', he concedes, 'we can hardly hope to develop Canada's role in world affairs.'[3] He doesn't seem to feel that the public has any greater part to play than to stand and wait, deferentially yet comprehendingly in the spectators' boxes.

It is institutional security from criticism that makes Quiet Diplomacy the natural ideology of the diplomatic caste. It gives a theoretical justification for the handling of all business by routine bureaucratic channels. If foreign policy is the private domain of the administrator, he need not take seriously clamour, interest group opinion, or, God forbid, Parliamentary interference. Public discussion of foreign policy problems is fine and even desirable, our diplomats will hasten to profess, so long as it does not disturb their professional activity.

The crucial link in this combination of institutional isolation and bureaucratic élitism is its endorsement by the leadership. Paradoxically the Liberal leaders bring an unprecedented background of experience to their handling of foreign affairs. Yet Mr Pearson, the Nobel Prize winner, has turned the 'unobtrusive oil can' tactics, which led to his own international successes in the mid-fifties into a dogma which frustrates the continuation of this early record. Mr Martin, for all his concern for his public image, is unable to convey to the nation a convincing and unambiguous understanding of what Canada can achieve internationally and has not been able to transmit the growing public concern for foreign policy questions into revised governmental policies. Nor has he shown any sign of opening the major issues of foreign policy, such as the decision to renew the NORAD agreement, to public debate in parliament. Institutions, ideology, and leadership: we have here a troika of conditions that require basic reforms and changes. Yet remedies cannot be solely of relevance to our foreign policy. We face a general problem of Canadian democracy—the responsiveness of governmental policy and the civil service to public scrutiny and control. Reforms needed in this area of public policy are needed in other branches as well:

All bureaucracy is conservative, but the conservatism of diplomatic bureaucracy is in a class by itself. The ethos of diplomacy is an ethos of suspicion—suspicion tempered by skepticism, snow tempered by ice. The foreign service officer is a naysayer in statecraft, the abominable no-man of diplomacy. His mission in life is to preserve the status quo from those who propose to alter it.[4]

As James Eayrs points out, the problem of foreign policy change is the problem of subjecting bureaucratic inertia to some reasonable form of public control.

Let the Public In

The first step is to open the process of policy-forming so that the expression of expert, informed, and articulate opinions can have a major impact on foreign policy making. Yet in this age of McLuhan, our channels for public participation in politics are still using a Walter Bagehot technology. Gallup polls give irregular insights into public views on simplified issues, but their findings are ignored unless politically exploitable. A partial solution is to put the measuring of attitudes on a regular and scientific basis, possibly by a research institute that would, by continuous sampling, make 'what public opinion wants' no longer a subject for guesswork. More important, structural change such as the activation of the parliamentary committee on foreign affairs, as suggested by Griffiths, could institutionalize the public scrutiny of foreign policy in a way compatible with the parliamentary system. To be meaningful the committee would need a full-time research staff and would have to be able to require testimony from expert and interested groups as well as diplomats. While such a watchdog committee could not actually make policy, the defence committee hearings on tri-service unification have proved that basic public issues can be brought out into the open for thorough airing. The hearings would also provide our diplomats with a link to articulate opinion; they would start to see themselves as public servants rather than tight-lipped agents.

Another by-product would be important, if intangible. Coverage of the committee hearings by mass media would help give the public a sense of being involved in this hitherto exclusive area of policy. Other ways should be initiated to increase the public's interest in foreign policy.

If our foreign activity is to have the strength of public participation, the public must be sufficiently informed. Never has the man-in-the-street been so exposed by instant communications to international events, so bombarded with journalistic commentary and academic debate. Never has he had such a high level of education to absorb this information. But the data on Canadian foreign policy with which the public could come to policy conclusions is not made available. The change that is needed here is less quantitative than qualitative. To make public opinion aware of Canada's foreign policy problems, mass media and newspaper reports must relate their analysis of foreign affairs to Canadian external activity.

Civil Masters or Civil Servants?

To change from a quiet to a more independent approach to our foreign policy will require a transformation of the values of the practitioners, the diplomats in the Department of External Affairs. So long as the personnel of External Affairs maintain a secretive, distrustful attitude towards the public, an independent foreign policy is doubly stymied. An informed, alert public opinion cannot be developed if extensive, relevant information is not made regularly and easily available. As long as External Affairs maintains its Mandarin mystique explicitly tied to Quiet Diplomacy and anti-communism, the civil servants would be likely to block the implementation of an alternative foreign policy, even if the Government should desire it.

To change our diplomats from civil masters to civil servants will require a change in their ideology. A partial measure is to modify the environment they enter when they are recruited into the service so that the values they absorb conform to the desire of the public and the views of the leadership. In France, for example, recruits to all branches of the upper civil service receive three full years of practical and theoretical training at the National Administration School where they absorb the dynamic, nationalist values of the French state and so start their career as activist, not conservative, civil servants. The excellence and dynamism of the French civil service is one of the principal reasons for the impact of de Gaulle's foreign policy in Europe. Rather than have our new diplomats absorb willy-nilly the smug, conservative attitudes of the established bureaucracy, an introductory training programme—needed in any case to improve technical and linguistic competence—could give them an awareness of the role that the political leadership wants Canada to play and a consciousness of the challenge of achieving these goals in a democratic framework.

To prevent the diplomats from becoming cut off from public and informed opinion they need continual 'professional retraining' just as any doctor or engineer. Sabbatical leaves for research and senior staff officer courses are needed if our international crisis managers are to keep up intellectually with the rate of change of the crises they are entrusted to manage.

Leadership from the Top

No change in our diplomats' value system and no structural reform will be very productive without a third innovation: dynamic leadership. The muddling through of the quiet approach will continue until Canada's leaders realize that determination and a clear articulation of political objectives are needed to turn potentiality into reality. Canada is wealthy, strong, and developed. It does not need the mountain-moving voluntarism of Mao Tse-Tung. It simply needs a leadership that can make it clear to the public—if not in a little *Red Book* at least in a *White Paper*—what role Canada can play and how its objectives are to be achieved. This would give a sense of direction to the unusual talents in our diplomatic service and harness the force of public opinion behind this effort.

Partnership with Quebec

It is finally necessary to remove the uncertainty overshadowing the future of confederation. Although Quebec nationalism has made a major contribution to the development of a more independent Canadian activity, particularly in starting an aid programme to the French-speaking African states, the open diplomatic warfare between Ottawa and Quebec that broke out in conjunction with de Gaulle's visit to Quebec is rapidly becoming self-destructive.

It is time to come to some firm decision whether or not Quebec can satisfy its international aspirations as a special province in the federation acting both through Ottawa and autonomously in its areas of provincial jurisdiction. This is essentially an issue for Quebeckers to decide, though their compatriots can reasonably urge that the debate be fair and full before any irrevocable step is taken. It is for the French-Canadian intellectuals to spell out the costs and benefits of special status in the federation versus complete separation. Their English-speaking colleagues can point out, however, why they would like Quebec to stay in the effort to develop a new foreign policy. Not only does Quebec's wealth add strength to Canada's foreign power. More important, Quebec's culture and technology makes it possible for the total Canadian international effort in the under-developed world to have a unique impact. But the only finally convincing argument is the demonstration that Ottawa can mount a foreign policy that would be more independent and more effective than the foreign role that Quebec could play by itself, as a single state.

Quiet diplomacy has failed to provide this proof.

It is our belief that an independent foreign policy could give this proof to French and English Canadians alike by, first, rejecting its lingering anti-communism and downgrading the cold war alliances while, second, redirecting its resources and redefining its priorities to a determined support for the political, economic, and social needs of the developing countries—both through its multilateral diplomacy in international organizations and by directly making Canada a 'great power in foreign aid'.[5]

The Public Should Choose

We need more open diplomats, we need more public participation in policy-making. But most of all we need to choose: between the quiet, continental foreign policy we have followed in the main over the past decade and an independent foreign policy.

At a time when the Government is showing some quiet doubts about wisdom of its foreign policy approach, the expression of articulate opinion on this matter can have a significant effect. You, the reader, can write to your Member of Parliament. More simply you can answer and return the appended questionnaire that is designed to elicit your views on the policy questions raised in these pages. The answer received before 1 June 1968 will be tabulated and made public after being sent to the Prime Minister and the Minister of External Affairs. By returning this questionnaire, you can indicate to our leadership or to potential leaders waiting for the sign how you want the choice between quiet diplomacy and an independent foreign policy to be made.

Notes

1. Interview published in *Maclean's*, July 1967, 52.
2. Unpublished paper presented to the ULSR by Roman March, Carleton University.
3. Marcel Cadieux, 'La Tache du Sous-Secrétaire d'Etat aux Affaires extérieures', *International Journal* 22, 3 (Summer 1967): 527.

4. James Eayrs, *Fate and Will in Foreign Policy* (Toronto: Canadian Broadcasting Corporation, 1967), 50.

5. A phrase coined by Escott Reid in a speech to the Kiwanis Club, Toronto, 27 September 1967, when he argued that Canadian aid should be expanded from $300 million to $1 billion in five years.

Update
The Choices That Were Made and Those That Remain

Stephen Clarkson

Re-reading 'The Choice To Be Made'—the conclusion to the book, *An Independent Foreign Policy for Canada?* that I edited four decades ago after organizing a year-long process of discussions between many Canadian diplomats and a cross-disciplinary group of younger academic colleagues—gave me a strange feeling. *Plus ça change*. And much has changed in Canada's international, continental, and domestic context. *Plus c'est la même chose*. And much also remains the same in our seemingly eternal debate about Canada's role in the world.

The Context: Plus ça change

Let's pass in review how things were back then, what's happened since, and how they are now in the three scales that condition the country's foreign policy: the global, the continental, and the domestic.

GLOBAL BALANCE OF FORCES

Forty years later, the global balance of forces then are almost unrecognizable compared to today. Then, in the late 1960s, the Cold War standoff between East and West seemed frozen forever.

Although some non-aligned countries in the developing world kept their distance from both camps, Canada, which was on the flight path for long-range bombers and intercontinental missiles between the Soviet Union and the United States, had no choice but to support the Pentagon's strategy however mad—and the Mutually Assured Destruction on which the United States' second-strike nuclear-retaliation doctrine was, literally, MAD. Even when outrage at the United States's imperialist efforts to force its will on Vietnam had Canadians demonstrating by the thousands outside American consulates, Ottawa dissented from Washington's policy at its peril, since the fear of US economic retaliation was the ever-present subtext of Canada's international disagreements with Uncle Sam.

Since then, with the collapse of the Soviet Union, the United States passed from being the hegemonic entity of the West—its capitalist partners had supported Washington's construction of a liberal global order after the Second World War—to being the hegemonic entity of the world: in 1995, the launch of the World Trade Organization (WTO) created a global economic order using a made-in-the-USA rule book to which almost every country willingly subscribed.

Having been invited, on Pierre Trudeau's watch, to join the Economic Summit, the exclusive club of the seven most powerful states, Canada had been an actively contributing participant as the new trade régime was negotiated.

Although its relative power in the global hierarchy declined with the rise of China, India, and Brazil, Ottawa occasionally managed to take the lead in brokering multilateral agreements such as the International Criminal Court and the treaty banning anti-personnel landmines, even in the face of Washington's opposition.

Now, following 11 September 2001, when the United States subordinated its economically hegemonic role to its militarily imperialist persona, which unilaterally and arbitrarily tried to spread American values in the Middle East by force, poles of resistance have sprung up. The future economic colossus, China, is even threatening America's sense of energy security by buying a share in Alberta's oil resources.

Based as it was on evident misinformation and miscalculation, Washington's rogue behaviour in Iraq generated such dismay among the Canadian public that the country's political elite was obliged to back away from its default position of supporting the United States. And, even though Paul Martin vowed to repair the relations with the George W. Bush administration that he felt had been imprudently broken by his predecessor, Jean Chrétien, he was impelled by the public's distaste for Rumsfeld militarism to decline support to the US National Missile Defense program.

CANADA'S POSITION ON THE CONTINENT
Much has changed in Canada's political economy position in North America. In the late 1960s, Canada was striving to find ways to reduce the bleeding caused by its US-owned economy by constructing a more nationally focused market that would be less vulnerable to damaging American actions.

Since then, a decade's experimentation with a more nationally focused industrial strategy flamed out in the early 1980s with the ambitious but disastrously timed National Energy Program. John Turner's self-immolation in the 1984 federal election handed power to Brian Mulroney who, having sworn to give Washington the benefit of

the doubt, proceeded to join with then-President Ronald Reagan to sign a declaration of economic disarmament called the Canada–United States Free Trade Agreement (CUFTA). CUFTA locked Ottawa into a set of rules designed to subordinate the country's resources and manufactured production to the needs of the American economy.

Once Washington had established precedents to foreclose Canadian economic autonomy, it expanded the continental scope of what Ronald Reagan called the economic constitution of North America by including Mexico in this integrative régime. With the North American Free Trade Agreement (NAFTA) extending the WTO's massive and intrusive rules, Canada found itself saddled with an external constitution that sounded the death knell of an independent Canadian capitalism capable of competing with the United States. Canada's wealth remains dependent on pumping oil (for which the US thirst is insatiable), developing other economic niches (which are complementary but not competitive with US industries), hewing wood (which the US resists buying beyond the point that threatens rival US forestry interests), and, probably, drawing water (that is, diverting water southwards, an issue that is already on the agenda in the Great Lakes and south-western states).

Now, following close to two decades of border-lowering economic integration, Canada has been hit with Washington's latest strategic doctrine, a 'war on terror' focused on a border-raising, national security priority. Whereas Canadian leaders were able to dissent over the American position on Iraq, they have no freedom to diverge over its border policies because, in the Bush administration's view, security trumps trade. If Ottawa does not satisfy Washington that the Canada–US boundary is secure against terrorists—meaning that its immigration policies, its anti-terrorism secret policing, and its passport control processes meet with the approval of the Department of Homeland Security—the economic arteries that now flow from North to South will be blocked.

CANADA'S DOMESTIC SCENE

By 1968, the federal and provincial governments had put in place the health care system that was to become, with the Canadian flag, a defining element of Canada's national identity.

Since then, the relatively generous system of social-policy support for the unemployed, the poor, single parents, and the aged, which had been nurtured during the Trudeau years, came under attack by neoconservative budget slashing. The public's passion for health care, however, convinced politicians to restore those financial cuts. Meanwhile, Trudeau's immensely popular Charter of Rights and Freedoms gave millions of non-British and non-French immigrants a sense of security that theirs was not a second-class citizenship.

Now, differences between Canadian and American values grow ever greater. In sharp contrast to the fundamentalist conservatism espoused in the White House, the US Supreme Court, and the Congress, the Canadian government has followed the Canadian Supreme Court's lead by legalizing same-sex marriage and decriminalizing the possession of marijuana. These attitudinal differences underpin the continuing debate within Canada over its own foreign policy.

The Debate: Plus c'est la même chose

Canadian attitudes have changed little; Canadians remain anxiously obsessed with how to get along with their one and only neighbour in the face of its sometimes laudable but often destructive behaviour. As they look overseas, they remain worried about their standing in the rest of the world and how best to contribute to resolving its most urgent issues.

Interested academics, along with a limited number of journalists and civic-minded citizens, study how to understand these problems. The analytical and normative positions resulting from this consideration continue to fall into two distinct schools of thought, generating a debate that seems as irreconcilable as it is eternal.

Because its global, continental, and domestic context has changed, so too have the goalposts for the debate about Canada's foreign policy choices moved. Because the Cold War's demise has relieved Ottawa of the imperative to support the United States on the major issues, the foreign policy field it faces is considerably broader. But because the WTO and NAFTA have tied one hand behind the government's back and because there are very few economic sectors that remain under Canadian ownership and control, the field is also much shorter. Nevertheless, there are still two main schools of thought, two teams, as it were, which rally their supporters to propound opposing positions.

CONTINENTALISTS

A century ago Canadian imperialists expounded the view that the Dominion of Canada's prime goal should be to retain its connection with the British empire in order to guarantee its military security, its economic well-being, and its cultural identity. They reflected the interests of exporters who shipped their produce to Great Britain, importers who shipped consumer goods back across the Atlantic, the banking community that financed this commerce, and the intellectuals whose careers depended on nourishing their links with Oxford and Cambridge in the 'mother country'.

At that time, nationalists who wanted autonomy from the Empire looked to the United States as a progressive haven, relations with which could help burnish the Dominion's prospects as a self-sufficient and fast-growing, but more autonomous, society.

Four decades ago, the pattern had shifted: pro-British imperialists had become pro-American continentalists. Those wanting to extend relations with the United States were the dominant resource and manufacturing corporations for which continental integration promised economic salvation. Continentalists, as 'The Choice To Be Made' explained, admonished Canadians to support US foreign policy whether it was right or wrong. As the hearth of freedom in the Cold War, Washington should not be criticized. Furthermore, Canada's influence in the world depended on proving its influence in Washington's corridors of power. Being on the inside—pulling our own weight, being seen as sound—was the precondition for being effective in international forums. Even when we disagreed with Washington, we were advised not to speak our mind lest we risk being punished. Continental integration should be accelerated, they argued, since the interdependence of the two economies provided Canada with some insurance against Washington's arbitrary action since; if it tried to punish Canada, the United States would really be harming its own interests.

Since then, the same logic pushed Ottawa to negotiate CUFTA and NAFTA and abandon the previous strategy of developing a self-standing economy.

Now, in the aftermath of 11 September 2001, Canadian continentalists have made the same arguments. Ottawa should support US military policy in Iraq and the National Missile Defense not because these are sensible policies but because Canada might be punished for not toeing the American line. Canada's global influence depends on being seen as insiders in Washington where our advice is heeded. Criticizing American policy, they argue, will only alienate our American interlocutors and be self-defeating.

NATIONALISTS

The economic nationalist position has long been ambivalent. While admired by some for its great social, technological, and intellectual achievements, the United States was also seen as a threat to Canadian security. Interdependence really meant a dependence that shut down the possibility for creative action abroad. Rather than practicing 'quiet diplomacy', nationalists felt that Ottawa should develop a public diplomacy that spoke its mind. This could be valuable itself in buttressing Canadians' sense of their bilingual and multicultural identity.

Since then, nationalists have been mainly on the losing side of the debate. While they could take some comfort from Pierre Trudeau's occasional forays on the world scene and from Brian

Mulroney's defiance of both Margaret Thatcher and Ronald Reagan over apartheid in South Africa, they had to mourn their two defeats over free trade and resign themselves to the country's economic-policy castration and consequently to its ever-closer and dependent integration in the American system.

Lloyd Axworthy's surprisingly successful ventures in low-cost niche diplomacy—the International Criminal Court and the land mine treaty—proved the nationalist view that public diplomacy could produce effective foreign policy. But the Department of Foreign Affairs and International Trade had been too drained of funds, personnel, and morale from years of neoconservative budget-cutting for Axworthy's muscular 'damn-the-torpedoes' approach to continue under other leadership.

Now, the nationalists enjoy a clear, if temporary advantage. The American application of unilateral, preemptive war in Iraq has proven such a patent disaster that 'ready-aye-ready' solidarity with George Bush has almost no traction outside the boardrooms of the Canadian Council of Chief Executives (CCEE). Even the CCCE has been consternated by Washington's blatant disregard of its NAFTA commitments in defying dispute panel rulings that remanded US countervailing and antidumping duties levied against Canadian softwood lumber exports. Other examples of Washington's unprincipled protectionism, most glaringly, its prolonged ban on imports of Canadian beef, make continentalist arguments a hard sell. Nevertheless, Canada remains locked into its external constitution, just as its negotiators intended. Advocates of greater autonomy have few power levers at their command.

In the final analysis, the Canadian foreign policy debate between continentalist and nationalists remains just as unresolvable as that between the ideological right and left in domestic politics. The two schools are rooted in different value systems and support opposing corporate and citizen interests. Deploying actual evidence has little effect. Turning to the reforms advocated four decades ago, it is clear that much of what I recommended then has actually been implemented. White papers have been written on foreign policy issues, Parliament's Standing Committee on Foreign Affairs and International Trade has held hearings across the country on the major issues facing Canada and produced substantial reports, and public opinion polls are constantly commissioned in order to take the electorate's pulse.

The mandarinate—the diplomatic elite which kept its foreign policy cards close to its vest—has vanished and its place of dominance over Canadian foreign policy has been assumed by trade policy analysts inspired by an equally exclusive and arrogant ideology. It was the reverse takeover of the old Department of External Affairs in 1982, when the trade commissioners were moved to Sussex Drive from the Department of Industry, Trade, and Commerce, which led to Canadian foreign policy being hijacked by a mania for free trade agreements. Similar to the old Ottawa mandarinate in their anti-democratic elitism, but inspired by a messianic and economics-based faith in neoconservative market deregulation, they drove out considerations of Canada's national interests as a global power in order to hitch the country to America's destiny.

Now that the future of the United States seems decidedly less rosy; now that India, Brazil, and even Mexico are moving up the power hierarchy behind China; now that many Canadians have taken the future into their own hands by operating across national borders in non-government organizations that are directly coping with pandemics and rebuilding failed states, the continentalist–nationalist debate has taken on a renewed relevance. If the United States has become a rogue imperial power whose policies exacerbate rather than remedy global warming, expand rather than contain nuclear proliferation, provoke rather than stifle terrorism, and speed rather than slow the spread of HIV/AIDS, there is a powerful argument to 'go around' the United States, as former Defense Secretary Robert McNamara recently urged the international community.

Many foreign policy choices have been made over the past four decades, but many still remain to be made day-by-day and year-by-year. Given the ineradicably deep gaps separating the normative positions of continentalists and nationalists, what choices Ottawa should make will continue to be debated. Forty years from now, it would be surprising if the debate had been definitively resolved. With luck, students and scholars in the middle of the twenty-first century will conclude that the choices made in this period contributed to averting the social, economic, and environmental disasters that were facing both Canadians and the world during this century's first decade.

4

Where Do We, Should We, or Can We Sit? A Review of Canadian Foreign Policy Literature

Maureen Appel Molot

Canadian foreign policy literature in large measure reflects the Canadian preoccupation with Canada's place in the world, a preoccupation with status, position, influence, and power. This theme of 'place' links otherwise very different strands of literature. The more traditional Canadian foreign policy perspective debates whether Canada is a 'middle' or 'principal' power,[1] and examines Canada's place in the world primarily from the perspective of diplomacy and international politics. The political-economy/economic nationalism literature addresses the question of Canada's global status principally in economic terms, and discusses whether Canada is dependent, part of the periphery, or part of the core.[2] The most important subtheme or corollary to this 'position' concern is Canada's relationship to the United States. This literature, also voluminous, examines various facets of bilateral ties across a spectrum of issues, from defence to economics. While diverse in perspective, what is common to much of this literature is its attention to the implications of this most critical of Canada's foreign relationships in terms of Canadian domestic and foreign policy decisions. Most recently, the literature on Canada–United States relations has focused largely on the decision to negotiate the Free Trade Agreement (FTA).[3]

The second major theme or organizing principle of Canadian foreign policy literature is policy formulation—that which investigates the way in which Canadian foreign policy is made and the role of institutions—governmental and non-governmental—in the process. Sometimes described as 'statist',[4] this literature is divided between that which discusses the efforts of diverse Canadian interest groups to influence foreign policy outcomes[5] and discussions that focus more directly on the state actors responsible for foreign policy decisions.[6] In its analysis of questions such as the degree of state autonomy in foreign policy decision-making, or the importance of bureaucratic politics, the process literature has emphasized the impact of domestic sources on policy outcomes and has tended to downplay, if not ignore, the importance of external or systemic forces.[7] Important though this literature is to an understanding of Canadian foreign policy, limitations of space preclude an analysis of the process literature and the paradigms which have structured its arguments.

Different interpretive and philosophical predispositions characterize the writing on Canadian foreign policy. Nonetheless, the primacy of the dual interests in position and process remains, a phenomenon that derives from history and the continuing intellectual interests of analysts of Canadian foreign policy. This legacy has definite strengths: it has produced a literature rich in debates from the perspectives of problem solving and critical theory.[8] But it is also a tradition which has been captured by its own preoccupations and has, therefore, remained highly descriptive, rarely posing questions about the implications of paradigm choice and paradigm debate for its endeavours. Moreover, it has left many important questions about Canadian foreign policy and Canada's place in the world unasked and, therefore, undebated. This essay is an effort both to review the sum of recent Canadian foreign policy literature and to pose a number of questions about possible new directions for Canadian foreign policy research. The selection of material and the organization of any review article are by definition subjective, and result in the discussion of some works to the exclusion of others. The lack of attention to the literature on defence policy, for example, is not a judgment of its importance, but rather a reflection of the author's interest in other questions.

International relations and the concerns of foreign policy have changed substantially over the last two decades as the issues on the global agenda increase in diversity. No longer are international relations courses structured solely around considerations of war and peace, arms control and disarmament, critical questions though these continue to be. Quite clearly, the definition of international relations has broadened to include a host of environmental and economic issues. Of significance among the latter are trade and tariff questions, and the organizations created to promote international trade, the new protectionism, technology transfer, the movement to regional trading blocs, the internationalization of production, and the rise of the Newly Industrializing Countries, to note but a few of the topics currently considered within the confines of the field. The rapidly growing interest in international political-economy during the late 1970s and 1980s has influenced the research agenda in Canada and elsewhere, as scholars began to examine the formulation of foreign economic policy and states' responses to global economic change and crises.[9] Among the results of this broadened definition of international relations has been a new focus on the conditions of state autonomy and paradigms of state–society relations, and the development of shared interests between Canadian foreign policy, now defined more broadly than ever to include foreign economic policy, and Canadian political-economy, as scholars undertake research on subjects of common concern.

Where Do We Sit?

THE MIDDLE POWER PERSPECTIVE

The debate over Canada's place in the global system has long galvanized Canadian academics, although the theoretical assumptions that structure it have often been more implicit than explicit. This is particularly true of the historic discussion of Canada as a middle power. In recent years, the debate has focused more on Canada's position within the global economy than on the country's involvement in military/security or international diplomacy questions. The original conception of Canada as a 'middle power' was the result of comparison—Canada was less 'powerful' than the United States, Britain, or France, and more so than most of the countries of the world. Precise categorization, however, was rarely specified.[10] Moreover, since much of this middle power literature was focused on Canada's dedication to and participation in the construction and maintenance of the postwar order, decisions on criteria for determining the effectiveness of this role bordered on the impossible. The genesis of the perspective lay in the functional concept of representation, developed in Ottawa during the Second World War, which asserted that absolute size alone was insufficient to determine participation in the councils of the war and postwar period. Rather, capacity for contribution, interest, and expertise should all play a role in decisions on representation.[11]

Concomitant with this view of Canada as a middle power was that of Canada's commitment to liberal internationalism.[12] In large measure the creation of foreign policy practitioners, liberal internationalism expressed in rhetoric and practice the assumption that Canada could have an impact on world affairs precisely through its activities as a middle power. What was recommended and analyzed was a Canadian praxis that emphasized support for international organizations, peace-keeping, promotion of international dialogue (and it was hoped agreement) in functional areas such as law of the sea and human rights, and concern to improve conditions in the Third World.

The perspective of liberal internationalism was clearly the predominant intellectual lens through which Canadian foreign policy was analyzed in the postwar period and for at least two decades after the war. Moreover, as I shall argue below, it remains a significant analytical perspective, though more for its hortatory connotations than its analytical rigor. It was also a perspective that distinguished Canadian foreign policy literature from that produced in the United States, where the realism of Henry Morgenthau[13] was the predominant paradigm. For many in Canada, realism was not only an alien paradigm but also one subject to much criticism by analysts who decried both its roots and its policy implications.[14] Nonetheless, for many Canadian practitioners and students of international relations, this realist paradigm was the one utilized in teaching courses on international relations. The Canadian experience of middle powermanship may have been useful to argue the limitations of a US-centered approach to analysis and as an organizing device for readers on Canadian foreign policy.[15] At the same time, however, the pre-eminence of the realist paradigm in the general international relations literature engendered tensions in Canadian analyses of global politics and of Canadian behaviour. With respect to the creation of and Canadian participation in NATO and NORAD, for example,[16] Canada may have insisted on the inclusion of Article 2 (about eco-

nomic cooperation) in the NATO charter, but the conception of the alliance and the explanation for Canadian participation lie in recognizing the realities of a bipolar world. Similarly, Canadian defence policies and many analyses of it are premised on superpower conflict.[17]

By concentrating on the analysis of instances of liberal internationalism or Canada's middle power status, Canadian foreign policy literature has tended to ignore considerations of national interest in Canadian action, despite emphasis in the larger international relations literature on precisely this issue. The result was a sense, intentional or not, that Canadian foreign policy decisions were altruistic. Whether it was 'the grain of economic interest',[18] or motives that captured other domestic considerations, Canadian foreign policy behaviour was motivated by the national interest in a stable, international order that would prevent or reduce conflict and promote economic growth.[19]

The tensions in Canadian foreign policy analysis between liberal internationalism and realism can perhaps be resolved through what Keating, following Hedley Bull and Martin Wright, has characterized as the 'Grotian perspective on the nature of international politics'.[20] This is an attempt at a nuanced view of interstate relations which combines a recognition of continuing interstate conflict, on the one hand, with at least a minimal commitment to the maintenance of international order, on the other. Although at one level this argument may be simply another way to express the liberal internationalist tradition, at another, it suggests the need to counterpoise the realist or Hobbesian conception of anarchy in a fashion that more appropriately captures not only the Canadian but also the global situations. Moreover, it provides a provocative, alternative intellectual formulation of one of the dominant traditions in Canadian foreign policy analysis.

For all the criticism of liberal internationalism by analysts as well as practitioners,[21] its continuing underlying attraction in the analysis of Canadian foreign policy is ironic. As Tucker noted in his discussion of Canadian foreign policy in the

Trudeau era, Trudeau may have spoken disparagingly of the idea of Canada as a middle power, yet, his stance on a range of issues, from North–South concerns to those of the environment and the diminution of global conflict, confirmed the perspective he disdained.[22] Part of the explanation for the attraction of liberal internationalism may be its resonance within much of the Canadian public, as submissions and presentations to parliamentary committees studying Canadian foreign policy since the mid-1980s reveal.[23] But equally significant is the belief among analysts and politicians in Canada's responsibility to actively promote an improved quality of life around the world. This is the theme of the Matthews and Pratt volume, *Human Rights in Canadian Foreign Policy*,[24] which examines Canada's record in promoting human rights in a variety of countries and international institutions, and an important component of the Holmes and Kirton book, *Canada and the New Internationalism*.[25] It is also the perspective that shapes much of the literature on Canada and international development,[26] and Canadian efforts to promote solutions to regional conflicts.[27] Two recent books edited by Cranford Pratt contrast realism with what is termed 'humane internationalism', and examine the ability of middle power internationalism to ameliorate conditions in the Third World.[28] Much of the aid and regional conflict resolution literature is critical of Canadian efforts: too much Canadian aid is tied; Canada ignores human rights infringements in its distribution of aid; the level of development assistance should not have been lowered; the Canadian state benefits more from aid than the recipients; there is a gap between Canadian rhetoric and its endeavours to reduce regional conflict.[29] But the basis for the assessment of Canadian performance is grounded in the expectation of an enduring Canadian commitment to international peace and justice.

THE PRINCIPAL POWER VIEW

A major challenge to the liberal internationalist explanation for Canadian foreign policy, one that also had its roots in the mainstream international relations literature, is Dewitt and Kirton's conception of Canada as a 'principal power'. The origins of this conception of Canada's status are twofold, a frustration with the middle power view of Canada because it did not capture the reality of Canadian capabilities and, second, the assessment that the realist view of the international system had to be rethought in terms of its appropriateness to a changed global environment.[30] Antecedents of the principal power formulation among Canadian foreign policy analysts were the arguments of James Eayrs, and Lyon and Tomlin that on many indices of national capability, Canada ranked not with the middle powers, but with those generally agreed to be major actors.[31] Dewitt and Kirton argued further that Canada's participation in international fora and its initiatives on issues necessitated a new interpretation of its position. Finally, in their view, the global system envisioned by the realists no longer existed. With American hegemony under challenge in an ever more complicated global environment, there was a need to reconceptualize the international system and to recognize the opportunities that these changes provided actors like Canada. In their advocacy of principal power status for Canada, Dewitt and Kirton identify the complex neorealist perspective within international relations theory.[32]

Although a stimulating interpretation of the Canadian position and an effort to link international relations theorizing with the study of Canadian foreign policy, the principal power formulation has not had a major impact on Canadian foreign policy analysis. The reasons for this lie both in the Dewitt-Kirton volume itself— the case studies which constitute an important part of their 'proof' lie outside the mainstream of Canadian foreign policy behaviour and the theory of complex neorealism is neither easily nor convincingly applicable to the Canadian experience—and in the lack of subsequent studies prepared to employ this paradigm which would permit additional critical evaluation of it. With the exception of Canadian political-economy literature, there has been little interest in recent years in macroanalyses of Canada's global status. At the same time, the conception of a more complex global environment, which offers opportunities for state action at a number of levels and in diverse locations, is now a given in our conceptions of the international system. Although *Canada and the New Internationalism* was cited above as reflecting the Canadian penchant for strengthening international institutions, at least some of the chapters in the volume have been influenced in their conception of world order by the ideas of complex neorealism.

THE ECONOMIC STRUCTURALIST PERSPECTIVE

The third tradition that has examined Canada's place in the world emanates from a very different intellectual perspective than the two discussed above. Variously described as the 'economic nationalist' or 'peripheral dependence' perspective,[33] this literature concentrates its attention on economic structure, primarily the level of foreign, direct investment in Canada, and on economic indicators, rather than diplomatic/military/security activity, to explain both Canada's global position and many of its policies. Proponents of this view of Canada include a wide variety of Canadian analysts from diverse disciplines as well as a host of public policy practitioners. The theoretical underpinnings of this approach are diverse, and include the writings of Harold Innis[34] and the application of dependency theory to the Canadian situation.[35] Its practical origins lie in the growing concern during the 1960s over American control of Canadian industry and the broad public policy implications of such control. While it is difficult to encapsulate a literature that is more disparate in its arguments than either the middle power or principal power depictions, in essence, most of this literature argues that the structure of the Canadian economy (high levels of foreign ownership, technological dependence, composition of exports) has produced a political-economy that resembles that of a less rather than a more developed state,

with the attendant limitations that such status imposes on state autonomy.[36] Juxtaposed to this view of Canada is a different, critical, economic perspective, one that describes the country not as dependent but the opposite—an imperial power in its own right, albeit a secondary one, that exported capital abroad.[37]

Much of the political-economy debate of the last few years on Canada's current position assumes a middle ground between the two views just expressed, arguing that, notwithstanding Canada's truncated industrial structure, the Canadian GNP, standard of living, competitive trade position, and growing international prominence of its capital make comparisons between Canada and Third World states questionable.[38] Moreover, the dependency perspective does not allow for the possibility of change in status over time. Resnick argues that although Canada might have been classified, following Wallerstein, as 'semiperipheral',[39] in the years prior to the Second World War, since 1945, there have been important changes in the indicators used to measure Canada's position; as a result, Canada should now be 'classified as one of the core countries in the world, in economic terms especially'.[40] All three of these economic structure categorization efforts have difficulties that stem from their theoretical assumptions. The dependency theorists so concentrated on Canada's relationship with the United States that they ignored Canada's position relative to the rest of the world. The argument that Canada is an imperialist power disregarded the importance for Canada of its bilateral relationship with the US. And the perimeter of the core perspective assumes too much from the increase in Canadian direct investment abroad, particularly in the US.[41]

The debate over Canada's status has never been confined solely to academic analysts. Two reports, one by the Canadian Government, the second, an annual international review of the competitiveness of a number of economies at varying stages of development, exemplify the challenges of the status discussion and the divergent assessments that it generates. *Competitiveness and Security*, the Mulroney government's green paper on Canadian foreign policy, presents a rather gloomy picture of Canada's international economic position, suggesting that the country's declining international competitiveness has rendered it vulnerable to a rapidly changing global economy.[42] Taking a very different perspective on Canada is the *World Competitiveness Report* (WCR) which, in its 1989 edition, suggests that Canada's international competitiveness ranking among twenty-two development market economies, as measured by nine different variables, had risen from sixth to fourth.[43] The point made by the WCR and by Canada's inclusion as a member of the G7 is that the country has considerable economic strength and potential; how that potential is harnessed and how industry adjusts to a rapidly changing global economy are issues that have been addressed frequently in recent years, particularly in the context of Canada–United States relations.

Where Do We Sit? Canada–US Ties

Given the level of Canadian trade dependence (approximately 30 per cent of the Canadian GDP) and trade concentration (close to 75 per cent of our trade is with the United States), a number of trends in the global economy during the 1980s generated questions about the appropriate future economic path for Canada. Among the more significant of these were the increase in US protectionism, exemplified by the passage of the 1988 Omnibus Trade and Competitiveness Act, the European Community's decision to move toward a single market by 1992, and uncertainties about the outcome of the Uruguay Round of GATT talks.[44] The importance of secure access to US markets catapulted the age-old question of Canada–US free trade to prominence once again in the context of the Royal Commission on the Economic Union and Development Prospects for Canada (the Macdonald Commission), and the commitment of the Mulroney government to improve Canada–US relations.[45] If regional trading blocs were one possible, future trade scenario,

Canada might have little alternative but to formalize what many already saw as extant: a North American trade entity.[46]

Canada–US relations have been analyzed from a variety of vantage points over the years.[47] One perspective, which might broadly be styled the economic nationalist school, takes as its point of departure Canada's economic (and military) dependence on the United States and the resulting constraints on Canadian sovereignty. This tradition, initiated in foreign policy terms by Clarkson's *An Independent Foreign Policy for Canada?*,[48] had its counterpart on the domestic and foreign economic policy sides in a number of publications, some of which fall under the rubric of the dependency approach within Canadian political-economy.[49] On the opposite side of the philosophical spectrum was the literature, produced primarily by economists, that criticized the concerns of those who decried high levels of American investment in Canada, the composition of Canadian exports, technological dependence, etc. Arguing that the tariff simply protected inefficient Canadian industry, proponents of what some termed the continentalist perspective maintained that economic prosperity would result from reduced government-imposed barriers to trade.[50] Less prominent, but still significant because they represented an effort to analyze bilateral relations using an international relations literature of some influence through the 1960s, were examinations of Canada–US relations that employed a regional integration framework.[51] The obvious differences between the experiences of the European Community and Canada–US—the number and relative size of participants and the formalized versus unconscious character of economic and political connections—made the application of a literature which focused on the measurement of progress toward a specific end problematic. At the same time, the theoretical and practical questions raised by the integration literature, among them the automaticity of the process and the necessity of political institutions to manage economic linkages,[52] exemplified the assumptions and concerns of proponents and opponents of closer bilateral ties.

The issues addressed by the latest bevy of publications on Canada–US free trade differ little at one level from those raised over the years about the evolving relationship. At the root of the discussion are differences in perspective that engender divergent attitudes about whether closer ties with the United States—now examined in much more focused terms—will be to Canada's benefit or detriment. As Woodside notes, the FTA collected in one document a host of 'longstanding issues in Canada–United States relations—the desirability of a continental energy policy and investment review, the proper role of US banks in the Canadian financial market, and the kind of industrial policy we should pursue . . .'.[53] While the FTA was under negotiation, a number of volumes either supporting or opposing freer trade with the US appeared.[54] At another level, when the provisions of the agreement became known, analysis could become much more specific. Thus, subsequent to the signing of the agreement, came publications analyzing the negotiation process, the provisions of the agreement (most notably the chapters on dispute settlement and energy), and whether Canada made too many concessions to obtain the agreement.[55]

It is far too early in the history of the agreement to even begin to contemplate an evaluation of the impact of free trade on Canada. Whether bilateral trade disputes increase or decrease in the future will only in part be a function of free trade. Equally significant will be how industry in Canada and the US adjusts to both the challenges of free trade and to increasing international competition. In a number of industries critical of the economic health of both economies, the immediate prognosis is for considerable adjustment, with the domestic political ramifications that this necessarily involves.[56] Also of relevance will be the outcome of the Uruguay Round of tariff talks, European progress toward 1992 and the stability of the global economy. Many of these important international political-economy issues went

unaddressed in the analyses of the FTA because the literature tended to preoccupy itself with the larger pro and anti questions.

Where Does Quebec Sit?

Location has also been a focus of some of the foreign policy literature emanating from Quebec. Generated by a particularistic concern with provincial place and a desire to legitimate the province's international role, there have been a number of books and articles which discuss the overall evolution of Quebec's international activities and its relations with specific countries. The Painchaud reader, noted in footnote 15 above, contains a section on Quebec's international relations; Albert Legault and Alfred O. Hero, Jr edited a volume exploring Quebec's links with Anglophone Canada, the United States, and the rest of the world;[57] Gerard Hervouet and Helene Galarneau with a team of contributors reviewed *La Présence internationale du Québec* over the years 1978 to 1983.[58] Among all of Quebec's international connections, perhaps none has received more attention than its ties with the United States as analysts have focused on a link which, in economic terms especially, is critical for Quebec.[59]

Does Location Matter?

Concern with Canada's status within the global system has produced a Canadian foreign policy tradition diverse in philosophical perspective yet rather narrow in the range of issues it has examined. While the question of position may be important, and recent work has demonstrated the increasing complexity of determining location, it reflects a fixation with either power or the lack thereof, which needs some rethinking. For the moment, at least, Canadian international relations scholars have turned away from debates on the appropriateness of prominent paradigms for the Canadian situation. Though power is clearly a central concept in the international relations literature, there are limits to the intellectual progress that can emanate from grand theory.

Moreover, the attention to position has led to the neglect of a host of other issues of relevance. Perhaps most crucial has been the relative lack of attention from a Canadian perspective to the evolving global system and what this means for Canada across a range of foreign policy topics. Cognizant of the theoretical impact of regime literature over the last decade, it is noteworthy that there has been no analysis of Canada's behaviour in international economic and other institutions as what Lake describes as a 'system supporter',[60] particularly given the liberal internationalist tradition in Canadian scholarship. Has Canada consciously assumed the role of system supporter in the GATT or the IMP, and has this role altered with the passage of time? Are there limits to supportership? Does the regime paradigm of analytical utility have a Canadian perspective, or does it exemplify a theoretical preference at variance with Canadian interests? Though there has not

been space in this essay to review the literature on foreign policy formulation, it is suffice to note that here, too, there is an enormous potential research agenda, particularly with respect to foreign economic policy where state autonomy is arguably more restricted because of the mobilization of domestic interests. Are changes in the global economy increasing the constraints under which foreign policy is made and, therefore, by implication, reducing the significance of domestic interests? The growing overlap in research interests between scholars of foreign and domestic policy, produced by the development of international political economy on the one hand, and the revival of Canadian political-economy on the other,[61] enhances opportunities for new understanding. In sum, although a review of Canadian foreign policy literature demonstrates its richness, it also illustrates the urgency of new intellectual challenges.

Notes

For their helpful comments and revision suggestions, I am grateful to Tony Porter and two anonymous reviewers.

1. The literature on Canada as a 'middle power' is vast. Some of it will be noted briefly below in the discussion of the internationalist perspective in Canadian foreign policy. Among the more prominent examples of this perspective are: John Holmes, *The Better Part of Valour: Essays on Canadian Diplomacy* (Toronto: McClelland and Stewart, 1970); Holmes, *Canada: A Middle-Aged Power* (Toronto: McClelland and Stewart, 1976); J. King Gordon, ed., *Canada's Role as a Middle Power* (Toronto: McClelland and Stewart, 1966); Denis Stairs, *The Diplomacy of Constraint: Canada, the Korean War and the United States* (Toronto: University of Toronto Press, 1974); Annette Baker Fox, *The Politics of Attraction: Four Middle Powers and the United States* (New York: Columbia University Press, 1977). The conception of Canada as a 'principal' power is that of David

Dewitt and John Kirton, *Canada as a Principal Power* (Toronto: John Wiley & Sons, 1983).

2. Among the relevant works here are: Stephen Clarkson, ed. *An Independent Foreign Policy for Canada?* (Toronto: McClelland and Stewart, 1968); Clarkson, *Canada and the Reagan Challenge* (Toronto: James Lorimer & Co., 1982, 1985); Glen Williams, 'Canada in the New International Political Economy' in Wallace Clement and Glen Williams, eds, *The New Canadian Political Economy* (Montreal: McGill Queen's University Press, 1989), 117–39; Williams, 'Canada and the International Political Economy', *Studies in Political Economy* 25: 107–40; Philip Resnick, 'From Semiperiphery to Perimeter of the Core: Canada's Place in the Capitalist World Economy', *Review* 12, 2 (Spring 1989): 263–97.

3. Literature supportive of the FTA includes Gilbert Winham, *Trading with Canada: The Canada–US Free Trade Agreement* (New York: Twentieth Century Fund Paper, 1988); Richard Lipsey and Robert York, *Evaluating the Free Trade Deal* (Toronto: C.D.

Howe Institute, 1988); Richard Lipsey and Murray Smith, *Taking the Initiative: Canada's Trade Options in a Turbulent World* (Toronto: C.D. Howe Institute, 1985); Bernard Landry, *Commerce sans frontières: Le sens du libre-échange* (Montreal: Editions Québec Amérique, 1987); John Crispo, ed., *Free Trade: The Real Story* (Toronto: Gage, 1988). Among the books critical of the FTA are: Duncan Cameron, ed., *The Free Trade Papers* (Toronto: James Lorimer & Co., 1986); Cameron, ed., *The Free Trade Deal* (Toronto: James Lorimer & Co., 1988); John W. Warnock, *Free Trade and the New Right Agenda* (Vancouver: New Star Books, 1988). Among the volumes that attempt to evaluate the issue and contain both supportive and critical positions are: Michael Henderson, ed., *The Future on the Table: Canada and the Free Trade Issue* (Toronto: Masterpress, 1987); Marc Gold and David Leyton Brown, eds, *Trade-Offs on Free Trade: The Canada–US Free Trade Agreement* (Toronto: Carswell, 1988); Alan Maslove and Stanley Winer, eds, *Knocking on the Back Door: Canadian Perspectives on the Political Economy of Freer Trade with the United States* (Halifax: Institute for Research on Public Policy, 1987).

4. Elizabeth Riddell-Dixon employs this terminology to describe some of the more recent process literature. 'State Autonomy and Canadian Foreign Policy: The Case of Deep Seabed Mining', *Canadian Journal of Political Science* 21, 2 (June 1988): 297.

5. Among the more prominent examples here are Elizabeth Riddell-Dixon, *The Domestic Mosaic: Interest Groups and Canadian Foreign Policy* (Toronto: Canadian Institute for International Affairs, 1985); David Taras and David H. Goldberg, eds, *The Domestic Battleground: Canada and the Arab–Israeli Conflict* (Montreal: McGill-Queen's University Press, 1989); many of the books and articles that discuss Canadian foreign policy with respect to Southern Africa and Latin America, for example, or Canadian aid and human rights policies, implicitly or explicitly focus on interest-group views and demands.

6. The major 'process' volume is Kim Richard Nossal's *The Politics of Canadian Foreign Policy*, 2nd ed. (Toronto: Prentice Hall, 1989). Also useful is Denis Stairs and Gilbert Winharn, eds, *Selected Problems in Formulating Foreign Economic Policy* (Toronto: University of Toronto Press, 1985). Among the relevant articles are Nossal and M. Atkinson, 'Bureaucratic Politics and the New Fighter Aircraft Decisions', *Canadian Public Administration* 24, 4 (Winter 1981): 531–62; Nossal, 'Analysing the Domestic Sources of Canadian Foreign Policy', *International Journal* 39, 1 (Winter 1983–4): 1–22; John Kirton and Blair Dimock, 'Domestic Access to Government in the Canadian Foreign Policy Process 1968–1982', *International Journal* 39, 1 (Winter 1983–4): 68–98; Kirton, 'The Foreign Policy Decision Process' in M.A. Molot and B.W. Tomlin, eds, *Canada Among Nations 1985: The Conservative Agenda* (Toronto: James Lorimer & Co., 1986), 25–45; Kirton, 'Foreign Policy Decision Making in the Mulroney Government' in B.W. Tomlin and M.A. Molot, eds, *Canada Among Nations 1988: The Tory Record* (Toronto: James Lorimer & Co., 1989), 21–38; Harald Von Riekhoff, 'The Structure of Foreign Policy Decision Making and Management' in B.W. Tomlin and M.A. Molot, eds, *Canada Among Nations 1986: Talking Trade* (Toronto: James Lorimer & Co., 1987), 14–30 .

7. This argument is made by Michael Hawes in 'Structural Change and Hegemonic Decline: Implications for National Governments', in David G. Haglund and Michael Hawes, eds, *World Politics: Power Interdependence and Dependence* (Toronto: Harcourt Brace Jovanovich, 1990), 198.

8. These categorizations of theory are those of Robert W. Cox, 'Social Forces, States and World Orders: Beyond International Relations Theory', *Millenium* 10, 2 (1981): 126–55.

9. The volume of books and articles on these subjects is enormous. Readers will always disagree on the salience of particular works; however, among the more influential non-Canadian focused works are Peter Katzenstein, *Between Power and Plenty* (Madison: University of Wisconsin Press, 1978); Peter Gourevitch, *Politics in Hard Times* (Ithaca: Cornell University Press, 1986); Helen Milner, *Resisting Protectionism* (Princeton: Princeton University Press, 1988); Michael Piore and Charles Sabel, *The Second Industrial Divide* (New York: Basic

Books, 1984) to list but a few. Among the relevant Canada-centred publications are Duncan Cameron and François Houle, eds, *Le Canada et la nouvelle division internationale du travail/Canada and the New International Division of Labour* (Ottawa: University of Ottawa Press, 1985); John Holmes and Colin Leys, eds, *Frontyard Backyard: The Americas in the Global Crisis* (Toronto: Between the Lines, 1987); Rianne Mallon, *The Politics of Industrial Restructuring: Canadian Textiles* (Toronto: University of Toronto Press, 1984), again to cite but some of the literature on this broad topic.

10. Dewitt and Kirton list the comparison countries in *Canada as a Principal Power*, 22–3. Nossal also notes the difficulties in defining middle power in *The Politics of Canadian Foreign Policy*, 2nd ed., 46–50. These authors, as well as Michael Hawes discuss the middle power/internationalist perspective in some detail. Michael Hawes, *Principal Power, Middle Power, or Satellite: Competing Perspectives in the Study of Canadian Foreign Policy* (Toronto: York University Research Programme in Strategic Studies, 1984), 3–8.

11. Nossal, *The Politics of Canadian Foreign Policy*, 47–9; Dewitt and Kirton, *Canada as a Principal Power*, 17–21.

12. Liberal internationalism connotes an approach to international politics and the global system that stresses opportunities for conflict resolution and accepts a real role for international institutions and non-major powers such as Canada. Juxtaposed to liberal internationalism is realism, which sees power in zero-sum terms and assumes a system of continuing interstate conflict in which nation-states egoistically pursue their own interests.

13. Hans Morgenthau, *Politics Among Nations; The Struggle for Power and Peace*, 5th ed. (New York: Alfred A. Knopf, 1973).

14. See, among others, John Kirton, 'Realism and Reality in Canadian foreign policy', *International Perspectives* (January/February 1987): 3–8; Axel Dorscht et al., 'Canada's International Role and "Realism"', *International Perspectives* (May/June 1986): 6–9 and (September/October 1986): 6–9; and papers delivered at the conference on 'The

Consequences of Paradigm Hegemony in the Study and Practice of International Relations in Canada', Carleton University, 9–11 October 1986.

15. In a reader edited by Paul Painchaud, *De Mackenzie King à Pierre Trudeau: quarante ans de diplomatie canadienne* (Quebec: Les Presses de l'Université Laval, 1989), the growth of Canada's international activities is discussed in terms of three spheres in which Canada has been active: global, within the western alliance, and in the north–south system. For an earlier reader which adopted a similar format see Painchaud, ed., *Le Canada et le Québec sur la scène internationale* (Quebec: Universite Laval, 1977). The Quebec perspective on foreign policy will be noted briefly below.

16. For a recent discussion on the background to NORAD and Canadian and American perspectives on cooperation and distance, see Joseph T. Jockel, *No Boundaries Upstairs: Canada, the United States and the Origins of North American Air Defence* (Vancouver: UBC Press, 1987).

17. For a recent analysis of Canadian defence policy see D.W. Middlemiss and J.J. Sokolsky, *Canadian Defence: Decisions and Determinants* (Toronto: Harcourt Brace Jovanovich, 1989). The appropriateness of a neutralist position for Canada is debated in Claude Bergeron et al., *Les choix géopolitiques du Canada: l'enjeu de la neutralité!* (Montreal: Editions du Méridien, 1988). Tom Keating and Larry Pratt's *Canada, NATO and the Bomb: The Western Alliance in Crisis* (Edmonton: Hurtig Publishers, 1988) examines the history of Canada's participation in NATO and the importance of a multilateral approach to Canadian security. Although events in the last year in particular necessitate a new analysis of superpower relations, the Mulroney government's white paper on national defence, *Challenge and Commitment* (Ottawa: Supply and Services Canada, 1987), assumed a bipolar world. The Conservative government's foreign policy green paper adopted a neorealist view of the world. See *Competitiveness and Security* (Ottawa: Supply and Services Canada, 1985), 10–12.

18. Reg Whitaker, 'The Cold War and the Myth of Liberal Internationalism', Paper presented at the

annual meetings of the Canadian Historical Association and the Canadian Political Science Association, 8 June 1986, 6.

19. Tom Keating, 'Making a Virtue of Necessity: Perspectives on Canada's Defence and Foreign Policies', Paper presented to the conference on 'The Consequences of Paradigm Hegemony in the Study and Practice of International Relations in Canada', Carleton University, 9–11 October 1986, 16.

20. Keating, 'Making a Virtue of Necessity . . .', 12.

21. Among the foreign policy practitioners, the most outspoken critic of the conception of Canada as a middle power was Prime Minister Trudeau. See, among others, Nossal, *The Politics of Canadian Foreign Policy*, 51–2, and Michael Tucker, *Canadian Foreign Policy: Contemporary Issues and Themes* (Toronto: McGraw Hill, 1980).

22. Ibid. Hawes, *Principal Power*, 6–9, and Nossal, *The Politics of Canadian Foreign Policy*, 51–2, also suggest the continuing salience of this view of Canadian behaviour.

23. See Report of the Special Joint Committee on Canada's International Relations, *Independence and Internationalism* (Ottawa: Queen's Printer, 1986) and Report of the Standing Committee on External Affairs and International Trade on Canada's Official Development Assistance Policies and Aid Programs, *For Whose Benefit?* (Ottawa: Queen's Printer, 1987).

24. Montreal: McGill-Queen's University Press, 1988.

25. Toronto: Canadian Institute for International Affairs, 1988.

26. See, for example, Martin Rudner, 'New Dimensions in Canadian Development Assistance Policy', in B.W. Tomlin and M.A. Molot, eds, *Canada Among Nations 1988: The Tory Record* (Toronto: James Lorimer & Co., 1989), 149–68; Cranford Pratt, 'Ethics and Foreign Policy: The Case of Canada's Development Assistance', *International Journal* 43, 2 (1988): 264–301; John Hendra, 'Fit to be Tied: A Comparison of the Canadian Tied Aid Policy with the Tied Aid Policies of Sweden, Norway and Denmark', *Canadian Journal of Development Studies* 8, 2 (1987): 261–81.

27. See, for example, Chris Brown, 'Canada and Southern Africa: Autonomy, Image and Capacity in Foreign Policy' and Tim Draimin and Lisa North, 'Canada and Central America' both in M.A. Molot and F.O. Hampson eds, *Canada Among Nations 1989: The Challenge of Change* (Ottawa: Carleton University Press, 1990), 207–24, 225–43.

28. Cranford Pratt, ed., *Middle Power Internationalism: The North South Dimension* (Montreal: McGill-Queen's University Press, 1990) and Cranford Pratt, ed., *Internationalism Under Strain: The North–South Policies of Canada, the Netherlands, Norway and Sweden* (Toronto: University of Toronto Press, 1989).

29. See the sources cited in footnotes 25 and 26 as well as Kim Richard Nossal, 'Mixed Motives Revisited: Canada's Interest in Development Assistance', *International Journal* 43, 2 (1988): 264–301, who argues that Canada's development assistance program is designed primarily to benefit the interests of policy formulators; the interests of beneficiaries are of secondary importance.

30. *Canada as a Principal Power*, 36–46.

31. James Eayrs, 'Defining a New Place for Canada in the Hierarchy of World Power', *International Perspectives* (May/June 1975): 15–24; Peyton Lyon and Brian Tomlin, *Canada as an International Actor* (Toronto: Macmillan of Canada, 1979). Also reflecting this perspective is Norman Hillmer and Garth Stevenson, eds, *Foremost Nation: Canadian Foreign Policy and a Changing World* (Toronto: McClelland and Stewart, 1977).

32. Complex neorealism is an analytical perspective in international relations which accepts the primacy of politics (as does realism), but which goes beyond standard realism to recognize the existence of international order based on the convergence of interests among actors. See Dewitt and Kirton, *Canada as a Principal Power*, 36–46. This perspective bears some resemblance to the Grotian view outlined above, although with greater emphasis on the realist side of the argument.

33. The first term is that of Hawes, *Principal Power, Middle Power or Satellite*, 20–6; the second, that of Dewitt and Kirton, *Canada as a Principal Power*, 28–36. As subsequent paragraphs will indicate, the economic structuralist perspective has mostly

depicted Canada as being 'dependent' on the US because of the structure of its economy. This literature has been influenced by the arguments of Latin American dependency theorists such as Andre Gunder Frank.

34. Innis was particularly concerned about the impact on Canada of staples dependence, especially when this came to focus heavily on the United States. H.A. Innis, 'Economic Trends in Canadian–American Relations' in Mary Q. Innis, ed., *Essays in Canadian Economic History* (Toronto: University of Toronto Press, 1956), 233–41.

35. The first to do so was Kari Levitt, *Silent Surrender: The Multinational Corporation in Canada* (Toronto: Macmillan, 1970). As Canadian political-economy experienced a revival in the late 1960s and after many scholars adopted the dependency perspective to portray the Canadian situation.

36. Among the proponents of this view are Wallace Clement, *Continental Corporate Power* (Toronto: McClelland and Stewart, 1977); Clement, *Class, Power and Property: Essays on Canadian Society* (Toronto: Methuen, 1983); Daniel Drache, 'The Crisis of Canadian Political Economy: Dependency Theory vs. the New Orthodoxy', *Canadian Journal of Political and Social Theory* 7, 3 (Fall 1983): 25–49; Michael Claw, 'Canadian Political Economy and the International Underdevelopment and Dependency Debate', Canadian Political Science Association papers, Ottawa 1982.

37. The major proponents of this view are Steve Moore and Debi Wells, *Imperialism and the National Question in Canada* (Toronto: Moore, 1975). Jorge Niosi discusses Canada's role as a capital exporter in contradistinction to the view of Canada as part of the periphery. *Canadian Multinationals* (trans. of *Les multinationales canadiennes*, Toronto: Garamond Press, 1985).

38. Among the more prominent proponents of this view are Glen Williams, *Not For Export: Towards a Political Economy of Canada's Arrested Industrialization*, updated ed. (Toronto: McClelland and Stewart, 1986); Williams, 'On Determining Canada's Location Within the International Political Economy', *Studies in Political Economy* 25 (Spring

1988): 107–40; Philip Resnick, 'From Semi-periphery to Perimeter of the Core: Canada's Place in the Capitalist World Economy', *Review* 12, 2 (Spring 1989): 263–97; William Carroll, *Corporate Power and Canadian Capitalism* (Vancouver: UBC Press 1986). An element of Resnick's argument is the changed position of the United States. For a discussion of the latter, which also includes Canada, see Bertrand Bellon and Jorge Niosi, *L'industrie américaine: fin de siècle* (Montreal: Boréal Express, 1987). A review of these diverse perspectives can be found in Raymond Hudon, 'Locating Canada in the International System', Paper prepared for the conference on 'Paradigm Hegemony and International Relations in Canada', Carleton University 9–11 October 1986. A more recent review essay on Canada in the international political economy is Glen Williams's 'Canada in the International Political Economy', in Wallace Clement and Glen Williams, eds, *The New Canadian Political Economy* (Montreal: McGill-Queen's University Press, 1989), 116–37.

39. Immanuel Wallerstein, *The Modern World System: Capitalist Agriculture and the Origins of the European World-Economy in the Sixteenth Century* (New York: Academic Press, 1974).

40. Resnick, 'From Semiperiphery to Perimeter of the Core', 273. Resnick discusses the indices of classification and the reasons for the change in Canada's position, 273–92.

41. For this latter point, I am indebted to Tony Porter.

42. Department of External Affairs, *Competitiveness and Security: Directions for Canada's International Relations* (Ottawa: Minister of Supply and Services, 1985). For reviews of the document see Maureen Appel Molot and Brian W. Tomlin, 'The Conservative Agenda' in Molot and Tomlin, eds, *Canada Among Nations 1985: The Conservative Agenda* (Toronto: James Lorimer & Co., 1986), 3–24, and Canadian Institute of International Affairs, *Behind the Headlines* 42, 6 and 43, 1 (1985).

43. *European Affairs*, 1989. See, particularly, the summary table on page 117. The 1990 report has moved Canada down to 5th place. *Globe and Mail*, 20 June 1990, 83.

44. For a discussion of the challenges the 1990s present for Canada, see Lorraine Eden, 'Two Steps Forward, One Step Back: Into the 1990s' in M.A. Molot and F.O. Hampson, eds, *Canada Among Nations 1989: The Challenge of Change* (Ottawa: Carleton University Press, 1990), 135–62.

45. For a review of the history of the idea, see J.L. Granatstein, 'Free Trade Between Canada and the United States: The Issue That Will Not Go Away' in Denis Stairs and Gilbert Winham, eds, *The Politics of Canada's Economic Relationship with the United States*, Volume 29, Royal Commission on the Economic Union and Development Prospects for Canada (Toronto: University of Toronto Press, 1985). For statements supportive of bilateral free trade prior to the Mulroney government's decision, see Economic Council of Canada, *Looking Outward: A New Trade Strategy for Canada* (Ottawa: Information Canada, 1975) and Standing Senate Committee on Foreign Affairs, *Canada–United States Relations*, particularly Volume 3 (Ottawa: Minister of Supply and Services, 1982).

46. Since mid-1989, there has been growing discussion about a Mexico–US free trade agreement and its possible implications for Canada as well as a North American free trade agreement involving all three countries. See, for example, Ignacio Trigueros, 'A Free Trade Agreement Between Mexico and the United States?' in Jeffrey J. Schott, ed., *Free Trade Areas and US Trade Policy* (Washington: Institute for International Economics, 1989), 225–70; Gerado M. Bueno, 'A Mexican View' in William Dicbold Jr, ed., *Bilateralism, Multilateralism and Canada in US Trade Policy* (Cambridge, MA: Ballinger Publishing Company, 1988), 105–27; Michael Hart, 'A North American Free Trade Agreement: The Elements Involved', Paper presented to the conference entitled 'Foro Internacional: Mexico y sus Perspectivas de Negociacion Comercial con el Exterior', Mexico City, 11–15 June 1990.

47. A relatively recent, broad overview of the relationship which examines a host of bilateral issues is Charles F. Doran and John H. Sigler, eds, *Canada and the United States: Enduring Friendship, Persistent Stress* (Englewood Cliffs: Prentice-Hall Inc., 1985).

A similar overview of the stresses of the relationship is David Leyton-Brown, *Weathering the Storm* (Toronto: Canadian–American Committee, 1985).

48. Toronto: McClelland and Stewart, 1968.

49. For example, D. Godfrey and M. Watkins, *From Gordon to Watkins to You* (Toronto: New Press, 1970); Abraham Rotstein and Gary Lax, *Independence and the Canadian Challenge* (Toronto: Committee for an Independent Canada, 1972); and Ian Lumsden, ed., *Close the 49th Parallel* (Toronto: University of Toronto Press, 1970). More recent proponents of this critical view of bilateral relations, in addition to those cited in footnote 3, include Stephen Clarkson, *Canada and the Reagan Challenge*, updated edition, (Toronto: James Lorimer & Co., 1985) and Melissa Clark-Jones, *A Staple State: Canadian Industrial Resources in Cold War* (Toronto: University of Toronto Press, 1987).

50. For a review of both perspectives, see Glen Williams, *Not For Export*, Chapter 7, and Kim Nossal, 'Economic Nationalism and Continental Integration: Assumptions, Arguments and Advocacies' in Stairs and Winham, eds, *The Politics of Canada's Economic Relationship with the United States*, 55–94. Among the economists who were the most articulate proponents of the liberal economics perspective are Harry Johnson, *The Canadian Quandary* (Toronto: McGraw Hill, 1963); H.E. English, *Industrial Structure in Canada's International Competitive Position* (Montreal: Private Planning Association of Canada, 1964); and R.J. and P. Wonnacott, *Free Trade Between the United States and Canada* (Cambridge: Harvard University Press, 1967).

51. The integration literature, which itself stems from two different perspectives (neofunctionalist and transactional), is huge. Its focus, sparked by the move toward a common market in Europe, is on the efforts of the diverse economics to form a larger economic and possibly political unit. The major analytical instance of use of the integration framework in North America is Andrew Axline et al., eds, *Continental Community? Independence and Integration in North America* (Toronto: McClelland and Stewart, 1974).

52. Charles Pentland, 'North American Integration and the Canadian Political System' in Stairs and Winham, eds, *The Politics of Canada's Economic Relationship with the United States*, 97.

53. Kenneth Woodside, 'The Canada–United States Free Trade Agreement', *Canadian Journal of Political Science* 22, 1 (March 1989): 157.

54. See volumes cited in footnote 3. For a review article on some of these publications, see Woodside, 'The Canada–United States Free Trade Agreement', 155–70. Andre Donneur and Panayotis Soldatos edited a volume that juxtaposed the alternatives of 'diversification–continentalism'. *Le Canada entre le monde et les États-Unis* (Toronto: Captus Press, 1988).

55. Marc Gold and David Leyton-Brown, eds, *Trade-Offs On Free Trade*; Duncan Cameron, ed., *The Free Trade Deal*; Peter Morici, ed., *Making Free Trade Work: The Canada–US Agreement* (New York: Council on Foreign Relations, 1990).

56. For a discussion of a number of industries in a 'North American' context, see 'The North American Political Economy', *International Journal* 42, 1 (Winter 1986–7). Adjustment questions join studies of foreign and domestic economic policy. Among the latter are François Houle, 'L'état canadien et le capitalisme mondial: stratégies d'insertion', *Canadian Journal of Political Science* 20, 3 (September 1987): 467–500; Michael Atkinson and William Coleman, *The State, Business, and Industrial Change in Canada* (Toronto: University of Toronto Press, 1989); Rianne Mahon, *The Politics of Canadian Industrial Restructuring: Canadian Textiles* (Toronto: University of Toronto Press, 1984); and a number of the studies done for the Royal Commission on the Economic Union and Development Prospects for Canada.

57. 'Le nationalisme québécois à la croisée des chemins', *Choix* 7 (Quebec: Centre québécois de relations internationals, 1975).

58. Quebec: Centre québécois de relations internationales.

59. See 'Les relations économiques Québec–Etats-Unis', *Études Internationales* Special Issue 2, 1 (March 1971); and Alfred O. Hero, Jr, and Louis Balthazar, *Contemporary Quebec & the United States 1960–1985* (Cambridge, MA: Center for International Affairs Harvard University and University Press of America, 1988).

60. 'Supporters' are middle-sized countries which do not challenge the hegemony but which have some influence on outcomes in the international system. David Lake, 'International Economic Structures and American Foreign Economic Policy, 1887–1934', *World Politics* 35 (July 1983): 517–34. Michael Hawes argues that 'supportership' deserves considerable attention in international relations research. Michael Hawes, 'Structural Change and Hegemonic Decline: Implications for National Governments' in *World Politics: Power, Interdependence and Dependence*, 207–9.

61. In an article entitled 'CFP (Comparative Foreign Policy) and IPE: The Anomaly of Mutual Boredom', *International Interactions* 14, 1 (1988): 17–26, Rosenau comments on the gap between the foreign policy and international political-economy literature. The problem of field distance is not unique to Canada.

5

Of Playing Fields, Competitiveness, and the Will to Win: Representations of Gender and Globalization

Claire Turenne Sjolander

As Canada enters a new millennium, the role of international trade has reached an unprecedented level of importance in the strengthening of our economy. . . . For the first time, particular attention is being placed on the unique challenges faced by women owners of export-oriented small- and medium-sized businesses (SMEs). . . . [This] report serves as a flag . . . that the barriers to trade confronting women-owned SMEs are often distinctive. At the same time it applauds the professionalism and dedication of a rapidly growing number of women entrepreneurs that are overcoming these hurdles daily in the international marketplace. (Rayman, 1999: 2)

By the mid-1990s, Canadian policymakers had begun to recognize that women entrepreneurs were a significant feature of the changing Canadian economy. Almost as many businesses were being started by women as by men. The start-up rate of women-owned businesses had become nearly equal to that of men (Marchi, 1999b), and had grown at a rate of twice the national average (Eggleton, 1997). These businesses led by women were creating jobs at four times the national average (Marchi, 1999b; Eggleton, 1997). By the end of the 1990s, 30 per cent of all businesses in Canada

were owned or operated by women, and they provided 1.7 million jobs—more than Canada's top 100 companies combined (Marchi, 1999b). As former Trade Minister Sergio Marchi noted when he addressed the Canada–USA Businesswomen's Trade Summit in May 1999: 'Quite simply, women are fuelling the growth in small- and medium-sized enterprises . . . in this country and contributing both to our balance of trade and to our national prosperity. And in this era of globalization and interdependence, Canada's national prosperity is increasingly linked to our success in international markets' (Marchi, 1999b). As the Minister had said in an earlier speech, 'Clearly, the world of business is no longer just a man's world' (Marchi, 1997).

Nevertheless, in many respects (indeed, in most), the Minister was wrong. As Marianne Marchand has written, gender operates on at least three interconnected levels: the individual (through the social construction of physical male and female bodies), the collective (through the interactions among and between men and women structured in terms of gender roles and expectations), and the ideational or ideological (through the gendered representations of different social spheres, processes and practices, and the relative value placed on each) (Marchand, 2000: 223,

226, n4). For the Minister, the physical presence of a growing number of women entrepreneurs signalled the end to the maxim that business is a man's world and changed a preconception as to the gender-exclusive nature of business.[1] Whether or not international trade is a man's world, however, depends not only on the number of women who operate export industries, but also on the social practices in the business of international trade, and most significantly for this chapter, about the representation—or the discursive construction—of international trade. This representation of international trade confirms that while women entrepreneurs may be involved in business in greater numbers, the way in which business is represented has not changed. The business of international trade remains a gendered world, even if it is no longer the exclusive preserve of men.

This chapter examines the ways in which globalization, in particular, international trade, has been constructed, or represented, in Canadian foreign policy. It argues that this construction has been founded on a number of analogies centred on the jungle and competitive sports. These analogies begin with the premise that globalization is a jungle 'out there', which necessitates negotiation of multilateral trade and investment laws (to tame the jungle). These multilateral laws become the 'rules of the game', and international trade is transformed imperfectly into a 'competitive game' which countries, firms, and individuals play to 'win'. However, the sports analogies which prevail in the construction of globalization and international trade define the terrain of trade in very masculine terms. Sports analogies are gendered, and this has implications for policy—particularly at a time when some of the efforts of the Department of Foreign Affairs and International Trade (DFAIT) to respond to the challenges of globalization have led to the formulation of policies designed to encourage the participation of women entrepreneurs in international trade.

Globalization is a gendered series of processes—it functions in a gendered manner and has gendered consequences. The discursive construction of international trade, however, has effectively limited the capacity of the Canadian government to see globalization in gendered terms; to use Marchand's typology, it has been unable to respond to issues of gender at an ideational or ideological level (given that it participates in the construction of the gendered trade world at the ideational level), and rather, responds to gender at the individual level—with some acknowledgement of a collective concern. As a result, issues of gender and international trade are translated into the observation that while women entrepreneurs have become an engine of growth for an often stagnant Canadian economy, they remain under-represented in international trade (Marchi, 1997). The Canadian government, concerned about Canada's capacity to compete in a globalizing economy, became determined to change that. The 'man's world' of international trade was to be opened up to 'the incredible dynamism of women entrepreneurs' (Marchi, 1997).

Globalization, Multilateralism, and the 'Rules' of the 'Game'

The restructuring of the global marketplace has been a central theme in Canadian foreign policy for at least two decades. First given tangible expression in the negotiation of the Canada–US free trade agreement, the apparently immutable reality of a globalizing world has surfaced repeatedly as an imperative force that is driving, and to a large extent defining, Canada's foreign policy. Globalization has been invoked as the unquestioned and unquestionable justification for economic and financial deregulation, the liberalization of trade and investment, and deficit and debt reduction—and the consequences for spending on social and other programs has often been hastily dismissed as part of this 'new' reality. Paying close attention to discourse, however, reveals that globalization can be, and has been, constructed as many things, and thus it is imperative to understand the way in which the term has been and is defined as a backdrop for the expression of Canadian foreign policy. What becomes clear through an examination of ministerial speeches and policy pronouncements is that globalization has been presented as a series of expansive processes taking place 'out there' which limit state action. These processes are often threatening, or at least potentially so, and the international marketplace conceals the unknown dangers of a global jungle. Such a representation of globalization and of trade, however, has particular consequences for our capacity to imagine alternative foreign policies, consequences which are seen strikingly in attempts to respond to issues relating to gender and the global economy.

One of the most compelling—and revealing—assessments of the nature and significance of globalization was offered by International Trade Minister Pierre Pettigrew in a speech before the Global Forum 2000. Reflecting upon the implications of citizen unrest during the December 1999 World Trade Organization (WTO) meetings in Seattle, Washington, Pettigrew painted a sombre picture of globalization. Globalization, he argued, 'is the result of technological advances, trade liberalization and deregulation'; it leads to a world where 'corporations can decide to carry out a given industrial function in a given geographic region for economic reasons, notwithstanding any political considerations.' Globalization 'ignores political borders and merges economic spaces'. It is best described as 'a stateless power' defined in the horizontal processes and structures of the marketplace, 'at once intoxicating and fearsome to watch as it gradually replaces the vertical power of the state' (Pettigrew, 2000b). In Pettigrew's interpretation, globalization is a force outside the state, with which states are confronted and threatened. Globalization produces an international marketplace where the 'law of the jungle' often prevails (Pettigrew, 2000a; Marchi, 1999c), and the Canadian government, and Canadian exporters, are confronted by the perils that hide within it.

The portrayal of globalization existing outside the state, a force 'out there', is reminiscent of early realist writings, where the space inside the state was controlled by rules and laws, while the space outside the state was anarchic—a Hobbesian state of nature—where the rules of the jungle, and might equals right, prevailed. As in these early writings, Pettigrew's portrayal of globalization is possible because the state and the market are each assigned their own spheres, the one independent of the other. In this way, Pettigrew is able to argue that in an earlier era, a 'too exclusively' *political state* committed blunders because of its inherent inability to read the market's signals, whereas globalization has witnessed the emergence of a 'too exclusively' *economic market*, equally incapable of reading the state's signals (Pettigrew, 2000b). The state and the market are distinct, but the fundamental restructuring of the economic marketplace brought about by globalization has in turn led to a change, if not a diminution, in the role and capacity of the state.

Pettigrew's analysis, though fuelled by the protests in Seattle, is not in itself new.

In January 1995, the then-Trade Minister, Roy MacLaren, was musing about how globalization was 'somehow circumventing and diminishing the influence of national governments'. The restructuring of the global economy was not mainly a by-product of state regulation or even deregulation; rather, 'trade liberalization is following as much as leading the underlying economic trends'. For MacLaren, quoting Marx (of all economists!), 'technology shapes the course of history', and information technology as an autonomous force was leading the processes of globalization to which states were then compelled to react (MacLaren, 1995). Trade Minister Sergio Marchi also invoked globalization as a force 'out there' to which the state must respond or suffer the consequences of its refusal to do so, when he asked whether 'Canadians [are] prepared to accept the decline in our standard of living that would be sure to result from trying to hide from globalization' (Marchi, 1998; see also Axworthy, 1999).

The jungle which is globalization envelops us all, and the brave must confront it. Failure to do so inexorably leads to marginalization and defeat.

Seen from this perspective, globalization becomes a significant and potentially determining factor in foreign policy. The state is not a principal architect of the processes underway; rather, it is confronted by the global economic restructuring brought about by revolutionary technological change, and it must adapt to the best of its abilities. The state is not part of globalization *per se*, but it cannot escape its exigencies. Globalization, in a sense, is the antithesis of the state; the anarchic realist international system it reinforces in the economic sphere—the globalization jungle—is the antithesis of the rule of law of the Western, liberal state. Trade Minister Pettigrew expressed this viewpoint most succinctly when he reported an encounter with protestors at the WTO meetings in Seattle. 'They said, "We hate globalization." I looked at them and said, "I am a member of a government. It is far more difficult for me to accept globalization because globalization is threatening us. You are globalization"' (Pettigrew, 2000b). Globalization, even as manifested in the uneven capacity of protestors to use information technology to co-ordinate transnational political action, is beyond the control of the territorial state, and the state is at its mercy, trying its best to respond.

Of course, this picture of globalization belies the extent to which the entire post-war economic order has been constructed by states and the international organizations as they have given voice to their interests at a global level. This is not to suggest that there is no reciprocal relationship between states, transnational corporations, and the technological changes that have facilitated processes of economic restructuring, nor is it to suggest that states bear exclusive responsibility for the fundamental economic changes underway. But to diminish the extent to which states and the international financial and economic institutions have been key players in orchestrating trade, financial, and investment liberalization and deregulation is to be more than somewhat disin-

genuous. To the extent that globalization has become the jungle out there, states and international organizations have fostered its development. The portrayal of globalization as a jungle, however, conditions the kind of foreign economic-policy responses chosen by states. Jungles can never be fully tamed; those who flourish in the face of its perils are individuals of skill and cunning, often possessing special expertise and daring. To face the jungle of globalization, governments must facilitate the activities of national Tarzans. Those sectors of the economy that hope to succeed in the jungle must be 'hardened', having been fully tempered by exposure to international competition. As Marchand notes in the case of a similar discussion of the Dutch economy, the notion that export sectors must be tough or hard in the face of the perils of globalization 'evokes elements associated with contemporary hegemonic masculinity: facing tough competition, taking on responsibilities and the use of new technologies' (2000: 222).[2] The Tarzans of globalization are constructed as men.

Paradoxically, Canada's role in the international financial and economic institutions is not one which political leaders seek to disavow, even in their discussions of the challenges posed by globalization. Rather, Canadian participation in the structuring of the post-war economic order is heralded as an attempt to devise a response to the externally imposed restructuring processes known as globalization. Canadians, we are reminded, have been 'team players' and active members in—at times, architects of—a wide variety of multilateral economic forums, including the General Agreement on Tariffs and Trade (GATT, now the World Trade Organization, or WTO), the International Monetary Fund, the World Bank, and the G7 (now the G8).

In keeping with Canadian traditions, the maintenance and strengthening of multilateral institutions is presented as the key to the challenges—the jungle—posed by globalization; while the state may be overwhelmed by global economic restructuring and may find that its capacity is limited by the exigencies of economic change, answers are to be found in the structures already in place. In some respects, this is an interesting sleight of hand; the very states and institutions which played a crucial role in setting the liberalization of the global economy in motion are seen as those most likely to control the genie, if not to put him back in the bottle. Former Finance Minister Paul Martin, testifying before the Standing Committee on Foreign Affairs and International Trade, explained the current situation as follows: 'Globalization poses new and difficult questions that no single government can resolve by itself. This means if we're going to address the challenges that are posed by modern globalization, we're going to have to find ways to promote cooperative solutions', solutions that, for Martin, are to be found in the reform of the Bretton Woods institutions.

Such a commitment to working collectively resonates well with the traditional Canadian commitment to multilateral practices and negotiations. While it might be a little strong to suggest, as did Sergio Marchi, that 'multilateralism is part of the Canadian DNA' (Marchi, 1998), the Canadian propensity to seek out collective forums for the discussion of international problems is well documented and serves as a pillar of Canadian foreign policy. The Chrétien government's foreign policy statement, *Canada in the World*, underscored this historical commitment when it emphasized the importance of the multilateral economic system for Canada: 'The system has, on the whole, worked well for us and has demonstrated an impressive capacity to adjust to changing times and pressures. Moreover, Canada has worked hard to protect and promote our interests through the international economic system, a system that we have shaped to a very significant extent' (DFAIT, 1995). The newly appointed foreign affairs minister, John Manley, was already pointing to this tradition within days of assuming his new responsibilities: 'Canada has a strong multilateralist tradition. . . . We must reaffirm our commitment to multilateralism and

focus on updating international institutions in order to ensure their continuing relevance in the face of new global realities' (Manley, 2000).

In the era of globalization, the need for multilateral solutions framed within the context of international financial or economic institutions is defended because these alone can define the 'rules of the game' that are badly needed to tame the jungle out there. The analogy is pervasive; the new global economy needs rules and referees, and multilateral solutions are the only ones that might work to the advantage of states, including (and perhaps especially) Canada. Canada is committed to a 'rules and order-based system' (Manley, 2000), and such a system will only emerge from a renewed effort to strengthen multilateral institutions. The need for rules is a profound motivator for Canadian foreign policy; over and over again, the Canadian government, through the speeches of its ministers and its policy statements, reiterates this observation. Multilateral rules are the only way to guarantee that Canada has a chance to compete successfully in the global marketplace. The multilateral rules are necessary to guarantee that the workings of the global economy will be fair and that, by extension, Canadians will have a reasonable shot at success. Pierre Pettigrew has underscored this relationship between multilateral rules and fairness on a number of occasions, though never more strongly than when he argued, 'We needed—and we still need—to have a system of international trade governed by the rule of law, not the law of the jungle; a system where disputes are settled based not on the size of your economy or the strength of your military but according to a predictable set of agreed multilateral rules that determine the rights and obligations of the parties. A system that levels the playing field' (Pettigrew, 2000a). The anarchic realist jungle must be tamed by laws and rules.

What becomes clear in the discourse of a rules-based regime governing international economic restructuring is that the rules are intended as the framework for a competitive global economic game—on a playing field that cannot be level without the clear elaboration of rules and of mechanisms to enforce them. The promotion and negotiation of multilateral rules ensuring a more 'level playing field' and the flourishing of fair competition thus becomes a central pillar of Canadian foreign policy. The rules of the game are the only mechanism that can bring the jungle of globalization under control, and Canadian foreign policy must ensure that the rules are fair. This games or sports analogy is a constant in speeches dealing with the multilateral economic and financial institutions, although some statements carry the analogy much further than others. Two examples serve to illustrate this point. In his speech to the Ottawa-based Centre for Trade Policy and Law in 1998, Sergio Marchi bemoaned the growing opposition to the negotiations for Multilateral Agreement on Investment (MAI). He justified the need to participate in this multilateral process by making reference to the sports world of many Canadian children. 'You know, anyone who played hockey as a kid or who has children playing hockey now will remember what every good coach drills into young players: "You can't score if you don't shoot." The same is true of international trade negotiations: You can't score a good deal if you don't take your best shot at negotiating it' (Marchi, 1998). In the same vein, former Finance Minister Paul Martin commented before the House of Commons Standing Committee on Foreign Affairs and International Trade: 'Hockey, Mr Chairman, is a wonderful game. It's fast paced, free wheeling, and sometimes risky. It's the players that make the game, not the referees. But that being said, hockey without rules and referees wouldn't be hockey. It would be high-speed, high-risk, high-stakes anarchy. Unfortunately, without rules and referees, that is what the international financial system all too often resembles.'[3] Whether or not the international financial or economic system is truly comparable to a game of hockey, the point is clear. The globalized economic order is a competitive one (a jungle), taking place on a playing field

that is only at times level, and in need of multilateral rules and international referees, without which smaller players (like Canada) confront unfair, and therefore unacceptable, risks. Without referees, hockey is not hockey—it is the anarchy and the peril conveyed by the jungle imagery. Rules and referees turn the jungle into a playing field, where competitors are able to display their skill, protected, at least in part, from the perils of the untamed jungle.

The use of sports imagery as a shorthand for the global economy does not end with the discussion of the multilateral economic order. The name Team Canada for the Chrétien government's policy response to the challenges confronting small- and medium-sized firms attempting to participate in the global economy further emphasizes the image of sports. It is not necessarily bad to think in terms of a team; much can be said that is positive about teamwork and collaboration. However, the imagery of a team also signals competition, battle, and victory or defeat. There are winners and there are losers in the globalized economy, and one way to enhance one's chances of victory is to make certain that you are playing for the best possible team. The speeches of federal ministers are therefore also filled with statistics supporting the claim that the Canadian team is one of the best: *Time* magazine describes Canada as an 'exporting superhero' (Marchi, 1999c); a 'leading US magazine' refers to the 'Maple Leaf Miracle', and *The Economist* calls Canada a 'fiscal virtuoso' (Marchi, 1999a). In a speech to the Ireland–Canada Business Association, Sergio Marchi went so far as to congratulate the two winning teams of the global economy—the 'Celtic Tigers' and the 'Maple Leaf Miracle'—encouraging them to 'form the partnerships that will allow both of our nations to prosper in new and exciting markets' (Marchi, 1999a). Images of on-field camaraderie and locker-room celebrations are evoked; even picturing the team jerseys does not require much imagination.

So what does this all mean? After all, it is not difficult to make the claim that the global economy is an arena of increasing competition, that states have lost (by choice or otherwise) some of their capacity to soften the blow of international competition, and that the multilateral system might provide the best guarantee for smaller states that they too will have a place in the global marketplace, that they will be able to find their way in the jungle. If discourses coloured by the analogy of sports, with its playing fields, fierce competitions, and victory celebrations for the best teams, conveys the reality of the global economy, what is the objection? The answer is twofold. First, as we will see, sport in modern western society remains a fundamentally gendered expression of those societies, and sports analogies perpetuate this gendered experience of the modern Western world. Second, and more important, this image of the global economy both camouflages important truths about the structure and functioning of that economy in the era of globalization and makes the state less able to imagine policies that might mitigate the gendered nature of globalization. In important respects, the articulation of Canadian foreign policy alternatives in response to some of the challenges of globalization has become a prisoner to the gendered logic of a sports analogy.

Sport and Gender

Understanding gender requires an appreciation of the fact that 'gender is socially constructed, producing subjective identities through which we see and know the world; and . . . that the world is pervasively shaped by gendered meanings. That is, we do not experience or "know" the world as abstract "humans" but as embodied, gendered beings' (Peterson, 1992: 9). Such an understanding of gender as a social construct inevitably leads us to an analysis of social relations and of the ways in which the world (and in this case, international trade policy more specifically) is characterized by particular and often persistent rules and discursive practices. These rules and practices are not simply neutral abstractions that facilitate international life, but rather are themselves gendered, 'con-

struct[ing] and reproduc[ing] notions of masculinity and femininity and associated power differentials' (Prügl and Meyer, 1999: 5).

Foreign policy in general is not a field of study in which analyses of gender are prevalent, and Canadian foreign policy is no exception. The place of and for women is often secondary, if it exists at all, in foreign policy statements and policies. The international system is a place where the histories of diplomats, soldiers, and heads of state prevail, and these histories, and the discourses that represent them, are predominantly those of men. It is within this context that the sport analogy that is prevalent in Canadian discourses on discussions of multilateralism and the global economy assumes its significance, for sport is part of a social and political culture, and its symbols reinforce a particular understanding of social order. That order is neither trivial nor neutral; rather, the culture of sport 'generates, reworks, and affirms an elitist, masculine account of power and social order' (Burstyn, 1999: 4).[4]

The masculine bias of sport is quite clear. Despite some progress over the past three decades, male sports are still much better funded than female sports, they receive far more media attention, and they enjoy far greater public support. 'Athletics have long been the province of men. In the Western world, not only have men dominated the playing fields, but athletic qualities such as aggression, competitiveness, strength, speed, power, and teamwork have been associated with masculinity. For many men sport has provided an arena in which to cultivate masculinity and achieve manhood' (Cahn, 1994: 3). Burstyn puts it more bluntly: 'While many girls and women are athletic, women are not organized in and through sport such that it serves as an economic, cultural, and associational backbone for their gender interests. These are functions sport plays with respect to men as a gender, indeed as a gender class' (Burstyn, 1999: 8). Thus the symbolism of sport and the role sport plays in defining a gendered order speak to women in very different ways than to men.

Acknowledging that sport is a gendered construct in modern societies does not necessarily tell us very much about the implications of that gendered construct, or why it is a problem. The answer is to be found in some of the 'athletic qualities' identified above, and the way in which they organize society and are celebrated in particular patterns of order:

> The problem—if the myriad difficulties of modern sport can be connected in one phrase—is that Sport . . . divides people in ways that are often destructive and antisocial. Sport divides people against themselves. It separates children from children, men from women, men from men, and community from community. Sport models and exacerbates social conflict and encourages antisocial and undemocratic values. And it does this most centrally through its inflection of gender, particularly its offering of ideal types and behaviours for men. (Burstyn, 1999: 27)

Sports divides people; it encourages individualist behaviour, competition, and coercion—and these 'athletic qualities' are a gendered expression of what is important to success. 'The athletic world of power, speed, and pain is an expression of the masculine ideals of our culture' (Pronger, 1990 as cited in Burnstyn, 1999: 8). In this respect, the analogy of sport 'fits' particularly well with the logic of globalization, for 'the rhetoric of competition has been tied up with the rhetoric of the market since Adam Smith proposed his invisible hand' (Burstyn, 1999: 43). Competition is central to sport, it is central to the processes considered intrinsic to globalization, and it is central to the discourses about the global economy and Canada's place within it.

As we have seen above, the sports analogy closes the circle between globalization and competition— Canada must be able to compete, and to win, on a level playing field, defined by clear, 'sporting' rules. Tarzan must be able to demonstrate his skills, cunning, and superiority in an ordered jungle. As a model for social order or for the global economy, however, competition has its problems:

Competition, often praised as one of the most important lessons sport teaches, is at bottom a hostile dynamic based in a mentality of scarcity. It can be seen as rationalized hostility because it is based on a zero-sum equation . . . The victory of one party entails loss by the other. The competitive relation, embodying hostility, is rehearsed over and over again through the rituals of childhood and youth sport. It is . . . celebrated by culture and the mass media. The message is simple: doing one's best is measured in doing better than others and in getting more (love, respect, stuff) as a reward. In the core men's sports, doing better usually means being more physically aggressive. Children's empathetic and cooperative impulses are thwarted through the culture of physical competition, and their narcissism and aggression rewarded. (Burstyn, 1999: 43)

In the global economy, winning comes at someone else's expense. Winning must mean doing better than others because the global economy is a zero-sum game defined by scarcity—the jungle may be tamed by rules, but it remains a jungle nonetheless. Helping Canadians to win internationally must be a foreign policy goal of government, for losing is unthinkable. The analogy is problematic in at least two ways. First, the notion of competitiveness as a value in and for itself obscures the nature of the global economy, in particular the interests that reside there. 'Where the idea of competition once represented the aspirations of bonded individuals against a fixed feudal order, today it cloaks the interests of huge transnational corporations, many times more powerful than the old monarchies and aristocracies. As the mechanism seen to guide the market, the idealization of competition by sport has approached sanctification' (Burstyn, 1999: 43). The 'individuals' who are successful in the competitive game are very often huge transnational firms, whose advantages far outweigh the individual skills and talents of the individual competitor. Second, in concealing the nature of the interests residing in the global economy through this insistence on individual preparation, skill, and achievement, the sports analogy of competition also conceals the extent to which the operation of the global economy is in itself gendered and reproduces the gendered social order. The celebration of competition and sport is also a celebration of socially constructed men; it is men who are the warriors, men who are the entrepreneurs, men who are the competitors, and men who are the risk-takers. It is men who define the 'game' of the globalized economy, and masculine values prevail; '[m]others should take care of nappies, clothes and food; fathers are for money, sport and punishment' (*The Economist*, 1996 as cited in Burstyn, 1999: 44).

The focus on competition, even within a set of defined rules (although the rules are never perfect, and an element of risk—the perils of the jungle—prevails), drives analysis of the global economy to the level of the individual, whether it be an individual person, firm, or even country. As in sport, the competitive basis of the global economy drives players who wish to be successful to train—to acquire the *individual* skills and assets required in order to extract the biggest pay-off from playing the game. As in any game, the assumption is clear: identify your skills and talents, practise hard, and invest the effort required in order to perfect those areas where you are lacking, seek mentors who can point out your weaknesses and suggest remedies, work hard, and you will succeed. While the portrayal of the competitive game is inherently gendered, its representation as such reduces policy responses to globalization to the level of the individual players in the game and to the strengthening of individual teams. Failure is a failing of the individual (person, firm, or country), who has not been daring enough, cunning enough, knowledgeable enough, dedicated enough, or tough enough. Nowhere does this discursive construction of international trade and the global economy allow policy makers or even critics to ask whether this game is itself being played with a stacked deck that requires the labour of the non-competitive marginalized 'losers' in order to guarantee the success of the entrepreneurial 'winners', as we will see below.

The gendered nature of the global economy, however, is well-documented. Cynthia Enloe's groundbreaking work, *Bananas, Beaches and Bases*, documents the way in which the exigencies of the global economy (whether in the growth of export-processing zones or in the austerity programs promoted by the International Monetary Fund) not only have a greater impact on women than on men, but are dependent upon the willingness of women to adapt to them. For example, the adoption of IMF austerity measures depends on the capacity of women to respond to those measures:

> A government's ability to maintain its legitimacy [after IMF austerity measures have been adopted] depends at least in part on the capacity of families to tolerate those measures, specifically on the capacity of women to stretch their budgets, to continue to feed, clothe, and care for their families. . . . A dynamic is [thus] set up around ideas about what women will and will not do, the actual material conditions of their lives, and the policies produced by international organizations and foreign governments. This dynamic both sustains and is dependent on assumptions about what are considered the appropriate roles and qualities of women, and women of particular races, in specific times and places. (Whitworth, 2000: 96)

The 'hard-edged' policies associated with the IMF austerity measures, the notion of 'getting one's financial house in order' so that a national economy may be able to compete better in the global economy (and thus to raise export revenues), conceal the gendered reality of the impact of such policies as they deploy gendered representations of that reality.

In a similar vein, the celebration of the new world of global finance evokes—as Marianne Marchand has written eloquently—'images of adventurous, risk-taking, fast-paced, globetrotting young men' (2000, 223). The new risk-taking warriors of the global economy are the most potent symbols of globalization, and yet the image projected by global finance conceals the gendered nature of this industry:

> What is often overlooked, however, is that this same global financial community cannot function without the existence of an internationalized service economy in both the private and public spheres: for instance, large groups of migrant women (and men) are employed in the global financial centres of London, New York, and Hong Kong as domestic help, nannies, gardeners, etc.; alternatively, migrant women (and men) may find themselves cleaning the offices of Chase Manhattan and similar banks at night; and increasingly, it is also possible for women to find work in the Philippines or India as data-entry clerks for large companies abroad. (2000: 223)

Global finance rests on the emergence of this feminized internationalized service economy, and yet the representation or discursive construction of this apex of globalization conceals the reality underpinning its operation. As a symbol of this economy, George Soros is the picture of the victorious male warrior who has succeeded through his daring, skill, and competitive edge—the jungle's new Tarzan. The women (and men) who provide the services that make his success possible are invisible, as are the gendered power relationships enshrined therein—and yet, these are critical to the global financial economy. The logic inherent in the competitive sports analogy would suggest that domestic workers, for example, need only work harder, work longer hours, and hone their competitive skills in order to succeed in the international marketplace; in fact, however, the international marketplace could not function without such domestic workers.

DFAIT and Women Entrepreneurs

The Canadian government, in particular the Department of Foreign Affairs and International Trade, has been largely unable, and often unwilling, to consider the ways in which the global economy has a fundamentally gendered nature,

and that global economic restructuring has a consequential gendered impact. From the perspective of the discursive representations of the global economy echoed by Canadian policy makers, however, a failure to grasp this reality within a policy context is unsurprising. In fact, the sports analogy that drives the discursive construction—and therefore conceptual understanding—that characterizes almost all discussion of the global economy makes it all but impossible to understand globalization in broader structural terms. Calls to pay attention to the gendered nature of globalization and to the gendered consequences of global economic restructuring are inevitably answered with the question of 'what do (individual) women need to help them to perform more effectively in the global marketplace?'. The gendered reality of globalization is obscured by the logic of competition, winners and losers, and the rules of the game, which reinforces the bias toward the analysis of individual circumstance at the expense of the whole—of an analysis of globalization as a series of processes that depend upon gender to function. This is not to say, of course, that there is no worth in attempting to understand how individual women have confronted the jungle of the global economy. Such a response, however, does not address questions of gender and globalization, but rather, focuses attention on (individual) women in international trade. To return to Marchand's typology, the gendered ideational or ideological level of understanding of globalization defined in a sports analogy of competition fosters a gendered individual—and to some extent, narrowly collective—response.

In April 1997, the Organization for Economic Co-operation and Development (OECD) held a conference called 'Women Entrepreneurs in Small and Medium Enterprises: A Major Force in Innovation and Job Creation'. The OECD was motivated in large part by the same observations as those made by Canadian trade ministers, namely, that 'women-owned SMEs . . . are growing at a faster rate than the economy as a whole', yet, that despite this, 'the economic potential of women entrepreneurs remains partly untapped' (OECD, 1997). The purpose of the conference was to assess the problems confronting women entrepreneurs and to facilitate the growth and development of the SMEs that they head. Billed as a 'true world economic summit on women entrepreneurs in SMEs' (OECD, 1997), the conference was the most significant international event to that point to focus on the specific issues and problems confronting women entrepreneurs in business, and in international trade.[5] This OECD conference initiative, motivated in part by the emerging reality of women's greater entrepreneurial participation in the Canadian market, also coincided with a series of measures by the Canadian government to facilitate women entrepreneurs' access to international markets.

These Canadian initiatives took a variety of forms. The trade commissioner's staff at the Canadian Embassy in Washington inaugurated the Canadian Women's International Business Initiative to provide women entrepreneurs with information and business contacts needed in order for them to pursue export opportunities in the mid-Atlantic states of the United States (Eggleton, 1997). The centrepiece of this enterprise was the first ever Canadian Women's Trade Mission to Washington in November 1997 (Marchi, 1999b)—a women-only 'Team Canada'. Following upon this Team Canada mission, Minister Marchi announced the establishment of a public–private-sector consortium of individuals and organizations, the Trade Research Coalition (TRC), whose mandate was to 'gather information which clarifies the degree and type of participation by Canadian businesswomen in the trade environment, particularly in the US market; and to propose recommendations, policies, measures and activities to promote export development by businesswomen' (Trade Commissioner Service, 1997). Significantly, the TRC was also to report on the 'barriers which may have limited' the 'success' of women entrepreneurs in gaining access to the US and international markets.

The new women-focused activities of DFAIT did not end there, however. In June 1998, International Trade Minister Sergio Marchi introduced 'Businesswomen in Trade', the first website created especially for Canadian women exporters (DFAIT, 1998),[6] which offered electronic access to a broad range of business information in Canada and internationally. The website was also designed to facilitate networking between the businesswomen. The first women-only Team Canada mission spawned several others, including the Canadian Women's Mission to the World Bank and the Inter-American Development Bank in Washington in March 1998, the Businesswomen's Mission to Chicago in January 1999, the Businesswomen's Mission to Los Angeles in March 1999, and the Women's Information Technology Mission to the Federal Office Systems Exhibition in Washington in April 1999 (Marchi, 1999b). In March 1999, the TRC published its report *Beyond Borders: Canadian Businesswomen in International Trade* (DFAIT, 1999; Orser et al., 1999); a parallel study of US businesswomen was being published in the United States—*A Snapshot of Selected US Women Owned Exporting Firms* (Marchi, 1999b). Both reports profiled the experiences of businesswomen in international trade, and both served as the basis for discussion at the first Canada–USA Businesswomen's Trade Summit held in Toronto in May 1999. The recommendations of that summit on the opportunities for, and barriers to, enhanced participation by women in international markets formed part of the basis for discussion at the 'Women Entrepreneurs in SMEs: Realising the Benefits of Globalisation and the Knowledge-based Economy', the OECD conference held in Paris in November 2000. The OECD made it clear that although women's entrepreneurship was generally growing in the OECD countries, the impetus for the OECD's attention to the issue came from North America: 'In some countries, *for example the United States and Canada*, women-owned businesses are increasing at a very rapid pace' (OECD, 2000; emphasis added). The OECD went on to note, 'In an era of global economic integration, this significant economic and social development is of growing interest to practitioners and policy makers worldwide' (OECD, 2000).

In order to assess more carefully the nature and significance of these initiatives, it is worthwhile to turn our attention to the *Beyond Borders* report published by the Trade Research Coalition.[7] In many respects, *Beyond Borders* details the assumptions about women in international trade that have motivated Canadian government policy. As mentioned earlier, the TRC was a private- and public-sector consortium made up of individuals representing various interests, although three-quarters of the members were drawn from different government departments (including DFAIT, Status of Women Canada, and Industry Canada). This consortium's activities were sponsored by a number of private- and public-sector organizations, including DFAIT, the Royal Bank of Canada, the Export Development Corporation, the Canadian Institute of Chartered Accountants, Status of Women Canada, Industry Canada, the Certified General Accountants of Canada, Lever Enterprises (a firm specializing in international commercial development and finance), and the Women Entrepreneurs of Canada (a national association for established women business owners, founded in 1992).

The study began with two related premises: that exports, which constitute 40 per cent of Canadian gross domestic product, are a leading source of new jobs, and that the 1990s witnessed an unprecedented increase in the number of women becoming business owners. Taken together, and given the need identified by the Canadian government in the establishment of its Team Canada initiative to stimulate export activity among small- and medium-sized businesses, the report sought to identify the 'conditions that assist the development of export business; [the] major impediments to the development of export business for women business owners in Canada; [the] strategies and tactics used by Canadian development of trade relationships, and [the]

awareness of and satisfaction with existing public and private sector initiatives that related to export promotion' (Orser et al., 1999).[8]

The study presents a profile of women entrepreneurs involved in export activities. The majority were born in Canada (75 per cent), did not describe themselves as a member of a minority group (93 per cent), were highly educated (28 per cent had a graduate degree, 43 per cent have a college diploma or university degree, 18 per cent had some college or university education), had founded their own firm (88 per cent), were living with a spouse or partner (69 per cent),[9] were unilingual (60 per cent), had never worked outside of Canada (62 per cent), and sold products rather than services (64 per cent) (Orser et al., 1999). It is clear, and hardly surprising, that the profile of these women does not suggest the average Canadian woman.

The atypical profile of these women, mostly white and highly educated, underlines the individualist bias of the government response that stems quite naturally from the understanding of globalization as a competitive game. Canada's best potential players must be sought out in order to strengthen the team. It is the activities of *some* women in international trade that are being examined, and not the relationship between women and international trade in any broader sense. When asked about the nature of the challenges facing women entrepreneurs in engaging in international trade, the respondents pointed to the cost of developing such markets, the difficulties in setting up distribution channels, in finding local partners, obtaining information about foreign markets, and in complying with the regulations of foreign governments (Orser et al., 1999). These challenges were not framed by the respondents in gendered terms; it is as likely that SMEs headed by men would confront the same difficulties.

The survey did, however, push respondents to identify specific gender challenges relating to exporting. Roughly three-quarters of the participants did report on some gender-specific aspects to the business challenges they faced. These were primarily defined in terms of cultural and interpersonal differences, focusing in particular on the attitudes of the people the exporter dealt with. The comments of respondents referred to: 'a perceived lack of respect by male business owners; businessmen who explicitly refuse to do business with a woman; bravado, physical gestures and chauvinism; clients who verify the female business owner's decision through a male member of staff; perceived gender discrimination by Canadian lending institutions; the assumption that the business is owned by a man; differences in management experience and style of doing business; and different or more limited professional networks' (Orser et al., 1999). Businesswomen also complained of not being taken seriously, or of having their ability, experience, and background minimized because of their gender. Family issues were also identified as a gender-specific challenge, including the logistical hurdles posed by family responsibilities and the potential limitations on travel for mothers of 'young children' (Orser et al., 1999). What is perhaps most telling about the discussion of gender-specific challenges, however, are the recommendations for responding to them—the shared 'tricks of the trade' offered as assistance to other businesswomen in similar situations. The report presents a list of these 'hints' for handling gender-specific problems: avoiding personal or phone contact in certain countries through the exclusive use of e-mail; ignoring slights; insisting that customers must deal with them if they want to do business; building their own credibility; avoiding social events if the purpose of the event might be misconstrued; having a male employee handle certain firms or customers; changing business cards to clarify ownership of the firm; working with Canadian trade commissioners as interlocutors; and consciously hiring male employees and subcontractors (Orser et al., 1999).

These gender-specific challenges, and the solutions to which they give rise, are undoubtedly perfectly accurate and reasonable assessments of the situation for women entrepreneurs as they engage, or attempt to engage, in international trade. They are also the stories of *individual* women, and of their strategies as *individuals* for overcoming some of the gendered consequences of their business participation, consequences which are largely understood to be the result of the collective, rather than ideational, level at which gender can be constructed. As these women reflected on the ways in which the construction of gender in the interactions between men and women affected them—women perceived to be less competent, less credible, and less worthy than their male colleagues—the ideational or ideological context in which they find themselves remains unexplored. The 'game' of international trade, with its rules of competition and winning, is their mantra as well. *Beyond Borders* paints a picture of a community of women business owners prepared to share their expertise and experience in order to help others to 'train', or to practise, in order to win at the game of international business. As one of the respondents noted, in her experience: '[w]omen have a problem with the concept of making money. . . . And with selling themselves and thinking as a business. . . . So it's making that transition . . . that you're . . . selling a service and you're developing a quality service but it's all right to charge for it. It's all right to market it. It's all right to hustle' (quoted in Orser et al., 1999). It's all right to play the competitive game to win. The role of government, and thus the consequent objective of Canadian policy, is to become a better coach or personal trainer, in order to enhance the performance of its winning athletes. From websites to women-only Team Canada missions, the way to address gender and globalization is to respond to the requirements of individual women and women-led firms so that they might be more successful in the export game. The individualist logic of a gendered competitive sports analogy drives the government response in that direction; when globalization is seen as a competitive game, it is inconceivable that its gendered nature and consequences would be uncovered.

The extent to which trade, and women's places

as exporters, becomes defined in terms of the competitive sports analogy is reinforced by the publication of the *Beyond Borders* summary document (Rayman, 1999). Here, the academic prose and carefully crafted research results are translated into a glossier publication that highlights the main findings of the study. What is striking, and in many respects disturbing, is the addition of illustrations designed to enhance the portrayal of women in international trade. Of the seven women portrayed in the publication, only one is engaged in what might be considered a business activity: she is talking on her cell phone. The other six images are engaged in various sporting activities: speed skating, volleyball, running hurdles, a foot race on an athletic track, a soccer match, and a celebration of an athletic team victory. These women are all competing, displaying in their determined faces and in their athleticism that they too possess the qualities such as aggressiveness, competitiveness, strength, speed, power, and teamwork that have been associated with masculinity, and which are deemed to be necessary for success in the globalization jungle— even if that jungle has been tamed by international rules. One woman, the head of a freight forwarding company in Toronto, commented in the summary report that, given the lack of women in the transportation industry, 'I found some of the people were negative about me in business. I knew I could do it and that's what I did. . . . Now they accept me because they see that I know what I am doing and I can be just like one of them' (Arlene Singroy, quoted in Rayman, 1999: 19). The quite logical response to the gendered representation of globalization is to learn the rules of the game and to play as well as possible—to be a skilled, cunning and knowledgeable Tarzan, just like one of them.

Conclusion

The identification of globalization as a perilous condition existing 'out there' to which governments are subject builds a conceptual prism for the Canadian government. The jungle of globalization must be tamed in order to ensure that those who venture forth into the wild can survive, and taming the jungle becomes a pressing need because withdrawal and hiding from it are not options. The means for doing this taming are multilateral rules (despite the fact that some of these rules fostered the growth of the jungle in the first instance), and these rules turn the jungle into a competitive game. Without rules and referees, there can be no game, just as, to return to Paul Martin's analysis, without the rules and referees of hockey, there is only anarchy, not hockey. Faced with the jungle that they have partly created, states and international financial and economic organizations create the rules to ensure fairness, but the jungle remains an arena for competition and for the survival of the most talented, cunning, and skilled.

The study of Canadian foreign policy has not been characterized by attention to the gendered construction of the key concepts that dominate the foreign policy discourse and agenda. Sensitivity to the gendered construction of discourse, however, allows us to interpret Canadian foreign policy in a different light—and allows us to ask how the conceptualization of globalization as a competition defined by certain multilateral rules drives policy in a particular direction. If globalization is a game, then the policy responses to it are almost naturally to be found in assisting the players to succeed, and in so doing, strengthening the team. What this analysis allows us to see, however, is the way that conception of the global economy discourse conceals its underlying gendered nature, and thereby privileges responses that target individual women rather than seek to address its foundations. In deploying a discourse that conceals the nature of globalization, links between foreign policy and issues of labour standards, human rights, and welfare support are never made. The consequences for foreign policy of seeing globalization as gendered are potentially transformative: women working in sweatshops in developing countries, or immigrants doing piece work for desperation-level wages in Toronto, become part of globalization. Human rights policies become part of international trade. Labour standards become part of international trade. And international trade becomes something other than sport.

These sports analogies, however, are neither trivial nor neutral. Sports and sport culture celebrate the masculine values of individual skill, power, aggression, and speed, just as the contemporary global economy celebrates the victories of its most successful entrepreneurs. Microsoft becomes Bill Gates rather than a multi-billion dollar corporate empire, and it is he who is celebrated for having been tougher and stronger than his rivals in business and trade, whatever rules of fair play may have been broken along the way. Such an analogy brings with it its own logic, however: the individualistic focus on competition conceals the power of today's largest corporations, as well as the fundamentally gendered nature of the global economy. Using such a pervasive analogy to define globalization, the Canadian state is reduced to devising strategies to help Canadians, including women entrepreneurs, win on the global playing field. Trying to respond to more

fundamental challenges posed by globalization is inconceivable because globalization has been defined as an incontrovertible reality 'out there', to be faced by only the most skilled players. This observation should neither be construed as a critique of the government's trade policy *per se*, nor as a dismissal of the possible benefits of helping women become more proficient exporters. Nor is this observation in any way a criticism of women exporters themselves, for they, like others, have learned to succeed in a harsh and competitive environment. Rather, this analysis suggests that the government's deaf ear that has often greeted women's groups when they raise issues of the gendered nature of the global economy is unlikely to change, because at least from the government's perspective, the state is doing everything it can and should do. When globalization is seen as a competitive game, those who complain about its effects simply are not aggressive enough, or have not worked or trained nearly hard enough. Only a broader perspective on gender and international trade moves us beyond the individualistic competitive game, and makes it possible to appreciate the long-term unsustainability of continuing to play hockey in the jungle.[10]

Notes

1. It is important to note that the existence of women in business-ownership activities in no way tells us whether they had chosen to become entrepreneurs, or had been driven to seek self-employment as their only option during the massive restructuring of the Canadian economy, with its particular impact on women.

2. For a similar argument analysis of finance and credit, see Marieke de Goede (2000).

3. It is interesting that Martin emphasizes the need for referees and rules for the game to be considered hockey. Referees create a particular kind of order and enforce rules which in themselves are hardly neutral-the construction of 'playing fields', and the extent to which they are 'level' depends upon the rules and the enforcement mechanisms put into

place, Martin could just as easily have promoted the image of shinny as the 'real hockey' representative of international finance and the global political economy, but had he done so, he would have denied the existence of a space for political action in taming the hockey 'jungle'.

4. In the way in which sport is being discussed in this chapter, sport is much more than the athletic competition itself; it is much more than a 'game' for those who play, and 'entertainment' for those who do not. Sport is not somehow separate from society, nor does it transcend or have '"nothing to do with" politics and social conflict' (Allison, 1993: 5). Sport is not reducible to the 'physical activities and game forms that have promoted personal well-being, community coalescence, and social equality'

(Burstyn, 1999: 4); rather, through the power of its symbols, it plays a significant role in shaping our understanding of modern society.

5. This is not to say that the 1995 Beijing World Conference on Women did not address issues of the global economy or of women's place within it. The 1997 OECD Conference represented the first major international discussion among *economic* bureaucracies focused exclusively on the issues relating to women as entrepreneurs.

6. The URL for DFAIT's 'Businesswomen in Trade' website is http://www.inforexport.gc.ca/businesswomenl menu-e. asp.

7. The research for *Beyond Borders* was conducted by a team of academics, led by Barbara Orser, President of Equinox Management Consultants Ltd (Ottawa) and Adjunct Professor of Business at Carleton University, and including Eileen Fischer (York University), Rebecca Reuber (University of Toronto), Sue Hooper (Asia Pacific Foundation), and Allan Riding (Carleton University).

8. The study's results were compiled using rigorous social science methodologies. Criteria were established in order to select appropriate participants for the study, including firms employing fewer than 500 full-time employees, actively involved in exporting, or planning to become actively involved, which were owned or partially owned by a woman who had equity capital at risk in the venture, was responsible for the strategic direction of the business, and has the authority to make decisions, including export decisions. From a list of more than 1,000 contacts, 735 firms met the screening criteria for eligibility. Data were obtained from 254 faxed survey responses, 54 in-depth telephone interviews, focus group sessions with experienced women entrepreneurs and telephone consultations. A total of 67 women business owners were involved in the focus group sessions and telephone consultations (Orser et al., 1999).

9. Although 69 per cent of the women reported living with a spouse or partner, only 17 per cent of women business owners reported having to pay for daycare services for children, or for elderly or disabled relatives (Orser et al., 1999).

10. I am indebted to Ann Denholm Crosby for pointing this out.

References

Allison, L. 1993. 'The Changing Context of Sporting Life', *The Changing Politics of Sport*. Manchester: Manchester University Press.

Axworthy, L. 1999. 'Message from the Honourable Lloyd Axworthy, Minister of Foreign Affairs to the Hague Appeal for Peace', 13 May.

Burstyn, V. 1999. *The Rites of Men: Manhood, Politics, and the Culture of Sport*. Toronto: University of Toronto Press.

Cahn, S.K. 1994. *Coming on Strong: Gender and Sexuality in Twentieth-Century Women's Sports*. New York: Free Press.

de Goede, M. 2000. 'Mastering "Lady Credit": Discourses of Financial Crisis in Historical Perspective', *International Feminist Journal of Politics* 2, 1 (Spring): 58–81.

DFAIT. 1999. 'Marchi Welcomes New Data on Businesswomen Exporters.' Press release 49, 8 March. Available at http://www.dfait-maeci.gc.ca/english/news/press_releases/ii_press/99_049-e.htm

———. 1998. 'Marchi Launches Internet Site Dedication to Canadian Businesswomen.' Press release 150, 8 June. Available at http://www.dfait-maeci.gc.ca/english/news/press_releases/98_press/98_150e.htm.

———. 1995. 'The Promotion of Prosperity and Employment', in *Canada in the World*. Ottawa: Publishing, Public Works and Government Services Canada. Available at http://www.dfait-maeci.gc.ca/english/foreignp/cnd-world/chap3.htm.

Eggleton, A. 1997. Notes for an Address by the Honourable Art Eggleton, Minister for International Trade, on the Occasion of the International Conference on the World Association of Women Entrepreneurs. Toronto, 3 May.

Enloe, C. 1989. *Bananas, Beaches and Bases: Making Feminist Sense Out of International Relations*. London:

Pandora.

MacLaren, R. 1995. Statement 95/2. 'Canada's Trade Policy for the 21st Century: The Walls of Jericho Fall Down'. Notes for an Address by the Hon. Roy MacLarn, for International Business, University of Toronto, Toronto, 18 Jan.

Manley, J. 2000. Notes for an Address by the Hon. John Manley, Minister of Foreign Affairs, to the Third Annual Diplomatic Forum 'Canada's Foreign Policy Agenda and Priorities', Winnipeg, 20 Oct. Available at http://198.103.104.118/minpub/Publication.asp?/FileSpec=/Min_Pub_Docs/103808.htm.

Marchand, M. 2000. 'Gendered Representations of the "Global": Reading/Writing Globalization', in R. Stubbs and G.R.D. Underhill, eds, *Political Economy and the Changing Global Order*. Don Mills, ON: Oxford University Press.

Marchi, S. 1999a. 'Notes for an Address by the Honourable Sergio Marchi, Minister for International Trade to the Business Networking Luncheon co-hosted by the Ireland-Canada Business Association and the Can. Embassy', Dublin, 14 June. Available at http://198.103.104.118/minpub/Publication.asp?FileSpec=/Min_Pub_Docs/101433.htm.

———. 1999b. 'Notes for an Address by the Honourable Sergio Marchi, Minister for International Trade to the Canada–USA Businesswomen's Trade Summit, Toronto, 18 May. Available at http://198.103.104.118/mipub/Publication.asp?FileSpec=/Min_Pub_Docs/100232.htm.

———. 1999c. 'Canada and the World Trade Organization: Opening Opportunities around the World'. A Statement by the Honourable Sergio Marchi Minister for International Trade to the House of Commons Standing Committee on Foreign Affairs and International Trade, 9 May, Ottawa. Available at http://198.103.104.118/minpub/Publication.asp?FileSpec=/Min_Pub_Docs/100222.htm.

———. 1998. 'Notes for an Address by the Honourable Sergio Marchi, Minister for International Trade, to the Centre for Trade Policy and Law', 13 Feb. Ottawa. Available http://www.dfait-maeci.gc.ca/english/news/statements/98_state/98_008e.htm.

———. 1997. 'Notes for an Address by the Honourable Sergio Marchi, Minister for International Trade, to

the Luncheon for William Daley, US Secretary of Commerce, Offered by the Canadian Businesswomen's International Trade Mission'. 13 Nov. Available at http://198.103.104.118/minpub/Publication.asp?FileSpec=/Min_Pub_Docs/101766.htm.

OECD. 2000. *Women Entrepreneurs in SMEs: Realising the Benefits of Globalisation and the Knowledge based Economy*. Available at http://www.oecd.org/dsti/sti/industry/smes/news/women2000.htm.

———. 1997. OECD Conference on Women Entrepreneurs in Small and Medium Enterprises. Available at http://www.oecd.org/dsti/sti/industry/smes/act/smeconf.htm.

Orser, B., et al. 1999. *Beyond Borders: Canadian Businesswomen in International Trade*. Complete Research Report. Available at http://www.infoexport.gc.ca/businesswomen/book/menu-e.asp.

Peterson, V.S., ed. 1992. 'Introduction', *Gendered States: Feminist (Re)Visions of International Relations Theory*. Boulder: Lynne Rienner.

Pettigrew, P.S. 2000a. 'Notes for an Address by the Honourable Pierre Pettigrew, Minister for International Trade, to the Canadian Bar Association'. 19 May. Ottawa. Available at http://198.103.104.118/minpub/Publication.asp?FileSpec=/Min_Pub_Docs/103416.htm.

———. 2000b. 'Notes for an Address by the Honourable Pierre Pettigrew, Minister for International Trade, on Seattle: A Collision Between Two Worlds to the Global Forum 2000'. 15 May. Washington, DC. Available at http://198.103.104.118/minpub/Publication.asp?FileSpec=/Min_Pub_Docs/103338.htm.

Prügl, E., and M.K. Meyer. 1999. 'Gender Politics in Global Governance', in *Gender Politics and Global Governance*. Lanham, MD: Rowman and Littlefield.

Rayman, R. 1999. *Beyond Borders: Canadian Businesswomen in International Trade*. Summary Report. Available at http://www.infoexpert.gc.ca/businesswomen/beyond_borders/report-e.pdf.

Trade Commissioner Service. 1997. *Businesswoman in Trade—News and Press Releases: Trade Research Coalition*. Ottawa: Department of Foreign Affairs and International Trade. Available at http://www.info

export.gc.ca/businesswomen/news-trc-e.asp.

Whitworth, S. 2000. 'Theory and Exclusion: Gender, Masculinity, and International Political Economy', in R. Stubbs and G.R.D. Underhill, eds, *Political Economy and the Changing Global Order*. Don Mills, ON: Oxford University Press.

6

Hegemony and Foreign Policy Analysis: The Case of Canada as Middle Power

Mark Neufeld

Introduction

It has become commonplace in the discipline of international relations to observe that changing conditions in the global order demand new analyses of that order. The dissolution of the Soviet bloc and the lingering global economic downturn are both touted as developments requiring new appraisals and prognoses. Equally important, this realization has its parallel at the (meta-)theoretical level; it is increasingly accepted that the failure of students of world politics to anticipate and account for the sea-changes of the past few years cannot be divorced from a discussion of the way in which world politics has been studied. Simply put, what is required is not just new analysis, but new ways of analyzing; not merely re-examination of global structures and processes, but critical exploration of alternatives to the dominant theoretical traditions and analytical frameworks that have guided our thinking about world politics.[1]

It is the intent of this paper to pursue this theme with regard to the analysis of Canadian foreign policy in the context of a changing global order. The alternative tradition that will be the focus is one which is derivative of neo-Marxist theories of the state—an approach to foreign policy which

Cranford Pratt has termed 'dominant class theory'.[2] It will be argued that the 'dominant class theory' approach to the study of Canadian foreign policy, as articulated by Pratt and others, can be strengthened and enhanced through the integration of Gramscian-inspired theorizing—in particular, the notion of 'hegemony'. I will illustrate this point in terms of the notion of Canada as a 'middle power'. Before moving to a discussion of the relevance of the Gramscian notion of hegemony, and to its usefulness in conceptualizing discourse around the notion of 'middlepowermanship', however, I will briefly examine recent developments in the theoretical mainstream which also take up the question of new ways of analyzing in relation to the notion of Canada as a 'middle power'.

Relocating Canada as a Middle Power: Neorealist Directions

In a review of scholarly literature on Canadian foreign policy, Maureen Appel Molot has argued that what distinguishes that literature is a preoccupation with Canada's 'location' in the international system.[3] Typical has been the notion of Canada as a 'middle power' which informed traditional analyses of Canada's place in the world in terms of diplomatic practice and influence, and, more recently, with reference to Canada's position within the global economy.[4]

With reference to the wider academic literature, Molot identifies two liabilities attached to this approach. First, in concentrating analysis on Canada's middle power status, and the attendant 'selfless' character of Canadian foreign policy, this approach has 'tended to ignore considerations of national interest in Canadian action, despite emphasis in the larger international relations literature on precisely this issue'.[5] Furthermore, argues Molot, given the centrality of the analysis of international regimes during the 1980s,

> it is noteworthy that there has been no analysis of Canada's behaviour in international and other institutions as what Lake describes as a 'system supporter', particularly given the liberal internationalist tradition in Canadian scholarship. . . . Does the regime paradigm of analytical utility have a Canadian perspective, or does it exemplify a theoretical preference at variance with Canadian interests?[6]

In this regard, it is significant that recent works coming out of the theoretical mainstream have attempted to address both these issues. Of particular note is Andrew Cooper, Richard Higgot, and Kim Nossal's *Relocating Middle Powers: Australia and Canada in a Changing World Order*,[7] where an effort is made to relate Canadian foreign policy initiatives during the 1980s to the issue of 'national interest'. More importantly, the authors frame the question of Canada as middle power not in terms of its location, but rather in terms of an approach to diplomacy, 'geared to mitigating conflict and building consensus and cooperation'.[8] Drawing heavily upon the very regime literature highlighted by Molot, they argue that middle power diplomacy

> will fix on mediatory and consensus-building activities, especially such activities as building reformist coalitions to bring about change within existing regimes or creating 'foundational coalitions' to establish new regimes.[9]

It must be recognized that, in terms of the mainstream study of Canadian foreign policy, *Relocating Middle Powers* represents important progress. In emphasizing the centrality of Canada's 'national interest', this approach demonstrates that power and interest cannot be ignored; as such, it provides an effective counter to the idealist-inspired myth of Canadian 'exceptionalism' in foreign policy practice. Furthermore, by drawing on the regime literature the approach makes several important contributions. First, by integrating the concept of international regimes[10] it becomes possible to take a more differentiated view of the international context in which foreign policy is made and implemented.[11] Secondly, the notion of regimes opens the door to the integration of interpretive methodologies and explicitly normative concerns.[12] And finally, it allows for the conceptualization of greater autonomy for international actors—of particular relevance when the object of foreign policy analysis is a non-superpower.

It must be acknowledged, however, that the neorealist/regime-oriented approach represented by *Relocating Middle Powers* suffers from important liabilities as well. First, neorealism's neglect of the important role played by social forces and societal structures in determining state action leads to an exaggeration of the autonomy of the state bureaucracy in foreign policy making.[13] Furthermore, neorealism's focus on the 'national interest' lends legitimacy to policies in place, obscuring the degree to which state policy may serve some parts of the 'nation' better than others. A parallel critique can be directed at regime theory, where the clear predilection to support the basic principles of the Liberal International Economic Order (LIEO) obscures the degree to which that order serves the interests of some individuals and groups better than others.

As a consequence, it must be recognized that the neorealist/regime-oriented approach to the study of foreign policy is not a neutral one. In every case, the object of analysis—i.e., the liberal-capitalist state, or the LIEO—becomes something to be accommodated and not challenged. In short, despite its strengths, the neorealist/regime-oriented approach to the study of Canadian foreign policy can be understood as a form of 'traditional theory', seeking to facilitate the smooth working of existing social and political arrangements.[14] Accordingly, here the focus will be on the development of a more 'critical' form of foreign policy analysis—an approach that, instead of accepting the status quo, seeks to challenge the 'ideologically frozen relations of dependence'[15] that sustain it.

The Dominant Class Model and Canadian Foreign Policy

Although marginalized within mainstream foreign policy analysis, it is important to note that efforts to develop a critical approach to the study of foreign policy have been made. One of the most important is Cranford Pratt's exploration of the relevance of the 'dominant class model'. Following Pratt, the defining characteristics of the dominant class model can best be understood in terms of an alternative answer to the question 'How can one best conceptualize theoretically the interaction of government and society in the making of Canadian foreign policy?' In contrast to neorealism's emphasis on the autonomy of the bureaucracy in constructing policies in the 'national interest', the dominant class approach suggests that

> the capital-owning class in any capitalist state is the dominant class and that the policies of the state reflect and perpetuate that dominance.[16]

Accordingly, notes Pratt, dominant class theory approaches the study of foreign policy by concentrating

> on the widely pervasive bias in policy towards the interests of the dominant class. Sometimes this bias operates through the structural constraints identified by the structural theorists and sometimes through the network of linkages identified by the

so-called instrumental theorists. Through the power which the dominant class has to shape social attitudes and values, its influence extends far beyond those cases where structural determinant or direct class influence can be demonstrated. It can thus claim to be a powerful theory even while abandoning any aspiration to reduce to class terms the whole range of internal factors which influence policy formation.[17]

The dominant class theory approach has a number of strengths. First, dominant class theory, like neorealism, is able to attribute a considerable degree of autonomy to the state; unlike neorealism, however, which must be content to affirm the universal pursuit of power, dominant class theory is able to identify the specific goals pursued by the state apparatus: the reproduction of the capitalist relations of production. Secondly, dominant class theory acknowledges the crucial legitimizing function of an accepted dominant ideology that 'provides a rationale for the private and severely unequal ownership of capital.'[18]

At the same time, it must be conceded that the dominant class approach suffers from some lacunae. First, the dominant class approach as articulated by Pratt is limited to being a theory of 'foreign policy', thus leaving largely unanswered the question of how its emphasis on class society at the domestic level relates to the larger global context. Secondly, to the degree that dominant class theory is derivative of structuralist Marxist theories of the state, it is prone to the same weaknesses as structuralist Marxism itself, the most serious of which is the over-emphasis on determining structures, and the corresponding neglect of human agency.

Accordingly, this paper will seek to build upon the strengths of dominant class theory by means of Gramscian-inspired theorizing at two specific levels. To begin, I will draw upon the Gramscian approach to the study of world order to sketch out the global politico-economic setting of Canadian foreign policy. This is necessary for two reasons. First, a focus on the global setting makes clearer how the emphasis on class society at the domestic level relates to the larger global context. Secondly, attentiveness to the material context of Canadian foreign policy is vital if the discursively-oriented analysis which follows is not to descend into linguistic idealism.[19]

Consistent with the Gramscian emphasis on the importance of ideas, I will analyze the public discourse surrounding Canadian foreign policy at the domestic level. Specifically, I will focus on the regulative ideal of 'middle power'. It is important to stress that no fixed meaning is attached to this term. 'Middle power' (and the attendant notion of 'middlepowermanship') will be approached as an 'essentially contested concept', whose definitional content in any given context is a product of efforts by societal agents to define key terms in public discourse in a way consistent with the political project they support. In certain contexts, those articulating a vision corresponding to the interests of the dominant class (e.g., government leaders, mainstream intellectuals) may enjoy a relatively free hand in defining key terms. In others, the understanding of key terms in public discourse may be hotly contested by oppositional forces within society as part of the larger effort to give voice to political aspirations directly contradictory to the interests of societal elites. Accordingly, while the particular definitional content of the notion of 'middle power/middlepowermanship' must be seen in relation to its material context, it should not be seen as merely the 'effect' of that context; rather, its politico-normative content is the product of creative social agents in pursuit of concrete political projects.

Conceptualizing the Global Context of Canadian Foreign Policy

It is necessary to distinguish the Gramscian notion of hegemony from that of (neo)realism. In the neorealist framework, states are understood to be the principal actors in the international realm. Given a context of 'anarchy'—that is, an absence of a central authority with a monopoly on the legitimate use of force—states compete with one another in an ongoing struggle for power. The distribution of capabilities (power) across the units (states) is the key variable in explaining outcomes in the international system.

Accordingly, in neorealist terms international orders may be understood as hegemonic or non-hegemonic. They are hegemonic to the degree that a preponderance of power on the part of one state (the hegemon) allows it to dominate other states, thereby serving as a rough approximation of a central authority. Hegemonic international orders in this sense have been seen as the necessary precondition for a liberal international economy embodying the norms of openness and nondiscrimination.[20]

In contrast, the Gramscian notion of hegemony assumes a capitalist world economy in which relations between classes is a key explanatory variable.[21] The role and activities of social structures, from firms to states to international organizations, are understood in terms of class relations. As in the case of neorealism, hegemony can be applied to an analysis of the international realm. In this case, however, hegemony is understood to involve not dominance of one state by another, but rather the institution and maintenance of a world order that serves the interests of the dominant class of the dominant state while at the same time it serves the interests of the dominant classes of other states as well.[22]

As such, a hegemonic order is characterized by the fact that the dominant power presents that order as consistent with the common interest. As Robert Cox notes, in a hegemonic world order

a leading nation's conception of the world becomes universalized to the point where its own leaders stand by the universalized principles when they conflict with particularist domestic interests.[23]

Thus, in contrast to the neorealist approach, the Gramscian notion of hegemony allows us to conceptualize not two but three distinct categories of world order: i) a hegemonic world order, defined by a duly recognized leader whose actions are understood to serve the 'common interest' (i.e., those of the dominant social classes at home as well as associated elements in other states); ii) a non-hegemonic order in which a single state dominates other actors in pursuit of its own 'national' interests; and iii) a non-hegemonic order in which power is sufficiently diffused so that no single state dominates all others.

The Gramscian-derived notion of hegemony is not limited to the level of the international order, however. In terms of core states, at least, hegemony at the international level has its parallel in hegemony at the domestic level, where dominant classes make real concessions (always within limits) to subordinate classes to achieve broad societal consent for their leadership.

A hegemonic world order, then, implies relations of hegemony in the international/interstate realm coupled with hegemonic relations at the level of civil society in core states. Such an order, moreover, has important consequences in terms of the understanding of the behavioural norms and institutions established to regulate the world order, whether it be a question of inter-state conflict or forces of civil society acting across borders. Significantly, these norms and institutions are not identified with the narrow interests of specific states or social classes, but rather take on a semblance of universality and, therewith, an aura of legitimacy.[24]

In terms of the post-war period, one can speak of a hegemonic world order extending from the end of the Second World War to the mid-1960s. In this period, the United States established a world order built around norms and institutions that John Ruggie has termed the 'compromise of embedded liberalism'—i.e., a Keynesian welfare state combined with a liberal(izing) international economic order—all stabilized under the overarching structure of the cold war.

By the end of the 1960s, however, the bases for a stable American-led hegemony were beginning to erode. The expectation of continuing economic growth and rises in productivity, which had been central to the stability of the hegemonic order as the means of moderating both inter- and intrastate conflict, proved more and more questionable. Indeed, the very components of the 'compromise of embedded liberalism' came increasingly into conflict one with another.[25] Finally, the rise of East–West detente robbed the Soviet threat of much of its mobilizing efficacy.

As a consequence, hegemony began to dissolve not only at the international level, but also in domestic terms. In the United States, for example, hegemony began to unravel as the legitimacy of the American state and the order it represented came to be seen as open to question, a process clearly visible in the growing public opposition to US government policy in South-East Asia, as well as the increasingly vocal civil rights movement.[26]

Given the centrality of the leading state in the maintenance of any hegemonic order, the nature of the foreign policy of that state is a good indicator of the robustness of hegemony. As Cox notes,

the evidence of the decline of hegemony is to be sought less in loss of power than in a tendency towards unilateralism in furtherance of specific interests.[27]

In point of fact, by the 1980s the change in the nature of the global order was clearly visible in the shift in US foreign policy. Specifically, the Reagan administration's response to the undermining of American moral superiority and universalism took the form of 'nationalist assertiveness', most clearly evident in the abandonment of multi-lateral consultative leadership, typifying hegemony, in favour of an unrepentant unilateralism—a trend which, arguably, remains very much present in US foreign policy into the present. Thus, the US remains dominant in the system at present. However, it must be remembered that, in contrast with neorealist notions of hegemony, in Gramscian terms US dominance is a sign of a non-hegemonic world order qualitatively different from the hegemonic pax-Americana that preceded it.

Canada as a Middle Power: The History of a Concept

The early successes of Canada as a middle power were attributable to our skill in producing sound ideas for the general rather than just the Canadian interest. This is the way to be listened to.

—John Holmes[28]

It was in the context of the American-led hegemonic order that the character of post-war Canadian foreign policy first took shape. Given Canada's status as a core state, the Canadian capitalist class enjoyed clear benefits in its association with American-led efforts toward liberalization in trade and investment regimes. Domestically, of course, concessions were extended to subaltern classes—in the form of the welfare state—to provide a stable basis for capitalist class hegemony within Canadian society.

It was also in this context that the regulative ideal of Canada acting in the world as a 'middle power' first came into prominence. To begin, it is important to note that as a regulative ideal guiding state action, middlepowermanship was nested in a complex of assumptions about the global order shared by Canada's politico-economic elite. Pratt identifies the following two assumptions as key:

i) the most serious threat to international peace and global human welfare was international communism and the strength of the United States was the primary bulwark against its spread;

ii) the international economic order and its major institutions operate to the substantial advance of all participants therein, that consequently no significant injustices or indefensible inequalities were due to the international economic relationships.[29]

It was these assumptions which provided 'the underlying unity to such seemingly disparate policies as Canada's membership in the North Atlantic Treat Organization, its close military and defence productions links with the United States, its expanding aid programme, its active role in peace-keeping, and its effective participation in international institutions. . . '.[30]

Upon the foundation of these assumptions, then, the notion of 'middle power' was erected. As a regulative ideal, 'middle power' must be understood in terms of both levels of the global order. In terms of the international level, middlepowermanship directed the Canadian state to play a prominent role in multilateral fora, particularly in terms of international organizations associated with the North Atlantic community, and the Bretton Woods and UN systems. In this way, the notion of 'middle power' oriented the Canadian state to a role supportive of the hegemonic global order in two critical senses: i) by fulfilling an important role of facilitator and mediator, Canada helped to defuse potential conflicts which, if not addressed, might have undermined the stability of the global order,[31] and ii) by showing itself willing to sacrifice short-term national interests for the greater good, Canada helped to reinforce the notion that the global order was in fact not a narrowly 'American' order, but one which truly represented the 'common interest'.[32]

In terms of the construction of hegemony at the domestic level the notion of 'middle power' played an important function as well. First, in its stability-reinforcing role of facilitator at the international level noted above, the Canadian state helped to create an environment conducive to economic growth. It was upon this growth that the compromise of the liberal welfare state—the cornerstone of hegemony within core states like Canada—depended. Secondly, the image of 'middle power', with its attendant emphasis on Canada as a responsible member of the international community, was crucial in creating a domestic consensus in support of extensive involvement in the maintenance of the international order. As Holmes has noted, in the immediate post-war context the notion of 'middle power' served the important function of 'encouraging a wallflower people to get responsibly involved in keeping the peace and unleashing the world economy'.[33] Finally, in representing Canada's selfless activism in the international realm as the natural expression of Canadian society as a whole, middlepowermanship reinforced the notion that the social order within Canada's borders was an essentially just one, and deserving of widespread public support.

It is clear, then, that in its original formulation, the regulative ideal of 'middle power' was framed in terms of dominant class interests and in tune with a hegemonic global order. Nor is it surprising, given such an understanding of the origins of this formulation, that in a context of declining hegemony (both internationally as well as within core states) already discernible during the 1960s, this definition of middle power would progressively lose its value both as a guide for action and as a source of legitimacy.

An episode which demonstrates clearly the change that declining American hegemony had for the regulative ideal of 'middlepowermanship' is the Johnson administration's hostile reaction to Pearson's suggestion, made in his 1965 speech at Temple University, that the United States suspend its bombing of North Vietnam. The most cursory reading of the text of Pearson's speech will confirm the degree to which the speech reflected an uncritical acceptance of the US administration's view of the conflict—i.e., that 'the US intervened to help South Vietnam defend itself against aggression . . .', that 'its motives were honourable, neither mean nor imperialistic . . .' that 'its sacrifices have been great and . . . were not made to advance any selfish American interest.'[34] The implicit criticism of US policy can only be described as gentle, while Pearson's justification for the suggestion—that a temporary suspension of bombing might induce the North Vietnamese leaders to make significant concessions while allowing them to save face—was hardly radical.[35]

Most importantly, however, criticism of US policy was consistent with the notion of 'middle power' situated within a context of pax-Americana, and with Canada's efforts in support of

Western interests in Indochina during the 1950s, which 'enabled us to differ from the United States without opposing the interests of the United States as we saw them'.[36] In this case, however, American hegemony was sufficiently threatened (both domestically and internationally) that the Johnson administration felt no more willing to extend concessions to associated elements in an allied state than it did to the North Vietnamese themselves. The generosity of spirit which marks a hegemon's relations with its allies during a stable hegemony had given way to a close-minded siege mentality reflective of hegemony in decline. The consequence for Canadian foreign policy was profound. As Holmes notes, 'Among the casualties [of the Vietnam war] has been the Canadian belief in its role as a middle power.'[37]

Accordingly, as the 1960s came to an end, a growing dissatisfaction with the regulative ideal of 'middle power' could be discerned within government circles. And since that time, efforts to find an alternative formulation, which would both safeguard dominant class interests as well as achieve public acceptance, have been a regular feature of Canadian political discourse.

The first such effort was made by the newly-elected Trudeau government, which initiated a review of foreign policy, the result of which was a series of papers, collectively entitled *Foreign Policy for Canadians*.[38] There is no question that this report was designed to revise the terms in which foreign policy was understood.

What is most notable about *Foreign Policy for Canadians* was the explicit rejection of the essence of 'middlepowermanship'. 'Public disenchantment' [read, 'elite dissatisfaction'] with Canada's foreign policy, stated the report, was directly attributable to 'an over-emphasis on role and influence' [read 'middlepowermanship'] resulting in an 'obscuring [of] policy objectives and actual interests'.[39] It was 'misleading', argued the report, 'to base foreign policy on an assumption that Canada can be cast as the "helpful fixer" in international affairs', a role which 'no longer corresponds with international realities'.

There is no natural, immutable or permanent role for Canada in today's world, no constant weight of influence. Roles and influence may result from pursuing certain policy objectives . . . but they should not be made the aims of policy. To be liked and to be regarded as good fellows are not ends in themselves; they are a reflection of but not a substitute for policy.[40]

It can be argued that the effort to redefine the regulative ideal for Canada's foreign policy away from the image of selfless internationalism to an explicitly self-focused pursuit of 'national aims and interests in the international environment' was a logical response to a changing international environment marked by a hegemonic order in decline. The erosion of hegemonic pax-Americana allowed increasingly little scope for a middle power foreign policy characterized, at least in part, by a stance of 'loyal opposition'.[41]

Significantly, the break with 'middlepowermanship' promoted by *Foreign Policy for Canadians* met with considerable resistance in many parts of the attentive public. In some quarters this resistance was motivated by a continuing allegiance to the traditional notion of 'middle power', and the attendant 'selfless' character of Canadian foreign policy. For others, however, the rejection of the alternative promoted by *Foreign Policy for Canadians* was grounded in a deeper-level dissatisfaction with the basic assumptions common both to the notion of a self-interested foreign policy as well as to the traditional practice of 'middlepowermanship'.

Indeed, it was public questioning of the traditional assumptions about the international order by emerging oppositional social groupings which led, outside of official circles, not to an abandonment, but to a substantive redefinition of the notion of 'middle power'. Pratt has referred to this social grouping, which arose in the context of declining hegemony, and remains active into the present context, as the 'counter-consensus'.[42] What distinguished the members of the counter-consensus was their rejection of the principal

assumptions informing elite discourse about the global order, voicing criticism, in explicitly ethical terms, of both the militarism associated with the Cold War as well as the workings of the international economy which they saw as systematically disadvantageous to the Third World.

Indeed, radicalization and expansion of the social base of the 'counter-consensus' through the 1970s and 1980s, most recently in the context of anti-free trade struggles, led to increased emphasis on the links between disarmament, economic development and wealth re-distribution, environmental policy, and democratization at the global level with radical change at the domestic level. In this respect the 'counter-consensus' can be understood as forming part of an emerging 'counter-hegemonic bloc'.

Of particular importance for the discussion here is the fact that the counter-discourse of the 'counter-consensus' gave new life to the regulative ideal of Canada as a 'middle power'. Significantly, the links of the earlier notion of 'middle power' to support for an American-led hegemonic order were severed. Rather, 'middle power' was recast to signify the influence enjoyed by a country like Canada, and the potential such influence offers to effect radical progressive change in terms of disarmament, economic development and wealth re-distribution, environmental policy, and democratization of the foreign policy-making process:

> The outline of a global community, in which the planet's resources could be managed by institutions practising fairness and stewardship, is coming into view. . . . People who sense the power and creativity of our time now demand a safer, saner world in which governments, using the levers in hand, generate the production of the goods of life, not the weapons of death. As this constitutes an enormous challenge to Canada, this land so blessed in space, resources, technology, ability and reputation throughout the world. *The rise of middle-power influence* with the end of superpower enmity provides Canada with an unprecedented opportunity to work for the development of global security structures.[43]

It is not hard to appreciate how this oppositional understanding of 'middle power', were it to achieve widespread acceptance, could pose a serious threat to dominant class interests at both the domestic and international level. Accordingly, it is not surprising to observe that the regulative ideal of 'middlepowermanship'— if not the term itself[44] resurfaced in the reviews of foreign policy conducted by the Mulroney government beginning in the latter half of the 1980s. What is equally noteworthy, however, is that the definitional content of the revived notion of 'middle power' in official discourse differed significantly, not only from that of the counter-consensus, but also from the traditional notion of 'middle power' associated with the heyday of pax-Americana. No longer was the notion of 'middle power' designed to motivate 'a wallflower people' to active participation in the management of a hegemonic global order. Rather, now 'middlepowermanship' was defined in a way consistent with Holmes's observation, made in the 1980s, that if there was still a point in seeing Canada as a middle power, it was 'to discipline ourselves':

> . . . we still need guidelines to cling to and knowing one's strength remains a sound principle. If we are now more discriminating and calculating in our estimates of our own as well as others' powers, so much the better. Scepticism about spreading our good offices too wide may have induced a sense of proportion about the number of rescue missions, crusades, or moral interventions a country of twenty-five million can conduct at one time. Our moral majority may want the government to pass judgement on every misbehaviour in the world, and no doubt they will feel better if we do so, but it is the surest way to undermine the beneficent role of the middle power.[45]

In this regard, it is striking that beginning with the 1985 review of Canadian foreign policy, *Competitiveness and Security*, through the report of the Special Joint Committee on Canada's International Relations (*Independence and Internationalism*), the response of the government of Canada

to the report of the Special Joint Committee (*Canada's International Relations*), and to the Defence White Paper of 1988–9, concessions to the 'counter-consensus' that Canada must work in multi-lateral fora in the interests of peace and justice[46] were consistently twinned with observations about the limits to Canada's power and influence, and about the restrictions the international environment places on Canada's latitude of action. Accordingly, and notwithstanding the fact that 'our values dictate that we help the poor, the hungry and the politically abused',[47] Canadians were admonished to discipline their expectations, and accept the simple and unavoidable truth: 'We do not have the resources to do all we would like in international affairs.'[48] In short, the 'limitationist' conception of 'middle power' was a call to abandon exactly the kind of progressive activism entailed by the definition of 'middle power' proffered by the counter-consensus (even while paying it lip service), in favour of an orientation more in keeping with existing power and privilege in Canadian society and in the global order.

Conclusion

The limitationist notion of 'middle power' was an elite attempt to succeed—as the image of Canada as a self-interested, utility maximizer had not—in garnering widespread public support for government foreign policy initiatives while retaining sufficient flexibility to work in the service of dominant class interests. Accordingly, the limitationist notion of 'middle power', which first achieved prominence in the Mulroney years, has also become a regular feature of official discourse since the election of the Chrétien government in 1993.[49] The Liberal government statement, *Canada in the World*, for example, repeats the pattern established in the 1980s by twinning affirmations of 'exceptionalism' in Canada's foreign policy record:

> Canada's history as a non-colonizing power, champion of constructive multilateralism and effective

international mediator, underpins an important and distinctive role among nations as they seek to build a new and better order.

with thinly veiled admonishments to limit expectations of progressive action in the future:

> While Canadians strongly support an active foreign policy, they also have a realistic view about the challenges ahead and the constraints—especially financial constraints—that we face. . . . [Accordingly] We will not do everything we have done in the past, nor shall we do things as we have done before.[50]

In a similar vein, renewed enthusiasm in policy circles for peace-keeping, often represented as the quintessential expression of the Canadian tradition of 'middlepowermanship',[51] can be seen as a strategy to appeal to public sentiment while dampening expectations for progressive action. Specifically, a focus on peace-keeping i) appeals to public sentiments which support a progressive role for Canada in the international realm, while ii) serving as a justification for high levels of military spending, thereby deflecting calls for a 'peace dividend'. In terms of the international order, middle power as peacekeeper makes Canadian military forces available to serve the larger agenda of 'global riot control' increasingly important in a non-hegemonic world order marked by US dominance.[52]

At the same time, it is far from certain that these efforts will be successful. For while government pronouncements in favour of peace-keeping and multilateralism may be more effective in garnering public support than the notion of a self-interested foreign policy in the national interest associated with *Foreign Policy for Canadians*, it is doubtful whether such a limited conception of middle power will, in the long run, satisfy the demands of the counter-consensus. Nor is it at all clear in what sense even a limitationist notion of 'middle power' can serve as an effective guide for policy-making in a post-hegemonic world order marked by i) American unilateralism, ii) the lack

of a unifying external threat (absent the Soviet menace), and iii) increasing economic insecurity derivative of an unregulated global economy. Accordingly, it would seem more likely that the issue of Canada's behaviour on the world stage will remain strongly contested, and a potential flash-point within the larger debate surrounding the proper role of the Canadian state in an era of globalization.

Ironically, recent events would suggest that political leaders are finding even the limitationist notion of 'middle power' too prone to incite expectations of progressive policy initiatives. It is noteworthy that, despite the call for the promotion of Canadian values such as human rights in *Canada in the World*, more recent statements have sought to distance government policy from that orientation by down-playing the importance of human rights records in determining Canada's trade relations.[53] Ultimately, political leaders may be tempted to distance themselves from even the limitationist notion of 'middle power' to ensure sufficient latitude for the defence of dominant class interests, much as they have broken with the basic tenets of the welfare state. What is not clear is how public acceptance of the former can be achieved any more easily than the latter.

Finally, although too cursory an overview to be more than suggestive, the exploration of Canada and middlepowermanship effected here lends support to the argument that Gramscian theorizing—and in particular, the notion of hegemony—is a valuable adjunct to the dominant class approach to foreign policy analysis, To begin, it is compatible with—and, indeed, reinforces—dominant class theory's inherently critical orientation. Additionally, it provides a means of relating the global context to foreign policy-making, as well as a space for agency in terms of the construction of meaning through discourse. As such, the Gramscian approach is a viable alternative to realist-oriented theorizing, and deserves serious consideration in the search for analytical frameworks adequate to the contemporary world order.

Notes

I would like to thank Leo Panitch, Fred Judson, Harriet Friedman, and especially, Tony Porter for their comments on earlier drafts, as well as the Social Science and Humanities Research Council of Canada for financial support. An earlier version of this paper was prepared for the conference 'Canada and the World', held in May 1993 at the Centre for International and Strategic Studies, York University.

1. For a discussion of this theme in relation to theorizing about world politics more generally, see Mark Neufeld, *The Restructuring of International Relations Theory* (Cambridge: Cambridge University Press, 1995).

2. Cranford Pratt, 'Dominant Class Theory and Canadian Foreign Policy: the Case of the Counterconsensus', *International Journal* 39, 1 (Winter 1983–4): 99–135.

3. Maureen Appel Molot, 'Where Do We, Should We, or Can We Sit? A Review of Canadian Foreign Policy Literature', *International Journal of Canadian Studies* 1, 2 (Spring–Fall 1990): 77–96.

4. As a counterposition within the mainstream literature, see the literature on Canada as a principal power, in particular, David Dewitt and John Kirton, *Canada as a Principal Power* (Toronto: John Wiley & Sons, 1983).

5. Molot, 'Where Do We . . .', 80.

6. Ibid., 86, 87.

7. (Vancouver: University of British Columbia Press, 1993). See also A. Clair Cutler and Mark W. Zacher, eds, *Canadian Foreign Policy and International Economic Regimes* (Vancouver: UBC Press, 1992).

8. Cooper et al., *Relocating Middle Powers*, 174.

9. Ibid., 174.

10. The classic definition is that of Krasner, where regimes are defined as 'implicit or explicit principles, norms, rules, and decision-making procedures around which actors' expectations converge in a given area of international relations'. Stephen D. Krasner, 'Structural Causes and Regime Consequences: Regimes as Intervening Variables', in S. Krasner, ed., *International Regimes* (Ithaca, NY: Cornell University Press, 1983), 2.

11. For example, by distinguishing between economic and strategic contexts.

12. On this point, see Friedrich Kratochwil and John Gerard Ruggie, 'International Organization: A State of the Art on the All of the State', *International Organization* 40, 4 (1986): 753–5.

13. Critiques of the propensity of neorealist theorizing to reify the state, and thereby underplay (if not negate completely) the role of social forces are, of course, standard within critical theorizing about world politics. One of the best remains Richard Ashley, 'The Poverty of Neorealism', in Robert Keohane, ed., *Neorealism and Its Critics* (New York: Columbia University Press, 1986), 255–300. For a parallel critique, which targets Kirton and Dewitt's neorealist re-conceptualization of Canadian foreign policy, see Pratt, 'Dominant Class Theory', 108–115.

14. On the distinction between 'traditional' and 'critical' theory, see Max Horkheimer, 'Traditional and Critical Theory', in Horkheimer, *Critical Theory: Selected Essays* (New York: Continuum, 1989), 188–243.

15. Jürgen Habermas, *Knowledge and Human Interests*, trans. Jeremy J. Shapiro (Boston: Beacon Press, 1971), 310.

16. Pratt, 'Dominant Class Theory', 104.

17. Ibid., 116.

18. Ibid., 105.

19. In this I follow Fredric Jameson in affirming that while history 'is inaccessible to us except in textual form', history is nonetheless 'not a text, nor a narrative, master or otherwise'. Rather, 'history is what hurts', and 'its alienating necessities will not forget us, however much we might prefer to ignore them.' See Jameson, *The Political Unconscious* (New York: Cornell University Press, 1981), 35, 102.

20. The most developed formulation of this position is that of 'hegemonic stability theory'. See Robert Keohane, *International Institutions and State Power* (Boulder: Westview Press, 1989), esp. Chapter 4. See also David Lake, 'Leadership, Hegemony, and

the International Economy: Naked Emperor or Tattered Monarch with Potential?' *International Studies Quarterly* 37, 4 (December 1993): 459–89.

21. The pioneer in this regard is, of course, Robert Cox. For a good overview of the relevance of Gramscian theorizing for the study of world politics, see Stephen Gill, ed., *Gramsci, Historical Materialism, and International Relations* (Cambridge: Cambridge University Press, 1993).

22. One of the outcomes of such a global order is the internationalization of what were, originally, domestic forces. As Cox notes, such an order 'would most likely give prominence to opportunities for the forces of civil society to operate on the world scale (or on the scale of the sphere within which hegemony prevails).' See Robert Cox, 'Gramsci, Hegemony and International Relations: An Essay in Method', in Gill, *Gramsci, Historical Materialism and International Relations*, 61. General agreement between representatives of the dominant classes of core states on politico-economic arrangements and strategies is often achieved by means of a semi-formal, institutionalized bargaining process located within Northern-controlled international organizations. In this regard, one can also speak of an internationalization of the dominant classes of core states not only in material terms, but also in terms of class consciousness. See Stephen Gill, *American Hegemony and the Trilateral Commission* (Cambridge: Cambridge University Press, 1990).

23. Robert Cox, 'Middlepowermanship, Japan, and Future World Order', *International Journal* 44, 4 (Autumn 1989): 829.

24. As Cox has noted: 'The rules and practices and ideologies of a hegemonic order conform to the interests of the dominant power while having the appearance of a universal natural order of things which gives al least a certain measure of satisfaction and security to lesser powers', 'Middlepowermanship', 825.

25. As Cox notes, the crisis of hegemony 'became apparent at the level of the world economy in the conjunction of oil shocks, disarray in the international monetary system, the international transmission of inflation, and the downturn in growth in the advanced capitalist countries that also had consequential negative effects for Third World trading partners.' See 'Middlepowermanship . . .', 829.

26. Ibid., 829–31.

27. Ibid., 829.

28. John Holmes, 'Most Safely in the Middle', *International Journal* 39, 2 (Spring 1984). Reprinted in J.L. Granatstein, ed., *Towards a New World: Readings in the History of Canadian Foreign Policy* (Toronto: Copp Clark Pitman, 1992), 100.

29. See Cranford Pratt, 'Dominant Class Theory', 120–1. To these two assumptions, shared by leading decision-makers both north and south of the 49th parallel, can be added a third, more distinctly Canadian notion, deriving from Canada's status as a non-superpower, namely that the national interest is best served by 'an orderly and predictable world environment that embod[ies] some limits to the ambition and the reach of dominant powers'. See Cox, 'Middlepowermanship', 824.

30. Pratt, 'Dominant Class Theory', 121. For a discussion of the seamier side of Canadian diplomacy in the service of Pax Americana, see Noam Chomsky, 'The Drift Towards Global War', *Studies in Political Economy* 17 (Summer 1985): 5–31.

31. It will be remembered that the Pearsonian innovation of 'peace-keeping' was prompted by the desire to regulate a conflict between core states during the Suez crisis. Specifically, the Canadian peace-keeping contribution allowed for a resolution of the potentially destabilizing rift between France and Great Britain, on the one hand, and the United Slates on the other. In short, it can be argued that from the beginning the principal function of peace-keeping has been to contribute to the maintenance of order and stability within the hegemonic sphere—a goal very much in keeping with the 'national interest' of a non-superpower.

32. It can be argued that Canada's political leadership was not always completely consistent in this regard. One of the corollaries of middlepowermanship was the principle of functionalism, according to which countries, such as Canada, should be allotted a seat at the table in international organizations to the degree to which they contributed. This principle,

while achieving some success in deterring the great powers from appropriating all decision-making power to themselves, clearly contradicted liberal international principles of global governance (i.e., the formal equality of all states) by arguing, in effect, that there should be a further differentiation between secondary and lesser powers. The cost of advocating a principle of global governance which hardly lent itself to the claim of representing the 'common interest' was that at the first meeting of the UN General Assembly. Australia, and not Canada, won a seat on the Security Council. See Tom Keating, *Canada and World Order* (Toronto: McClelland and Stewart, 1993), Chapter 1.

33. Holmes, 'Most Safely in the Middle', 90.

34. *Mike: The Memoirs of Lester B. Pearson, Vol. 3* (Toronto: Toronto University Press, 1975), 138.

35. Indeed, it is very much in keeping with classical realism's skepticism about solving political problems with military means, and its emphasis on the need to find diplomatic solutions to political conflicts. See Gordon Craig and Alexander George, *Force and Statecraft: Diplomatic Problems of Our Time*, 2nd ed. (Oxford: Oxford University Press, 1990), Part II.

36. Holmes, 'Canada and the Vietnam War', in J.L. Granatstein and R.D. Cuff, eds, *War and Society in North America* (Toronto: Thomas Nelson, 1971), 190.

37. John Holmes, 'Canada and the Vietnam War', 191.

38. Ottawa: Secretary of State for External Affairs, 1970.

39. *Foreign Policy for Canadians*, 8.

40. Ibid., 8.

41. See Mark Neufeld and Sandra Whitworth, 'Imag(in)ing Canadian Foreign Policy', in Glen Williams and Wallace Clement, eds, *The New Canadian Political Economy* (Montreal: McGill-Queen's Press, 1989).

42. Pratt defines the 'counter-consensus' as 'internationally minded public interest groups', which exist in substantial number, and which have traditionally been 'peripheral to decision-making in Canadian public life'. Within this group, Pratt includes church-related organizations like Project Plough-

shares, the Canadian Council for International Co-operation, Oxfam, the Canadian Catholic Organization for Development and Peace, Ten Days for World Development, the Inter-Church Committee on Human Rights in Latin America, the taskforce on the Churches and Corporate Responsibility, as well as secular organizations such as disarmament, peace, or Third World solidarity groups. One should also include organized labour, as well as extraparliamentary opposition groups such as the National Action Committee.

43. *Transformation Moment: A Canadian Vision of Common Security,* The Report of the Citizen's Inquiry into Peace and Security (Co-published by Project Ploughshares and the Canadian Peace Alliance: March 1992), 6, emphasis added.

44. As Cooper et al. note, in December 1991, Barbara McDougall, Canada's Secretary of State for External Affairs, described Canada's foreign policy in middle power terms without, however, employing the term itself. See *Relocating Middle Powers*, 184, note 37.

45. Holmes, 'Most Safely in the Middle', 102.

46. Now refurbished with the new title of 'constructive internationalism'.

47. *Competitiveness and Security*, 43.

48. Joe Clark, 'Foreword', *Competitiveness and Security*.

49. Interestingly, under the Liberals, the term 'middle power' itself has been resurrected. In early November 1993, for example, the new Foreign Affairs Minister, André Ouellet, promised a foreign policy review with explicit reference to the tradition of 'middlepowermanship': 'It's clear Canada's foreign policy must be reviewed in the context of the end of the Cold War. . . . It also has to be reviewed in the context of Canada's capacity, as a *middle power*, to play an important role at the United Nations. . . .' *Toronto Star*, Friday, 5 November 1993, emphasis added.

50. *Canada in the World* (1995), 8, 9.

51. A recent discussion of Canadian peace-keeping under the rubric of 'middlepowermanship' is to be found in *Meeting New Challenges: Canada's Response to a New Generation of Peacekeeping*, Report of the Standing Senate Committee on Foreign Affairs (February 1993). For a critical look at the use of

the image of Canada as peacekeeper, see Stephen Dale, 'Guns N' Poses', *This Magazine* 26, 7 (1993), 11–16.

52. See Michael T. Klare, 'The Pentagon's New Paradigm', in Micah Sifry and Christopher Cerf, eds, *The Gulf War Reader* (New York: Random House, 1991), 466–76.

53. In this regard, note Foreign Affairs Minister André Ouellet's insistence that 'to try to be a Boy Scout on your own, to impose your own rules on others when indeed nobody else is following it is absolutely counterproductive and does not lead to any successful future.' *Globe and Mail*, Tuesday, 16 May 1995, A11.

Selected Bibliography

Comprehensive Texts

Cohen, Andrew. 2003. *While Canada Slept: How We Lost Our Place in the World*. Toronto: McClelland and Stewart.

Cooper, Andrew F. 1997. *Canadian Foreign Policy: Old Habits and New Directions*. Scarborough, ON: Prentice-Hall.

English, John, and Norman Hillmer, eds. 1992. *Making a Difference? Canada's Foreign Policy in a Changing World Order*. Toronto: Lester.

Granatstein, J.L., ed. 1986. *Canadian Foreign Policy: Historical Readings*. Toronto: Copp Clark Pitman.

Keating, Tom. 2002. *Canada and World Order*, 2nd ed. Don Mills, ON: Oxford University Press.

Michaud, Nelson, and Kim Richard Nossal, eds. 2001. *Diplomatic Departures: The Conservative Era in Canadian Foreign Policy, 1984–93*. Vancouver: UBC Press.

Munton, Don, and John Kirton, eds. 1992. *Canadian Foreign Policy: Selected Cases*. Toronto: Prentice-Hall.

Nossal, Kim Richard. 1997. *The Politics of Canadian Foreign Policy*, 3rd ed. Scarborough, ON: Prentice-Hall.

Tucker, Michael. 1980. *Canadian Foreign Policy: Contemporary Issues and Themes*. Toronto: McGraw-Hill Ryerson.

Welsh, Jennifer. 2004. *At Home in the World: Canada's Global Vision for the 21st Century*. Toronto: HarperCollins.

Canada Among Nations, an annual edited volume, is organized around a timely theme. It is a product of the Norman Paterson School of International Affairs at Carleton University, and is currently published by McGill-Queen's University Press.

Academic Journals

Articles on Canadian foreign policy can be found in many peer-reviewed academic journals around the world. That being said, however, there are three journals that specialize in the study of Canadian foreign policy. The Canadian Institute for International Affairs, founded in 1928, is Canada's oldest association for the discussion of international events and Canada's place in the world. The CIIA publishes two prominent publications: *International Journal* and *Behind the Headlines*. *International Journal* is a quarterly journal that has published since 1946 and has been the starting point of many of the most important debates in Canadian foreign policy. *Behind the Headlines*—an associated publication of *International Journal*—is also a quarterly publication that produces short topical and provocative opinion pieces. *Canadian Foreign Policy*, now in its eleventh year, is published by the Norman Paterson School of International Affairs at Carleton University. This particular journal includes formal articles from practitioners, academics, and media representatives, as well as roundtable discussions, documents, and book reviews.

Literature Reviews and Perspectives on Canadian Foreign Policy

Black, David R., and Heather A. Smith. 1993. 'Notable Exceptions? New and Arrested Directions in Canadian Foreign Policy Literature', *Canadian Journal of Political Science* 26, 4 (December): 745–75.

Blanchette, Arthur E., ed. 1994. *Canadian Foreign Policy 1977–1992: Selected Speeches and Documents*. Ottawa: Carleton University Press.

————. 1980. *Canadian Foreign Policy 1966–1976: Selected Speeches and Documents*. Ottawa: Carleton Library.

————. 1977. *Canadian Foreign Policy 1955–1965: Selected Speeches and Documents*. Ottawa: Carleton Library.

Hawes, Michael K. 1984. *Principal Power, Middle Power or Satellite? Competing Perspectives in the Study of Canadian Foreign Policy*. Toronto: York University Research Programme in Strategic Studies.

Nossal, Kim Richard. 2000. 'Home-Grown IR: The Canadianization of International Relations', *Journal of Canadian Studies* 35 (Spring): 95–114.

Stairs, Denis. 1994. 'Will and Circumstance and the Postwar Study of Canadian Foreign Policy', *International Journal* 50, 1 (Winter): 9–39.

Middle Power Perspectives

Axworthy, Lloyd. 2003. *Navigating a New World: Canada's Future*. Toronto: Vintage.

Andrew, Arthur. 1993. *The Rise and Fall of a Middle Power*. Toronto: Lorimer.

Chapnick, Adam. 2000. 'The Canadian Middle Power Myth', *International Journal* 55, 2 (Spring): 188–206.

Cooper, Andrew F., Richard A. Higgott, and Kim Richard Nossal. 1994. *Relocating Middle Powers: Australia and Canada in a Changing World Order*. Vancouver: UBC Press.

Dewitt, David B. 2000. 'Directions in Canada's International Security Policy: From Marginal Actor at the Centre to Central Actor at the Margins', *International Journal* 55, 2 (Spring): 167–87.

Holmes, John W. 1976. *Canada: A Middle-Aged Power*. Ottawa: Carleton Library; Toronto: McClelland and Stewart.

————. 1970. *The Better Part of Valour: Essays on Canadian Diplomacy*. Ottawa: Carleton

Library; Toronto: McClelland and Stewart.

Pratt, Cranford, ed. 1990. *Middle Power Internationalism: The North–South Dimension.* Montreal: McGill-Queen's University Press.

Principal Power Perspectives

Dewitt, David B., and John J. Kirton. 1983. *Canada as a Principal Power: A Study in Foreign Policy and International Relations.* Toronto: John Wiley and Sons.

Eayrs, James. 1975. 'Defining a New Place for Canada in the Hierarchy of World Powers', *International Perspectives* (May–June): 15–24.

Hillmer, Norman, and Garth Stevenson, eds. 1977. *A Foremost Nation, Canadian Foreign Policy in a Changing World.* Toronto: McClelland and Stewart.

Hampson, Fen Osler, and Maureen Appel Molot. 1998. 'The New Can Do Foreign Policy', pp. 23–55 in Fen Osler Hampson and Maureen Appel Molot, eds, *Canada Among Nations 1998: Leadership and Dialogue?* Don Mills, ON: Oxford University Press.

————. 1996. 'Being Heard and the Role of Leadership', pp. 3–20 in Fen Osler Hampson and Maureen Appel Molot, eds, *Canada Among Nations 1996: Big Enough To Be Heard?* Ottawa: Carleton University Press.

Hampson, Fen Osler, Michael Hart, and Martin Rudner. 2000. 'A Big League Player or Minor League Player?', pp. 1–25 in Fen Hampson, Michael Hart, and Martin Rudner, eds, *Canada Among Nations 1999: A Big League Player?* Don Mills, ON: Oxford University Press.

Kirton, John. 2002. 'Canada as a Principal Summit Power: G7/8 Concert Diplomacy from Halifax 1995 to Kananaskis 2002', pp. 209–32 in Norman Hillmer and Maureen Appel Molot, eds, *Canada Among Nations 2002: A Fading Power.* Don Mills, ON: Oxford University Press.

————. 1999. 'Canada as a Principal Financial Power: G7 and IMF Diplomacy in the Crisis of 1997–99', *International Journal* 54, 4 (Autumn): 603–24.

Lyon, Peyton, and Brian Tomlin. 1979. *Canada as an International Actor.* Toronto: Macmillan of Canada.

Satellite Power Perspectives

Clarkson, Stephen. 2002. *Uncle Sam and Us: Globalization, Neoconservatism, and the Canadian State.* Toronto: University of Toronto Press.

————. 1985. *Canada and the Reagan Challenge: Crisis and Adjustment, 1981–85.* Toronto: Lorimer.

Doran, Charles. 1996. 'Will Canada Unravel?' *Foreign Affairs* 75 (September/October): 97–109.

Grant, George. 1965. *Lament for a Nation: The Defeat of Canadian Nationalism.* Toronto: McClelland and Stewart.

Hampson, Fen Osler, and Maureen Appel Molot. 2000. 'Does the 49th Parallel Matter Anymore?', pp. 1–27 in Fen Osler Hampson and Maureen Appel Molot, eds, *Canada Among Nations 2000: Vanishing Borders.* Don Mills, ON: Oxford University Press.

MacLeod, Alec. 2000. 'Hobson's Choice: Does Canada Have any Options in its Defence and

Security Relations with the United States', *International Journal* 55, 3 (Summer): 341–54.

Molot, Maureen Appel, and Norman Hillmer. 2002. 'The Diplomacy of Decline', pp. 1–33 in Norman Hillmer and Maureen Appel Molot, eds, *Canada Among Nations 2002: A Fading Power*. Don Mills, ON: Oxford University Press.

Critical Approaches

Howard, Peter, and Reina Neufeldt. 2000. 'Canada's Constructivist Foreign Policy', *Canadian Foreign Policy* 8, 1 (Fall): 11–38.

Keeble, Edna, and Heather A. Smith. 1999. *(Re)Defining Traditions: Gender and Canadian Foreign Policy*. Halifax: Fernwood Publishing.

Neufeld, Mark. 1999. 'Democratization in/of Canadian Foreign Policy: Critical Reflections', *Studies in Political Economy* 58 (Spring): 97–119.

Roussel, Stephane, and Charles-Phillipe David. 1998. 'Middle Power Blues', *American Review of Canadian Studies* 28 (Spring/Summer): 131–56.

Sjolander, Claire Turenne, and David Black R. 1996. 'Multilateralism Re-constituted and the Discourse of Canadian Foreign Policy', *Studies in Political Economy* 49 (Spring): 7–36.

Sjolander, Claire Turenne, Heather A. Smith, and Deborah Stienstra, eds. 2003. *Feminist Perspectives on Canadian Foreign Policy*. Don Mills, ON: Oxford University Press.

Stienstra, Deborah. 1994. 'Can the Silence be Broken? Gender and Canadian Foreign Policy', *International Journal* 50, 1 (Winter): 103–27.

External Factors and Canadian Foreign Policy

Canadian foreign policy is greatly affected by two different aspects of the international environment: 1) the international system in which Canada must operate (geography, anarchy, polarity, etc.); and 2) Canada's place in that international system. The first aspect of the international environment comprises sets of variables that are givens, 'in the sense that every foreign policy maker must confront them without being able to challenge them easily or rapidly'.[1] The second aspect of the international environment was discussed in the articles on middle power, principal power, and satellite power in Part I. Part II focuses on the different external actors that Canada confronts in the international system. Canada's relationship with these external actors provides it with a number of constraints and opportunities in conducting its foreign policy.

This history of Canadian foreign policy, since the end of the Second World War, has been the tension between bilateralism[2] and multilateralism. From pre-confederation until 1945, Canada's foreign policy was a balancing act between two different bilateral relationships: the United Kingdom and the United States. Since 1945, it has been a balancing act between a bilateral relationship with the United States and a multilateral impulse through international organizations. At times, Canada has sought to distance itself from the United States, such as the Third Option initiative of the early 1970s, but at other times Canada has sought greater collaboration with the Americans, such as the decision to pursue a comprehensive trade agreement in the 1990s. This section explores this tension by focusing on Canada's relationship with the United States and the United Nations.

Canada's geography, security, economy, and culture are all inexorably intertwined with the United States. Over $2 billion in trade and half a million people cross the border each day. There also exists a vast collection of ties between family, friends, interest groups, sports leagues, and businesses on both sides of the border. These connections have been formalized in a number of different institutions including the International Joint Commission (IJC), Permanent Joint Board on Defence, NORAD, and North American Free Trade Agreement (NAFTA). Further complicating matters is the power imbalance that exists between Canada and the

United States. While the US is the world's only superpower with great wealth and military might, Canada is a medium-sized country with only roughly 10 per cent of its neighbour's population and economic size. Given the massive multi-disciplinary, but asymmetrical, relationship that exists between Canada and the United States, it is safe to say that no international issue is more fraught with dangers for the Canadian government.[3] When Prime Ministers become too close to American Presidents, such as Louis St Laurent and Dwight Eisenhower or Brian Mulroney and Ronald Reagan, they are criticized for abandoning Canadian autonomy. However, when they become too distant, such as John Diefenbaker and John Kennedy, Pierre Trudeau and Richard Nixon, or Jean Chrétien and George W. Bush, they are criticized for abandoning Canadian security and economic interests.

Don Barry explores the complexity of the bilateral Canadian–American relationship in Chapter 7. Ottawa and Washington have traditionally avoided linkage, as Robert Keohane and Joseph Nye wrote in 1977, because of the large number of non-state actors, the huge volume of interactions, the complexity of the relationship, and the absence of military coercion.[4] However, since 9/11 a 'big idea' has been promoted by different groups on both sides of the border that would explicitly link greater security integration (what America wants) with greater economic integration (what Canada wants). This 'big idea' meshes two of Canada's key foreign policy objectives: physical security and economic prosperity. Barry concludes, like Keohane and Nye did 30 years ago, that the 'sheer size and complexity' of the relationship would make negotiation of the 'strategic bargain' difficult to achieve and that Canada, as the weaker of the two parties, would therefore be negotiating from a position of weakness.

A second set of external factors exist as international organizations. Canada is a great supporter of international organizations and belongs to most universal organizations (United Nations, World Bank, World Trade Organization, International Monetary Fund, International Criminal Court), regional organizations (North Atlantic Treaty Organization, Organization of American States, North American Free Trade Agreement), and historic/linguistic organizations (Commonwealth and Francophonie). Tom Keating has argued that Canada's interest in multilateral institutions has been due to both external sources (Canada's middle power position, trade dependency, and as a counterweight to the US) and domestic sources (activist Canadian politicians and officials, public opinion, and civil society).[5] It would be nice for a full examination of Canada's participation in a range of international organizations, but space limitations restrict us to a single chapter on the most important of these international organizations: the United Nations. This problem is partially alleviated by the inclusion of a significant discussion on other international organizations in other sections of this book: Duane Bratt and NATO (Chapter 14), John Kirton and the G7/G8 (Chapter 18), and Elizabeth Smythe and the WTO (Chapter 19).

Canada is frequently viewed, at least by Canadians, as a leader at the UN. Elizabeth Riddell-Dixon, in Chapter 8, partially agrees with this sentiment when she writes that 'Canada shows great leadership within the UN in launching initiatives, developing policies, and generating ideas.' However, she also notes 'it has frequently been less effective in establishing priorities among these initiatives, policies, and ideas and in committing the resources necessary to implement them.' The gap between agenda-setting and implementation is addressed through an examination of the Brahimi Report on UN peace operations, the International Criminal Court, the Responsibility to Protect, human rights, and sustainable development.

Notes

1. Kim Richard Nossal, *The Politics of Canadian Foreign Policy*, 3rd ed. (Scarborough, ON: Prentice-Hall, 1997), 8.
2. This has also been called continentalism or regionalism.
3. For a historical account see Lawrence Martin, *The Presidents and the Prime Ministers: Washington and Ottawa Face to Face: the Myth of Bilateral Bliss, 1867–1982* (Toronto: Doubleday, 1982).
4. See Robert O. Keohane and Joseph S. Nye, *Power and Interdependence: World Politics in Transition* (Boston: Little, Brown and Company, 1977).
5. Tom Keating, *Canada and World Order: The Multilateralist Tradition in Canadian Foreign Policy*, 2nd ed. (Don Mills, ON: Oxford University Press, 2002), 1–16.

7

Managing Canada–US Relations in the Post-9/11 Era: Do We Need a Big Idea?[1]

Donald Barry

The remarkable growth of Canadian–US economic integration, combined with the security implications of the 11 September 2001 terrorist attacks on the United States, have brought the management of Canada–US relations into sharp focus. The most important challenge facing Canadian decision-makers is how to respond to the new security environment while ensuring the uninterrupted flow of people and commerce across the 8,893-kilometre common border. The dimensions of the challenge became apparent in the immediate aftermath of 11 September, when the United States virtually closed its borders in reaction to the attacks. Quick action by the Canadian government led to the 'Smart Border Declaration' in December 2001 to secure the border while facilitating the flow of low-risk travellers and goods. Building on the declaration in November 2004, Ottawa and Washington launched a 'New Partnership in North America', that set out an agenda to promote security, prosperity, and quality of life.[2] And in March 2005, Canada, the US, and Mexico announced a 'Security and Prosperity Partnership of North America', which outlined a broad plan to strengthen security and economic relations among these three countries that draws heavily upon the earlier initiatives.

Some observers argue that bolder action is required to deal with US security concerns and to protect Canada's access to the US market. Economist Wendy Dobson proposes that Ottawa strike a 'strategic bargain' with Washington that would see Canada support US objectives on border security, immigration, and defence in return for a customs union or common market arrangement.[3] Allan Gotlieb, a leading observer of Canada–US relations and a former Canadian ambassador to the United States, argues for an integrated approach to trade and security subsumed within a binding 'North American community of law'.[4] The Canadian Council of Chief Executives calls for the establishment of a coordinated approach to trade, immigration, energy, security, and defence that would transform 'the *internal border* into a shared checkpoint within the Canada–United States economic space'.[5] An Independent Task Force on the Future of North America recommends the 'establishment by 2010 of a North American economic and security community, the boundaries of which would be defined by a common external tariff, and an outer security perimeter'.[6] The common theme running through these proposals is that security and trade are closely linked and that explicit trade-offs can be made between them.

The 'big idea' approach is not new. It extends and formalizes the partnership paradigm that constituted the framework for the management of Canada–US relations during the early years of the Cold War. This essay explores the history of the concept from its high point during the Cold War, through then-Prime Minister Brian Mulroney's attempt to restore the paradigm in the mid-1980s, to efforts to apply it to the current conduct of Canada–US affairs. The essay argues that the erosion of international conditions sustaining the approach, the proliferation of issues and actors in Canada–US relations, and institutional changes on both sides of the border limit the application of the concept. That incrementalism, exemplified in the Smart Border and the Canada–US and North American Partnership initiatives, provides a sounder basis for the management of the relationship.

The Partnership Paradigm

The partnership paradigm informed the conduct of Canada–US relations during the first two decades after the Second World War. Created by the Soviet threat, the partnership was managed in a quiet, pragmatic way by government elites who held compatible worldviews, were in firm control of their governmental processes, and who were in a position to sustain trade-offs that were crucial to the stability of the relationship. The United States gave Canada favourable economic treatment in return for Canada's willingness to maintain an open investment climate and to contribute to continental and North Atlantic defence.[7] During the Cold War years, Canada received a variety of concessions from the United States; for example, Washington allowed Marshall Plan recipients to buy Canadian goods with US dollars and exempted Canadian oil from domestic import quotas and Canadian softwood lumber from import restrictions. This regime was backed up at the official level by a common 'diplomatic culture' that 'placed great emphasis on consultation, exchange of information, personal friendship, informal communication, and easy access to points of decision'.[8] On occasion, bureaucrats prevented issues from arising as a result of misunderstandings at the political level. For instance, US and Canadian officials sidelined a study of the feasibility of bilateral free trade requested by President Dwight Eisenhower in 1953 because of the objections of the St Laurent government.

By the mid-1960s the Cold War conditions sustaining the partnership approach had begun to erode. Cracks began to appear early in the decade when the Diefenbaker government dragged its feet in putting Canadian forces on alert during the Cuban Missile Crisis and reneged on its commitment to acquire nuclear warheads for its weapons systems. In 1963, the Pearson government imposed a take-over tax on non-resident purchases of Canadian companies and the Kennedy administration introduced an interest equalization tax on US capital outflows to ease chronic balance-of-payments problems. The Canadian tax was quickly withdrawn and Canada was ultimately exempted from the US measure, but the actions created concern on both sides of the border. The following year, the Pearson and Johnson governments commissioned two former senior officials, Arnold Heeney and Livingston Merchant, to study and make recommendations for improving the relationship. Their report, 'Principles for Partnership', published in July 1965, called for the 'maintenance and strengthening of the partnership', stressing the importance of 'intimate, timely and continuing consultation on all matters of mutual concern'.[9]

The report passed almost unnoticed in the United States, but it was heavily criticized in Canada. Ironically, concern focused on its preference for 'quiet diplomacy' rather than the partnership concept that informed it.[10] However, the partnership paradigm masked a growing Canadian dependence on the United States. In response to emerging pressures, Ottawa took steps to protect key economic and cultural sectors, including banking and broadcasting, although when Washington moved to deal with continuing balance of payments difficulties, Ottawa sought and received exemptions that were not granted to other US allies and trading partners.

By the end of the decade Canadian concerns that the country had become too dependent on the United States were matched by American concerns that the United States had become too generous with its friends and that it ought to take a more self-centered approach to the rest of the world. As both countries began pursuing more nationalistic policies it became more difficult, or perhaps it no longer seemed necessary, to continue the trade-offs that were central to the partnership approach. In any case, the Trudeau government's decision in 1969 to halve Canadian military forces in Europe doubtless made it easier for the Nixon administration to deny Canada its customary exemption in imposing a 10 per cent surcharge on all dutiable imports as part of a major restructuring of US foreign economic policy in August 1971.

Comme les Autres

In 1972, both governments formalized their new approaches. President Nixon declared 'that mature partners must have autonomous independent policies', thereby indicating that the United States no longer considered it necessary to give special concessions to Canada.[11] The Trudeau government said that it would aim to reduce Canada's 'vulnerability' to the United States through the 'Third Option', consisting of internal measures to strengthen the Canadian economy and culture, and diversification of external economic relations to counterbalance ties to the United States.[12]

Despite the new approaches, economic and cultural linkages between the two countries continued to grow, bringing more issues and interests into play and further complicating the management of the domestic politics of their interaction. In addition, Canadian provinces and the US Congress, both of which were highly responsive to their own constituencies, became more visible

players. Canada's provincial governments, following the example of Quebec, showed a new determination to exercise their constitutional responsibilities to the full. In the United States, dominance of foreign policy by the executive, with the support of a handful of key congressional leaders, gave way to a more decentralized system in which a democratized Congress became an increasingly important player. The result was a more open, less predictable legislative process and a tighter connection between domestic and foreign policies. The tradition of close bureaucratic cooperation between Ottawa and Washington was also affected by these developments.

This could be seen clearly by the mid-1970s. In 1974, Pierre Trudeau and Gerald Ford reaffirmed the importance of effective management of the relationship. But the following year, the departing US ambassador to Canada observed that relations had deteriorated during his tenure. He called attention to a growing negative reaction toward Canada within American business and congressional circles as a result of restrictive Canadian policies on television advertising, energy, and foreign investment, and because of Saskatchewan's takeover of US-owned potash operations in the province. Ford and Trudeau, as well as Henry Kissinger, the US Secretary of State, and Allan MacEachen, the Canadian Secretary of State for External Affairs, challenged the ambassador's characterization, but US State Department officials endorsed it.[13]

The warming trend at the executive level continued under the Trudeau and Carter governments. Similar international outlooks, declining economic prospects, a global energy shortage, and the election of a separatist government in Quebec focused both governments' attention on the benefits of closer relations. But cooperation fell victim to Carter's inability to manage the domestic politics of the conduct of US policy toward Canada, exemplified in the administration's failure to secure Senate ratification of the East Coast fisheries agreement. In the fall of 1980 Canada's ambassador to the United States warned that 'the pendulum' had 'begun to swing in the wrong direction', coupling this with a call for more US attention to the relationship.[14]

Relations deteriorated further under the Trudeau and Ronald Reagan governments. The worldviews of Ottawa and Washington had seldom been more different. The Reagan administration's policies were aimed at shoring up US national and continental strength in the face of unsettled global economic conditions and worsening relations with the Soviet Union. The administration sought to do this by reducing government intervention at home and increasing US power abroad. The Trudeau government attempted to focus international attention on the North–South dialogue while simultaneously reducing Canada's dependence on the United States by increasing Canadian control over the economy and expanding ties with Mexico and other oil-producing and newly industrializing countries.

With a decisive victory in the Quebec referendum in May 1980 behind it, the Trudeau government introduced the National Energy Program (NEP), which was designed to restructure economic and political power in Canada, to increase Canadian ownership of the US-dominated energy industry, and to strengthen the existing Foreign Investment Review Agency (FIRA) that regulated foreign investment in the country. These actions provoked strong reactions from US energy interests, their legislators, and the Reagan administration. Canada had its own concerns about US policies, including the handling of the East Coast fisheries treaty, acid rain, and the effects of the Reagan administration's mounting budget deficits. On the international front, the two governments were frequently at odds over East–West relations. However, the early tensions gave way to more cooperative relations as the two governments, alarmed by the deterioration, developed a new determination to manage the relationship more effectively. An important sign was the decision of External Affairs Minister MacEachen and Secretary of State George Schultz in 1982 to begin quarterly meetings to review the bilateral

agenda.[15] After abandoning its nationalistic economic policy in the wake of the global recession of the early 1980s, Ottawa sought sectoral free trade negotiations with the United States. The Reagan administration responded favourably. The discussions were not successful, but they drew attention to the possibility of concluding a more comprehensive trade agreement.

Reviving the Partnership Paradigm

Prime Minister Brian Mulroney, who assumed power in September 1984, saw closer trade and investment relations with the United States as the key to Canada's prosperity. He sought to revive the partnership paradigm, and offered the United States foreign policy and defence support and more liberal investment laws with the expectation that the Reagan administration would give Canada a sympathetic hearing on economic issues. Good personal relations with the president were seen as crucial.[16] At their first summit, shortly after Mulroney's election, the two leaders agreed to meet on an annual basis and to maintain the quarterly meetings between the external affairs minister and the secretary of state. Regular summits would continue under Mulroney and Reagan's successor, George Bush, although they would be informal affairs in keeping with the new president's style. However, the quarterly meetings between the Canadian and American foreign ministers were discontinued in 1991.

A dramatic improvement in East–West relations made it easier than expected for the Mulroney government to support the Reagan administration's policies. Ottawa temporarily boosted Canada's defence spending and when it mattered, Mulroney supported, or at least did not oppose, US actions to protect important interests. Mulroney's government also dismantled the NEP and replaced FIRA with the more liberal Investment Canada. But Reagan, although a strong president, was not able to provide the favourable economic treatment Mulroney sought. Accordingly, maintaining the partnership façade,

Ottawa increasingly attempted to exploit Canada's interdependence with the United States while subjecting US power to legal constraint.

In September 1985, Mulroney proposed that the two governments begin free trade negotiations. Reagan welcomed the overture, which further-thered his long-held goal of closer North American cooperation.[17] But in order to secure fast-track authority from Congress to negotiate the agreement, he had to agree to act on the US lumber industry's complaints about Canadian softwood lumber exports that comprised an increasing share of the US market.[18] The 1989 Canada–US Free Trade Agreement (CUSFTA) and its successor, the 1994 North American Free Trade Agreement (NAFTA)—between Canada, the United States, and Mexico—reached during the Bush presidency, improved Canada's access to the US market and established dispute settlement arrangements to help check the whimsical application of US trade remedy laws.

However, the unwillingness of the United States to agree to uniform trade laws because of pressure from special interests and their allies in Congress gave rise to a series of disputes over issues such as softwood lumber and agricultural products. These disputes would become a continuing source of friction in the relationship. Moreover, the tendency of US special interests to look to their congressmen and senators for redress in the face of what the special interests charged were unfair Canadian trade practices, and the willingness of the legislators to respond, escalated the political significance of the disputes. As a result, the disputes became politicized at the official level as well. When Canada successfully challenged unfavorable US trade tribunal decisions, US special interests groups often refused to accept defeat and persuaded their legislative supporters to change US laws or renew pressure on Canada. The result was that Ottawa and affected Canadian interests, fearing the costs of drawn out battles, in Jeffrey Simpson's words, were forced into negotiating 'a series of strategic retreats'.[19] By the time Mulroney left office in June 1993, a pub-

lic backlash against what many regarded as his excessively close relationship with his US counterparts led his successor, Kim Campbell, to distance herself from the style, if not the substance, of her predecessor's approach.

Business-like Relations

Prime Minister Jean Chrétien came to office in November 1993 promising to bring a more business-like perspective to the relationship. In a pointed reference to Mulroney's unusually close relations with Reagan and Bush, he observed, 'Business is business and friendship is friendship, and the two cannot be confused.'[20] Chrétien and President Bill Clinton developed a warm, though less ostentatious, relationship than their predecessors. This was made easier by the fact that their governments shared 'a fundamental compatibility' in their foreign and domestic policy outlooks.[21] To be sure, Foreign Affairs Minister Lloyd Axworthy's 'human security' initiatives on such matters as anti-personnel landmines and the International Criminal Court raised hackles in some quarters of the administration and Congress. However, the Canadian embassy in Washington, headed by Chrétien's nephew, Raymond Chrétien, worked with the prime minister's foreign policy team to contain differences.[22] Ongoing trade disputes over such issues as softwood lumber proved more difficult to manage. In June 1999, the Chrétien government revisited its strategy for dealing with the United States. It agreed to step up efforts to lobby US legislators by cabinet members and parliamentarians. Follow-up action, however, was limited.[23]

Meanwhile, in response to growing pressures of trade and travel, Ottawa began pressing Washington for joint measures to improve the management of the border. The first step was taken in 1995 when Chrétien and Clinton signed the 'Canada–United States Accord on Our Shared Border' to upgrade customs and immigration cooperation. Two years later they launched a 'Border Vision Initiative' to facilitate information sharing and coordination between Canadian and US customs and immigration authorities, and a 'Cross-Border Crime Forum' to further cooperation in dealing with organized crime. In 1999, they established the 'Canada–US Partnership Forum' in order to foster dialogue among governments, border communities, and other stakeholders on border management and policies. Although these measures increased bilateral cooperation, according to George Haynal, 'resource constraints and the lack of national priority attached to these efforts kept change within narrow limits.'[24]

Management of border relations was also complicated by an emerging US tendency that began with NAFTA, to view Canada–US relations in trilateral, rather than bilateral, terms. This could be seen in congressional efforts to deal with certain issues by taking a common approach to Canada and Mexico even though there are substantial differences between the United States' southern and northern borders.[25] In 1996, Congress passed the Illegal Immigration Reform and Immigrant Responsibility Act, Section 110 of which required all foreigners to be registered when entering or leaving the United States. The provision was aimed at Mexico, but Canada was included, reportedly because legislators feared protests from Hispanic Americans if stronger actions were taken against Mexico than Canada.[26] Concerned that the system would lead to gridlock at the Canada–US border, US businesses, border state legislators, and Canadian authorities mounted a sustained lobbying effort to overturn the provision. Matters became complicated in December 1999 when US customs officers arrested Ahmed Ressam, an Algerian living illegally in Canada, as he tried to enter the United States from British Columbia with bomb-making materials in his car. The lobbying effort was ultimately successful, but the incident brought the Canadian refugee policy under scrutiny. Canadian officials floated the idea of a perimeter security system that would see the two countries harmonize visa requirements and share intelligence information, and the US ambassador

to Canada also mused about a North American security system, but no action was taken.

The election of Vicente Fox as president of Mexico in July 2000 provided more evidence of the changing continental landscape. During his election campaign Fox promoted the concept of a North American community among the three countries. Modelled loosely on the European Union, it would include a common market, a regional development policy, free movement of peoples, and a common currency.[27] Fox discussed the scheme with Chrétien in Ottawa the following month, but the prime minister offered no encouragement, saying 'We have the United States, which is enormous, and two countries that are much smaller on either side. [I don't think] we can apply European rules.'[28]

George W. Bush, the new US president, appeared to have his own North American agenda. To the consternation of some Canadians, he announced shortly after his inauguration in January 2001 that he would make his first foreign visit to Mexico. Canadian authorities arranged for Chrétien to visit Washington just before Bush's trip. The priority Bush accorded to Mexico should not have come as a surprise. As former state governors (Bush of Texas and Fox of Guanajuato), the two leaders were well acquainted and they recognized that there were pressing border problems that needed to be addressed. Bush also knew that 35 million Spanish-speaking Americans (20 million of whom are of Mexican descent) had become a significant force in US electoral politics. At the end of their meeting, Bush and Fox said that they wanted to work with Canada 'to consolidate a North American economic community' that would include a common approach to energy resources—a matter of special interest to the Bush administration.[29] In April, Bush, Fox, and Chrétien agreed to create a North American Energy Working Group to explore ways of facilitating North American energy trade, although in Canada's view, NAFTA made a continental policy unnecessary.[30]

Shortly thereafter, Paul Cellucci, the US ambassador to Canada, suggested that the three countries expand their ties in a 'NAFTA-plus' arrangement that would include harmonized border controls, immigration, law enforcement, energy, and environmental policies. The goal would be to create a security perimeter that would result in more open borders among the three countries. John Manley, the Minister of Foreign Affairs, reacted cautiously, saying that Ottawa preferred to approach border issues on a bilateral basis by means of administrative changes.[31]

Aftermath of 11 September 2001

The al-Qaeda terrorist attacks on New York and Washington elevated security to the top of the US policy agenda. Following the attacks, Washington briefly shut down its airports and seaports and highly detailed inspections by US customs officials at land borders resulted in long traffic delays, forcing some Canadian companies temporarily to close their operations. Prime Minister Chrétien created an Ad Hoc Cabinet Committee on Public Security and Anti-Terrorism, headed by Manley, to map out Canada's policy. He also set the tone for the government's response, declaring that although Ottawa would stand with Washington in the struggle against terrorism, 'the laws of Canada will be passed by the Parliament of Canada.'[32]

However, the government's reaction was complicated by widespread criticism of Canadian security policies by US media outlets and politicians, which were fueled by false reports that the terrorists had entered the United States via Canada. Attorney General John Ashcroft, citing the Ressam case, called the Canada–US border a 'transit point' for terrorists and announced plans to strengthen security along the northern border.[33] (He later admitted that Canadian officials had provided information leading to Ressam's arrest.[34]) The Canadian business community called for the creation of a continental security perimeter to exclude potential terrorists. 'We have to make North America secure from the outside,' said the president of Canadian Pacific Ltd, 'We're going to lose increasingly our sovereignty, but necessarily so.'

Canada sometimes presses its sovereignty 'a little too far', added the chief executive officer of Enbridge Inc.[35] The Coalition for Secure and Trade-Efficient Borders, consisting of forty business groups from the manufacturing, transportation, and resource sectors, lent its support to the security perimeter idea, as did the Canadian Chamber of Commerce.[36] Significantly, US businesses, not wanting to be seen as out of step with Washington's security priorities, were noticeably silent.[37]

Manley rejected the security perimeter approach, and stated that he preferred to deal with 'specific areas of concern' rather than integrate Canada's policies with those of the United States. 'Working closely with the United States does not mean turning over to them the keys to Canadian sovereignty,' he said. Manley added, 'Perimeter implies NAFTA. . . .I think it makes the problems, whatever they are, much more complex if you try and do two borders at once.'[38] President Bush appeared to agree, telling Chrétien, 'You pass your laws; we'll pass our laws.'[39] The goal, as Michael Kergin, Canada's ambassador to the United States, put it, would be to create a 'zone of confidence' that would see the two governments adopt parallel measures that would meet each other's concerns.[40] Border relations with Mexico would be approached in a similar way.

Manley became the point man in discussions with the newly appointed US Homeland Security Adviser, Tom Ridge, with whom he soon developed a close working relationship. As Ridge had not yet assembled his team of advisers, an experienced Privy Council Office Borders Task Force, operating under the direction of Manley's cabinet committee, took the lead in drafting an action plan to strengthen border security. The draft became the basis of the Smart Border Declaration signed by Manley and Ridge on 12 December 2001.[41] The aim of the declaration was to ensure the security of the border and to expedite the movement of low-risk shipments and travellers. The declaration was accompanied by a 30-point Action Plan that included the development of common biometric identifiers for permanent resident cards and travel documents, expedited clearance for pre-approved travellers, visa policy coordination, a safe third country agreement for refugee claimants, prescreening of air passengers, compatible immigration databases, border infrastructure improvements, complementary commercial processing systems, joint posting of customs officers at seaports, integrated border and maritime enforcement, intelligence sharing, and exchange of fingerprint data.[42] Ottawa's December 2001 budget allocated $7.7 billion over five years to improve border infrastructure and enforcement, and $1.2 billion to boost the country's military, which had been weakened as a result of earlier budget cuts. Washington committed $10.7 billion to improving security along the US–Canada and US–Mexico borders.[43] In March 2002, American and Mexican authorities signed a 'Border Partnership Agreement', modelled on the Smart Border Declaration.[44]

The Canadian government also made good on its commitment to the war on terrorism, deploying a naval task force to the Persian Gulf as part of US-led operations against al-Qaeda terrorists and the Taliban government in Afghanistan that sheltered them. In addition, it dispatched a battle group to operate alongside US forces in the country, although the commitment was not renewed beyond the initial six-month tour of duty because Canada's over-stretched military was unable to provide a replacement unit. Still, Ottawa contributed the fourth-largest military contingent to the Afghanistan campaign. In August 2003, Canada assigned troops to the International Security Assistance Force (ISAF) to protect the new government of Afghanistan, taking command of the force for a six-month period beginning in February 2004.[45]

Although the Smart Border Declaration set an agenda for border management, the determination of the administration and of Congress to forge ahead with US security priorities affected negotiations. President Bush's 2003 budget requested funding for a revived system, to be in place by 2005, to record the entry and exit of all foreigners arriving in and departing from the United States. The measure became law in May 2002, after Congress passed the Enhanced Border Security and Visa Entry Reform Act.[46] But by the summer of that year there were signs that the step-by-step approach set out in the Smart Border Declaration was gaining currency, although some US measures would provoke controversy.[47]

When Manley and Ridge met to review progress in late June, they noted advances in intercepting high-risk travellers, the deployment of fast-track programs for low-risk travelers (NEXUS) and commercial shipments (FAST), intelligence sharing, and the establishment of joint customs teams at Canadian and US ports. They also initialed a 'Safe Third Country Agreement' to prevent asylum shopping by requiring refugee seekers to make their claims in whichever of the two countries they entered first.[48] Progress was sufficiently encouraging that when the Global Business Forum called for closer North American integration, Ambassador Cellucci offered no support, saying that the debate 'on whether we need to have a more formal economic union like Europe, whether we need the border or we should have a monetary union . . . those are big questions that involve sovereign issues and I do not want the progress we are making on a smart, secure border to get held up because of this.'[49]

In December 2002, Manley and Ridge announced that the Smart Border Declaration would expand to include measures such as the sharing of airline passenger lists and other forms of intelligence, exchange of criminal files by the RCMP and the FBI, and joint Canada–US customs facilities and databases.[50] In addition, Canadian and American defence authorities established a Binational Planning Group that gave the Canadian military a link to the recently created Northern Command (Northcom). Northcom was part of a US internal military reorganization to command American forces responsible for defending the United States, Canada, Mexico, and parts of the Caribbean. The planning group was charged with developing contingency plans for

Canada–US responses to terrorist attacks and other crises, and with coordinating maritime surveillance and intelligence sharing. The arrangement would also allow Canadian and US forces to cross the border in emergency situations with the permission of the host government.[51]

As well, Ottawa appeared to be abandoning its earlier misgivings about participating in the Bush administration's planned ballistic missile defense system. Russia's apparent acquiescence in the abrogation of the 1972 Anti-Ballistic Missile treaty reportedly eased Canadian fears that the system would undermine international arms control efforts. The government was also concerned that unilateral deployment by the United States would usurp the surveillance and warning functions of the North American Aerospace Defense Command (NORAD), the joint military command structure responsible for protecting the two countries against air and space attack.[52] However, a widely reported FBI alert for five men of Middle Eastern descent, who allegedly entered the United States from Canada with fake documents shortly before Christmas 2002, led to new charges of inadequate Canadian security in US media and congressional circles. The alert turned out to be based on false information and was subsequently withdrawn. And US cabinet members, including Secretary of State Colin Powell, Homeland Security Secretary Ridge, and Attorney General Ashcroft, expressed confidence in Canadian procedures. Still the episode showed that there were lingering perceptions that Canadian security was lax and that there would be substantial pressure on US authorities to take strong measures on the northern border if a real terrorist threat by way of Canada ever materialized.[53]

The Canadian government's handling of relations with the United States came under more scrutiny in March 2003 when Chrétien declared that Canada would not join the US-led war against Saddam Hussein's regime in Iraq without the backing of the United Nations. Ottawa was skeptical of Washington's claims that the regime had weapons of mass destruction and ties to al-Qaeda.[54] Canadian public opinion was solidly

behind the government's decision. However, business interests feared the action and anti-American outbursts from members of the governing party that accompanied it, would damage relations with the United States. 'If Americans don't see us as a close ally, they will want to treat us as something else,' said Thomas d'Aquino, head of the Canadian Council of Chief Executives. 'The question is, what is the something else?'[55] The business community's fears appeared to be confirmed when Ambassador Cellucci, on instructions from the White House, publicly criticized Canada for not supporting the United States in the war.[56] The speech paralleled similar criticism of the Mexican government by the US ambassador to that country. In follow-up comments, Cellucci reproached the government for not repudiating Liberal MPs, including the Minister of Natural Resources, for personal attacks on President Bush, and warned that 'short-term strains' could result.[57] The White House appeared to lend substance to the ambassador's criticisms in mid-April, when it announced that Bush had decided to cancel a planned visit to Ottawa that was to take place on 5 May. Cellucci pointedly noted that the visit would have occurred had Canada participated in the war.[58]

Meanwhile, early in April, one hundred of Canada's top business leaders travelled to Washington under the auspices of the Canadian Council for Chief Executives in an attempt to mend fences with the Bush administration. It quickly became apparent that although Canadian–US relations were strained, the economies of the two countries were so closely intertwined that reprisals would be very difficult to undertake. As Richard Perle, a member of Secretary of Defense Rumsfeld's Defense Policy Board and an outspoken critic of Canadian policy, put it, 'even if people wanted to be punitive . . . . It could damage us as well.' One participant blamed 'overheated rhetoric' for exaggerating the economic consequences of Chrétien's decision.[59] Underscoring the fact that relations between the two countries were operating effectively despite the chill at the top, Cellucci revealed that Canadian citizens would be exempted from the planned US entry–exit registration system—a long-sought Canadian objective. And returning to a central theme in the Bush administration's policy, he reasserted Washington's interest in working with Ottawa and Mexico City to establish a North American energy market.[60]

The following month, however, the prime minister joined in the criticism of the Bush administration, pointedly referring to Washington's growing deficit and its harmful effect on the global economy. He also contrasted the administration's stand on social policy issues with those of his government. Challenged by opponents, the prime minister defended his right to speak out and noted that he had not taken offence at Cellucci's frequent criticisms of Canada's defence spending.[61] Condoleezza Rice, Bush's National Security Adviser, warned that it would 'take some time' to repair the damage caused by the attacks on the administration.[62]

Underlining the Chrétien government's paradoxical habit of criticizing the administration while cooperating with it on most issues, Ottawa announced in late May that it would begin discussions with Washington on Canada's possible participation in ballistic missile defence.[63] Defence minister John McCallum defended the action, saying that if Canada failed to join the missile defence program, there was 'a risk' that it would be 'gradually excluded from key aspects of continental defence'.[64] Shortly thereafter, the House of Commons passed an Alliance party motion calling on the government to give NORAD responsibility for 'any system developed to defend North America against ballistic missiles'. In a show of defiance, 38 Liberal MPs joined Bloc Québecois and New Democratic Party members in voting against the measure on the grounds that it could lead to the deployment of weapons in space.[65] Public opposition to the Bush administration's policies was also growing. An opinion poll released in early July reported that although Canadians viewed the United States positively, most had an unfavourable assessment of President Bush. Continuing instability in Iraq in the aftermath of the war and the failure to find

banned weapons or to establish a connection between Saddam Hussein and al-Qaeda contributed to this outlook. More that 70 per cent of Canadians polled thought Chrétien had been right in opposing the war and that Bush had knowingly used unreliable intelligence to justify the invasion. A spokesman for the polling firm observed that the findings went beyond Iraq to question 'the credibility of the US administration', and would make it more difficult for Bush 'to get Canadian support for any platform'.[66]

Martin and Bush

Paul Martin succeeded Jean Chrétien as prime minister in December 2003. Martin had signalled his intention to establish 'a more sophisticated relationship' with the United States 'based on informed dialogue, shared values and respect for our differences'. The Bush administration welcomed his appointment. 'We're really looking forward to a dialogue with Canada again,' said an administration official.[67] Shortly after taking office, Martin took steps to improve the coordination of Canadian policy toward the United States. He created a cabinet committee to oversee government policy and established a Department of Public Safety and Emergency Preparedness, headed by Deputy Prime Minister Anne McLellan, to take charge of intelligence, border security, public health, and disaster response. But with the public uneasy about the Bush administration's policies and a general election in the offing, Martin's officials warned the White House to 'expect some mixed signals' from the prime minister 'even if his overall intention remains to improve bilateral ties'.[68] Pointing to Canada's commitment to provide $300 million in reconstruction aid to Iraq, Martin criticized the administration's decision to bar countries that had not participated in the war from bidding on primary contracts funded by Washington. He also condemned US authorities' treatment of Mahar Arar, a citizen of Canada and Syria who had been arrested as a suspected terrorist in New York in September 2002 while en route to Canada. The United States had sent Arar to Syria where he was imprisoned and tortured for several months before the Canadian government secured his release. Syrian officials found no evidence against him.[69]

Bush invited Martin to Washington for an early meeting but the prime minister opted for a discussion on the fringe of a summit of Western Hemisphere leaders in Monterrey, Mexico in mid-January 2004.[70] At the meeting, Martin reportedly promised closer security cooperation with Washington while Bush confirmed that Canadian firms would be eligible to compete in a second round of US-sponsored reconstruction contracts. The two leaders approved a non-binding protocol by which each government would inform the other of any planned deportation of its citizens and consult at the other's request. Bush also said the United States would work with Canada to reopen the border, which had been closed to live Canadian cattle and certain beef products following the discovery of a case of bovine spongiform encephalopathy, or mad cow disease, in Alberta in May 2003. Both sides agreed that the relationship was off to a good start. The prime minister is 'a straightforward fellow, who's easy to talk to', said Bush. Martin described the president as someone who is 'very frank' and 'looks for solutions to problems'.[71]

Shortly thereafter, Martin's defence minister, David Pratt, wrote to Secretary Rumsfeld seeking to negotiate 'a Missile Defence Framework Memorandum of Understanding . . . with the objective of including Canada as a participant in the current US missile defence program'.[72] Parliament endorsed the move although, ominously, 29 Liberal MPs joined Parti Québécois and New Democratic Party members in opposing the talks.[73] The government also announced that it would forgive $750 million in Iraqi debt and that a contingent of Canadian troops would remain on duty with the International Security Assistance Force in Afghanistan after Canada's commitment ended in August 2004.[74]

Building on planning efforts begun under Chrétien's government, Martin's officials began developing proposals to expand security and eco-nomic collaboration with the United States.[75] The proposals, which were made public by the prime minister's parliamentary secretary, Scott Brison, in a speech in Washington in March, envisaged closer cooperation through administrative and regulatory change based on the Smart Border model. The measures included harmonization of government regulations; review of rules of origin requirements; common standards for electronic commerce, energy, and environmental cooperation; and business mobility, and would be open to participation by Mexico. Designed to circumvent congressional involvement at a time when protectionist pressures in the United States were on the rise and to avoid stirring up anti-Bush sentiment in Canada, the proposals fell short of the grand bargain favoured by big idea enthusiasts. The emphasis, as one commentator put it, was on making 'tangible progress in areas where a lack of cross-border co-ordination has a substantial impact'.[76]

With Martin scheduled to visit Bush in Washington at the end of April, Ottawa announced new defence and security initiatives. Martin said the government would commit $7 billion to upgrade Canada's military, a move the Bush administration welcomed. In addition, Deputy Prime Minister McLellan released a new national security policy embracing intelligence, energy management, public health, transportation, border security, and international security. Some $690 million would be allocated to upgrade maritime security, government computer networks, passports, security agency staffing, and intelligence assessment. A security roundtable would be set up to liaise with minority groups, especially Arab and Muslim Canadians, who were concerned about the impact of government anti-terrorist measures. As well, a new secretariat would be opened at Canada's embassy in Washington to expand contacts with US legislators.[77]

At his meeting with Bush, Martin touted Canada's contributions to North American security and defence, and pledged assistance in helping to rebuild failed states. Bush praised Canada's role in the ISAF in Afghanistan and the UN stabilization mission in Haiti, which was created to maintain order after President Jean-Bertrand Aristide fled the country. He also said that he wanted the US border open to Canadian cattle 'as quickly as possible'.[78]

The anticipated Canadian general election, which took place on 28 June, reduced Martin's government to minority status. Despite the government's weakened position, Martin indicated that Ottawa would soon make a decision on ballistic missile defence. With a number of Liberal MPs prepared to join the Bloc Quebécois and New Democrats in opposing Canada's participation, the new Conservative Party would play a pivotal role if parliamentary approval were required.[79]

On 5 August, in a move that ensured NORAD's continuing importance in aerospace defence, Ottawa and Washington agreed to share data from the organization's early warning system with Northcom, the US command responsible for missile defence. Bill Graham, the new defence minister, characterized the decision as a necessary but not inevitable step toward participation. 'We're keeping all options open', he said. The government's announcement promised that Parliament would have 'input' on the issue.[80]

Graham began making the case for Canadian participation. He acknowledged that missile defence was unpopular in Canada but argued that the issue was 'not about American domestic politics. It's about North American security. We can't afford to draw a border between Canada and the United States when it comes to defence of the continent.'[81] Seeking to capitalize on the government's problems, Conservative leader Stephen Harper said his party would not commit itself on missile defence until it had seen the details of any Canada–US agreement. Martin agreed to Harper's demand for a vote in the House of Commons on Canada's participation.[82]

The Martin government's ability to fashion a parliamentary consensus on missile defence was further complicated by the Bush administration's failure to respond to Canadian concerns about US trade protectionism. American restrictions on beef exports, challenges to wheat sales, the ongo-

ing softwood lumber dispute, and the refusal of Congress to yield to a World Trade Organization (WTO) ruling to repeal the Continued Dumping and Subsidy Offset Act of 2000 (Byrd Amendment) intensified Canadian dissatisfaction with Bush's policies. The Byrd amendment allowed Washington to give to domestic companies duties from foreign firms deemed to be trading unfairly with the US, thereby complicating the resolution of Canada–US trade disputes. Indeed Martin had already called for changes to NAFTA to strengthen the capacity of the dispute settlement panel to deal with trade complaints. But recognizing that the United States might seek to renegotiate other provisions of the agreement, he subsequently backed away from his stand.[83]

Bush was returned to power in the US presidential election on 2 November. He quickly accepted Martin's invitation to visit Canada, viewing it as an opportunity to begin improving relations with key allies following the divisive Iraq war. Ambassador Cellucci hinted that Bush would welcome an invitation to address Parliament. However, the announcement that the visit would take place on 30 November–1 December brought renewed criticism of the president. Not wanting to risk being heckled, Bush decided to travel to Halifax on 1 December to belatedly thank Atlantic Canadians for sheltering stranded US air travelers following the 2001 terrorist attacks.[84]

In an apparent effort to ease Martin's difficulties over missile defence, Cellucci, who had been pressing the government to act, said that Washington did not expect a quick decision. 'We're not going to put any time limit on this,' he commented. 'We expect that [the debate] will proceed and we will be waiting to see what the decision is.' Administration officials told their Canadian counterparts that Bush would not raise the issue in his discussions with Martin. And at an Asia Pacific Economic Cooperation (APEC) meeting in Chile prior to the Ottawa summit, Bush indicated that he would ask the US Office of Management and Budget to launch a review process leading to the opening of the border to Canadian cattle.[85]

A New Partnership in North America

At their meetings in Ottawa, Bush and Martin discussed security, defence, and economic issues, with the president surprising the prime minister by pressing Ottawa to join the missile defence program, despite all indications that the US was willing to wait for Canada's decision.[86] The principal outcome of the deliberations was a joint statement on 'A New Partnership in North America', which committed the two countries to 'deepening' their cooperation, working 'bilaterally to address Canada–US priorities' and 'with Mexico on issues of trilateral concern'. Described by Martin as 'an agenda in which our two nations will cooperate in a practical way towards common goals' of security, prosperity and quality of life, the statement set out a series of priorities including improved intelligence sharing, law enforcement, security infrastructure, passports, maritime surveillance and defence, NORAD renewal, regulatory reform, reduction of rules of origin costs, energy efficiency, environmental and public health coordination, advancement of democracy, response to humanitarian crises, enhancement of multilateral institutions, that completion of the Doha Round of WTO trade negotiations, and free trade in the Americas.[87] Deputy Prime Minister McLellan and Foreign Affairs minister Pierre Pettigrew would work with US ministers to provide detailed proposals on how to advance the plan by June 2005.[88]

In his speech in Halifax, Bush pledged to 'reach out' to American allies, but he defended his government's foreign policy, citing the 11 September 2001 attacks as evidence of the need to confront threats before they materialize. He also renewed his call on Ottawa to participate in the missile defence system. Martin agreed that Canada shared 'many ideals' with the United States but cautioned the president not to expect automatic Canadian support for his policies. Although Ottawa would work closely with Washington in continental defence, it would not necessarily participate in missile defence.[89]

Bush's intervention intensified the missile defence debate in Canada. With opposition growing, Martin said that he would seek written assurance that the program would not lead to the weaponization of space. He added that Canada would not help fund the system, nor would it allow the United States to install interceptor missiles in Canada. At the same time, Martin quietly dispatched a senior government official to Washington to assure US authorities that the government had not made a final decision. The official reportedly told the Americans that Canada would sign on to the program.[90]

While Martin was grappling with missile defence, Bush was dealing with the effects of congressional involvement in economic policy-making. The failure of Congress to meet a December 2004 deadline for repeal of the Byrd Amendment prompted Ambassador Cellucci to take the unusual step of encouraging the Canadian government to impose sanctions on the United States. 'Getting Congress to act, and repeal a law that is passed, is not an easy thing to do,' Cellucci said. 'I suspect that it will take the imposition of sanctions by Canada and other countries to get the Congress to act.'[91]

To be sure, there was movement on the mad cow issue in late December when the US Department of Agriculture proclaimed new rules that would reopen the border to live cattle under 30 months of age. But the discovery of two new cases of the disease in Washington State and Alberta, both involving Canadian cattle, gave American opponents new ammunition. Although US agriculture officials were satisfied with Canadian control measures, in March 2005 a district judge in Montana granted an injunction that put the plan on indefinite hold. The US Senate backed the judge's action by passing a resolution to keep the ban in place. The injunction was overturned by a US federal appeals court in July 2005.[92] Shortly after, however, Washington's willingness to meet its international trade obligations was again called into question when the Bush administration declared that it would not comply with a NAFTA Extraordinary Challenge Committee ruling that declared US penalties on Canadian softwood lumber imports illegal and ordered the repayment of $5 billion in duties.[93]

Meanwhile, the missile defence issue had come to a head in February 2005 when Martin decided that Canada would not join the program. Public opposition, the uncertain prospect of approval by Parliament, and sharp divisions within the womens' and Quebec wings of the Liberal caucus and party prompted him withhold support. In order to offset the negative effect of the decision, the announcement would be made after the government's budget, which would increase military spending by $12.8 billion over five years. Canadian officials privately informed their American counterparts in Ottawa and at a NATO summit meeting in Brussels that Canada would not participate, but Martin did not broach the issue with Bush. In a sign of displeasure, Condoleezza Rice, Bush's new Secretary of State, called off plans to visit Canada in mid-April and the president himself held off returning Martin's phone call to discuss a planned meeting of the three North American leaders in Waco, Texas, on 23 March. The meeting, initiated by the United States, was designed to bring Mexico into North American cooperation arrangements.[94]

If the Bush administration was disappointed by Martin's decision on missile defence, the Canadian public overwhelmingly approved. An opinion poll conducted in mid-March reported that two-thirds of those surveyed supported the action. Ironically, only Conservative party supporters thought Canada should take part. A polling firm representative observed that the opposition had more to do with Bush's foreign policy, particularly regarding the war in Iraq and US trade actions, than with missile defence.[95]

Waco Summit Extends Partnership to Mexico

Although business interests pressed for a 'major initiative' at the Waco summit, Canadian, US, and Mexican authorities had a more limited goal in mind. As a US official put it, 'The intention will be to focus on things that can be done without legislation in any of the three states.'[96] Seeking to influence the deliberations, the Canadian, US, and Mexican co-chairs of an Independent Task Force on the Future of North America—sponsored by the Canadian Council of Chief Executives, the US Council on Foreign Relations and the Mexican Council on Foreign Relations—issued a statement calling for the creation of a North American community with a continental security perimeter and a common external tariff within five years. The group's Canadian chair, John Manley, who was Deputy Prime Minister in Jean Chrétien's government had supported a pragmatic approach to continental cooperation, urged Martin, Bush, and Fox to 'think big' in their deliberations.[97] However, the Canadian and US governments continued to play down the prospect of far-reaching change. 'This will be a comprehensive agenda that builds on previous accomplishments—such as the Smart Borders Action Plan—and sets a work plan that outlines where action will be taken, challenges diminished, and opportunities seized,' said Martin.[98]

At the end of the Waco summit, Martin, Bush, and Fox announced the creation of a 'Security and Prosperity Partnership of North America' to advance common objectives. The agreement, which superseded the Canada–US New Partnership in North America, was 'trilateral in concept . . . allowing any two countries to move forward on an issue', while creating 'a path for the third to join later'. It contained commitments to advance common security and prosperity goals, including border security and bioprotection strategies; strengthened infrastructure and facilitation of cargo and travellers; improvements to maritime and aviation security; regulatory reform; cooperation in energy, transportation, financial services, and technology; and environmental and food safety collaboration. But it stopped short of committing the three governments to a North American security perimeter, a common external tariff, or improved trade dispute resolution measures. Ministerial-led working groups would consult with stakeholders in developing work plans that would 'set specific, measurable, and achievable goals' and 'implementation dates'. The initial report would be due within 90 days, with subsequent reports to follow on a semi-annual basis.[99]

The leaders went out of their way to differentiate their approach from that of grand bargain proponents. 'We're not talking about a big bang, we're talking about big progress,' said Martin. 'We are three sovereign nations—jealous of our sovereignty—but we recognize that sovereignty is stronger if North America is competitive and compatible.'[100] A senior US State Department official was even more emphatic: 'The "Security and Prosperity Partnership" is not an effort to launch a new "big idea" in North America,' the official observed. 'NAFTA was and remains the "big idea". Indeed, the Security and Prosperity Partnership recognizes that one of the foundations of NAFTA's success has been integrating our trade and our markets while maintaining our distinct sovereignties and national identities.'[101]

In late June, senior Canadian, American, and Mexican ministers issued their first report on initiatives, both planned and already under way, some carried out trilaterally others on a Canada–US or Mexico–US basis. Progress had been made in facilitating electronic commerce, liberalizing rules of origin, public health and safety protection, labeling of textiles and apparel, entry of temporary workers, migratory bird protection, harmonized approaches to mad cow disease, aviation navigation safety, prosecution of smugglers, border infrastructure, science and technology cooperation, and port and cargo security. Future plans included the establishment of a single North American Trusted Traveller Program to accommodate frequent travellers, common standards for visitor visa screening and processing, a trilateral Regulatory Cooperation Framework to streamline regulations, a North American Steel Strategy to enhance steel industry competitiveness, an Automotive Partnership Council of North America to make recommendations on developing an integrated auto sector, and a sustainable North American energy economy to promote the long-term supply and use of energy.[102]

The Big Idea Critique

Critics contend that only a big idea can address US security concerns and protect Canada's access to the American market. They argue that management of the border requires a stronger basis than administrative interpretation, which is vulnerable to the uncertainties of politics and unforeseen crises.[103] As Wendy Dobson sees it, 'Small ideas or temporizing will get lost in the highly diffused (and highly focused) US political system. Staying with the status quo will see our sovereignty eroded when we are forced to react to, rather than shape, our assertive neighbour's initiatives.'[104] Allan Gotlieb says, 'For any initiative to succeed . . . . It must be bold, it must come from Canada, and it must be espoused at the highest level. It must be comprehensive so as to allow trade-offs and broad constituencies to come into play. It must address the US agenda as well as ours.'[105] William Robson, a supporter of the big idea, adds that 'a simultaneous commitment by leaders on both sides to address each other's principal economic and security concerns offers an overarching bi-national payoff. Especially for Canadians who doubt their ability to capture US attention on economic grounds alone, negotiations on economic and security issues at once have obvious attractions.'[106] Given its stake in the outcome, Thomas d'Aquino asserts, the business community must take the lead in building support for a new paradigm as it did when it campaigned for the Canada–US and North American free trade accords.[107]

Although the various grand bargain schemes differ in some respects, all are based on the assumption that only an integrated approach to economic and physical safety can provide an effective basis for managing Canada–US relations. Dobson's big idea would see Canada improve border security, tighten immigration policy, accelerate energy and resources development, and increase contributions to continental defence in exchange for expanded access to the US market in the form of a customs union or common market. This would be managed by 'functional co-operative mechanisms'. Dobson discounts the possibility that increased co-operation would undermine Canada's distinctiveness, arguing that the two countries would be equal partners. 'Harmonization may be proposed, but the other partner has a say in whether the proposal is accepted,' she contends.[108]

Gotlieb's North American community of law would subject political power to the rule of law in Canada–US relations. It would include a common external tariff; abolition of trade remedy laws; binding rules for the free movement of people, goods, and investment; mutual recognition of standards; immigration rules; a common security perimeter, and increased defence co-operation. The community of law would not require overarching political architecture, although 'in a few areas, joint institutions might help the smooth functioning of the common space.'[109]

The North American Security and Prosperity Initiative, championed by the Canadian Council of Chief Executives, calls on Ottawa to adopt 'a comprehensive strategy for strengthening its economic and security partnership with the United States', with Mexico joining in when it is in a position to do so. The strategy would require negotiations on a wide range of issues, resulting in 'a single overarching agreement', or 'a series of interlocking and mutually supporting agreements'. Key elements would include a common external tariff or customs union, suspension of trade remedy measures, an improved dispute settlement process, regulatory convergence, full labour mobility, a comprehensive resource security pact containing a common energy strategy, improved border management with expanded infrastructure, common security procedures for processing immigrants and refugees, joint watch lists and visa requirements, and enhanced defence cooperation. Joint commissions, modelled on the Canada–US International Joint Commission (IJC), would facilitate policy coordination and resolve problems.[110]

The Independent Task Force on the Future of North America envisages a continental security perimeter with an expanded NORAD adding responsibility for land and naval defence, a North American border pass with biometric identifiers, a joint border action plan with harmonized visa and asylum regulations, additional customs facilities, infrastructure, and information-sharing. The plan also includes a common external tariff, a permanent tribunal for adjudicating trade and investment disputes, a unified approach to unfair trade practices, review of sectors excluded from NAFTA, a North American Competition Commission, a North American regulatory plan, a continental resource strategy, a move to full labour mobility, an economic development plan for Mexico, and increased educational exchanges. Annual North American summit meetings would oversee implementation of the plan. A North American Advisory Council of eminent persons outside government would function as a source of advice and ideas, while a North American Interparliamentary Group would provide legislative input.[111]

Assessing the Big Idea

It is improbable that a grand bargain could be achieved or that it would be in Canada's interest. As the Conference Board of Canada observes, the sheer size and complexity of the Canada–US relationship 'would make one sweeping "grand bargain" extremely difficult to negotiate'. Moreover, big negotiations 'often do not favour the weaker party'.[112] For example, Richard Falkenrath, a former US Homeland Security official and member of the Independent Task Force on the Future of North America, has argued that because the United States has a greater interest in security than economic collaboration, it should press Canada to cooperate 'across an even broader range of national and homeland security issues' than the Task Force recommended, 'including nuclear and ballistic missile threats', as a condition for closer trade ties.[113] Even so, it is far from certain what steps Ottawa could take that would cause Washington to forego its own security measures. As Kathleen Macmillan points out, 'The big worry about big ideas is that we will end up capitulating in areas where we pay a price in terms of our policy sovereignty only to find out that, down the road, the US remains unsatisfied.'[114] In practice, negotiations would have to be disaggregated into more manageable elements, and the deals struck would reflect the relative bargaining strengths of the two countries. As well, it is highly unlikely that Ottawa and Washington would be willing to hand over control of politically sensitive issues to International Joint Commission-like institutions. The two sides have used the IJC to make recommendations and decisions on technical issues, but they have not been prepared to extend this to political matters.[115]

In addition, as Prime Minister Mulroney discovered when he attempted to revive the partnership paradigm in the 1980s, while American presidents continue to play an indispensable role in the management of the relationship, they no longer have the necessary leverage *vis-à-vis* Congress to implement the trade-offs that are central to the approach. Matters such as trade remedy laws that were not resolved in the Canada–US and North American free trade agreements when circumstances were relatively favourable would be even harder to settle in today's difficult trade environment. Moreover, 'on specific issues', Bill Merkin, a former US trade negotiator, observes, 'if it makes domestic political sense any administration is usually willing to temporarily set aside its free-trade principles.'[116] The Bush administration's response to the NAFTA Extraordinary Challenge Committee's ruling on softwood lumber shows that Washington is willing to do so even at the expense of its international obligations. A chastened Allan Gotlieb warned that the action 'risks the stability of the legal framework supporting the world's largest trading relationship'. He called on Ottawa to resort to high-level diplomatic means to try to resolve the dispute.[117]

Nor is there any evidence that US special interests and their legislative allies would be more willing to compromise on such matters if the agenda were broadened to include border security and transit. For example, border state legislators, who have been Canada's traditional allies on transboundary issues, are now among the most vocal supporters of strong US security measures. As Barrie McKenna stated: 'It's hard to imagine what would make any of these people embrace a plan to virtually do away with the border.'[118] At the same time, Canada's capacity to respond to US priorities is constrained by the government's minority status, the administration's failure to respond to Canadian trade concerns, and public opposition to Bush's policies. Jeffrey Simpson notes that '[i]t's hard for a government to expend political capital at home to work closely with an administration abroad that the public does not like.'[119]

As well, unlike Reagan, Bush appears to have little interest in big ideas for the Canada–US relationship. In any case, it would be politically difficult for the United States to deepen ties with Canada without involving Mexico. The Bush administration needs a good relationship with the Fox government to advance its own goals, including energy security, and to shore up support among Hispanic American voters. However, differing issues and levels of engagement among the three countries will likely preclude elaborate, formal arrangements in the near future. What we are more likely to see are limited forms of collaboration, together with overlapping bilateral initiatives that could lay the groundwork for further cooperation among the three countries.

The success of the Smart Border initiative supports the Conference Board's view that '[a]n incremental approach, working out the individual bilateral issues in the context of clear strategic objectives, will give Canada the best opportunity to renew the relationship between the two countries.'[120] By identifying aims Washington and Ottawa shared, and shaping the agenda in a way that incorporated US interests, Ben Rowswell observes, John Manley persuaded Tom Ridge 'to agree that a secure border not only blocks out terrorists but keeps the North American economy ticking by facilitating the lifeblood of cross-border travelers and trade. Canada may have a greater relative interest in "economic security" and the US in "public security" but in the final analysis both countries share both goals.'[121] The follow-up bilateral New Partnership in North America and trilateral Security and Prosperity Partnership of North America agreements have deepened and widened the cooperative arrangements the Smart Border accord set in motion.

Incrementalism will not resolve all Canada–US issues, but it does allow Canada and the United States (and Mexico) to pursue shared goals in ways that create confidence in the each other's actions while giving both sides the flexibility to pursue individual policies as their interests dictate. Canada can also exercise its right to challenge arbitrary US actions in international venues, as it has done in NAFTA and the WTO on softwood lumber. Moreover, incrementalism is an approach on which both Ottawa and Washington can agree.

Notes

1. This chapter is an expanded version of the paper 'Managing Canada–US Relations in the Post-9/11 Era: Do We Need a Big Idea?', originally published in CSIS *Policy Papers on the Americas*, XIV, Study 11 (November 2003) © 2003 by the Center for Strategic and International Studies, Washington, DC. All rights reserved. I would like to thank Chris Sands for his comments on an earlier draft.

2. Office of the Prime Minister, 'Joint Statement by Canada and the United States on Common Security, Common Prosperity: A New Partnership in North America', 30 November 2004. Available at http://www.pm.gc.ca/eng/news.asp?id=341.

3. Wendy Dobson, 'Shaping the Future of the North American Economic Space: A Framework for Action', *C.D. Howe Institute Commentary* 162 (April 2002).

4. 'Managing Canada–U.S. Relations in the Post-9/11 Era'; Allan Gotlieb, 'A North American Community of Law', *Ideas That Matter* 2, 4 (2003): 25–30.

5. Thomas d'Aquino, 'Security and Prosperity: The Dynamics of a New Canada–United States Partnership in North America', Presentation to the annual general meeting of the Canadian Council of Chief Executives, 14 January 2003. Available at http://www.ceocouncil.ca (hereafter Security and Prosperity Presentation).

6. Richard N. Haass, 'Foreword', in *Building a North American Community: Report of the Independent Task Force on the Future of North America*. The task force

was chaired by Pedro Aspe, former Secretary of the Treasury of Mexico in the Salinas government; John Manley, former Foreign Minister, Minister of Finance and Deputy Minister of Canada in the Chrétien government; and William Weld, former Governor of Massachusetts. It was sponsored by the Council on Foreign Relations in association with the Canadian Council of Chief Executives and the Consejo Mexicano de Asuntos Internacionales, May 2005, vii. Available at http://www.cfr.org/publication.html?id=8102.

7. To be sure, explicit linkages across issue areas were rare, with President Lyndon Johnson's support for the Autopact Agreement in 1965, reportedly in return for the Pearson government's role in establishing a UN peace-keeping force in Cyprus being one of the few examples cited. Rather, the trade-offs generally took the form of contextual linkages wherein each side attempted to accommodate the other's priorities when it was in a position to do so in the interest of maintaining the partnership. See Robert Bothwell, *Canada and the United States: The Politics of Partnership* (Toronto: University of Toronto Press, 1992), 93, and Charles F. Doran, *Forgotten Partnership: US–Canada Relations Today* (Baltimore: The Johns Hopkins University Press, 1984), 20–25, 36–41.

8. Kal J. Holsti and Thomas Allen Levy, 'Bilateral Institutions and Transgovernmental Relations Between Canada and the United States', in Annette

Baker Fox and Joseph S. Nye, eds, *Canada and the United States: Transnational and Transgovernmental Relations* (New York: Columbia University Press, 1971), 291.

9. US Department of State, *Principles for Partnership: Canada and the United States* (Washington, DC: US Department of State, August 1965).

10. Donald Barry, 'The Politics of "Exceptionalism": Canada and the United States as a Distinctive International Relationship', *Dalhousie Review* 60, 1 (Spring 1980): 125–6.

11. Quoted in Roger F. Swanson, ed., *Canadian–American Summit Diplomacy, 1923–1973: Selected Speeches and Documents* (Toronto: McClelland and Stewart, 1975), 298.

12. Hon. Mitchell Sharp, 'Canada–U.S. Relations: Options for the Future', *International Perspectives* (Autumn 1972).

13. Barry, 'The Politics of "Exceptionalism"', 130.

14. Quoted in Canadian Press, 'Canada envoy chides U.S. insensitivity', *Calgary Herald*, 3 October 1980.

15. See Joseph T. Jockel, 'The Canada–United States Relationship After the Third Round: The Emergence of Semi-Institutionalized Management', *International Journal* 40, 4 (Autumn 1985): 689–715.

16. Confidential source. See also L. Ian MacDonald, *Mulroney: The Making of the Prime Minister* (Toronto: McClelland and Stewart, 1984), 304–6.

17. See Donald Barry, 'The Road to NAFTA', in *Toward a North American Community? Canada, the United States, and Mexico*, ed. Donald Barry (Boulder, CO: Westview Press, 1995), 3–14.

18. G. Bruce Doern and Brian W. Tomlin, *Faith and Fear: The Free Trade Story* (Toronto: Stoddart, 1991), 35–9.

19. Jeffrey Simpson, 'When it comes to trade, the Americans just never give in or give up', *Globe and Mail*, 16 February 1996; confidential source.

20. Quoted in Edward Greenspon, 'PM pledges new style of rule', *Globe and Mail*, 5 November 1993.

21. John Kirton, 'Promoting Plurilateral Partnership: Managing United States–Canadian Relations in the Post-Cold War Period', *American Review of Canadian Studies* 24, 4 (Winter 1994): 464.

22. Confidential source.

23. Robert Fife and Giles Gherson, 'Cabinet to intensify lobbying of Congress', *National Post*, 30 June 1999.

24. George Haynal, 'Interdependence, Globalization and North American Borders', *Policy Options* 23, 6 (September 2002): 21.

25. Christopher Sands, 'Fading Power or Rising Power: 11 September and Lessons from the Section 110 Experience', in *Canada Among Nations 2002: A Fading Power*, eds, Norman Hillmer and Maureen Appel Molot (Don Mills, ON: Oxford University Press, 2002), 49–73.

26. Drew Fagan, 'Canada: stand on guard', *Globe and Mail*, 4 December 2001.

27. April Lindgren, 'Fox seeks close ties with Canada', *Calgary Herald*, 5 July 2000.

28. Quoted in Heather Scoffield, 'Chrétien Rejects Mexico's Vision', *Globe and Mail*, 23 August 2000.

29. The White House, Office of the Press Secretary, 'Joint Statement by President George Bush and President Vicente Fox Towards a Partnership for Prosperity', 16 February 2001. Available at http://www.whitehouse.gov/news/releases/2001/02 (accessed 18 November 2003).

30. Steven Chase, 'New pact on energy not needed, Ottawa says', *Globe and Mail*, 6 August 2001.

31. Mike Trickey, 'U.S. ambassador favours closer links with Canada', *Calgary Herald*, 30 June 2001; Alan Toulin and James Baxter, 'Border divides Liberal ranks', *National Post*, 3 August 2001.

32. Quoted in Shawn McCarthy and Campbell Clark, 'Canada will make its own laws, PM vows', *Globe and Mail*, 20 September 2001.

33. Quoted in John Ibbitson and Campbell Clark, 'Canada and U.S. tighten borders', *Globe and Mail*, 26 September 2001.

34. Daniel LeBlanc, 'Canada praised for tip to U.S. on Ressam', *Globe and Mail*, 4 December 2001.

35. Quoted in Murray Campbell and Lily Nguyen, 'Security perimeter backed', *Globe and Mail*, 15 September 2001.

36. Nancy Hughes Anthony, 'Resolving U.S. border-fears vital for Canadian business', *Calgary Herald*, 15 October 2001; Heather Scoffield, 'Business coalition pushes for common border rules', *Globe*

and Mail, 3 December 2001.

37. Confidential source.

38. Quoted in Paul Wells, 'We don't pull our weight: Manley', *National Post*, 5 October 2001.

39. Quoted in Steven Frank and Stephen Handelman, 'Drawing a Line', *Time* (Canadian edition), 8 October 2001, 45.

40. Quoted in Shawn McCarthy, 'Manley doubts perimeter idea', *Globe and Mail*, 5 October 2001.

41. House of Commons Standing Committee on Foreign Affairs and International Trade, *Partners in North America: Advancing Canada's Relations with the United States and Mexico* (Ottawa: House of Commons, December 2002), 167–8.

42. Government of Canada, 'Canada and the United States Sign Smart Border Declaration', *News Release*, 162, 12 December 2001.

43. House of Commons Standing Committee on Foreign Affairs, *Partners in North America*, 168.

44. The White House, 'U.S.–Mexico Border Partnership Agreement', 22 March 2002. Available at http://www.whitehouse.gov/infocus/usmxborder/22points.html (accessed 18 November 2003).

45. Department of Foreign Affairs and International Trade, 'Canada's Actions Against Terrorism Since September 11th—Backgrounder', 10 October 2002. Available at http://www.dfait-maeci.gc.ca/can-am/main/menu-en.asp (accessed 9 January 2003); Daniel LeBlanc, 'Canada takes Afghan mission', *Globe and Mail*, 13 February 2003.

46. Lisa M. Seghetti, 'Border Security: U.S.–Canada Border Issues', Congressional Research Service Report for Congress, 8 July 2002. Available at http://www.usembassycanada.gov/content/can_usa/border_crs_070802.pdf (accessed 18 November 2003).

47. Perhaps the most notable example was the introduction of the US National Security Entry–Exit Registration System (NSEERS), which required citizens of Canada and other countries or dual nationals born in Iran, Iraq, Libya, Sudan, and Syria to be photographed, fingerprinted, and interviewed when entering the United States. The zealous application of the law by US immigration inspectors drew charges of racial profiling and prompted Ottawa to issue a travel advisory to affected Canadians. Washington subsequently modified the policy so that place of birth would no longer automatically trigger a special interrogation. Elizabeth Thompson, 'Racial profiling by U.S. denounced', *Calgary Herald*, 31 October 2002; Mike Trickey, 'U.S. backs down on security plan', *Calgary Herald*, 1 November 2002.

48. Campbell Clark, Estanislao Oziewicz, and Tu Thanh Ha, 'Canada–U.S. agree to "safe third country" refugee pact', *Globe and Mail*, 29 June 2002.

49. Quoted in Angelo Persichilli, 'Cellucci says Canada–U.S. relationship "a role model for the world"', *Hill Times*, 7 October 2002.

50. Department of Foreign Affairs and International Trade, 'Governor Ridge and Deputy Prime Minister Manley Issue One-Year Status Report on the Smart Border Action Plan', 6 December 2002. http://www.dfait-maeci.gc.ca/can-am/menu-en.asp (accessed 17 December 2002).

51. US Department of Defense, 'Unified Command Plan Responsible for the U.S., Canada, and Mexico and Parts of the Caribbean', *News Release* 188-02, 17 April 2002; Department of National Defence, 'Enhanced Canada–U.S. Security Cooperation', *News Release* BG-02.041, 9 December 2002.

52. Daniel LeBlanc, 'Canada open to missile-shield discussions', *Globe and Mail*, 10 December 2002; Daniel LeBlanc, 'Canada gets short shrift at NORAD', *Globe and Mail*, 31 May 2003.

53. Sheldon Alberts, 'Canada needs to fix image in U.S.: Liberals', *National Post*, 9 January 2003.

54. For a discussion of Canadian and US policies toward the war see my 'Chrétien, Bush, and the War in Iraq', *The American Review of Canadian Studies*, 35, 2 (Summer 2005): 215–45.

55. Quoted in Eric Reguly, 'Iraq stance will burn Canada', *Globe and Mail*, 20 March 2003.

56. A. Paul Cellucci, 'Speech by U.S. ambassador to Canada to the Economic Club of Toronto', Toronto, 25 March 2003.

57. Quoted in Gloria Galloway, 'U.S. envoy scolds Canada', *Globe and Mail*, 26 March 2003.

58. Canadian Press, 'Envoy links Bush snub to war policy', *Toronto Star*, 17 April 2003.

59. Quoted in Sinclair Stewart, 'Rift over Iraq expected to heal', *Globe and Mail*, 7 April 2003.

60. Shawn McCarthy, 'U.S. plans border exemption for Canada', *Globe and Mail*, 17 April 2003; Shawn McCarthy, 'Forgive, forget; it's good for business', *Globe and Mail*, 18 April 2003.

61. Robert Fife, 'Chrétien says he's better than Bush', *National Post*, 28 May 2003; Robert Fife, 'Chrétien sticks to his guns at shot at U.S. economy', *Calgary Herald*, 29 May 2005.

62. Quoted in Peter Morton, 'It will take some time to mend this fence', *National Post*, 31 May 2003.

63. Aileen McCabe and Robert Fife, 'Ottawa opens up to missile talks', *Calgary Herald*, 30 May 2003. (David Frum, Christopher Sands, and others have argued that the Chrétien government's grudging cooperation with the Bush administration has not earned it any credit with Bush. See, for example, David Frum, 'Why Mulroney gets Bush's red carpet', *National Post*, 14 December 2002.)

64. Daniel LeBlanc, 'Canada gets short shrift at NORAD', *Globe and Mail*, 30 May 2003.

65. Daniel LeBlanc, 'Missile Defence gets boost in House', *Globe and Mail*, 3 June 2003.

66. Shawn McCarthy, 'Canadians vote Bush least liked president', *Globe and Mail*, 12 July 2003; Wallace Immen, 'Canadian public skeptical of war in Iraq, poll shows', *Globe and Mail*, 19 July 2003.

67. Bruce Cheadle, 'Grits' criticism of GOP hurting Martin, MP says', *Globe and Mail*, 7 September 2004; Stephen Handelman, 'Agenda for Canada', *Time* (Canadian edition), 17 November 2003, 31.

68. Drew Fagan, 'On the balance beam', *Globe and Mail*, 7 January 2004.

69. Jeff Sallot and Paul Koring, 'Martin wades into spat over U.S. contracts', *Globe and Mail*, 11 December 2003; Jeff Sallot, 'Martin reminds Washington to respect Canadians' rights', *Globe and Mail*, 26 November 2003; DeNeen L. Brown and Dana Priest, 'Chrétien Protests Deportation of Canadian', *Washington Post*, 6 November 2003.

70. Drew Fagan, 'Canada, U.S. seal Arar deal', *Globe and Mail*, 13 January 2004.

71. Susan Delacourt, 'Vibes were very, very good', *Toronto Star*, 14 January 2004.

72. Canada, Department of National Defence/CF, 'Letters Exchanged on Missile Defence', 15 January 2004. Available at http://www.forces.gc.ca/site/Fucus/Canada-US/letter_e.asp; Jeff Sallot, 'Motion defeated to break off missile talks with U.S.', *Globe and Mail*, 25 February 2004.

73. Jeff Sallot, 'Motion deferated to break off missile talks with U.S.', *Globe and Mail*, 25 February 2004.

74. Daniel LeBlanc, 'Martin Forgives Iraqi debt', *Globe and Mail*, 24 January 2004; Mike Blanchfield, 'Canada to keep troops in Kabul', *Calgary Herald*, 31 January 2004.

75. See Graham Fraser, 'Plan would give U.S. a say in our energy', *Toronto Star*, 9 January 2003; Drew Fagan, 'Is it time for a summit?' *Globe and Mail*, 14 January 2003; Steven Chase and Greg Keenan, 'Canada, U.S. consider one steel market', *Globe and Mail*, 1 February 2003; Drew Fagan, 'PM looks at closer relations with U.S.', *Globe and Mail*, 24 February 2004.

76. Drew Fagan, 'Brison maps out proposals for closer U.S. ties', *Globe and Mail*, 1 April 2004.

77. Jeff Sallot, 'Ottawa unveils security plan to beef up defences', *Globe and Mail*, 28 April 2004.

78. Susan Delacourt, 'Bush, Martin promise closer ties', *Toronto Star*, 1 May 2004; Sheldon Alberts, 'Historic meeting strikes a balance', *Calgary Herald*, 1 May 2004.

79. Canadian Press, 'Martin tells U.S. ambassador decision on missile defence pending', 11 July 2004.

80. Drew Fagan, 'Canada opens door for missile shield', *Globe and Mail*, 6 August 2004.

81. Mike Blanchfield, 'We "will regret" snubbing missile plan', *canada.com News*, 23 September 2004.

82. John Ward, 'Shield hot topic in Canada', *Chronicle-Herald*, 4 October 2004.

83. Patrick Brethour, 'Tycoons join PM to paint the town red', *Globe and Mail*, 8 July 2004; confidential source.

84. Brian Laghi, 'Martin decries MP's "unacceptable" antics', *Globe and Mail*, 19 November 2004; Tim Harper and Susan Delacourt, 'Bush to thank Halifax', *Toronto Star*, 25 November 2004; Alan Freeman, 'U.S. sets about mending fences', *Globe and Mail*, 27 November 2004.

85. Jeff Sallot, 'Missile defence not a "deal-breaker", Cellucci says', *Globe and Mail*, 4 November 2004; Brian Laghi, 'Bush does not expect Canada to rubber-stamp missile plan', *Globe and Mail*, 9 November 2004; Peter Baker, 'Bush Doctrine Expected to Get Chilly Reception', *Washington Post*, 23 January 2005; Graham Fraser, 'Bush starts plan to end beef ban', *Toronto Star*, 21 November 2004.

86. Tim Harper and Susan Delacourt, 'Missile pitch stuns Martin', *Toronto Star*, 1 December 2004.

87. The White House, Office of the Press Secretary, 'Remarks by President George W. Bush and Prime Minister Paul Martin in a Joint Press Availability', 30 November 2004; Office of the Prime Minister, 'Joint statement by Canada and the United States on common security, common prosperity: A new partnership in North America', 30 November 2004.

88. Bruce Campion-Smith, 'Leaders pledge secure border, better traffic flow', *Toronto Star*, 1 December 2004. (In October Martin and President Vincente Fox had launched a more limited 'Canada–Mexico Partnership' described as 'a high-level public–private forum' to 'strengthen bilateral economic and policy cooperation and promote private and public sector dialogue at senior levels'. It would function as 'a mechanism for identifying policy areas in which [the two countries] can facilitate cooperation and enhance opportunities for economic development and investment'. Canada, Office of the Prime Minister, 'Joint Statement by Canada and Mexico: A commitment to our common future', 26 October 2004. Available at http://www.pm.gc.ca/eng/news.asp?id=296.

89. The White House, Office of the Press Secretary, 'President Discusses Strong Relationship with Canada', 1 December 2004. Available at http://www.whitehouse.gov/news/releases/2004/12/print/20041201-4.html; Office of the Prime Minister, 'Address by Prime Minister Paul Martin at Pier 21', 1 December 2004. Available at http://www.pm.gc.ca/eng/news.asp?id=345; Richard Foot, 'Join missile shield, Bush urges', *Calgary Herald*, 2 December 2004.

90. Graham Fraser and Tonda MacCharles, 'PM wants missile deal in writing', *Toronto Star*, 15 December 2004; Robert Fife and Anne Dawson, 'Martin rules out funds for U.S. missile defence shield', *Calgary Herald*, 15 December 2004; Robert Russo, 'PM will back missile plan, Cellucci says', *Globe and Mail*, 10 January 2005.

91. Steven Chase, 'Sanctions may be the only way to sway Congress: Cellucci', *Globe and Mail*, 23 December 2004.

92. Gina Teel and Jim Gransbery, 'U.S. court blocks cattle', *Calgary Herald*, 3 March 2005; Dawn Walton and Barrie McKenna, 'U.S. Senate backs border ban on Canadian beef', *Globe and Mail*, 4 March 2005; Dave Ebner, 'U.S. ruling raises hope for end to cattle ban', *Globe and Mail*, 15 July 2005.

93. Steven Chase, 'U.S. brushes off Canada's NAFTA softwood victory', *Globe and Mail*, 11 August 2005.

94. Sean Gordon and Bruce Campion-Smith, 'It's no to missile plan', *Toronto Star*, 25 February 2005; Brian Laghi and Jane Taber, 'It was not an easy decision to make', *Globe and Mail*, 25 February 2005; Susan Delacourt, 'Bush phone call surprises Martin', *Toronto Star*, 6 March 2005; confidential source.

95. Alexander Panetta, 'PM gets thumbs-up on missile defence', *Chronicle-Herald*, 23 March 2005.

96. Alan Freeman, 'NAFTA partners mull summit', *Globe and Mail*, 19 January 2005.

97. Tim Harper, 'Fortress America' sparks new fears', *Toronto Star*, 15 March 2005. See also Chairman's Statement, Independent Task Force on the Future of North America, 'Creating a North American Community', n.d.

98. Canada, Office of the Prime Minister, 'Prime Minister to attend meeting of North American leaders', *News Release*, 21 March 2005. Available at http://www.pm.gc.ca/eng/news.asp?id=441.

99. Office of the Prime Minister, 'Security and Prosperity Partnership of North America Established', 23 March 2005. Available at http://www.pm.gc.ca/eng/news.asp?id=443.

100. John Ivison, 'Relationship nowhere near consummation', *National Post*, 24 March 2005.

101. Linda Jewell, Deputy Assistant Secretary of State, 'The Current State and Future Prospects for U.S. Studies in Canada: Towards a National Strategy

Perspectives on the United States—The View of the U.S. Government', Remarks to the US Studies Conference, Montréal, 6 May 2005. Available at http://www.usembassycanada.gov.

102. *Security and Prosperity Partnership of North America*, Report to Leaders, June 2005. Available at http://www.fac-aec.gc.ca/spp/spp-menu-en.asp.

103. Canadian Council of Chief Executives, 'The North American Security and Prosperity Initiative: Background, Questions and Answers', March 2003, 8. Available at http://www.ceocoun cil.ca/English/ Publications/reports/apr3-03.pdf (accessed 18 November 2003).

104. Wendy Dobson, 'Trade can Brush in a new border', *Globe and Mail*, 21 January 2003.

105. Allan Gotlieb, 'A grand bargain with the U.S.', *National Post*, 5 March 2003.

106. William B.P. Robson, 'The North American Imperative: A Public-Good Framework for Canada–U.S. Economic and Security Cooperation', *C.D. Howe Institute Commentary*, 204 (October 2004), 25.

107. Canadian Council of Chief Executives, 'Security and Prosperity: Toward a New Canada–United States Partnership in North America', January 2003, 1–2. Available at http://www.ceocouncil.ca /English/Publications/reports/jan-2003.pdf.

108. Dobson, 'Shaping the Future of the North American Economic Space', 29.

109. Gotlieb, 'A North American Community of Law', 30.

110. 'New Frontiers: Building a 21st Century Canada–United States Partnership in North America', A Discussion Paper of the Canadian Council of Chief Executives, April 2004, 26. Available at http://www.ceocouncil.ca/en/view/?docu ment_id=312&area_id=1; Thomas d'Aquino, 'Security and Prosperity'; Thomas d'Aquino 'Beyond Free Trade—A Canada—United States

Partnership for Security and Prosperity', Notes for remarks in Dallas, Tucson, Phoenix, Cleve-lend, and Buffalo, 24 February–3 March 2005. Available at http://www.ceocouncil.ca/ en/view/? area_id=1&document_id=393.

111. *Building a North American Community, Report of the Independent Task Force on the Future of North America.* Available at http://www.cfr.org.

112. David MacDuff, *Course Correction: Advice on Canada's Future Foreign Policy* (Ottawa: The Conference Board of Canada, 2003), 6.

113. Richard A. Falkenrath in *Building a North American Community*, 37.

114. Proceedings of the Standing Senate Committee on Foreign Affairs, Issue 2: Evidence, 3 February 2003. Available at http://www.parl.gc.ca/37/2/ parlbus/commbus/senate/com-e/FORE-E/02eva-e.htm?Language=E&Parl=37&Ses=2&comm _id=8 (accessed 20 November, 2003).

115. Doran, *Forgotten Partnership*, 12–13.

116. Barrie McKenna, 'Looming U.S. vote poses trade dilemma for Canada', *Globe and Mail*, 10 May 2004.

117. Allan Gotlieb, 'The dos and don'ts of softwood lumber', *National Post*, 20 August 2005.

118. Barrie McKenna, 'Canadian CEOs' border vision unlikely to fly in nervous U.S.', *Globe and Mail*, 17 January 2003.

119. Jeffrey Simpson, 'There is little for Canadians to admire', *Globe and Mail*, 1 December 2004.

120. Charles A. Barrett and Hugh Williams, 'Renewing the Relationship: Canada and the United States in the 21st Century', *Briefing*, February 2003, 3.

121. Ben Rowswell, 'McLellan's U.S. Challenge', *Toronto Star*, 18 December 2003.

8

Canada at the United Nations in the New Millennium

Elizabeth Riddell-Dixon

We have entered a new century and a new millennium with a new US President, whose unilateral impulses appear stronger than his commitment to the United Nations. In contrast, Canada views the UN as a vital tool for promoting an equitable international community based on international law; hence the UN continues to be the most important multilateral institution for Canada. It is, therefore, not surprising that Canada's macro-level priority relating to the UN is to ensure that the organization functions effectively, with the US as a co-operative participant. Canada shows great leadership within the UN in launching initiatives, developing policies, and generating ideas. It has frequently been less effective in establishing priorities among these initiatives, policies, and ideas and in committing the resources necessary to implement them.

In the past 17 months, two developments have preoccupied the UN agenda; the desire to counter terrorism in the aftermath of 11 September and, more recently, the need to 'manage' the US in the wake of its unilateral threats to wage war against Iraq in retaliation for the latter's non-compliance with UN resolutions to disarm. The world did not change on 11 September 2001 when the terrorists attacked the US. It did, however, bring home to the people and governments in the US and Canada what is a daily reality for many around the world. The events of 11 September profoundly affected perceptions of vulnerability, especially among northern countries, with the result that counterterrorism measures became the Security Council's number-one preoccupation and continued to be so until President Bush issued his threat of unilateral action against Iraq. At that point, the chief focus became trying to persuade the US to abandon its unilateral stance and to work co-operatively through the Security Council.

Although Canada has worked from the sidelines to promote the development and implementation of counterterrorism provisions and to persuade the US to work through the Security Council, it has not been a principal player in either case. The task of addressing these two very high-profile issues has been the responsibility of the Security Council—a body of which Canada is not currently a member. The issues are, nonetheless, of great importance to Canada. Furthermore, the preoccupation with them has made it more difficult for Canada to pursue some of its own priorities, including promoting the International Criminal Court and the Canadian-sponsored 2001 report, *The Responsibility to Protect.*

The chapter will begin with a brief examination of the two dominant issues on the Security Council agenda before examining Canada's success in realizing its priorities in the areas of peace operations (including reforms to the Security Council), human security (especially the responsibility to protect and international impunity), human rights, and sustainable development. All come under the rubric of peace and security, broadly interpreted to include not only security for states but, more importantly, security for civilians—not just from the dangers of physical violence but also from the untold suffering that results from dire poverty, environmental degradation, and poor health. Some observations about Canadian leadership at the UN are also offered.

The United States and Iraq

In his speech to the General Assembly on 12 September 2002, US President George Bush issued his definitive threat to go to war against Iraq if the latter failed to comply with UN resolutions to disarm. The US decision to confront Iraq directly, instead of referring the matter to the Security Council—the international body authorized under international law to deal with international peace and security—threatened the credibility of the Security Council. Most members of the UN, including Canada, are skeptical of the American motives in making the threat. No evidence has been presented linking the Iraqi government to the terrorist attacks on the US. There are also questions to be asked about timing: why did President Bush decide to take action in September 2002? Iraq's non-compliance with UN resolutions is not new—it was all too apparent in the late summer and early autumn of 1990 when Iraq refused to withdraw from Kuwait—and the ongoing problem of Iraq's violations of UN resolutions is well-known. It has been suggested that the threat of war is motivated by electoral concerns: President Bush would rather campaign for re-election as a war President than as a recession President.

The first positive breakthrough came when the Bush administration backed down from proceeding with unilateral action and returned to the negotiating table, a move prompted by both international and domestic factors. International opinion clearly favoured a multilateral solution and the vast majority of UN members opposed a unilateral attack on Iraq. Within the US, public opinion polls showed that most citizens were opposed to going to war alone (CBS *News World*, 2002a, 2002b).

The negotiations among the permanent members of the Security Council took place at the highest political levels. In particular, France and the UK and, to a lesser extent, Russia deserve a great deal of credit for negotiating a solution acceptable to all permanent members of the Security Council. Credit is also due to the negotiating skill of Colin Powell, US Secretary of State. On 8 November 2002, the Security Council unanimously[1] approved Resolution 1441, which requires Iraq to disarm or face serious consequences. The resolution called for UN arms inspectors to be sent back into Iraq to determine if Iraq is complying with UN resolutions. The inspectors are authorized to make such determinations and they will report to the Security Council. What will happen after the inspectors submit their reports remains to be seen. The US claims that it can act against Iraq under Security Council Resolution 678, adopted on 29 November 1990 and authorizing member states to 'use all necessary means' to expel Iraq from Kuwait. The resolution provided the international sanctioning for Operation Desert Storm. Canada and most of the UN membership say that a new Security Council resolution would be necessary to authorize a fresh attack—Iraq, after all, has had no presence in Kuwait since the Gulf War.

Canada is concerned about how little thought has been given to the aftermath of a war. The war, itself, would likely be short-lived. Iraq was much more powerful in 1991 and even then the war was over in a few months. Iraq lost most of its armed forces in 1991 and it has been under sanctions for the past 12 years. In addition, its finances, at least to some extent, have been controlled by the UN. As a result, Iraq has been weakened and defeating it would not be the most difficult task; the much tougher challenge would be trying to rebuild the country after a war. Who would replace Saddam Hussein? How could democracy he implemented? How could the differences between Shiite and Sunni Muslims be reconciled? How would the position of the Kurds be addressed? Would there be a Kurdish uprising that would trigger a civil war in Turkey?

The crisis over Iraq raises many vital issues: the credibility and viability of the UN, the American commitment to work within the UN, the threat of war, and the overwhelming prospects of peace-building in the aftermath of a war, Canada, along with most members of the UN, would prefer to ensure that the inspectors are able to fulfill their mandates and that the UN takes measures necessary to ensure compliance. War against Iraq is not a preferred option, most particularly because of the dire consequences that would follow. Yet in this debate, Canada can only support from the sidelines because it is not privy to the major negotiations taking place in the Security Council. Likewise, and for the same reasons, Canada has not been a key player in the counterterrorism campaign-the other major preoccupation of the Security Council.

Counterterrorism

The UN reacted quickly to the 11 September terrorist attacks and undertook a range of activities to counter terrorism. Twelve counterterrorism treaties have been developed under the auspices of the UN—two within the last year. Prior to 11 September, only the UK and Botswana had ratified all the treaties. Now 24 countries, including Canada, have ratified all 12. On 28 September 2001, the Security Council passed its landmark resolution 1373, which forbids countries from harbouring terrorists, from providing a safe haven for their funds, or from permitting the raising of funds for terrorist activities within their borders.

Furthermore, states are obliged to ensure that anyone planning, financing, or participating in terrorist activities is brought to justice. On the same day the Security Council also established a Counter-Terrorism Committee, as recommended in Resolution 1373. The Committee is the most important international body for determining the needs of countries in fulfilling their treaty obligations and their responsibilities under Resolution 1373. The Committee monitors compliance, holds countries accountable, and provides support and advice when changes are required. A major impediment to the implementation of the resolution is the lack of domestic infrastructure in many countries to allow them to fulfill their obligations, such as monitoring capital flows. Thus, Canada and the UN have been concerned with capacity-building.

Canada has been clear in asserting that terrorism is a problem requiring global solutions and, hence, that the UN is the pre-eminent organization to address the issue. For Canada, the response to terrorism must be global, both in the sense that all countries must participate in finding solutions and in the sense that efforts to combat terrorism must encompass a broad range of areas—not just border and airport security but also the conditions that foster terrorist sentiments. Canada's objectives are, therefore, to have the international community, working through the UN, committed to addressing both the direct threats of terrorism and the conditions propitious to its development.[2] In order to have a global response to terrorism it is necessary to develop common assessments of the threats, as well as common values and interest in addressing the problem in all its dimensions.

In addition to having ratified all 12 counterterrorism treaties, Canada is one of the countries most in compliance with Resolution 1373. Canada's Philippe Kirsch chaired the working group that drafted the most recent of the 12 counterterrorism treaties: the International Convention for the Suppression of the Financing of Terrorism and the International Convention for the Suppression of Terrorist Bombings. Two fur-ther treaties are contemplated: a treaty on nuclear terrorism and a comprehensive convention on terrorism. Canada has devoted considerable effort to making them a reality, but in both cases the negotiations are stalemated. Debates over the nuclear terrorism treaty tend to pit the nuclear powers, which are in favour of prosecuting others but want exemptions for their own troops, against members of the non-aligned movement, which fear the treaty would prejudice the debate on the legality of nuclear weapons and undermine the advisory opinion provided by the International Court of Justice in 1996 declaring nuclear disarmament to be required under international law. Negotiations of a comprehensive convention on terrorism have floundered over definitions of 'terrorist', which reflects the old controversy over who is a terrorist and who is a freedom fighter. It was possible to get agreement on the 12 existing conventions because they criminalize certain types of activities without defining a terrorist. Through the Human Security Program, Canada has assisted countries in developing the legisla-tion necessary to fulfill their obligations under the 12 counterterrorism treaties.

In addition to supporting UN efforts to combat terrorism, Canada has been active in adopting counterterrorism measures unilaterally and in co-operation with the US. In October 2001, Canada passed two new bills. The Anti-Terrorism Act con-tains measures to 'identify, prosecute, convict and punish terrorists; provide new investigative tools to Canadian law enforcement and national secu-rity agencies; and ensure that Canadian values of respect and fairness are preserved through stronger laws against hate crimes and propaganda' (DFAIT, 2002a: 3). The Public Safety Act is designed to 'increase the government's capacity to prevent terrorist attacks, protect Canadians, and respond swiftly should a significant threat arise' (Ibid.). An Ad Hoc Cabinet Committee on Public Security and Anti-Terrorism was established to strengthen Canada's capacity to combat terrorism and ensure public security. The Committee is

chaired by Deputy Prime Minister John Manley. In December 2001 the Canadian government approved a budget of $7.7 billion to be spent over five years 'to enhance security for Canadians and make Canada's borders more secure, open and efficient' (DFAIT, 2002b: 3). The same month, Canada and the US signed the Smart Border Declaration and the Action Plan, which outlined provisions for sharing information and co-ordinating activities to combat terrorism while keeping the border open to legitimate trade. There is no doubt that combating terrorism has been a major priority for the Canadian government since 11 September, as evidenced by the direct involve-ment of the most senior levels of government and the extensive resources allocated to the campaign.

The threat of terrorism has not only preoccu-pied the Security Council for most of the past 17 months but has also had a profound effect on how the UN and its member states conduct busi-ness. The UN no longer receives mail directly. Instead the mail is rerouted to a clearinghouse in Florida to be checked for the anthrax virus before being delivered to the UN. Canada is by no means alone in facing this threat and, like others, has changed some of its standard business proced-ures. For example, far greater use is now made of e-mails and faxes to minimize the amount of mail received at the Canadian mission.

Although counterterrorism and the crisis resulting from Iraq's failure to prove that it has dis-armed are receiving most of the media attention, the UN is far more than the current preoccupations of the Security Council. The media focus on debates at the UN headquarters in New York and generally ignore the work being done in other parts of the system, which is at least as important and which has become all the more salient in the post-Cold War era. One cannot talk about social peace and social justice without referring to the International Labour Organization. The World Health Organization is central to the fight against HIV/AIDS and other pandemic diseases. Discussions of social and political turmoil must involve the High Commissioner for Refugees and the High

Commissioner for Human Rights. The International Telecommunication Union is central to addressing issues of high technology. The UN is a multi-institutional tool with the capacity to address problems in a functional way. A narrow focus on New York, to the exclusion of UN bodies based elsewhere, fails to present a comprehensive or accurate picture. Even in New York, the Security Council's current preoccupations are only part of the story. They have, for example, in no way dampened Secretary-General Kofi Annan's commitment to implementing the Millennium Development Goals. Canada's chief ongoing priorities at the UN are closely related to several areas outlined in these goals. In particular, they pertain to peace operations, human security, human rights, and sustainable development.

Peace Operations

The 2000 *Report of the Panel on Peace Operations* (the Brahimi Report—named after the panel's chair, Lakhdar Brahimi) was welcomed by most analysts as a realistic, doable plan for improving peace operations in several interrelated areas of activity: conflict prevention (early warning and peace-building capacity), peace-keeping (realistic mandates, adequate resources to fulfill mandates, more secure funding, enhanced quality and quantity of training for all participants, and the rapid deployment of experts as well as troops), peace-making, and the reform of UN bodies involved with peace operations, particularly the Department of Peacekeeping Operations and the Department of Political Affairs. The Brahimi Report reflected many Canadian objectives, including providing troop-contributing countries with a larger voice in the Security Council's decision-making process, enhancing the UN's rapid reaction capability (e.g., equipment, experts, logistical improvements), and strengthening the civil police component in peace operations.

Since the Security Council is the executive body responsible for international peace and security, its effectiveness is closely linked to the efficacy of peace operations. Two of Canada's three top priorities during its 1999–2000 term on the Security Council related to the latter's reform: making it more effective and credible, and making it more transparent and accountable (DFAIT, 2001: 3–4). Of particular concern to Canada was the regular failure to hold meaningful consultations with troop-contributing countries.

Democracy requires that elected national governments are responsible for decisions made about how and when their troops are deployed. The Security Council has traditionally operated in a very autocratic way and has frequently made decisions—including the decision to change the mandate of a mission—without consulting the troop-contributing countries. For example, the Security Council expanded the mandate of the Sierra Leone mission after troops were already in the field, requiring them to control the country-side. The troops of the contributing countries, India and Jordan, did not have the capability to control the countryside so each country recalled its troops. This completely undesirable situation strengthened the arguments being made by Canada and other troop-contributing countries for the Security Council to hold more regular and more co-operative meetings with them. On 13 June 2001, the Security Council unanimously adopted Resolution 1353, in which it undertook to keep troop-contributing countries fully informed of the mandates for missions and to hold meetings with them:

> in particular, when the Secretary-General has identified potential troop-contributing countries for a new or ongoing peace-keeping operation, when considering a change in, or renewal or completion of a peace-keeping mandate, or when there is a rapid deterioration in the situation on the ground, including when it threatens the safety ad security of United Nations peacekeepers. (UN Security Council, 2001: 6)

The meetings, which can be held either publicly or privately, may be called at the request of the contributing states. Significant progress has been made: the Security Council is now meeting more regularly and more co-operatively with the troop-contributing countries. There is, however, still room for improvement as the substance of the consultations is rarely well reflected in policy outcomes.[3]

Although Security Council decision-making is by no means transparent, the Council is holding more meetings to which the broader UN membership is invited. For example, it held open meetings on women and security in October 2002, on human security in December 2002, and on children and armed conflict in January 2003. The Security Council is also introducing greater transparency into its operations. Resolution 1441 was circulated in advance to the broader UN membership before being adopted by the Security Council. This move was a complete departure from traditional practice.

The Brahimi Report also recommended the development of rapid deployment capability—an objective long advocated by Canada. In 1996 seven states responded to a Danish initiative to establish a brigade-size, rapid deployment force, known as the Stand-by High Readiness Brigade (SHIRBRIG).[4] It was established in close co-operation with the UN Secretariat and both bodies continue to work closely. The SHIRBRIG aims to deploy 1,000 to 5,000 troops quickly (i.e., in 14 to 30 days) after the Security Council has authorized a peace operation under Chapter Six of the Charter. The SHIRBRIG is designed to be a stop-gap measure to secure a conflict area in the period between the Security Council authorizing a peace operation and the arrival of the larger UN mission. Participation in the SHIRBRIG is entirely voluntary and member states decide whether to deploy on a case-by-case basis. The missions are sent for a maximum of six months.

The SHIRBRIG was not used during the first four years of its existence. To be fair, it took time to marshal a force of sufficient size and caliber, to undertake the necessary pre-deployment planning and training, to develop common operating procedures, and to ensure that members were contributing equipment that was mutually compatible. The slow start, however, was not good for credibility. The SHIRBRIG was first deployed in the autumn of 2000, after the Security Council had decided to establish a mission for Ethiopia and Eritrea, under Chapter Six of the Charter. The deployment of Dutch, Canadian, and Danish personnel took some 90 days—well beyond the 30-day target specified in the Brahimi Report. It took only three days for the Canadian cabinet to authorize the deployment of Canadian troops but it took significantly longer for the Dutch parliament to approve the deployment of its troops. Once the approvals were secured there were greater delays—the Canadian troops spent 25 days travelling by sea because Canada had no airlift capability. The SHIRBRIG's first six-month mission to Ethiopia and Eritrea was considered a success and it was redeployed in May 2001.

Canada would like to see the SHIRBRIG improved in two respects. First, its membership needs to be more geographically representative. At present there are no southern members. Two southern states have observer status: Senegal, which never attends the SHIRBRIG meetings, and Jordan, which comes regularly and reports back to the Group of 77. There is increasing support among the SHIRBRIG members to abolish the observer category and to force the current observers either to join or to stop attending the meetings. Canada and Sweden strongly opposed such a move on the grounds that it is important to have greater southern involvement. It is also much better to have Jordan reporting back to the Group of 77 so the latter knows what is happening from one of its own members rather than hearing reports from northern states, whose accounts might be regarded with suspicion. The Steering Committee—the SHIRBRIG's executive organ—has compiled a list of countries to approach about becoming members.[5]

Second, Canada would like to see the SHIRBRIG mandate expanded so that it can be used not only in peace-keeping operations carried out under

Chapter Six of the UN Charter operations, but also enforcement missions under Chapter Seven, such as Sierra Leone and the Congo. There is, however, great opposition to expanding the SHIRBRIG mandate. The Netherlands has threatened to pull out of the SHIRBRIG if the latter's mandate is expanded to include Chapter Seven missions. At a meeting a year ago in Copenhagen, the Steering Committee agreed on a compromise: the SHIRBRIG would remain a Chapter Six instrument but its deployment to Chapter Seven missions could be considered on a case-by-case basis. Although Canada has not changed its position on expanding the mandate to include Chapter Seven missions, it realizes that it would be futile to push further on this issue at this time. Instead, it is concentrating on trying to enhance the versatility of the SHIRBRIG and to promote strategies to enhance the capacity of peacekeepers.

In February 2002, Canada organized a 'lessons learned' exercise in New York, which drew over 100 participants from all the major peace-keeping countries, the UN Secretariat, and the General Assembly's Special Committee on Peacekeeping Operations. Its report concluded that deployment to Ethiopia and Eritrea had been fairly rapid and effective, although securing national approval for troop deployments needed to be expedited and procedures for transferring authority from the SHIRBRIG to the incoming UN force needed to be improved. The report, nonetheless, provided a ringing endorsement of rapid deployment. In January 2003 Canada began a one-year term as president of the SHIRBRIG; hence it is now well positioned to seek progress on its key objectives, including enhancing the SHIRBRIG's capacity and expanding its membership.

The main weakness of the Brahimi Report was the failure to include an implementation plan. Consequently, there was the very legitimate fear that its recommendations would be shelved. The Special Committee on Peacekeeping Operations was, in fact, ready to shelve the report on the grounds that more study was necessary and the Secretariat had to be convinced of the need to table an implementation plan. As vice-chair of the Special Committee, Canada's Michel Duval effectively negotiated behind the scenes to lay the groundwork for the eventual adoption of the Brahimi recommendations for enhancing UN peace-keeping capacity.[6] The latter were controversial, especially since they required new resources, including the creation of over 200 additional staff positions. The Group of 77 quickly saw the predominantly northern desire to enhance the effectiveness of peace operations as an opportunity to bargain for additional resources for economic development and made its acceptance of the Brahimi recommendations conditional on receiving corresponding increases in the resources allocated to economic development. To court southern allies, Canada lobbied hard among major southern troop-contributors—states with vested interests in ensuring that peace operations received adequate resources. The Special Committee on Peacekeeping Operations moved from its initial insistence that the report needed more study—a position that would, at best, have seriously delayed implementation and, at worst, have resulted in the report being shelved—to working for its implementation. Canada got agreement that the recommendations would be adopted as a package and not negotiated individually. In March 2002, the Special Committee adopted most of the Brahimi Report's recommendations for enhancing UN peace-keeping capacity. Their acceptance was made possible by the combined backing of member states, the Secretariat, and the Secretary-General. To secure this level of support required effective diplomacy and hard work by Canada and its like-minded allies.

All but one of the new staff positions recommended to enhance peace-keeping capacity have been adopted. The Group of 77 remains resistant to creating the position of a gender adviser on peace-keeping.[7] Some of its members say the position is unnecessary because the UN already has a Special Adviser for Gender Issues and the Advancement of Women. Others reject the concept of gender and still others resist because the position is seen to reflect northern—rather than southern—priorities. Canada remains firmly committed to the creation of the position for practical as well as symbolic reasons. Its existence would highlight the importance of gender analysis to sound policy. Nonetheless, Canada chose not to push this issue when the other provisions were to be adopted for fear of reopening debate on all the Brahimi recommendations. Having the Brahimi recommendations for improving peacekeeping accepted is a significant victory. Canada and its like-minded allies are now working to ensure that these recommendations are reflected in the mandate of each new peace mission.

Human Security

Promoting human security was one of Canada's three principal goals when it served on the Security Council in 1999–2000. Canada defines human security as 'a people-centred approach to foreign policy which recognizes that lasting stability cannot be achieved until people are protected from violent threats to their rights, safety or lives' (DFAIT, 2002d: 1). Human security became a central pillar of Canadian foreign policy under Lloyd Axworthy and it has continued to be so. In June 2000, the Department of Foreign Affairs and International Trade established the Human Security Program, which funds projects around the world that 'strengthen the ability of the global community to respond to threats to Human Security and support peaceful governance' (DFAIT, 2002c: 1).

Canada brought the concept of human security to the Security Council in spite of the skepticism expressed by many countries about putting the protection of civilians on the agenda. Canada, along with its like-minded allies, continues to promote human security whenever it gets the opportunity, particularly in the General Assembly, the Human Rights Commission, and the Executive Committee of the Office of the High Commissioner for Refugees. Of the five pillars that comprised Canada's platform on human

security when it sat on the Security Council, highest priority is now given to the protection of civilians and good governance, which includes addressing international impunity.[8]

ADDRESSING INTERNATIONAL IMPUNITY

No one accused of genocide or crimes against humanity should be exempt from prosecution. Three sets of international institutions are designed to deal with international impunity: the International Criminal Court, the International War Crimes Tribunals for the Former Yugoslavia and Rwanda, and the special courts being established to deal with war crimes in Sierra Leone and Cambodia.

The International Criminal Court (ICC) is the first permanent international court dedicated to trying cases of genocide, war crimes, and crimes against humanity. The ICC has two main objectives: to punish those who have committed genocide, war crimes, and crimes against humanity; and to deter further perpetrators of such crimes. The Court is intrinsically important to international law and justice. Its very existence reflects a shift from a laissez-faire attitude to impunity to an increased demand for accountability.

Although it became an independent institution on 1 July 2002, when the Rome Statute of the International Criminal Court entered into force, the Court was developed under the auspices of the UN. The ICC's Preparatory Commission was a UN body, chaired by Canada's Philippe Kirsch. Canada, along with the EU, played a pivotal role in creating the ICC. Canada established a group of likeminded states at the start of the Rome Conference, which it continues to chair. Membership in the group has grown from some 20 states to over 60 states, including members of the European Union, Australia, New Zealand, Norway, Argentina, South Africa, and Lesotho. Canada and other members of the group remain strongly committed to making the Court an effective tool of international justice and to getting as many states as possible to ratify the enabling statute. The pro-ratification campaign has met with considerable success and 87 states have ratified. Canada has organized numerous conferences and workshops to educate countries so they will have the legislation in place necessary to fulfill their obligations under the statute. At home, the Canadian government has adopted the legislation necessary to make the Canadian legal system compatible with the fulfillment of its commitments under the ICC. In his speech to the Assembly of States Parties in September 2002, Canadian Foreign Minister Bill Graham committed Canada to spending $1.5 million over the next year on projects promoting ratification and implementation of the ICC statute (DFAIT, 2002e: 4). Most of these funds will be drawn from the Human Security Program.

At its first session, held 3–9 September 2002, the Assembly of States Parties adopted instruments developed by the Preparatory Commission that are necessary to the functioning of the Court. Judges and prosecutors were elected in February 2003. Once elected, the judges chose from among their numbers Philippe Kirsch of Canada as the president of the ICC. Canada had nominated Kirsch as a candidate for the bench with the hope that he might also be elected as the ICC president.

The success in creating the ICC has been undermined by President Bush's formal rejection of it. The US actively opposes the ICC on the grounds that American soldiers and government officials could be subjected to politically motivated accusations and trials. In response, Canada and other like-minded states have pointed out that the ICC is designed to complement—not replace—national courts. An individual accused of war crimes, crimes against humanity, or genocide can only be brought before the ICC if the courts of his/her own country are unable or unwilling to try the case. As a result, the ICC would only have jurisdiction to prosecute US officials and members of its armed forces if US courts failed to try them.

Initially, the US sought complete exemptions for all US citizens—a position that ran contrary to Canada's belief that no one should be above the law. When most states were unwilling to accede

to its demand for exemption, the US took the draconian measure on 30 June 2002 of vetoing the renewal of the mandate for the UN peace operations in Bosnia. Canada's Permanent Representative to the UN, Paul Heinbecker, wrote to the British chair of the Security Council, asking for an open meeting at which the Security Council could hear the views of the broader UN membership on this issue. When nothing came of the request, Heinbecker sent a second letter, which he circulated throughout the UN. These efforts generated enough pressure from the broader membership and from sympathetic members of the Security Council to prompt the Council to hold a meeting in July, at which delegates from some 50 countries criticized the US stance. The US has since backed away from seeking an automatic exemption. Instead, it seeks to limit its exposure by referring to Security Council Resolution 1422 (July 2002), which, in turn, refers to Article 16 of the ICC statute. Article 16 allows for the deferral of investigations pertaining to UN peace-keeping missions. It was intended to be used in complex peace negotiations where, in order to get key officials to attend the talks, it was necessary to guarantee that they would not be prosecuted during the peace process. The US has interpreted this provision as a blanket deferral—an interpretation that goes against the spirit and the letter or the law. Under Resolution 1422, the deferral has to be renewed each year; hence the issue will be revisited in July 2005. The outcome, as Heinbecker noted, was 'a two-thirds victory for the US and a one-third victory for Canada'.

The US seeks to negotiate bilateral agreements with all members of the UN. Although fewer than 15 mostly small states have entered into such agreements with the US, the American efforts in this regard may have a chilling effect on ratification. Some countries that appeared to be moving towards ratification are now backing away, although the overall number of ratifications keeps increasing. Canada is continuing to promote the ICC and to encourage ratification. Within the UN, support for the ICC appears to be growing, as it is often mentioned in UN resolutions and in Kofi Annan's speeches.

In contrast to the ICC, the International War Crimes Tribunals for Rwanda and the Former Yugoslavia are not permanent and their mandates are geographically limited. Both are functioning with little need for outside involvement. The Security Council is, however, still active in two regards. First, its support is essential because it alone has the authority to pressure governments to ensure that individuals accused of war crimes and crimes against humanity are prosecuted. Second, Security Council involvement is necessary to develop exit strategies. The tribunals are expensive[9] but establishing timetables for completing their work is problematic. A backlog of cases, for example, waits to be tried by the International War Crimes Tribunal for Rwanda. The situation with Yugoslavia is complicated because some of the key accused—including Radovan Karadzic and Ratko Mladic—have yet to be apprehended. In addition, there is an ongoing, low-intensity conflict in Macedonia that may produce additional cases for the tribunal.

Unlike the tribunals established for Yugoslavia and Rwanda, the special courts for Sierra Leone and Cambodia are not being created by the Security Council. The Security Council held informal negotiations to get processes moving and passed resolutions highlighting the importance of establishing them, but it did not pass a resolution setting up the court for Sierra Leone nor will it do so for a Cambodian court. Neither is yet functioning but the court for Sierra Leone is close to being operational. It was set up under a bilateral agreement between the UN Secretariat and the government of Sierra Leone, with support from funding countries. Canada has provided significant support. In addition to furnishing $2 million, it established a Management Committee—an informal mechanism to secure funding and to provide guidance on the court's functioning, budget, and the hiring of its officials. Fifteen states have now volunteered to serve on the Management Committee, which is chaired by Canada.

Establishing a court for Cambodia has been much more problematic. The Cambodian people want closure and the court would be an important part of that process. In contrast, the government has not been co-operative, largely because its leader was formerly in the Khmer Rouge and he does not appear keen to have the court proceed. In this case, it is necessary to find balance between what is achievable, given the past Khmer Rouge associations of many government officials, and what is compatible with the criteria of international justice. The process has been further complicated by the unhelpful positions of China and Vietnam, which appear to value their trade with Cambodia more than international law and justice. They seem unwilling to risk alienating Cambodia by supporting UN efforts to establish the court.

Australia took the lead in proposing a resolution to set up the court but Cambodia refused to co-sponsor it, thereby indicating an unwillingness to co-operate. Without Cambodia's co-sponsorship, the resolution could not succeed and had to be abandoned. Cambodia might be willing to co-sponsor a resolution if the mandate of the court is severely restricted, but this would seriously undermine the court's efficacy. Consequently, plans for the Court are on hold, much to the chagrin of Canada, Australia, the Netherlands, and, to some extent, the US. A UN resolution was recently passed requesting the Secretary-General to restart the talks but the outcome of these efforts is uncertain at this point. If a special court were to be set up for Cambodia, it is expected that Canada would contribute money and officials, as it has done in Sierra Leone.

In addition to the current frustrations in dealing with Cambodia, Canada is concerned that UN credibility not be harmed by the functioning of the special courts. The UN's reputation would be damaged if the trials were seen to be shams, which is unlikely to happen in Sierra Leone but is a distinct possibility with Cambodia, especially since Cambodia wants each trial chamber to be dominated by Cambodian judges. The UN would also come under criticism if the courts ran out of money before completing their mandates. Blaming the UN for its members' lack of political will is a long-standing, although unfair, practice. The UN Secretariat did ask for three years of guaranteed funding for the special court for Sierra Leone but countries were unwilling to make this length of commitment.

RESPONSIBILITY TO PROTECT

In December 2001 the Canadian-sponsored Commission on Intervention and State Sovereignty submitted its report, *The Responsibility to Protect*, to Secretary-General Kofi Annan, who had it circulated as an official UN document. The report begins with two basic principles (ICISS, 2001: xi). First, the sovereign state bears primary responsibility for protecting its people. Second, in cases where a state is either unwilling or unable to protect its people from serious harm, the international responsibility to protect takes precedence over a deference to the principle of non-interference. Military intervention is seen as justified in cases where there is either large-scale loss of life or large-scale ethnic cleansing. The Security Council is designated as the appropriate body to authorize military intervention in such cases. The report refocuses attention away from debates over the degree to which sovereignty should remain sacrosanct to the duty to protect people when their state is unwilling or unable to do so.

Translating the recommendations of the report into action is recognized to be a longer-term project and Canada has yet to decide on the degree to which specific norms need to he adopted. Canada does, however, want the report to receive careful consideration and expects follow-up action by the Security Council, so that in future it is better prepared to act and the horrors of the Rwandan genocide are not repeated.

Canada is pursuing a two-track strategy to ensure that the report is not ignored: promoting it within UN circles, both in New York and Geneva; and building support for it in civil society. Although it is early in the process, there are some reasons for optimism. In May 2002 the Security Council held a retreat, during which a session was held on *The Responsibility to Protect*. Kofi Annan is a strong supporter of the report and he regularly incorporates its language into his speeches. Canada's Permanent Representative to the UN, Paul Heinbecker, has held consultations on a technical resolution to ensure that the report is given further consideration by the member states and that the Secretariat facilitates this consideration. From the consultations, it is evident that even such a modest resolution would face resistance from some southern countries, which argue that the issues raised in the report require further discussion. As a result, Canada has decided to organize events in New York to facilitate further discussions before officially tabling a resolution on *The Responsibility to Protect*.

In addition to promoting the report within UN circles, Canada recognizes that the longer-term implementation of the report will require cultivating the support of civil society. Canada is encouraging the establishment of NCO networks similar to those that existed for the landmines campaign. Canada's efforts in this regard have received some financial support from large US foundations, including the MacArthur Foundation. On 4–6 November 2002 the Canadian government held a conference for Parliamentarians for Global Action, at which some 100 parliamentarians discussed *The Responsibility to Protect* as well as the International Criminal Court. Other conferences and events to promote the report are scheduled to be held in all regions of the world.

The timing of the report affected its reception both positively and negatively. The report deals with prevention, intervention, and rebuilding—all of which are relevant to today's crises. Afghanistan exemplifies what can happen when a situation is ignored. Conditions deteriorated and religious extremists took control, thus creating a situation ripe for the development of Osama bin Laden's al-Qaeda operations. Afghanistan also exemplifies the need to rebuild and to create the conditions for a lasting peace in the future. Having the report released as the campaign in Afghanistan was being waged heightened its relevance.

In some ways, however, timing has not been propitious. The current preoccupation with the Iraq situation is making it harder for Canada to promote *The Responsibility to Protect* because some states fail to distinguish between the situations addressed in the report, in which a state is unable or unwilling to protect its people, and the current situation, in which a functioning state is defying UN resolutions requiring it to disarm. The Iraqi government has committed grave human rights violations against its own citizens, but this is not the primary motivation for President Bush's threat of war. Canada is devoting time and energy to explaining the distinction between the Iraq crisis and the conditions being addressed in *The Responsibility to Protect*, when it would prefer to be expounding on the merits of the report's recommendations. The utility of the report depends on the implementation of its recommendations. The international community has yet to respond to the gross violations of human rights, including the loss of life, that are taking place today in Zimbabwe and the Ivory Coast, where the governments are clearly unwilling or unable to protect their peoples from serious harm. Intervention into such dangerous situations would be costly. Failure to act indicates that the report's recommendations are not being taken seriously.

Human Rights

Canada is a world leader in promoting the development of international human rights norms. It has proposed more resolutions than any other state at the Commission on Human Rights and has been very active in promoting the establishment and implementation of norms on a broad range of issues, including women's rights (especially the elimination of violence against women and reproductive rights), children's rights (especially education and protection in armed conflict), freedom of expression, impunity, indigenous peoples, and gender mainstreaming. The events of 11 Sep-

tember make human rights more important than ever, as the link between the deprivation of human rights and terrorism is recognized. Yet the past 17 months have been extremely difficult and challenging for those concerned with human rights. Highly contentious political debates over the Middle East preoccupied participants at the World Conference Against Racism and at the annual meetings of the UN Commission on Human Rights.

Preparations for the Conference Against Racism, which was held in Durban from 31 August to 7 September 2001, had been long and arduous. At the conference, the US and Israel walked out because their efforts to have anti-Israeli language deleted from the text were being thwarted. Canada was the first country to speak after the Declaration and Programme of Action were adopted, expressing agreement with most of their provisions but dissociating itself from the passages on the Middle East—a stance that left it fairly isolated. The discomfort of the Canadian delegation was exacerbated when its speech was booed by NGOs. The latter were unwilling to see criticisms of Israel's treatment of Palestinians derail support for the many important issues on which critical progress had been made, such as protecting migrants and refugees from discrimination and intolerance, declaring slavery a crime against humanity, and promoting gender equality (Human Rights Watch, 2001: 1). Thus Canada—a country that prides itself on promoting human rights and that enjoys relatively good relations with NGOs—was unable to endorse fully an important human rights document, much to the consternation of many southern countries and most NGO participants. The outcome at Durban is all the more lamentable because issues of racism, including racial profiling, are all the more important after 11 September.

Just as the Durban conference was diverted from its central purpose by geopolitical discussions on the Middle East, debates about the Middle East permeated all debates at the March 2002 session of the Commission on Human Rights. About half of the time available at the session was spent on the Middle East situation, which, as Marie Gervais-Vidricaire of the Global Affairs Bureau at DFAIT has noted, left little time for the numerous remaining items on the agenda.

In addition to the preoccupation with the Middle East, two other developments have caused Canada concern. The African states have become much more unified in collectively opposing discussion of their members' human rights records, especially if such discussion could be construed as criticism. As a result, it is extremely difficult to address grave human rights abuses taking place in countries such as Zimbabwe and Sudan. The chair of the Commission on Human Rights rotates among the regions and it is now Africa's turn to preside. The African states nominated Libya—a country with an abysmal human rights record[10]—and it was elected in January 2003. So the prospects for the March 2003 session of the Commission on Human Rights are not rosy. Conflict in the Middle East has been intensifying, not diminishing, thus much of the debate is likely once again to focus on the politics of that region and, to make matters worse, Libya will be in the chair.

A further challenge has been to prevent backsliding, especially in the area of women's reproductive rights. Canada was particularly disturbed by the tough stand taken by the US at the UN Special Session on Children in May 2002. At the Johannesburg World Summit on Sustainable Development, Canada once again had to struggle to prevent the Vatican and the US from rolling back progress achieved at previous conferences and summits.

In an otherwise rather gloomy picture, there were, nonetheless, a few important bright spots. Human rights comprise one of the six categories of objectives outlined in the Millennium Development Goals. In 2000, the UN Security Council unanimously passed a resolution on women, peace, and security that recognized 'the urgent need to mainstream a gender perspective into peace-keeping operations'.[11] The mandates of the International Criminal Court and the International War Crimes Tribunals for Rwanda and the Former Yugoslavia all explicitly require that sexual crimes against women be considered when deciding on the jurisdiction and when judging cases. The Optional Protocol to the Convention on the Rights of the Child on the Involvement of Children in Armed Conflict, which came into force in February 2002, was seen as a major breakthrough in the campaign to protect children affected by armed conflict. It seeks to limit their involvement and raises the minimum age for recruitment to 18. Canada continues to pressure for ratification and has contributed funds from the Human Security Program to promote this objective. Also in 2002, the Economic and Social Council established the Permanent Forum on Indigenous Issues to address indigenous concerns pertaining to economic and social development, education, health, human rights, culture, and the environment. Its 16 members include eight indigenous-nominated experts and eight government-nominated experts. Canada's indigenous groups welcomed the new body, and a Canadian, Wayne Lord, has been elected as one of the government-nominated experts.

Within UN circles there is growing disillusionment with holding further mega-conferences on human rights. The meetings themselves are costly and the follow-up is weak. A breadth of substantial norms now exists; hence, the focus needs to be on implementation, not on further norm development. Canada strongly endorses this focus.

Sustainable Development

Sustainable development is defined as 'development that meets the needs of the present without compromising the ability of future generations to meet their own needs' (World Commission on Environment and Development, 1987: 43). Intrinsically important in its own right, sustainable development is also closely linked to the other issue areas discussed in this chapter. Economic rights comprise a set of human rights as exemplified by the Convention on Economic, Social and Cultural Rights, one of six principal treaties in the human rights regime. The link between terrorism and economic privation was made apparent in President Bush's National Security Strategy,[12] as well as in Prime Minister Chrétien's speech of 16 September 2002 to the General Assembly (PMO, 2002: 2). The relationship between peace and development is well established:

> It doesn't get more basic than this: without peace, there can be no lasting development. It is no coincidence that half of the 47 countries with the lowest human development index have experienced serious conflict in the past decade, and that 15 out of 20 of the least-developed countries have been involved in violent conflict. (Brown, 2000: 1)

The linkage between peace and development is also clearly depicted in the Brahimi Report, *The Responsibility to Protect*, and the Carnegie Commission's 1997 report, *Preventing Deadly Conflict*.

The World Summit on Sustainable Development (WSSD) was held in Johannesburg, South Africa, 26 August–4 September 2002. Its objectives were to provide further strategies and mechanisms for implementing the recommendations of the 1992 World Conference on the Environment and Development, to identify fresh challenges and the means of addressing them, and to stimulate greater global commitment to sustainable development. Although the WSSD was the largest-ever single gathering of heads of state and government, US President Bush refused to attend. Colin Powell represented the US and, while it would have been more encouraging to have had presidential participation, Bush's absence did not have any significant impact on the Summit's success.

Canada went into the Summit with five priorities: to promote better health and environmental safeguards and to recognize the interrelationship between them; to develop, and to ensure the implementation of, innovative strategies for pro-

moting sustainable development and partnerships, especially those involving the private sector; to produce sustainable communities, particularly in cities where population growth is greatest and where infrastructures are frequently inadequate to match this growth; to promote stewardship and conservation, especially of the natural resource sectors but also of parks and the Arctic; and to improve international environmental governance.

The Summit established targets for increasing access to clean water and adequate sanitation; increasing access to energy for those currently without; improving health; enhancing agricultural productivity; and better safeguarding biodiversity and better managing the world's ecosystems. Some of these issues (e.g., health and agriculture) were already being addressed within the UN system but needed a higher profile, and the linkages between them needed to be made more explicit. Other issues, in particular water and energy, had received little attention. No UN bodies are devoted to safeguarding water or to ensuring that all peoples have access to sustainable sources of energy. In dealing with all five issues and addressing the linkages between them, the Summit made significant contributions. It also made important headway in developing and expanding mechanisms to ensure partnerships to promote sustainable development among northern and southern countries, the private sector, and NGOs. Prior to the Summit, over 220 such partnerships, with a total of US $235 million in resources, had been identified and an additional 60 were announced in the course of the Summit (WSSD, 2002: 1).

The success of the WSSD was due in large measure to being able to incorporate provisions negotiated in other forums into its Declaration on Sustainable Development and Plan of Implementation. The Millennium Development Goals had been developed by the UN Secretariat without being widely negotiated by member states. They set targets to be achieved by 2015, which include halving extreme poverty and hunger;

ensuring that all girls and boys receive primary education; promoting gender equality and empowering women; reducing child mortality by two-thirds; decreasing maternal mortality by three-quarters; combating HIV/AIDS and other pandemic diseases; promoting sustainable development (in particular, access to clean water and significantly improving the lives of slum dwellers); and developing partnerships for development, involving northern and southern states, the private sector, and NGOs. Although the goals had been championed by Secretary-General Kofi Annan, they had not been heartily endorsed, let alone implemented, by member states. At the WSSD, the Millennium Development Goals were refined, given higher profile and greater credibility, and endorsed by member states and the NGO community.

The balance struck between northern and southern interests at the March 2002 Monterrey Conference on Financing for Development was adopted at the WSSD. Southern countries agreed to create the conditions necessary for development within their respective countries, including commitments to democracy, good governance, and human rights. In turn, northern states promised to increase foreign aid, assist with debt relief, encourage southern trade, and promote investment in the South.

The chapter on Africa in the Johannesburg Plan of Implementation drew heavily on the New Partnership for Africa's Development. At the G8 Summit in June 2002, Canada, with support from the UK and France, was successful in making African development a major focus. The Summit adopted the G8 Africa Action Plan, which served as a further impetus for the WSSD chapter on Africa.

The Doha ministerial meetings of the World Trade Organization are much more focused on development issues than any previous trade round has been. They are discussing such critical issues as agricultural subsidies, which frequently prevent southern sales to major northern markets, and southern access to patent medicines.

While the details of such agreements remain to be worked out, the need to make progress on these development issues was recognized at the Doha meetings and subsequently at the WSSD.

At the WSSD, the importance of the Kyoto Protocol to the United Nations Framework Convention on Climate Change was affirmed and Prime Minister Chrétien committed Canada to ratifying it. The Summit also benefited from documents produced by the OECD and the UN's five regional economic commissions, as well as its own preparatory meetings.

The WSSD realized many Canadian objectives. Its documents contain strong language linking the environment and human health. The impact of the former on the latter had never been as clearly defined before. Canada led the campaign to get commitments to address the social, political, and environmental problems associated with mining, which comprises the principal export sector for many southern countries. Canada also led the efforts to get recognition of the need for further work on chemicals and the environment. After a tough struggle, Canada, with support from Norway, Australia, Switzerland, and the EU, managed to prevent fundamentalist Islamic states, led by Egypt, as well as the US and Argentina, from rolling back progress made on reproductive rights at previous negotiations.

As president of the UN Environment Program since 2001, Canada's Minister of the Environment, David Anderson, is credited with getting the campaign to improve international environmental governance launched. At the WSSD, some countries within the Group of 77, including Venezuela, India, and Indonesia were eager to roll back the provisions for good governance that had been adopted at Monterrey. Again, a reneging on previous agreements was prevented. Furthermore provisions were included for improving the financing of the UN Environment Program and for improving its linkages with other UN bodies working on environmental issues.

Although most of Canada's priorities were reflected in the Summit documents, there were a few disappointments. The treatment of globalization is not as substantial as it might have been and Canada would have preferred stronger language on good governance. For example, it would have liked even more concrete recommendations to enable the UN Environment Program to co-ordinate its work more effectively with other UN bodies. Overall, the WSSD was a success, both in terms of UN and Canadian objectives.

Leadership

The issue of Canadian leadership arises in many chapters in this book. Leadership can be defined in many ways, ranging from entrepreneurial leadership (forming like-minded coalitions, engineering agreements, and facilitating the negotiation of compromise solutions), to intellectual leadership (offering fresh ideas, new perspectives, and creative ways of conceptualizing problems), to providing resources to translate the ideas into concrete, effective programs (Young, 1991: 281). Canada is well known for its entrepreneurial leadership. As noted in this chapter's discussion of peace operations, human security, human rights, and sustainable development, Canada has an excellent record of forming coalitions with like-minded slates. It is not, however, always very willing to share the credit for new ideas and initiatives with its like-minded allies. Ministers' names often become associated with a new idea, which makes it harder for Canada to share the limelight. At times, it needs to be more sensitive to the frustration that other countries may feel when their contributions are not fully recognized publicly.

Canada has been, and it continues to be, one of the world's foremost intellectual leaders at the UN. Recent examples include the campaign to create the International Criminal Court and Canadian sponsorship of the International Commission on Intervention and State Sovereignty. Canada has also been a leader in promoting gender equity and the rights of children. Overall, Canada's intellectual leadership is highly commendable. However, a cautionary note is in order. Canada proposes a great many ideas but at times quantity seems to prevail over quality and the need for more clearly defined priorities is evident. Canada's initial human security agenda was incredibly broad, comprising five pillars: the protection of civilians, peace support operations, conflict prevention, governance and accountability, and public safety. It would be hard to think of many issues that would not come under at least one of the pillars. They could include eliminating landmines, promoting economic development, organizing anti-malaria campaigns, ensuring adequate food distribution, countering terrorism, limiting the use of child soldiers, and even installing traffic lights to curtail accidents. Examples of excellent human security priorities for Canada include assisting a broad range of countries to develop the domestic legislation and the structures necessary to facilitate good governance, to combat international terrorism, and to comply with the statute of the ICC. For the international community to function well, it is essential that each member state have a well-functioning system of governance based on international law.

In many cases, Canada's intellectual leadership has not been matched at the implementation stage. Speeches by Canadian officials to the UN laud Canada's contributions to peace-keeping, yet concerns are increasingly being raised as to whether the rhetoric continues to be supported by action. Canada now ranks thirtieth in terms of contributing peace-keeping troops to UN operations, while many of the top 20 contributors are southern states. Canada refused to send troops to Sierra Leone, largely for fear of casualties and the political consequences that would follow. This fear has been heightened after four Canadians were killed by 'friendly fire' in Afghanistan. Canada's failure to deploy to some of the world's most serious crises, most of which are in Africa, raises questions about its commitment to non-European conflicts.

Canada can, and does, justifiably claim to offer intellectual leadership, which is based on its long and distinguished history of participation in UN peace-keeping missions. Its past record and its experience are internationally recognized. Canada also contributes experts and significant funding to peace-building. Does Canada need to continue to contribute peace-keeping troops to be seen as a peace-keeping country? Will a failure to send troops hurt Canada's reputation abroad and its credibility in peace-keeping decision-making at the UN? Are intellectual and entrepreneurial leadership and the contribution of non-military resources sufficient?

Patterns of strong intellectual leadership not being matched at the implementation stages are evident in other areas of endeavour. Canada asserts the need to implement the Millennium Development Goals, while the percentage of its gross national income devoted to international development assistance remains far below the international target of 0.7 per cent. Giving only 0.22 per cent of gross national income, Canada ranks nineteenth out of 22 OECD donor countries. At the Monterrey conference Prime Minister Chrétien promised to double Canadian overseas development assistance by the end of the decade. Time will tell if this commitment is realized. Canada has ratified the Kyoto Protocol but it has the third highest per capita emissions of greenhouse gases of northern countries. As Denis Stairs has pointed out, there are indeed cases where Canada's rhetoric exceeds its performance (Stairs 1999, 339).

Conclusion

Although we have entered a new millennium and the specifics of the issues preoccupying the UN are somewhat different from those taking precedence at the end of the twentieth century, developments at the UN, and Canada's foreign policies, are better characterized as part of an ongoing historic progress than as something brand new. US unilateralist impulses and Canada's desire to keep the US participating multilaterally are themes that have been present since the creation of the UN in 1945. Canada's chief preoccupation during the Korean War was maintaining the integrity of the

UN. As such, it sought both to discourage the LJS from proceeding unilaterally and to keep the UN from becoming a tool of US foreign policy (Keating, 2002: 34). Today there is the struggle to have the US address Iraqi non-compliance through the Security Council. US unilateralism is very much in evidence in the US refusal to ratify the ICC statute, the Kyoto Protocol, and the Convention on the Prohibition of the Use, Stockpiling, Production, and Transfer of Anti-Personnel Mines, and on Their Destruction.

Yet, in spite of the gloom cast by the threat of terrorism, the threat of an impending war with Iraq, and the potential long-term consequences of such a war, the picture is not all bleak. In 2001 Kofi Annan and the UN won the Nobel Peace Prize in recognition of their contributions to world peace and the promotion of human rights and their efforts to combat new challenges, such as HIV/AIDS and international terrorism. Annan has worked to streamline the UN, to clarify and improve its priorities, and to better allocate resources to coincide with priorities. Significant progress has been made on many other fronts, especially in the development of norms and procedures to increase the efficacy of peace operations and to ensure that those who have committed crimes against humanity do not escape punishment. The responsibility to protect represents a major conceptual shift from a preoccupation with preserving state sovereignty to a focus on protecting people. The finances of the UN have improved largely because the US has paid a significant amount—although not all—of its arrears. In his 12 September speech to the UN, President Bush committed the US to participating in UNESCO after an absence of 19 years. US support for the UN has ebbed and flowed over the decades and there is every reason to expect the pattern to continue. Coping with the American Colossus involves persuading it to work as a co-operative participant within the system rather than having it gravitate to the extremes of either acting unilaterally or seeking to reduce the UN to being a tool of its foreign policy, both of which threaten the UN's credibility and viability.

Notes

Much of the research for this chapter was drawn from interviews with federal public servants. In particular, I would like to thank Richard Ballhorn, Director General, Environment and Sustainable Development Affairs Bureau, DFAIT; Susan Brown, Chief, Peace-building Unit, CIDA; Terry Cormier, Director, International Crime Division, DFAIT; Marie Gervais-Vidricaire, Director General, Global Affairs Bureau, DFAIT; Paul Heinbecker, Ambassador and Permanent Representative of Canada to the United Nations; John Holmes, Director, UN Human Rights and Economic Law Division, DFAIT; Vanessa Kent, Peacekeeping Desk Officer, Regional Security and Peacekeeping Division, DFAIT; Patricia Lonie, Director General, International Organizations Bureau, DFAIT; Isabelle Massip, Director, UN Commonwealth Affairs Division, DFAIT; Mark Molner, Canadian Ambassador to Ireland; and Peter Taylor, Deputy Director, United Nations Section. The author acknowledges assistance from the Office of Research Studies, University of Western Ontario.

1. Kofi Annan's effective diplomacy is credited with ensuring that even Syria supported the resolution.
2. 'Address by Prime Minister Jean Chretien on the Occasion of the United Nations General Assembly High-Level Plenary Debate on the New Partnership for Africa's Development', New York, 16 September 2002. Available at http://pm.gc.ca/default.asp? Language+E&Page'newsroom&Subnewyorkne pad20020916_e (accessed 9 January 2003). Also CBC News Online, 'Chrétien Interview on September 11', 16 September 2002. Available at http://www.cbc.ca (accessed 9 January 2003).
3. See General Assembly, 'Special Committee of Peacekeeping Operations Ends Two-Day Debate on Need for Rapid Deployment of Peace Operations', Press release, GA/PK/175, 12 Feb. 2002. Available at: http://www.un.org/News/Press/docs/2002/GAP K175.doc.htm (accessed 28 November 2002).
4. Those with full membership in the SHIRBRIG includes Austria, Canada, Denmark, Italy, the Netherlands, Norway, Poland, Romania, and Sweden. Five other countries (Finland, Lithuania,

Spain, Portugal, and Slovenia) also participate. For a more comprehensive analysis of the SHIRBRIG, see Peter Langille, *Bridging the Commitment–Capacity Gap: A Review of Existing Arrangements and Options for Enhancing UN Rapid Deployment* (Wayne, NJ: Centre for UN Reform Education, 2002), esp. 50–9.
5. The list of potential members includes Ghana, South Africa, Uruguay, Japan, Thailand, and Slovakia.
6. The most important proposals in the Brahimi Report pertain to conflict prevention. Yet these recommendations have been more rhetoric that reality.
7. Some southern countries, such as Fiji, speak out in favour of gender mainstreaming. For example, see the speeches by Amraiya Naidu to the Special Committee of Peacekeeping Operations, General Assembly, 'Special Committee of Peacekeeping Operations Ends Two-Day Debate on Need for Rapid Deployment of Peace Operations', 1, 8.
8. In 1998 Canada and Norway created the Human Security Network. The Network's current membership includes Austria, Canada, Chile, Greece, Ireland, Jordan, Mali, the Netherlands, Norway, Slovenia, Switzerland, and Thailand. South Africa participates as an observer. See George MacLean, 'Building on a Legacy or Bucking Tradition? Evaluating Canada's Human Security Initiative in an Era of Globalization?', *Canada Foreign Policy* 9, 3 (2002): 65–83; and the human security website of the Department of Foreign Affairs and International Trade. Available at http://www.humansecurity.gc.ca.
9. For example, the 2002–3 budget for the International War Crimes Tribunal for the Former Yugoslavia is US $223,169,800. UN, International War Crimes Tribunal for the Former Yugoslavia, 'ICTY Key Figures: General Information', 4 December 2002, 6. Available at: http://www.un.org/icty/glance /keyfig-e.htm (accessed 16 January 2003).
10. The list of human rights abuses committed by the government of Libya includes extrajudicial and summary executions, the systematic use of torture, arbitrary arrests, and long-time detention without trail. Human Rights Watch, 'Libya Confirms Why it

is Wrong for UN Rights Chair', Press release, August 2002, 1.

11. UN Security Council, S/2000/1044, 31 Oct. 2000, 2. Available at http://www.frauen.spoe.at/download/uno_resolution.pdf. The resolution set important standards and principles. Unfortunately, it has not been effectively implemented.

12. According to the US National Security Strategy, 'poverty, weak institutions, and corruption can make weak states vulnerable to terrorist networks and drug cartels within their borders.' US, *The National Security Strategy of the United States of America, Washington*, Sept 2002, 3. Available at http://www.whitehouse.gov/nsc/nss.pdf (accessed 12 January 2003).

References

Brown, Susan. 2000. *Why Conflict Prevention?* Ottawa: CIDA.

Canadian Parliament. 2000. Crimes Against Humanity and War Crimes Act. Ottawa, 29 June.

CBS News. 2002a. 'War with Iraq: Americans in No Hurry'. New York. 7 October. Available at http://www.cbsnews.com/stories/2002/10/06/opinion/polls/main 524496.shtml (accessed 9 January 2003).

———. 2002b. 'Americans Worry About Iraq'. New York. 7 November. Available at http://www.cbsnews.com/stories/2002/11/02/opinion/polls/printable527933.shtml (accessed 9 January 2003).

Department of Foreign Affairs and International Trade (DFAIT). 2002a. 'Canada's Actions Against Terrorism Since September 11th—Backgrounder'. Ottawa. Available at http://wwwdfait-maeci.gc.ca/can-am/menu-en.asp?act=1&did=10&did=1684 (accessed 10 January 2003).

———. 2002b. 'Canada–US Cross Border Crime and Security Cooperation'. Ottawa. Available at http://www.canadianembassy.org/border/crime-en.asp (accessed 10 January 2003).

———. 2002c. 'Human Security Program'. Ottawa. Available at http://www.humansecurity.gc.ca/pshe.asp (accessed 4 December 2002).

———. 2002d. 'Human Security Program: Human Security Program in Brief'. Ottawa. Available at http://www.humansecurity.gc.ca/psh_brief.e.asp (accessed 4 December 2002).

———. 2002e. 'Notes for an Address by the Honourable Bill Graham, Minister of Foreign Affairs to the Assembly of States Parties, International Criminal Court'. New York. 9 September. Available at http://www.un.int/canada/s-09sep2002Graham.htm (accessed 30 October 2002).

———. 2001. Statement by Ambassador Paul Heinbecker, Ambassador and Permanent Representative of Canada to the United Nations on 'Canada and the UN Security Council: Putting People First, An Overview'. March. Available at http://wwwun.int/canada/html/s-march2001/heinbecker.htm (accessed 30 October 2002).

Gervais-Vidricaire, Marie. 2002. Interview with the Director General, Global Affairs Bureau, DFAIT. Ottawa. 15 November.

Heinbecker, Paul. 2002. Interview with the Ambassador and Permanent Representative of Canada to the Untied Nations. Waterloo, ON. 8 November.

Human Rights Watch. 2001. 'Anti-racism Summit Ends on Hopeful Note: Progress Amid Controversy', New York. 10 September. Available at http://www.hrw.org/prss/2001/09/wcar0910.htm (accessed 9 December 2002).

International Commission on Intervention and State Sovereignty. 2001. *The Responsibility to Protect*. Ottawa: International Development Research Centre.

Keating, Tom. 2002. *Canada and World Order: The Multilateralist Tradition in Canadian Foreign Policy*, 2nd ed. Don Mills, ON: Oxford University Press.

Organization for Economic Co-operation and Development (OECD). 2003. 'Net ODA in 2001 as a Percentage of GNI'. Available at http://www.oecd.org/phf/M00037000/M00037873 .pdf (accessed 23 January 2003).

Prime Minister's Office (PMO). 2002. 'Address by Prime Minister Jean Chrétien on the Occasion of the United Nations General Assembly High-Level

Plenary Debate on the New Partnership for Africa's Development'. New York. 16 September. Available at http://pm.gc.ca/default.asp?Language+E&Page=newsroom&Sub=newyorknepad20020916_e (accessed 9 January 2003).

Stairs, Denis. 1999. 'Canada and the Security Problem: Implications as the Millennium Turns', *International Journal* 54, 3: 386–403.

United Nations Security Council. 2001. Resolution 1353. S/2001/573. 13 June. Available at http://www.un.org/News/Press/docs/2001.doc.htm (accessed 11 November 2002).

World Commission on Environment and Development. 1987. *Our Common Future*. Oxford: Oxford University Press. Available at http://www.gerio.org/edu/pcsd/endnotes.html (accessed 19 January 2003).

World Summit on Sustainable Development (WSSD). 2002. Johannesburg Summit 2002, Johannesburg. September. Available at: http://www.johannesburgsummit.org/html/whats_new/feature_story39.html (accessed 18 December 2002).

Young, Oran. 1991. 'Political Leadership and Regime Formation: On the Development of Institutions in International Society', *International Organization* 45, 3.

Selected Bibliography

Bothwell, Robert. 1992. *Canada and the United States*. Toronto: University of Toronto Press.

Chapnick, Andrew. 2005. *The Middle Power Project: Canada and the Founding of the United Nations*. Vancouver: UBC Press.

Cooper, Andrew F. 2004. *Tests of Global Governance: Canadian Diplomacy and United Nations World Conferences*. Tokyo: United Nations University Press.

Granatstein, J.L., and Norman Hillmer. 1994. *From Empire to Umpire: Canada and the World to the 1990s*. Toronto: Copp Clark Longman.

———. 1992. *For Better of Worse: Canada and the United States to the 1990s*. Toronto: Copp Clark Longman.

Holmes, John W. 1981. *Life with Uncle: The Canadian–American Relationship*. Toronto: University of Toronto Press.

Keating, Tom, and Larry Pratt. 1988. *Canada, NATO and the Bomb: The Western Alliance in Crisis*. Edmonton: Hurtig Publishers.

Kirton, John. 2001. 'Guess Who is Coming to Kananaskis? Civil Society and the G8 in Canada's Year as Host', *International Journal* 57, 1 (Winter): 101–22.

MacMillan, Margaret O., and David S. Sorenson, eds. 1990. *Canada and NATO: Uneasy Past, Uncertain Future*. Waterloo, ON: University of Waterloo Press.

McKenna, Peter. 1995. *Canada and the OAS: From Dilettante to Full Partner*. Ottawa: Carleton University Press.

Potter, Evan H. 1999. *Transatlantic Partners: Canadian Approaches to the European Union*. Ottawa: Carleton University Press.

Rochlin, James. 1994. *Discovering the Americas: The Evolution of Canadian Foreign Policy Towards Latin America*. Vancouver: UBC Press.

Simpson, Erika. 2001. *NATO and the Bomb: Canadian Defenders Confront Critics*. Montreal: McGill-Queen's University Press.

Stairs, Denis. 1999. 'Global Governance as a Policy Tool: The Canadian Experience', pp. 67–85 in *Globalization and Global Governance*, Raimo Väyrynen, ed. Lanham, MD: Rowman and Littlefield.

Taylor, Rupert, ed. 1995. *Canada in Action: Canada and the G7*. Waterloo, ON: Taylor Publishing.

Thompson, John Herd, and Stephen J. Randall. 2000. *Canada and the United States, Ambivalent Allies*. Montreal: McGill-Queen's University Press.

PART III

Domestic Factors and Canadian Foreign Policy

Part III examines the relevance of domestic influences on Canada's international relations. Studies of foreign policy are often problematic given the separate realms these issues occupy. The term 'foreign' implies a context in which theories of international relations or global political economy might apply. The 'policy' aspect, however, draws attention to public administration or public policy frameworks. Other approaches look to transcend levels of analysis by incorporating second-image reversed models or two-level games. The first two chapters of this section, which are reprinted from the Winter 1983–4 edition of *International Journal*, represent the first serious attempt to address these questions in the context of Canadian foreign policy.

Kim Richard Nossal's 'classic' contribution presented in Chapter 9 touches on many of these questions. First, he starts with the distinction between state and civil society and acknowledges the difficulty in compiling a comprehensive list of relevant actors. Nossal then moves on to evaluate empirical, liberal, Marxist, and statist theories of the democratic state for insight into the relationship between societal forces and governments. After laying this groundwork Nossal identifies what he believes are the two main reasons for the 'domestication' of Canadian foreign policy. Specifically, policy-makers must now deal with 'low' issues of politics, in addition to traditional peace and security concerns. As a result, domestic groups seek greater access to the policy process. Nossal, however, concludes that theories of the democratic state do not provide an adequate model for understanding these realities. He instead proposes a 'modified statist' approach, which accepts that societal pressures have some impact on the state. Although Nossal ultimately marginalizes the relevance of non-state actors in his conclusion, this chapter introduces basic parameters for better understanding domestic forces in this policy area.

Or does it? The remaining chapters in Part III both question and reinforce these conclusions. Cranford Pratt's response to Nossal in Chapter 10, for example, argues that a 'dominant-class' approach offers a better understanding of domestic factors. Despite affirming statist conclusions, Pratt suggests that the interests of the dominant class in Canada are consistent with élites in other states. Therefore, what is required is the creation of a counter-consensus to challenge these entrenched values. The importance of Pratt's work should not be underestimated. In fact, his discussion of dominant-class theory goes beyond Nossal's flirtation with Marxist analysis and instead includes a wide range of variables related the construction of knowledge, class, ideology, and political culture. The absence of ethical and normative considerations in Canadian foreign policy is also highlighted. The influence of Pratt on future scholars, such as Mark Neufeld (Chapter 6) is both important and obvious.

Despite this praise, the remaining chapters in Part III embrace an institutional perspective in the study of Canadian foreign policy. Paul Gecelovsky argues that the prime minister has decisive control in the formulation of Canada's international relations. In contrast, John English evaluates the relevance of legislative considerations, especially in terms of Parliament. Chris J. Kukucha, on the other hand focuses on the increasing relevance of the provinces both in terms of the formulation of Canadian foreign policy and the impact of non-central governments on the evolution of international norms and standards. The obvious weakness of Part III is its failure to include further critical analysis as well as its exclusion of a wide range of scholarship on the democratization of Canadian foreign policy. Having said that, however, other critical approaches are included elsewhere in this volume.

9

Analyzing the Domestic Sources of Canadian Foreign Policy

Kim Richard Nossal

Canada's external behaviour is affected not only by power and capability, but also by the values, interests, and preferences of individuals, groups, and classes in Canadian society. How one sees the impact of 'domestic sources' on Canadian foreign policy depends very much on which set of empirical lenses one uses. This article seeks to examine the different approaches to the study of domestic sources of foreign policy in a democratic system by examining contending empirical theories of democratic behaviour.

At the bottom, the study of domestic sources of foreign policy is bound up in one of the most fundamental issues of empirical democratic theory: how best to analyze the relationship between the governors and the governed, or, to use the terminology followed in this article, between the state and civil society. On this critical issue, there is more disagreement than consensus.

There is agreement that individuals in civil society have interests, values, and policy preferences; that members of civil society, as individuals or in groups, may be disposed to make their interests and preferences known to the state. The key actors in civil society and the means of communicating preferences may be readily enumerated. Society may be differentiated into classes with similar characteristics, such as a common relationship to the means of production, or groups with common material or ideological interests. Interest associations, including groups with common economic interests, business firms, citizens' groups, political parties, churches, and unions are the groups that dot civil society's landscape. They communicate their interests, values, and policy preferences to officials of the state through public opinion polls, the media, lobbying of different sorts, mass demonstrations, personal communications, and, of course, through voting.

There agreement ends. For example, little consensus exists on what constitutes 'the state' or even on whether the distinction between the state and civil society is at all analytically useful.[1] Certainly there is no accord on the relative importance of the diverse elements in civil society for the making of policy in a democratic state. For example, elections are an integral part of the form and structure of a democratic system. For some, the electoral behaviour of citizens in democratic society is a pivotal force in explaining how and why the state acts as it does. For others, by contrast, elections are dismissed as part of the superstructure of a capitalist society, having no importance for our understanding of policy outcomes. Similarly, for some, class in capitalist society assumes paramount importance in the analysis of public policy; others, however, treat the impact of class relations on policy with indifference. In short, what marks different conceptions of how to understand the impact of societal sources of policy is divergence over the relative influence assigned to elements within civil society.

Empirical Theories of the Democratic State

Normative liberal democratic theory stresses notions of the equality of all citizens; individual consent to be governed; the sovereignty of the 'people', or all citizens; representative institutions of governance; and the paramountcy of constitutionalism. Central to the successful functioning of liberal democracies is the willingness of the governors to pay obeisance to (if not believe) the idea that 'public men are proud to be servants of the state and would be ashamed to be its masters', as Winston Churchill put it to the United States Congress in December 1941. Thus, the focus of normative theory is on how the state ought to behave, and how it ought to respond to the desires and interests of the governed. Empirical democratic theory, by contrast, attempts to explain the actual relationship between society and democratic governments. Three broad theories of the state can be identified: liberal, marxian, and statist.

LIBERAL VARIANTS
Pluralism
The pluralist interpretation of policy-making comes closest to the normative ideal. Pluralism assumes that civil society comprises numerous centres of interest—and of power. All citizens, individually or in groups, have an equal opportunity to affect government decisions, and thus each centre of power is considered an important explanatory variable for governmental policy. The behaviour of the state is characterized as reflecting an aggregation of the diverse interests and preferences of civil society. The political process is likened to a marketplace: political lead-

ers compete for votes and for support from the citizenry by structuring their policies either on the basis of demands or on the rule of anticipated reaction. Other forms of the paradigm focus on the importance of differences in power between groups: those groups with the weightiest political resources secure their objectives. In its essence, however, pluralism characterizes the state as a passive reactor to any and all societal demands.[2]

Neopluralism
This model developed as a critique of the more overtly *liberal* assumptions of pluralism. Like pluralists, neopluralists assume that the behaviour of the state is shaped by societal actors and their preferences; they differ from pluralists in their assumption that while all have an equal opportunity to express their policy preferences to the state, some actors are more equal than others in their ability to translate their preferences into state action. As one student has characterized the neopluralist canvas: 'The effective demand group universe is composed of relatively small, hierarchically organized, financially well-endowed groups.'[3] The focus of neopluralism is on elite groups and their preferences, not on the mass of citizens. Understandably, this paradigm accords little weight to public opinion or electoral behaviour in explaining policy outcomes.[4]

Corporatism
This strand of liberal theory focuses on the style of interest intermediation found in a number of European democracies. In countries like Austria, the Netherlands, and Norway, interest group leaders are given functional representation on numerous private-sector/public-sector committees, councils, and boards established to provide advice to the government in key policy issue-areas. The authority to regulate or control certain areas of public policy is exercised not by the state, but by the interest group itself. The legitimate position of these functional interest group leaders gives them a powerful voice in shaping policy. Under the corporatist model, the most important groups in civil

society are these interest association elites, whose institutionalized sharing of authority with the state effectively constrains state officials.[5]

MARXIAN VARIANTS

For marxian analysts, the behaviour of the democratic state is inexorably tied to the capitalist mode of production and to the inherent conflict between the dominant or hegemonic class—those who control capital—and other classes in society. Although those who adopt a class analysis are rarely in agreement about what constitutes a marxist theory of the state,[6] two dominant variants can be identified.

Instrumental Marxism[7]

This variant sees the state as the governing instrument of the bourgeoisie. In its most unrefined form, the model adheres to Marx's and Engels' assertion that 'the executive of the modern state is but a committee for managing the common affairs of the whole bourgeoisie.' The behaviour of the capitalist state, the primary premise of Marxism argues, always coheres to the interests of the dominant class. It is important to stress that, as Leo Panitch points out, instrumentalism does not imply that the state acts on the instructions of the bourgeoisie: this is 'a caricature which fails to distinguish between the state acting on *behalf* of the bourgeoisie and its acting on their *behest*'.[8] Rather, the 'social character' of officials of the modern state is stressed—how governmental officials share the same background as the capitalist class, and how close contacts, social and familial, are maintained. Other manifestations of societal interests—interest groups, political parties, public opinion, elections—are assumed to be inconsequential in explaining the actions of government. Look to the interests of the dominant class, the instrumentalist argues, and one will find the root cause of state behaviour.

Structural Marxism

Rather than casting the state as an instrument of the dominant class, structuralists take a different tack. Structuralism attempts to explain in marxian terms why the democratic state often adopts policies contrary to the putative interests of the bourgeoisie (social welfare legislation is an oft-cited example). This model, usually associated with Nicos Poulantzas,[9] begins by recognizing that the capitalist class, while dominant *vis-à-vis* other classes in society, is not a monolithic whole with but one, readily identifiable, interest. Rather, the bourgeoisie is beset by internal conflicts based on the differentiated complexities of modern capitalism. For example, the interests of importers diverge from those of exporters; the demands of small business differ considerably from those of large enterprises which differ again from those of multinational corporations; financiers and manufacturers may not always agree on policy. In other words, the interests of these different segments, or 'fractions', of the capitalist class are sufficiently divergent that there can be no common interest of the capitalist class that the state is mirroring. In this model, the state, 'solidly embedded, structurally and functionally, within capitalist relations of production',[10] does have its own interest—in the preservation of the capitalist mode of production and the maintenance of the structures necessary for capital accumulation and reproduction. But given the clash of interests within the dominant class, the state has to assume a 'relative autonomy' *vis-à-vis* the bourgeoisie, to mediate intra-class conflict, and to perpetuate the dominance of the bourgeoisie as a whole. In other words, the state acts not on the short-term interests of the capitalist class, or any segment thereof, but defines its own notion of the national interest, a definition that ensures the long-term interests of the capitalist system writ large. Thus policies that would appear to be contrary to the interests of the capitalist class are adopted by the state, not only to give the system legitimacy in the eyes of other classes, but ultimately to avert the collapse of the system through disaffection or revolution.

STATISM

The unifying theme of the variants of liberal and marxian theories of the democratic state is that the state's behaviour is understandable only by reference to the interests of civil society. Structural marxists, it is true, predict that the state will be relatively free to define its own interests. But such a definition is inexorably predicated on the notion of societal interests, with the state cast in the paternalistic role of acting on occasion to save capitalists from their own short-sighted greed. These variants differ fundamentally, of course, in the relative weights they accord to different groups in society. However, the idea that the state might have interests of its own, separate and independent of the interests of groups or classes within civil society, would be dismissed as absurd by marxians and heretical by liberals.

But such is the central premise of the statist, or state-centric, model.[11] Statists make four assumptions about the relationship between the state and civil society that differ markedly from both liberal and marxian variants.

First, officials of the state, as a group of men and women charged with the making of authoritative decisions for the polity, will have their own interests and preferences. Public officials, whatever their 'social character', whatever their relationships with members of dominant classes or politically resourceful groups, are not automata, slavishly pursuing—consciously or unconsciously—the interests of others.

Second, the statist approach focuses on the interests of the state as a variable separate from the interests of civil society. Society-centred explanations of public policy deny, implicitly or explicitly, that state officials could develop interests independently of the configuration of dominant interests, including the capitalist mode of production, in civil society. By contrast, statism assumes that the preferences of the democratic state may indeed be divergent from the interests or preferences of civil society.

Third, the statist approach assumes that if the preferences of the state and civil society diverge, the state will act on *its* preferences, not on those of civil society. To do this successfully, it may be necessary for officials to work to shift values, attitudes, or preferences within civil society until they are consonant with those of the state. Statism assume that public

officials will not be hesitant to engage in such activity, Churchill's declarations notwithstanding. In short, the state is assumed to be *autonomous* in that its actions will accord fully with its preferences.

Fourth, statism assumes that the government has the *power* to prevail in any conflict of interest between state and society. Public officials have access to the resources of the state, which can be used to withstand public pressure, or the importunities of élites. These resources can be used to de-fuse or mould opinion, or to mobilize societal support for state preferences.

Importantly, statism does not assume that 'the state' is a cohesive, monolithic unit. Divergences over policy will occur within the apparatus of state, with those officials with the weightiest political resources prevailing. Policy is assumed to be the result of 'governmental politics'[12]—the struggle for power within government among officials for adoption of policies which fit their particular conception of the national interest.

By contrast with other paradigms, the statist model predicts a minimal role for domestic groups in the policy-making process. The state does not seek guidance or direction from groups within society; rather, it seeks to use domestic sources for the pursuit of its own interests.

These contending paradigms offer starkly different predictions about the importance of domestic sources for foreign policy-making. On the one hand, pure statism argues that the state is fully autonomous vis-à-vis society, acting always on its, not civil society's, preferences. This model predicts minimal importance for the interests, values, and attitudes of society as a source of foreign policy. By contrast, the other paradigms predict *some* level of societal constraint on the behaviour of the state.[13] This latter group, however, evinces no agreement about the relative potency of groups within civil society.

The Analysis of Canadian Foreign Policy

It might be expected that the favoured paradigm for the analysis of Canadian foreign policy would be one of the liberal models, because much of the literature stresses how far Canada's external relations have been 'domesticated' since the late 1960s. The jargon is decidedly misleading, however, bearing no relationship to the usual dictionary definition of the term. Rather, the domestication of Canadian foreign policy refers to two inter-related phenomena.

First, domestication refers to an assumed shift in the issues confronting foreign policy decision-makers. No longer, the argument runs, is Ottawa's agenda dominated by the traditionally 'external' issues of war and peace, of military and security affairs. Rather, policy-makers now must grapple with such 'low' policy issues as fisheries, civil aviation, pollution, energy, refugees, technology transfer, investment and capital flows, debt and currency management, cultural and communications policy, maritime law, tariffs and non-tariff barriers, and so on. These issues, it is argued, are more 'domestic' than the 'high' policy issues, mainly because they have a more direct bearing on the livelihood of citizens.

Second, the domestication of Canadian foreign policy also refers to the process of allowing more input into the shaping of 'low' policy by those domestic groups affected by these issues. The practice of wider consultation, and of giving functional groups representation on Canadian delegations to international conferences or negotiations, it is argued, is indicative of this trend.

These inter-related elements of domestication of Canadian foreign policy have both normative and empirical connotations. They conform, in their essence, to liberal views of the policy process. Perhaps because of the coincidence between its precepts and normative theories of the democratic state, domestication has attained the status of orthodoxy. This is reflected in both government and academic circles.

The strongest proponent of domestication has been the state itself. Its public pronouncements have tended to stress both strands of domestication, as the following selections indicate. 'The traditional distinction between foreign policy and domestic policy implies a hard and fast dividing-line that no longer exists', the secretary of state for external affairs asserted in 1979.[14] So too has there been insistence that public participation was an important element in policy formulation. The 1970 white paper was insistent that the government's foreign policy decisions would find their wellsprings in the aspirations, needs, and desires of civil society.[15] In 1979, Allan Gotlieb, the undersecretary of state for external affairs, spoke of 'those who contribute to policy formulation—e.g. parliamentarians, provincial officials, journalists, academics, business or labour leaders' and claimed that the government was 'conscious of the fact that, in an open society like ours, the interests and concerns of the public as a whole must be reflected in foreign policy'.[16] Two years later Gotlieb would write of Canadian policies on the law of the sea and the Arctic ecology that: 'La participation publique à l'élaboration de la politique canadienne dans ces domaines a surpassé tout ce qui s'est fait dans le passé. Les intérêts en jeu étaient ceux des Canadiens eux-mêmes et ce, de façon très directe dans certains cas.'[17]

It is perhaps indicative of the orthodoxy that state officials are inclined from time to time to call for greater public participation in the foreign policy process. As Flora MacDonald, Joe Clark's Secretary of State for External Affairs, stated in 1979: 'Foreign policy must not be the exclusive preserve of the few, inside or outside government . . . I have stressed, and cannot stress enough, the importance I attach to parliamentary and public input in our foreign policy review.'[18] Allan MacEachen, in August 1983, promised greater public input and involvement in the policy-making process.[19]

The orthodoxy of domestication tends to be reflected in the academic literature. '[I]n the 1970s', Michael Tucker has noted, 'to a degree greater than hitherto, Canadian publics had an influence on policies or decisions . . . In the main this heightened influence can be seen as the product of the advent of the new economic and environmental issues in Canadian foreign policy.'[20]

Denis Stairs concluded that the growth of 'functional international politics' in the 1970s was in part responsible for 'the growing importance of publics in the foreign-policy process'.[21] Likewise, Cranford Pratt has written of the wider basis of participation by the public partly as a result of 'the great increase in the importance of economic matters in foreign policy issues'.[22] David Dewitt and John Kirton argue that Canadian foreign policy after 1968 is marked by the high salience of domestic groups, particularly interest groups, labour unions, the media, and the business community: '[I]t is clear that the degree of private-sector . . . participation has shown a steady increase and that official Ottawa has been responsive to these interests.'[23]

The orthodoxy of domestication conforms closely to the expectations of liberal models of influences on state behaviour, and, not incidentally, conforms as closely to the dominant bourgeois ideology in Canadian society. Similarly, societal constraints (of an admittedly different sort) are central to all strands of marxian analysis. However, none of the three paradigms outlined above is well represented in explanations of Canadian foreign policy. Marxian analyses of the external behaviour of the Canadian state leave large analytical holes; despite the orthodoxy of domestication, societal-constraint assumptions are not employed in the analysis of Canadian foreign policy in quite the way liberal theory expects. Nor is there a pure statist tradition in the analysis of Canadian foreign policy.

POLITICAL ECONOMY APPROACHES

While there is in Canada a rich political economy tradition, and an active community of marxian scholars, there is ironically a paucity of marxian analysis of Canadian foreign policy.[24] Studies using a class approach to foreign policy tend to be highly selective, concentrated in three major foreign policy areas—Canadian–American relations, foreign economic policy, and international development assistance.[25] These areas bear directly on the processes of capital accumulation and

reproduction and thus fit well an analytical approach that centres on the structural needs of a capitalist mode of production. But many of the foreign policy actions of the Canadian state have little or nothing to do with capital accumulation. On how we may explain such behaviour of the state, marxian analysis is largely silent.[26] Because a state apparatus with interests separate from civil society is a theoretical impossibility in marxian terms, and because liberal explanations of state behaviour are held to be empirically incorrect, we are left in an analytical vacuum.

A significant strain of the political economy approach to the making of Canadian foreign policy, both marxian and non-marxian, should be mentioned at this juncture. Those models that cast Canada as a weak, penetrated, and dependent nation-state in the international economy implicitly or explicitly deny a significant role for domestic sources.[27] 'In Canada', Linda Freeman notes, 'the dominant class is not Canadian . . . [K]ey decisions are made outside the country.'[28] A comparable perspective underwrites numerous studies of foreign policy in Canada. The Canadian government is assumed to have little autonomy *vis-à-vis* the international system: its decisions therefore are made within parameters set by external actors, notably the United States. The implication is clear: the configuration of domestic forces in Canada pales into analytical insignificance in this model.[29]

LIBERAL APPROACHES

Paradoxically, those students of foreign policy in Canada who use neither a marxian nor a political economy approach tend to share liberal expectations about the behaviour of the state, but rarely use models of analysis that conform with such normative expectations. Thus, pluralist explanations of state behaviour enjoy even less prominence in the literature on Canadian foreign policy than marxian analyses. No analyst has characterized the external behaviour of the Canadian state as stemming from the configuration of demands or pressures from civil society.

The state is never characterized as a passive reactor, or as a mere processor of societal demands. Neopluralist or corporatist assumptions may be applied to particular issue-areas or in specific case studies,[30] but there are few non-marxian students who explicitly say: look only to civil society to understand why the state behaves as it does.

Indeed, it is indicative of this paradox that the impact of domestic groups on foreign policy is assumed, a priori, to exist: the role and impact of domestic groups continue to be examined, even though a common conclusion is that domestic groups do not play a significant role in shaping the external behaviour of the state.[31]

THE STATIST APPROACH

There are few students of Canadian foreign policy who would adopt a purist state-centric approach. I noted earlier that some of the assumptions of the governmental, or bureaucratic, politics model formed part of the statist model: do, therefore, bureaucratic politics enthusiasts use statist assumptions?

It is true that there are some similarities between the models. The governmental politics paradigm characterizes policy as (to use Allisonian terms) a 'resultant' of 'pulling and hauling' between participants in the policy-making process (i.e., state officials). These officials have independently formulated policy preferences, which are derived from three inter-related aspects: ideological beliefs and conceptions of the national or public interest; desires to protect the health of the organizations to which they belong; and personal career interests. Officials seek to act on these preferences, their success in translating their preferences into state behaviour being dependent on positional authority and personal influence.[32] In short, there is some congruence between statism and the governmental politics paradigm.

But the bureaucratic politics model is not statist; by contrast, it assumes definite linkages between state officials and civil society. Politicians are assumed to have constraints and imperatives imposed upon them by (among other things) the periodic requisites of the electoral contest; bureaucrats are likewise assumed to be linked and constrained by their clients in the private sector—those citizens to whom services are rendered. Officials of the provincial state apparatus are also assumed to be linked to their subnational civil societies. In short, the governmental politics model, while its precepts may usefully be applied to a statist paradigm, is essentially cast within a societal-constraint framework.

Dewitt and Kirton are the only students of Canadian foreign policy to claim to be statists. They argue that their 'complex neo-realist' paradigm follows the 'statist tradition' of Krasner in predicting a strong, impermeable, and autonomous state.[33] Such a claim must, however, be strongly doubted, for there is a significant logical inconsistency in their position. 'Complex neo-realism' claims to predict autonomy; but it also predicts

> a much larger and richer role for a broader array of domestic actors. It suggests that Canada, as a principal power, has the surplus capability in the international system that enables its government to respond to the demands of its own society . . . Organized labour, associational interest groups, the provincial governments, and the media thereby come to play significant roles in the foreign policy process . . . The private corporate sector . . . has an enhanced influence in the decision-making process.[34]

Such pluralist assumptions are strongly at odds with the requisites of a state-centric approach.

A MODIFIED STATIST MODEL

Dewitt and Kirton argue that, to understand Canadian foreign policy, one should look to the state *and* look to civil society. Such a position is clearly not statist, for it places too much emphasis on the receptivity of the state to the interests of civil society. But neither is it entirely liberal, for officials are assumed to have values of their own making, policy preferences that emerge not from civil society, but from within the apparatus of state. In this, their mixed model conforms to the dominant method of analyzing the relationship between domestic sources and the external behaviour of the Canadian state.

The major histories of Canadian external policy[35] provide a selective, but not unrepresentative, sample of the mode of analysis dominant in explanations of Canadian foreign policy. It could be suggested that these works are framed within an empirical paradigm for explaining state behaviour that falls between the stools of statism and liberalism. C.P. Stacey, John W. Holmes, and James Eayrs all focus on the state and the often contending attitudes of its officials as the source of Canadian foreign policy.[36] In many respects, the behaviour of the state as outlined in these histories conforms to the precepts of Nordlinger's and Krasner's 'autonomous' paradigm. Officials, elected and bureaucratic, have their own conceptions of the national interest, as well as organizational and personal interests. They have definite ideas about what Canada's foreign policy should or should not be. And when these ideas are thought to run against societal preferences, officials use their authority and the resources of the state to help convince society of the rightness of the state's preferences.[37] These officials are never assumed to be automata acting on behalf of any group or class within society—however coincident their 'social character' (socio-economic status and educational achievement) is with that of the dominant class. The process of policy-making is anything but 'open'. On the contrary, officials jealously guard their prerogatives to make decisions autonomously: the decision process is tightly controlled; access is restricted; secrecy is pervasive; little input or participation by groups or individuals in civil society is welcomed.[38]

However, while Stacey, Holmes, and Eayrs do not characterize the state as a passive reactor to societal demands, neither do they assume that it is fully 'autonomous' in a statist sense. Rather, the state is assumed to be constrained and impelled by societal preferences. Their work suggests a modified statist paradigm. What assumptions does such a model make about the impact of societal preferences on foreign policy making?

Civil Society and Foreign Policy Behaviour

A modified statism would begin by rejecting the purist position that the autonomy of the state should be cast in absolute terms. In other words, it would begin by accepting the notion of degrees of autonomy of the state from civil society, just as societal-constraint models implicitly accept variance in degrees of constraint (and do not insist, for example, on absolute conditions of permeability).

Such an initial assumption would allow conclusions to be drawn about the levels at which the state may seek (and enjoy) autonomy, and the levels at which it is constrained. Denis Stairs uses the work of James J. Best's examination of public opinion to posit four levels at which foreign policy may be affected by public opinion: administration-setting, policy-setting, agenda-setting, and parameter-setting.[39] These categories can be used in a wider context to assess how the external behaviour of the state may be affected by the preferences of actors and elements in civil society writ large.

The administration, or implementation, of foreign policy may be constrained or impelled by societal preferences. However, most modern states, including Canada, are sufficiently impermeable to preclude widespread administration-setting by civil society in foreign policy. The explanation, as Stairs notes, lies partly in the traditional secrecy surrounding the actual administration of external policy and partly in the nature of foreign policy itself with its emphasis on diplomacy and negotiation. A modified statist interpretation would stress the state's autonomy at this level of policy behaviour. While officials might be inclined to consult affected groups in civil society in the process of international negotiations or even to engage in corporatist interest intermediation, this is done more to de-fuse potential criticism than to ensure that the administration of policy directly conforms to the interests of these groups.[40]

At a higher level, societal preferences may determine what policies are to be pursued by the state. In other words, the pressure of public opinion, specific interest associations, or other groups determines the state's specific policy choices. Again, a modified statist perspective would argue that at this level, the state retains considerable latitude. It is rare that the state will be confronted with a united preference on a single policy issue: as long as there is division (as surely there always will be), the state can rationalize *its* choice. As the deputy minister for foreign policy, de Montigny Marchand, said so candidly in 1983: 'We [the government] can listen and we can accommodate, to some extent we can even manage certain contradictions, but we cannot avoid the overriding need for a policy which is a coherent synthesis of national interests and priorities . . . There will be times when government exercises its leadership somewhat ahead of public opinion.'[41]

The third level is the setting of the policy agenda: determining those issues deemed important enough by society to warrant government action. At this level, less stress is placed on the autonomy of the state, and more importance placed on the ability of certain groups in civil society—notably the print and electronic media—to structure the issues with which the government must deal. Governments in Canada do not choose which issues will receive media attention, but few issues given wide attention can be ignored.[42] Nor do governments choose how society will react to issues. Prime Minister Pierre Trudeau's reaction to questions put to him in 1968 about Canadian assistance to the victims of the Nigerian civil war is indicative of his surprise that such an issue would be raised: 'You have the funniest questions. We haven't considered this as a government.'[43] Similarly, the Trudeau government was taken by surprise when so many Canadians reacted vigorously to plans to test the cruise missile in Canada: what might have passed as a routine feature of Canadian–American defence co-operation escalated into a major political issue.

However, while the state may not be able to choose its own agenda, it is still assumed to have some autonomy in choosing how to deal with issues on the agenda. For example, media attention and public opinion may ensure that there will be a reaction from Ottawa to a particular external event. But a wide latitude to choose the response of the state's own choosing will exist, particularly when there is likely to be no unified societal preference pressing the government to take a specific course of action.

At the most general level, civil society can define acceptable policy actions. Parameter setting has 'the effect of establishing certain limits on what the policy-makers are actually able to do— able, that is, within the range of what they regard as acceptable, or tolerable, political and other costs. Such opinions can serve, in short, to confine the policy community's range of politically workable choices.'[44] At this level, the state is assumed to be constrained by the parallelogram of societal preferences at any given time. However, Stairs stresses both the essential *negativity* of this process and the wideness of its scope. First, he argues that the preferences of civil society writ large will act to rule out certain policy options rather than to establish general courses of action that the government must follow. Second, the parameters of 'acceptable behaviour' established by civil society will always be exceedingly broad. Indeed, they tend to be so broad that it is unlikely that state officials will be unanimously agreed on a policy that falls outside this range of 'acceptable behaviour' ascribed to civil society.[45]

Importantly, if state behaviour *were* to fall outside the limits of acceptable behaviour, society is assumed to have both the willingness and the ability to punish at least those officials of the state who are susceptible to electoral retribution. This single feature of democratic systems is assumed to be a sufficiently powerful deterrent to constrain elected officials and, because of hierarchical relationships between the elected leadership and the bureaucracy, their civil servants. In this, a modified statist paradigm conforms to a Burkeian view of representative democracy, in which elected officials are entrusted with the autonomy to make policy on the understanding that there is periodic accountability to the electorate.

In other words, such a view of the impact of domestic sources on foreign policy holds that, the orthodoxy of domestication notwithstanding, the state enjoys (to borrow a phrase) relative autonomy *vis-à-vis* civil society. Only at the outer limits of a broad band of acceptable behaviour will the state's actions not diverge from societal preferences.

Conclusions

This paper has argued that despite the claims that are made about the domestication of Canadian foreign policy, and despite the dominance of a liberal ideology in Canada, the external behaviour of the Canadian state is assumed by many scholars to be more autonomous of civil society than either liberal or marxian theories of the democratic state would suggest.

Canada's secretary of state for external affairs, Allan MacEachen, was reported to have said at the height of the cruise testing controversy in December 1982 that the 'growing public pressure against the tests has no bearing on the Government's thinking.'[46] 'I find the implications of that statement,' Margaret Laurence wrote, 'very chilling indeed.'[47] Laurence was clearly referring to the normative implications of MacEachen's statement and the government's subsequent behaviour on the cruise missile issue. It might be noted, however, that the cruise missile controversy also holds important implications for the contending empirical theories of the impact of domestic sources of foreign policy in a democratic system.

Notes

1. In this paper, the definition of the state follows Eric A. Nordlinger: 'all those individuals who occupy offices that authorize them, and them alone, to make and apply decisions that are binding upon any and all segments of society . . . [This definition] differentiates between public officials and public employees—those individuals who hold publicly funded positions that do not involve them in authoritative decisions.' (All other individuals, including employees of the state, comprise civil society.) Nordlinger, *On the Autonomy of the Democratic State* (Cambridge, MA: Harvard University Press, 1981), 11.

2. The classic formulations of pluralist theory are: Robert A. Dahl, *Who Governs* (New Haven, CT: Yale University Press, 1961); David B. Truman, *The Governmental Process: Political Interests and Public Opinion* (New York: Knopf, 1951); see also the discussion in Nordlinger, *Autonomy of the Democratic State*, 151–7; Stephen D. Krasner, *Defending the National Interest: Raw Materials Investments and US Foreign Policy* (Princeton: Princeton University Press, 1978), 26–30.

3. Nordlinger, *Autonomy of the Democratic State*, 158.

4. Theodore J. Lowi, *The End of Liberalism: Ideology, Policy and the Crisis of Public Authority* (New York: Norton, 1969).

5. J.J. Richardson and A.G. Jordan, *Governing under Pressure: The Policy Process in a Post-Parliamentary System* (Oxford: Martin Robertson, 1979).

6. For a recent discussion of different approaches which concludes by eschewing the search for a general theory, see Bob Jessop, *The Capitalist State: Marxist Theories and Methods* (New York: New York University Press, 1982); see also John Holloway and Sol Picciotto, eds, *State and Capital: A Marxist Debate* (London: Edward Arnold, 1978), especially the introduction.

7. See Ralph Miliband, *The State in Capitalist Society* (New York: Basic Books, 1969) for an exposition of instrumentalism.

8. Leo Panitch, 'The Role and Nature of the Canadian State', in Panitch, ed., *The Canadian State: Political Economy and Political Power* (Toronto: University of Toronto Press, 1977), 4; emphasis in original.

9. Nicos Poulantzas, *Classes in Contemporary*

Capitalism (London: New Left Books, 1975); also, Jessop, *Capitalist State*, 153–91.

10. Nordlinger, *Autonomy of the Democratic State*, 120.

11. The following discussion is drawn from three key proponents of statist theory. Stephen Krasner posited a statist approach in *Defending the National Interest* (Chapters 1 and 9). A superior statement of theory, more extended and more carefully drawn out, is presented in Nordlinger, *Autonomy of the Democratic State*. See also Theda Skocpol, *States and Social Revolutions* (New York: Cambridge University Press, 1979), which takes the marxian proposition of the relative autonomy of the state further in an examination of how, at the time of the French, Russian, and Chinese revolutions, these states pursued policies quite at variance with the interests of the dominant classes. One of the limitations of her analysis, however, is that none of her examples had a democratic form.

12. There is, as I will argue, a congruence between the statist approach and the governmental, or bureaucratic, politics paradigm espoused by such analysts as Graham T. Allison (see his *Essence of Decision: Explaining the Cuban Missile Crisis* [Boston: Little Brown, 1971], chapter 5). For Nordlinger's view, see *Autonomy of the Democratic State*, 49.

13. In the work of statists like Nordlinger, the dichotomy between statism and the societal-constraint models is perforce starkly drawn in an either/or fashion, with autonomy assumed to be an absolute condition: either the state is autonomous, or it is not. Anything less than autonomy ipso facto becomes constraint. Thus, for pure statists, notions of the 'relative autonomy' of the state are held to be miscast, for the state can no more be relatively autonomous than a woman can be relatively pregnant.

14. Canada, Department External Affairs, Statements and Speeches 79/6, 5 March 1979, 4.

15. *Foreign Policy for Canadians* (Ottawa: Information Canada, 1970), booklet 1.

16. Statements and Speeches 79/11, 15 February 1979, 7.

17. Alan [*sic*] E. Gotlieb et Léonard H. Legault, 'Droit et diplomatie: nouvelles frontières du Canada',

Politique internationale 12 (Été 1981), 282.

18. Statements and Speeches 79/22, 30 October 1979, 1–2.

19. *Globe and Mail*, 23 August 1983, 8.

20. Michael Tucker, *Canadian Foreign Policy: Contemporary Issues and Themes* (Toronto: McGraw-Hill Ryerson, 1980), 41.

21. Denis Stairs, 'Public Opinion and External Affairs: Reflections on the Domestication of Canadian Foreign Policy', *International Journal* 33, 1 (Winter 1977–8): 149.

22. Cranford Pratt, 'Canadian Foreign Policy: Bias to Business', *International Perspectives* (November/December 1982): 3.

23. See David B. Dewitt and John Kirton, *Canada as a Principal Power* (Toronto: John Wiley & Sons, 1983), table 1.1, 20; also 193.

24. The fifteen essays in Panitch, ed, *Canadian State*, are indicative of this activity; however, it is telling that no essay on foreign policy was included in this collection.

25. Wallace Clement, *Continental Corporate Power: Economic Linkages between Canada and the United States* (Toronto: McClelland and Stewart, 1977); Kari Levitt, *Silent Surrender: The Multinational Corporation in Canada* (Toronto: Macmillan, 1970); Harley D. Dickinson, 'Canadian Foreign Aid', in John Allan Fry, ed., *Economy, Class and Social Reality* (Toronto: Butterworths, 1979), 97–119; Glen Williams, *Not For Export: Towards a Political Economy of Canada's Arrested Industrialization* (Toronto: McClelland and Stewart, 1983); Linda Freeman, 'The Political Economy of Canada's Foreign Aid Programme', Paper presented to the Canadian Political Science Association, Montreal, June 1980.

26. There are notable exceptions: see John W. Warnock, *Partner to Behemoth: The Military Policy of a Satellite Canada* (Toronto: New Press, 1970); similarly, Cranford Pratt employs what he terms a 'dominant class' approach. See 'Bias to Business' and 'Canadian Policy towards the Third World: The Search for a Paradigm', University of Toronto Development Studies Programme, working paper A.2, March 1983.

27. The 'peripheral-dependence' model is outlined in

Dewitt and Kirton, *Canada as a Principal Power*, 28–36.

28. Freeman, 'Political Economy of Canada's Foreign Aid Programme', 3.

29. The literature in this mode ranges from a crude caricature of the Canadian government as an agent of United States imperialism (see some of the articles in Ian Lumsden, ed., *Close the 49th Parallel Etc.: The Americanization of Canada* [Toronto: University of Toronto Press, 1970]) to careful and thoughtful analyses of the Canadian–American relationship (indicative would be the essays in Andrew Axline et al., eds, *Continental Community?: Independence and Integration in North* America [Toronto: McClelland and Stewart, 1974]). For a useful critique of the different approaches, see John H. Redekop, 'A Reinterpretation of Canadian–American Relations', *Canadian Journal of Political Science* 9, 2 (June 1976): 227–34.

30. For example, Tareq Y. Ismael argues that Canada's postwar mid-East policies have been largely fashioned by domestic actors, notably the Jewish community in Canada: 'Canada and the Middle East', in Peyton V. Lyon and Tareq Y. Ismael, eds, *Canada and the Third World* (Toronto: Macmillan, 1976), esp. 266–9. See also Stephen Greene and Thomas Keating, 'Domestic actors and Canada–United States fisheries relations', *Canadian Journal of Political Science* 13, 4 (December 1980), 731–50.

31. Tucker, *Canadian Foreign Policy*, 30–15; Donald Barry, 'Interest Groups and the Foreign Policy Process', in A. Paul Pross, ed., *Pressure Group Behaviour in Canadian Politics* (Toronto: McGraw-Hill Ryerson, 1975), 117–47; Robert O. Matthews, 'The Churches and Foreign Policy, *International Perspectives* (January/February 1983): 18–21; Denis Stairs, *The Diplomacy of Constraint: Canada, the Korean War, and the United States* (Toronto: University of Toronto Press, 1971), 326–9; Stairs, 'Publics and Policy-makers: The Domestic Environment of the Foreign Policy Community', *International Journal* 26, 1 (Winter 1970–1): 221–48.

32. Michael M. Atkinson and Kim Richard Nossal, 'Bureaucratic Politics and the New Fighter Aircraft Decisions', *Canadian Public Administration* 24, 4

(Winter 1981): 531–62; Tucker, *Canadian Foreign Policy*, 60–72.

33. Dewitt and Kirton, *Canada as a Principal Power*, 197–8 and fn 4.

34. Ibid., 168–9.

35. C.P. Stacey, *Canada and the Age of Conflict: A History of Canadian External Policies, I: 1867–1921* (Toronto: Macmillan of Canada, 1977), and *II: 1921–1948* (Toronto: University of Toronto Press, 1981); John W. Holmes, *The Shaping of Peace: Canada and the Search for World Order, 1943–1957* (2 vols; Toronto: University of Toronto Press, 1979, 1982); James Eayrs, *In Defence of Canada* (5 vols; Toronto: University of Toronto Press, 1964–83).

36. James Eayrs makes his assumptions explicit: 'Since statesmen stress determinism, historians by stressing free will may bring their assessment back in balance. That is why this study . . . is introduced by a discussion not of the political culture or the Precambrian Shield—important as such factors are—but of some leading personalities and the policies they espoused.' *In Defence of Canada, III: Peacemaking and Deterrence* (Toronto: University of Toronto Press, 1974), 4.

37. For example, the government's campaign in the late 1940s to secure approval for a peacetime alliance is a good example of this: see ibid. *IV: Growing Up Allied* (Toronto: University of Toronto Press, 1980), 51–62.

38. See Franklyn Griffiths, 'Opening up the policy process', in Stephen Clarkson, ed. *An Independent Foreign Policy for Canada?* (Toronto: McClelland and Stewart, 1968), 110–18.

39. 'Domestication of Canadian Foreign Policy', 130–8. It should be noted that Stairs orders these categories differently.

40. For a statist interpretation of how the state uses co-option to enhance its autonomy, see Nordlinger, *Autonomy of the Democratic State*, 118–43.

41. De Montigny Marchand, 'Foreign Policy and Public Interest', *International Perspectives* (July/August 1983): 9.

42. For a discussion of the media, see Dewitt and Kirton, *Canada as a Principal Power*, 180–1; Denis Stairs, 'The Press and Foreign Policy in Canada',

International Journal 33, 2 (Spring 1976): 223–43.

43. Stairs, 'Domestication of Canadian Foreign Policy', 131, fn 6.

44. Ibid.

45. Three examples, drawn from different eras in Canada's history, demonstrate the improbability that a course of action falling outside these parameters will enjoy unanimous support within the state apparatus, One could argue that there were putative societal preferences for Canadian involvement in the Boer War in 1899, and in the Second World War in 1939, and for continued participation in the North Atlantic Treaty Organization (NATO) in 1969. Sir Wilfrid Laurier's disposition not to send Canadian troops to fight for the British cause was met with substantial and immediate resistance within his cabinet; the disposition of O.D. Skelton, Mackenzie King's under-secretary of state for external affairs, to have Canada remain neutral in September 1939 was dismissed by the prime minister; and the disposition of key members of the Trudeau government to revise substantially Canada's commitment to NATO enjoyed anything but unanimous support within the state.

46. *Globe and Mail*, 10 December 1982.

47. Margaret Laurence, 'Foreword', in Ernie Regehr and Simon Rosenblum, eds, *Canada and the Nuclear Arms Race* (Toronto: James Lorimer, 1983), xii.

10

Dominant Class Theory and Canadian Foreign Policy: The Case of the Counter-Consensus

Cranford Pratt

Paul Pross, a leading student of Canadian pressure groups, has written that 'the real problem in the study of Canadian pressure groups lies not in the paucity of the literature, but in the poverty of its analytical approach.'[1] Others, perhaps seeking to make the same point, have spoken of the need to develop an appropriate theoretical framework for the study of the relationship between society and the state. This is argued from both the left and the right.[2] Their point is surely correct. Almost all social scientists, whether knowingly or not, work within established theoretical approaches, which set their basic assumptions and indicate what are the important questions and the key relationships to study. Often this choice of an approach is implicit and unexamined, determined by inclination, interest, ideology, and temperament. It is better that this choice be the product of reflection and openly articulated.

This essay attempts to take this injunction seriously. It will compare the explanatory power in regard to the domestic determinants of foreign policy of the two main theoretical approaches to the study of the national determinants of government policies in Canada. The first of these approaches is statist theory which assumes that in the formation of government policy the state has

a wide measure of autonomy from the society and that therefore the main national determinants of policy are likely to be internal to the government decision-making process; the second approach, dominant class theory, also assumes significant state autonomy but sees the state as heavily influenced by structural and class factors in ways that will favour capitalism in Canada and as especially attentive to the interests of the dominant class and its attitudes and values. My conclusion is that a dominant class theory is the more powerful, the more suggestive, and the more illuminating of these two theories.

To develop this argument, I will not only offer a general comparison of these two theories but I will as well 'test' each of them by asking how it would serve as a theoretical framework for the study of an interesting new phenomenon in Canadian public life: the counter-consensus. In recent years there has emerged in Canada a substantial number of internationally minded public interest groups which are in serious opposition to many components of the present consensus which underlies Canadian foreign policy. These anti-consensus groups are an interesting and important development in Canadian public life. While in no way marginal to Canadian society, they are certainly peripheral to decision-making in Canadian public life and have very little impact upon it. Statist theory and dominant class theory suggest quite different explanations of this fact, each having different implications as well for the work of these groups. Because class is not directly relevant to the positions they advocate, the anti-consensus groups provide a particularly appropriate case study for an essay that argues that dominant class theory is superior to statist theory.

The argument will be developed in three sections: first, a comparative assessment of the application of statist and dominant class theories to the domestic determinants of Canadian foreign policy; second, a description of the counter-consensus; and third, a consideration of the comparative utility of these two theories for the study of the counter-consensus.

Theoretical Approaches to the Study of the Domestic Determinants of Foreign Policy

The most fundamental distinction within the literature that seeks to explain foreign policy is between explanations which emphasize international factors and those which are concerned with internal factors. This difference is so central and has such ramifications that it is legitimate to attach that overworked word, paradigm, to these two basically different theoretical approaches. Yet foreign policy has in fact both international and national determinants. Neither of the two paradigms is therefore exhaustive: each represents a different primary focus or interest, a different judgment about what is significant. In addition to this distinction, one can discern different theoretical streams in each paradigm. These may be subdivided according to whether or not they assume that the state enjoys a fair measure of autonomy vis-à-vis societal forces in the identification and pursuit of its foreign policy objectives. Each of these four groups, in turn, has right and left variants. These various approaches to the study of Canadian foreign policy are summarized in Table 10.1. In some cases they represent actual major schools of writing on Canadian policy and in others theoretical approaches to the study of state-society relations that have not been used as yet to any significant degree in regard to foreign policy.

There are four approaches within paradigm A, the international paradigm. The *liberal internationalist* approach assumes that Canadian foreign policy can best be understood if Canada is seen as a middle power which seeks to contribute to international peace and stability by advocating and supporting an increasing institutionalization of international relations in ways that would ensure a major role for Canada.[3] The *radical nationalist* approach is marked by the conviction that. Canada has failed to follow a foreign policy sufficiently independent of the United States and

Table 10.1   Approaches to the Study of the Determinants of Canadian Foreign Policy

	Paradigm A Primary concern with international factors	Paradigm B Primary concern with internal factors
High levels of state autonomy	(1) Liberal internationalist (2) Radical nationalist (3) International realist	(5) Statist (6) Dominant class/Structuralist
Low levels of state autonomy	(4) Dependency (left and right)	(7) Pluralist (8) Dominant class/Instrumentalist

looks to an upsurge of populist nationalism to overcome the determinants that have so far shaped policy.[4] The *international realist* approach views each state as seeking to maximize its security, its advantages, and its ability to influence within a largely anarchic international system. The *dependency* approach sees Canadian polices as heavily influenced by Canada's economic, cultural, and military dependence upon the United Stales but, unlike the radical nationalist approach, does not see this dependence as likely to be overcome by political nationalism.[5] A right variation of this, clearly identifiable amongst economists, acknowledges many of these same factors but does not see them as threatening.[6]

These four approaches are each important within the literature on Canadian foreign policy. Nevertheless, and not surprisingly, none of them provides a reasonable framework for the study of the domestic determinants of foreign policy. Their basic preoccupation is with determinants that are international and systemic rather than with societal and governmental factors. They offer no hypotheses about the role of domestic determinants in foreign policy except the obvious one, by implication, that international influences are the more significant.

In contrast to the approaches of paradigm A, those within paradigm B are precisely about the internal influences upon foreign policy. These four approaches are in effect rival theoretical answers to a common question: 'How can one best conceptualize theoretically the interaction of government and society in the making of Canadian foreign policy?'

Statist approaches assume that the bureaucracy has a significant autonomy in determining government policy. They therefore concentrate upon the dynamics of the decision-making process within the government, explaining policies as a product of intra-government bargaining and discussion. For the statist, the state plays a major initiating role, identifying desirable policies through its own internal procedures, promoting support for these policies, and then executing them.

Frequently, these policies are presented as representing the national interest. This approach is often presented in contradistinction to the pluralist approach.

The *dominant class/structuralist* approach is an application to the study of foreign policy determinants of an influential body of writing on the state which has developed in the last decade.[7] Its most central proposition is that the capital-owning class in any capitalist state is the dominant class and that the policies of the state reflect and perpetuate that dominance. Of the two major variants of this approach, the dominant class/structuralist approach concedes to the state an important relative autonomy from the dominant class. It thus has much in common with the statist approach: both see the state as having a significant autonomy which enables it to pursue ends which it determines itself. However, in explaining what constitutes the heart and substance of these ends, dominant class theorists suggest that any contemporary capitalist state will, for compelling structural reasons, seek to maintain its unity and to ensure the reproduction of its conditions of production. It 'must' do this for otherwise it will disintegrate as a capitalist state. The autonomy of the state can thus be counted upon to be exercised in ways to meet these structural necessities.

This autonomy, which extends to autonomy even from the major fractions of the dominant class, is seen in this theory to be essential to the management of a contemporary capitalist state. One or more fractions of the capitalist class, if not constrained, might very well so push the pursuit of its specific interests that the stability of the whole system is jeopardized. Only a strong government enjoying a relative autonomy will be able to control the intra- and inter-class struggles and thereby to manage the politics and economy of a modern capitalist state to the permanent long-term advantage of capitalism. This hypothesis is not contradicted by evidence of severe disagreement between the state and major fractions of the dominant class. That might only illustrate the dominant class reasserting its authority over a wilful state or, alternatively, an unresolved struggle between major fractions of the dominant class. Only if the state persisted successfully with policies that undermined capitalism, and were so intended, would it unavoidably constitute a serious challenge to the theory.

A final component of this approach is the important role it provides for ideology. A capitalist state, and particularly a democratic one, will be far more stable if the distribution of property and the ownership of capital are largely unquestioned. The acceptance of a dominant ideology that provides a rationale for the private and severely unequal ownership of capital is clearly an enormous asset to a capitalist state; it thereby legitimates what would otherwise be likely to divide the society deeply.

While a dominant class/structuralist approach has not yet been much used in the study of Canadian foreign policy, its implications are clear. It would expect foreign policy to reflect the central preoccupation with stability and the preservation and advancement of capitalism that it identifies generally as the state's role in a capitalist society.

Pluralist theories of a democratic state start from the multitude of structures which citizens have created in pursuit of their interests. These groups are many, their memberships overlap, and their purposes are cross-cutting. Through these groups, every bit as much as through political parties, individuals express their needs politically. Effective democracy therefore requires constant mediation between these groups so that there will be a working consensus about the major issues of public policy, which will be acceptable to a substantial portion of the population. Political parties, of course, play a major role in this process, but their integrating and mediating work must be supplemented by extensive interaction between interest groups and government officials. Thus, active interest groups are functionally necessary to modern democracy. A pluralist theory of the determinants of foreign policy would therefore focus primarily on the inputs to policy-making from the plural society and on how these are then melded into policies acceptable to that society.

The *dominant class/instrumental* approach views those exercising power in the state as a section of the dominant class.[8] The intimacy of their links with the property-owning class and the corporate sector and the great influence wielded by the latter provide this approach with its main explanation for the bias of policy towards the interests of the dominant class. The main determinant of Canadian foreign policy for this school would be societal, as is also true for the pluralists. However, in this instance one class, the capitalist class is seen to have largely absorbed the bureaucracy and to use its wealth and power to influence policy-making greatly to its own advantage. Thus a dominant class/instrumental theory offers a critical, left perspective to an approach which, like pluralism, locates the key actors and initiators in society itself rather than within the machinery of the state.

In deciding which of these theoretical approaches is more appropriate for studies relating to domestic influences on foreign policy, most scholars are likely to ask questions along these lines:

1. Which approach is most applicable to the specific policies to be studied and most suggestive and illuminating about them?
2. Which has the broader explanatory power?
3. Which is the more persuasive, that is, which offers explanations that do not sound fanciful but are congruent with one's own understanding of the processes involved and thus convincing?
4. Which is adequately parsimonious, that is, which offers a broad explanatory hypothesis that illuminates relationships and suggests linkages that had been concealed by the very density and complexity of reality?

When one applies these or similar tests to choosing a theoretical approach for the study of domestic determinants of foreign policy, one must discard pluralist theory. Pluralist theory provides an inflated perception of the importance of interest groups. It is now conventional but valid wisdom to point out that government typically does far more than merely mediate between the various pressures and demands emanating from society. It takes many more policy initiatives and is far more manipulative of public opinion than pluralist theory allows. This is true in most fields of policy. It is especially true in regard to foreign policy.

Nor does pluralist theory do justice to the hard fact that the interest groups which are effective in Canadian society are in fact not widely representative. Instead, the interest groups from one sector—the corporate sector—are by far the most influential. These interest groups have an intimacy of access, an acceptability, and an influence in policy-making circles which representatives of the poor and the working class never achieve. Few pluralists deny this fact. However they struggle to diminish its significance. Robert Presthus, for example, acknowledges it explicitly.[9] Nevertheless, for him the value to society as a whole of the accommodation that is accomplished by elites is not undermined by the fact that many interest groups are left out of the process. His references to this bias within the system are few and brief and nearly always diminishing of its importance. For example:

> The perhaps inevitable inequalities in political resources among interest groups mean that the government, to some extent, is pushed into the anomalous position of defending the strong against the weak. While the government elite plays an equilibrating role in welfare areas, much of its energy is also spent reinforcing the security and growth of interests that already enjoy the largest shares of the net social product. Here again, the fundamental problem is the unequal distribution of political resources that characterizes all societies.[10]

This is a revealing passage. Presthus' theory leads him to focus upon elite accommodation. Thus even while he acknowledges the class bias of the system, the bias is not seen as at all central. It reflects a maldistribution of political resources that is perhaps universal. It may be regrettable, but it is probably unavoidable. It is therefore briefly acknowledged and subsequently ignored.

For the reasons I have outlined, pluralist theory has little explanatory power and is not persuasive. It provides an ideologically attractive way to view the operation of constitutional democracy, but it conflicts too markedly with widely acknowledged features of such a political system to be useful. The crucial choice of theoretical approaches for our purposes therefore is between statist theory and dominant class theory,[11] and the balance of this essay is concerned with this choice.

A COMPARISON OF STATIST THEORY AND DOMINANT CLASS THEORY

Statist theory has a number of attractive advantages as a theoretical framework for the study of the internal determinants of Canadian foreign policy. It provides a truer portrait of the power and role of the bureaucracy than does pluralist theory and therefore possesses a basic verisimilitude. Its emphasis on the decision-making processes within the public service has been very productive of fresh research. Empirical studies conducted under its influence have revealed the crucial importance of quite specific bureaucratic concerns to many major policy decisions. A further important feature of this approach is that it combines effectively with an international realist theory. International realists, as was argued above, are primarily concerned to identify the international determinants of foreign policy. However they are likely as well to wish to explain how these international factors actually influence policy. A statist theory can therefore be a natural companion to an international realist theory. The latter hypothesizes how changes in the international system will call forth foreign policy changes, and the former provides an approach to the internal determinants of foreign policy which can be used to explain how the international systemic determinants are actually translated into concrete policies.

A recent work on Canada's foreign policy, *Canada as a Principal Power*, provides an illustration of this approach. A major concern of the authors, David Dewitt and John Kirton, is to explain the shift in the 1970s from a Canadian foreign policy reflecting liberal internationalism to a more narrowly self-serving one. They find their explanation in the decline of United States hegemony within the Western world. They argue that for as long as that hegemony was unquestionable, Canadian policy sought to protect Canadian influence in Washington and to internationalize the handling of major world issues in order, inter alia, to increase Canada's international role. Since the late 1960s, however, the United States has had to share that dominance with a limited number of 'principal powers' that can no longer be fully overshadowed by the United States. These powers now have an opportunity to order the international system in ways that will maximize the advantages to them. Thus, the relative decline of United States power *vis-à-vis* that of the West European states and Japan provided the opportunity, and growing economic strength the capacity, for Canada to move toward its more complex, more self-centred, more bilaterally structured foreign policy of the late 1970s and early 1980s.

Kirton and Dewitt are also concerned with how foreign policy decision-makers accomplished this change. International systemic changes open up opportunities for policy change, but the decision to make these changes must somehow arise from within the state's processes. For Dewitt and Kirton, the bureaucratic decision-makers are the key actors who decide whether and how a state decides to respond to the shifts in the distribution of power within the international system. It is this linking of the intellectual concerns of the international realist and those of the student of bureaucratic politics which gives the book its breadth and its power. For Kirton and Dewitt, shifts in the international distribution of power provided Canada with the opportunity to increase national advantage through important changes in its for-

eign policy. The senior bureaucracy of the foreign service, because it is professionally competent, recognized this opportunity and initiated a restructuring of the decision-making process which produced the policy changes appropriate to the changed international environment.

Dewitt and Kirton thus provide a theoretical framework that is very ambitious in the range of the phenomena it seeks to explain. In their effort to develop a theory that will straddle both international systemic and governmental factors, however, they lose in persuasiveness what they gain in coverage. Intriguing as is their argument, it is for this reader at least finally unconvincing. Their attempt to move from international systemic changes, through bureaucratic organizational development, to policy outcome is too mechanistic to be persuasive. They largely omit classes, political parties, interest groups, the media, and public opinion save as phenomena that the bureaucracy has to manage and to manipulate. They deal only awkwardly with Parliament, cabinet, and prime minister, for despite their formal supremacy over the bureaucracy, these institutions are seen as yielding the central role in policy-making to the bureaucracy. Because of this excessive depoliticization of their analysis of the determinants of policy, the policy outcomes they study do not seem to me to have been adequately explained. The policy changes are not deducible from the systemic changes alone.[12] An explanation of these policy consequences requires as well a detailed analysis of domestic determinants.

Perhaps a specific example may clarify this criticism of the Kirton and Dewitt analysis. It is convincing to argue, as they do, that the decline in United States hegemony has affected what Canada can accomplish internationally. It is not convincing to argue, as they also do, that the decline in liberal internationalist policies and the rise of a more assertive narrow economic nationalism in Canada are a consequence of this international systemic change. There does not seem to be any good reason why, if it so wished, Canada could not use for liberal internationalist objectives any increased influence which it has as a consequence of international systemic changes. The explanation of why it has not done so must be sought in significant part in the operation of domestic determinants. Dewitt and Kirton do not totally ignore this domestic factor, but they deal with it only in the most general and briefest fashion. Their theory leads them astray by suggesting that international systemic and bureaucratic factors are by far the most important influences.

Two features of statist theory explain this failure to provide an adequate theory of the internal determinants of foreign policy. The first is the absence of any detailed analysis of the relationship between the bureaucracy and society. Statists accept that interests and values influence the bureaucracy's choice of policy objectives, but they lack a developed theory of the determinants of the interests and values which shape the decisions taken by the bureaucracy. This is an important weakness. It greatly lessens the utility of statist theory as a framework for the study of the determinants of foreign policy.

The force of this criticism can also be illustrated from Dewitt and Kirton's *Canada as a Principal Power*. They analyze in great detail the changes in the decision-making procedures which were introduced in the late 1970s to permit the senior bureaucracy to take advantage of the new Opportunities for Canada which became available as a consequence of shifts of power in the international system. They analyze hardly at all the determinants of what the senior bureaucrats do with the increased capacity to influence international affairs which, in their view, Canada has gained. Nevertheless, one can put together from their occasional references a coherent picture of the assumptions which they appear to be making. In their view the bureaucrats will (or at least should?) seek to promote Canada's national interest. That national interest is not the total set of Canadian policies. It is rather a set of premises, perceptions, and policy-relevant priorities that is desirable, comprehensive, inter-related, internally 'prioritized,' and general.[13] Their definition of the

national interest is very similar to that of Stephen Krasner for whom government policies which relate to general societal goals, persist over time, and are given a consistent ranking of importance constitute the national interest.[14]

Kirton and Dewitt define the national interest to embrace both interests and values. The interests and values which are reflected in foreign policy are, however, discussed in only very general terms as a configuration of military, economic, social, and cultural concerns which has evolved historically.[15] These values, they write, 'are general to society and the state and produced by the chief executive group and central co-ordinative structures'; 'interests are primarily the preserve of society, while values reside primarily in the state.'[16] That is the sum total of their reflections on the role of values in the determination of foreign policy. Because the important questions for them are the international systemic and bureaucratic political ones, Dewitt and Kirton make the enormous assumption, without any analysis, that the values which a society projects on the international scene are a configuration of concerns which have evolved historically, which is its national interest, and which the state expresses. This begs many issues which are important to students of state/society relations. How can one assume in a class society that the state will express societal values rather than either dominant class interests or narrow bureaucratic interests? How can one assume that the bureaucracy will provide an accurate and acceptable configuration of societal values?

A second feature of statist theory, which prevents it from providing a suitable framework for analyzing the domestic elements of foreign policy, lies in an intriguing ambivalence in statists' writing about the concept of 'the national interest.' If it is merely a label to be applied to the objectives being pursued by government, it is inappropriate for scholarly purposes for the term implies what such a definition would deny, namely that the policies have a legitimacy which is a consequence of their intrinsic merit. If, however, the 'national interest' is taken to represent a set of superior objectives that desirably should but may not be the goal of government policies, then the concept is unusable for there is no clear test of which policies are in the national interest.

Krasner and, following him, Dewitt and Kirton seek to avoid this unpromising choice by treating the national interest as an empirically discoverable but politically and ethically superior selection of the policies which a government actually pursues. Although they give to the national interest a rather rigorously empirical meaning, in fact they also can be said to endorse the judgment that the policies, which they call the national interest, are in fact in the nation's interests. Kirton and Dewitt never discuss this issue directly. However their references to the national interest as it has been articulated by the bureaucratic process are always uncritical and flattering. For example, they stress the importance to Canada of co-ordinating structures which will integrate and transcend society's inputs, achieving a durable, interrelated, and comprehensive policy.[17] Later they refer to the need for a government to control internal cleavages in order 'to impose a transcending framework of values and priorities.'[18] They suggest that Canada's 'possession of a surplus margin of capability allows for and prompts an effective debate within society about the purposes for which that power should be employed.' They go on to say that 'the stress on national interest and initiative emphasizes the desirability of considering domestic sources' and that 'the result is a highly dispersed and evenly balanced process, in which all types of institutions and those organizations whose strength is based on population, resource, or technological capabilities have substantial impact.'[19] Although they welcome this increase in community activity in regard to foreign policy, they nevertheless herald the achievement of greater bureaucratic control of foreign policy making as 'the culmination of a trend within Ottawa towards an over-arching conception of the national interest.'[20] They thus make the enormous simplifying assumption that

the bureaucracy receives all these inputs from society in an 'evenly balanced process' and produces, through its own structures and at arms length from society, policies which will promote the national interest. It does seem fair to conclude therefore that they attribute to a bureaucratically created foreign policy a superior political and ethical validity.[21] It is thus natural to their viewpoint and consistent with it for them to give to such a policy the value-loaded title, the national interest.

To put this second criticism of statist theory bluntly, the theory goes beyond the argument that the bureaucracy exercises significant autonomy in policy formation to offer as well an ideological rationalization for this very heavy concentration of power in the hands of senior civil servants. We have come to recognize the ideological character of the comforting assumptions of pluralist theory. We need also to recognize the ideological nature of the assumption in statist theory that bureaucratically produced policies represent the national interest.

At first glance, a dominant class theory might also seem to have little to recommend it as a theoretical framework for a study of the domestic determinants of Canadian foreign policy. Certainly a dominant class theory cannot be fully comprehensive. It cannot explain without strain and convoluted argument the full range of foreign policies. (Thus, for example, strategic policies are better analyzed in international realist terms.) Nor can a dominant class theory easily translate into class terms such internal determinants of real importance to foreign policy as ethnicity and nationalism. Finally, in its more doctrinaire variants, dominant class theory tends to view measures that are advantageous to groups outside the dominant class as clever concessions made by that class to legitimize its role. A doctrinaire dominant class theory would seem to rule out the possibility that constitutional democracies, while certainly still having a dominant class, have nevertheless made progress in varying degrees towards achieving integrated societies with shared perceptions of national goals and have in their political institutions the bases for some counterbalancing of the power of the dominant class. The acceptance by subordinate classes of the policies produced in constitutional democracies need not be entirely due to manipulation and false consciousness. A dominant class theory that implies this is the case may thereby augment its claim to universality, but it loses its persuasiveness and begins to appear fanciful.

A non-doctrinaire variant of dominant class theory can take all these points in its stride. Such a variant would be a middle-level theory, which identifies a marked bias in policy towards the interests of the dominant class as an important influence upon much foreign policy. Such a theory need not aspire to be holistic or universal—to claim to offer a comprehensive theory that adequately covers the whole of foreign policy or which encompasses all the domestic determinants of foreign policy. What it thereby loses in universality, it will gain in relevance and persuasiveness.

Such a variant of dominant class theory concentrates on the widely pervasive bias in policy towards the interests of the dominant class. Sometimes this bias operates through the structural constraints identified by the structural theorists and sometimes through the network of linkages identified by the so-called instrumentalist theorists. Through the power which the dominant class has to shape social attitudes and values, its influence extends far beyond those cases where structural determinants of direct dominant class influence can be demonstrated. It can thus claim to be a powerful theory even while abandoning any aspiration to reduce to class terms the whole range of internal factors that influence policy formation. Finally, a dominant class theory of this sort can accommodate within it the view that democratic societies can achieve a measure of shared national objectives through their constitutional processes.[22] While recognizing this possibility, a dominant class theory would nonetheless caution that the dominant class, through its control of the media and of the major political companies, is able substantially to influence decision-making within constitutional democracies.

As a theoretical framework for the study of the internal determinants of foreign policy a non-doctrinaire dominant class theory of the sort here outlined has several important advantages over a statist theory:

1. Although it shares with statist theory the correct identification of the fact that the state enjoys a significant autonomy in the exercise of its authority, dominant class theory does not give to this fact a favourable ideological gloss.

2. It offers a hypothesis, missing from statist theory, about the determinants of the goals and objectives that a bureaucracy will seek to pursue in the exercise of the autonomy conceded by both theories. This is a point of real significance. If in fact the bureaucracy has such autonomy in the formulation of policy, the determinants of the use to which it puts that autonomy are centrally important to any study of the making of foreign policy. Dominant class theory offers hypotheses about these determinants; statist theory does not.

3. It is consistent with the powerful evidence that there is indeed in Canada a dominant class and that this class has an influence within the political system which no other sector of Canadian society enjoys. To find evidence of this dominant class bias, one need but recall the personal and financial links between the corporate sector and the two major political parties, the links between senior civil servants and the corporate sector, and the ideology which is largely shared by the dominant class and the senior bureaucracy.[23]

The argument of this paper now moves to an examination of the comparative value of statist theory and dominant class theory to the study of an important new phenomenon, which is here called the counter-consensus.

The Counter-Consensus

A substantial cluster of groups has emerged in the last fifteen years in Canada which are, on basically humanitarian grounds, in profound opposition to many components of Canadian foreign policy. As well, many institutions that have in the past either supported Canadian foreign policy, or at least avoided criticism of it, have begun to oppose it. A major example of such institutions is, of course, the Canadian churches that have become far more active in these mailers. Expressions of opposition to official policies have not been confined to foreign policy issues, as is illustrated by the recent direct challenge to government economic policies and their underlying ethic by the Social Affairs Commission of the Canadian Conference of Catholic Bishops.[24] Nevertheless, it appears that the groups, including the churches but extending far beyond them, which challenge the security and foreign policies of the government are particularly active.

These groups are not special interest groups that take positions reflecting their own economic interests or ethnic background. Rather they are groups opposed on ethical grounds to important elements of Canadian foreign policy. During the past fifteen years in which these groups have multiplied, they have tended to focus on specific issues. Nuclear disarmament, human rights, international equity, and solidarity with oppressed peoples have been the most frequent themes. However, there has gradually emerged a recognition that they are united in support of a consensus counter to that which currently sustains Canadian foreign policy. This counter-consensus involves a new view of the sources of international tension and how these tensions can be managed and a different sense of Canada's opportunities and responsibilities internationally.

These anti-consensus groups do not, of course, encompass all the public interest groups concerned about or involved in international issues. Many organizations which take an active interest in international issues or are involved in international service activities do not take positions on public issues. This is true, for example, of the Canadian Institute of International Affairs and the Canadian Red Cross. However, many groups have gradually begun to oppose individual Canadian foreign policies on grounds that suggest a fundamentally different reading of Canadian interests and obligations. I think, for example, of Project Ploughshares, the Canadian Council for International Co-operation, Oxfam, the Canadian Catholic Organization for Development and Peace, Ten Days for World Development, the Inter-Church Committee on Human Rights in Latin America, the Taskforce on the Churches and Corporate Responsibility, many of the World Outreach Committees of the Conferences of the United Church, and the myriad of local organizations concerned either with nuclear disarmament or with solidarity with oppressed Third World peoples. The list is a very long one.

Many of these groups were launched and are supported by national institutions, most particularly by the churches. They are thus too respectable and too substantial to be ignored, in particular by a Department of External Affairs and a Liberal government which are heirs of the internationalism of Lester Pearson. Moreover these organizations bring to issues a high level of expertise and detailed knowledge: for example, both the Inter-Church Committee on Human Rights in Latin America and the Taskforce on the Churches and Corporate Responsibility have excellent sources of information through their network of Christian contacts. Their representations to government are, therefore, both well informed and seriously considered.[25] Finally, these groups have persisted in their commitments over a number of years.

Most of these groups regard lobbying government as secondary to their main activities—public education work and consciousness-heightening activities within the community. In any case these groups are coming to the view that their disagreement with the government is sufficiently severe that their lobbying is likely to have little effect.

This judgment is correct. The government has evolved a range of techniques for dealing with these public interest groups which are much more exercises in public relations, in the erosion of dissent, and in the co-option of dissenters than real consultations. These include granting formal interviews with senior officials or a minister, the indirect sponsorship of new 'non-government' organizations whose activities and membership can be influenced more easily than genuine non-government organizations, and consultations with select and unrepresentative groups.[26]

The existence of groups who profoundly disagree with the assumptions on which Canada's current foreign policy is based contrasts with the two decades after the war during which there was markedly little serious dissent over Canadian foreign policy. Then there was a very wide consensus in Canada about its place and its responsibilities in the international arena. That consensus supported an internationally activist role for Canada. It had, in retrospect, severe limitations; above all, for many it was permeated with cold war ideology. But it did see Canada as appropriately and desirably playing a creative mediatory role in international affairs.

The wide consensus supporting Pearsonian internationalism was based upon many shared assumptions, but there were four which were perhaps most basic to the shaping of Canadian policies towards the issues that were later to absorb the attention of the anti-consensus groups. The first of these was that the most serious threat to international peace and global human welfare was international communism and that the strength of the United States was the primary bulwark against its spread. The second assumption was that this threat was often better checked by imaginative development assistance than by increased military aid. Thus, while the Atlantic military alliance was necessary, it was for many not a sufficient answer to the challenge of communism. A third assumption was the belief that poor countries, with initial support from the rich, could advance their economics to the point where their subsequent growth would be self-generated and they would therefore no longer be in need of support. Finally, it was believed that the international economic order and its major institutions operated to the substantial advantage of all participants therein; as a result it could be assumed that no significant injustices or indefensible inequalities were due to international economic relationships. These assumptions provide the underlying unity to such seemingly disparate policies as Canada's membership in the North Atlantic Treaty Organization, its close military and defence production links with the United States, its expanding aid programme, its active role in peace-keeping, and its effective participation in international institutions and in the Commonwealth.

That broad consensus had begun to disintegrate by the middle of the 1960s. It has now almost vanished. Instead there are, I think, three clearly distinguishable sets of attitudes which compete with each other. The first is the Canadian equivalent of the American New Right. It is, in a sense, the narrow nationalist mirror image on the right to the humanitarian internationally minded counter-consensus. It has emerged as a force in Canadian politics much more slowly than in the United States, but it is no longer insignificant. Several of its number were candidates for the leadership of the Progressive Conservative party, and one of its ablest, Sinclair Stevens, has been made the External Affairs critic in Brian Mulroney's shadow cabinet. The Fraser Institute is its intellectual think tank, and Barbara Amiel and C-FAR are its articulate vulgarizers. Its worldview is marked by a virulent anti-communism. It places primary responsibility for the underdevelopment of Third World societies squarely upon the leadership, culture, and social practices of those societies about whose poverty it feels little can be done. Its primary concern in regard to the Third World is to check the spread of communism. To that end military aid to reactionary regimes is likely much more effective than technical or capital assistance for development purposes. This group therefore opposes most foreign aid, favours military assistance to anti-communist military regimes, is unconcerned with the inequities within the international order, and looks uncritically to the United States to sustain the dominance of the Western world.

The second set of basic attitudes prevalent in Canada today is that which is embedded in the new official consensus that supports the foreign policy that has evolved in the last fifteen years. Although this new and narrower consensus is a derivative of Pearsonian internationalism, it has shed much of its predecessor's more liberal traits. Four components of this new official consensus need be identified for the purposes of this paper.

First, there is a continuation of the earlier preoccupation with the perceived threat from international conununism.[27] Second, there is a lingering remnant of Pearsonian internationalism. This is identifiable, for example, in the reaffirmation of a foreign aid target of 0.7 per cent of Canada's gross domestic product it is present as well in Mr Trudeau's recurrent personal initiatives on North–South issues, in Canada's activity at the United Nations Commission on Human Rights, and in recent policy decisions concerning Central American refugees.

However, counterbalancing this element, and indeed overwhelming it, is a particular responsiveness to Canadian corporate interests narrowly conceived.[28] This third component of the new Canadian foreign policy consensus has become by far its most important feature. In 1970, the Trudeau government's paper, *Foreign Policy for Canadians*, identified the pursuit of Canadian economic growth and the promotion of international social justice as two of the six basic objectives of Canadian foreign policy. One obligation of policy-makers, therefore, was to achieve an effective balancing of these two objectives. But even at the time it was clear that Canada was tending to sell short its concern for social justice in its pursuit of economic gain. For example, *Foreign Policy for Canadians* affirmed strongly a revulsion against the systematic practice of racial discrimination in South Africa, but it also com-

mented that there were 'better than normal opportunities for trade and investment' in South Africa. For that reason, Canada's policy towards South Africa was marked even then by a comparatively forthright rhetoric combined with trade and economic policies which strengthened and reinforced the oppressing regime. Since that time, apart from a brief show of concern in December 1977, there has been an erosion of resolve about Canadian policies towards South Africa, a continuing dilution even of the weak measures already taken.[29]

This shift is important. Hostility to oppression and racism, a responsiveness to extreme human needs, and concern for human rights, for democratic institutions, for social justice, for tolerance and inter-community mediation are genuine components of the Canadian political culture. They are, however, not irrevocably entrenched within it. There are counter-tendencies as well in the culture which recurrently threaten their prominence. This is especially true in regard to international issues. Canada has often failed to give expression in its foreign policy to the liberal and humane component of Canadian attitudes and values. That foreign policy should reflect these attitudes and values was indeed acknowledged in *Foreign Policy for Canadians*, and they are reflected in the rhetoric of the government on North–South economic issues and at the United Nations Human Rights Commission. But they have had little effect on policy. Moreover, in recent years, even when a humane policy was articulated, the government quietly drained it of much of its substance. For example, Canadian aid policy in 1975 affirmed that the Canadian International Development Agency (CIDA) would concentrate its aid on projects that would help the poor in the Third World to increase their incomes.[30] In reality, CIDA has not been able to do this because it has never been able to get rid of the requirement that 80 per cent of bilateral Canadian aid must be spent on Canadian goods and services. As long as its aid is tied in this way, Canada cannot get involved in aid projects that would reach the poorest. It cannot, for example, develop the rural projects that would help poor peasants, because such projects would never have a high Canadian import content.[31]

A further example of the narrowing of the focus of Canadian policy to what is immediately advantageous economically is provided by Canadian policy towards arms sales. Canada has long affirmed a forthright policy regarding the international sale of military and strategic goods. Canada will not sell them, we are told, to countries that represent a military threat to itself, to countries engaged in or under immediate threat of hostilities, to countries to which United Nations resolutions forbid the export of arms, and to regimes considered to be wholly repugnant to Canadian values. It is enormously disheartening to those who have moved towards the counter-consensus to discover how that policy has been diluted. In particular, the commitment not to sell arms to regimes under imminent threat of hostilities or to regimes repugnant to Canadian values has been interpreted with depressing narrowness. For example, Canada has sold transport aircraft to the Chilean military junta at the same time as it has voted for resolutions condemning the regime's extreme violations of human rights. More recently, it has been ready to sell transport aircraft to Honduras, a country very close to a state of war with Nicaragua, a country from which American-trained anti-Sandinista rebel forces make major incursions into Nicaragua. Information about such sales is very hard to come by. When the Canadian churches were finally sure of their facts and challenged the government on such sales, the reply was that Canada had been assured by the Honduran government that the aircraft were wanted for transporting relief to refugee camps. The minister was careful not to say that he would monitor this use or that he was satisfied that this was the purpose of the purchase. Later the government announced that the sales would not take place, but gave as the reason that De Havilland had withdrawn the request for permission to make the sale. There was similar

equivocation in regard to the sale of transport aircraft to Chile. These sales to Chile were rendered acceptable to the government by an assurance from the Pinochet regime that the aircraft would be used for scientific work in the Antarctic.[32] As this paper is being written, the Taskforce on the Churches and Corporate Responsibility has ferreted out the information that the government has approved the sale of De Havilland Twin Otter aircraft to Guatemala, ostensibly for the promotion of rural development and without regard to the actual activities of this regime in the rural areas and to the fact that this aircraft may be converted for military purposes. Canada's policy, in reality, is to sell military equipment to almost any government as long as it will promise to use the equipment only for peaceful purposes.

A final illustration of the force of this aspect of the new consensus is that Canada has abandoned any serious effort to play a significant mediating role in the interest of equity and justice in North–South negotiations. When the chips are down, whatever the earlier rhetoric of the prime minister, at the multilateral trade negotiations and the innumerable negotiations for a new international order Canada has pursued minor trade objectives and small national advantages rather than the promotion of equity and justice.

The fourth component in the new and narrower consensus underlying Canadian foreign policy is the near exclusion from it of ethical considerations. There is very little talk now, as there was in *Foreign Policy for Canadians*, of a need to reflect Canada's liberal and humanitarian values in its foreign policy, lest these values atrophy at home. The Economic Council of Canada, a good window on the dominant ideological trends in Canada, views humanitarian concerns almost entirely as the responsibility of individuals. 'Moral arguments', it blandly asserted in 1978, 'seldom constitute sufficient reason for action between states.'[33] The 1979 discussion papers of the Department of External Affairs also reflected this drastic 'privatization' of ethical obligations. Those papers acknowledged humanitarian concerns only to the extent that some sections of the public press them upon government and for that reason they become a factor to be weighed in the policy-making process. The promotion of social justice was not presented as one of the primary objectives of policy, as it had been nine years before in *Foreign Policy for Canadians*. Indeed the 1979 discussion papers carefully suggest that humanitarian 'impulses' (a revealing diminishing choice of words) may in fact be an obstacle to the identification of Canadian interests. To give effective expression to ethical concerns is no longer seen as one of the major objectives of Canadian foreign policy.[34]

In addition to the new right and the narrower official consensus, a third set of basic attitudes towards Canadian foreign policy has emerged. It is this set of altitudes which I call the counter-consensus. It has three core components.[35]

The first and most fundamental characteristic of the counter-consensus is the belief that the ethical obligations of Canadians extend beyond Canada's borders. It represents a breaking out of the national mould in which loyalties and ethics are largely confined by the established consensus. For some this belief grows out of a fundamental ethical universalism. However for many the internationalization of ethical obligations has resulted from their increased awareness of global poverty and oppression and from the links with overseas peoples through trade, travel, and service abroad. It is a commonplace in ethical theory that for most individuals meaningful obligations are operative only between peoples that belong in some sense to a common community. If contact with others is totally lacking, there is for most people an artificiality and thinness to any efforts to establish duties and obligations towards them. However, as links develop between peoples, the awareness of interdependence and common humanity grows and with that there also develops an awareness of new and wider duties and obligations.

As the world has become more interdependent and information more easily available, people know much more of the suffering of others. In consequence a sense is gradually emerging that indeed people do have duties beyond national borders. There is, for example, a growing acknowledgment of a human obligation, despite a numbing concern still for the sanctity of sovereignty, to act internationally against widespread starvation, extrajudicial executions, systematic torture, or extensive detentions without trial. Along with this sensitivity to basic human rights there is the imperative, presented for example by the Brandt Commission, to be far more responsive to what the commission called the obligations of global solidarity.[36] Finally, and at this time most important, are the challenges to official policy-makers which come from the network of peace and disarmament movements. These concerns over disarmament, over basic human rights, and over international equity constitute an upsurge of cosmopolitan values, to follow Stanley Hoffmann's revival of an attractive terminology.[37] This constitutes the first core component of the counter-consensus in Canada.

The second component of the counter-consensus is the conviction that something is profoundly remiss in the ways in which the superpowers seek to maintain their security and thereby to ensure peace. There is a widening rejection of the further accumulation and continuing development of nuclear weapons by the great powers. Whatever sense the nuclear build-up makes to strategists, it makes no sense to these people. They refuse to accept that the world must continue to waste the resources which are now poured into nuclear armament. They also refuse to accept that ways cannot be found to de-fuse the suspicion and fear with which each side views the other, and they seek to undermine the mood of defiant confrontation that marks the superpower relationship. Critics can fairly argue that the peace groups are much divided on the policy consequences of their positions. Yet their 'truth' may still be sound: there may well be something profoundly pathological and eventually disastrous about a culture which persists in the further accumulation of nuclear weapons and which deals with the main international division between the great powers primarily in terms of crude and total confrontation. To recognize a pathological condition, even if one cannot yet prescribe a cure, is nevertheless an advance over indulging in complex ratiocinations for the pathology in which one is locked.

The third component of the counter-consensus is a recognition that poverty in the Third World is significantly augmented by features of the international economic system which benefit the rich and which the rich will not see changed. The counter-consensus thus accepts on grounds of equity an obligation to support significant changes in the international economic order.

Such then are the main features of the counter-consensus—the phenomenon in which this article is interested. What then is the most useful theoretical framework to use in studying it?

Statist Theory, Dominant Class Theory, and the Study of the Counter-Consensus

Earlier in this article I suggested that a modified dominant class theory was a more appropriate theoretical framework than statist theory for the study of the domestic determinants of foreign policy. A comparison of the light shed on the counter-consensus by each of these theories suggests the same conclusion.

As noted earlier, the anti-consensus groups that constitute the counter-consensus have been largely unsuccessful in their efforts to influence government policies on the issues of major concern to them. This section considers how statist theory and dominant class theory would explain this failure and what each explanation implies about how these organizations might increase their influence. It concludes with a comparison of how suggestive each theory is of hypotheses relevant to further research on the counter-consensus.

Statist theory implies that when organized groups fail to have an impact upon government that failure is due to one or more of the following three reasons. First of all, the groups may not have sufficient popular support to compel the attention of the senior bureaucracy. Second, they may have

been ineffective lobbyists. Third, they may be aloof from the historical traditions of their society and therefore less likely to have an impact upon a bureaucracy seeking to articulate a national interest which, in the view of statist theory, is in significant part historically determined. The latter possible reason for the comparative failure of interest groups is clearly irrelevant to many of the anti-consensus groups in Canada as they are integral to the country's historical traditions. Statist theory would therefore have to explain their failure largely in terms of the ways in which they have sought to influence government. Statist theory would, no doubt, also add that the more popular support these groups secure the more likely they will be able to command the attention of government. However, as so many of the interest groups which are successful in their relations with government represent very few people and make no effort to generate popular support, the main implication of statist theory would have to be that the anti-consensus groups could do much to improve their performance with government by following the tried and proven tactics of already successful lobbyists. Thus, for example, they need to cultivate carefully their personal links with senior decision-makers, they need to sustain continuous intensive lobbying in Ottawa, they must define objectives which would entail but marginal shifts in policy, and they must avoid open controversy with government officials.

In contrast, the variant of dominant class theory set out earlier in the article would hypothesize that the counter-consensus, whatever its strength, would be very unlikely to have effective access to decision-makers in Ottawa because it does not represent any important fraction of the dominant class. Moreover, the dominant class theory would suggest that the anti-consensus groups will encounter persistent hostility from the government, to the extent, which is significant, that their concerns run counter to the interests of the dominant class or are hostile to the ideology which that class, the two major political panics, and the senior civil service very largely share. This dominant class theory would nevertheless suggest that the anti-consensus groups may be able from time to time to win acceptance for some liberal and humanitarian policy changes. This possibility is held out by the theory because it allows that in part government policies express shared values within the national community. However the theory implies that these victories will not be numerous because the objectives of the anti-consensus groups run counter to the interests and ideology of the dominant class.

The tactics suggested for the counter-consensus by dominant class theory include lobbying, public education, and consciousness-raising. The primary activities will be the latter two for the main objective must be to make public opinion increasingly sensitive to the values and attitudes which the counter-consensus champions. However, lobbying will also have its role, partly because it has consciousness-heightening and public educational consequences, but also because, from time to time, liberal and humanitarian appeals may strike responsive chords within government.

These expectations of dominant class theory fit the experience of counter-consensus groups more accurately than do those of statist theory. The anti-consensus groups have in fact encountered persistent rejection of their major proposals. They have been received by government in ways much more designed to manage and manipulate the relationship than to create genuine dialogue leading to an increasing responsiveness. Their experience in no way suggests that lobbying after the manner of special interest groups would make any significant difference in their work. The concern of the anti-consensus groups is for more fundamental change. This requires activities primarily directed to the community itself. While it is of course true, as both theories suggest, that a more substantial popular following would augment the influence of the anti-consensus groups, the dominant class theory's perception of a sustained rejection of their viewpoint because it runs counter to the interests of the dominant class does seem a more accurate rendering of their experience to date.[38]

The dominant class theory also passes a further test more successfully than statist theory. It offers more illuminating and more convincing hypotheses about how these anti-consensus groups are likely to develop. It thus is a more useful approach for research. Indeed, as I have suggested, because statist theory does not have any developed ideas about the domestic determinants of foreign policy, it can offer few if any hypotheses relevant to the prospects and potential or the counter-consensus. In marked contrast, the following comments relating to the counter-consensus follow in an unforced fashion from the dominant class theory developed earlier.

1. It provides a realistic theoretical perspective on how the Canadian government and bureaucracy are likely to view anti-consensus groups. This perspective suggests that these groups must anticipate from government hostility, caution, and an arm's-length relationship, in marked contrast to the intimate close relationships which the government has with the corporate sector.[39]

2. It draws attention to the importance of ideology in the formation of government policies, foreign policy included. This is a vastly understudied issue. Yet unquestioned values and unexamined hypotheses about international politics are an important determinant of many major policies.[40] We know very little about how systems of ideas about social causation, historical processes, and social objectives become part of the assumptions on the basis of which social classes or other groups understand their world and determine their objectives. It is in this very area that many of the anti-consensus groups seek to have their impact. A dominant class approach at least encourages the examination of this factor. Moreover it does not rule out the possibility that political and educational activities can initiate a shift in the operating assumptions on which a government

bases its policies. However, our dominant class theory does offer the warning that these assumptions often reflect or are compatible with the interests of the dominant class so that resistance to change is likely to be persistent and strong.

3. It suggests that it will be illuminating to investigate the extent to which the main objectives of the anti-consensus groups run counter to the interests of the dominant class. If that is the case, as in large part it almost certainly is, then this theoretical approach will anticipate that these groups will face many more difficulties than would otherwise be the case. The situation is more complicated in regard to nuclear disarmament and peace objectives. It is true that a strong hostility towards communism is a major feature of the ideology of the dominant class. It is also true that the armament industry itself is an important part of that class. Nevertheless, peace and nuclear disarmament are compatible with many of the most obvious of the economic interests of the dominant class. This suggests that this aspect of the counter-consensus viewpoint may be able to penetrate the thinking of the dominant class with less difficulty than those elements that seem directly to contradict the interests of that class.

4. Approaching a study of the counter-consensus from within the framework of a dominant class theory would underline the importance of the fact that the anti-consensus groups are seeking to shift values and attitudes across all classes. The ideas and the interests of the dominant class constitute important and special barriers to this effort because they are so influential within government. However, there is no reason to expect that it would be much different were a different class to become the dominant class. The anti-consensus groups are engaged in a different effort. They are striving to increase the responsiveness in Canada to values that have long been a component of its political tradition and to have them reflected more vigorously in its foreign policy. They are therefore unlikely to be successful if instead they embraced the view that the dominant class is the primary obstacle to be overcome.

Concluding Remarks

It remains to summarize the argument that has been developed. Dominant class theory, it is argued, offers a more appropriate theoretical approach for the study of the domestic determinants of Canadian foreign policy than does statist theory. This proposition was investigated first in general terms and then with specific reference to the study of the counter-consensus in Canada on foreign policy. In each case a non-doctrinaire dominant class theory was shown to be more persuasive and more illuminating than statist theory. Further evidence that a dominant class theory of this sort is the appropriate framework for the study of the counter-consensus is provided by the fact that structural obstacles, ideological bias, and dominant class interests are already clearly discernible in the government's response to the representations of the anti-consensus groups, and these groups in turn are experiencing their relationship with government and defining their own activities in ways which are more compatible with dominant class theory than with statist theory. Finally, dominant class theory generates more interesting and illuminating hypotheses for further research on the counter-consensus than does statist theory.

Notes

The author wishes to express his appreciation in particular to Professors Janice Stein and Franklyn Griffiths for their insightful comments on an earlier draft of this article.

1. Paul Pross, 'Pressure Groups: Adaptive Instruments of Political Communication', in Pross, ed., *Pressure Group Behaviour in Canadian Politics* (Toronto: McGraw-Hill Ryerson, 1975), 4.

2. Nicos Poulantzas, in his celebrated exchange with Ralph Miliband in the *New Left Review* over ten years ago, argued, inter alia, that Miliband had failed to develop an alternative theoretical framework to that employed by the pluralist theorists whom he was criticizing. Their exchange is reprinted in Robert Blackburn, *Ideology in the Social Sciences* (New York: Vintage Books, 1973). Robert Presthus also emphasizes the need for a comprehensive theory in his *Elite Accommodation in Canadian Politics* (Toronto: Macmillan, 1973).

3. This approach, which dominated the literature on Canadian foreign policy for the twenty-five years after 1945, is summarized perceptively and sympathetically in David Dewitt and John Kirton, *Canada as a Principal Power* (Toronto: John Wiley, 1983), 17–28.

4. In Canadian public life this approach has been represented in particular by the Committee for an Independent Canada. Amongst the most important academic books in this tradition are Stephen Clarkson's *Canada and the Reagan Challenge* (Toronto: James Lorimer, 1983) and John Hutcheson's *Dominance and Dependency: Liberalism and National Policies in the North Atlantic Triangle* (Toronto: McClelland and Stewart, 1978).

5. The seminal book in this tradition has been Kari Levitt's *Silent Surrender: The Multinational Corporation in Canada* (Toronto: Macmillan, 1968). More recently, the most influential is probably Wallace Clement's *Continental Corporate Power: Economic Elite Linkages between Canada and the United States* (Toronto: McClelland and Stewart, 1977).

6. Stephen Clarkson exposes the ideological component in the anti-nationalism of many Canadian economists in his 'Anti-nationalism in Canada: The Ideology of Mainstream Economics', *Canadian Review of Studies in Nationalism* 5 (Spring 1978).

7. Amongst the most influential writings that take this approach to the state are Nicos Poulantzas, *Political Power and Social Classes* (London: New Left Books, 1975), Claus Offe, 'Structuralist Problems of the Capitalist State', in Klaus Von Begme, ed., *German Political Studies* (Beverly Hills: Sage, 1974), and James O'Connor, *The Fiscal Crisis of the State* (New York: St Martin's Press, 1973). The most important example of this approach applied to Canada is Leo Panitch, ed., *The Canadian State: Political Economy and Political Power* (Toronto: University of Toronto Press, 1977).

8. Ralph Miliband is perhaps the best-known and most influential writer who has taken this approach: see his *The State in Capitalist Society* (London: Weidenfeld & Nicolson, 1969). In Canada this approach to the study of state–society relations has been powerfully employed in a number of major studies, including in particular John Porter's *The Vertical Mosaic* (Toronto: University of Toronto Press, 1965) and Wallace Clement, *The Canadian Corporate Elite* (Toronto: Macmillan, 1975).

9. Presthus, *Elite Accommodation in Canadian Politics*, particularly chapter 10.

10. Ibid., 349.

11. This is now a commonplace observation. These are the two approaches in which much interesting work on the state is currently being done. Stephen Krasner, in his *Defending the National Interest: Raw Materials Investments and US Foreign Policy* (Princeton: Princeton University Press, 1978), and Eric Nordlinger, in his *On the Autonomy of the Democratic State* (Cambridge, MA: Harvard University Press, 1981), both see these two approaches as having important elements in common and each see the choice of theoretical approaches as being essentially between them.

12. There is, in their analysis of the policy changes of the last few years, a tendency to accept that because policy changes have accompanied or followed international systemic changes, they therefore illustrate what their theoretical analysis would lead one to expect. Yet it is not clear why 'complex neo-realism', to use their term for their theory, should suggest these policies. Much in the section, 'the era of bilateralism' (*Canada as a Principal Power*, 76–84) suggests to this reader a *post hoc ergo propter hoc* argument.

13. Ibid., 418.

14. Krasner, *Defending the National Interest*, 13.

15. Dewitt and Kirton, *Canada as a Principal Power*, esp. 36–40.

16. Ibid., 418.

17. Ibid., 45.

18. Ibid., 197.

19. Ibid., 45–6.

20. Ibid., 232.

21. So also, I think, does Krasner. That would seem to be the clear implication of his complex argument on pages 44–6 in *Defending the National Interest*.

22. Ralph Miliband, in his *Marxism and Politics* (London: Oxford University Press, 1979) accommodates this recognition quite effectively within a dominant class theory.

23. I develop this argument more fully in my 'Canadian policy towards the Third World: a basis for an understanding', *Review of Political Economy* 13 (1983).

24. *Ethical Reflections on the Economic Crisis* (Ottawa: Episcopal Commission for Social Affairs, Canadian Conference of Catholic Bishops 1983).

25. For a collection of statements by a variety of interchurch structures including the two just named, see the appendices to Robert Matthews and Cranford Pratt, eds, *Church and State: The Christian Churches and Canadian Foreign Policy* (Toronto: Canadian Institute of International Affairs, 1983).

26. I discuss these various ways by which the government manages its relations with public interest groups in my 'Canadian Foreign Policy: Bias to Business', *International Perspectives* (November–December 1982): 3–6.

27. This preoccupation was central in the background papers prepared under the aegis of the Conservative government's secretary of state for external affairs, *Canada in a Changing World: The Global Framework* and *Canada in a Changing World: Canadian Aid Policy*, dated 30 November 1979, eventually printed in Standing Committee on External Affairs and National Defence, *Minutes of Proceedings and Evidence*, 32nd Parl., 1st sess., no. 3, 10 July 1980.

28. I develop this argument in my 'Canadian Policy Towards the Third World: A Basis for an Understanding.'

29. For a full demonstration of this erosion and dilution, see 'Canadian Policy Towards Southern Africa: Brief from the Taskforce on the Churches and Corporate Responsibility', *Canadian Journal of African Studies* 16, 1 (1982) and 'Canadian Policies towards South Africa: An Exchange Between the Secretary of State for External Affairs and the Taskforce on the Churches and Corporate Responsibility', edited and with a commentary by Cranford Pratt, *Canadian Journal of African Studies* 17, 3 (1983).

30. *Strategy for International Development Cooperation, 1975–1980* (Ottawa: Canadian International Development Agency, 1975).

31. For a thorough and depressing appraisal of Canadian aid policies since 1975, see *In the Canadian Interest: Third World Development in the 1980s* (Ottawa: North-South Institute, 1980), 5–18.

32. This whole story is fully documented in the 1982 annual report of the Taskforce on the Churches and Corporate Responsibility.

33. *For a Common Future: A Study of Canada's Relations with the Developing Countries* (Ottawa: Economic Council of Canada, 1978), 31.

34. Readers can reflect upon whether in the last decade Canadian policies regarding unemployment, welfare, land social services have borne out the warning in *Foreign Policy for Canadians*, that values not applied beyond Canadian borders are likely in time to atrophy within Canada.

35. What follows is, unavoidably, my personal effort to distill the core elements in the position of a very wide range of public interest groups. It no doubt needs additional refinement. However I hope it is sufficiently accurate to justify the argument that the counter-consensus is an important and quite radical innovation in Canadian public life.

36. The Brandt Commission, although stressing that rich and poor states had many mutual interests, recognized that little could be accomplished internationally to reform the operation of the international economic order if the rich countries failed

to respond to moral imperatives as well: *North–South: A Programme for Survival* (London: Pan Books, 1980).

37. Stanley Hoffmann, *Duties Beyond Borders* (Syracuse: Syracuse University Press, 1981).

38. An interesting illustration of this is the fact that on two occasions when an earlier version of the argument of this essay was presented to conferences, which included representatives of the churches and other anti-consensus groups, it was strongly supported by them. See the forthcoming summary of the proceedings of the first of these occasions, a conference organized by the Canadian Institute of International Affairs and the Paterson School of International Affairs, held in Ottawa in June 1982, on the subject: Canadian Interest Groups and Canadian Foreign Policy. The proceedings of the second conference have been published as Robert Matthews and Cranford Pratt, eds, *Church and State: The Canadian Churches and Canadian Foreign Policy*.

39. I develop this point at some length in 'Canadian Foreign Policy: Bias to Business', 3–7.

40. As I write this article, I am reminded again of the great force of this point by James Eayrs' superb dissection of the thinking and decision-making of Canadian policy-makers in the mid-1950s in regard to Vietnam. What struck this reader above all was the degree to which Canadian policies were influenced by an unexamined premise that international communism was a monolithic force guided from Moscow and threatening 'the free world' wherever it gained an influence. *In Defence of Canada, Vol. V: Indochina: Roots of Complicity* (Toronto: University of Toronto Press, 1983).

11

Of Legacies and Lightning Bolts: The Prime Minister and Canadian Foreign Policy

Paul Gecelovsky

Introduction

The purpose of this chapter is to examine the role played by the prime minister in the formulation of Canada's foreign policy. Other contributors to this volume have looked at the influence of parliament (English), the provinces (Kukucha), the 'dominant class' (Pratt), and the state (Nossal). What these contributors have, for the most part, overlooked is that the prime minister is the key person in deciding both the direction and the content of Canada's foreign policy. Therefore, the prime minister can override the interests of these other actors and have Canada pursue a foreign policy of his or her liking. In the making of Canada's foreign policy, the prime minister is *primus* without *pares*, to borrow from Donald J. Savoie.[1] To demonstrate that the prime minister has no equal in setting the content and course of Canada's foreign policy, the paper is divided into two parts. The first part examines the powers possessed by the prime minister while the second looks at the constraints within which the prime minister operates. It will be shown that the former outweigh the latter significantly and that, furthermore, the constraints are only constraints if the prime minister allows them to stop him or her

from acting. In short, the powers possessed by the prime minister are decisive.

Powers of the Prime Minister

The prime minister possesses a vast range of powers. This chapter focuses on only those powers possessed that are relevant to the formulation of Canada's foreign policy. The discussion of these powers is divided between those possessed by the office of the prime minister—the role or positional variable—and the extent or degree to which a prime minister seeks to distinguish the international behaviour of his or her government from other administrations—the idiosyncratic variable.[2]

In examining the role or positional variable four main constitutional powers need to be addressed. The first power of office to be discussed concerns the power of appointment. The prime minister has the authority to name persons to various positions within the state including, inter alia, ministers, deputy ministers, ambassadors, and high commissioners. Who ultimately sits in the foreign minister's chair and for how long is, in large part, determined solely by the prime minister. While the department charged with maintaining Canada's foreign relations was created in 1909, it was not until 1946 that the prime minister relinquished the position of Secretary of State for External Affairs (SSEA) to another minister.[3] Louis St-Laurent was coaxed out of retirement by then-Prime Minister William Lyon Mackenzie King to become the first person, other than the prime minister, to hold the external affairs portfolio. It needs to be noted that King believed that in giving up the position of SSEA to St-Laurent, King was jettisoning the mundane chores of departmental administration and management while freeing up time to deal with the more important foreign policy concerns of the state; St-Laurent was to do the housekeeping while King focused on diplomacy. Since the naming of St-Laurent in 1946, successive prime ministers have appointed others to be responsible for the foreign affairs portfolio.

Appointing others to be responsible for Canada's international behaviour does not mean that those holding the office of prime minister were not interested or influential in setting both the tone and course of Canada's foreign policy. It is the prime minister who establishes the parameters within which the foreign minister operates and determines what leeway the occupant of the foreign minister's chair is given. This setting of the boundaries is accomplished through various means including the active involvement of the prime minister in any departmental matter of his or her choosing. The prime minister may discharge what Don Johnston, a former minister in the Trudeau government, has referred to as 'lightning bolts'.[4] That is, the prime minister is able to change the content and direction of Canada's policy at his or her discretion without consultation with a minister, Cabinet, or departmental officials. What the prime minister says is policy. A lightning bolt was fired in late 1997 by then-Prime Minster Chrétien when he decided that Canada would commit forces to help protect those attempting to escape the violence in the Great Lakes region of Africa. Andrew Cooper has argued that Canadian involvement in the region came as a result of Aline Chrétien watching television news

coverage of the atrocities while she and the prime minister were on a weekend getaway at their cottage in Quebec. Also influencing the prime minister's decision to intervene was information obtained from his nephew, Raymond Chrétien, who had served as a United Nation's Special Envoy to the Great Lakes region in 1996 and as Canada's Ambassador to Zaire (with joint accreditation to Rwanda, Burundi, and the Congo) in the late 1970s.[5] The actions of Jean Chrétien demonstrate that it is the prime minister who ultimately decides which issues or crises are important for Canada and how Canada will respond.

Besides direct involvement in foreign policy, the prime minister is also able to establish boundaries by setting the parameters a foreign minister must follow to appoint more senior ministers to the foreign affairs troika. Since 1982, the responsibility for Canada's foreign affairs has fallen to a troika of ministers, including the minister of foreign affairs, the minister of international trade and the minister of international co-operation.[6] Within this triad of ministers, the minister of foreign affairs is usually the most senior, followed by the minister of international trade and, finally, the minister of international cooperation is the most junior. There have been occasions, however, when the prime minister has appointed a more junior parliamentarian to the foreign minister portfolio. This occurred in 1989 when then-Prime Minister Brian Mulroney was dissatisfied with the overly cautious approach to foreign policy exhibited by then-Secretary of State for External Affairs Joe Clark. Mulroney replaced Clark with the more junior Barbara McDougall. Concurrent with this move, Mulroney moved Michael Wilson from finance to international trade, and replaced John Crosbie as Minister for International Trade. Monique Landry maintained her position as the minister responsible for the Canadian International Development Agency, the third member of the triad. With these moves, Wilson assumed the position of lead minister in the foreign affairs troika, not McDougall.[7] The main effect of this cabinet shuffle was that for the remainder of Mulroney's term in office, trade issues dominated Canada's foreign relations and the control over Canada's foreign policy effectively shifted to the prime minister and the Prime Minister's Office (PMO); the foreign minister lacked any real freedom of action.

A third way in which the prime minister outlines the parameters of permissibility for foreign ministers is through the issuing of mandate letters. Mandate letters are given to all ministers upon their being sworn into cabinet and also to those who have been assigned to a new portfolio as a result of a cabinet shuffle. A mandate letter will outline the issues and areas of importance on which the minister is to focus. The letters most often span only two or three pages and are prepared by officials in the Privy Council Office after they have consulted with relevant members of the PMO and the Deputy Minister(s) affected by the change. As Savoie has noted, there are two basic types of mandate letters. The first form of mandate letter is the 'Don't call us, we'll call you' letter which, in effect, tells a minister to do nothing but maintain the status quo and stay out of trouble. The second type of mandate letter outlines the major challenges and the specific objectives the minister is to concern himself or herself with during his or her tenure.[8] The mandate letters effectively set the terms on which the minister is to serve in the appointed position.

A fourth manner in which the prime minister sets the boundaries for the foreign minister is through the appointment of senior civil servants. Since Pierre Trudeau entered office in 1968, prime ministers and their staffs have become increasingly involved in the appointment of senior civil servants at the rank of deputy minister. All deputy minister appointments are vetted by the prime minister and the PMO to determine the applicant's suitability for the position. All deputy ministers are also given mandate letters upon their appointment. This is done, in part, to ensure that the minister and the deputy minister are both working from the same set of priorities and expectations, as determined by the prime minister.

A second constitutional power of the office possessed by the prime minister in addition to the power of appointment and of relevance to our discussion concerns the design of the administrative structures of government. The prime minister is the architect of government, and as such, he or she has the authority to create, redesign, amalgamate, and/or eliminate departments. This power has been used most recently by Prime Minister Paul Martin when, in January 2004, only one month after assuming office, he separated the Department of Foreign Affairs and International Trade into Foreign Affairs Canada (FAC) and International Trade Canada (ITCAN). In this move, Martin undid the 'consolidation and re-organization' initiatives of the Trudeau 1980–3 government; Trudeau's actions had integrated sections of the Departments of Industry, Trade and Commerce, and Employment and Immigration with the Department of External Affairs.[9]

Though it does not hold the same degree of importance as structural changes to administrative departments, the prime minister also has the authority to change the names of government departments. Brian Mulroney exercised this power in June 1989 when he changed the name of the Department of External Affairs, as it had been known since its 1909 creation, to External Affairs and International Trade Canada. Prime Minister Chrétien wasted little time in further changing the name of the department when he renamed it the Department of Foreign Affairs and International Trade on 5 November 1993, only one day after assuming office. Finally, as noted above, Prime Minister Martin changed the name once again to FAC and ITCAN. Concurrent with the changes in the department's name has come a change in the title of the minister's position from secretary of state for external affairs from 1909 to 1993 and, thereafter, minister of foreign affairs.

In addition to the constitutional powers of appointment and the design of administrative structures, the prime minister also has the constitutional authority to mould the processes of decision-making within his or her own administration. This power is demonstrated clearly by a comparison of the decision-making processes instituted by Prime Ministers Trudeau and Mulroney. While a full rendering of these contrasting decision-making styles is beyond the scope of this chapter, it is necessary to highlight some of the key characteristics of each prime minister's approach. When he assumed the role of prime minister in 1968, Trudeau wanted to inject a greater degree of discipline and rationality into the government's decision-making system. He was critical of what he regarded as the 'partisanship' and the 'incremental drift' of the Pearson era.[10] To overcome these problems, Trudeau implemented a series of changes to the committee system. Decisions were to be channelled through a number of committees at various levels of government; they were to be the result of debate and deliberation by numerous persons throughout government. The objective of implementing a more structured and formalized decision-making process was to have decisions made on a more rational basis than had been done previously. Decisions were to flow from the application of reason to the problem at hand to the best possible course of action for Canada under the prevailing conditions. Decisions would not be quick and immediate but rather slow and deliberate.

Conversely, the primary concern for Brian Mulroney was for a 'policy and a process that succeeds', that is, one that would be 'popular with the Canadian public'.[11] Replacing a concern for rationality was the concern for whether or not a decision had 'political appeal'.[12] Mulroney's philosophy of political leadership stressed the 'accommodation of interests' over the Trudeau's concern for an 'interplay of ideas'.[13] Further, Mulroney's background as a labour negotiator meant that he was more comfortable working out solutions to problems on a one-to-one basis with ministers or other heads of state.

The final variable to be addressed concerns the plenipotentiary power possessed by the prime minister. The prime minister has the authority to negotiate and sign international agreements. This power was first put to use in 1923 with the negotiating and signing of the Halibut Treaty with the United States, the bilateral treaty that established fishing for Pacific Halibut would not occur from November to February to help preserve fish stocks. More recently, the authority of the prime minister to negotiate, sign, and ratify treaties that concern those subjects that are within the ambit of provincial authority has been called into question. Decisions of the Supreme Court of Canada have not fully or clearly articulated the extent of the prime minister's authority to act as an agent of the provinces in the international realm.[14] The current state of affairs is that the prime minister may negotiate, sign, and ratify international treaties but he or she cannot force provinces to implement those agreements or be bound by the provisions of the ratified agreements. What the prime minister may do, however, is focus the public's attention on an issue. In other words, the prime minister may put the issue on the agenda of the provinces. A recent example of this concerns Canada's negotiating, signing, and ratifying the Kyoto Protocol. Facing pressure from the provinces, industry, and even some from within his party, then-Prime Minister Chrétien moved forward with the ratification of the Protocol. Chrétien went so far as staking the continuation of his government on the ratification of the legislation in the House of Commons by declaring Kyoto a motion of confidence. In a clear demonstration of the prime ministers plenipotentiary power, the Kyoto Protocol was ratified by Parliament in December 2002 providing what Kathryn Harrison has called a 'triumph' for the prime minister.[15]

Having considered the four constitutional powers of the office of the prime minister relevant to the discussion of foreign policy-making (the power of appointment, to design administrative structures, to design decision-making processes, and plenipotentiary authority), this discussion now moves to analyze the idiosyncratic component of prime ministerial authority. In particular, this section focuses on the prime minister's own predilections—the set of objectives that the prime minister seeks to fulfill during his or her time in power. All prime ministers have a sense of what is to be accomplished during the term in office. They want to leave a legacy for future generations; they want to make a difference. A prime minister, however, cannot do everything that he or she wants to do and so he or she must choose a few main policy objectives on which to focus the resources of the state. This 'strategic prime ministership', as it has been termed by Thomas Axworthy, the former principal secretary to Pierre Trudeau, aids both the prime minister and the PMO in staying on track and in 'saying no to hundreds of other requests' not related to the prime minister's strategic policy agenda.[16] While the prime minister's strategic policy agenda will be primarily shaped by domestic issues, prime ministers usually have a couple of policy priorities that they seek to have met in the area of Canada's foreign policy.

The continuation of the policy of apartheid in South Africa was just such a priority concern for Prime Minister Mulroney. Although the issue of apartheid played an insignificant role in the 1984 election campaign wherein Mulroney and the Progressive Conservative Party captured a majority of seats in the House of Commons, the increasing violence within South Africa in the fall of 1984 brought the issue to Mulroney's attention. The newly elected prime minister, as Kim Richard Nossal has averred, 'demonstrated a visceral and intensely personal anger at the institutionalized racism of apartheid'.[17] This palpable anger was evident in public statements, speeches, and interviews given by Mulroney in this period. The anger was also demonstrated in the use of increasingly punitive measures adopted by the Canadian government, including the possibility of breaking diplomatic relations with South Africa. Mulroney attempted to lead both the Commonwealth and the Group of Seven (G7) in adopting a stronger position towards South Africa. Canadian resources were employed to move the leaders of member states of these organizations to adopt a stricter stance towards South Africa. Mulroney even used his position as chair of the Commonwealth Heads of Government Meeting in Vancouver in 1987 and as host of the G7 Summit in Toronto in 1988 to press these organizations to assume a more censorious position regarding apartheid. The prime minister, however, was 'rebuffed' in his efforts. Fearful of becoming a 'lightweight' and losing 'all capacity for exercising influence in other areas of interest to Canada',[18] Mulroney retreated from his 'gut commitment to fight for stronger measures'[19] to be imposed on South Africa. The end result of Mulroney's efforts, and a significant portion of the foreign policy legacy of his government, is that the policies of his government towards South Africa are believed by many to have worked to bring about an end to the system of apartheid.[20]

For those persons who have had the opportunity to plan their retirement from the prime minister's chair, the ability to focus the resources of the state on a few priority issues has allowed them to better plan their legacies. Prior to his retirement in December 2003, Prime Minister Chrétien used his position as host of the G8 Summit in 2002 'to ensure that African concerns would have their full place' in the discussions.[21] Chrétien's focus on Africa meant that discussions at the Kananaskis Summit would not be overtaken by discussions regarding the 9/11 terrorist attacks on the United States and the debates concerning the proper response to the acts of terrorism and how to quell the terrorist threat. Steven Langdon has noted that it was 'Canadian leadership' that moved the G8 to adopt an Action Plan for Africa at Kananaskis and that Canada's commitments to Africa were 'particularly specific and enthusiastic'.[22] This action by Canada, moreover, was the result of Chrétien's 'deep sense of personal engagement and a strong sense of identification with issues of poverty in Africa'.[23] Knowing that the G8 Summit in Kananaskis was to be his last as host, Chrétien used this occasion to help build a legacy of compassion.

Constraints on a Prime Minister

While the prime minister possesses an array of powers that enable him or her to dominate the policy-making process, there are a number of constraints that may act to inhibit a prime minister from getting his or her way.

The first, and most important, constraint on a prime minister is time. The prime minister's schedule at the best of times is hectic; he or she attends to Cabinet business, Parliament, the legislative calendar, party caucus, party fundraising and other functions, and government and patronage appointments. Added to this list is the amount of time taken up with consultations and meetings with personal staff, the principal secretary, the clerk of the Privy Council Office, individual ministers, provincial premiers, foreign heads of state, and business leaders. On top of this already crowded schedule, the prime minister must make time for constituency matters and for maintaining contact with members of the riding association. A prime minister, then, must be careful with his or her time because there are always issues and people who seek to have 'just a few minutes'. If a prime minister does not prioritize, he or she will soon fall victim to 'political overload', that is 'a pervasive sense of urgency and an accompanying feeling of being overwhelmed both by events and the number of matters needing attention'.[24] To avoid overload, a prime minister needs to be selective with his or her time and focus only on those issues on his or her strategic policy agenda.

In addition to time, there are a number of issues with which all prime ministers have had to be concerned and which operate as constraints on the freedom of manoeuvrability. Donald Smiley has referred to these as the 'enduring axes' of Canadian politics. They are: French–English relations, regionalism, and Canada–US relations. The first two are important because they deal with national unity, always a primary concern for any prime minister. The first, moreover, is a foreign policy concern because Quebec has, since the mid-1960s, pushed for recognition abroad as an independent actor in foreign affairs.[25] In relations with other states of importance to Quebec, especially other French-speaking states, the prime minister will be cognizant of the position of Quebec on the issue(s) at hand—a position most likely at variance with that of the federal government—and the ramifications of the Canadian position on Quebec and on politics within that province.

In terms of Canada–US relations, the bilateral relationship affects all of Canada's international behaviour. This is not to argue that Canada's relationship with the United States determines Canada's foreign policy but rather that the bilateral relationship is an important factor in decision-making. For example, John Holmes argued that it was 'the fact of American policy' that hampered Canada's recognition of the People's Republic of China as the government of China,[26] a position favoured by Canada since 1949 when Mao Zedong and the Chinese Communist Party first came to power. The 'fact' to which Holmes was referring, and what prevented Canada from moving forward on recognition until 1970, was that communist states were seeking to expand their influence and needed to be 'contained' in both their geographic boundaries and international influence. A similar 'fact of American policy' is operative today. It is the 'fact' that terrorism is a serious threat to the American homeland from which the United States needs to protect itself. According to US policy, the protection of the US begins outside its borders. To this end, Canada has instituted a number of measures including legislation dealing with terrorism, a new Smart Border Agreement with the US, and a restructuring of the civil service to create a Department of Public Safety and Emergency Preparedness. The prime minister needs to be aware of any action that Canada takes that might be construed as not being in line with the US war on terror and the prime minister will need to weigh the benefits of the action against its costs in terms of its deleterious effect on the bilateral relationship.

The media is another constraint on the prime minister's freedom of action in foreign affairs because it helps to set the public's agenda. The media, by focusing attention on certain events or issues, attaches a sense of importance to those events or issues for Canadians. What is often referred to as the 'CNN effect' is a result of the power of that television network's all-day every-day coverage of news events to shape the public's agenda. Media coverage of events works as a constraint on a prime minister's power when the public, as a result of media coverage of an event or issue, presses for its prime minister to take action when he or she may not necessarily want to do so. In short, problems arise when the public's agenda differs from the prime minister's strategic agenda.

That events happening in far-off places would strike a chord with a significant portion of the Canadian populace and that they would press their government for action was demonstrated by the Ethiopian famine crisis of 1984 and 1985. In this case it was the televised media's coverage of the famine and the images of children starving on the evening news that moved Canadians to become active in grassroots campaigns and to push their government to respond to the catastrophe.[27] The televised media's coverage of the famine moved the issue onto the public agenda, and then onto the prime minister's agenda.

The ability of the public to move the government to respond to a particular issue or event is heightened if either a large or well-organized domestic group or industry is involved. An example of the former is Canada's response to the Tiananmen Square massacre on 4 June 1989. In May 1989, Chinese students and workers began holding demonstrations in Tiananmen Square to press their government for changes. After six weeks, the Chinese government's patience had worn out and they ordered force to be used to clear the Square. During this period, demonstrations were held in all major Canadian cities in support of the Chinese students and workers. A number of pro-democracy groups were formed in larger Canadian cities with a sizable Chinese population (i.e. Vancouver and Toronto). These groups were very vocal and active in pushing the Canadian government to support the demonstra-

tors and they pressed the Canadian government to adopt stern measures in response to the Chinese government's decision to use violence to quell the demonstrations. The Mulroney government's response was a series of measures that was stricter than most Western states, including the United States. Part of the reason for this reaction has to do with the size and organization of the Chinese Canadian community.[28]

Canada's involvement in the creation of the Kimberley Process stems from the increasing importance of the diamond industry to Canada, especially to the economies of the North. In 2003 Canada was ranked sixth as a producer of diamonds in terms of volume and ranked fifth in terms of export value.[29] The Kimberley Process is a certification scheme for rough diamonds to ensure that diamonds from areas of conflict—blood diamonds—are excluded from the legitimate diamond market. In a series of reports in 2000, released by civil society organizations on the impact of blood diamonds on the conflicts in Africa, one report was of particular importance for our discussion. This report was produced by a Canadian civil society organization—Partnership Africa Canada—and it brought the issue of blood diamonds to the attention of Canadians.[30] The combination of pressure from both the diamond industry and civil society organizations put the issue on the agenda of the Chrétien government.

Moving attention away from the media and public opinion, there are three additional constraints on a prime minister's power. Each of these remaining constraints derives from the workings of the Canadian system of parliamentary government; they are institutional factors. The first institutional constraint concerns whether or not the prime minister commands a majority in the House of Commons. The issue of support from the House is only problematic should the prime minister not command a majority in that body. Then, the prime minister needs to be cognizant of the level of support within the House for his or her initiatives in both domestic and foreign policy. In the case of a minority government, the prime minister's freedom of action may be somewhat circumscribed by the composition of the House. In such a case the prime minister is not without a certain degree of power over the House; no party leader would want the Government to fall over a matter of little importance to the Canadian public, and much of Canada's foreign policy falls within the ambit of minimal importance to Canadians. In fact, it is rare for a foreign policy issue to dominate Canadian politics and even more rare for a foreign policy issue to be more than a peripheral factor in a general election. There are, of course, instances when a foreign policy issue is of importance to a particular riding, or even a few ridings within a region, but seldom does an issue move beyond regional significance to affect a national campaign. For example, a new border crossing connecting Windsor, Ontario with Detroit, Michigan would help to speed up the movement of trucks between Canada and the United States and, thereby, increase the attractiveness of cross-border commercial relations. In addition, the increase in the movement of trucks would help to reduce air pollution in Windsor caused by trucks idling on city roads. However, the issue of a new border crossing has little electoral salience beyond Windsor's border, even though the Windsor–Detroit link is the major commercial thoroughfare for Canadian exports to the US and, as such, is an issue of importance to all Canadians.

A second institutional constraint on the prime minister derives from the role of Opposition parties in the House of Commons. The main role of Opposition parties is to find fault with the Government and to provide an alternative choice for Canadians in the next general election. To this end, the Opposition parties use Question Period and other occasions to demonstrate the weaknesses of the current regime, and especially of the prime minister. Each Opposition party puts forward an alternative agenda, including a different foreign policy platform, to be implemented should one of them win the next general election and form the Government. Other than putting forward an alternative to the present Government and attempting to uncover ministerial misdeeds or departmental indiscretions, the Opposition parties have little that they can do to effect change in Canada's foreign policy.

A final institutional constraint on the prime minister exists in the form of the provinces. The workings of federalism and the need for federal–provincial co-operation in a range of foreign policy-related issues limits the range of possible choices for a prime minister. This issue is covered in greater detail in Chapter 13.

Conclusion

In examining the various constraints under which a prime minister operates it is important to note that none of them are decisive. The only caveat from this is the last constraint concerning the provinces. There are areas of constitutional responsibility accorded to the provinces in the Constitutional Act (1982) and through the decision of the courts on which a prime minister may not tread. Given this, none of the other constraints discussed present an insurmountable challenge to the authority of the prime minister. All of the obstacles presented herein may be overcome by a prime minister who has the determination and desire to do so. It is a question of political will. A prime minister can use the powers of office to discharge lightning bolts to deal with unplanned events or crises and plan his or her legacy by focusing on a few key issues. In short, if a prime minister has the will, he or she can have his or her way.

Notes

1. Donald J. Savoie, *Governing From the Centre: The Concentration of Power in Canadian Politics* (Toronto: University of Toronto Press, 1999).

2. James N. Rosenau, 'Pre-theories and Theories of Foreign Policy', in R.B. Farrell, ed., *Approaches to Comparative and International Politics* (Evanston:

Northwestern University Press, 1966), 43.

3. From 1909 to 1993 the minister was known as the secretary of state for external affairs. After 1993 the minister became the minister of foreign affairs.

4. As cited in Savoie, 319.

5. Andrew Cooper, 'Between Will and Capabilities: Canada and the Zaire/Great Lakes Initiative', in Andrew F. Cooper and Geoffrey Hayes, eds, *Worthwhile Initiatives: Canadian Mission-Oriented Diplomacy* (Toronto: CIIA Irwin, 2000), 64–78.

6. While the names of the various ministerial positions within the troika have all changed over the years, the troika has consistently comprised ministers responsible for foreign relations (i.e. political, security, and consular issues), international trade, and international development (i.e. the Canadian International Development Agency).

7. Charlotte Gray, 'New Faces in Old Places: The Making of Canadian Foreign Policy', in Fen Osler Hampson and Christopher J. Maule, eds, *Canada Among Nations 1992–93: A New World Order?* (Ottawa: Carleton University Press, 1992), 15–28.

8. Savoie, 137.

9. Kim Richard Nossal, *The Politics of Canadian Foreign Policy*, 3rd ed. (Scarborough, ON: Prentice Hall, 1997), 245–7.

10. Peter Aucoin, 'Organizational Change in the Machinery of Canadian Government: From Rational Management to Brokerage Politics', *Canadian Journal of Political Science* 19, 1 (March 1986): 3–27.

11. John Kirton, 'Managing Global Conflict: Canada and International Summitry', in Maureen Appel Molot and Brian W. Tomlin, eds, *Canada Among Nations 1987: A World of Conflict* (Toronto: James Lorimer, 1988), 23.

12. Andrew F. Cooper, *In Between Countries: Australia, Canada, and the Search for Order in Agricultural Trade* (Montreal and Kingston: McGill-Queen's University Press, 1997), 188.

13. Aucoin, 17.

14. For a cogent discussion of this issue, see Christopher J. Kukucha, 'From Kyoto to WTO: Evaluating the Constitutional Legitimacy of the Provinces in Canadian Foreign Trade and Environmental Policy', *Canadian Journal of Political Science* 38, 1 (March 2005): 129–52.

15. As cited in Kukucha, 148.

16. Thomas S. Axworthy, 'Of Secretaries to Princes', *Canadian Public Administration* 31, 2 (Summer 1988): 247–64.

17. Kim Richard Nossal, *Rain Dancing: Sanctions in Canadian and Australian Foreign Policy* (Toronto: University of Toronto Press, 1994), 106.

18. Nossal, *Rain Dancing*, 250.

19. Linda Freeman, *The Ambiguous Champion: Canada and South Africa in the Trudeau and Mulroney Years* (Toronto: University of Toronto Press, 1997), 286.

20. See Freeman, *The Ambiguous Champion* and Nossal, *Rain Dancing*.

21. Robert Fowler, 'Canadian Leadership and the Kananaskis G8 Summit: Towards a Less Self-Centred Foreign Policy', in David Carment, Fen Osler Hampson, and Norman Hillmer, eds, *Canada Among Nations 2003: Coping with the American Colossus* (Don Mills, ON: Oxford University Press, 2003), 219.

22. Steven Langdon, 'NEPAD and the Renaissance of Africa', in Carment, Hampson, and Hillmer, eds, 249–50.

23. Langdon, 251.

24. Donald J. Savoie, 'The Federal Government: Revisiting Court Government in Canada', in Luc Bernier, Keith Brownsey, and Michael Howlett, eds, *Executive Styles in Canada: Cabinet Structures and Leadership Practices in Canadian Government* (Toronto: University of Toronto Press, 2005), 26.

25. See Louis Belanger, 'The Changing World Order and Quebec's International Relations: An Analysis of Two Salient Environments', in Michael J. Tucker, Raymond B. Blake, and P.E. Bryden, eds, *Canada and the New World Order: Facing the New Millennium* (Toronto: Irwin, 2000), 163–84.

26. John Holmes, *The Better Part of Valour: Essays on Canadian Diplomacy* (Toronto: McClelland and Stewart, 1970), 215.

27. Andrew F. Cooper, Richard A. Higgott, and Kim Richard Nossal, *Relocating Middle Powers: Australia and Canada in a Changing World Order* (Vancouver: UBC Press, 1994), 23.

28. See Paul Gecelovsky, 'The Canadian Response to the Tiananmen Square Massacre', *Canadian Foreign Policy* 8, 3 (Spring 2001): 75–98.

29. See Chair's Report to Plenary, Kimberley Process Plenary meeting, Gatineau Quebec, Canada, 27–29 October 2004. Available at http://www.kimberley process.com:8080/site/.

30. Ian Smillie, L. Gberie, and R. Hazleton, *The Heart of the Matter: Sierra Leone, Diamonds, and Human Security* (Ottawa: Partnership Africa Canada, 2000).

12
The Member of Parliament and Foreign Policy

John English

For most of Canadian history, Canada's House of Commons had no committee on foreign affairs. When Paul Martin arrived in Ottawa in 1935, fresh from studying international affairs in Geneva and international law at Harvard, he discovered there was little that a government backbencher interested in foreign affairs could do to express that interest. He quickly made friends with some members of the bureaucracy who shared his foreign policy interests. One of them, Norman Robertson, encouraged him to ask a question in the House on Japanese politics. He did so and discovered quickly, in his own words, 'from the expression' on Mackenzie King's face 'that [he] had pulled a boner'. Mackenzie King, Martin later recalled, 'did not encourage private members to speak out on international relations'. The Foreign Affairs portfolio remained within the Prime Minister's Office until 1946; no separate committee on foreign affairs would be established until 1949, when King left office (Martin, 1983: 181).

Things are better now for private members. There is a Committee on Foreign Affairs and International Trade, and the Liberal Party Red Book of 1993 called for a participatory foreign policy in which members of Parliament played a central role. 'A Liberal government', the Red Book

declared, 'will also expand the rights of Parliament to debate major Canadian foreign policy initiatives, such as the deployment of peace-keeping forces, and the rights of Canadians to regular and serious consultation on foreign policy issues' (Liberal Party of Canada, 1993: 109). Following another Red Book undertaking, the Liberal government, after the 1993 election, established a Special Joint Committee of the Senate and the House of Commons to Review Canadian Foreign Policy. The government responded specifically to the recommendations of the report and accepted many of them. The parliamentary committee has also produced significant reports on a range of matters, from circumpolar co-operation to child labour and government assistance to small business exporters, and, in this Parliament, the Multilateral Agreement on Investment. The Red Book commitment to consult Parliament before significant foreign policy decisions are made was initially met through House of Commons debates on each commitment, but, lately, the committee has held the debates and has received expert testimony from Foreign Affairs officials and others. The device has worked well and seems to command non-partisan support.

Until the mid-1980s, committees could study

specific questions only when a minister authorized them to do so. This practice sometimes had embarrassing consequences. One committee chair noted for his controversial views waited for over a year for a minister's authorization. One day the phone call from the minister finally came. The minister asked that the committee undertake hearings on a highly significant topic. The chair quickly called together the committee. Just as the committee was assembling, the party whips rushed in and announced: 'The House has been dissolved.' The minister laughed last and no doubt heartily. In 1983 and 1985, however, committees gained the authority to meet year-round and determine their own agenda. Committees now have great freedom to choose topics and to study them with vigour and appropriate assistance. When one considers that Mackenzie King would not even allow a committee on foreign affairs to exist, one realizes that such independence is important for the MP interested in foreign policy questions.

There are other apparent improvements. When Paul Martin reflected on his colleagues in 1935 and those elected in Trudeau's first government in 1968, he claimed that the latter group was far more interested in broader questions and international aspects of Canadian politics than the members in 1935. The concern of the first Trudeau class was no longer the local post office or the appointment of a customs inspector. Today, the class of 1968 seems parochial when compared with members elected in 1993. In 1970, in a Parliament of 263 members, 16 were born outside of Canada, 26 had studied outside of Canada, and 17 had worked outside of Canada. In 1994, in a Parliament of 295 members, 29 were born outside of Canada, 50 studied outside of Canada, and 22 had worked outside of Canada. Canada now enjoys a Parliament with many members with international experience, a committee structure that permits considerable freedom, and assistance far beyond the wildest imaginings of Paul Martin in 1935. Why, then, do so many members of Parliament echo his frustration of those earlier times?

The statistics mask many differences as well as the major limits that face the Canadian Member of Parliament, especially when compared with his/her counterparts in the United States and Great Britain. He/she faces such limits because of the character of the Canadian Parliament, the type of background MPs possess, the nature of constituency politics, the diversity of the Canadian population, and the committee system of Parliament.

Canada's Parliament meets approximately 60 per cent of the year, except in election years when the number of days in session drops considerably. The majority of members do not live in Ottawa but rather commute weekly to their homes, often many hours distant. The availability of virtually unlimited air passes makes this vagabond life possible, but it also makes sustained focus on particular issues most difficult. When one member of Parliament read Jack Pickersgill's memoir, *Seeing Canada Whole*, published in 1994, he remarked on how much more interaction there was among members in Pickersgill's day when committees were not interrupted by votes in the House and, most significantly, when members lived too far from home to permit them to fly home on weekends or, more accurately, on Thursday afternoon to return on Tuesday morning.

Members now have passes allowing them to fly anywhere in Canada with or without spouse or children, but they have neither budget nor 'points' that would permit them to travel outside of Canada. In Parliament itself, the multi-party system and, in this Parliament, the narrow majority means that much time is occupied with voting, procedural matters, and other time-consuming parliamentary tasks. Moreover, party discipline prevents the kind of initiatives available to American congressmen and senators. Bill Richardson's active personal diplomacy as a congressman, which led to his appointment as the American UN ambassador, would not have been possible for a parliamentarian in Canada. One finds Richardson's counterparts in Britain, Germany, and especially Scandinavia, where less stringent rules on legislators' activities make personal diplomacy possible and where legislative tenure has tended to be much longer. Indeed, some Scandinavian legislators are absent for months at a time on international work.

Recent academic research supports this argument. David Docherty's *Mr Smith Goes To Ottawa* concludes that 'Parliament acts to push members away from the capital and to pull them towards their local ridings.' The result is they spend more time in their constituencies 'at the expense of their more parliamentary-based responsibilities'. This tendency is particularly marked by recently elected members and is less prevalent among senior members, of whom there have been few recently (Docherty, 1997: 203).

Canadian MPs today have considerable interest in foreign policy, but when compared with their counterparts of 25 years ago they have, on the whole, less international background in terms of their education or work experience, limiting their understanding of the contemporary international system. Certainly, more have been born outside the country and in countries not represented in previous Parliaments. In 1970, seven of the 16 non-Canadian births were from Britain and five from the United States. In 1994, six of the 29 were born in Britain but only two in the United States. There were five from Asia and five from Italy alone. Members can speak of the Punjab, Croatia, Hungary, Armenia, and other countries with personal experience lacking in previous decades. The partisan nature of this experience tends to make government and opposition leaders nervous.

In the Parliament elected in 1993, the Official Opposition was a party dedicated to Quebec separation. The practice of earlier times, even in the days of Mackenzie King, of taking opposition members to international conferences became difficult, if not impossible, to follow. In the Parliament of 1949, several private members from the Liberals, the Conservatives, and the CCF attended the UN in the fall for six weeks. The technique was cleverly used by Lester Pearson to create non-partisan support for his foreign policy initiatives, even with John Diefenbaker in the early 1950s (English, 1993: 213–14). That practice rarely occurs now. In part, the explanation lies in the character of recent Parliaments. Bloc Québécois members, it was feared, might use the occasion of international gatherings or activities to promote the cause of separation. In the Parliament elected in 1997, the Official Opposition, the Reform Party, is wary not only of foreign travel by Members of Parliament but also of the cost of Canadian internationalism. The Reform Party refuses to 'pair', a practice whereby a member of the governing party and of the opposition agree to be absent for parliamentary votes, that allowed some independent initiatives by members. In some senses, the Reform Party reflects the isolationist tendencies found among neo-conservatives in the United States, who regard international institutions and commitments with deep suspicion. This mood and attitude have been largely absent from the Canadian House of Commons since the 1930s.

In the case of the Liberal Party, one finds many members with extensive international experience and interests. However, most of those members find their place in the cabinet or as parliamentary secretaries. Although Prime Ministers Mulroney and Chrétien both reduced the size of the cabinet, the current cabinet is only slightly smaller than in the early Mulroney days. When over 35 members of the Liberal parliamentary group are part of the ministry, it means that nearly all of the Liberals with strong foreign affairs background are part of the government. About 25 of the remainder are parliamentary secretaries, whose workload and other activities prevent them from working in a sustained way on foreign policy issues. Parliamentary secretaries, for example, are forbidden to accept payment for travel to attend conferences outside of Canada and have no independent budgets to carry out such work.

These constraints are worth noting, but they are probably less important than constituency demands. Because of improvements in transportation and communication, the member of Parliament is now closer to his/her constituency than ever before. Indeed, it is astonishing to think that most constituencies had no members' offices until the 1970s. Members shared a secretary in Ottawa, and that secretary apparently could deal with most of their correspondence. The private member now has an office in the constituency, a personal office in Ottawa, and a staff of four or five employees. Free long distance telephone and fax are available, as well as electronic mail. In Parkinsonian fashion, the work has expanded to meet the staff available. Docherty's surveys of recent members revealed that members spend over two-fifths of their working time on constituency affairs (Docherty, 1997: 178). Today, the average MP in an urban constituency in Toronto, Vancouver, Calgary, and many other smaller cities receives approximately 100 calls per day. According to Toronto MP Dennis Mills, over three-quarters of his calls deal with immigration. In this sense, there is involvement with aspects of Canada's relations with other countries, but that involvement is very specific. In many cases, the presence of significant ethnic communities profoundly influences not only the interests but also the origins of MPs. Although Canada has always had members who have spoken for the interests of other nations such as Israel and Ireland, recent Parliaments have seen an explosion of the 'special interest' politician.

At the first meeting of candidates on foreign policy that I attended as a candidate just before the 1988 election, we began to talk about 'issues' when one of the senior members blurted out: 'The only Canadian foreign policy issue which matters in my constituency is an independent Punjab.' The candidates were not so startled as one might expect, for many had fought nomination battles where the support of the Sikh community was a valuable commodity. Indeed, Liberal membership lists before the 1988 and 1993 elections and the 1990 leadership convention bore testimony to the involvement in the party of Canadians from various areas who,

unlike most Canadians, did have strong views on foreign policy issues in their area of origin. At my own nomination battle in 1987, the Kitchener Liberal Association had about 3,000 members, of whom about 800 were of Greek or Cypriot origin and about 600 of Sikh background. Their willingness to come out to vote on a cold December night was much more pronounced than was the case for other association members.

The diversity of the Canadian population has had several effects on the Member of Parliament's interest in foreign policy. On the one hand, it has created the special interest MPs described above and particular focus on issues such as locating a Canadian consulate in Amritsar. On the other hand, it has provided new resources that draw Canadian attention to areas previously ignored and give Canada a capacity it earlier lacked when members were overwhelmingly French or British in origin. There are now lively debates about Greek and Turkish issues in which members of Greek origin and others with considerable Turkish populations in their ridings take their respective sides. On the whole, these debates probably have little impact on policy, but they are not ignored. Numerous international parliamentary associations now reflect these interests. The Reform Party generally refuses to participate in their activities, and many others regard their activities with a skeptical eye. For many years, overseas trips have been the method for purchasing loyalty for both government and opposition since party whips decide who participates. Whatever their political purpose, these associations are the principal contact that private members have with international fora.

The major associations receive parliamentary funding, although these funds have been much reduced since 1993. No longer can members take spouses and fly business class, and rarely is there a full delegation. Indeed, Canadian delegations to such parliamentary groups as the North Atlantic Assembly or the Parliamentary Assembly of the Organization for Co-operation and Security in Europe are smaller than those from countries of much less international weight. Moreover, there are problems of balance: there is a funded Canada–Israel Parliamentary Association but no Arab counterpart. Even more troubling are other associations, usually termed 'friendship groups', which have neither parliamentary funding nor sanction. The Canada–Taiwan Friendship Group creates obvious problems, if not for the members who take their spouses on first-class flights to first-class hotels in Taipei. The televised sight of Canadian MPs cavorting in the streets at a presidential rally during the last election in Taiwan no doubt horrified the Asia-Pacific desk at Foreign Affairs.

Some members devote much of their time to parliamentary association work and find it extremely rewarding. Senior members, often with earlier ministerial experience and less concern about re-election, tend to become chairs of these groups. Charles Caccia, for example, has given strong leadership to the Canada–Europe group. His extensive network of connections with European parliamentarians provided valuable assistance to the government during the 'Turbot War' with Spain. Similarly, another former minister, Sheila Finestone, prodded the Inter-Parliamentary Union to consider the land mine ban in 1997. Members of Parliament, however, share places with senators who have more freedom and, in recent times, more funds to participate in these associations. Although senators and MPs tend to work well together, the tendency of non-Canadians to treat the senators as the 'senior' delegate members irks those from the Commons. Other difficulties arise from the time constraints on Canadian members, especially when parliamentary majorities are narrow or non-existent. The Council of Europe, at which Canada gained observer status, has 60 days of meetings each year. One Danish parliamentarian told me that she spent about 80 days per year on parliamentary association business. Such a commitment would be unacceptable in Canada to one's caucus, one's colleagues, and, almost certainly, one's constituency. For Canadians, the substance of parliamentary association business does not merit the

time of such commitments even though Europeans believe that in their case it does.

It could be argued that Canada does have a direct interest, similar to that of European parliamentarians, in creating links with the United States Congress. The Canada–United States parliamentary group, established, surprisingly enough, by John Diefenbaker, meets regularly for approximately three days to discuss bilateral issues. Discussions have been lively, but the group is less active than it was in the 1980s and certainly cannot be said to be an important component of the bilateral relationship. In the 1980s Peter Dobell, the founder of the Parliamentary Centre, which provides assistance to many groups, called for more exchanges and closer contact because of the growing importance of Congress. Legislators, he argued, have an 'instinctive' respect for each other, which could be useful in Washington where legislators traditionally have distrusted diplomats (Dobell, 1992: 131). His argument was cogent but had little effect. Canadian and American legislators meet rarely and accomplish little of substance together. North American integration may parallel Europe in some respects but not at the legislative level.

For most MPs, foreign policy in the sense one encounters in academic circles is of little concern or interest. There have been major debates on foreign policy issues in the 1990s. One thinks immediately of the Gulf War debate, when many members gave eloquent speeches and revealed serious study of the issue. There have also been good debates on peace-keeping commitments since the Liberals were elected in 1993, and many private members have spoken passionately and well on human rights issues. Reform MP Keith Martin's focus on land mines has been rightly lauded, and Liberal MP Paddy Torsney's interest in women's issues on the international level is well known. But in the hundreds of pages of Hansard, these moments are relatively rare.

The most significant focus on foreign policy occurs in the Committee on Foreign Affairs and International Trade. That committee, chaired by

Bill Graham, a distinguished international lawyer, has had two subcommittees in recent times. One deals with trade matters, the other with human rights concerns. According to the Liberal whip, more Liberal members ask to be members of the Foreign Affairs Committee than any other committee. Since 1994, after the Special Joint Review Committee reported, the Foreign Affairs Committee has carried out numerous special studies, most of which have been well received by the media. Some have enjoyed unanimous support, a rare quality for committee reports in recent years and an indication that normal partisan spirits abate in foreign affairs discussions. According to Peter Dobell, the Foreign Affairs Committee has been highly innovative and, in many ways, has created new possibilities for parliamentary committees (1997).

Nevertheless, there are many difficulties with the committee's operation. Some are specific to it; others are common to the Canadian committee system. Specifically, the Foreign Affairs and International Trade Committee has a vast territory to survey but little time to contemplate the details. Three ministers—Foreign Affairs, International Trade, and International Co-operation—report before the committee, as do two secretaries of state (Asia-Pacific and Africa and Latin America). Ministerial appearances are brief and offer little time for detailed questioning. Moreover, departmental business plans and estimates are complex and vague. The most determined parliamentary efforts to find out what, for example, Canada is doing in and about southern Africa are exercises in fact-finding futility. Because of the range of issues, the committee is often required to 'fight fires' and respond to immediate demands. Although the committee under Graham's able leadership has carried out some important and valuable studies, long-range thinking and analysis about Canada's foreign policy priorities have given way to the urgent though not necessarily most prescient issues. A high turnover of committee membership means that final consideration of studies occurs after many of the committee members who heard witness testimony have left.

Graham's frustrations are expressed in a broader sense in a report of the Liaison Committee of Committee Chairs of the 35th Parliament, which he chaired. In this report, the chairs of committees reviewed the current effectiveness of committees in carrying out their functions. The review made several interesting observations. Reports, it claimed,. had little impact on policy. Indeed, the situation may have been better before 1985 when committees could not set their own agendas. In those days, 'Ministers who had proposed orders of reference, usually paid close attention to the committee's report because they and their advisers had selected areas of policy where the government was undecided on how best to proceed and was looking for advice.' Moreover, committee members of all parties proceeded on the assumption that their work would be taken seriously by the government since the government commissioned it (Liaison Committee, 1997: 9).

Even more troubling is the claim that the new power to select subjects of inquiry has meant that the committees pay less attention to the estimates than they did before 1985. A separate report by the Standing Committee on Procedure and House Affairs came to the same conclusion and issued an even more strongly worded recommendation that departmental estimates be given more than perfunctory attention. In the 35th Parliament, several members of the Foreign Affairs Committee tried to discover a way to examine CIDA estimates effectively. After taking advice from independent experts on development assistance, they considered focusing on one country and examining CIDA assistance in detail, but the task was beyond the capacity of a committee whose budget is meagre and whose members' time is limited. In assessing the reasons for the lack of 'conscientious scrutiny of proposed expenditures', the subcommittee on procedure and house affairs pointed to problems with 'rules and structures' (House of Commons, 1996: 81).

The Liaison Committee report, however, suggested the problems are not merely technical. Here some comparisons were made. According to the report:

> Compared to many other legislatures, where committee members have greater security of tenure, this practice of substantial change in committee membership mid-way through a Parliament inevitably means that Canadian members lack the acquired background and the institutional memory that contribute greatly to the quality of committee work. (1997: 11)

The Canadian House has other unique problems. There are only 12 committee rooms to serve 19 committees, and the need for interpretation (translation) is absent in other parliaments. Although the multiparty system was not mentioned, the need to deal with five parties rather than two or three, as is the case in the United States and Britain, obviously complicates committee work. There are not only more parties but also more interest groups, and the demand to hear witnesses exceeds the time available to members. Those who appear before committees often find audiences that are a fraction of the full committee. There is, very simply, neither world enough nor time for adequate committee work (Liaison Committee, 1997: 11).

The private member in Canada has a shorter political life expectancy than his/her British counterparts and therefore less ability to undertake separate initiatives. In comparison with American congressmen, the Canadian MP lacks the staff, budget, and independence to carry out foreign policy initiatives or even sustained study of a foreign policy issue. Rewards in the constituency for foreign policy interest, with the notable exception of highly ethnic ridings, are rare. Moreover, in the view of the private member, the Canadian bureaucracy is unsympathetic to such initiatives and considerably stronger than its American counterpart. Whether true or not, the comment

of a first-term Liberal member—'If the bureaucrats don't buy it, it's dead'—is a widely held opinion among private members on both sides of the House (Docherty, 1997: 234).

The rise of non-governmental organizations allows the bureaucracy to argue that there is an alternative to Parliament in gauging and understanding popular opinion. At the first National Forum on Canadian Foreign Policy, MPs were initially not invited despite the clear statement in the Red Book that the Forum would include 'representation from Parliament and non-governmental organizations, and members of the general public who have an interest or involvement in world affairs' (Liberal Party of Canada, 1993: 109). The chair of the Foreign Policy Review, Jean Robert Gauthier, complained loudly. Nevertheless, at some sessions at the 1994 forum, members of Parliament were not permitted to speak. At one session, the MPs took seats at the back of the room while others gathered around the central table. Someone asked the chair: 'Who are those people at the back?' She replied rather sternly: 'They are members of Parliament. They may stay but cannot speak.' Although NGO representatives and academics were vocal, Canada's elected representatives were stifled. The ambiguity of public representation was clear.

In summary, the Canadian MP is tied tightly to his/her constituency, and most have few incentives to pursue an interest in foreign policy issues unless there is a distinct constituency connection. Nevertheless, foreign affairs debates bring out the best in parliamentarians, and the Foreign Affairs Committee is prestigious for members. This contradiction probably signals that the present does not predict the future, just as it does not reflect the past. The upheavals of the Canadian party system in the past decade are mirrored in Parliament, a Parliament that is clearly in transition. For now, the fragmented Parliament brings a fragmented focus when Canadian parliamentarians look beyond their boundaries.

References

Canadian Parliamentary Guide. 1970, 1993, 1994.

Dobell, Peter. 1992. 'Negotiating with the United States', in J.L. Granatstein, ed., *Towards a New World: Readings in the History of Canadian Foreign Policy*. Toronto: Copp Clark Pittman.

Dobell, Peter, and Lynda Chapin. 1997. 'Renewal at the House of Commons', Parliamentary Government (November).

Docherty, David. 1997. *Mr Smith Goes to Ottawa: Life in the House of Commons*. Vancouver: UBC Press.

English, John. 1993. *The Worldly Years: The Life of Lester Pearson 1949–1972*. Toronto: Knopf.

Liaison Committee of Committee Chairs. 1997. 'Report of the Liaison Committee on Committee Effectiveness'. Parliamentary Government (September).

Liberal Party of Canada. 1996. *A Record of Achievement: A Report on the Liberal Government's 36 Months in Office*. Ottawa.

———. 1993. *Creating Opportunities: The Liberal Plan for Canada*. Ottawa.

Martin, Paul. 1983. *A Very Public Life: Volume 1. Far From Home*. Ottawa: Deneau.

Pickersgill, J.W. 1994. *Seeing Canada Whole: A Memoir*. Toronto: Fitzhenry and Whiteside.

Standing Committee on Procedure and House Affairs. 1996. 'The Business of Supply: Completing the Circle of Control'. Ottawa.

13

Expanded Legitimacy: The Provinces as International Actors

Christopher J. Kukucha

The international activity of Canadian provinces has a direct impact on Canada's foreign policy and the evolution of regime-based norms and standards. Quebec's nationalist objectives, for example, resulted in the province's formal representation in la Francophonie and its challenge of Canada's role in the North Atlantic Treaty Organization (NATO). In contrast, other provinces traditionally focused on tourism, the development of export markets, and immigration issues, usually in the form of foreign offices and trade promotion initiatives. The expansion of international agreements, such as the General Agreement on Tariffs and Trade (GATT), and the North American Free Trade Agreement (NAFTA), into areas of domestic policy space, however, created greater legitimacy for provincial foreign engagement. Specifically, because of federal–state clauses in both GATT and NAFTA, and a degree of domestic constitutional ambiguity, the federal government became increasingly aware of provincial pressures in the negotiation and implementation of these commitments. These developments contributed to an increasingly complex policy process. It is also clear, however, that Canadian provinces have a direct impact on the final content of foreign trade agreements, most notably in terms of subsidies, services, agriculture, energy, and softwood

lumber. Several provinces also pursue cross-border linkages with American states with similar results. Having said that, most aspects of provincial foreign policy remain functional in nature and do not directly challenge Ottawa's international legitimacy.

For the most part, there is only a limited range of literature focusing on provincial foreign policy. Some studies examine questions of centralization and decentralization within Canadian federalism. Douglas Brown and Earl Fry, for example, have suggested that a decentralized federal system allows central governments to manage the foreign policy initiatives of provinces, states, and cantons.[1] Kim Nossal has also argued that Ottawa remains firmly in control of Canada's global trade relations.[2] Grace Skogstad, Michael Hart, Bruce Doern, and Brian Tomlin, on the other hand, have pointed out that both levels of government value institutional linkages that facilitate greater communication and cooperation.[3] Other contributions, however, investigate a broader range of issues. Stephen de Boer has questioned the potential for a greater provincial role in North American integration. Economic studies by John Helliwell, John McCallum, Michael Anderson, and Stephen Smith have reviewed trade patterns, particularly in terms of North American regional economies and the global exports of the provinces.[4] Comparatively, much has also been written on the political and economic foreign policy of Quebec although little or no attention has been directed at other provincial governments.[5] Therefore, it is clear that these contributions do not comprehensively engage issues of process and change related to the international activity of Canadian provinces.

Provincial International Legitimacy and the Canadian Constitution

Canada is one of the few federal states without clearly defined constitutional parameters regarding the international activity of non-central governments. In fact, the only reference to international relations in the 1867 British North America Act (BNA) is Section 132, which grants the Dominion the authority to *implement* treaties negotiated by Great Britain. Over time, however, Ottawa gained increasing autonomy in its foreign affairs, and in some cases this has had direct implications for Canadian provinces. As these issues were opened to judicial interpretation three sections of the BNA Act became increasingly more important: the treaty-making power, the trade and commerce power, and the Peace, Order and Good Government (POGG) clause. In terms of the treaty-making power, the 1937 *Labour Conventions* decision by the United Kingdom's Judicial Committee of the Privy Council (JCPC) established the precedent that Ottawa had the power to *negotiate* international treaties but it did not have the right to *implement* agreements in areas of provincial jurisdiction. Despite initial concern that the ruling would limit federal autonomy, the Supreme Court of Canada did not subsequently use *Labour Conventions* in favour of either level of government, preferring instead to maintain a balance between federal and provincial authority in this issue area.[6]

Judicial review of the trade and commerce power also followed a similar pattern. In 1867 Parliament was given exclusive control over the regulation of trade and commerce in Section 91(2). The difficulty, however, was that provinces were granted jurisdiction over property and civil rights, which includes the regulation of contracts through which international trade is conducted. Although the 1891 *Citizens Insurance Company v. Parsons* case appeared to confirm Ottawa's control over international trade, later questions were raised regarding the regulation of products that were consumed locally and traded internationally. As with *Labour Conventions*, however, the Supreme Court did not use trade and commerce to entrench federal or provincial power. Instead, it reaffirmed 'there was no federal power to regulate a single trade or business. And, it indicated that issues . . . must be determined on a careful case-by-case basis.'[7]

A third means of interpreting federal authority is the POGG clause. In comparison to trade and commerce or the treaty making power, judicial interpretation of POGG is less defined, especially in terms of economic and environmental issues. For Canadian provinces, the most relevant Supreme Court decision is *Crown Zellerbach* (1988). In this case, the forest company was accused of dumping wood waste into the Pacific Ocean. Although existing federal legislation defined 'sea' as an extension of provincial internal waters the Court ruled that POGG allowed Ottawa to extend control into areas of jurisdiction not explicitly defined in the BNA Act when these issues were deemed to be matters of 'national concern'.[8] Despite this, *Crown Zellerbach* has also not served as an extensive precedent for federal control. Not only did the decision set specific conditions for federal intervention but the Court was also deeply divided with Justice La Forest dissenting on the basis that marine pollution was not distinct enough to qualify as a matter of national concern.[9] Subsequent cases, such as *Friends of the Oldman River Society* (1992) and *Canada v. Hydro Quebec* (1997), reinforced this federal–provincial balance. Therefore, as a result of these rulings there is a level of constitutional ambiguity that grants Canadian provinces international legitimacy, especially in terms of foreign trade and environmental policy.[10]

Quebec Nationalism and Provincial International Activity

Quebec, more than any other province has an extensive history of international activity. According to Nossal, Quebec's foreign policy is linked to its 'desire to project abroad some sense of the province's cultural and linguistic attributes that distinguish francophone Québécois from other Canadians'.[11] As a result, Quebec has openly challenged 'the government of Canada, especially in the francophone world, demanding to represent internationally the francophones of North America'.[12] Surprisingly, Quebec was not the first province that pursued an enhanced international role in the immediate post-war period. During the 1950s British Columbia actively protected its interests in the negotiation of the final Canada–United States Columbia River Treaty. By the 1960s, however, Quebec had re-opened a foreign office in Paris and demanded its officials be given the 'rights and privileges' granted to regular consular officers. In response, the French government extended diplomatic immunity to the Quebec delegation; the following year the province opened a second office in London. In 1964 an international division was established in the province's Department of Trade and Commerce. As an extension of these initiatives an exchange program was also established between Quebec's Department of Youth and a similar French organization for 'young civil servants and technicians'.[13]

Quebec's first formal international agreement was an educational exchange negotiated with France in 1965, which many Québécois viewed as legitimizing the province's international status. French president Charles de Gaulle supported this perception with his famous 1967 Montreal speech when he stated 'Vive Montréal, vive le Québec, vive le Québec libre, vive le Canada français, vive la France.'[14] Provincial objectives were further clarified in the 1965 Gérin-Lajoie doctrine, which

argued that Quebec had the right to pursue international objectives consistent with its cultural identity or in constitutionally defined areas of jurisdiction. In fact, it was the publication of Gérin-Lajoie that reinforced Quebec's attempts to gain independent membership in international francophone organizations. Gabon, with the encouragement of the French government, directly extended an invitation to Quebec in February 1968 for an international education conference. The following year, Canada was represented by a joint-delegation at francophone conferences in Congo due to a cooperative agreement between Ottawa and Jean-Jacques Bertrand's provincial government. Although France threatened to boycott subsequent meetings in Niger unless Quebec received its own formal invitation a compromise was reached when the African government issued invited both levels of government. Due to the earlier co-operative agreement, however, Canada continued to be represented by only one group of officials.[15]

Quebec's interest in external affairs increased with the election of René Lévesque's Parti Québécois (PQ) in November 1976. Most notably, the PQ attempted to use foreign policy as a means of generating support for an anticipated referendum on Quebec independence. Specifically, the PQ government continued to 'project the image of an independent international actor by attempting to acquire the symbols of statehood, such as diplomatic immunity for its representatives abroad, or "participating-government" status at international summits'.[16] The PQ also made statements on human rights issues, such as South African apartheid, and strongly criticized federal policy in matters judged to be harmful to Quebec interests. In addition, the party considered an independent defence policy for a sovereign Quebec, including the province's potential withdrawal from both the North Atlantic Treaty Organization and the North American Aerospace Command (NORAD).[17]

There were three significant developments that motivated Quebec to re-evaluate its international role in the 1980s. The first was a loss of support from the French government. Specifically, Paris had started to seriously question the legitimacy of Quebec's foreign activities and was wary of further damaging its deteriorating relationship with Ottawa. The arrival of Brian Mulroney as prime minister in September 1984, the resignation of Lévesque in October 1985, and the PQ's subsequent defeat in provincial elections the following month, created a greater shift in federal–provincial relations. In fact, Mulroney and the new Liberal government of Robert Bourassa quickly negotiated an agreement that allowed both Quebec and New Brunswick formal representation at the first la Francophonie summit in Paris. Finally, Washington made it explicitly clear that a unified Canada was essential to continental security and economic prosperity.[18]

Although the defeat of the PQ made the issue of separatism a moot point it did not eliminate tension between Ottawa and Quebec City. At the beginning of the 1990s, for example, Bourassa publicly requested that proposed la Francophonie reforms not weaken Quebec's status in the organization. The newly elected PQ government of Jacques Parizeau, prior to the Marrakech Ministerial Conference in December 1996, further reiterated this position. Although this created the potential for a significant backlash from other members, the 1999 summit in Moncton, New Brunswick expanded Quebec's standing in la Francophonie to include all ministerial meetings, something that Ottawa had challenged the previous year.[19] Not surprisingly, the United States also remained an ongoing concern for the PQ during the Parizeau era. The 1995 referendum again raised questions in Washington related to both economic and security issues. Ultimately, President Bill Clinton adopted an approach similar to that of Jimmy Carter during the 1980 referendum: that while Washington valued its longstanding relationship with Canada, this issue was an internal Canadian matter. Secretary of State Warren Christopher, however, did make statements suggesting that an independent Quebec

could face difficulties in securing US investment and negotiating a new NAFTA partnership. These comments were not well received in Quebec, and the provincial government sent a formal letter to Washington protesting interference in the domestic politics of a sovereign state.[20]

Support for Quebec separatism and the province's foreign policy agenda was further bolstered by the success of the Bloc Québécois (BQ) in the federal election of 1993. In a March 1994 address to the United Nations Lucien Bouchard, the leader of the BQ, made it clear that separatism was once again at the forefront of Quebec's political agenda. Bouchard also made a point of trying to include federal representatives during the trip in the hopes of gaining tacit legitimacy for Quebec's international aspirations. In response to American concerns related to trade and investment, Bouchard further stressed that it would be 'business as usual' if Quebec gained independence.[21] In subsequent comments Bouchard suggested that 'British Columbia and Alberta could also go their own way if Quebec was to separate.'[22] Not surprisingly, officials from both Ottawa and Washington challenged these conclusions. In fact, the Canadian Ambassador to the United States, Raymond Chrétien, stated, that 'on many occasions, many Americans told him . . . that [Quebec] would not be treated on preferential terms.'[23] Even Quebec's delegate general in New York, Reed Scowen, told Bouchard 'that he was wrong to claim he represented the interests of all Quebec'.[24]

Although Bouchard continued to embrace issues of sovereignty and international legitimacy after he became premier of Quebec similar problems remained, especially in terms of economic relations with the United States. Critics, for example, argued that Quebec separation would have implications related to membership in both NAFTA and the World Trade Organization (WTO). First, there were provisions in international law that allowed Canada, the United States, and Mexico to block Quebec's accession to NAFTA. There were also questions as to whether or not an independent Quebec would have its own custom tariff, related to the imposition of duties on imports. Furthermore, the United States also made it clear it would seek further concessions if an independent Quebec attempted to join NAFTA or the WTO. In the words of one observer: 'until those negotiations were completed, [Quebec] would remain outside the North American trading system with none of the advantages that accrue to NAFTA members.'[25] The province could opt for its own customs regime but 'until it secured admission to the NAFTA . . . there would be no automatic right of most favoured nation treatment for Quebec-origin goods and services.'[26] In addition, Quebec would also have to implement a series of visible tariffs and attempt to negotiate separate agreements with each of its trading partners in the hopes of regaining most of the benefits it currently has under NAFTA.[27]

Provincial Foreign Offices

As part of its nationalist objectives, Quebec was the first province to establish a series of foreign provincial offices. In fact, Quebec's initial international presence dates back to 1882 with the appointment of Hector Fabre as the province's agent-general in Paris. In 1911 Quebec also opened a 'commercial' office in Britain, which was followed by a provincial posting in Brussels in 1915. Ontario's first office, on the other hand, was in London in 1918. As Nossal points out, many of these offices were in response to Ottawa's efforts to increase federal representation abroad. In 1868 the Dominion Agency for Emigration was opened in London and several other immigration offices were established throughout Europe. By 1907 twelve trade commissions were located in such diverse locations as Yokohama, Sydney, Cape Town, and Mexico City. Nossal makes it clear, however, that these federal and provincial officials were 'not diplomats in anything but the most superficial sense. They were not accorded diplomatic status; nor, notably, were they representatives of a government with an independent

international personality, capable of conducting an independent foreign policy.'[28]

Most provincial offices, in a pattern to be repeated in subsequent years, were closed by the 1930s. Quebec terminated its Paris office in 1912 and the province's presence in Brussels and London ended in the 1930s. However, following the Second World War, the provinces began to revisit the idea of foreign delegations. In 1945 Ontario re-opened its London office and established a further presence in Chicago (1953), New York (1956), and Los Angeles and Cleveland (1967). The province also opened offices in Europe and Asia, including Milan (1963), Stockholm (1968), Brussels, Vienna, and Tokyo (1969), Frankfurt (1970), and Mexico City (1973). Quebec, on the other hand, posted a delegation in New York in 1941 and added several offices in subsequent years, including Brussels (1972), Tokyo (1973), Mexico City (1980), and Buenos Aires (1998).

It is important to note, however, that several provincial governments did not pursue a similar international strategy in the post-war period. Alberta, for example, limited its offices to London (1948), Los Angeles (1964), and Tokyo (1970). Comparatively, other provinces had either no interest or an 'idiosyncratic' approach to overseas representation. New Brunswick opened a London office in 1970, and subsequently established a presence in Hamburg and Boston, all of which were terminated by the 1990s.[29] Manitoba posted representatives in Minneapolis in 1975 and Saskatchewan opened and closed a series of offices in the late 1980s in a variety of cities, including London, Zurich, Hong Kong, Minneapolis, and New York.[30] Nova Scotia also recalled its delegation from London, but maintained a trade and investment presence in Boston until 2002.[31] British Columbia had various contacts in the Pacific Northwest and California. Regardless, by the 1990s the majority of these offices, including those from Ontario and Quebec, became targets for provincial budget cuts.[32]

Continuing the trend of opening and closing

offices, Mike Harris announced in 2001 that his Conservative government planned 'to open Ontario missions in New York, Shanghai, Tokyo, Munich, and London'.[33] The province also opened, and closed, offices in several American cities, including Boston and Atlanta. The Liberal government of Dalton McGuinty has established the London and Tokyo delegations first announced by the Conservatives, and has expressed further interest in New Delhi and Los Angeles.[34] Alberta is expanding its list of foreign representation, with offices in Beijing, Hong Kong, Tokyo, Seoul, Taipei, Mexico City, and European postings in London and Munich. Additionally, Alberta has established missions in Washington, DC, and Portland, Oregon.[35] For the most part Alberta and Ontario follow similar organizational models and work to ensure that these delegations are part of larger Canadian consulates. Not surprisingly, Quebec has also maintained its international presence with 25 offices in 17 countries.[36] These include general delegations in Brussels, London, Mexico City, New York, Paris, and Tokyo. A less comprehensive range of services is available in Buenos Aires, Boston, Chicago, and Los Angeles. Government bureaus, on the other hand, are in Barcelona, Beijing, Damascus (Immigration Office), Hong Kong (Immigration Office), Miami, Munich, Shanghai, Vienna (Immigration Office), and Washington, DC ('Tourism' Office). Finally, Quebec also has trade branches in Atlanta, Berlin, Rome, Santiago, Seoul, and Taipei, including additional business agents in Lima, Milan, and Hanoi.[37]

Trade Promotion

Trade promotion is another aspect of provincial foreign policy. In addition to international offices, trade missions are the most common example of promotional activity. Most provinces were active participants in federal initiatives, such as Jean Chrétien's Team Canada program. Other provinces, however, have organized independent trade missions. In the 1990s, for example, Alberta

targeted the Pacific Rim with the goal of diversifying its trade relations. Ontario also recently completed its first trade mission to Asia in two decades, which consisted of provincial officials and business representatives in the technology, tourism, and education sectors. In addition to Asia, Ontario has targeted India and more traditional trading partners in Japan and Western Europe, in sectors such as life sciences, information and communication technology, automobiles and parts, construction and architecture, environmental technologies, and the aerospace industry.[38] New Brunswick has also recently focused on trade promotion as part of its international strategy. In addition to the United States, New Brunswick has pursued export markets in China, Germany, the UK, Japan, Mexico, Eastern Europe, and members of la Francophonie. In addition to trade missions, the province also organizes training for both exporting companies and members of the provincial bureaucracy.[39]

Despite the significance of provincial trade missions it is important to keep these efforts in perspective. During Ontario's 2005 Asian tour Premier McGuinty attempted to lower expectations by stressing that the mission was not focused on 'announce-ables' (actual contracts) but on educating the Chinese about the province's economic potential. There was also no shortage of critics during Ralph Klein's first trade mission to Asia in 1993. In fact, many observers felt the most symbolic moment of the trip was the premier's attempt to sell Drummond Beer to the Japanese.[40] More recently, however, the Alberta government has acknowledged that numerous barriers exist in its attempts to diversify trade relations in Asia, despite a subsequent trade mission to China in 1997. These include a lack of railway infrastructure to transport international exports through British Columbia and capacity problems in coastal ports. As one provincial observer suggested, 'it is highly unlikely that Alberta will ever enjoy any substantial economic success in Asia. Whether we like it or not we are too far away and have little of real value to offer their consumers.'[41]

Therefore, Alberta relies on other methods of advancing provincial trade interests, including the protection of oil and gas exports in international trade agreements, reductions in tariffs in the agricultural sector, and an ongoing commitment to foreign trade offices, which is second only to Quebec.[42]

Expanding the International Agenda: Implications for Canadian Federalism

Unlike trade promotion, 'trade policy' is a distinctly separate matter, related to the negotiation and implementation of international commitments. In this case, a slightly different relationship between Ottawa and the provinces has evolved, primarily over issues of consultation and participation. This reality is a result of both international and domestic developments. Numerous foreign trade agreements at the international level now include areas of provincial jurisdiction such as services, agriculture, alcohol, government procurement, health and safety standards, energy, environment, and labour issues. In the 1970s the United States also began targeting provincial investment and subsidy programs in a wide range of sectors, including fish products, pork, softwood lumber, automobile production, and Michelin tires. It was also during this period that Washington condemned the nationalization of American-owned potash firms by the Saskatchewan government and Quebec's takeover of Asbestos Corporation. Domestically, as noted earlier, previous judicial rulings by the JCPC and the Supreme Court of Canada enhanced the international legitimacy of Canadian provinces.[43] Provincial governments were also becoming concerned with federal policy initiatives that marginalized sub-national interests, such as the National Energy Program (NEP). As a result, several provinces—especially Quebec, Ontario, Alberta—began to demand a more inclusive role in the formulation of Canadian foreign trade policy.

In response to these pressures Ottawa attempted to institutionalize the interests of the provinces within the federal bureaucracy. During this period, External Affairs was re-organized to include a new Federal Provincial Coordination Division (FPCD). While the department was originally created to monitor the activities of Quebec, it soon became responsible for keeping the provinces informed of all relevant Canadian international initiatives. It was also expected to co-ordinate provincial activity and provide assistance for provincial foreign missions.[44] As External Affairs, became more comfortable with the international activity of the provinces, however, the 'political' need to monitor these initiatives diminished. The Privy Council Office (PCO), as a result, took control of most responsibilities formerly under the administration of the FPCD and although External Affairs continued to maintain a federal–provincial office, it was, in the words of one official, 'little more than a man and a boy'.[45]

At the same time, however, Ottawa began using 'executive federalism' to coordinate matters of principal concern.[46] The first evidence of this can be seen by reviewing the outcome of the Tokyo Round of the GATT. Given the scope of the negotiations, the federal government required the support of the provinces in order to successfully negotiate a binding international agreement under the GATT's 'federal state clause'. At the beginning of the Tokyo Round, however, the only formal mechanism for provincial input was the Canadian Trade and Tariffs Committee (CTTC), which was responsible for gathering briefs from business, unions, consumer groups, the provinces, and other interested parties. In order to better represent regional interests a more direct forum for the provinces was established in 1975 with the creation of an ad hoc federal–provincial committee of deputy ministers. In August 1977, a Canadian Coordinator for Trade Negotiations (CCTN) was appointed with the mandate to coordinate information from the provinces, the federal bureaucracy, industry, and other non-governmental organizations.

In the spring of 1985, the premiers of British Columbia, Alberta, Saskatchewan, and Manitoba all announced their support for 'full provincial participation' in the upcoming negotiations for the proposed Canada–United States Free Trade Agreement (FTA). Ultimately, the provinces were unable to secure representation in the Trade Negotiations Office (TNO), headed by Simon Reisman, but a commitment was made to continue consultation within the CCTN. Shortly after the implementation of the FTA, the CCTN became the Committee for the Free Trade Agreement (CFTA); each province had one official representative on the committee. Ottawa also set up a series of consultative committees with various provincial departments to address sectoral concerns and on-going trade irritants and similar committees were established for the stalled Uruguay Round. During negotiations for the North American Free Trade Agreement, the CFTA remained in place but Ottawa and the provinces also agreed to create the Committee for North American Free Trade Negotiations (CNAFTN).[47]

Ultimately, the CNAFTN process evolved into the CTRADE committee system for international trade. The current CTRADE system involves a series of meetings between Ottawa and the provinces that occur four times a year. In recent years one of the annual CTRADE meetings has also been scheduled outside of Ottawa. Initially, some provinces expressed concerns with the content and quality of information available through CTRADE. More recently, however, the federal government has attempted to improve access to information and the agenda-setting process. There is now a secure website and draft documents are made available to the provinces in areas of provincial jurisdiction. According to some officials the last two chairs of CTRADE also prioritized provincial input due to the complexity of current negotiations, especially in areas such as services.[48]

At the same time there is ongoing pressure from specific provinces, such as Quebec and Alberta, for a more formalized role in the policy process. Quebec, for example, has previously supported a European Union (EU) model, in which member states are direct participants in EU

negotiating teams. Alberta has also called for the institutionalization of federal–provincial relations outside of CTRADE, most notably as part of the evolving Council of the Federation framework. Of specific concern to the federal government is the possibility of a formal voting formula process that could restrict Canada's options in international negotiations. Enthusiasm for a more formalized structure is also not shared by other provinces. Some provincial governments want to maintain the informal and flexible structure that currently exists while others are concerned about the need for additional bureaucratic resources and expertise. As a result, it would appear that substantial alteration to the existing CTRADE system is unlikely in the near future.[49]

Evaluating Provincial Economic Interests

Not surprisingly, Canadian provinces protect sectoral interests that are crucial to regional and provincial political economies. Therefore, Atlantic Canada prioritizes fishing, agriculture, and shipbuilding; Quebec attempts to maintain its agricultural marketing boards; and Ontario focuses on manufacturing. These provincial interests have a direct impact on Canadian foreign trade policy, particularly in relation to international trade agreements. Pressure from Quebec, for example, contributed to Canada's contradictory approach to agriculture during both the WTO and NAFTA negotiations. Specifically, Ottawa promoted the liberalization of grains and red meats because of the market advantage enjoyed by western provinces, but protected dairy and poultry, which are vital to the economy of Quebec. Alberta, in response to the National Energy Program (NEP), also ensured that energy provisions in NAFTA guaranteed its exports of oil to the United States. In some cases provincial interests are considered so important that separate international agreements are negotiated. The automobile industry in Ontario, for example, motivated Ottawa to negotiate the Canada–United States Auto Pact in 1965. British Columbia's reliance on softwood lumber also resulted in the

Canada–United States Memorandum of Understanding in 1986 and the bilateral Softwood Lumber Agreement (SLA) in 1996. Therefore, provincial economic interests not only influence Canada's foreign trade policy, but also the evolution of international norms and standards.

Canadian provinces can also directly influence specific provisions in international trade agreements. During the Uruguay Round negotiations, for example, there was considerable pressure from the United States to alter Article 2.2 of the WTO Agreement on Subsidies and Countervailing Measures (SCM). Article 2.2, which states that 'the setting or change of generally applicable tax rates by all levels of government entitled to do so shall not be deemed to be a specific subsidy for the purposes of this Agreement' was targeted by Washington because it desired to reduce the practice of state subsidies, which create significant competition in the American market. Canada, however, opposed this position because of the threat it posed to regional and provincial subsidy programs in Canada. As one official pointed out: 'the US proposal would have made provincial programs countervailable and all provinces, not simply Ontario and Quebec opposed it. The simple reason is that regional subsidies extend beyond agriculture in Canada and provincial governments did not want other programs targeted.' The other important factor was the fact that 'regional subsidies in the US are primarily state driven programs, whereas in Canada the provinces rely almost exclusively on funding from the federal government.'[50]

Another specific interest for provincial governments is trade in services. In terms of NAFTA, pressure from Canadian provinces was directly reflected in Annex I and Annex II of the agreement. Annex I excluded all provincial health measures in existence prior to 1 January 1994 relating to national treatment, most-favoured nation (MFN) status, and local presence requirements. As Mark Crawford has noted, this reservation immediately excluded most health services as the 'basic nature of provincial schemes have not

changed since 1994'.[51] The difficulty, however, is when provinces, such as Alberta, threaten to pursue a system with greater access to privately funded services. The Supreme Court of Canada's decision on 9 June 2005 to strike down Quebec's prohibition of private health insurance also has the potential, based on the language of Annex I, to open these services to the NAFTA dispute process. The Annex II 'Social Service Reservation', on the other hand, could maintain the protection of provincial practices. Specifically, Annex II excludes social services 'established or maintained for a public purpose'.[52] As a result, Canadian officials have argued that Annex II includes 'private-delivery' of 'publicly-funded' services. Ultimately, it was British Columbia that pushed for a clear definition of social services in NAFTA. The BC government was especially critical of Ottawa's approach to Annex II negotiations. The advocacy of provincial officials in this policy area resulted in 'public education, public training, health, and child care' being included in provisions related to cross-border services and investment'.[53]

British Columbia also argued for a broader exemption related to Article 1.3 of the WTO's General Agreement on Trade in Services (GATS). These provisions excluded services provided by regional and local governments 'supplied neither on a commercial basis, nor in competition with one or more service suppliers'.[54] As Crawford points out, British Columbia was the only province to dispute what it believed was the narrow definition of the exemption. Other federal and provincial officials argued that the existing language of Article 1.3 could be 'interpreted broadly' and suggested the recognition of the 'right to regulate' and 'due respect for national policy objectives' in the GATS preamble protected non-central interests.[55] Although Article 1.3(c) states that all competition should be 'economically rational as well as legally and practically possible' Anthony VanDuzer has also argued that health and education services are likely 'within the exclusion'.[56] Regardless, in the case of GATS the BC government had an impact on Canada's negotiating position but did not alter the language of the WTO agreement.

In the current Doha Round a wide range of services are again open to negotiation. In the decade following the GATS, however, most provinces have developed clear priorities related to service-based industries. Specifically, provincial officials have reviewed existing legislation and are now aware that 'decisions made at GATS negotiations have the potential to constrain the policy-making capacity of their respective governments, and want to make sure that their specific interests are both protected and addressed.'[57] Most provincial governments, however, make a distinction between 'defensive' and 'offensive' interests. Defensive considerations require ongoing support for government regulatory capacity, especially in the area of health and education. Offensive interests, on the other hand, are service-based issues potentially benefiting from a reduction of market barriers, such as GATS Mode IV, or business travel. In Ontario, for example, there is obvious sensitivity to defensive concerns, but the province also supports greater Mode IV liberalization, especially in relation to professional services, such as architecture, engineering, management, and accounting.[58] At the same time, however, there is reluctance to expose tour guide services, given the interdependent nature of regulatory controls tied to municipal jurisdiction, and fishing, hunting, and other licence requirements.[59] Regardless, it is also important to remember that WTO rulings related to GATS are limited. In fact, only 12 of 332 complaints dating back to 1995 are in direct reference to services.[60]

Provinces and Cross-Border Functional Relations

Provinces engage in a wide range of cross-border activity, including issues related to the environment, transportation corridors, water management, security, road maintenance, and fire-fighting. This activity takes place in a number of formal and informal settings. The first, and most obvious,

contact exists at the executive level in United States regional associations, such as the New England Governor's Conference (NEGC) and the Western Governor's Association (WGA). Additionally, members of provincial and state legislatures interact in similar forums, including the Council of State Governments-West (CSG-West). The majority of these associations limit participation to members of government but some, such as the Pacific Northwest Economic Region (PNWER) are also open to business and non-governmental interests. These associations also have varying mandates. Some are limited to trade, while others address economic, security, environment, and social considerations.

The oldest example of these linkages occurred in Atlantic Canada. In fact, the first meeting between Eastern Canadian premiers and New England Governors was during the summer of 1973, primarily to discuss energy issues. This forum was subsequently formalized as the Conference of New England Governors and Eastern Canadian Premiers (NEGECP) following the first oil crisis in October of that year.[61] Participants include governors from New England states and the premiers of Newfoundland and Labrador, Nova Scotia, New Brunswick, Prince Edward Island, and Quebec. As Ross Gittell and Charles S. Colgan have pointed out, the meetings provide a 'vehicle for sharing ideas and advancing mutual interests of the states and provinces. . .and represent a level of cooperation that is extraordinarily rare around the world'.[62] In fact, a wide range of issues are addressed in this forum, including tourism, minor trade irritants, transportation issues, and economic development. Energy, as noted above, has received the most attention, especially during the 1970s and 1980s. The NEGECP has also established a number of committees to study regional issues, including, the environment, transportation, energy, and trade and globalization.

It is clear, however, that some provinces place a greater priority on the committee system because of a lack of bureaucratic resources and an agenda that does not always focus on Canadian interests. The exception to this was transporta-tion issues following the terrorist attacks of 11 September, at which time there was considerable pressure from the NEGECP committee to imple-ment new border procedures, such as the Smart Border Accord. The activity of non-central gov-ernments, however, does not always yield tang-ible results. According to an official from New Brunswick, the failure to implement the accord east of Montreal sparked a great deal of action 'by state and provincial officials as they attempted to influence both Washington and Ottawa to recon-sider this position, although with little success'.[63] There is also the reality that some provinces in Atlantic Canada have started to focus on other regional forums. New Brunswick, for example, has become an active participant in the Eastern Regional Conference of the Council of State Governments. The province also recently signed a comprehensive Memorandum of Under-standing (MOU) with Maine and a more specific agreement with North Carolina on knowledge-based industries. This is in addition to its other bilateral agreements with Maine related to high-way maintenance, bridge maintenance, and man-agement of the St Croix Waterway.[64] For the most part, however, other provinces do not share the same interest as New Brunswick.[65] Competing economic priorities, including lobsters, blueber-ries, and potatoes, also limit the incentive for stronger linkages.[66]

In evaluating cross-border functional relation-ships in central Canada it is important to make a distinction between Ontario and Quebec. Both provinces are associate members of the Council of Great Lakes Governors (CGLG), but Quebec's ties to Atlantic Canada, and the importance of hydro-electricity are such that its cross-border ties are more extensive. In fact, when reviewing Ontario's activity it is limited to a narrow range of water management issues within the CGLG, specific trade disputes, assorted functional agreements, and direct ties with US state representatives.[67] The newly elected Liberal government of Dalton McGuinty, however, has prioritized closer linkages

with US states. For the most part, this has occurred at the executive and official level, including a bilat-eral meeting with the governor of Georgia in 2005. The assistant deputy minister and other officials in the Ministry of Economic Development and Trade (MEDT) have also developed contacts in several American states, in particular New York and Pennsylvania. For the most part, however, Ontario's cross-border relations are primarily driven by issue specific concerns.[68]

Quebec, on the other hand, has a number of well-developed cross-border relations, which are the result of provincial energy interests and its par-ticipation in the NEGECP. Therefore, the province has a historic commitment to these linkages that does not exist in Ontario. In fact, much of the motivation to participate in the NEGECP was to secure a stable market for Quebec's energy exports.[69] Although energy remains a crucial issue for Quebec this forum also expanded its focus fol-lowing 11 September. At the 2002 NEGECP meet-ings in Quebec City, for example, trade, security, and environmental issues were on the agenda. Quebec Premier Bernard Landry even pointed to Europe as a possible regional model for future con-sideration.[70] At the same time, however, there are Quebec officials that view the Conference of Governors and Premiers as a forum driven by American interests.[71] Although Quebec is currently a member of the conference's sub-committee on trade and globalization, formed in 2000, provincial officials cite minimal interest from US representa-tives unless it focuses on cross-border infrastruc-ture projects.[72] Quebec has therefore pursued other institutionalized linkages in the region, including annual bilateral 'summits' with New York, dating back to 1983. Although energy issues were often on the agenda, the focus of these meetings shifted to security and transportation issues following the 2001 terrorist bombings, especially in relation to improved border crossings.[73]

The provinces of Manitoba, Saskatchewan, Alberta, and British Columbia also have cross-border linkages with American states. Saskat-chewan is an associate member of the Midwestern

Legislative Conference (MLC), a regional forum linked to the Council of State Governments Midwest. For the most part the MLC focuses on functional issues, such as economic development, the environment, education, health and human services, and natural resources and energy. The MLC, however, also has a Mid-West Canada Relations Committee that was first created in 1991. For the most part Saskatchewan's participation in the MLC is limited to the roundtable sessions where discussion focuses on an eclectic range of issues, including country of origin labelling, nursing homes, public pensions, legislative ethics, and affordable health insurance for small business. Saskatchewan's motivation for participating in the MLC is based on the recognition that in order to protect provincial interests contact must extend beyond the executive level. At the same time, however, Saskatchewan is realistic about its goals in this forum, and recognizes the marginal interest and limited bureaucratic resources in American states.[74]

Although Manitoba recently joined the MLC the province has historically emphasized cross-border linkages within the Western Governors Association. For the most part, the mandate of the WGA is similar to other regional associations and focuses on issues related to the environment, economic development, and other topical matters. For approximately the last decade, the premiers from Canada's western provinces have attended the WGA's annual meeting, but not as formal members of the association. Instead, the WGA has a working relationship with the Western Premiers Conference (WPC). For Manitoba Premier Garry Doer, the WGA primarily serves as a means of trade promotion but it has also facilitated formal cross-border functional agreements, such as the Memorandum of Understanding on Drought and Wildland Fires signed in September 2003. As part of this initiative Doer also represented provincial interests in a joint-study, *Enhancing Cross-Border Cooperation to Fight Forest Fires*, which dealt with issues outlined in the final agreement.[75] In addition, Manitoba has negotiated bilateral MOU's with

several US states and municipalities. The province, for example, recently completed a series of agreements with Minnesota related to economic development, trade, tourism, water issues, and education. In addition, the province signed an MOU with Texas on trade and economic development and engaged in preliminary discussions with California on clean energy strategies. Manitoba also signed a recent MOU on bio-science technology with the city of Atlanta.[76] In partnership with New Brunswick, Manitoba officials participated in a joint-trade mission to Texas in January 2005.

Among the western provinces, Alberta has the most prolific agenda related to cross-border functional issues. In fact, the province is associated with the WGA, the Council of State Governments West (CSG-West), the Pacific Northwest Economic Region, the Rocky Mountain Trade Corridor, the Montana–Alberta Bilateral Advisory Council (MABAC), and the CanAm Border Trade Alliance. In terms of the WGA, Alberta has also entered into agreements on cross-border technical issues, the most recent being a protocol 'Governing the Siting and Permitting of Interstate Electric Transmission Lines in the Western United States', signed in June 2002;[77] an addendum to the initial protocol was negotiated by Alberta in April 2004. Another example of Alberta's cross-border regional agenda is its involvement in PNWER. Formed in 1991, the association engages a diverse range of issues, including, agriculture, energy, forestry, infrastructure, sustainable development, tourism, transportation, the environment, health care, telecommunications, and workforce development. Although Alberta's primary interest in PNWER is the development of export markets it has also used the forum to address other issues, such as CANAMEX, a proposed trade corridor through Alaska, the Yukon, BC, Alberta, Montana, Idaho, Utah, and Nevada to the Mexican border. Following 11 September, PNWER also focused on issues aimed at preventing the disruption, or slowdown, of cross-border shipping and business travel.[78] Finally, Alberta also has bilateral agreements with a number of border-states and is a member of the Montana Alberta Bilateral Advisory Council.[79]

British Columbia's interest in cross-border functional issues has increased in recent years. In fact, BC is now associated with the WGA, CSG-West, PNWER, and the International Mobility and Trade Corridor (IMTC). Not surprisingly, BC's influence is often linked directly to the mandate and membership of these organizations. In the WGA BC has articulated provincial concerns related to the Canada–US softwood lumber dispute. In addition, BC has also signed bilateral agreements with other WGA members—most notably Idaho and Montana—on environmental protection and conservation.[80] The CSG-West, which is primarily a professional development forum for US legislators, focuses on fiscal affairs, trade and transportation, water, energy, natural resources, and southern border issues. Unlike the WGA, BC has official standing within CSG-West. British Columbia became an 'associate' member in 2000 but, despite its enhanced status, BC has limited influence.[81] As with the WGA and CSG-West, PNWER is viewed by provincial officials as a means of influencing American state legislatures on matters of international trade. In recent years, for example, a dispute between Oregon, British Columbia, and Alberta regarding horticultural producers and provincial phytosanitary restrictions was addressed within PNWER.[82] Whistler, BC hosted the first PNWER meeting held outside of the United States in July 2001. Finally, issues of cross-border access for BC are primarily addressed in the IMTC or as part of the Peace Arch Crossing Entry (PACE) and CANPASS programs.[83]

Although it is difficult to deny the relevance of provincial cross-border relations, it is also important to not overstate these developments. One problem is the differing levels of commitment to these regional forums throughout Canada. In Atlantic Canada, the majority of activity is driven by New Brunswick because of its shared border with the United States. In Central Canada, Quebec's interest is a result of historic ties related to the export of energy, although the province has

recently prioritized border access issues, especially with New York. Ontario, on the other hand, is active in several forums but appears to approach cross-border functional relations in a more ad hoc and reactionary capacity, focusing attention on trade disputes and Great Lakes water management issues. Comparatively, Western Canada has a more diverse range of relationships but arguably, with the exception of Alberta, these ties are relatively new and untested. These forums also have different mandates and, not surprisingly, are driven by American interests which, since 2001, have focused on a narrowing list of concerns, primarily border access, security, and trade promotion. Another issue limiting the importance of state–province relations is the obvious dominance of Congress in the formulation of trade policy in the United States. Limited bureaucratic resources on both sides of the border further weaken the potential impact of these linkages. Finally, it is impossible to ignore the overall lack of knowledge and interest in Canada among American legislators and bureaucrats outside a very selective range of issues, at both the state and federal level.

Conclusion

The expanding range of interests related to provincial foreign policy has both domestic and international implications. In Canada, the federal government has often struggled with Quebec's international activity due to the province's nationalist agenda. As a result, Quebec has secured official standing in la Francophonie and at times has directly questioned Canada's role in NATO. Historically, other provinces focused on the opening of foreign offices and issues such as tourism, immigration, and the pursuit of export markets. As international trade agreements became increasingly intrusive, however, this created challenges for Ottawa in the negotiation and implementation of these commitments. Although CTRADE was an attempt to facilitate dialogue with the provinces, the result was an increasingly complex domestic policy process. In addition, pressure from provincial governments has influenced the evolution of international norms and standards, especially in terms of services, agriculture, energy, softwood lumber, and the negotiation of subsidies. Cross-border ties with American states have also resulted in a number of sub-national agreements and initiatives. Although it is difficult to deny the increasing legitimacy of provincial foreign activity it is important to note that these actions do not threaten the federal government's ability to speak for Canada at the international level.

Notes

1. Douglas M. Brown and Earl H. Fry, eds, *States and Provinces in the International Economy* (Berkeley: University of California Press; Kingston, ON: Queen's University Institute of Governmental Studies Press and Institute of Intergovernmental Relations, 1993).

2. Kim Richard Nossal, 'The Impact of Provincial Governments on Canadian Foreign Policy', in *States and Provinces in the International Economy*, 241.

3. Grace Skogstad, 'International Trade Policy and Canadian Federalism: A Constructive Tension?', in Herman Kakvis and Grace Skogstad, eds, *Canadian Federalism: Performance, Effectiveness, and Legitimacy* (Don Mills, ON: Oxford University Press, 2002); G. Bruce Doern and Brian Tomlin, *Faith and Fear: The Free Trade Story* (Toronto: Stoddart Publishing, 1991); and Michael Hart, *Decision at Midnight: Inside the Canada–US Free-Trade Negotiations* (Vancouver: UBC Press, 1994).

4. Stephen de Boer, 'Canadian Provinces, US States and North American Integration: Bench Warmers or Key Players?', *Choices: Canada's Options in North America* 8, 4 (November 2002): 2–24; John F. Helliwell, *How Much Do National Borders Matter?* (Washington, DC: Brookings Institution Press, 1998); John McCallum, 'National Borders Matter: Canada–US Regional Trade Patterns', *The American Economic Review* 85, 3 (June 1995): 615–23; and Michael A. Anderson and Stephen L. Smith, 'Canadian Provinces in World Trade: Engagement and Detachment', *Canadian Journal of Economics* 32, 1 (February 1999): 22–38.

5. Louis Sabourin, 'Special International Status for Quebec?', in Stephen Clarkson, ed., *An Independent Foreign Policy for Canada?* (Toronto: McClelland and Stewart, 1968); Louis Bélanger, 'The Domestic Politics of Quebec's Quest for External Distinctiveness', *American Review of Canadian Studies* 32, 2 (Summer 2002); and Luc Bernier, 'Mulroney's International "Beau Risque": The Golden Age of Quebec's Foreign Policy', in Nelson Michaud and Kim Richard Nossal, eds, *Diplomatic Departures: The Conservative Era in Canadian Foreign Policy, 1984–93* (Vancouver: UBC Press, 2001).

6. Robert G. Richards, 'The Canadian Constitution and International Economic Relations', in Douglas M. Brown and Murray G. Smith, eds, *Canadian Federalism: Meeting Global Economic Challenges?* (Kingston: Queen's University Institute of Intergovernmental Relations, 1991), 58–9.

7. Ibid., 62.

8. Ian Robinson, 'The NAFTA, the Side Deals, and Canadian Federalism: Constitutional Reform by Other Means', in Ronald L. Watts and Douglas M. Brown, eds, *Canada: The State of the Federation 1993* (Kingston: Queen's University Institute of Intergovernmental Relations, 1993), 214.

9. Gerald Baier, 'Judicial Review and Canadian Federalism', in *Canadian Federalism*, 27; and Peter W. Hogg, *Constitutional Law of Canada: 1998 Student Edition* (Scarborough: Carswell, 1998), 417.

10. Christopher J. Kukucha, 'From Kyoto to the WTO: Evaluating the Constitutional Legitimacy of the Provinces in Canadian Foreign Trade and Environmental Policy', *Canadian Journal of Political Science* 38, 1 (March 2005): 129–52.

11. Kim Richard Nossal, *The Politics of Canadian Foreign Policy* (Scarborough: Prentice-Hall Canada, 1985), 199–200.

12. Elliot J. Feldman and Lily Gardner Feldman, 'The Impact of Federalism on the Organization of

Canadian Foreign Policy', in M.W. Westmacott and R.D. Olling, eds, *Perspectives on Canadian Federalism* (Scarborough: Prentice-Hall Canada, 1988), 268.

13. Sabourin, 'Special International Status for Quebec?', 104.

14. Nossal, *The Politics of Canadian Foreign Policy*, 205.

15. Kim Richard Nossal, *The Politics of Canadian Foreign Policy*, 3rd ed. (Scarborough: Prentice Hall, 1997), 326; and Bélanger, 'The Domestic Politics of Quebec's Quest for External Distinctiveness', 200.

16. Nossal, *The Politics of Canadian Foreign Policy*, 203.

17. Stéphane Roussel and Charles-Alexandre Théorêt, 'A "Distinct Strategy"? The Use of Canadian Strategic Culture by the Sovereignist Movement in Quebec, 1968–1996', *International Journal* 59, 3 (Summer 2004): 564.

18. Nossal, *The Politics of Canadian Foreign Policy*, 3rd ed., 204–5.

19. Bélanger, 'The Domestic Politics of Quebec's Quest for External Distinctiveness', 202.

20. Earl H. Fry, 'Quebec's Relations with the United States', *American Review of Canadian Studies* 32, 2 (Summer 2002): 329.

21. Graham Fraser, 'Bouchard Carries "S" Word to U.S.: Bloc Québécois Leader Visits UN, Bluntly Talks of Separation', *Globe and Mail*, 2 March 1994, A1.

22. 'U.S. Might Seek to Annex West, Bouchard Says: Americans Won't Resist Breakup, Bloc Leader Tells Business Group', *Globe and Mail*, 30 May 1994, A1.

23. Julian Beltrame, 'U.S. Officials Warned Bloc Boss Over Entry to NAFTA, Diplomat Says', *Vancouver Sun*, 11 March 1994, A15.

24. Graham Fraser, 'Bouchard Reassures U.S. Audience on Sovereignty', *Globe and Mail*, 3 March 1994, A3.

25. Lawrence L. Herman, 'The PQ Can't Count on Easing Quebec into NAFTA', *Globe and Mail*, 8 July 1994, A21.

26. Ibid.

27. For more detailed discussions of economic considerations relevant to Quebec sovereignty please see, Pierre-Paul Proulx, 'Some Comments on Earl Fry's Discussion of the Economic Dimension of Quebec, Canada, and United States Relations', *American Review of Canadian Studies* 26, 4 (Winter 1996):

607–18.

28. Nossal, *The Politics of Canadian Foreign Policy*, 3rd ed., 236.

29. Personal interview, 2 June 2003. The federal, provincial, and industry officials interviewed for this study spoke on the condition of anonymity with the understanding there would be no direct quotations without permission. Future references will cite only the date of these meetings. Locations are excluded given the small number of officials working in this policy area (to best ensure confidentiality).

30. Personal interview, 28 May 2003.

31. Personal interview, 29 May 2003.

32. Kim Richard Nossal, 'The Administration of Provincial International Activities: Provincial Missions Abroad', Paper presented at The Administration of Foreign Affairs conference, Hull, QC, 3 November 2001, 3–5; and Kim Richard Nossal, 'Anything but Provincial: The Provinces and Foreign Affairs', in Chris Dunn, ed., *Provinces: Canadian Provincial Politics* (Peterborough: Broadview Press, 1996), 506.

33. Nossal, 'The Administration of Provincial International Activities', 5.

34. Personal interview, 31 August 2005.

35. Alberta Economic Development, *International Offices*. Available at http://www.alberta-canada.com/aed/index.cfm (accessed 30 September 2005).

36. Jean Charest, 'Canada and the US: Change and Continuity', *International Journal* 60, 2 (Spring 2005): 325.

37. Quebec, Ministry of International Relations, *Quebec Offices Abroad*. Available at http://www.mri.gouv.qc.ca/en/action_internationale/representations_etranger/representations_etranger.asp (accessed 30 September 2005).

38. Sarah McGregor, 'McGuinty's Trip to China Set on Making Business Contacts, Not Announcements', *Embassy: Canada's Foreign Policy Newsweekly*, 21 September 2005, 9.

39. Brian Abeda, 'New Brunswick Looking Beyond U.S. Relationship: Maritime Province Eyes New Markets in France and China', *Embassy: Canada's Foreign Policy Newsweekly*, 21 September 2005, 12.

40. In a press conference at the Canadian embassy in

Tokyo Klein told the Japanese media that 'back home he was regarded as something of a connoisseur of beer'. For more information on Klein's attempts to market Alberta beer in Japan, please see Mark Lisac, 'Diplomatic Debut for Alberta Beer in Tokyo', *Edmonton Journal*, 9 November 1993, C7.

41. Personal interview, 24 January 1994.
42. Christina Leadlay, 'Alberta–Asia Trade Will Need Infrastructure Improvements', *Embassy: Canada's Foreign Policy Newsweekly*, 21 September 2005, 13.
43. Kukucha, 'From Kyoto to the WTO', 129–52.
44. Peyton Lyon, 'The Provinces and Canada Abroad', in Don Munton, ed., *Groups and Governments in Canadian Foreign Policy, Proceedings of a Conference, Ottawa, Canada, 9–11 June 1982* (Toronto: Canadian Institute of International Affairs, 1985), 27–28; and Feldman and Feldman, 'The Impact of Federalism on the Organization of Canadian Foreign Policy', 268–72.
45. Personal interview, 11 February 1994.
46. Donald V. Smiley, *Canada in Question: Federalism in the Eighties*, 3rd ed. (Toronto: McGraw-Hill Ryerson, 1980); and Donald V. Smiley, *The Federal Condition in Canada* (Toronto: McGraw-Hill Ryerson, 1987).
47. Personal interview, 11 February 1994; Personal interview, 21 February 1994; Personal interview, 23 February 1994; Doern and Tomlin, *Faith and Fear*, 128–30; Douglas M. Brown, 'The Evolving Role of the Provinces in Canadian Trade Policy', in *Canadian Federalism: Meeting Global Economic Challenges?*, 94–5; and Douglas M. Brown, 'The Evolving Role of the Provinces in Canada–U.S. Trade Relations', in *States and Provinces in the International Economy*, 114.
48. Personal interview, 28 August 2001; Personal interview, 9 October 2001.
49. Skogstad, 'International Trade Policy and Canadian Federalism', 171.
50. Personal interview, 9 February 1994.
51. Mark Crawford, 'Truth or Consequences? The Law and Politics of the GATS Health Care Debate', Paper presented at A Review of Canada's International Policies conference, Norman Patterson School of International Affairs, Ottawa, Ontario, 7 November 2003, 18.
52. Ibid., 19.
53. Personal interview, 2 August 2004.
54. World Trade Organization, *Annex 1B General Agreement on Trade in Services*, 15 April 1994, 3. For a summary of Canada's interpretation of this position, please see International Trade Canada, *Trade in Services: WTO—Trade in Services*. Available at http://www.dfait-maeci.gc.ca/tna-nac/TS/gats-negotiations-en.asp (accessed 10 March 2005).
55. Mark Crawford, 'Truth or Consequences? The Law and Politics of the GATS Health Care Debate', *Canadian Foreign Policy* 12, 2 (Fall 2005): 105–6.
56. J. Anthony VanDuzer, *Health, Education and Social Services in Canada: The Impact of the GATS*. Available at http://www.dfait-maeci.gc.ca/tna-nac/documents/health-edu-ss-gats-en.pdf (accessed 11 June 2005), 78.
57. George Kourakos, Yves Poisson, and Lynn Decarie, *Trade in Services: An Opportunity for Canada* (Ottawa: Public Policy Forum, 2003), 13.
58. Personal interview, 30 May 2002.
59. Kourakos, Poisson, and Decarie, *Trade in Services*, 16.
60. Personal interview, 31 August 2005. Of the 13 cases, three had direct reference to Canada, including *Certain Measures Affecting the Automotive Industry*, *Certain Measures Concerning Periodicals*, and *Measures Affecting Film Distribution Services*. Other important decisions involved the export of bananas to the European Community and the supply of offshore gambling services to the United States (*Regime for Importation, Sale and Distribution of Bananas*, and *Measures Affecting Cross-Border Supply of Gambling and Betting Services*).
61. Nossal, *The Politics of Canadian Foreign Policy*, 3rd ed., 303.
62. Ross Gittell and Charles S. Colgan, 'New England Regionalism: Economic Motivations and Barriers', in Stephen G. Tomblin and Charles S. Colgan, eds, *Regionalism in a Global Society: Persistence and Change in Atlantic Canada and New England* (Peterborough, ON: Broadview Press, 2004), 130.
63. Personal interview, 2 June 2003.
64. Ibid.

65. Personal interview, 29 May 2003.

66. Personal interview, 28 May 2003; Personal interview, 29 May 2003.

67. De Boer, 'Canadian Provinces, US States and North American Integration', 9–11, 18–19.

68. Personal interview, 31 August 2005.

69. Gittell and Colgan, 'New England Regionalism', 130–1.

70. Martin Lubin, 'Strains Between Governments at the Top, Hands Across the Border at the Base: The Role of Subnational Governments During the Bush-Chrétien Era and Beyond', *Canadian–American Public Policy* 54 (September 2003): 31.

71. Personal interview, 4 June 2003.

72. Ibid.

73. Lubin, 'Strains Between Governments at the Top, Hands Across the Border at the Base', 29–30.

74. Personal interview, 31 May 2004.

75. Western Premiers and the Western Governors Association, *Memorandum of Understanding on Enhancing Cross-Border Cooperation to Fight Wildland Fires*, 14 September 2003.

76. Personal interview, 2 June 2004.

77. Western Governors Association, et al., *Protocol Among the Members of the Western Governors Association Governing the Siting and Permitting of Interstate Electrical Transmission Lines in the Western United States*, 23 June 2002.

78. Alberta, International and Intergovernmental Affairs, *US Pacific Northwest–Alberta Relations* (Edmonton: Government of Alberta, 2004).

79. Alberta, International and Intergovernmental Affairs, *Montana–Alberta Relations* (Edmonton: Government of Alberta, 2004).

80. British Columbia, Idaho, and Montana, *Environmental Cooperation Arrangement*, September 2003.

81. Personal interview, 19 December 2002.

82. Ibid.

83. Theodore H. Cohn, 'Transportation and Competitiveness in North America: The Cascadian and San Diego–Tijuana Border Regions', in Heather N. Nicol and Ian Townsend-Gault, eds, *Holding the Line: Borders in a Global World* (Vancouver: UBC Press, 2005), 205–8.

Selected Bibliography

Brown, Douglas and Murray Smith, eds. 1991. *Canadian Federalism: Meeting Global Challenges?* Kingston, ON: Queen's University Institute of Intergovernmental Relations.

Burton, B.E., W.C. Soderlund, and T.A. Keenleyside. 1995. 'The Press and Canadian Foreign Policy: A Re-examination Ten Years On', *Canadian Foreign Policy* 3 (Fall): 51–69.

De Boer, Stephen. 2002. 'Canadian Provinces, US States and North American Integration: Bench Warmers or Key Players?' *Choices: Canada's Options in North America* 8 (November): 1–24.

English, John. 1992. *The Worldly Years: The Life of Lester Pearson. Vol II: 1949–1972.* New York: Knopf.

Gotlieb, Allan. 1991. *'I'll be With You in a Minute, Mr Ambassador': The Education of a Canadian Diplomat in Washington.* Toronto: University of Toronto Press.

Granatstein, J.L., and Robert Bothwell. 1990. *Pirouette: Pierre Trudeau and Canadian Foreign Policy.* Toronto: University of Toronto Press.

Halton, Dan. 2001. 'International News in the North American Media', *International Journal* 56, 3 (Summer): 499–515.

Head, Ivan, and Pierre Trudeau. 1995. *The Canadian Way: Shaping Canada's Foreign Policy, 1968–1984.* Toronto: McClelland and Stewart.

Hilliker, John. 1990. *Canada's Department of External Affairs, Vol. 1: The Early Years, 1909–1946.* Montreal: McGill-Queen's University Press.

Hilliker, John and Donald Barry. 1995. *Canada's Department of External Affairs, Vol. 2: Coming of Age, 1946–1968.* Montreal: McGill-Queen's University Press.

———. 1994. 'The PM and the SSEA in Canada's Foreign Policy: Sharing the Territory, 1946–1968', *International Journal* 50, 1 (Winter): 162–88.

Kirton, John. 1978. 'Foreign Policy Decision-Making in the Trudeau Government: Promise and Performance', *International Journal* 33, 2 (Spring): 287–311.

Kukucha, Christopher J. 2005. 'From Kyoto to the WTO: Evaluating the Constitutional Legitimacy of the Provinces in Canadian Foreign Trade and Environmental Policy', *Canadian Journal of Political Science* 38, 1 (March): 129–52.

———. 2003. 'Domestic Politics and Canadian Foreign Trade Policy: Intrusive

Interdependence, The WTO and the NAFTA', *Canadian Foreign Policy* 10, 2 (Winter): 59–86.

Lackenbauer, P. Whitney, ed. 2002. *An Inside Look at External Affairs During the Trudeau Years: The Memoirs of Mark MacGuigan*. Calgary: University of Calgary Press.

Lortie, Marc, and Sylvie Bedard. 2002. 'Citizen Involvement in Canadian Foreign Policy: The Summit of the Americas Experience 2001', *International Journal* 57, 3 (Summer): 323–40.

McNiven, James D., and Dianna Cann. 1993. 'Canadian Provincial Trade Offices in the United States', pp. 167–84 in Douglas M. Brown and Earl H. Fry, eds, *States and Provinces in the International Economy*. Berkeley: University of California Press; Kingston, ON: Institute of Governmental Studies Press and Institute of Intergovernmental Relations.

McRae, Rob. 2001. 'Human Security, Connectivity, and the New Global Civil Society', pp. 236–49 in Rob McRae and Don Hubert, eds, *Human Security and the New Diplomacy: Protecting People, Promoting Peace*. Montreal: McGill-Queen's University Press.

MacDonald, Laura C. 2002. 'Governance and State-Society Relations: The Challenges', pp. 187–223 in George C. Hoberg, ed., *Capacity of Choice: Canada in a New North America*. Toronto: University of Toronto Press.

Mace, Gordon, Louis Bélanger, and Ivan Bernier. 1995. 'Canadian Foreign Policy and Quebec', pp. 119–44 in Maxwell A. Cameron and Maureen Appel Molot, eds, *Canada Among Nations 1995: Democracy and Foreign Policy*. Ottawa: Carleton University Press.

Matthews, Robert. 1983. 'The Churches and Foreign Policy', *International Perspectives* (January/February): 18–21.

Michaud, Nelson. 2002. 'Bureaucratic Politics and the Shaping of Policies: Can We Measure Pulling and Hauling Games?' *Canadian Journal of Political Science* 35, 2 (June): 269–300.

Munton, Don, and Tom Keating. 2001. 'Internationalism and the Canadian Public', *Canadian Journal of Political Science* 34, 3 (September): 517–49.

Nossal, Kim Richard. 1996. 'Anything But Provincial: The Provinces and Foreign Affairs', pp. 503–18 in Christopher Dunn, ed., *Provinces: Canadian Provincial Politics*. Peterborough: Broadview Press.

———. 1995. 'The Democratization of Canadian Foreign Policy: The Elusive Ideal', pp. 29–43 in Maxwell A. Cameron and Maureen Appel Molot, eds, *Canada Among Nations 1995: Democracy and Foreign Policy*. Ottawa: Carleton University Press.

———. 1994. 'The PM and the SSEA in Canada's Foreign Policy: Dividing the Territory, 1968–1993', *International Journal* 50, 1 (Winter): 189–208.

———. 1984. 'Bureaucratic Politics and the Westminster Model', pp. 120–7 in Robert Mathews, et al. eds, *International Conflict and Conflict Management: Readings in World Politics*. Scarborough: Prentice-Hall.

Pearson, Geoffrey A.H. 1994. *Seize the Day: Lester B. Pearson and Crisis Diplomacy*. Ottawa: Carleton University Press.

Rempel, Roy. 2002. *The Chatter Box: An Insider's Account of the Irrelevance of Parliament in the Making of Canadian Foreign and Defence Policy*. Toronto: Dundurn.

Riddell-Dixon, Elizabeth. 1985. *The Domestic Mosiac: Domestic Groups and Canadian Foreign Policy*. Toronto: Canadian Institute of International Affairs.

Skogstad, Grace. 2002. 'International Trade Policy and Canadian Federalism: A Constructive Tension', pp. 159–77 in Herman Bakvis and Grace Skogstad, eds, *Canadian Federalism: Performance, Effectiveness, and Legitimacy*. Don Mills, ON: Oxford University Press.

Stairs, Denis. 2001. 'The Changing Office and the Changing Environment of the Minister of Foreign Affairs in the Axworthy Era', pp. 19–38 in Fen Osler Hampson, Norman Hillmer, and Maureen Appel Molot, eds, *Canada Among Nations 2001: The Axworthy Legacy*. Don Mills, ON: Oxford University Press.

Taras, David, ed. 1985. *Parliament in Canadian Foreign Policy*. Toronto: Canadian Institute of International Affairs.

Thordarson, Bruce. 1972. *Trudeau and Foreign Policy: A Study in Decision-Making*. Don Mills, ON: Oxford University Press.

Wolfe, Robert, ed. 1998. *Diplomatic Missions: The Ambassador in Canadian Foreign Policy*. Kingston, ON: Queen's University School of Policy Studies.

PART IV

Security

Adam Smith famously wrote that government has three main responsibilities: 1) enforcing rules of conduct within society, 2) settling disputes between its members, and 3) protecting society from external attack. The primary purpose of a country's foreign policy, then, is Smith's last responsibility—the protection of its citizens. Canada is in an unusual circumstance. It has only the United States as a neighbour and war between the two countries is inconceivable. In many respects Canada remains, in the words of Liberal Senator Raoul Dandurand at the League of Nations in 1924, 'a fire-proof house, far from inflammable materials'. Due to its favourable geographic situation, Canada has also felt an obligation to help build a more secure world. This section of *Readings in Canadian Foreign Policy* examines how Canada's foreign and defence policies are used to protect its territorial integrity and political independence, as well as to contribute to international peace and security. As with the other sections in this volume, a comprehensive analysis of all security issues is impossible. For instance, there are no specific chapters on the Canadian military, Canada's non-participation in the American-led war on Iraq,[1] Canada and Ballistic Missile Defence, or the role of Canada in disarmament.

When Canadians are asked to identify Canada's principal role in maintaining international peace and security, the quick answer is always peace-keeping. Duane Bratt explores this significant aspect of Canadian foreign policy in Chapter 14. He emphasizes the difference between 'peace-keeping' and 'peace support operations' and identifies a gap that exists between the Canadian public's perception of peace-keeping and the reality of peace support operations. He also argues that Canada has moved away from UN operations and towards NATO-led operations.

The 1990s saw the gradual weakening of borders among many developed states. The EU had only minimal restrictions on individuals going from one member country to the next and NAFTA had opened up the Canadian–American and American–Mexican border for the freer flow of goods. In fact, much of the North American discussion in the late 1990s was about making cross-border traffic even easier.[2] This debate ended suddenly on 11 September 2001 when, in response to the terrorist attacks on the United States, the Americans closed their borders.

Since 9/11 the United States has taken significant steps to tighten border security, including along what used to be proclaimed as the 'longest undefended border'. Peter Andreas has referred to this as the 'Mexicanization of US–Canada border politics'.[3] The essential question of border security is straight forward: how to prevent terrorists and criminals from crossing the border, while simultaneously ensuring minimal restrictions on legitimate traffic? In Chapter 15, Chris Sands, an American expert on Canadian foreign policy, assesses Canadian–American border co-operation in the immediate aftermath of 9/11.

National security places the emphasis on protecting the state from external threats. This involves the hard power concepts of border security, intelligence gathering, and the ability to use military force. Human security, on the other hand, places the emphasis on the protection of individuals and communities. Human security seeks to expand the traditional definition of security by asserting that anything that endangers the individual is a security threat, including genocide, civil war, poverty, environmental degradation, the absence of the rule of law, and international war. Moreover, elements that are used for national security may actually damage human security. Examples include the use of military/police personnel as tools of repression, violations of civil liberties that occur in the process of protecting the state from external threats, and the heavy dependence of military groups on state resources that could otherwise be used for alleviating poverty.

Elements of human security have always been a part of Canadian foreign policy,[4] but the terminology and the attention paid to human security was largely due to the appointment of Lloyd Axworthy as Foreign Affairs Minister.[5] Axworthy's tenure as Foreign Minister (1996–2000) was a time filled with great initiatives in the area of human security. The successful campaign, known as the Ottawa Process, to craft, sign, and ratify the Anti-Personnel Mines Convention in 1997–8 was the crowning achievement. However, there were other successes, including his role in establishing the framework for the creation of the International Criminal Court, his work on controlling the trade in small arms and light weapons, his efforts to eliminate the use of child soldiers, and his attempts to protect civilians in times of conflict.

Axworthy's policies, and to a certain degree his personality, made him a lightning rod for criticism among many Canadian foreign policy scholars.[6] Many of the criticisms of human security come from those who suggest that it ignores the reality of international relations and minimizes the role of hard military power. In contrast, Ann Denholm Crosby, in Chapter 16, offers a criticism of human security from a gender-informed Gramscian approach. She supports the concept of human security, pointing out that it has a 'gendered nature of security policy decision making' that was advocated by the Voice of Women in the early 1960s. However, though Axworthy's articulation and implementation of human security 'gives the appearance of security having taken on a human face, it remains the face of power acting in its own interests behind the mask'. In particular, it remains 'rooted in international institutions and documents' and it masks the idea that 'security is dependent upon global market forces.'

Notes

1. For a good academic analysis of this question see Donald Barry, 'Chrétien, Bush, and the War in Iraq', *The American Review of Canadian Studies* (Summer 2005): 215–45.
2. See Fen Osler Hampson and Maureen Appel Molot, eds, *Canada Among Nations 2000: Vanishing Borders* (Don Mills, ON: Oxford University Press, 2000).
3. Peter Andreas, 'A Tale of Two Borders: The US–Canada and US–Mexico Lines after 9-11', in Andreas and Thomas J. Biersteker, eds, *The Rebordering of North America: Integration and Exclusion in a New Security Context* (New York: Routledge, 2003), 9.
4. See John English, 'In the Liberal Tradition: Lloyd Axworthy and Canadian Foreign Policy', in Fen Osler Hampson, Norman Hillmer, and Maureen Appel Molot, eds, *Canada Among Nations 2001: The Axworthy Legacy* (Don Mills, ON: Oxford University Press, 2001), 89–107.
5. Axworthy has written extensively on human security. For one of his earliest efforts see Lloyd Axworthy, 'Canada and Human Security: The Need for Leadership', *International Journal* 52, 2 (Spring 1997): 183–96. For an assessment of Axworthy's record see Fen Osler Hampson, Norman Hillmer, and Maureen Appel Molot, eds, *Canada Among Nations 2001: The Axworthy Legacy* (Don Mills, ON: Oxford University Press, 2001).
6. For a brief survey of some of these criticisms see Fen Osler Hampson and Dean Oliver, 'Pulpit Diplomacy: A Critical Assessment of the Axworthy Doctrine', *International Journal* 53, 3 (Summer 1998): 379–406; Kim Richard Nossal, 'Pinchpenny Diplomacy: The Decline of Good International Citizenship in Canadian Foreign Policy', *International Journal* 54, 1 (Winter 1998–9): 88–105; William W. Bain, 'Against Crusading: The Ethics of Human Security and Canadian Foreign Policy', *Canadian Foreign Policy* 6, 3 (Spring 1999): 85–98.

14

Warriors or Boy Scouts? Canada and Peace Support Operations

Duane Bratt

Canadians are in love with peace-keeping. Year after year, public opinion polls across all regions, classes, ages, and ethnicities show a consistently high support for peace-keeping.[1] While every country builds monuments to its great military victories and war leaders, only Canada has a prominent peace-keeping monument. In fact, at a ceremony marking the 10th anniversary of that memorial, then-Foreign Affairs Minister Bill Graham declared that 'for many Canadians, and in the eyes of the world, peace-keeping is fundamental to who we are as a nation.'[2] These comments were reinforced by historian Norman Hillmer who pointed out that peace-keeping fit 'the government's international objectives and appeal[ed] to a public anxious to believe that Canada could be the world's conscience, untainted by power politics and considerations of narrow or selfish interests.'[3] Peace-keeping is also publicly celebrated on another national symbol: the loonie.

What explains Canada's support for peace-keeping? Memories and pride related to Lester Pearson's role in inventing United Nations peace-keeping in 1956, for which he justifiably won the Nobel Peace Prize, is surely an important factor, but it cannot be the only one. There are, in fact, a number of reasons—ranging from broad inter-nationalist concerns to more narrow self-interested ones—that explain Canada's frequent participation in peace-keeping operations.[4] One obvious explanation for peace-keeping, and the one frequently cited by Ottawa, is altruism. Canadians see their country as the 'peaceful kingdom', and therefore they have an obligation to share their good fortune with those lands stricken by war. In the words of Graham, 'the maintenance of peace remains our highest international aspiration.'[5]

Peace-keeping is also celebrated as a way that Canada can defuse disputes before they can escalate into regional or global conflicts. Small wars quickly turned into large ones in 1914 and 1939; in both cases drawing Canadian soldiers to fight on the other side of the world. The fear that the Americans and Soviets might clash following the British–French–Israeli intervention into the Suez was the catalyst that motivated Pearson to recommend the establishment of a multinational force. The recent International Policy Statement also acknowledged the changing nature of contemporary peace-keeping. Specifically, 'as the boundary between domestic and international continues to blur, Canada's defence and security policy must change. Today's front lines stretch from the streets of Kabul and the rail lines of Madrid to our own

Canadian cities.'[6] Failed states—the location of many peace-keeping operations—are 'obvious breeding grounds for terrorist networks and organized crime, which can directly threaten the security of Canadians'.[7]

Pragmatically, peace-keeping has also been used as a means of acquiring some influence in international affairs. As a medium-sized country, participation in peace-keeping gives Canada a 'seat at the table'. Many UN missions have consisted of large numbers of Canadian troops. Furthermore, Generals Burns, Mackenzie, Dallaire, and Hillier have all commanded UN peace-keeping operations in Egypt, Bosnia, Rwanda, and Afghanistan respectively. Even when the table moves from the field to the decision-room, Canada has been able to retain its seat through peace-keeping. For example, Canada's contribution to peace-keeping has been a contributing factor to its election as a non-permanent member of the Security Council every decade. The fact that the Security Council has increasingly consulted with troop-contributing states ensures some influence for Canada even when it is not an elected member.

Another reason for Canada to pursue peace-keeping is its utility in differentiating itself from the United States. Much of the Canadian identity is forged through positive comparisons with its southern neighbours. It has become a cliché to note that the US fought wars but Canada has successfully played the role of a peacekeeper. 'Peace-keeping was so popular', J.L. Granatstein has argued, 'because it was something we could do and the Americans could not'.[8] Even though Canada and the United States have co-operated in several recent peace-keeping operations (Bosnia, Afghanistan, Haiti), the idea that Americans are 'warmongers' while Canadians are 'peacemongers' still has resonance.

Finally, Ottawa has used peace-keeping to facilitate national unity in a bilingual, multicultural country. If universal public health care can be seen as the great Canadian domestic myth that has bound the country, then peace-keeping is our great international myth. Both health care and peace-keeping have come to be seen as reflecting Canada's 'unique' social values of co-operation, goodwill, and tolerance. In many respects, Canada's substantial linguistic, cultural, and regional divisions make it a difficult country to govern. Therefore politicians are attracted to public policies, like peace-keeping, that possess a strong nation-wide consensus across all its divisions. A particularly important asset of peace-keeping is its popularity in both French-speaking and English-speaking Canada.

From Peace-keeping to Peace Support Operations

Despite Canada's commitment to peace-keeping, it is obvious that the general public does not understand what is involved in its modern context. For example, in a series of polls between 2002 and 2005, Canadians were asked the following question: 'Some people say that Canadian Forces should adopt a traditional peace-keeping role which means trying to keep the two conflicting sides apart. Others say that Canadian Forces should adopt a peace-making role, which might involve fighting alongside other UN troops to force peace in a disputed area. Which view is closer to your own?' In each poll, a majority of Canadians preferred the one with less potential for violence (the traditional peace-keeping role) than the one that has become more common (the peace-making role).[9] Canadians were attached to the memory and myth of peace-keeping, not the modern reality.

This is reinforced by the famous peace-keeping monument *Reconciliation*, which shows three soldiers: one using binoculars, one using a radio, and one standing on guard with a gun strapped over his shoulder. This gives an impression that peace-keeping is about observing and monitoring. Where are the landmines, snipers, rocket propelled grenades, armoured personnel carriers, and suicide bombers that are also real features of peace-keeping? It is not just the public who misunderstands the true nature of peace-keeping. Many politicians, some of them in senior positions, also fail to recognize exactly what was entailed in current peace-keeping operations. In announcing that Canada would contribute troops to the 1999 UN mission in East Timor, Prime Minister Jean Chrétien said 'we're always there, like boy scouts, somewhat. We're happy and Canadians love it. They think it is a nice way for Canadians to be present around the world.'[10] The image of peacekeepers as 'boy scouts with guns', while deeply resented by the Canadian Forces, is the image that many Canadians have of peace-keeping.

Traditional peace-keeping can be defined as 'the deployment of a United Nations presence in the field, hitherto with the consent of all the parties concerned, normally involving United Nations military and/or police personnel and frequently civilians as well. Peace-keeping is a technique that expands the possibilities for both the prevention of conflict and the making of peace.'[11] Based on this definition, as well as decades of UN practice, five principles of traditional peace-keeping can be derived: 1) organized and authorized by the United Nations; 2) provided with sufficient military and financial resources by member states; 3) having the consent of the parties concerned; 4) acting impartially; and 5) minimum use of force.

Traditional peace-keeping, as exemplified by the United Nations Emergency Force (UNEF) sent to the Suez in 1956, involved a multinational force, following a cease-fire, establishing and monitoring a buffer zone between two combating states. However, in the early years of the post-Cold War era, UN troops were deployed as the result of civil wars where there was no peace to be kept. In the process, peace-keeping operations began to greatly diverge from these five traditional principles and, as a result, peace-keeping operations increasingly became the responsibility of regional organizations (Western Sahara) or ad-hoc coalitions (the US-led intervention into Somalia). Though the UN often authorized these efforts, they were not subject to its oversight in any meaning-

ful capacity. In addition, some operations were fully or partially funded through voluntary contributions (Macedonia) instead of through the United Nations peace-keeping budget. There were also several operations (Somalia and Bosnia) where troops were deployed without the consent of the warring parties. The definition of impartiality was modified in the early 1990s to allow peacekeepers to enforce UN Security Council resolutions impartially (Somalia and Bosnia), rather than just acting as an impartial body between the combatants. Similarly, the definition of self-defence was also re-interpreted from self-defence of the person to self-defence of the mission, which contributed to a greater use of force in both the former Yugoslavia and Somalia. This transformation away from traditional peace-keeping has been called second generation peace-keeping.[12]

The transition from traditional to second-generation peace-keeping had a direct impact on Canadian peacekeepers. The increased use of force, for example, had ramifications for Canadian troops in the Medak Pocket (a Serb-populated enclave in Croatia), which became the biggest firefight for the armed forces since the Korean War.[13] As part of the United Nations Protection Force (UNPROFOR) in Yugoslavia, the Canadians had a mandate to create a zone of separation between the Croats and the Serbs. On 15 September 1993, Croatian forces attacked members of the 2nd Battalion of the Princess Patricia's Canadian Light Infantry (2PPCLI), who were trying to protect a Serb enclave in Medak Pocket. When the Canadians attempted to stop the Croatians from ethnically cleansing the area, they were met by machine-gun fire, grenades, and mortar shells. The Canadians returned fire, and for fifteen hours, the fighting raged. No Canadians were killed or seriously wounded, but the battle killed 27 Croat soldiers. The fact that Canada did not officially recognize this battle until 2002 when Governor-General Adrienne Clarkson awarded special commendation to the 2PPCLI battle group is a strong indication that the government did not want the public to understand the true nature of peace-keeping. Modern peace-keeping means the willingness to kill and to be killed, but as Carol Off has argued, Canadians are 'squeamish about war and like to think of the CF as peacekeepers not warriors'.[14]

Second generation peace-keeping was a useful way of distinguishing between previous operations and the new and more dangerous operations. However, the term 'second generation' also implies a complete linear break with the past. In fact, the UN operation in the Congo in the early 1960s was a 'second generation peace-keeping operation' and the deployment of UN forces along the Ethiopia–Eritrea border in 2000 was a 'traditional peace-keeping operation'. Therefore, the phrase that is now widely used is the more accurate 'peace support operations'. Peace support operations are in the middle of a continuum that has traditional peace-keeping at one end, and full-scale warfare at the other end. For example, the Canadian Forces distinguishes between traditional peace-keeping and observer operations (Suez and Ethiopia–Eritrea), combat operations (1999 Kosovo air war and the 1991 Gulf War), and complex peace support and stabilization missions (Bosnia and Afghanistan).[15] In addition to the changes in consent, impartiality, and the use of force, peace support operations have more complex mandates that include: monitoring/conducting elections, disarming/demobilizing troops, clearing landmines, assisting with the civil administration of a state, monitoring human rights, repatriating refugees, delivering/protecting humanitarian assistance, assisting in civilian police functions, monitoring no-fly zones, implementing comprehensive peace plans, protecting designated 'safe areas', and providing a secure environment. Thus, peace support operations are multifunctional with political, military, humanitarian, social, and economic components requiring soldiers to work with civilian experts and humanitarian relief workers.

This does not mean that soldiers become social workers. To the contrary, there is an ongoing need for a disciplined and well-equipped multinational force that is willing and able to use force. The environment of peace support operations can be quite hostile. They may encounter battle-hardened soldiers unwilling to give up their arms without a fight. Warlords, who have both arms and men trained to use them, may act as spoilers in the peace process; warlords have the ability to make the countryside or mountainous regions ungovernable. Terrorists can mingle with shoppers and children in urban settings; it is often impossible for soldiers to spot the difference between a suicide bomber and a street merchant until it is too late. News reports provide an almost daily description of the violence that can exist in peace support operations: Sarajevo's 'sniper alley', the Rwandan genocide, or rocket attacks in Kabul.

Canada and UN Peace Support Operations

As a result of this transition from peace-keeping to peace support there have been major changes in Canada's role. An obvious consequence has been the declining rate of its participation in UN operations. At one time, Canada was a member of every peace-keeping operation, in addition to being one of the largest troop contributors. Those days are long gone. Canada now ranks 34 on the list of UN contributors, with only 312 troops.[16] The UN has 18 on-going missions but Canada is participating in only eight. In most of those operations, Canada has provided only a token presence of less than 10 troops and/or civilian police officers. The exceptions are Haiti (3 troops and 81 civilian police) and the Golan Heights between Israel and Syria (191 troops).[17]

Two main factors explain why Canada supplies fewer troops to peace support operations. The first factor is external and is related to the number of new troop contributors. In the 'golden age' of peace-keeping from 1956–88 there were only a handful of consistent and large-scale participants: Canada, Ireland, Australia, Sweden, Austria, and India. Even as late as 1991, there were only 37 troop-contributing states, but in 2005 the num-

Table 14.1:   Selected List of Contributors to un Peacekeeping Operations (as of 31 August 2005)

Country	Rank	Number of Troops
Pakistan	1	9,881
Bangladesh	2	8,812
India	3	6,321
Nepal	4	3,565
Ethiopia	5	3,424
Ghana	6	3,320
Nigeria	7	3,175
Jordan	8	2,791
Uruguay	9	2,435
South Africa	10	2,320
China	17	869
France	21	600
United Kingdom	28	384
United States	29	344
Russia	30	331
Canada	34	312

Source: Adapted from United Nations, 'Ranking of Military and Civilian Police Contributions to UN Operations', (31 August 2005), retrieved October 7, 2005 from http://www.un.org/Depts/dpko/dpko/contributors/2005/aug2005_2.pdf.

ber had dramatically jumped to 106.[18] The increase is due to two non-traditional sources: developing countries and permanent members of the Security Council (see Table 14.1 for a ranking of troop contributing states).[19]

The fact that more countries are participating in peace support operations may explain the drop in Canada's overall ranking, but it has little to do with the decrease in its raw number of troops. That can be explained by the second factor: the steep decline in size of the Canadian military. Simply put, Canada lacks sufficient forces to maintain its previous levels of support. At the end of the Cold War, Canada's military was over 88,000, which allowed it to deploy 4,000–5,000 soldiers a year on peace support operations in the early 1990s. Today, due to extensive and sustained budget cuts at the Department of National Defence, Canada's military has dropped by almost half, and sits at just over 50,000. This has had an

obvious effect on the number of troops that can be deployed on missions.

To make matters worse, reductions of the Canadian Forces were not matched by a drop in operations. In fact, as the Canadian military was downsized its operational commitments were increased.[20] This high operational tempo led to calls for Ottawa to resist future deployments. In 2002, the Senate National Security and Defence Committee recommended a 'strategic retreat' from current operational levels. This would involve bringing home all overseas troops at the end of current operational rotations and suspending any new deployments for over two years. A 30-month operational moratorium would allow the Canadian Forces to regenerate, train, maintain, and upgrade equipment, and for frequently deployed troops to spend time with their families.[21] In September 2003, the Canadian Forces announced a 'regeneration period' that would require 'at least 12 months between overseas missions for all personnel'.[22] However, this policy would not affect international emergencies or domestic operations. The operational pause was done by reducing the number of troops in Bosnia and Afghanistan by half. In the Fall of 2004 the Canadian Forces had slightly less than 1,900 personnel deployed on operations, compared to the more than 3,300 that were deployed in Spring 2004.[23]

The Paul Martin government took a number of tentative steps to rebuild Canada's military capability.[24] It ordered replacements for the 40-year old Sea King helicopters and it committed to adding 5,000 Regular and 3,000 Reserve personnel. This allowed Canada 'to continuously sustain up to 5,000 personnel on international operations'.[25] The 2005 budget also promised to provide the Canadian Forces with almost $13 billion in new money over the next five years. These steps are an important signal that the years of budget cutting are over, but further resources need to be directed towards the military if Canada is going to regain its historic level of participation in peace support operations. Most especially, there is a dire need for upgrading Canada's strategic lift capability. Right now, Canada relies on ancient Hercules aircraft or rented Russian-built Antonovs to transport men and equipment around the world. If our forces cannot be promptly transported to operations, some of which are in remote parts of the world (Afghanistan or the Darfur region of Sudan), it makes it difficult to participate in peace support operations.

Canada has responded to its diminishing ability to put 'boots on the ground', by becoming an idea generator. In 1995, Canada advocated the creation of a UN rapid reaction force.[26] While many of the proposals contained in the Canadian report were ignored—most notably the idea of a 'vanguard force' that would respond immediately to crises—other ideas were adopted, for example, the establishment of a Security Council Troop Contributors Committee and the creation of a permanent UN situation room.

A second major idea has been the *Responsibility*

to Protect (*R2P*). In September 2000, as one of the last initiatives of former Foreign Minister Lloyd Axworthy, Canada launched the International Commission on Intervention and State Sovereignty. Co-chaired by former Australian Foreign Minister Gareth Evans and senior UN diplomat Mohamed Sahnoun, the Commission presented its final report—*The Responsibility to Protect*—to the UN in December 2001.[27] *R2P* argued that in extreme cases of human suffering due to civil war, insurgency, or genocide, the international committee has an obligation to by-pass state sovereignty and intervene into the country to protect the people. From December 2001–September 2005, Canada, in co-ordination with other likeminded states and non-governmental organizations, actively promoted *R2P*. A major diplomatic success occurred when the principle of *R2P* was captured in the final report of the UN's High-Level Panel on Threats, Challenges, and Change.[28] During the September 2005 special session on UN reform, the world's heads of state and government, albeit in a watered-down form, accepted the central idea of *R2P*,[29] therefore allowing the establishment of future peace support operations.

As the shift from peace-keeping to peace support operations has occurred, Ottawa has attempted to portray Canadian Forces as warriors instead of peacekeepers or boy scouts. When Lieutenant-Colonel Don Denne was deployed in 2003 to command the 2nd Royal Canadian Regiment battle group in Kabul, Afghanistan he complained, 'God, I hate it when they call us peacekeepers. We loathe the term, abhor it. Peace-keeping can turn into a general war situation in the snap of your fingers.'[30] This education campaign became louder when General Rick Hillier, the newly hired Chief of Defence Staff, asserted that members of the Joint Task Force 2 (JTF2)—Canada's elite commando unit that were deployed in Afghanistan—would target members of the Taliban, al-Qaeda, and other regional warlords. Hillier, in uncharacteristically blunt language, emphasized 'these are detestable murderers and scumbags'. Moreover, the Canadian Forces are 'not the public service of Canada, we're not just another department. We are the Canadian Forces, and our job is to be able to kill people.'[31] Hillier's comments were echoed by his civilian boss, Defence Minister Bill Graham. In a speech to the Montreal Council on Foreign Relations, Graham warned that 'Canadians should not have illusions: this is a very complex, very demanding, and very dangerous mission. The region in Afghanistan where our troops will be deployed is one of the most unstable and dangerous in the country. In fact, that is the reason why we've been asked to go, and why we've accepted.'[32]

There have also been doctrinal changes within the Canadian Forces to reflect the shift from peace-keeping to peace support operations. The two most relevant concepts are the 3-D approach and three-block war. The 3-D approach involves the co-ordination of the Department of Foreign Affairs (diplomacy), Department of National Defence (defence), and the Canadian International Development Agency (development). This approach was put to the test in Afghanistan.[33] Canadian diplomats, led by the extremely competent Canadian Ambassador Chris Alexander, assisted the Afghan people in rebuilding their institutions after over a quarter century of war. Canadian aid workers, both through CIDA and international NGOs, undertook humanitarian projects including building schools and wells. The Canadian Forces provided a secure environment that was allowing the other two groups to succeed in their work.

The Canadian Army has also adopted three-block warfare, a term first coined by American Marine General Charles Krulak. 'On the first block of the three-block war, we will deliver humanitarian aid or assist others in doing that. On the second, we will conduct stabilization or peace support operations. On the third, we will be engaged in a high-intensity fight. We must be ready to conduct these operations simultaneously and very close to one another. We must be prepared to conduct them in large urban centres and complex terrain.'[34] In Afghanistan, the Canadian Army has been working simultaneously in all three blocks: it has assisted CIDA in the distribution of millions of dollars in humanitarian assistance; it provided security for NGOs distributing humanitarian assistance; and it was engaged in fire fights against elements of the Taliban.

Embracing NATO

It has been mentioned that Canada has seemingly abandoned contributing troops to peace support operations. That is not exactly correct. A more accurate statement is that Canada has been reducing its commitment to United Nations peace support operations and embracing peace support operations under the auspices of the North Atlantic Treaty Organization (NATO). The largest peace support operations of the last ten years have been in Bosnia, Kosovo, and Afghanistan. In all three cases, these were commanded and controlled by NATO. Canada had been in Bosnia since 1992 as part of UNPROFOR. In 1995, as part of the Dayton Peace Accords that ended the war, UNPROFOR was replaced by a 60,000 strong US-led NATO Implementation Force (IFOR). Canada kept over a thousand troops stationed as part of IFOR and its successor, Stabilization Force (SFOR), from 1995–2000. Throughout this period, the Bosnian mission was Canada's largest troop deployment. Since 1999, Canada has also been participating in the Kosovo Force (KFOR), which is responsible for providing security in the area following the 1999 NATO–Serbia war.

Since 9/11, Canada's military focus has been Afghanistan. In December 2001 Canada's elite special operations unit JTF2 was dispatched to work with American and British Special Forces to apprehend or kill al-Qaeda and Taliban members. In February 2002 Canada deployed 750 members of the 3rd Princess Patricia's Canadian Light Infantry (3PPCLI) and a reconnaissance squadron from Lord Strathcona's Horse. From February–July 2002, 3PPCLI 'fought al-Qaeda and Taliban remnants, maintained security around Kandahar and its airport, explored sensitive areas. . . pro-

Table 14.2: Comparison of NATO and UN Peace Support Operations

Organization	Operation	Maximum Strength	Canadian Contribution
NATO	Bosnia (1995–2004)	60,000	1,000
NATO	Kosovo (1999–present)	46,000	1,470
UN	Former Yugoslavia (1992–5)	38,599	2,400
UN	Somalia (1993–5)	28,000	750
UN	Congo (1960–4)	19,828	421
UN	Cambodia (1992–3)	19,350	213
NATO	Afghanistan (2003–present)	12,400	2,000

Source: Data for NATO operations comes from http://www.nato.int; for UN operations from http://www.un.org/Depts/dpko/dpko/index.asp; and for Canada's contribution from http://www.forces.gc.ca/site/operations/current_ops_e.asp.

vided humanitarian assistance and demining services. . .and six CF snipers registered Canada's first confirmed combat killings since the Korean War.'[35] Canada took a six-month break from Afghanistan, but returned in February 2003 with a 2,000-strong contingent to join the NATO-led International Security Assistance Force (ISAF) that was based in Kabul. For six months, Canadian General Rick Hillier—now Chief of Defence Staff—commanded ISAF and Canada was the largest troop-contributor. Now that Afghanis have elected both a President (October 2004) and a National Assembly (September 2005), Canada is in the process of moving its contingent out of the capital and into the provinces. In February 2006 Canada deployed a 250-strong brigade headquarters and an army task force of about 1,000 soldiers in Kandahar as part of a Provincial Reconstruction Team. While Afghanistan has become a shining example of the capability of the Canadian Forces, it has not been painless. Illustrative of the increased danger of peace support operations, 17 Canadians have been killed while serving in Afghanistan.

Why has there been a policy switch between supporting UN operations and NATO operations? It is important to remember that NATO's participation in peace support operations has been fairly recent. For most of its history, NATO's role was to deter the threat posed by the Soviet Union

through a multilateral collective defence mechanism. When the Cold War ended, NATO began to cautiously shift away from planning and training to fight the Soviets to a new role in the international environment. In the early 1990s NATO provided military support for UN peace operations in the former Yugoslavia by using both its navy to enforce weapons embargoes and sanctions and its air force to provide air support and air strikes. Gradually it moved from assisting the UN to assuming leadership of IFOR/SFOR, which implemented the Bosnian peace settlement. If NATO had been conducting peace support operations for as long as the UN, it is likely that Canada would have supported both organizations somewhat equally.

The three NATO-led operations also rank as some of the largest peace operations in history, with Bosnia and Kosovo at numbers one and two (see Table 14.2). Table 14.2 also shows that Canada has deployed a sizeable number of troops to every large-scale operation. It is not so much a matter of which international organization commands the operation as it is the overall size of the operation. It is not surprising, then, that Canada would have sent a large number of troops to the NATO operations in Bosnia, Kosovo, and Afghanistan. An additional point to consider is the fact that Canadian troops were already engaged in the three locations prior to the creation of the NATO peace support operation: Canada had been in Bosnia for three years with UNPROFOR prior to IFOR/SFOR; Canadian CF-18s had flown sorties over Serbia as part of the 1999 NATO war prior to KFOR; and Canadian troops were fighting alongside the Americans in Afghanistan prior to ISAF. Given Canada's history in the region, it would have been almost impossible for Canada not to participate in the new NATO operation.

Canada, as one of its founding states, has been an important and committed member of NATO. It has consistently supported the major post-Cold War transformations in the organization: membership enlargement and functional expansion. By participating with traditional members (United Kingdom, France, etc.), new members (Hungary, Slovenia, etc.), and potential members (through partnership for peace arrangements) in new types of operations (peace support), Canada is providing concrete support for NATO initiatives.

Finally, Canada feels comfortable working with its fellow NATO members. After all, the decades of the Cold War provided innumerable amounts of multinational training. This has greatly facilitated the interoperability of NATO forces. Due to the increased risk of peace support operations, Canadian troops also prefer working with their NATO allies, rather than troops from the developing world, which make up the majority of UN troops. These troops have been criticized for a lack of proper military training and discipline and many developing world contingents, even some of the most experienced contributor states, arrive to missions without proper equipment. These deficiencies can be seen not just in terms of modern communication devices and armoured personnel carriers, but in a lack of machine guns and clothing. For example, the Kenyan delegation arrived in Bosnia in the early 1990s without winter clothing, and the Canadians, who are specialists in winter operations, had to give them some of their parkas and boots. The soldiers in Afghanistan frequently stated how refreshing it was to work with professional soldiers from the United States, Britain, France, or Belgium com-

pared to working with the Jordanians or the Nepalese.[36] The Canadian Forces sees NATO contingents as their peers; they do not see many of the UN contingents the same way. Even new-NATO countries, like Slovenia and to a lesser extent Hungary, are viewed as more competent than the average UN contingent.

Conclusion

This chapter has argued that there is a wide divergence between the Canadian public's perception of peace-keeping and the reality of peace support operations. A major transformation has occurred with new operations that are substantially more complex and dangerous. Canadian soldiers are no longer patrolling a relatively secure and safe green line between Turks and Greeks in Cyprus. Instead, they are in Afghanistan trying to rebuild a deeply impoverished and war-torn country while at the same time trying to root out al-Qaeda and Taliban forces. Canada has responded to these new challenges both in theory and in practice. The 3-D approach and three-block warfare concept are not just ideas; they are being implemented in Afghanistan.

The lack of money and manpower has undoubtedly reduced Canada's capability to participate in peace support operations. In response, Canada has begun to contribute in several ways. First, it has tried to make an intellectual contribution through the creation and promotion of ideas. This can be seen in the rapid reaction capability and the responsibility to protect initiatives. Second, Canada has stopped trying to send troops everywhere and is instead concentrating its forces in a few strategic operations where it can make a difference. During the 1990s, it was Bosnia, and since 9/11 it has been Afghanistan. This idea of concentrating our resources instead of spreading them across the globe was a major theme in Canada's 2005 International Policy Statement. It is easy to compare the decision to focus Canada's official development assistance on twenty-five countries,[37] with the decision to focus its military in only one or two operations. Finally, Ottawa has taken some initial steps at re-investing in the Canadian Forces.

A final theme of this chapter has been the noticeable shift in Canada's operational support from the UN to NATO. It is too early to tell whether this will be permanent change, or simply a coincidence due to having to choose between UN or NATO operational commitments. However, because of the possibility that NATO will become a global expeditionary force, and because of the close military ties that Canada has with the organization's other members, such as the Americans and the British, it is reasonable to believe that in the future Canada will tend to devote its limited military capability to NATO-led operations.

Notes

1. See Pierre Martin and Michel Fortmann, 'Canadian Public Opinion and Peacekeeping in a Turbulent World', *International Journal* 50, 2 (Spring 1995): 370–400 and Pierre Martin and Michel Fortmann, 'Public Opinion: Obstacle, Partner, or Scapegoat?' *Policy Options* (January–February 2001): 66–72.

2. Foreign Affairs Minister Bill Graham, 'Notes for an Address at the Peacekeeping Medal Ceremony', *Speeches* 2002/NA (Ottawa: DFAIT, 22 October 2002).

3. Norman Hillmer, 'Peacekeeping: Canadian Invention, Canadian Myth', in J.L. Granatstein and Sune Akerman, eds, *Welfare States in Trouble: Historical Perspectives on Canada and Sweden* (North York, ON: Swedish Canadian Academic Foundation, 1994), 159–70.

4. See Joseph T. Jockel, *Canada and International Peacekeeping* (Washington: Center for Strategic and International Studies, 1994), 13–23. For a more general discussion about why countries participate in peace-keeping see Laura Neack, 'UN Peacekeeping: In the Interest of Community of Self?' *Journal of Peace Research* 32, 2 (1995): 181–96.

5. Graham, 'Notes for an Address at the Peacekeeping Medal Ceremony'.

6. Canada, *Canada's International Policy Statement, A Role of Pride and Influence in the World* (Ottawa: Government of Canada, 2005), 12.

7. Ibid., 13.

8. J.L. Granatstein, 'Peacekeeping: Did Canada Make a Difference? And What Difference did Peacekeeping Make to Canada?', in John English and Norman Hillmer, eds, *Making a Difference? Canada's Foreign Policy in a Changing World Order* (Toronto: Lester, 1992), 232.

9. See Lane Anker, 'Peacekeeping and Public Opinion', *Canadian Military Journal* 6, 2 (Summer 2005): 27.

10. Mike Trickey and Mark Kennedy, 'Chrétien doubts Canada will send 600 soldiers: Forces prepare "like boy scouts" to fill request in East Timor', *The Ottawa Citizen*, 14 September 1999, A10.

11. Boutros Boutros-Ghali, *An Agenda for Peace* (New York: United Nations, 1992), 11.

12. There is a large literature on the transition from traditional peace-keeping and second generation peace-keeping. Some of the more important sources include: Marrack Goulding, 'The Evolution of UN Peace-keeping', *International Affairs* 69, 3 (1993): 451–64; John Mackinlay and Jarat Chopra, *A Draft Concept of Second Generation Multinational Operations 1993* (Providence: Thomas J. Watson Jr Institute for International Studies, 1993); William J. Durch, ed., *The Evolution of UN Peacekeeping: Case Studies and Comparative Analysis* (New York: St Martin's Press, 1993); and United Nations, *The Blue Helmets: A Review of United Nations Peace-keeping*, 3rd ed. (New York: United Nations, 1996).

13. See Carol Off, *The Ghosts of Medak Pocket: The Story of Canada's Secret War* (Toronto: Vintage, 2004) and Scott Taylor and Brian Nolan, *Tested Mettle: Canada's Peacekeepers at War* (Ottawa: Esprit de Corps Books, 1998), 123–43.

14. Quoted in Anker, 'Peacekeeping and Public Opinion', 28.

15. In addition to these three types of operations, the Canadian Forces also distinguish between maritime interdiction operations (Persian Gulf after the Gulf War and as part of the campaign against terrorism),

humanitarian assistance missions (the deployment of the Disaster Assistance Response Team to Sri Lanka), and evacuation operations (Haiti). Canada, *Canada's International Policy Statement: A Role of Pride and Influence in the World—DEFENCE* (Ottawa: DND, 2005), 28.

16. United Nations, 'Ranking of Military and Civilian Police Contributions to UN Operations', 31 August 2005. Available at http://www.un.org/Depts/dpko/dpko/contributors/2005/aug2005_2.pdf (accessed 7 October 2005).

17. United Nations, 'UN Mission's Contributions by Country', 31 August 2005. Available at http://www.un.org/Depts/dpko/dpko/contributors/2005/aug2005_5.pdf (accessed 7 October 2005).

18. 'Summary of Personnel Contributions to UN Peacekeeping Operations', *Peacekeeping & International Relations* 20, 3 (May–June 1991): 2, and United Nations, 'Ranking of Military and Civilian Police Contributions to UN Operations', 31 August 2005. Available at http://www.un.org/Depts/dpko/dpko/contributors/2005/aug2005_2.pdf (accessed 7 October 2005).

19. For more information on the effect of 'new' peacekeepers on Canadian policy see Duane Bratt, 'Niche-Making and Canadian Peacekeeping', *Canadian Foreign Policy* 6, 3 (Spring 1999): 78–81.

20. See the graph 'Increasing Demand vs Failing Capacity' in Canada, *Canada's International Policy Statement—DEFENCE*, 7.

21. Senate, Standing Committee on National Security and Defence, 'For an extra $130 bucks . . . Update on Canada's Military Financial Crisis: A View from the Bottom', November 2002.

22. Department of National Defence, *Report on Plans and Priorities: 2004–2005* (2004). Available online: http://www.vcds.forces.gc.ca/dgsp/pubs/rep-pub/ddm/rpp/rpp04-05/intro_e.asp.

23. Defence Minister Bill Graham, 'Speaking Notes for an Address at the Royal Canadian Military Institute Conference', *Speeches* 2004/NA. Toronto: 22 September 2004.

24. One of Martin's most important moves was the symbolic visit to the National Defence headquarters on his first day as Prime Minister. Incredibly, Jean Chrétien never set foot inside of Canada's Defence headquarters during his more than ten year tenure as Prime Minister, despite it being only blocks away from Parliament Hill.

25. Canada, *Canada's International Policy Statement—DEFENCE*, 3.

26. Canada, Department of Foreign Affairs and International Trade, *Towards a Rapid Reaction Capability for the United Nations* (Ottawa: DFAIT, 1995).

27. The International Commission on Intervention and State Sovereignty, *The Responsibility to Protect* (2001). Available at: http://www.iciss.ca/pdf/Commission-Report.pdf.

28. Report of the Secretary-General's High-Level Panel on Threats, Challenges, and Change, *A More Secure World: Our Shared Responsibility* (New York: United Nations, 2004).

29. UN Doc. A/Res/60/1. 16 September 2005.

30. Quoted in J.L. Granatstein, *Who Killed the Canadian Military?* (Toronto: HarperCollins, 2004), 173–4.

31. Daniel Leblanc, 'JTF2 to hunt al-Qaeda', *The Globe and Mail*, 15 July 2005, A1.

32. Minister of National Defence Bill Graham, 'The Canadian Forces Mission in Afghanistan—Canadian Policy and Values in Action', *Minister's Speech*. Montreal: 22 September 2005.

33. See DFAIT, 'Rebuilding Afghanistan'. Available at http://www.canada-afghanistan.gc.ca/menu-en.asp (accessed 15 October 2005).

34. Department of National Defence, 'Three-Block War', in *A Soldier's Guide to Transformation*. Available at: http://www.army.forces.gc.ca.

35. Grant Dawson, '"A Special Case": Canada, Operation Apollo, and Multilateralism', in David Carment, Fen Osler Hampson, and Norman Hillmer eds, *Canada Among Nations 2003: Coping with the American Colossus* (Don Mills, ON: Oxford University Press, 2003), 192.

36. Interviews with Canadian troops, Kabul, Afghanistan, November 2004.

37. Canada, *Canada's International Policy Statement: A Role of Pride and Influence in the World—DEVELOPMENT* (Ottawa: CIDA, 2005), 22–3.

15

Fading Power or Rising Power: 11 September and Lessons from the Section 110 Experience

Christopher Sands

The border between Canada and the United States is the natural flash point for bilateral disputes, and was violated regularly in the nineteenth and twentieth centuries: by US troops until 1815; by Fenian raiders; by agents of the Confederate States during the US Civil War; and by rum-runners during Prohibition. In recent years, the Canada–United States Free Trade Agreement and the North American Free Trade Agreement (NAFTA) gave many Canadians and Americans the hope that border barriers to the free flow of people and commerce between these two countries would gradually fade away thanks to economic integration. A previous volume in the *Canada Among Nations* series captured this spirit with the theme *Vanishing Borders* (Hampson and Molot, 2000).

Until 10 September 2001, scholars continued to wonder whether this border was relevant anymore. The following morning, the border made a comeback.

In just three months following the terrorist attacks on the World Trade Center in New York and the Pentagon in northern Virginia, the governments of Canada and the United States established new security procedures at the border between the two countries and took steps to improve co-operation between their respective law enforcement and national security agencies. The US Congress and the Canadian Parliament voted to authorize new funding for the wide array of officials—from customs inspectors and immigration agents to police and intelligence services—responsible for managing borders and conducting domestic counter-terrorist activities, and on 12 December 2001 US Homeland Security Director Tom Ridge and Canadian Foreign Minister John Manley met in Ottawa to endorse a joint action plan (Office of Homeland Security, 2001) further committing the two governments to negotiate on an additional 30 separate areas of potential bilateral co-operation, designed to reduce if not eliminate the risk of future terrorist attacks.

This chapter addresses three questions about the joint response of the United States and Canada on border-related issues after 11 September 2001. First, how was it that the two governments were able to agree on a common agenda so quickly? This was particularly surprising to many who saw relations between the George W. Bush administration and the government of Jean Chrétien begin awkwardly and remain relatively poor (Sands, 2001). Second, what does this experience suggest about the prospect for improved

Canada–United States relations? Is Canada perhaps entering into a new period of constructive partnership with the United States? Third, how do the Chrétien government's choices now affect Canadian interests in the longer term? Is this episode in the aftermath of the 11 September attacks on the United States an aberration, or does it have lasting significance for Canada's relations with the United States and the world?

To answer the first question, the two governments were able to agree on a consensus agenda for action on the border because they had been engaged in a vigorous debate over border management that dated back to 1993, yet had received relatively little public attention. This debate belied the widespread impression that the border was becoming less important due to trade liberalization. A succession of bilateral agreements was signed between 1993 and 2001 to improve cross-border co-operation. These agreements were negotiated partly in response to the attempts of the Congress to reform US immigration policy following the passage of the Customs Modernization Act of 1993—both measures designed to address concerns raised by members of Congress and their constituents during the debate over NAFTA. The Canadian government viewed one provision of the US legislation as potentially harmful to its trade with the United States: the Section 110 requirement that the US Immigration and Naturalization Service (INS) develop an automated entry and exit record system to track non-US citizens crossing all US borders, including the land borders.

The debate over Section 110 coincided with the emergence of serious terrorist activity in North America that gradually began to colour the US perception of the urgency and necessity of stricter measures to control access across its land borders. In order to appreciate the reaction of the governments to the 11 September attacks, it is necessary to trace these three strands: congressional attempts to reform US immigration policy; Canadian attempts to engage the US government in a bilateral dialogue on border management, which Canada hoped would divert the US from implementing the Section 110 provision; and the growing penetration of both societies by al-Qaeda terrorists that culminated in the 11 September attacks. The connections between these three efforts grew more intense over time, and together explain the swift reaction of the two governments to border security after 11 September. These recent events also offer the best indication of the likelihood of success of post-11 September co-operation and suggest something further about the future of bilateral relations in the years to come.

INS Modernization and the Shared Border Accord

The Customs Modernization Act of 1993 grew out of the concerns of many in Congress that the policing of US borders required improvement in order to cope with the growing pressures of trade and individuals crossing in and out of the United States with increasing frequency. Its passage was an important precursor to the congressional ratification of NAFTA and related implementing legislation in November of that year. At the time, modernization of the INS, along with that of the US Customs Service, the other major border enforcement agency of the US government, was also considered necessary and individual representatives and senators crafted language for an INS modernization bill. President Bill Clinton, seeking to stave off concerns related to the potential for a flood of immigration and trade once NAFTA took effect (and thereby to win over enough members of Congress to get NAFTA and related implementing legislation passed), ordered the temporary transfer of one-third of the Customs, INS, and Border Patrol agents working on the northern border with Canada to serve on the southern border with Mexico.

On 26 February 1993, the first attack on the World Trade Center in New York resulted in the death of six people and the injury of 1,042. A rented van packed with explosives was detonated while parked in a garage beneath one of the towers. The US Federal Bureau of Investigation (FBI) launched an investigation that linked the attack to a group of individuals recruited by Sheikh Omar Abdel Rahman, a blind Egyptian Muslim cleric who had been accused by the Egyptian government of involvement in the assassination of Egyptian President Anwar Sadat. Abdel Rahman sought asylum in the United States from what he claimed was political persecution by the Egyptian government related to these unproven charges, and the US approved his application in 1989, permitting Abdel Rahman to settle in New Jersey.

The FBI investigation of the first attack on the World Trade Center uncovered evidence that followers of Abdel Rahman were actively plotting to bomb a series of New York City landmarks, including the United Nations headquarters building, the George Washington Bridge, and the Lincoln and Holland tunnels. These plans were thwarted when Abdel Rahman and nine of his associates were arrested on 23 June 1993.

Tracing Abdel Rahman's movements from his arrival in the United States, the FBI discovered that he had travelled extensively to cities across North America from 1990 to 1993, preaching in mosques and Islamic community centres in Los Angeles, Chicago, Detroit, and also in Montreal and Toronto. The FBI sought and received help from the Royal Canadian Mounted Police (RCMP) in investigating Abdel Rahman's activity while in Canada. Both the FBI and RCMP suspected that Abdel Rahman had used these trips to recruit followers for terrorist attacks, seeing the sheikh as the organizer of both the first World Trade Center attack and the plot to bomb New York City landmarks. Neither the FBI nor the RCMP yet suspected these incidents were linked to the larger al-Qaeda terrorist network, and the focus remained on Abdel Rahman as the key figure.

On 14 September 1993 the first World Trade Center bombing trial began, and on 4 March 1994 four individuals connected to Abdel Rahman were convicted on all charges. On the strength of testimony and evidence presented in this trial, federal prosecutors indicted fugitive Ramzi Yousef as the ringleader who had planned the attack on the World Trade Center. There was insufficient evidence at the time to indict Abdel Rahman in the World Trade Center attack, but he remained in custody and was brought to trial on 9 January 1995 with nine others for participation in the plot to bomb New York City landmarks. On 7 February, Ramzi Yousef was arrested in Pakistan and subsequently extradited to face charges in the United States related to the first World Trade Center attack.

Two years after the shock of the first attack on the World Trade Center it appeared that all of those involved had been caught and were being brought to justice. If US officials had been surprised by the extent of the terrorist network they had uncovered in the United States, they still believed that they had uprooted it completely and that key figures Abdel Rahman and Ramzi Yousef would soon be in prison.

In February 1995, during a state visit by President Clinton to Ottawa, Clinton and Prime Minister Chrétien signed the US–Canada Shared Border Accord. This agreement included a series of measures to improve co-operation between customs and immigration officials in both countries. The emphasis of the Shared Border Accord was on customs, however, since the main challenge the two countries faced at the border was facilitating rapid growth in commercial traffic, and Canada Customs hoped to observe and even consult with their US counterparts on the implementation of the Customs Modernization Act with a view to developing common commercial documentation and electronic data interchange standards so that firms could minimize the amount of paperwork required on shipments moving across the border.

Section 110 and the Border Vision Initiative

On 4 August 1995 the Immigration in the National Interest Act of 1995 was introduced in the US House of Representatives as HR 2202. The bill was intended to become the counterpart of the

Customs Modernization Act of 1993, reforming an array of regulations and procedural requirements in the legislation governing the INS. When several amendments caused passage of the bill to be delayed, it was renamed the Illegal Immigration Reform and Immigrant Responsibility Act of 1996. The colourful title of the new bill reflected the style of the new Republican majority in the House in the 104th Congress, led by Speaker of the House Newt Gingrich of Georgia. The 104th Congress was elected in 1994, at the same time that California voters approved Proposition 187, restricting some public services to US citizens and excluding thousands of illegal immigrants, mainly from Mexico. California's tough new mood on immigration was reflected in the 104th Congress, which was determined to legislate significant immigration reforms as quickly as possible.

One key amendment to the immigration reform bill established the Section 110 provision, which required the INS to develop a system to document the entry and exit of non-US citizens at all border crossing points. The initial purpose of the Section 110 provision was to allow authorities to keep track of those individuals who attempted to cross into the United States illegally and repeatedly, some of whom were thought to be human smugglers who charged substantial fees for aiding individuals seeking to evade lawful immigration procedures. Documentation of those exiting would allow the INS to determine that court-ordered deportations had in fact taken place; the agency had no way to be certain whether such orders were complied with except in extreme cases where individuals were escorted to the border in custody—and in such cases, there was no way to tell if these individuals re-entered the United States subsequently.

The Section 110 provision was to apply to all non-citizens crossing the US borders. The language of Section 110 allowed for the development of an automated system to track entry and exit, but no new funding was appropriated for this purpose. To give the INS time to develop and put in place an adequate system to comply with Section 110, the legislation required that Section 110 be implemented within two years after the immigration reform bill was signed into law.

The principal concern of members of Congress sponsoring the immigration reform bill was illegal migration across the US border with Mexico, by both Mexicans and Central Americans who crossed through Mexico in the hope of entering the United States (Krouse and Wasem, 1998). However, there was also concern in Congress about illegal entry from Canada. The INS estimated that 15,000 people attempted to enter the United States from Canada illegally in 1995. Acknowledging that there were illegal immigration flows from the United States into Canada as well, the INS nonetheless estimated that 75 per cent of the illegal migration across the Canada–US border went from Canada into the United States and consisted mainly of third-country nationals (not Canadians) who passed through Canada always intending to end their journey in the United States (Beltrame, 1997).

Canadian government officials insisted that the Section 110 provision was not intended to affect those entering from Canada, and solicited statements from individual sponsors of the legislation to support this contention. The Canadian government argued publicly that the effect of implementation would be long lines at busy border crossings and the loss of billions of dollars in trade to the economies of both countries (Cooper, 2000). Congress did not exempt the Canadian border from the application of Section 110, and did not agree to exempt Canadians from the documentation requirement for non-US citizens. On 21 March 1996 the Illegal Immigration Reform and Immigrant Responsibility Act of 1996, including the Section 110 provision, was passed by the House of Representatives by a vote of 333–87. Senate passage followed in May 1996, and after a House–Senate conference in September worked out differences between the two versions of the bill as passed by each chamber, the immigration reform legislation was signed into law in October, establishing the deadline for full implementation of Section 110 as October 1998.

Just one year before the Act became law, in October 1995, Abdel Rahman and nine others were convicted of plotting to bomb New York landmarks. During the course of their trial, it was revealed that one of the accused, El Sayyid Nosair, was also the assassin of New York Rabbi Meir Kahane in 1990, and that Abdel Rahman himself had indeed played a part in the assassination of Anwar Sadat, for which both were also convicted. All 10 individuals received lengthy prison terms.

Less attention was paid to the case of Ahmed Saied Khadr, an Egyptian-born Canadian citizen who was arrested in Pakistan in connection with a truck bombing of the Egyptian embassy in Islamabad that killed 16 and wounded 50 people. Khadr held computer science degrees from the University of Ottawa and headed up the Canadian branch of Human Concern International, based in Gloucester, Ontario. He had travelled to Pakistan en route to Kabul, Afghanistan, where he sought to arrange the marriage of his daughter to Khalid Abdullah, an Egyptian guest of the Taliban regime. Prime Minister Chrétien raised Khadr's case with Pakistani Prime Minister Benazir Bhutto during a visit to Islamabad in January 1996, and requested his release given the weak case against him for direct involvement in the embassy bombing. In March 1996, the Pakistani government released Khadr, who returned to Canada where he faced no charges (Dahlburg, 1996).

On 17 July 1996, TWA Flight 800 exploded above the Long Island shoreline, killing all 230 passengers and crew shortly after the plane left New York's Kennedy Airport. Crash investigators suspected a link to terrorism, given the suddenness of the explosion, and lawyers for Ramzi Yousef feared that the TWA incident would prejudice the jury in his trial against him. Yousef was charged in a plot to place bombs on at least a dozen US passenger aircraft bound for Asia. Prosecutors claimed that there was ample evidence for conviction even without the TWA 800 tragedy, and on 5 September 1996 Yousef and two associates were convicted. Yousef went to prison while the prosecutors built a case against him for mas-

terminding the 1993 World Trade Center attack.

The Canadian government did not ignore the US immigration policy debate. Two bilateral agreements in 1997 demonstrated Canada's willingness to be part of the solution to US immigration concerns anywhere there was a proven link to Canada. In February, Canadian Solicitor General Herb Gray and US Attorney General Janet Reno announced the formation of two groups, the Canadian Anti-Smuggling Working Group and the Northeast Border Working Group, which would co-ordinate an intensified campaign by national immigration and law enforcement resources in each country to combat human and contraband smuggling through Ontario and Quebec into New York and some New England states. Gray and Reno indicated that the two working groups would share information and attempt to co-ordinate intelligence information between them. In addition to the smuggling of individuals from third countries such as India and China, the two countries shared a concern over illicit movement of small arms (mainly handguns from the United States to Canada) and illegal drugs (flowing in both directions).

In April 1997, the governments of Canada and the United States announced a new Border Vision Initiative during Prime Minister Chrétien's first state visit to Washington as Prime Minister. This joint effort aimed to facilitate greater information-sharing and co-ordination between Citizenship and Immigration Canada (CIC) and the INS, particularly at the land border, through intelligence-sharing on illegal migration. The Border Vision Initiative also began a dialogue between CIC and INS on the potential for co-ordination and consolidation of lookout lists, third-country visa requirements, joint overseas operations, and intelligence exchanges for background checks on third-country applicants. Consensus formed on many of the technical issues addressed by the two agencies under the aegis of the Border Vision Initiative, but action did not immediately follow on some of the most far-reaching items under consideration for want of either funding (particularly for new technology) or political support (where sovereignty concerns were flagged by either side). Nonetheless, both 1997 agreements represented progress towards bilateral immigration policy reform, nudged along by new legislation in the United States.

'Bombs in Brooklyn' and the Cross-Border Crime Forum

The harmonious mood of co-operation that followed the Chrétien–Clinton meeting in April 1997 gave rise to hopes that the Section 110 provision could be waived for Canada, or perhaps eliminated entirely. The era of good feeling on immigration was undermined by revelations from a US Department of Justice investigation less than a year later.

On 31 July 1997 New York City police raided a Brooklyn apartment and caught two men, Ghazi Ibrahim Abu Mezer and Lafi Khalil, in the act of preparing explosive devices that they intended to detonate in the New York City subway system. The police had been tipped off by an Arab-American neighbour who disliked the two and heard them talking in Arabic about their plans. It was clearly a lucky break that led to the prevention of the attack, rather than effective intelligence. Days later, a furious New York Mayor Rudolph Giuliani and US Senator Alphonse d'Amato wrote an open letter to President Clinton demanding that the INS explain how Abu Mezer and Khalil got into the United States.

At the US Department of Justice, of which the INS is a part, the department's Office of the Inspector General began an investigation of INS handling of the Abu Mezer and Khalil cases. Members of Congress voted in November 1997 to extend the deadline for the implementation of the Section 110 provision by a full year to October 1999, compromising with the Clinton administration and US business groups, which had advocated removing the deadline entirely (Krouse and Wasem, 1998).

Canada and the United States expanded their bilateral co-operation at the border with the establishment of the Cross-Border Crime Forum, which held its first meeting in Ottawa on 30 September 1997. Where the Border Vision Initiative fostered co-operation in immigration cases, the Cross-Border Crime Forum was created to encourage law enforcement agencies in both countries to work together more effectively to combat transnational crime, including smuggling, telemarketing fraud, money laundering, missing children, and cyber-crime. Two concrete steps were taken as a result of dialogue at the Cross-Border Crime Forum. First, a procedure for binational threat assessments was established. Second, a proposal to create Integrated Border Enforcement Teams (IBETS) was tested along the British Columbia–Washington border, where Canadian and US law enforcement personnel working for federal, state, and local governments could conduct investigations and enforcement operations, as well as training exercises together, overcoming jurisdictional issues pragmatically and prompting a heightened degree of information-sharing among all of the participating organizations.

The need for cross-border co-operation was underscored in February 1998, when Walter Cadman, INS Counterterrorism Coordinator, testified before the Senate Judiciary Committee that in 1996, illegal immigrants from 118 countries had attempted unlawful entry into the United States from Canada, and that Canada was becoming an important 'alternative gateway' for illegal migration (Cadman, 1998). Cadman also told senators that established human smuggling operations were being used by international terrorist and organized crime groups to obtain entry for their members to the United States, thereby eluding new measures to screen applicants and detect forged documents more thoroughly that had been instituted by the INS in response to the 1996 immigration reform legislation passed by Congress.

Cadman's testimony anticipated the findings of the investigation into INS handling of the Abu Mezer and Khalil cases by Michael Bromowich, the inspector general of the US Department of Justice (Bromowich, 1998). The Bromowich report, titled 'Bombs in Brooklyn', confirmed that Abu Mezer was a Palestinian born on the West Bank who had been arrested several times in Israel, which believed him to be a member of the Hamas organization. Abu Mezer received a student visa from the government of Canada in 1993, and shortly after arriving in Canada he applied for political refugee status based on fear of persecution in Israel, admitting his connections to Hamas members but denying participation in any terrorist activity. At that time, he also applied for a visa to enter the United States at the US Consular Office in Toronto but was denied. Subsequently, he began attempting to enter the United States illegally, and was arrested on three occasions in 1996 and 1997. On his third try, when US officials sought to return him to Canada, Canada refused him entry due to two felony convictions (for assault and credit card fraud, respectively) during his time in Canada. The Border Patrol then began deportation proceedings and the case went to court. Had Abu Mezer's connection to Hamas been established at the time of his asylum hearing, Bromowich argued, he would have been swiftly deported. However, the INS had not conducted a thorough check on Abu Mezer through available databases on international terrorists (where it would have found the Israeli charges that Abu Mezer was a Hamas member), and the State Department responded to the immigration court judge's request for information with a routine reply that the department had no information concerning the individual in question.

Bromowich's report shed unflattering light on the state of co-operation at the Canada–US border by immigration and law enforcement agencies:

[T]his case exposes pervasive and long-standing weaknesses in the immigration process that are not unique to this matter. First, Mezer's easy entry to Canada and his ability to remain there while he repeatedly attempted to illegally enter the United States demonstrates part of the difficulty in controlling illegal immigration into the United States.

Second, Mezer's case also shows the inadequacy of INS resources for preventing illegal immigration along the northwest border. With an average of four Border Patrol agents in the Lynden and Blaine stations covering 102 miles of the northern border, and no coverage of the border from midnight to morning, it is surprising that Mezer was apprehended once, much less three times, within approximately six months.

Third, the virtual impunity from prosecution that aliens face when they are caught illegally entering the United States is also made apparent by Mezer's case. Border Patrol statistics show that most illegal aliens who are apprehended entering the United States from Canada are voluntarily returned without any criminal or immigration consequences. Despite twice being caught attempting to enter the United States illegally within one week, Mezer was simply returned voluntarily to Canada each time. INS and law enforcement authorities do not normally prosecute or even detain aliens who are caught attempting to enter the United States, and they are typically returned to Canada voluntarily, able to try again any time. (Bromowich, 1998)

The Bromowich report's findings in the case of Khalil were equally disturbing, but did not relate to Canada.

Meeting in Washington in May 1998, participants in the second Cross-Border Crime Forum could hope for no better case study of the challenges that the two countries faced in improving co-operation and co-ordination among law enforcement and other agencies within, and across, the border.

Section 110 and the CUSP

On 7 June 1998 Ramzi Yousef was convicted and sentenced to life in prison for his role in the first World Trade Center attack. Two months later, US embassies in Dar es Salaam, Tanzania, and Nairobi, Kenya, were bombed. President Clinton accused al-Qaeda, the terrorist organization led by Osama bin Laden, of carrying out the attacks, and ordered cruise missile strikes on suspected al-Qaeda targets in Sudan and Afghanistan. US officials who previously considered Sheikh Abdel Rahman and Ramzi Yousef the masterminds behind past attacks on the United States began reviewing the evidence for possible links between these attacks and al-Qaeda. When Swissair Flight 111, originating at New York's Kennedy Airport and bound for Geneva, crashed off the coast of Nova Scotia on 2 September 1998, killing 229, investigators naturally looked to terrorism as a possible cause.

The summer of 1999 saw an easing of concern over illegal immigration into the United States. In July, citing the progress of federal immigration policy reform, California Governor Gray Davis announced that he was dropping an appeal of an earlier federal court ruling that had found much of the state's Proposition 187 unconstitutional (Nieves, 1999). That same month, Congress lifted the October 1999 deadline for implementation of the Section 110 provision of the 1996 immigration reform legislation as part of the Border Improvement and Immigration Act of 1998. The new Act belatedly provided the INS with rather modest funding for the development of an automated entry and exit control system to implement Section 110, and at the same time called for a study of the impact entry and exit controls would have on traffic facilitation at the major border crossing points-a concession to critics of Section 110 in the business community. It was a partial retreat from Section 110 implementation, although Congress revived the prospect that Section 110 controls might be imposed at a later date.

US and Canadian officials continued their joint efforts to improve the management of the border. In December 1998 the US Department of Justice and Canada's Justice Ministry announced the successful conclusion of a joint operation (called Project Othello in Canada and Operation Over the Rainbow in the United States) to break up human smuggling rings operating across the New York border with Ontario and Quebec.

The growing number and range of such initiatives, from focused enforcement operations to co-ordinated planning for border management and infrastructure, combined with concern over the potential collateral damage to the economies of border communities if Section 110 were implemented, resulted in the mobilization of local leaders to demand a role in the discussions that had largely remained exclusively between federal officials on both sides of the border (Meyers and Papademetriou, 2001). Ottawa and Washington responded with the Canada–United States Partnership (CUSP) Agreement, signed during President Clinton's state visit to Ottawa in October 1999, during which he dedicated the new US Embassy building. The CUSP pledged both governments to initiate a series of stakeholder consultations that would solicit ideas and input on border management from communities, interest groups, and businesses. The explicit purpose of the CUSP process was to redress a perceived imbalance towards security and enforcement improvements with renewed attention to traffic facilitation in the spirit of the 1995 Shared Border Accord, while bringing local input into the security dialogue as well. CUSP consultations were planned for 2000 in the east and west (CUSP 2000).

Before the first CUSP meetings could be held, international terrorism would again touch North America. On 31 October 1999 EgyptAir Flight 990, bound from New York to Cairo, crashed in the waters off Nantucket killing all 217 aboard. Although 'pilot error' was ruled the probable cause, US investigators again considered terrorism a potential factor in the crash. Then, in December 1999, Ahmed Ressam was arrested attempting to enter the United States With a carload of explosives and, he subsequently confessed, a plan to attack the Los Angeles International Airport to coincide with millennium celebrations. Ressam was an Algerian who had resided in Montreal since 1994 while his application for political asylum was adjudicated. His application was denied in 1998, and he was ordered deported, at which point he went underground and adopted a new identity with forged documents that indicated that he was Beni Antoine Norris, a Canadian citizen.

The Ressam case received more attention than any previous incident involving terrorism and the Canada–US border. In part, this reflected the growing concern in the United States over international terrorism and attacks on US targets. Canadian officials initially downplayed the significance of the Ressam case, arguing that he had been caught—proof that existing security measures were adequate. But many Americans noted that the arrest of Ressam owed more to luck and a sharp-eyed US border inspector, and his plan could very easily have succeeded. CIC officials claimed that at no stage were they aware of the connections between Ressam and Algerian terrorist groups or al-Qaeda—an admission that drew American public attention to the Canadian immigration and refugee system and to the limited financial and intelligence resources available to CIC officials, whose decisions on immigrants were now viewed as affecting the safety of US citizens as never before (Farley, 1999).

The heightened public anxiety in the United States that followed Ressam's arrest quickly led to fierce political recriminations. In Washington, the Federation for American Immigration Reform (FAIR) held a press conference on 20 December 1999 to attack congressional leaders who had voted to waive the deadline for Section 110 implementation for increasing the risk of terrorist attacks on US citizens (FAIR, 1999). The group singled out Senator Spencer Abraham of Michigan, the lone Arab American in the US Senate, for his efforts to repeal the Section 110 provision. 'It is gross negligence that national lawmakers, led by Senate Immigration Subcommittee chair Spencer Abraham, have been actively working to undermine effective border security', charged FAIR executive director Dan Stein in a press release. 'A measure enacted by Congress in 1996 would have required the Immigration and Naturalization Service to collect records on all arriving foreign visitors and match them with departure records. But it has been attacked and buried by Sen. Abraham and a handful of other politicians who put the interests of border merchants and ethnic commun-

ities ahead of the security of the American public' (FAIR, 1999). FAIR subsequently produced television ads attacking Abraham's position on immigration reform that ran during his 2000 campaign for re-election, in which he was defeated.

In January 2000, the Subcommittee on Immigration and Claims of the House Judiciary Committee held a hearing on Canada's immigration and border control policies and their affect on the United States. Representative Lamar Smith (R-Texas), one of the key sponsors of the Section 110 provision, chaired the hearing. In addition to three American witnesses (including this author), the Subcommittee heard from a roster of Canadian critics of the Chrétien government's security policies who testified to the chronic underfunding of the RCMP and the Canadian Security and Intelligence Service, and charged that the Liberal government was too beholden to support from immigrant communities in Canada to restrict immigration to meet US security concerns.

The increasingly ugly debate over US immigration policy and borders, which now included a debate over Canada's immigration and security policies, cast a shadow over the first and second rounds of stakeholder consultations under the CUSP, which were held in April 2000 in Niagara-on-the-Lake, Ontario, and Buffalo, New York, and in June 2000 in Vancouver, British Columbia, and Blaine, Washington. Participants in these sessions were briefed on the increased degree of bilateral co-operation by federal agencies along the border and raised a number of concerns, including the importance of maintaining a secure yet relatively open border for tourism, trade, and local economies (CUSP, 2000). Perhaps the most important outcome of the CUSP process was the demonstration of the strength of the grassroots constituency in both countries for improvements at the Canada–US border.

It was with the same positive spirit that Representative Lamar Smith introduced the Immigration and Naturalization Service Data Management Act of 2000 on 18 May; the bill won wide support, passed both houses of Congress, and was signed into law by President Clinton on 15 June 2000—less than one month later. The new Act built on the immigration reform legislation of 1996 and 1998 by authorizing significant new funding for the development of information technology solutions for implementing the Section 110 provision, attempting to improve the quality of information gathered by those entering and exiting the United States to permit US Customs and INS inspectors at the border to implement better risk-management, focusing enforcement resources where the risk was higher, while facilitating the flow of low-risk individuals and commerce. The 2000 immigration law also expressed 'the sense of Congress that the Attorney General, in consultation with the Secretaries of State, Commerce, and the Treasury should consult with affected foreign governments to improve border management', an acknowledgement of the importance of consultation with neighbours in developing border management policies; it was a message Canada had wanted to hear.

In November 2000, test-implementation of a new electronic system called NEXUS began at the Blue Water Bridge crossing between Sarnia, Ontario, and Port Huron, Michigan. Under the NEXUS program, US Customs, the INS, CIC, and Canada Customs developed a common data form, allowing travellers and shippers in both countries to file the same personal information form. Individuals would then receive a NEXUS card with biometric support that would enable the bearer to access an expedited inspection and clearance lane, since NEXUS participation allowed the four agencies to confirm the individual as low risk and in the process gather more information about the person than was possible in the normal inspection interview. The program test was suspended in the wake of the 11 September attacks.

The Lessons of the Section 110 Experience

The most contentious aspect of US immigration policy reform from the perspective of Canada–US relations was the Section 110 provision, and charges that the failure to implement this provision contributed to the vulnerability of the United States to terrorist attacks before and on 11 September itself were the most incendiary of many levelled against proponents of improved co-operation between Canada and the United States in managing the border. On 10 October, Representative Virgil Goode (R-Virginia) introduced a bill calling for the immediate implementation of the Section 110 provision by the INS along both US land borders (introduced as HR 3077).

Yet the Section 110 provision was a failure from nearly every perspective. For its proponents, Section 110 failed because it was never implemented; its design had proven too controversial, too cumbersome and expensive to administer, and too extreme a response to what generally seemed to be the problem of illegal immigration and not terrorism. For its critics, including Canada, the flaws of Section 110 were immediately apparent. But even today the provision is not dead, despite the considerable time and energy spent by the broad coalition of government officials, business groups, and non-governmental organizations to stop it. After 11 September, the shadow of terrorism is certain to colour the US immigration policy debate, making the revival of the debate over Section 110 or a successor measure a possibility.

On 12 December 2001 the two governments endorsed the 30-point Smart Border Declaration (Office of Homeland Security, 2001). In it, the governments of Canada and the United States pledge to improve co-operation, develop new, joint procedures, share more intelligence information, and implement specific reforms to immigration, inspection, and traffic management practices at the border. It is a complex and ambitious agenda, but as can be seen from the foregoing discussion, the Smart Border Declaration is not a new beginning so much as a new commitment of political will and adequate funding to follow through on good ideas that had languished for want of both prior to 11 September.

Will the Smart Border Declaration succeed in improving the security and efficiency of the

Canada–US border while decisively forestalling measures like Section 110, where previous efforts have met with only partial success? It is still too early to answer this question, but the success of current efforts will depend to a considerable extent on whether or not leaders in both Canada and the United States have learned key lessons from their Section 110 experiences. Specifically, there are four important lessons for each side.

US Lesson 1: Security measures cannot ignore economic concerns

After 11 September, the desire of the US Congress that the INS better document who is crossing US borders does not appear to have been so unreasonable. Yet domestic US economic interests, including some of the largest US corporations, rely heavily on cross-border production and resisted the Section 110 mandate. If the proponents of Section 110 had been able to accommodate the Concerns of the business community, the requirement might have been successfully implemented. In other words, powerful economic interests can and will fight back if security measures come at a disproportionate economic cost.

US Lesson 2: Underfunded mandates are more difficult to implement

When the US Congress ordered the INS to develop a plan to implement the Section 110 requirement, it did not make significant new funding available to the INS to finance implementation. As a result, the INS had to consider the lowest-cost options for implementation—even paper forms, similar to those handed out to passengers arriving by air and sea. Critics of Section 110 pointed out that technologies already developed would allow the required information to be transmitted electronically for frequent border crossers through transponders or smart cards issued by the two governments. In fact, US and Canadian border agencies were experimenting with such systems on a limited basis throughout the debate over Section 110—ultimately leading to the test implementation of the NEXUS program. But in fairness to the INS, lack of

funding for a major expansion of such programs prevented consideration of viable high-tech alternatives that would permit better data collection without sacrificing border facilitation.

A further barrier to successful Section 110 implementation was inadvertently created through understaffing by US agencies at the Canadian border. The Clinton administration in 1994 ordered the temporary reassignment of one-third of the personnel at the Canadian border to the US–Mexican border to handle the anticipated surge in traffic prompted by NAFTA. Subsequently, these staffers were not replaced, and so US agencies working on the Canadian border were forced to inspect growing traffic volumes with a shortage of trained personnel. At busy ports, such as Detroit–Windsor and Buffalo–Fort Erie, college students and schoolteachers seeking supplemental income were hired to staff US inspection booths in order to reduce backups. Stretched as they were by understaffing, US agencies at the border were in no position to cope with the additional requirement of individual entry and exit documentation imposed by Congress.

US Lesson 3: Canada and Mexico are not the same

Since NAFTA took effect, there have been frequent attempts by Washington policy-makers to approach certain issues with one US policy for both Canada and Mexico. In Congress, the need to build coalitions in support of legislation often requires representatives and senators from northern and southern border states to work together, further encouraging the harmonization of practices at both borders. Yet the relative openness of the Canada–US border permits firms to employ just-in-time inventory management practices that make manufacturing and service operations vulnerable to border delays to a far greater extent than at the US–Mexico border, where longer inspection and clearance times are the norm. Failure to account for different border conditions and concerns was a key flaw in the design of the Section 110 provision of the 1996 immigration reform.

US Lesson 4: Unilateral approaches are more difficult to implement

Underscoring the previous lesson, the requirement that the INS record individual exit data at the borders as well as entry data effectively doubled the potential effort required to implement the Section 110 provision. Had the United States sought Canadian co-operation from the outset, Canadian officials might have been persuaded to gather entry data that could be shared with the United States—effectively allowing Canada to collect exit data for the US along the land border. As the series of bilateral agreements between 1993 and 2001 indicate, Canada was willing to work with the United States to improve border security throughout this period, making it reasonable to expect that Ottawa would have been willing also to co-operate with the United States in data collection at the border—something that the 2000 immigration reform legislation belatedly acknowledges. As it was, Canada fought the implementation of the Section 110 provision and many Canadians viewed the measure with hostility.

The Chrétien government, which encountered considerable US resistance in its attempt to turn back Section 110, also stands to learn important lessons from the Section 110 experience.

Canadian Lesson 1: Economic concerns do not trump security concerns

The mirror image of the US lesson, it became clear to Ottawa that despite the value of bilateral trade to both countries, members of Congress and US officials responsible for security at the border would not be deterred by economic arguments alone. One analysis suggests that the US is concerned mainly about security at the border, while Canada is concerned mainly about the economic impact of border management (Shea, 2001). This is too simplistic: in reality both countries are concerned with both goals, and the Section 110 debate proved that the two concerns could stalemate action if not reconciled.

Canadian Lesson 2: Canada has a credibility gap on security issues in the United States

Canadians did not consider themselves to be lax when it came to security, even after several incidents suggested that international terrorists were abusing Canadian openness and tolerance to gain access to the United States. The tendency of Canadians to respond to US criticism by touting Canada's supposedly superior tolerance of diversity further undermined Canadian credibility with Americans, who interpreted such rhetoric as evidence that their northern neighbours did not understand the extent of the danger posed by terrorism. Throughout the debate over Section 110 the American stereotype of Canadians as well-intentioned but naive Boy Scouts collided with Canadian stereotypes of Americans as gun-toting Rambo clones, and yet instead of cancelling one another out, the effect of these two shallow generalizations, when combined with increasing evidence of terrorist activity in North America, was to erode Canadian credibility on security questions. The result was that Canada repeatedly found itself placed on the defensive by critics in the United States who questioned Canada's resolve to fight terrorism.

Canadian Lesson 3: Trilateral solutions are problematic for Canada, but tempting for the United States

For some Canadians, the contrast between the US–Canada border and the US–Mexico border is so stark that there does not seem to be a polite way of pointing out the differences, since comparisons are inevitably so unflattering to Mexico. Yet in the face of a US tendency to trilateralize issues following NAFTA, Canada runs the risk of seeing the United States opt for the lowest-common-denominator approach to its borders rather than seeking to duplicate the 'best-practice' policies of the Canada–US border on the US–Mexico border. With the majority of congressional leaders now representing the populous southern states, the mental image of borders for many in Congress is the US–Mexico border. The Section 110 debate demonstrated the extent to which Canada must be prepared to educate US leaders about the US northern border.

CANADIAN LESSON 4: PARTICIPATION IN US DOMESTIC DEBATES IS OPEN TO THE CANADIAN GOVERNMENT AND ITS DOMESTIC CRITICS

The Canadian government was pleased to forge alliances with US business and border community groups with a common interest in blocking implementation of the Section 110 provision. It was less pleased to discover critics of its policies could just as easily win a hearing in the United States. The Section 110 debate provided both governments with a foretaste of the complex political dynamics that will accompany deepening bilateral economic integration. Participation in the US political arena will work for and against Ottawa's agenda at different times—and frequently, in a concurrent fashion. This will make conflict resolution with the United States more difficult for Ottawa to manage.

While it is important not to judge either government too harshly on whether it has learned these lessons in the immediate aftermath of 11 September, given the enormity of the attacks and the psychological and emotional impact they have had on citizens of both countries, there are encouraging signs in the Smart Border Declaration and the conduct of Canada–US relations since then that leaders in both countries have indeed adapted their approach to consider some of these lessons.

First, the two governments have adopted a reasonably balanced approach to improving security while remaining sensitive to the economic impact of new security measures. The constituency tapped by the CUSP process, mobilized by the Section 110 debate, is quick to praise or challenge measures that do not meet this test. So, on the first lesson, Canada and the United States both earn high marks.

Second, both countries are approaching the border with the understanding that they must establish their respective bona fides. The United States is demonstrating a new seriousness by committing to the full funding of border improvement measures, rather than mandating that the INS and other border agencies somehow manage to do more with less. Canada, for its part, has acted quickly to redress the under-funding of its immigration courts and domestic security services, and has closed loopholes in its immigration laws that were exploited by Abu Mezer and Ressam. On this second lesson, Canada and the United States also receive high marks. However, the United States has thus far earned an incomplete grade—the old congressional practice of announcing the authorization of funds, to which significant preconditions are attached, and then appropriating far less can still not be ruled out. For the US to win applause, the promised money must actually be spent.

Third, since 11 September the two governments have clearly rediscovered room for bilateralism in their relationship. They have done so generally without precluding Mexico from participation in new border management practices, but recognizing at the same time that Canada and the United States have a stronger foundation of bilateral co-operation at the border on which to build, as well as established security and intelligence-sharing relationships through NATO, NORAD, the Permanent Joint Board on Defence, the International Joint Commission, and other institutions. Here, too, Canada and the United States deserve credit for appearing to have learned something from the Section 110 debate.

The fourth lessons remain problematic for both countries, for different reasons. It is not at all clear that the United States has abandoned its preference for managing the border unilaterally since 11 September. Indeed, in the absence of any clear Canadian initiatives or counterproposals for improving border security and fighting terrorism in North America, the bilateral co-operation since 11 September is impossible to distinguish from a combination of US unilateralism and Canadian acquiescence to the US agenda. At the same time, while Canada has sought to establish its good faith as a partner to the United States rather than assuming it is viewed by Americans as a reliable security partner, Ottawa continues to react with evident shock when comments declaring Canada's determination to resist US pressure, made by Canadian politicians for domestic consumption, are interpreted by US policy-makers as evidence that Canada is an unreliable ally.

These suggested lessons from the Section 110 experience will remain important as the 30 points of the Smart Border Declaration move from rhetoric to implementation. So soon after the events of 11 September, no judgment on whether these lessons have been learned can be deemed final—the early good marks can be rescinded and the areas where improvement still seems necessary can yet be turned around.

11 September and Canada–US Relations: What Next?

Thucydides observed that in human relations and affairs of state, the strong do what they can and the weak accept what they must. This is an apt description for Canada–US relations over border management issues since 1993. The United States government sought to institute a series of immigration policy reforms, while gradually awakening to the threat posed to its citizens by international terrorism on US soil. The Canadian government adopted a strategy of attempting to substitute bilateral dialogue and co-operation for unilateral US actions, often fighting a rearguard battle to stop Section 110 implementation. However, in the aftermath of 11 September, Canada's strategy seemed to change.

It seems obvious that, in this bilateral relationship, the United States will always be the strong state and Canada the weak state. Yet, as Keohane and Nye argued 25 years ago, the interdependence of Canada and the United States, which has grown with deepening economic integration, alters the power balance between the two countries (Keohane and Nye, 1977). Interdependence

renders Canada stronger and the United States weaker vis-à-vis one another. Canada is one of the few states in the international system to have a choice of whether it will act as a strong state or a weak state in its approach to the United States.

A strong state strategy for Canada would involve improving Canadian domestic security and implementing a creative counter-terrorism effort taken with or without US participation, simply because Canadian citizens are threatened by international terrorism, as is their way of life as part of the civilized world. Canada's national interest lies in maintaining the best possible relations with the United States, and so a strong Canada would naturally secure its borders and aggressively enforce its laws in all areas. To paraphrase Pierre Trudeau, to those who do not like the sight of men with guns and who wonder how far Canada will go, just watch and see.

A weak state strategy for Canada would consider the threat of international terrorism largely a US concern, and seek to placate US pressure with minimum efforts while husbanding Canadian sovereignty and avoiding commitments to undertake new responsibilities with regard to the defence of North America. To paraphrase William Lyon Mackenzie King, full security co-operation with the United States If necessary, but not necessarily full security co-operation with the United States.

Whether Canada opts for a strong state strategy or a weak state strategy will have a decisive impact on its relationship with the United States as the campaign against global terrorism continues, both in North America and overseas. From the US perspective, a Canada following a strong state strategy is a desirable partner; a Canada following a weak state strategy is an obstacle to progress towards greater security. Washington will approach Canada in coming years based on the posture Canada adopts towards the United States. The strategy that Canada chooses will determine whether the US learns the final lesson of the Section 110 experience and approaches the border in the spirit of bilateral co-operation or with non-negotiable demands. At the same time, Canada's choice will indicate whether it has learned from the Section 110 experience—that in the face of deepening integration the vulnerability of Canadian interests to the United States will continue to grow and that a weak state strategy, while appearing to preserve Canada's ability to take decisions independently within its own sovereign jurisdiction, will further weaken Canada's ability to defend its interests in the United States.

The theme of the 2002 volume of the *Canada Among Nations* series describes 'a fading power'. Readers will be tempted to see in this theme an indication that Canada will inevitably opt to continue pursuing a weak state strategy with regard to the United States, as it did in the debate over the border from 1993 onward, once the residual effect of the 11 September attacks has faded and the politics of Canada–US relations revert to a new normalcy. The Section 110 experience, however, suggests another possibility.

The turbulent nature of the Section 110 debate, and the high stakes for Canadian interests in particular, mobilized an array of new participants in the debate over border management. Many border communities, transnational firms, and non-governmental interest groups demanded a voice in a policy debate that seemed too important to be left to the federal governments—and many felt that the federal governments were making a mess of things instead of co-operating. State and provincial governments, too, came to question the way that Ottawa and Washington were bickering over the management of the border, and sought a role

for themselves to defend their own interests. The federal governments responded with the CUSP process, which further encouraged new players to become involved and demand to be heard.

In the weeks after 11 September, when Ottawa appeared to hesitate to declare its unconditional support for the United States, Canadian citizens, firms, and communities reacted instinctively to demonstrate their support in words and deeds. Provincial governments stepped forward to offer emergency relief and to co-ordinate with state law enforcement and security counterparts in homeland defence preparations. For millions of Canadians, Americans are friends, family, and business partners. The choice between international terrorists and helping a neighbour was simple, and most Canadians made it without equivocation or calculation of national interest.

Thanks to deepening interdependence through economic integration, Canada is not a fading power in the United States. It is instead a rising power, more important to Americans and their prosperity today than ever before in US history.

No, it is Ottawa that risks becoming a fading power today. If it continues to adopt a weak country strategy it will fade in its ability to represent and defend Canadian interests in the United States, while fading in its attractiveness as a partner for Washington in the management of cross-border issues. The lessons of the Section 110 experience and the debate over the border in recent years indicate that Ottawa does have a choice. So, too, do Canadians.

References

Beltrame, Julian. 1997. 'Canada to help stop illegal entry into US: Illegal immigrants cross porous border from Ontario, Quebec', *Ottawa Citizen,* 8 February.

Bromowich, Michael. 1998. *Bombs in Brooklyn: How Two Illegal Aliens Arrested for Plotting to Bomb the New York Subway Entered and Remained in the United States.* Washington: Office of the Inspector General, US Department of Justice, March.

Cadman, Walter D. 1998. Prepared Testimony of Walter D. Cadman, Counterterrorism Coordinator, Office of Field Operations, Immigration and Naturalization Service, before the Senate Committee on the Judiciary, Subcommitee on Technology, Terrorism and Government Information Regarding Foreign Terrorist Activities in the United States, 24 February.

Canada–US Partnership Forum (CUSP). 2000. *Building a Border for the 21st Century: CUSP Forum Report,* December.

Cooper, Andrew F. 2000. 'Waiting at the Perimeter: Making US Policy in Canada', in F.O. Hampson and M.A. Molet, eds, *Canada Among Nations 2000: Vanishing Borders*. Don Mills, ON: Oxford University Press.

Dahlburg, John-Thor. 1996. 'Legacy of Fear: Afghanistan's Mix of Faith, Terror—A Global Scourge', *Los Angeles Times*, 6 August.

Farley, Maggie. 1999. 'Canada's Lapses Kept Algerian Suspect Free', *Los Angeles Times*, 23 December.

Federation for American Immigration Reform (FAIR). 1999. 'Senator Abraham's Activities Have Increased the Risk of Terrorist Penetration, Says FAIR', Press release, Washington, 20 December.

Hampson, Fen Osler, and Maureen Appel Molot. 2000. 'Does the 49th Parallel Matter Any More?', in Hampson and Molot, eds, *Canada Among Nations 2000: Vanishing Borders*. Don Mills, ON: Oxford University Press.

Keohane, Robert, and Joseph Nye. 1977. *Power and Interdependence: World Politics in Transition*. Boston: Little, Brown.

Krouse, William J., and Ruth Ellen Wasem. 1998. 'Immigration: Visa Entry/Exit Control System', Congressional Research Service Report for Congress. Washington: Library of Congress, 26 August.

Meyers, Deborah Waller, and Demetrios G. Papademetriou. 2001. 'Self-Governance Along the US–Canada Border: A View from Three Regions', in Meyers and Papademetriou, eds, *Caught in the Middle: Border Communities in all Era of Globalization*. Washington: Carnegie Endowment for International Peace.

Nieves, Evelyn. 1999. 'California Calls Off Effort to Carry Out Immigrant Measure', *New York Times*, 30 July.

Office of Homeland Security. 2001. 'Action Plan for Creating a Secure and Smart Border', Washington: Executive Office of the President of the United States, 12 December. Available at http://www.whitehouse.gov/ news/releases/12/20011212-6.html.

Sands, Christopher. 2001. 'Canada and the Bush Challenge', *Canada Focus* 2, 1.

Shea, Andrew. 2001. *Border Choices: Balancing the Need for Security and Trade*. Ottawa: Conference Board of Canada.

Washington: Center for Strategic and International Studies, January. Available at http://www.csis.org/ americas/canada/focus/focus0101.html.

16

Myths of Canada's Human Security Pursuits: Tales of Tool Boxes, Toy Chests, and Tickle Trunks

Ann Denholm Crosby

> The Voice of Women is a fine example of a bunch of hens running around with their heads cut off.

> There was something pathetically foolish about the appearance at the Parliament Buildings in Ottawa the other day of a group of matrons styling themselves with the pompous and absurdly unappealing title of the Voice of Women.

> The world must pity this nation's fall so low with a government bedeviled by wailing women and afflicted with indecision.
> —*Media Reports, 1962 (NFB, 1992)*

In 1997 Minister of Foreign Affairs, Lloyd Axworthy claimed that human security 'includes security against economic privation, an acceptable quality of life, and a guarantee of fundamental human rights' and that these ends were to be realized through 'the rule of law, good governance, sustainable development and social equity' (1997: 84). Axworthy has argued further that human security pursuits are particularly suited to the exercise of soft power, that is, to 'negotiation rather than coercion, powerful ideas rather than powerful weapons, public diplomacy rather than backroom bargaining.' In promoting this agenda, Axworthy wrote, 'Our basic unit of analysis in security matters has shrunk from the state to the individual' (1998).

These are precisely the ideas held by the Voice of Women (VOW), that 'group of matrons' and 'wailing women' of the above quotations. The similar discourses, however, are embedded in very different understandings of security. The VOW perspective was, and is still, rooted in an understanding of the gendered nature of power relations and how these support a range of power hierarchies involving gender, class, race, and culture that make some peoples secure at the expense of others. The perspective supported by the Department of Foreign Affairs and International Trade (DFAIT) under Axworthy's tutelage, on the other hand, masks the Canadian government's understanding that security is dependent upon global market forces and belongs to those who comply with those forces, and particularly to those who ply the forces. Lost in the government's rationale for pursuing human security initiatives within the context of market forces is a historical analysis of the ways in which that market, and its promotion, creates or exacerbates insecurities for the non-elites of the world, both at home and abroad. Retained in the rationale, however, is the gendered nature of security policy decision-making as described by the VOW.

The debates about human, as opposed to state-centred, security practices that, in the past decade, have exercised politicians and bureaucrats from both DFAIT and the Department of National Defence (DND), as well as a range of interested observers and academics, are essentially about means rather than ends. They can be reduced to whether the Canadian state, in its pursuit of prosperity and employment, should tackle the related security issues with instruments from DFAIT's tool box of soft-power resources or with DND's toy chest of military technologies. Either way, the debate is implicitly about how to address with one hand the ills produced with the other, and it serves to disguise the fact that this is what is being done. Soft and hard power advocates are equally implicated in this act of prestidigitation, and in furtherance of the charade, both dip into the tickle trunk of disguises to dress their discourse and practice of human security in the garb of humanitarianism. Hence, although the disguise gives the appearance of security having taken on a human face, it remains the face of power acting in its own interests behind the mask.

The following exploration of DFAIT's human security agenda in the context of its primary foreign policy interests, and the debates about the relative merits of hard versus soft power, is set within the theoretical context of 'conditioning frameworks' as described by Ricardo Grinspun and Robert Kreklewich (1994), and against the backdrop of the Voice of Women's human security discourse and practice. The former allows for a Gramscian explanation of the disciplinary nature of neo-liberal forces, including how they reinforce the gendered nature of security policy; the latter provides an example of how alternative ideas about security arise from within civil society as a result of particular experiences of power relations, as well as an example of feminist critical thinking about security that anticipated contemporary writings on the subject.

The Voice of Women: A Civil Society Conception of Human Security[1]

The VOW was founded in 1960 when, as Kay Macpherson, a founding member, wrote, 'one of those far-off summit conferences between the US and the USSR . . . had failed; Khrushchev banged his shoe on the desk at the UN; an American U2 spy plane was shot down over the USSR; [and] the Cold War was rapidly getting hotter . . .' (1994: 89). At home, the Canadian government was 'afflicted with indecision' (NFB, 1992) over whether to accept US nuclear weapons on Canadian soil for use by Canadian forces in the East–West relations of nuclear deterrence. It was the gathering of 400 VOW members in Ottawa to petition the government not to accept the weapons that earned them the criticisms quoted above.

Anticipating the works of post-Cold War critical-security theorists,[2] the organization mounted a critique of Cold War state-centred security practices. The VOW perspective understood the state to be a part of the security problem in that not only were women disadvantaged within the institutions and structures of the state and thus less secure than men in both the public and private state realms, but the promotion of state interests through the use of military means created further insecurities, and not just for women. Vast sums of money were being spent on nuclear weapons that exposed all peoples to the possibility of a nuclear war and annihilation; the testing of these weapons exposed peoples to the health hazards of radioactive fallout; and the legitimation of the use of violence by the state in pursuit of state interests conditioned peoples to accept violence was an inevitable characteristic of relations between states. Their bottom line, however, was that the use of state violence through military means aggravated rather than addressed the conflicts among the world's peoples. Instead, the VOW held that negotiation, compromise, conciliation, and the building of trust among peoples and their governments, in other words, the tools of soft power, should be the means of choice for pursuing peaceful relations of global cohabitation.

Since its founding, the VOW has embarked on numerous campaigns which reflect their human security perspective. Throughout the Cold War, the organization consistently lobbied the government against military build-up and reliance on the use of force; its argument was that force, whether used or threatened, intensified and prolonged East–West tensions and mistrust. To demonstrate that the testing of nuclear weapons was a health hazard, the organization collected over 5,500 baby teeth from across the country and had them tested at the University of Toronto for the effects of radioactive fallout. As the Cold War raged in the 1960s, VOW hosted Russian women in Canada and visited the USSR on a number of occasions in efforts to build transnational channels of communication and trust. During the Vietnam War, the organization brought Vietnamese and American women together in Canada to discuss the war, its effects on both Americans and Vietnamese, and possible ways to bring it to an end. VOW has also worked against the use of nuclear power since the 1960s; lobbied representatives of NATO, the Warsaw Treaty Organization, and a range of international disarmament fora; and organized and attended numerous conferences throughout the world on peace, development, refugee, and health issues, building bridges with similarly inclined women in the process. In this way, the VOW's efforts to address Cold War security issues evolved, over the ensuing years, into attempts to also address inequities rooted in gender, class, race, and cultural hierarchies of power.

Representatives of the VOW were vilified in Ottawa in 1962, however, not only for their ideas and activism, for like those of the peace movement in general, these tended to be dismissed by the media as the noise of the 'frighteningly muddled', 'emotional', 'malinformed and misinformed', and representative of 'an unholy mixture of greedy opportunism, naive idealism and pious hypocrisy' (Crosby, 1998a: 169–70). Rather, VOW members were vilified primarily for stepping out-side their prescribed gender roles and behaviour, and thus flouting the public and private authority of men. As one member of the Ottawa delegation put it, 'men didn't let their wives go out like that, especially not to challenge government policy' (NFB, 1992). By publicly censuring these women for breeching gender norms and rules, the media both reinforced those norms and rules, and demonstrated the barriers to women's social, economic, and political mobility, as well as to their freedom of speech, association, and movement. The public ridicule demonstrated the gendered nature of power in Canada at the time, and the extent to which women's lives were compromised by the structures and relations of gender.

The VOW took up the challenges of the Cold War on their understanding that men and women in general had different ways of doing things, had different knowledge, and that these were derived from their differing experiences of, and roles within, the public and private realms of the state. Some VOW members held to the radical feminist belief that gender differences were biologically determined; others believed that they were learned. All, however, felt that they had a better understanding than men in public office of what constituted security and how it could be realized. Although they gave voice to and embodied the liberal feminist belief that a larger number of women in public office would lead to progressive change, the kind of egalitarian change that the VOW has struggled to establish in the organization and through its national and international activities, implies a critical feminist understanding of the socially constructed nature of gender relations and the links between gender, race, class, and cultural hierarchies of power.

This perspective, since articulated and nuanced by a number of feminist scholars working in the area of critical security studies,[3] holds that the societal norms, rules, traditions, and laws that have established women as nurturers, conciliators, compromisers, and the purveyors of subjective forms of knowing and being within the private realm of the state, and as secondary to men, have also assigned to men the characteristics of aggressiveness, competitiveness, individualism, and rational objectivity, the attributes thought to be required for the management of the public spheres of business, politics, and national security, the spheres that were understood to be appropriately populated by men. Within this gender construct, neither men nor women are able to explore, without social constraints, the spectrum of human characteristics and attributes in order to develop those expressions of being human with which they feel most comfortable; by the same token, neither the public nor private realms of the state is shaped by the range of human possibilities.

Thus, for VOW members it was not an inevitability of human nature that the realist perspective dominated the security ideas and practices of the Cold War era. Men had defined and shaped the security interests and relations of states and had done so from their gendered perspective which understood the dominant human characteristics to be those of themselves, of gendered males. States, run by statesmen, were therefore seen to embody the characteristics of the gendered male, and as such were understood as sovereign, unitary actors, pursuing self-interest competitively and aggressively, particularly in the anarchical international environment that they inhabited. Given these characteristics, a self-interested state's security depended on its ability to defend its interests and territory from the self-interested encroachment of other states. Although accommodation, negotiation, and conciliation were tools of the state, they were considered the tools of second-order human activities, as more appropriately women's way of doing things. Force and violence were the tools of the first, or dominant, order of human activity, and military means were therefore the ultimate guarantor of state security.

This perspective is self-perpetuating because it creates state relations of competitive self-interest dependent upon the use of force and violence, and practising these relations over time leads to the belief that they are the 'natural' relations among states.[4] The ideas and practices of state-

centred security pursuits are further reinforced because they are also functional for the interests sustained by the use of force and power, the interests that thrive on the pursuit of wealth and power within global cultural, political, and economic structures.[5] Hence, making states and their political, economic, and cultural interests secure, ultimately through the use of military force, is seen as tantamount to making people as citizens of states secure. Not incidentally in the practice of this understanding of security, gendered hierarchies of power are sustained, reinforced, and reproduced, as they in turn sustain, reinforce, and reproduce the relations of hierarchical power that privilege some peoples at the expense of others.

Despite the VOW's long history of attempting to redefine who security should be for, what it could consist of, and how it might be achieved, DFAIT claims that the government's efforts to promote a human security agenda are rooted in international institutions and documents: the International Committee of the Red Cross, the UN Charter, the Universal Declaration of Human Rights, the Geneva Conventions, and the 1994 UNDP Human Development Project (DFAIT, 1999). In this way, the Canadian government demonstrates how women's contributions to the making of a society's history are lost. In this case, however, the lack of recognition is a blessing in disguise for, from a VOW perspective and from that of a number of feminist critical-security scholars, the government has the concept wrong anyway. The difference in the two perspectives becomes apparent when the government's version of human security is viewed in relation to its dominant foreign policy interests.

DFAIT's Human Security Agenda

Since the Liberal government's 1994 Foreign Policy Review, Canadian foreign policy has been broadly defined by three objectives: 'the promotion of prosperity and employment; the protection of our security within a stable global framework; and the projection of Canadian values and culture.'⁶ Although presented as the 'three pillars' of Canadian foreign policy, the security and cultural pillars are little more than flying buttresses to the economic pillar. According to *Canada in the World*, the government's still relevant response to the foreign policy review, both domestic and international stability are rooted in the processes that 'reinforce' global prosperity, while Canada's role in promoting that prosperity is facilitated by the projection of Canadian values—'respect for human rights, democracy, the rule of law, and the environment . . . . After all, the document notes, "More prosperous people are able to maintain more mature and mutually beneficial economic partnerships with Canada, becoming increasingly open to our values and thus more active partners in building the international system."' Accordingly, the main thrust of Canadian foreign policy, which the document describes in considerable detail, is the promotion of rules-based forms of economic multilateralism at all levels and in all institutions of global governance. In keeping with this policy position, the Canadian government is active in the World Trade Organization, the International Monetary Fund, the World Bank, APEC, the OECD, and in the temporarily suspended MAI negotiations. In addition, DFAIT has pursued bilateral trade and investment arrangements on its own initiative and through its Team Canada partnerships with Canadian business.

Since from DFAIT's perspective, the security of the world's peoples is dependent upon the prosperity and stability provided by global market forces, it follows that the pursuit of prosperity for Canadians by promoting those global market forces is tantamount to pursuing prosperity, and hence security, for all peoples. This logic allows DFAIT to state quite simply that 'the promotion of prosperity and employment is at the heart of the Government's agenda.' Hence, one foreign policy pillar and two flying buttresses, and hence also, the Canadian version of the Western panacea for global ills—liberal democratic practices and neo-liberal markets.

Much has been written, however, about the ways in which global neo-liberal economic forces create insecurity for vast numbers of the world's peoples. As Susan Strange argues, for example, global market forces are largely responsible for the distribution of the world's goods, for determining who gets how much of the world's political, economic, social, and cultural resources and under what conditions (1996: 3–15). This, she claims, constitutes a shift in power from states to markets, a shift that has eroded the state's ability to perform a number of its traditional functions, including its ability to shape or stabilize its domestic economy, to set taxation standards, to impose wage and price controls, to determine trade policy, to control foreign investment, and to stabilize its currency. These constraints have created a widening economic gap within states between those who benefit from market-driven deregulation and those who do not. The state is caught, therefore, in a double bind. Not only is it restricted in its ability to manage its domestic economy and distribute resources on a stabilizing and equitable basis, but its pursuit of 'prosperity and employment' for Canadians within the global economy strengthens the very forces that tie its hands domestically.

At the same time, Strange holds that whatever power less- or non-industrialized states have enjoyed in the past is shifting upwards to the industrialized states, with the latter, although limited in their ability to influence global market forces, still better positioned than the former to realize their economic and political interests within that market. Thus, there are growing gaps in wealth and privilege amongst states and peoples in the international realm. Strange also argues that, because of these two market-induced shifts in power, there are now places where no power at all is being exercised, as evidenced by the contraction or absence of social, health, educational, and environmental programs.

According to a number of international political economy theorists (Strange, 1996: 44–65; Cox, 1999; Lipshutz, 1992), these market-induced shifts of power and authority are directly responsible for producing or exacerbating a range of insecurities for peoples, including those rooted in poverty, environmental degradation, resource depletion, and the inequitable distribution of political, economic, and social resources. In turn these insecurities produce others, including population movements, human rights abuses, conflicts between states, crime, prostitution, child soldiering, and arms trafficking. Axworthy has called this range of market-induced insecurities the 'dark side of globalization' (1999c). It is, however, precisely these insecurities that DFAIT's human security agenda is intended to address.

In essence, the government is attempting to address with one hand the ills it is causing with the other. In other words, DFAIT's human security agenda is meant to address the range of insecurities produced or exacerbated by global market forces even as the government's main foreign policy interest, the pursuit of prosperity and employment for Canadians through the global economy, serves to reinforce those forces. In this context, the best that the government can hope to accomplish with its human security policy is an easing of the symptoms of insecurity, not the root causes. However, because the state is constrained by market forces in implementing domestic remedial policies or circumscribing market interests, even its ability to ease the manifestations of market-induced insecurities is limited.

Human Security as a Conditioning Framework

Rather than constituting an alternative practice of security as imagined by the VOW and critical security theorists, the discourse and practice of human security as plied by DFAIT serve, in a manner similar to that described by Ricardo Grinspun and Robert Kreklewich, as a 'conditioning framework' for business as usual (Grinspun and Kreklewich, 1994: 34–7). Borrowing from Robert Cox, Grinspun and Kreklewich employ the concept of conditioning frameworks in relation to neo-liberal economic processes, specifically free

trade agreements. It is their contention that such agreements 'impose and lock-in neoliberal reforms' by promoting 'what Cox has defined as the "internationalization of the state".' This, is a 'global process whereby national policies and practices have been adjusted to the exigencies of the world economy of international production.' This process is 'largely élite-driven and rarely mandated by popular "free choice"'. Although there may appear to be 'free choice', the choices are restricted to policies that represent the interests of global market practices, and it becomes almost impossible to imagine any alternatives. Hence the reproduction of hegemonic neo-liberal ideas and practices. Inasmuch as global economic structures, like political structures, are gendered, as argued earlier, this too is reproduced through neo-liberal conditioning frameworks. Grinspun and Kreklewich further argue that conditioning frameworks can be formal or informal 'depending on whether or not the terms are prescribed in a legal agreement.' Informal frameworks do not involve legal agreements, and their 'effects are invisible (i.e., not spelled out explicitly to the public), although they are clearly observable'.

In this way, DFAIT's discourse and practice of human security can be understood as an informal conditioning framework for the pursuit of neo-liberal economic interests and processes in that human security is about security *within the context* of global market forces and the on-going efforts by the state to reinforce them. Market-induced insecurities are represented either as time-bound aberrations of that system rather than endemic to it, or as phenomena caused by 'failed or rogue states' or to ethno-nationalist programs rooted in historical hatreds, that is, to disorientations unrelated to the history and effects of the growing reach of Western political and economic interests. Moreover, by focusing on the plight of the individual in any of its various environments of insecurity, the government's human security perspective further conditions both itself and its citizens to see situations of insecurity in isolation from their causes. At the same time, both governments and individuals enjoy a sense of moral rectitude for trying to alleviate suffering instead of feeling responsible for having created or aggravated these insecurities. DFAIT's human security agenda, then, is a *restricted* set of policy choices adjusted to the exigencies of the world economy of international production and finance; and practising human security facilitates the on-going practice of market interests.

A range of what the Canadian government considers to be human security initiatives demonstrates this dynamic. Recognizing a need to bring 'greater "coherence" to [its] capacity to solve these interlinked and increasingly prominent [human security] issues' (Malone, 1999: 197), the government established a Global and Human Issues Bureau in 1995. Its responsibilities cover a range of 'functional issues' which sweepingly include 'the environment, human rights, children's questions (e.g., child labour, children in war, sexual exploitation of children) gender issues, youth, humanitarian policy, conflict prevention and peace-building, terrorism, crime and drugs, health, population, migration and refugees, as well as circumpolar and Aboriginal issues' (Malone, 1999: 197). The Canadian International Development Agency (CIDA), the funding agency for the Human Issues Bureau, also deals with many of these matters in its development assistance programs. Sixty per cent of CIDA's funding is from the Overseas Development Assistance (ODA) program, and the ODA budget was consistently cut throughout the 1990s; funding was increasingly targeted for the more developed of the developing countries and often tied to the World Bank's structural adjustment programs. 'Indeed, government policy towards developing countries since 1994 has focused almost exclusively on bilateral and multilateral trade and investment initiatives, meeting the primary foreign policy goal of *Canada in the World* of strengthening Canada's economic prosperity' (Draimin and Tomlinson, 1998: 145, 150–7).

The conclusion that most analysts reach after examining Canada's ODA and CIDA programs is that 'pressures from the private sector, the Prime Minister's Office and DFAIT continue to ensure that much Canadian aid is deployed to advance Canadian trade interests' (Pratt, 1998: 13). Similarly, Cranford Pratt argues that efforts to create new funding programs that might favour the Human Issues Bureau over CIDA 'could easily prove to be activities to promote Canadian trade rather than efforts to augment global human security' (1998: 12).

Nor has Canada been able to maintain its rhetorical commitment to human security concerns related to environmental degradation, as evidenced by its failure to meet the targets for reducing greenhouse gas emissions that it set for itself at the Kyoto Summit in 1997. Moreover, it has adopted the US position that 'developing nations . . . should bear the costs of transition to more environmentally friendly industrial technology' (Draimin and Tomlinson, 1998: 159). Again, trade and investment interests are the primary determinants of environmental policy. As Linda Reif concludes (1998: 281), 'The formation, content, and implementation of Canada's international commitments on environmental protection are, in the majority of sectors, being influenced by the economic interests of both government and civil society actors, the latter primarily in the commercial and industrial sectors.' To the extent that the federal government has domestic human security concerns, these are not well served either by cuts in federal funding to education, health, and a variety of social programs. These cuts serve to further deprive the already underprivileged in Canadian society while safeguarding the interests of the privileged. In other words, as the government's security focus has, in Axworthy's word, 'shrunk' from the state to the individual, so has the funding for domestic human security initiatives.

Whereas the VOW's understanding of human security depended upon the deconstruction of class, gender, and racial hierarchies of power, DFAIT's version reinforces all three, for it works to the advantage of those in control of global market forces, those being predominantly privileged white men from the industrialized West. At the same time, because those characteristics that have been constructed as stereotypically male are functional for the management of globalized political and economic processes, the system attracts people who have honed those characteristics and thus it remains gendered even as women enter the systems in increasing numbers and increasingly in positions of authority. When assuming positions of power under these conditions, women do not, for the most part, bring with them alternative understandings of security. Moreover, although their presence in positions of power indicates a weakening, particularly in the West, of the barriers to women's participation in public life, this does not translate into a weakening of gendered hierarchies of power in the globalized political economy. As Cynthia Enloe has documented so well (1993), women continue to be economically disadvantaged as compared to men, and this is especially so in industrializing or non-industrialized states. When doing business in these countries, western transnational corporations, carrying western understandings of gender construction, and supported by political and economic institutions dominated by western values, deem it appropriate to disproportionately disadvantage women simply because they are women.

In as much, then, as DFAIT's human security perspective disciplines both government and civil society to an understanding of security as dependent upon market forces, it simultaneously disciplines both to reinforcing gendered structures of power. In this way, DFAIT's version of human security acts as a conditioning framework for both market forces and for hierarchical relations of power rooted in an unequal valuing of peoples according to gender, race, class and or culture.

Finally, DFAIT's human security perspective also fails to address the concerns of both the VOW and critical-security scholars concerning the efficacy and ethos of military means for addressing conflicts among states. As examples of its success in pursuing human security initiatives, DFAIT cites the Ottawa Process that produced the Convention to Ban the Use of Anti-Personnel Landmines,

which was signed by 122 countries in December 1996; as well as Canada's role in establishing the framework for the International Criminal Court, its on-going efforts to control the trade in and use of small arms and light weapons, and its involvement in the issue of child soldiers. As Robin Jeffrey Hay points out, however (1999: 229), 'Save for the International Criminal Court, one would be hard pressed to point to any one of these issues that addresses the root causes of human insecurity.' Indeed, the flagship initiative, the convention to ban land mines, was successful in large part because it stigmatized a weapon rather than its users. States were applauded, and applauded themselves, for banning anti-personnel land mines when it was primarily states themselves that had produced, transferred, sold, stockpiled, and implanted them throughout vast regions of the world. Yet the ethos of state military practices emerged unscathed from the landmine campaign. What changed was the relegation of one weapon of questionable military utility to the junk heap of obsolescent military means. What did not change was the perception of the appropriateness of killing, and threatening to kill, others as a means of addressing problems (De Larrinaga and Sjolander, 1998; Beier and Crosby, 1998).

Still, when the Secretary-General of NATO spoke in Toronto in 1989 'about cooperation being better than confrontation', some VOW members took this as a sign that new ideas had 'penetrated the obsolete and inappropriate thinking of those in so-called high-places' (Macpherson, 1994: 137), ideas about the advantages of soft power over hard power. This conclusion only holds if the ends to which soft power are applied are significantly different than the ends pursued by hard power.

DFAIT's Tool Box of Soft Power Means

As Minister of Foreign Affairs, Lloyd Axworthy argued that 'in the conduct of international relations in a globalized, integrated world, . . . traditional military and economic might, while still important, do not have the over-whelming pre-eminence they once did.' Instead, he proposed, 'Skills in communication, negotiating, mobilizing opinion, working within multilateral bodies, and promoting international initiatives are increasingly effective ways to achieve international outcomes.' These are the tools, or methods, of 'soft power' and are, according to Axworthy, particularly suited to the problems of human security, the kinds of security issues that 'do not pit one state against another, but rather a group of states against various transnational challenges' (1998: 192).

In the same article, however, Axworthy went on to cite Joseph Nye's definition of soft power as 'the power to co-opt, rather than to coerce, others to your agenda and goals', and in another venue he added that the soft power means to these ends are, 'negotiation rather than coercion, powerful ideas rather than powerful weapons, public diplomacy rather than backroom bargaining' (1998a). In the language of peace research and feminist writings on the subject, this translates into bringing 'others to your agenda and goals' through structural, as opposed to direct, violence.[7] From Axworthy's perspective, then, the ends to which both hard and soft power are turned are the same and since for DFAIT, human security is to be found within the western forms of liberal democracy and the globalized market system, the promotion of both are the ends to which soft power is applied. Negotiation, powerful ideas, and public diplomacy are not tools for discovering and pursuing common definitions of what it means to be secure, but rather for bringing others to DFAIT's understanding of what constitutes security.

Moreover, Axworthy has noted that a soft power focus does not negate the need for hard power 'when conditions warrant' (DFAIT, 1999). Soft and hard power are understood as the flip sides of the same coin, the latter providing the muscle for the former when necessary. Thus, Axworthy was able to argue that the NATO bombings of both Bosnia and Kosovo were human security initiatives; 'concrete expression(s) of this human security dynamic at work.' In particular, the Kosovo initiative 'should serve to dispel the misconception that military force and the human security agenda are mutually exclusive' (Axworthy 1999b). Again, neither what constitutes security for others, nor the efficacy of bombing peoples into submission, is seen as a problem (Cox and Axworthy, 2000). Instead, the questions about the ethics of humanitarian interventions are settled in favour of those states with the power to intervene on the basis of their own understandings of security (Pasic and Weiss, 1997; Smith, 1998). Those states are also free to decide when soft power means have run their course, if they choose to employ them, and when and how to escalate their intervention to the use of military power.

Yet, despite this, soft power *still appears* to represent a more conciliatory, democratic, and egalitarian method of conducting relations amongst states and peoples and this *appearance* is supported by a number of DFAIT's soft power tools. One of these tools is fashioned out of a selective understanding of Canadian history and culture.

Canadians tend to imagine themselves as being particularly adept at plying the methods of soft power in support of human security pursuits. Aiding the destitute, diseased, displaced, and disoriented peoples of the world fits the image Canadians hold of themselves as 'helpful fixers' and a morally conscientious people. According to Cranford Pratt, there has been a consensus, at least since the 1970s, in the Canadian public domain 'that industrialized states have ethical obligations relating to global poverty' (1994b: 334). It is these images and beliefs that the government reflects when presenting its rationale for pursuing human security initiatives. 'Canada's history as a non-colonizing power, champion of constructive multilateralism and effective international mediator,' states *Canada World View* (DFAIT, 1998: Executive Summary, 1), ideally situates the country for 'an important and distinctive role among nations as they seek to build a new and better order.' Moreover, and in explicit reference to human security, the document declares that 'the concerns of Canadians about security issues are broader than those of self-interest. The desire to help others to build peace reflects some of the most deeply-held and widely-shared Canadian values' (DFAIT, 1998: Section IV, 1). Indeed, Axworthy and Taylor assert that Canada's history is one of 'attractive values, a reputation as an honest broker, skills at networking, a democratic tradition, and a willingness to work closely with civil society' (1998: 193).

Forgotten in this history, however, is the one Laura Macdonald (1995) describes of Canada as a colonizer by proxy in its political support of Britain's empire-building efforts, and its enjoyment of the fruits of colonialism through its Most Favoured Nation trade status with England. Forgotten, too, is the history of Canada's culturally insensitive missionary zeal at home and abroad, as well as the country's legacies of genocidal practices with respect to the First Nations peoples, of racism during and after the Second World War towards Jewish and Japanese people, and its history of endemic sexism and homophobia.[8]

Through this selective historical memory, Canadians are conditioned and condition themselves to support a human security agenda because it feels both right and Canadian from every angle: political, economic, social, and moral. In this way, attention is diverted from considerations of what it means to pursue a human security agenda *within* the context of global market forces. In this way too, the means of hard and soft power become separated in the national imagination. Traditionally, hard power, that is, military means, has been used in support of state-centred security pursuits, but when the government promotes the use of soft power in pursuit of human security, with both the tools and the agenda supposedly reflecting quintessentially non-aggressive Canadian values and culture, then the assumption is that new understandings of what constitutes security and for whom are coming into play. The government displays this assumption itself when it indulges in self-congratulation for its moral and sensitive human

security discourse and practices. But the ends to which both soft and hard power are directed are the same.

There is also an array of international institutions that provide legitimacy for Canada's human security agenda and in doing so prevent a deeper investigation of the ends that are being pursued. As mentioned earlier, DFAIT locates the origins of its human security policies in the International Committee of the Red Cross, the UN Charter, the Universal Declaration of Human Rights, the Geneva Conventions, and the 1994 UNDP Human Development Project. Variously, these, as well as Boutros Boutros-Ghali's *Agenda for Peace* and the UN's *Agenda 21* report, which emerged from the Rio de Janeiro conference on Environment and Development, cite environmental degradation, economic development, and human rights abuses as security issues; locate security as residing with the individual as well as the state; and call for partnerships between government and civil society in the pursuit of human security. Despite the controversial nature of the UN's humanitarian interventions in places such as Somalia, Haiti, Rwanda, and the former Yugoslavia, and whatever the *intent* of the UN documents, the international human security discourse legitimizes the Canadian government's particular human security understandings, including its efforts to inculcate with the same understandings, the range of multilateral bodies with which it is involved. Two examples of the latter are the government's efforts to use its seat on the Security Council in 1999–2000 as a forum for 'advancing Canada's agenda, especially integrating the human dimension—human security—into the council's work' (Axworthy, 1999a); and the government's role in 1998 in negotiating the Lysoen Declaration with Norway, which is designed to serve as the basis for building a human security network amongst 'like-minded countries and partners from civil society to promote respect for human rights and humanitarian law' on the understanding that 'a humane world is a safe world' (Axworthy and Vollebaek, 1998).

Finally DFAIT's partnerships with NGOs and activists working in issue areas involving aspects of human security also make it *appear* that the government has embarked on a new way to define and address security issues. Whereas the state tends to act behind closed doors in traditional security pursuits involving the military and issues of ' national interest', in human security pursuits it works in co-operation with NGOs and concerned citizens through both traditional and non-traditional diplomatic and civil society channels and fora.

Here, the anti-personnel landmine campaign is again informative as to the nature and limits of the state/civil society relationship. Because the goal of the lead NGOs in the Ottawa Process, the International Committee to Ban Landmines, and the International Committee of the Red Cross, was to remove anti-personnel land mines from military arsenals and use worldwide, they were not interested in mounting a critique of military practices in general.[9] The NGOs associated with the campaign that had a deeper understanding of the causes and contexts of human insecurity, and a related critique of military means in general, shelved those concerns in order to help achieve a landmine ban.[10] In this way, and by promoting the Convention as a humanitarian initiative, the *appearance* of systemic change was achieved while the power structures and ethos of military means remained unchallenged, and indeed were reinforced under the guise of humanitarianism.

Not surprisingly, the NGOs that *do not* challenge basic state interests are the ones that governments tend to consult, or more accurately, hear.[11] Consequently, both openness and a democratic consideration of the range of civil society concerns in human security issues are compromised and the wielding of soft power is not then all that it purports to be. Ironically, however, what human security and the exercise of soft power do purport to be can be used as a tool by those NGOs with a deeper critique of government activities. They can hold the government accountable to its own rhetoric on poverty alleviation, environmen-

tal integrity, and the full range of justice concerns, and in this way there is a potential for change.

While DFAIT's tool box of soft power means, then, support a rhetorical reframing of security issues, there is no substantive change in the ends being pursued. Soft-power means do not challenge the underlying government understanding that human security is security within the context of global market forces, and that military means are the ultimate guarantor of security as it is defined by the state according to state interests. Ultimately, it is not that the government's pursuit of economic prosperity has trumped its human security concerns, but rather that DFAIT's human security discourse and practice are cut from the same cloth of intentions as the government's economic pursuits. Using soft power means to alleviate human insecurities that are produced and reproduced by those pursuits does nothing to ameliorate the root causes of a vast array of human insecurities; rather it reinforces them, while at the same time rendering invisible the role Canada plays in exacerbating them.

Still, proponents of military means are not convinced of the efficacy of soft power, and the contest between hard and soft power proponents is another element in the framework that serves to condition Canadians and the security-policy-making community to a new way of conducting old-style security pursuits.

DND'S Toy Chest of Military Means

Advocates of military means are quite clear that the ends sought by both soft and hard power proponents are similar. David Haglund (1999: 176) argues that Canada's security interests are designed to support its trade and investment interests, while most who have joined the hard/soft power debate in favour of strengthening the former, are explicit about their concern for securing both states and peoples from non-traditional, as well as traditional, security threats and within the changing global environment of political, economic, cultural, and social relations.

Despite this agreement on ends, the attack by hard power proponents on the Axworthy Doctrine, as it is often described, is virulent. It has been referred to, in derogatory tones, as pulpit diplomacy, moral multilateralism, nickel diplomacy, Canada's Methodist phase of foreign policy, quasi-pacifism, boy scout imperialism, and foreign policy for wimps. This is name-calling, not argumentation, and is a sign that something more personal is at stake in the debate, that being the professionalism of the practitioners of military means, and by extension, the professionalism of their promoters. Since the government's budget for security programs is finite, the most direct challenge to military professionalism is financial, for a strengthening of DFAIT's soft power tools can impinge upon DND's ability to maintain, let alone strengthen its toy chest of military means. But the military is also being constrained in its professional role for a number of other reasons.

As one hard power proponent put it, 'profoundly unwise decisions over the past three years to "restructure" the military for what politicians and policy-makers in Ottawa foolishly believe will be a comparatively benign post-Cold War era . . . have done grave damage to Canadian power, position and influence over the "high" political issues on the global agenda' (Ross, 1996–7: 2). These 'unwise' decisions, according to Douglas Ross, include budget cuts to DND and decisions not to replace aging military equipment, and both have compromised the Canadian forces' ability to participate in high-risk peace-keeping on land, in the air and at sea, to undertake antisubmarine warfare, to effectively control Canadian waters, and to monitor and impede foreign traffic in the Arctic archipelago. In short, 'Canada has no credible military instrument to apply to international crises when they arise' (Ross, 1996–7: 4).

The Canadian military has also suffered from what some hard power proponents refer to as a series of 'public relations disasters' in relation to 'assorted misdeeds of Canadian military personnel' (Ross, 1996–7: 2 n.1) which Denis Stairs (1998: 548–9) lists as including:

Soldiers viciously torturing their prisoners. Soldiers and sailors crudely hazing their new recruits. Officers failing to enforce discipline and making exploitive use of their own expense accounts. Officers covering up. Officers and enlisted personnel alike abusing—even raping—their female colleagues and showing signs of racism and other forms of illiberal and intolerant disposition. The establishment as a whole failing to maintain the incomes of its personnel, and even the living quarters of its families, at a standard reasonable for our time. And so on.

Stairs is quick to argue that although these are all serious matters, they 'are *not* about "defence policy" or "security policy"' (emphasis in the original). Rather they are about the 'internal affairs' of the military and 'the behavior, treatment, and circumstances of individuals.' They are 'human interest' issues and examples of 'simple sinning'. The problem, he asserts, is that because the media have chosen to sensationalize them, the military fears it will lose respect in the public mind and therefore be disadvantaged in its competition for its share of the budget. 'The Art Eggletons of the world thus lose out to the Lloyd Axworthys of the world' (Stairs, 1998: 549–50).

In the zero-sum game of security budgets, then, the debate is about winning the means for the means, not the ends. With a bad press, aging and obsolescent equipment, the government making 'profoundly unwise' assessments of the global security environment, and the high profile of soft power means, the cards appear stacked against the military. To compound matters, the military's source of alliance toys is also drying up. Canadian troops have been removed from permanent deployment in Europe under the NATO command, and their access to US military means depends on the government's decision whether to participate in the American National Missile Defense program. Should Canada not participate, the Canadian military's role within NORAD, if not NORAD itself, will be seriously jeopardized. This would be a monumental blow to the military because it is through the joint Canada–US command that Canadian military personnel are able to participate in the planning and manning of the systems that project US power and interests worldwide (Crosby, 1998b).

Hence the vitriol on the part of the beleaguered hard power proponents. But more to the point, the debate contributes to the framework that conditions both the Canadian public and policy makers to the government's human security agenda. It does this in two ways. First, the debate about which means to use in combatting the fallout from the 'dark forces of globalization' treats the 'fallout', and therefore the market itself, as a given, thus rendering invisible the ways in which the market has been constructed out of specific interests, and the ways in which the government's security programs are designed to address the insecurities which that same government helps to create by supporting market forces. Hence it is possible for Canadians to believe that the government's foreign policy is solving, rather than creating, security problems both for themselves and others.

Second, the arguments in support of hard power means are, for the most part, so doctrinaire as to entrench the thinking of soft power advocates and to attract the uncommitted to their camp by default. In both instances, a deeper analysis of the security problem is bypassed. Describing, for example, acts of racism, rape, torture, murder, and cover-up performed by military personnel as 'simple sins' having no bearing on defence or security policy is fundamentally at odds with the perspective of a number of military analysts and critical feminist theorists who convincingly argue otherwise.

Since the end of the Cold War, some military analysts have noted the direction that military strategies have taken under the contemporary dual influences of arms-length, or stand-off, warfare and zero-tolerance, at least amongst the militaries of Western industrialized states, for 'friendly casualties'.[12] These analysts have argued that, as a result of both influences, military con-

flicts can no longer be defined as struggles of soldiers against soldiers, but rather as a 'struggle between one side's military might and the other side's civilian population', and that, accordingly, soldiers are now being trained, not as warriors but as killers. As a case in point they cite NATO's high-altitude bombings of Kosovo by pilots who flew high enough to avoid anti-aircraft fire but too high to distinguish between civilian and military targets. This, according to Gwynne Dyer, was 'a coward's strategy' and clearly representative of what a former US army officer has described as efforts to conduct a 'bloodless techno-war'.[13]

Similarly, the 'simple sins' of racism, rape, torture, and murder committed by members of the Canadian military were all acts of cowardice in that they were perpetrated by the relatively powerful, the victims being prisoners, women, youth, recruits, or members of racial minorities. As cowardly acts, they reflect the ethos of contemporary military training as described by Dyer and others. More generally, they substantiate the military ethos of the appropriateness of pursuing the interests of the powerful at the expense of the less so; the appropriateness, in other words, of the strong victimizing the weak. As such, and in contradiction to Stairs conclusions, the acts of 'simple sinning' arc quintessentially about 'defence policy' and 'security policy', for it is this ethos that is at work when the government mobilizes the military. This is precisely the point of the critical feminist scholars mentioned earlier. Mobilizing a military is also the mobilization of its ethos, and when that ethos is socially constructed out of gendered practices that deem it appropriate to secure some at the expense of others, then mobilizing that ethos is reflective of the state's understanding of what constitutes security and who it can be for. Mobilizing that ethos also reinforces the gendered understandings that support it.

In terms of the doctrinaire arguments employed by the proponents of hard power in support of their case, most treatises on the subject list the traditional threats to state security that are presently in existence and conclude, therefore, that traditional military means are required to address them, as though this were self-evident (Hampson and Oliver, 1998: 382–5; Stairs, 1999: 386–91; Ross, 1996–7: 8–19). It is not self-evident, however, to a growing number of security analysts, including some former realists.[14] Moreover, as proof of their arguments, hard power advocates cite the 'successes' of military undertakings in Bosnia, Kosovo, and the Persian Gulf, as though these too are self-evident 'successes', and as though 'success' is to be measured only in terms of the immediate interests of those with the preponderance of military means; this is another realist tenet that is being contested in the literature on the subject of what constitutes security, for whom, and by what means (Cox and Axworthy, 2000).

Rooted as they are in traditional realist thinking, and what perhaps can be called the super-realism of bloodless techno-war strategic thinking, these arguments not only fail to reveal the range of insecurities produced by the exercise of contemporary military means, but they also divert attention from the root causes of conflict and how these might be attacked by other than direct or structural force.

By contrast, the government's soft power arguments tend to explore alternative forms of conflict resolution, and that provides an opportunity for progressive change of the kind envisaged by vow and critical feminist theorists.

Human Security Prospects

In its pursuit of economic prosperity and employment for Canadians through trade and investment initiatives and the promotion of rules-based forums of political and economic multilateralism, the Canadian government reinforces the political, economic, and cultural forces of the global market. In so doing, it also reinforces the market related forces that create or exacerbate a wide range of insecurities for both states and peoples, at home and abroad, including all manner of inter- and intra-state conflicts rooted in the inequitable distribution of the world's resources, resource depletion, and environmental degradation. The government then attempts to correct these insecurities as though they were aberrations of the system and not endemic to it, thus distancing itself from its role in producing them, and further doing so by dressing its security practices in the discourses of human security, soft power, and humanitarianism.

Freed from the constraining influences of the Cold War relations of nuclear deterrence, these discourses are represented as quintessentially Canadian, reflecting the country's history, culture, and internationalist interests, with the 'successes' of human security initiatives taken to date cited as proof. The ideological content of the Canadian government's promotion of soft power means, the range of tools available and used in its practice, and the debate between hard and soft power proponents, all serve to deflect both vision and analysis from the causes of the insecurities that the government seeks to address, and its own role in producing them, as they also serve to condition Canadians to the view that new, meaningful, and moral *choices* are being made with regard to our role in global security relations. However, the ends of both soft power and hard power pursuits are similar. Both means are exercised in support of Canada's foreign policy agenda and goals, the former through processes of structural co-optation, the latter through practices of direct coercion.

This is not to argue that it matters little whether the government chooses to dress its security interests in the suits of diplomacy or the battle fatigues of the military, for it does matter. As compared to the vow understanding of human security, the government has it all wrong in that neither its discourse nor its practice substantively challenge gender, racial, class, or cultural hierarchies of power within which relative insecurities reside. For a number of reasons, however, even having it wrong opens spaces for change.

When the Canadian government's security interests are dressed in the character of soft power, not only are a wider range of policy tools available for addressing conflicts, but they are taken seriously, as compared to the often dismissive attitude of hard power proponents towards the use of soft power instruments. A soft power approach also includes more actors, many of whom are in civil society. This extends the range, density, and quality of the transmission of ideas and practices, increasing the range of alternatives and the opportunities for their serious consideration. By comparison, hard power approaches are generally limited to hard power players employed by the state, to a highly specialized set of hard power tools, and to closed-door decision making.

Furthermore, while hard-power tends to be exercised at arm's length, soft power means tend to be hands-on in terms of addressing security issues and thus actors are more likely to be brought into contact with the origins of insecurities, making it more difficult to ignore the root causes, and Canada's role in fostering them. In this way, spaces are opened for transformative change, for addressing the causes of insecurities rather than only the manifestations. Without intending to, DFAIT under the leadership of Lloyd Axworthy has opened spaces for these kinds of changes. Should both the discourse and practice of DFAIT's version of human security fall into decline, as now seems to be the case after September 11, one of the tragedies would be in the closing of these spaces.

Notes

1. Throughout, information about the VOW is taken from the National Film Board documentary (1992), Kay Macpherson (1994) especially pp. 89–149, and from my own 25-year involvement in the organization.

2. For non-feminist works of this ilk see Walker (1990), Paul (1999), Booth (1991), and George and Campbell (1990).

3. See for instance Tickner (1992b), Peterson (1992), and Stienstra (1994–5). For a discussion of the distinctions among various feminist perspectives, see Whitworth (1994) and Keeble and Smith (1999).

4. For discussions of the socially constructed nature of the realist perspective, see Murphy (1996), Rosenberg (1994), and Wendt (1992).

5. For discussions of the historical relationship between state security and economic interests, see Miller (1990) and Ruggie (1993).

6. All quotations in this and the following paragraph are from Canada, Department of Foreign Affairs and International Trade, *Canada World View*, 20 October 1998, Executive Summary, 1–2. This is a slightly edited update of *Canada in the World*, indicating the continuing relevance of that 1995 document. Details of DFAIT's economic and trade policy are in Section III of the document, 'The Promotion of Prosperity and Employment'.

7. In the peace research literature, see for example Galtung (1971). In the feminist literature see Peterson (1992), Enloe (1993), and Reardon (1985).

8. See also Stienstra (1994–5) and Whitworth (1995).

9. For the position of the ICBL, see Beier and Crosby (1998: 276–8). The ICRC is constitutionally unable to be involved in the politics of conflict and war, and although some members have voiced criticisms of military means, the organization's publication *Anti-personnel Landmines: Friend or Foe?* (1996) was a key resource document for the movement to ban land mines. It contains a chapter on military alternatives to landmines thus indicating ICRC's unwillingness to critique military means as part of the land-mine initiative.

10. These were mainly NGOs working on 'development' issues in mined communities. For references to their concerns see reports on various mine action forums in *An Agenda for Mine Action* (DFAIT, 1997).

11. See Raustiala (1997) for a discussion of this phenomenon as it also applies to environmental issues that are heavily populated by NGOs.

12. For the most recent, and extensive, Canadian writing on this topic see Ignatieff (2000).

13. For these arguments and their proponents, see Robinson (1999), particularly page 673. Hampson and Oliver (1998: 385) also attest to the penchant

for targeting civilians, particularly women and children, in contemporary military initiatives operations.

14. A former realist who has had a change of mind, for example, is Booth (1991).

References

Axworthy, L. 1999a. 'Human Security and Canada's Security Council Agenda'. Notes for an Address by the Minister of Foreign Affairs to the Société des Relations Internationales de Québec, Quebec City, 25 February.

———. 1999b. 'Kosovo and the Human Security Agenda'. Notes for an Address by the Honourable Lloyd Axworthy, Minister of Foreign Affairs, to the Woodrow Wilson School of Public and International Relations, Princeton University, 7 April.

———. 1999c. 'Message from the Honourable Lloyd Axworthy, Minister of Foreign Affairs to the Hague Appeal for Peace', 13 May.

———. 1998. Notes for an Address by the Minister of Foreign Affairs to the Canadian Institute of International Affairs Foreign Policy Conference, Ottawa, 16 October.

———. 1997. 'Canada and Human Security: The Need for Leadership', International Journal 53, 2 (Spring): 183–96.

Axworthy, L., and K. Vollebaek. 1998. 'Now for a New Diplomacy to Fashion a Humane World', Herald International Tribune, 21 October.

Axworthy, L., and S. Taylor. 1998. 'A Ban for All Seasons', International Journal 53, 2 (Spring): 189–203.

Beier, M., and A.D. Crosby. 1998. 'Harnessing Change for Continuity: The Play of Political and Economic Forces behind the Ottawa Process', in M.A. Cameron, R.J. Lawson, and B.W. Tomlin, eds, To Walk without Fear. Don Mills, ON: Oxford University Press.

Booth, K. 1991. 'Security and Emancipation', Review of International Studies 17, 4: 313–32.

Cox, R.W. 1999. 'Civil Society at the Turn of the Millennium', Review of International Studies 25, 1: 3–28.

Cox, R.W., and L. Axworthy. 2000. 'Correspondence: the Crisis in Kosovo', Studies on Political Economy 63 (Autumn): 133–52.

Crosby, A.D. 1998a. Dilemmas in Defence Decision-Making: Constructing Canada's Role in NORAD, 1958–96. Houndsmills, UK: Macmillan.

———. 1998b. 'Defining Security Environments for Global Governance: Canada and the US "Global Protection System"', Global Governance 4: 331–53.

de Larringa, M., and C.T. Sjolander. 1998. '(Re)presenting Landmines from Protector to Enemy', in M.A. Cameron, R.J. Lawson, and B.W. Tomlin, eds, To Walk without Fear. Don Mills, ON: Oxford University Press.

DFAIT. 1999. Human Security: Safety for People in a Changing World. Ottawa: DFAIT.

———. 1998. Canada World View. Ottawa, 20 October.

———. 1997. An Agenda for Mine Action. Ottawa, 2–4 December.

Draimin, T., and B. Tomlinson. 1998. 'Is There a Future for Canadian Aid in the Twenty-First Century?', in F. Hampson and M.A. Molot, eds, Canada Among Nations 1998: Leadership and Dialogue. Don Mills, ON: Oxford University Press.

Enloe, C. 1993. The Morning After: Sexual Politics at the End of the Cold War. Berkley: University of California Press.

Galtung, J. 1971. 'A Structural Theory of Imperialism', International Journal of Peace Research 8: 81–118.

George, J., and D. Campbell. 1990. 'Patterns of Dissent and the Celebration of Difference: Critical Social Theory and International Relations', International Studies Quarterly 34: 269–93.

Grinspun, R., and R. Kreklewich. 1994. 'Consolidating Neoliberal Reforms: "Free Trade" as a Conditioning Framework', Studies in Political Economy 43 (Spring): 269–93.

Haglund, D. 1999. 'Grand Strategy—or Merely a Geopolitical Free-for-all', in F. Hampson, M. Hart, and M. Rudner, eds, Canada Among Nations 1999: A Big League Player? Don Mills, ON: Oxford University Press.

Hampson, F., and D. Oliver. 1998. 'Pulpit Diplomacy:

A Critical Assessment of the Axworthy Doctrine', *International Journal* 53, 2 (Summer): 379–406.

Hay, R.J. 1999. 'Present at the Creation? Human Security and Canadian Foreign Policy in the Twenty-First Century', in F. Hampson, M. Hart, and M. Rudner, eds, *Canada Among Nations 1999: A Big League Player?* Don Mills, ON: Oxford University Press.

Ignatieff, M. 2000. *Virtual War: Kosovo and Beyond.* Toronto: Viking.

International Committeee of the Red Cross (ICRC). 1996. *Anti-personnel Landmines: Friend or Foe?* Geneva: ICRC.

Keeble, E., and H. Smith. 1999. *(Re)Defining Traditions: Gender and Canadian Foreign Policy.* Halifax: Fernwood.

Lipshutz, R. 1992. 'Reconstructing World Politics: The Emergence of Global Civil Society', *Millennium* 21, 3: 389–420.

Macdonald, L. 1995. 'Unequal Partnerships: The Politics of Canada's Relations with the Third World', *Studies in Political Economy* 47 (Summer).

Macpherson, K. 1994. *When in Doubt, DO BOTH: The Times of My Life.* Toronto: University of Toronto Press.

Malone, D. 1999. 'The Global Issues Biz: What Gives', in F. Hampson, M. Hart, and M. Rudner, eds, *Canada Among Nations 1999: A Big League Player?* Don Mills, ON: Oxford University Press.

Miller, L. 1990. *Global Order: Values and Power in International Politics.* Boulder: Westview Press.

Murphy, A.B. 'The Sovereign State System as Political-Territorial Ideal', in T. Biersteker and C. Weber, eds, *State Sovereignty as Social Construct.* Cambridge, UK: Cambridge University Press.

National Film Board. 1991. *The Voice of Women: The First Thirty Years.* Montreal.

Pasic, A., and T.G. Weiss. 1997. 'Yugoslavia's Wars and the Humanitarian Impulse', *Ethics and International Affairs* 11: 105–50.

Paul, D.E. 1999. 'Sovereignty, Survival and the Westphalian Blind Alley', *Review of International Studies* 25, 2 (April): 217–32.

Peterson, V.S., ed. 1992. *Gendered States: Feminist (Re)Visions of International Relations Theory.* Boulder: Lynne Rienner.

Pratt, C. 1998. 'DFAIT's Takeover Bid of CIDA: The Institutional Future of the Canadian International Development Agency', *Canadian Foreign Policy* 5, 2 (Winter): 1–13.

———. 1994. 'Humane Internationalism and Canadian Development Assistance Policies', *Canadian International Development Assistance Polices: An Appraisal.* Montreal: McGill-Queen's University Press.

Raustiala, K. 1997. 'States, NGOs, and International Environmental Institutions', *International Studies Quarterly* 41, 4: 719–40.

Reardon, B. 1985. *Sexism and the War System.* New York: Teachers College Press.

Reif, L. 1998. 'Environmental Policy: The Rio Summit Five Years Later', in F. Hampson and M.A. Molot, eds, *Canada Among Nations 1998: Leadership and Dialogue.* Don Mills, ON: Oxford University Press.

Robinson, P. 1999. 'Ready to Kill But Not to Die: NATO's Strategy in Kosovo', *International Journal* 54, 4 (Autumn): 671–82.

Rosenberg, J. 1994. *The Empire of Civil Society.* London: Verso.

Ross, D.A. 1996–7. 'Canada and the World at Risk', *International Journal* 52, 1 (Winter): 1–24.

Ruggie, G. 1993. 'Territoriality and Beyond: Problematizing Modernity in International Relations', *International Organization* 47, 1: 137–74.

Smith, M.J. 1998. 'Humanitarian Intervention: An Overview of the Ethical Issues', *Ethics and International Affairs* 12: 63–79.

Stairs, D. 1999. 'Canada and the Security Problem: Implications as the Millennium Turns', *International Journal* 54, 3 (Summer): 386–403.

———. 1998. 'The Media and the Military in Canada', *International Journal* 53, 3 (Summer): 544–81.

Stienstra, D. 1994–5. 'Can the Silence Be Broken? Gender and Canadian Foreign Policy', *International Journal* 50 (Winter): 103–27.

Strange, S. 1996. *The Retreat of the State: The Diffusion of Power in the World Economy.* Cambridge, UK: Cambridge University Press.

Tickner, J.A. 1992. *Gender in International Relations: Feminist Perspectives on Achieving Global Security.* New York: Columbia University Press.

Walker, R.D.J. 1990. 'Security, Sovereignty and the Challenge of World Politics', *Alternatives* 15: 3–27.

Wendt, A. 1992. 'Anarchy Is What States Make of It', *International Organization* 46, 2: 33–67.

Whitworth, S. 1995. 'Women, and Gender, in the Foreign Policy Review Process', in M.A. Cameron and M.A. Molot, eds, *Canada Among Nations 1995: Democracy and Foreign Policy*. Ottawa: Carleton University Press.

———. 1994. *Feminism and International Relations*. Houndsmills, UK: Macmillan.

Selected Bibliography

Axworthy, Lloyd. 1997. 'Canada and Human Security: The Need for Leadership', *International Journal* 52, 2 (Spring): 183–96.

Bell, Stewart. 2004. *Cold Terror: How Canada Nurtures and Exports Terrorism Around the World*. Toronto: Wiley.

Bratt, Duane. 2006. *The Politics of CANDU Exports*. Toronto: University of Toronto Press.

———. 1999. 'Nice-Making and Canadian Peacekeeping', *Canadian Foreign Policy* 6, 3 (Spring): 73–84.

Buckley, Brian. 2000. *Canada's Early Nuclear Policy: Fate, Chance, and Character*. Montreal: McGill-Queen's University Press.

Cameron, Maxwell A., Robert J. Lawson, and Brian W. Tomlin, eds. 1998. *To Walk Without Fear: The Global Movement to Ban Landmines*. Don Mills, ON: Oxford University Press.

Clearwater, John. 1998. *Canadian Nuclear Weapons: The Untold Story of Canada's Cold War Arsenal*. Toronto: Dundurn.

Dallaire, Romeo. 2003. *Shake Hands with the Devil: The Failure of Humanity in Rwanda*. Toronto: Random House.

Dewitt, David B., and David Leyton-Brown, eds. 1995. *Canada's International Security Policy*. Scarborough: Prentice-Hall.

Edgar, Alistair D., and David G. Haglund. 1995. *The Canadian Defence Industry in the New Global Environment*. Montreal: McGill-Queen's University Press.

Gammer, Nicholas. 2001. *From Peacekeeping to Peacemaking: Canada's Response to the Yugoslav Crisis*. Montreal: McGill-Queen's University Press.

Granatstein, J.L. 2004. *Who Killed the Canadian Military?* Toronto: HarperCollins.

Granatstein, J.L., and David Stafford. 1990. *Spy Wars: Espionage and Canada from Gouzenko to Glasnost*. Toronto: Key Porter Books.

Jockel, Joseph T. 1999. *The Canadian Forces: Hard Choices, Soft Power*. Toronto: Canadian Institute of Strategic Studies.

———. 1994. *Canada and International Peacekeeping*. Washington: Center for Strategic and International Studies.

Legault, Albert. 1999. *Canada and Peacekeeping: Three Major Debates*. Clementsport: Canadian Peacekeeping Press.

Legault, Albert, and Michel Fortmann. 1992. *A Diplomacy of Hope: Canada and Disarmament, 1945–1988,* trans. Derek Ellington. Montreal: McGill-Queen's University Press.

Mackenzie, Lewis. 1993. *Peacekeeper: The Road to Sarajevo.* Vancouver: Douglas & McIntyre.

Morrison, Alex, ed. 1992. *A Continuing Commitment: Canada and North Atlantic Security.* Toronto: Canadian Institute of Strategic Studies.

Morton, Desmond. 2003. *Understanding Canadian Defence.* Toronto: Penguin.

———. 1999. *A Military History of Canada: From Champlain to Kosovo.* Toronto: McClelland and Stewart.

Nossal, Kim Richard. 1994. *Rain Dancing: Sanctions in Canadian & Australian Foreign Policy.* Toronto: University of Toronto Press.

Roach, Kent. 2003. *September 11: Consequences for Canada.* Montreal: McGill-Queen's University Press.

Sloan, Elinor C. 2005. *Security and Defence in the Terrorist Era: Canada and North America.* Montreal: McGill-Queen's University Press.

PART V

Trade and Other Economic Issues

Until the last decade only a small number of academics focused on Canada's foreign trade and economic policy. The end of the Cold War, the negotiation of the Canada–United States Free Trade Agreement (FTA), the North American Free Trade Agreement (NAFTA), the creation of the World Trade Organization (WTO), the prominence of the G7/8, the launching of the Doha Round, and the failure of the Multilateral Agreement on Investment (MAI), all contributed to increased interest and awareness in this policy area. The nature of trade and investment also changed during this period. Specifically, Canada faced new challenges related to the relevance of non-traditional issues, such as services, subsidies, labour, and the environment. The increasing fluidity of financial capital and the intrusiveness of these commitments into areas of domestic policy space also made it increasingly difficult for federal and provincial officials to respond to these developments. Three prominent authors with extensive background in this issue area are included in Part Five. Although there are notable omissions—namely Michael Hart, Gilbert Winham, Sylvia Ostry, Robert Wolfe, Grace Skogstad, Bruce Doern, and Thomas Courchene—these three chapters offer a wide spectrum of approaches to better understand Canadian foreign trade and economic policy.

At first glance, Brian Tomlin's examination of the FTA appears dated, however, it is a 'classic' contribution that engages Canadian foreign trade from a policy perspective. Specifically, Tomlin adopts John Kingdon's policy stream approach in an attempt to explain how the FTA became a priority for the Mulroney government. His argument suggests that particular problems and solutions, combined with reinforcing political pressures, produced a favourable policy environment for the FTA. This included a growing desire within the foreign policy bureaucracy to secure United States export markets in response to increasing American protectionist measures. Domestic fiscal issues also contributed to Canada's decision, as did industry and interest group support. Therefore, Tomlin concludes that 'policy entrepreneurs' were able to take advantage of these conditions to successfully promote the FTA.

John Kirton's review of the G8 provides an update of the principal power thesis introduced in Chapter 2. In fact, Kirton examines the relevance of the G8 by adopting traditional theoretical approaches to the study of Canadian foreign policy. He concludes that Canada's role in this forum has directly contributed to the evolution of international norms and standards. Therefore, Ottawa no longer relies on the G8 to 'constrain' the United States but instead actively uses the institution to seek coalitions with like-minded governments in the pursuit of a global financial order consistent with Canadian priorities. Kirton argues that Canada's foreign policy is not ad hoc and reactionary, as many critics suggest. Instead, the federal government has the capacity and expertise to pursue issues vital to its national interest.

Finally, Elizabeth Smythe's discussion of Canada and the negotiation of WTO investment rules suggests that although the European Union was viewed as the main catalyst for including investment in the Doha Round, Canada also supported these negotiations. Unlike Kirton, however, Smythe makes it clear that Canada was not able to influence this international economic regime to reflect its interests. This was due to negative public opinion related to NAFTA's Chapter 11 provisions and the potential limitations a WTO agreement would place on the ability of states to regulate in the public interest. Significant divergence between WTO members on the issue also contributed to its removal from the Doha agenda.

17
Leaving the Past Behind: The Free Trade Initiative Assessed

Brian W. Tomlin

In mid-summer of 1985, Brian Mulroney was meeting with senior officials in his office on Parliament Hill. The occasion was a discussion of an advance copy of the report of the Royal Commission on the Economic Union and Development Prospects for Canada, chaired by Donald S. Macdonald, who had been a minister in Pierre Trudeau's Cabinet. The report contained a recommendation for the establishment of a free trade arrangement with the United States. According to those in attendance, Mulroney recognized the opportunity it presented for a bold policy initiative, and he relished the idea of using a former Liberal cabinet minister to give bipartisan legitimacy to the initiative. The volumes of the report arranged on his desk, Mulroney spread his hands over them and told the officials present in his office that summer day that he would use the report to beat Liberal party leader John Turner in the next election.

The decision to negotiate free trade was a fundamental policy shift on the part of the Canadian government, and it was certainly unanticipated at the beginning of the 1980s, even by those at the centre of the policy process. Few would have predicted that within three years Canada would propose sectoral free trade and that, two years later,

it would offer to negotiate a comprehensive free trade agreement with the Americans. This decision involved a basic redefinition of Canada's relationship with the United States and represented a fundamental change in policy. In this chapter I want to (1) explain how the issue of Canada's trade relations with the United States made its way to the top of the Mulroney government's decision agenda and (2) demonstrate the need to understand the policy process that led Canada to propose to the United Slates that the two countries negotiate a bilateral free trade agreement.[1]

To accomplish this, I use a policy model, developed by John Kingdon,[2] that is directed at understanding both agenda-setting and the development of policy alternatives, the two key elements that require explanation here. Kingdon conceives the policy process as consisting of three separate 'streams' that, largely independently of one another, flow through and around government: problems, policies, and politics. At certain critical times, these three streams come together, and it is at that juncture that major policy change can occur.

I will examine the process by which particular solutions became joined to particular problems and how this, when combined with favourable political forces, produced free trade. Kingdon argues that this coupling is most likely to occur when policy windows—defined as opportunities to advocate particular proposals—are opened, either by the appearance of compelling problems or by events occurring in the political stream. I begin my analysis with a more complete outline of the model and its elements.

Streams in the Policy Process

How do certain problems surface on the government's policy agenda? And why is a particular policy alternative selected to address a particular problem? For Kingdon, the answer lies in the analysis of the three process streams flowing through the public policy system: streams of problems, policies, and politics.

PROBLEMS

It is a fact that governments pay attention to some problems and not others, which obliges us to ask how it is that certain problems capture the attention of important people in and around government and, thereby, secure a place on the governmental agenda.[3] Kingdon argues that objective indicators of the presence of a problem are important but that they require a focusing event to push them onto a governmental agenda.[4] Such an event may arise from the occurrence of a crisis, the creation of a symbol, or the personal experience of a policy-maker. Finally, problem identification is more likely to occur when government officials receive feedback about the inadequacy of existing policies and programs. All of these characteristics may be present, however, and a problem may still not make it on to the government's policy agenda. This is because the policy process consists of more than a stream of problems waiting to be identified; it also includes a stream of policy alternatives that must ultimately be linked to problems.

POLICY PROPOSALS

Kingdon argues that ideas about policy alternatives circulate in communities of specialists, both inside and outside government.[5] Advocates for particular proposals or ideas are policy entrepreneurs who are defined by their willingness to invest resources (time, energy, and occasionally money) in order to secure a future return (desired policies, satisfaction from participation, or career rewards). This process of creating alternatives for policymakers to consider proceeds independently of the process of problem identification. However, viable alternatives must exist before a problem can secure a solid position on the decision agenda. Even in this circumstance, problems and their alternative solutions exist alongside the political stream, which also exerts influence on the policy process.

POLITICS

In Kingdon's model, developments in the political stream have their most powerful effects on agendas. The stream is composed of elements related to the electoral, partisan, and pressure group considerations of politicians and those who serve them. An important component of the political stream is what Kingdon refers to as the national mood—gleaned from mail, media, and lobbyists, among other sources—which can provide fertile ground for certain ideas. Organized political interests are also important to those in government in so far as they all point in the same direction, thus providing a powerful impetus to move on that course. Turnover and jurisdiction within government are also important in as much as agendas are significantly affected by changing incumbents and by turf battles.

POLICY WINDOWS

Much of the time these three streams—problems, policies, and politics—flow through the policy system on largely independent courses. However, the streams come together at critical times, with the result being that a problem is recognized, a solution is developed and available within the policy community, a political change makes the time right for policy change, and potential constraints are not severe. This joining of the streams is most likely to occur when a policy window opens, and policy entrepreneurs play a critical role in what Kingdon calls the 'coupling of the streams', which occurs at this time. Typically, a policy window opens because the policy agenda is affected by a change or event in the political stream or by the emergence of a pressing problem that captures the attention of government officials.[6]

This model of agenda setting and policy alternative specification is designed to help us 'find pattern and structure in very complicated, fluid, and seemingly unpredictable phenomena'.[7] However, it is a highly probabilistic model—one that explicitly leaves room for a residual randomness in the way events will unfold in any particular policy episode. In addition, it is historically contingent: the direction of change depends heavily on initial conditions, and events may develop in different ways depending on how they happen to start. Nevertheless, it provides us with a comprehensive representation of the enduring streams in the policy process and alerts us to the critical ingredients that increase the likelihood of policy change. I will now apply the model to an analysis of how the trade issue rose to the top of the decision agenda and to an analysis of why a Canada–US free trade agreement became the preferred policy alternative for the Mulroney government.[8]

The Evolving Problem Stream

While the decision to negotiate free trade was taken by the Conservative government, this fundamental policy shift originated in the unprecedented conditions of crisis and conflict that marked the early 1980s. The majority Liberal government elected in 1980 had adopted an ambitious national policy agenda designed to enhance the resources and visibility of the federal government. The National Energy Program (NEP) was a central element in this overall strategy, one that had highly negative consequences for foreign investors in the Canadian oil and gas industry. When the government also announced its intention to extend the mandate of the Foreign Investment Review Agency (FIRA) in the regulation of direct foreign investment, the howls of outrage from the American business establishment turned the guns of the Reagan administration on Canada. American plans for retaliatory measures targeted the Canadian Achilles heel of trade dependence on the United States.[9]

This acute conflict, and the sense of vulnerability it created for Canadians and their government, represented a turning point for Canada in its relations with the United States. The United States had overtly threatened the security of access to a market on which Canada was overwhelmingly dependent, with profound implications for employment and investment. This stimulated a reassessment, on the part of both business and government, of the value to Canada of secure and enhanced access to the US market, an assessment that would take place within the context of an economic recession more severe than any experienced since the Great Depression of the 1930s.

The government reassessment was undertaken through a task force, organized initially through the Department of Industry, Trade, and Commerce (ITC) but subsequently shifting to the Department of External Affairs (DEA), where it was placed under the direction of Derek Burney, assistant under-secretary for trade and economic relations in External Affairs.[10] This was the first, but would certainly not be the last, time that Burney would be in a position to play a crucial role in the free trade initiative. A concurrent review of the Canada–US relationship was also initiated by External Affairs. As the trade task force conducted its review during 1982, the emerging economic crisis guaranteed that the threat to secure access to the American market for Canada's exports would be defined as the central problem for Canadian trade policy. In consultations with representatives of the Canadian business community and provincial governments, the task force was repeatedly told that the central goal of any trade policy should be to 'get the Canada–US relationship right'. The US market was fundamentally important to Canadian economic well-being, and preservation of that market required stability in the Canada–US relationship. In particular, the government had to find a means to protect Canadian exporters from the application of US trade remedies, primarily anti-dumping and countervailing duties, to Canadian exports.

The decline in trade that accompanied the recession also made trade policy a central preoccupation for the Reagan administration. However, from Washington's perspective, the problem was the unfair trading practices of its major trading partners, a problem made more serious, or at least more visible, by the severity of the recession, which added significantly to protectionist pressures, prompting a greater willingness in the United States to move more aggressively to curb imports. By the time the Mulroney Conservatives came to power in 1984, they faced a mounting tide of US protectionism. There was an increase in the number of investigations of Canadian export practices under the American countervailing duty process as well as the introduction of specific legislation in Congress that would limit Canadian exports to the United States.[11]

For the Conservatives, the problems with trade compounded the problem they faced in the Canadian economy. The minister of finance, Michael Wilson, was convinced by his officials that the economy was in a state of profound malaise, for which there could be no easy cure. In the fall of 1984, Wilson agreed with senior Finance officials that Canada could no longer tax or spend its way out of its economic troubles; instead, the country would have to grow its way out of the problems that beset the economy, and the key to this growth was a significant increase in Canadian trade.

In this way, the Canadian trade policy problem evolved over the first half of the decade, until, by the time the Mulroney government seized the trade issue, the problem was overwhelmingly defined in terms of the threat that US trade remedy action posed to Canadian exports as well as in terms of the need for enhanced and secure Canadian access to the US market. As this prob-

lem redefinition occurred, policy entrepreneurs inside and outside government gradually moved the option of comprehensive bilateral free trade onto the menu of policy alternatives that would be presented to the government. I now turn to the story of how ideas about policy alternatives shifted from the 1980 revival of the Third Option—a short-lived effort in the 1970s to promote the restructuring of the Canadian economy and to diversify Canada's foreign economic relations—to bilateral free trade.

Developments in the Policy Stream

The 1982–3 review by the External Affairs task force was an important first step in this shift. It was the crisis in the economy that ensured that the task force examination of Canada's trade policy would centre on securing access to the US market. And the Canadian business lobby saw to it that the negotiation of some form of trade liberalization arrangement was put forward as an option for consideration. Leading advocates included the Business Council on National Issues (BNCI), made up of major corporations operating in Canada, and the Canadian Manufacturers' Association (CMA). During 1982 and 1983, the president of BNCI, Thomas d'Aquino, was active in advocating negotiations for a comprehensive trade agreement as a means to guarantee access to the US market. Equally important, however, was the influential CMA's reversal of its long-standing opposition to free trade with the United States.

In its report,[12] the task force played it absolutely safe and reaffirmed the centrality of the multilateral GATT (General Agreement on Tariffs and Trade) system for Canada. Secondarily, however, it also raised the prospect of pursuing *sectoral* free trade arrangements with the United States as an additional option for the government to consider. The sectoral option was not without precedent, since Canada already had three sectoral free trade agreements with the United States, covering automobiles, defence materials, and agricultural machinery. In fact, in 1981, Canadian embassy officials in Washington, with Ottawa's knowledge, informally discussed broader sectoral free trade arrangements with officials in the Office of the US Trade Representative (USTR). This initiative was part of the Canadian effort to resolve the conflict with the United States over the NEP and FIRA. It did not proceed, however, because of opposition from within the ITC in Ottawa, which still carried the trade mandate at that time. Despite these precedents, free trade was a sensitive political issue in Canada. The pride of place given by the task force to the GATT undoubtedly eased the task of the Liberal minister for international trade, Gerald Regan, who received the report and saw to its acceptance by Cabinet.

Regan was a free trader from Nova Scotia, and it was the sectoral initiative that caught his attention. While stressing the report's reaffirmation of the GATT with his cautious Cabinet colleagues, Regan persuaded them to go along with its sectoral option as well, despite the suspicions of the 'nationalist' group in the Liberal Cabinet. With Cabinet endorsement in hand, Regan turned the report upside down at its presentation at a press conference in August 1983. Seizing on its most controversial element, he announced the demise of the Third Option and proclaimed the government's intention to pursue a limited free trade agreement with the United States. Regan's proclamation did not by any means reflect mainstream thinking in External Affairs. The concurrent review of the Canada–US relationship that was prepared for the deputy minister for foreign relations had reaffirmed the basic tenets of the Third Option. That report was overtaken by events, however. It was the trade policy review that provided the opening for fundamental change in Canadian–American relations as sectoral free trade negotiations became the preferred option of the Liberal government of Pierre Elliott Trudeau.

The task of implementing the sectoral initiative from the Canadian side fell to Tony Halliday, an experienced trade official in External Affairs. In February 1984, he and his counterparts in USTR were ready to bring Regan and the US trade representative, William Brock, together in Washington where they identified four sectors upon which officials from the two countries could focus. By June, however, little progress had been made in these preliminary discussions, principally because USTR was unable to bring American industries on board. Although Regan and Brock agreed to explore alternative sectors, nothing further was decided on the question of whether and when to begin formal negotiations.

The election of Mulroney and the Conservatives in September 1984 provided an opportunity for advocates of a comprehensive agreement with the United States to promote their idea to a new government. During their first few months in government, the Tories began to sketch the principal dimensions of what would become the Conservative policy agenda. In an economic and fiscal statement presented by Wilson to the House of Commons in November 1984, the government identified its priorities of economic renewal and national reconciliation. Wilson also tabled a policy agenda, setting out a strategy for economic renewal. One element of the strategy was increased and secure access to markets for Canadian exports, especially in the United States. Referring to sectoral free trade, the Finance agenda noted: 'This initiative has generated public interest in exploring broadly-based bilateral arrangements with the US.'[13]

The Conservatives were still some distance from free trade at this early stage in their mandate, however. The Finance economic renewal statement had not been prepared especially for the Conservatives but was begun in May 1984 while the Liberals still held power. Nor was the concept of 'broadly-based bilateral arrangements' cleared through Trade Minister James Kelleher, who was not consulted on the Finance statement. Nevertheless, the autumn of 1984 saw pressures mount for the government to pick up the free trade agenda. Canadian business organizations engaged in a vigorous lobbying effort to shore up support for a comprehensive free trade arrangement, and their position was given serious attention by a government committed to making Canada a better place to do business.[14]

Also circulating in Ottawa at this time was a C.D. Howe Institute study of Canada's trade options, co-authored by Richard Lipsey, one of Canada's most respected economists.[15] Following publication of the study, Lipsey and Wendy Dobson, then head of the C.D. Howe Institute and later associate deputy minister of finance in Ottawa, launched what, for a think tank, was an unprecedented personal lobby to promote the free trade option among key ministers, their staffers, and senior members of the bureaucracy. Their efforts, along with the trade policy studies prepared by the Macdonald Commission, helped to shatter many of the prevailing myths about free trade. In particular, they vigorously argued that, rather than representing a complete break with the Canadian past, the free trade option was quite consistent with Canada's commitment to trade liberalization throughout the postwar era.

Changes in the Political Stream

The importance of politics—particularly the elements of turnover and jurisdiction—in the process that led to the joining of the trade problem and policy streams was apparent even before the election of the Conservatives. The outcome of the 1982–3 trade policy review was fundamentally affected by the major reorganization of ITC, which was undertaken in January 1982 in order to integrate federal industrial and regional development policies. As a result, the trade elements of ITC were split off and integrated into a reorganized Department of External Affairs as a new trade and economic wing reporting to its own minister for international trade. Consequently, in the spring of 1982 the trade policy review was shifted to an External Affairs task force. This shift was important, since the free trade option had less chance of emerging from ITC, with its mandate to protect and nurture Canadian industry. In addition, it created an important role for Derek Burney as manager of the task force.

The fact that the new Conservative government was looking to establish a policy agenda made it particularly receptive to the arguments in favour of a comprehensive free trade agreement. In the event, the first, and very important, act of policy entrepreneurship came from an unlikely source: Donald Macdonald, chairman of the Royal Commission on the Economic Union and Development Prospects for Canada. Established by Trudeau in 1982, the Macdonald Commission was examining Canada–US free trade as part of its study of the Canadian economy. Although the commission had neither completed its studies nor framed its conclusions, Macdonald nevertheless announced in November 1984 that he favoured free trade between Canada and the United States as the principal long-term solution to Canada's economic problems.

Acknowledging that Canadians might be nervous about maintaining their sovereignty in a free trade arrangement with the United States, Macdonald nonetheless argued: 'If we do get down to a point where it's going to be a leap of faith, then I think at some point Canadians are going to have to be bold and say, yes, we will do that.'[16] Macdonald's call for a 'leap of faith' was a big news item in Canada. And because it was bipartisan and seemingly authoritative, his conversion provided important momentum to the free trade option at a critical juncture as the new government was considering its options. This endorsement was followed by a series of government reports and consultations that moved the Mulroney Cabinet ever closer to a final commitment to negotiation.

The first of the reports was the product of a review of trade policy options initiated by Derek Burney in the Department of External Affairs. That review generated sharp conflicts, both in External Affairs and in the Department of Regional Industrial Expansion (DRIE), the successor to the ITC. The conflict resulted from opposition to Burney's determination to put the comprehensive free trade option before the government. From a DRIE perspective, trade liberalization would threaten Canadian industries supported by an average tariff that was roughly double that of their American competition. In External, the opposition centred on traditional concerns over political autonomy. In the end, Burney was forced to override opposition from the most senior administrative levels of his own department, which wanted to suppress the free trade discussion. His task force presented comprehensive free trade as one of the options for Canada in the report prepared for Kelleher. Because the trade minister did not share the reluctance of his senior officials to consider all of the options available to Canada in its relations with the United States, he released the report in January 1985.[17]

This government discussion paper, while acknowledging the importance of multilateral trade liberalization, confirmed the need to seek enhanced and secure access to the US market. To this end, the paper suggested that some form of bilateral trade arrangement should be considered, and it set out the options available to Canada. These were the status quo, sectoral arrangements, a comprehensive trade agreement (the Conservative euphemism for free trade) to remove tariff and non-tariff barriers on substantially all bilateral trade, and a bilateral framework to discuss means to improve and enhance trade relations (a BNCI proposal). Although the paper was careful to avoid identifying a preferred option, it rejected the status quo as inadequate, sectoral arrangements as unattainable, and the BNCI framework as unnecessary.[18] Clearly the government was edging down the path to comprehensive free trade negotiations.

Another policy window was about to open in March 1985 in Quebec City at the so-called Shamrock Summit between Mulroney and Reagan, and policy entrepreneurs were ready to take advantage of it. The Shamrock Summit was orchestrated in exquisite detail by Prime Minister's Office (PMO) staffer and Mulroney confidant Fred Doucet. Working closely with Doucet was Derek Burney, who oversaw the drafting of the trade declaration to be issued by the prime minister and the president. Although the declaration contained no explicit statement of bilateral trade policy by either government, it did call for an examination of ways to reduce and eliminate existing barriers to trade. Mulroney and Reagan instructed Kelleher and Brock to report in six months on mechanisms to achieve this end.

Following the summit declaration, Burney's External Affairs task force proceeded to flesh out the free trade option in preparation for the presentation of a recommendation to Cabinet. It continued to encounter considerable opposition to a comprehensive agreement both within External Affairs and other departments. However, it was apparent that Canadian business was now solidly behind the initiative, and this could make all the difference in Cabinet, especially with support from Wilson in Finance. With Canadian business on side, and with the backing of key ministers, Burney was determined to press ahead, despite continued opposition from senior officials.

The politics of the trade issue were right in other respects as well. Free trade was not only congruent with the government's agenda for economic renewal; it also served the Conservative priority of national reconciliation. The western provinces had been deeply disaffected over the NEP, and Mulroney and his minister of energy, Patricia (Pat) Carney, wasted little time in undoing the NEP through the Western Accord. There was also substantial support for free trade in the west, especially Alberta, long a stronghold of Conservative support. Alberta's Conservative premier Peter Lougheed, a strong supporter of the free trade option, was the principal exponent of western grievances, and he held close counsel with Mulroney on the trade issue throughout this period. His support was important in shoring up Mulroney's resolve as the time for decision approached.

Also important was the surprising degree of support for free trade in Quebec, home to a substantial number of inefficient Canadian industries that were the least likely to survive the elimination of protective barriers. The province's long-standing opposition to trade liberalization had been an essential element in shaping Canadian trade policy. All that changed, however, with the willingness of the Quebec business establishment to support free trade. This support would reinforce Mulroney's strategy to consolidate the Conservative landslide he had achieved in the province in 1984 and, thus, turn the political tables on the Liberals.

Mulroney's path to the free trade decision was also smoothed by the presence of Tory governments in most of the remaining provinces, with the notable exception of Ontario. These premiers were ideologically sympathetic to the pro-market approach of the federal party, and they were deeply concerned about American protectionism. As a result, they were generally positive about negotiating a comprehensive trade agreement for enhanced and secure access to the US market, assuming, of course, that an agreement left untouched such 'non-trade' shibboleths as agricultural marketing boards and regional development grants.

A Policy Window

Thus, in the summer of 1985, the streams in the policy process had come together—a problem had been recognized, a solution had been developed and put forward, and a political change had made the time right for policy change. And policy entrepreneurs, both inside and outside government, were ready to take advantage of the policy window that was created by the coupling of these streams. By August, Kelleher was concluding the report on trade relations that he had been directed to prepare following the Shamrock Summit, and he made a preliminary oral presentation to Cabinet's Priorities and Planning Committee at its meeting in Vancouver. Although up to this point in the decision process Cabinet had engaged in no serious comprehensive discussion of the free trade issue, and despite lingering uncertainties on the part of some ministers, the committee moved quickly to confirm the decision the prime minister had already taken to seek

comprehensive trade negotiations with the United States.

Shortly after the 5 September 1985 release of the Royal Commission report, to ensure that free trade would be tied to Macdonald, the prime minister indicated, in reply to a question in the House of Commons on 9 September, that the government had decided to pursue 'freer' trade with the United States. On 26 September, Mulroney told the Commons that he had telephoned Reagan to ask him to explore with Congress Canada's interest in pursuing negotiations to reduce tariffs and non-tariff barriers between the two countries. This call, and the formal written proposal that followed on 1 October, finally brought to an end four years of policy transformation in Canada.

This reconstruction of events between the decision to undertake a trade policy review in September 1981 and the September 1985 request for negotiations makes it clear that there was nothing inevitable about the Mulroney government's decision to seek free trade with the United States. In its beginnings, the free trade issue was the Liberals' legacy to the Conservative government, for it was they who had placed it on the governmental agenda. That legacy was nurtured and developed by a small, and relatively isolated, group of External Affairs officials led by Derek Burney and supported by key ministers in the Conservative Cabinet who were determined to move the trade issue onto the government's decision agenda. The framing of the problem that needed to be addressed was also critical to the policy process surrounding the issue. The policy papers prepared for ministers by Burney and his External Affairs group focused relentlessly on the trade policy problem of securing access to the US market in the face of growing American protectionism. Canadian business support for free trade was also directed to the need to secure access to their largest market and to escape US trade remedy actions against Canadian exports.

Free trade is more than trade policy, however. It can also serve as an industrial policy to bring about economic restructuring and adjustment. And it was primarily as an industrial policy, loosely defined, that free trade was advocated as the principal long-term solution to Canada's economic problems by the Macdonald Commission. According to the commission's analysis, the source of Canada's economic problems could be found in a manufacturing sector producing at too high a cost for too small a market. Free trade would at once expand the market and remove the protective barriers that insulate inefficient firms from competition. These firms would either adjust, by becoming larger and more competitive, or die. The result would be an increase in total national production. This analysis of industrial policy and its free trade prescription may represent sound economics, but it does not represent sound politics. With fewer but larger firms producing more, there are still likely to be large numbers of disaffected individuals and groups who have been 'adjusted' out of jobs and out of business. It is for this reason that protectionist measures—first tariffs, then non-tariff barriers—have enjoyed such popularity with politicians in all countries.

For ministers, the central problem facing Canada was security of access to the country's major market. A comprehensive trade agreement with the United States offered an appealing, if politically sensitive, trade policy solution to the problem. Had the problem been defined primarily in terms of an uncompetitive manufacturing sector, however, then it is likely that a proposal for an industrial policy to subject the economy to a sudden cold shower through free trade would have been viewed as a considerably more risky venture. But these hard economic facts were not laid out for the prime minister because he never received a comprehensive briefing from his senior trade officials on the economics of bilateral free trade.

The way the problem was framed for Mulroney helps explain why this otherwise cautious prime minister would take such a leap of faith. As a trade policy, free trade offered the prospect of secure access to the American market. Although it carried some domestic political risk, the prospect of reducing protectionist harassment in Canada's dominant trade market would make that risk worthwhile. As an industrial policy, however, the removal of barriers to trade offers the potential for market gains but at the risk of potential industry losses. Since the free trade option was framed as a means to achieve secure market access rather than as an equation of gains and losses, it offered a more palatable choice to policy-makers.

This reconstruction of events also makes it clear that the joining of the problem and policy streams alone would have been insufficient to drive this fundamental shift in policy. Change in the political stream was necessary as well. First, of course, was the timing of the failure of the sectoral initiative and the 1984 federal election, which produced Mulroney's majority government. In these circumstances, the significant partisan advantages that free trade offered the Conservatives made the option of comprehensive negotiations attractive. Mulroney was determined to offer a clear alternative to the centralizing, interventionist policies of the Trudeau Liberals and to build a lasting power base for his party. A policy that was market-oriented and had broad appeal in western Canada and Quebec served both ends. The summer of 1985 also saw Mulroney and his ministers under fire for a lack of clear direction and purpose. Free trade offered the prospect of immediate partisan advantage to a government in search of a major policy upon which to fix. Finally, when the problem, policy, and politics streams were joined, key policy entrepreneurs took advantage of the policy window (i.e., d'Aquino and Lougheed aligned critical business and political interests, while Burney moved the policy process inexorably towards free trade).

Conclusion

As noted at the outset of this chapter, the decision to negotiate a free trade agreement with the United States was a fundamental policy shift on the part of the government of Canada. It is equally clear, however, that this shift in policy was not the product of a Conservative determination to fashion an agenda of major policy departures. There were significant changes under way in all three of Kingdon's policy streams: the problem was redefined to emphasize the need to ensure secure access to the US market; the range of policy alternatives was expanded incrementally to include comprehensive free trade; and, of course, the electoral, partisan, and interest group dimensions of the political stream had shifted.

In hindsight, it is clear that there was nothing inevitable about the Conservative decision to seek free trade with the United States; rather, it was the product of the alignment of a complex array of conditions in three largely autonomous policy streams—conditions that evolved over a four-year period. Moreover, this alignment simply created windows of opportunity for key policy entrepreneurs who happened to be skilful enough, and lucky enough, to be able to exploit them before they closed. Free trade was not, therefore, a Conservative idea whose time had come; rather, it was a policy that had been thrust onto the agenda through a series of conjunctions of events and that was finally chosen as the result of cold political calculation.

Notes

1. When Mexico requested bilateral free trade negotiations with the United States, Canada overcame its initial reluctance and decided to seek trilateral negotiations to create the North American Free Trade Agreement (NAFTA). See Maxwell A. Cameron and Brian W. Tomlin, *The Making of NAFTA: How the Deal Was Done* (Ithaca: Cornell University Press, 2000).

2. John W. Kingdon, *Agendas, Alternatives and Public Policies* (New York: HarperCollins, 1995). Kingdon's model is a revised version of the 'garbage can' model of policy choice, advanced originally in Michael Cohen, James March, and Johan Olsen, 'A Garbage Can Model of Organizational Choice', *Administrative Science Quarterly* 17 (March 1972): 1–25. The analytical framework and concepts presented here are drawn from Brian W. Tomlin, 'On a Fast-Track to a Ban: the Canadian Policy Process', *Canadian Foreign Policy* 5, 3 (1998): 5–7.

3. On problem definition and agenda setting, see David Rochefort and Roger Cobb, eds, *The Politics of Problem Definition* (Lawrence, KS: University Press of Kansas, 1994); Deborah Stone, 'Causal Stories and the Formation of Policy Agendas', *Political Science Quarterly* 104, 2 (1989): 281–300.

4. Kingdon, *Agendas*, 90.

5. On policy communities, see Paul Sabatier and Hank Jenkins-Smith, eds, *Policy Change and Learning* (Boulder, CO: Westview, 1993); Michael Atkinson and William D. Coleman, 'Policy Networks, Policy Communities and the Problems of Governance', *Governance* 5, 2 (1992): 154–80; and Peter Haas, 'Introduction: Epistemic Communities and International Policy Co-ordination', *International Organization* 46, 1 (1992): 1–35.

6. Michael Howlett, 'Predictable and Unpredictable Policy Windows: Institutional and Exogenous Correlates of Canadian Federal Agenda-Setting', *Canadian Journal of Political Science* 31, 3 (1998): 495–524. For a critique of Howlett's analysis, see Stuart Soroka, 'Policy Agenda-Setting Theory Revisited: A Critique of Howlett on Downs, Baumgartner and Jones, and Kingdon', *Canadian Journal of Political Science* 32, 4 (1999): 763–72.

7. Kingdon, *Agendas*, 224.

8. The following analysis is drawn from G. Bruce Doern and Brian W. Tomlin, *Faith and Fear: The Free Trade Story* (Toronto: Stoddart, 1991).

9. Stephen Clarkson, *Canada and the Reagan Challenge* (Toronto: James Lorimer, 1982).

10. Michael Hart, Bill Dymond, and Colin Robertson, *Decision at Midnight: Inside the Canada–US Free Trade Negotiations* (Vancouver: UBC Press, 1994).

11. David Leyton-Brown, 'Canada–US Relations: Towards a Closer Relationship', in Maureen Appel Molot and Brian W. Tomlin, eds, *Canada Among Nations 1985: The Conservative Agenda* (Toronto: James Lorimer, 1986).

12. Canada, *Canadian Trade Policy for the 1980s: A Discussion Paper* (Ottawa: Department of External Affairs, 1983).

13. Canada, *A New Direction for Canada: An Agenda for Economic Renewal* (Ottawa: Department of Finance, 1984), 33.

14. On the role of the Canadian business community, see Doern and Tomlin, *Faith and Fear*, chap. 3.

15. Richard Lipsey and M. Smith, *Canada's Trade Policy Options* (Toronto: C.D. Howe Institute, 1985).

16. *Globe and Mail*, 19 November 1984.

17. Canada, *How to Secure and Enhance Access to Export Markets* (Ottawa: Department of External Affairs, 1985).

18. David Leyton-Brown, 'Canada–US Relations: Towards a Closer Relationship', in Molot and Tomlin, eds, *Canada Among Nations 1985*, 182.

18
Canada as a G8 Principal Power

John Kirton

Introduction

In its definitive statement on Canadian foreign policy on 7 February 1995, then-Prime Minister Jean Chrétien's government boldly declared: 'Canada can further its global interests better than any other country through its active membership in key international groupings, for example, hosting the G7 Summit this year and the APEC Summit in 1997' (DFAIT, 1995).[1] The statement further presented the G7 as a forum that allowed Canada to exercise world leadership, to reform international economic and financial institutions, and to successfully secure its shared values in the world.[2]

Such far-reaching claims are easily dismissed by those who treat the annual G7 (and, since 1998, the G8) Summit as little more than a great 'global hot tub party', with Canada merely 'being there' to bask in the reflected glory of the great (Keating, 1993; Wood, 1988).[3] This first school of thought, in peripheral dependant (PD) fashion, argues that the 'summits provided a sensation of power without its reality' while Canadian efforts to shape the agenda 'resulted in little, if any, success' (Keating, 1993: 196).

A second school highlights Canada's ineffective activism in the G8 (David and Roussel, 1998).

Andrew Cooper, Richard Higgott, and Kim Nossal (1993) acknowledge, in good liberal-internationalist (LI) fashion, that Trudeau 'did get North–South issues onto the agenda' at his 1981 Summit, that 'Canada focused on presenting the Cairns position', and moved 'well in front of its G7 partners . . . to move these states into adopting a more coercive policy towards South Africa'. But Canada was unable to shape Summit outcomes or ensure their success in the wider world.[4]

A third school of thought sees the G8 as a malevolent constraint on Canada because it takes attention and policy away from the United Nations (UN) and other multilateral institutions at the heart of the LI vision of Canada's proper place in the world (Helleiner, 1995; Nossal, 1998; Lovbraek 1990).[5] In pure PD fashion, it is the G8, and the US through it, that influences Canada, inducing it to adopt positions preferred by the capitalist major powers rather than the humane middle powers, of the world.

A fourth school sees the G8 as an institution for influence in Canadian foreign policy. This more complex neo-realist (CNR) view points to a significant Canadian role in, and beneficial results from, the G8 (Gotlieb, 1978; Artis and Ostry, 1988; Ostry, 1986; Ostry et al., 1991; Dobson,

1991, 1991a, 1994; Macmillan and Delvoie, 1999, Fowler, 2003, Haynal, 2005, Black, 2005).

The evidence of Canada's performance within the G8 suggests the even more far-reaching argument that the G8 has become an effective centre of global governance, thus allowing Canada as an equal first-tier member, to Canadianize the global order in accordance with its national interests and distinctive national values at home (Dewitt and Kirton, 1983). It shows Canada's effective diplomacy of concert through the G8 in global governance as a whole. The advent of the G7 in 1975 moved Canada from the traditional, UN-based 'diplomacy of constraint' to the modern, G8-centred 'diplomacy of concert' (Stairs, 1974). The G8 has allowed Canada to move beyond assembling coalitions of like-minded middle powers in the broadly multilateral forums of the UN to constrain the predominant US. It has thrust Canada into assembling issue- and interest-specific coalitions of fellow major democratic powers in a flexible, leader-driven, plurilateral concert to shape world order in accordance with Canadian interests and values, often over the opposition of such powerful imperial partners as the UK and US. Propelling Canada's rise as a G8 principal power have been the emergence of a new global intervulnerability, the failure of the 1994–5 multilateral organizations in response to the shocks they breed, and the growth of the G8 as a democratic concert offering the concerted power, constricted participation, common principles, and political control lacking in increasingly obsolescent institutions. Canada has increasingly used its relatively invulnerable, well connected position in the summit to reinforce its major power presence, assert its national interests, form fluid interest- and issue-based partnerships, prevail in its positions, and secure international compliance and domestic acclaim, and a world order in its image. Canada has come to behave regularly as a leader, steadily shifting from defensive to offensive forms of leadership, and shaping the G8-centred system global order as a result.

An Overview of Canada's Summit Contribution

Canada's growing position as a principal summit power first appears in its performance as a modestly and increasingly successful summit host. The 1981 Montebello Summit earned a C, Toronto in 1988 a C–, and Halifax in 1995 and Kananaskis in 2002 both earned a B+ (Bayne, 2000: 195; Bayne, 2003). Canada's B– average places it above the overall summit average of C+. Canada's B+ grades for Halifax and Kananaskis are the third highest grades in the summit's history and the highest since the Cold War's end in 1989 (Bayne, 2005; Kirton and Takase, 2002). A count of the specific, actionable, future-oriented 'commitments' that each summit produces shows a similar rise (Kokotsis, 1999). Pierre Trudeau's Montebello Summit produced 40 commitments, Brian Mulroney's Toronto Summit dropped to 27, but Chrétien's Halifax Summit in 1995 soared to 76 commitments and his second Summit, in Kananaskis in 2002, produced an historic high of 188 (Kirton and Takase, 2002, 267).

Canada has also secured its priority objectives at each of the annual summits since 1995 to a relatively high degree, with an average grade of B+ (G8 Research Group, 2003). Canada further complies with its summit commitments to a high and rising degree, usually ranking second only to Britain in the high compliance club. Moreover, Canada's more powerful partners, notably the United States and France, have also increased their compliance in recent years (von Furstenberg and Daniels, 1991; Kokotsis, 1999; Kirton and Kokotsis, 2004).

Canada has also made a substantial contribution to the development of global governance through the G8. Canada mounted a major comprehensive and inclusive program of UN and Bretton Woods reform at Halifax in 1995. At the ministerial level, Canada's 1981 Montebello Summit created the Trade Ministers Quadrilateral, the first stand-alone G7 forum for ministers not regularly involved at the summit itself (Cohn, 2002).

On 12 December 1995, in response to the sarin gas attacks on the Tokyo subway and other terrorist attacks, Canada founded the G7's Ministerial Meeting on Terrorism. In 1999 it founded the G20 finance ministers to cope with the globalized financial crises of the time (Kirton, 2001, 2005a). In late 2001, it hosted the first meeting of the Global Health Security Initiative, which gathered the ministers of the G7 and Mexico. In 2002 Canada established the G8 Ministerial Meeting for Development Co-operation and the G8 meeting of parliamentary presidents.

Canada as a Successful Summiteer, 1975–94

Canada's emergence as an equally influential principal power in an effective G8 concert can be understood by examining Canada's 1975–94 summit diplomacy along five dimensions. These are, first, Canada's presence in becoming a full member of all G8 groups; second, its participation, by equally asserting positions based on Canada's national interest and distinctive value-based positions, agendas, and program initiatives; third, its partnerships, by joining and creating coalitions with any other member, against any other members, as interests and values direct; fourth, its prevalence with these coalitions to produce the summit's collective directions and decisions, and; fifth, its public acclaim for its G8 diplomacy and achievements.

At one end of the spectrum formed by these five factors lies a pattern of diplomacy that can be labelled the 'diplomacy of support'. Here, in PD fashion, Canada is present in G8 forums through US support alone, relies on American initiative, supports American-led coalitions, and acquiesces in and adjusts to American-generated G8 decisions, in ways the Canadian public and media recognize and dislike. At the other end lies a pattern that can be labeled the diplomacy of concert. Here, in CNR fashion, Canada is present and participating over American opposition, joining or initiating coalitions against America, and securing collective endorsements of some magnitude, in ways that mobilize support at home. In between lie the LI patterns of the diplomacy of constraint and compromise within the concert.[6]

In regard to presence, Canada has secured a full, top-tier, permanent, and equal presence in every component institution of a rapidly expanding G8 system. Despite resistance from France, which hosted and controlled the invitation list for the first summit, Canada asserted and achieved its desire for membership prior to the first gathering at Rambouillet in 1975. While Canada was not physically present at Rambouillet, Canada had secured a prior promise from Henry Kissinger, on behalf of President Gerald Ford, that the United States would host a second summit that Canada would attend. All other summit members save France supported Canada's inclusion. Canada's first-tier presence has been reinforced at the ministerial level.[7] Canada became a charter member of all the G7/8 stand-alone ministerial forums— trade in 1981, foreign ministers in 1984, G7 finance ministers in 1986, and the 1990s additions for labour, environment, and much else. At the official level, a similar expansion and inclusion took place.

Canada has also proven to be an unusually active participant in both the preparations for, and discussions at, the annual summit.[8] Canada has increasingly shaped the summit's agenda, consistently pressing political-security, north–south, human rights, environmental, and trade concerns.[9]

In 1976 Canada was assigned the lead on an important issue of energy, where Canada's specialized capabilities loomed large. Pierre Trudeau sought to broaden the G7's treatment of this issue from oil and gas to nuclear energy and its political-security extension, nuclear proliferation, and succeeded in 1997. He was also among the summit leaders in putting East–West political-security issues on the summit agenda, succeeding most clearly when he hosted in 1981.

Canada also quickly took the lead on North–South issues, sympathetically raising southern concerns. North–South relations was the centrepiece theme of Montebello in 1981. The G7's initiatives on debt relief for the poorest countries were born when Canada next hosted, at Toronto, in 1988. Under Brian Mulroney's leadership, Canada also encouraged the summit to take up issues of democratization and human rights, first against South African apartheid in 1987 and against China over the Tienanmen Square massacre in 1989 (Kirton, 2004).

Since the 1980s Canada, along with Germany and Italy, emphasized the environment as a special interest, notably over-fishing of high seas straddling stocks. Throughout, Canada has concentrated on the core economic domain of trade, and has used the G7 for promoting multilateral trade liberalization, reducing export subsidies and protectionism, and building strong multilateral rule-based trade institutions and regimes.

When all of these issues are considered together, Canada has broadened the summit agenda, transforming it from an institution dealing with limited economic issues within the G7 and industrialized North to include once domestic issues within the North and the North's economic, political, and security issues with the communist East and with the developing South. Canada has from the start sought to make the G8 a forum for not just G8 governance but for full global governance as well.

In forging partnerships within the G8, Canada is usually neither a supporter of American initiative nor a mediator of Franco-American differences but an advocate of positions based on Canada's national interests and distinctive national values, backed by an ad hoc coalition of countries in each case.[10] Within this fluid and free-forming array there has been a tendency for Canada to combine less with historic partners and powers—notably the United States, Britain, and France—and more with the rising powers and the permanently excluded UN Security Council Permanent Five countries of Germany, Italy, and Japan. The classic North Atlantic 'Anglo-Saxon triumvirate' of America–Britain–Canada has combined on trade liberalization

issues, notably agricultural subsidies in 1986 and the Uruguay Round's completion in 1990–1. However, Canada and Britain more typically join with France, against the US, in a Commonwealth–Francophonie coalition on matters of development, debt, African, and North–South issues. The advent of French president François Mitterrand in 1981 permitted the 'francophone twins' to flourish on political issues, notably East–West security in 1983, with quiet German encouragement, and strong sanctions against the Peoples Republic of China over Tiananmen in 1989 and 1990.

Increasingly, Canada's alignment with the three rising non-traditional partners of Italy, Germany, and Japan has risen to the forefront. Italy and Canada have been arrayed together as the 'outer two' positioned against the 'inner five' over agenda and membership issues, notably on the production of a formal political declaration in 1980–1, a statement on South Africa in 1987, enlargement of the G5 finance ministers group in 1986, and membership in the Bosnian Contact Group in 1994.

Canada and Germany have often been in the lead on political issues, such as skyjacking in 1978, East–West reassurance in 1983–4, and assistance to the former Soviet Union and Central and Eastern Europe in 1990. Germany, Canada and, at times, Italy—with French support in 1989—have formed the vanguard ecological triumvirate within the G8, as in the creation of a G7 environment ministers forum in 1992, 1994, and 1995.

The Canadian–Japanese G8 partnership has been slower to develop (Kirton, 1998), yet the P5-excluded coalition of Canada, Germany, Italy, and Japan sprung to life with the Cold War's end. Since 1999, the four have been the pioneers of the G8's conflict prevention agenda, over the resistance of the Russians and above all the French (Kirton and Stefanova, 2003). The latter fear that the G8 will replace the UNSC—where they enjoy a more secure P5 position—as the effective centre of global security governance (Kirton, 2000a). Finally, at Genoa in 2005 Canada joined with Japan and

Russia in a new North Pacific triangle that agreed to ratify the Kyoto Protocol and bring it into effect, even though the US stayed out (Kirton, 2004).

Through this pattern of fluid coalition diplomacy and strengthening partnerships with the rising G7 partners, Canada was increasingly able to prevail. In 1977, Trudeau finally succeeded in putting nuclear proliferation on the table and enlarging the agenda to embrace North–South relations and human rights. He did so by using his assigned lead on energy, conceived of as hydrocarbons, to take the discussion into nuclear energy, then nuclear proliferation, and then nuclear arms control.

Canada followed by working with host Germany to devise a regime to deal with aircraft hijacking at the Bonn 1978 Summit.[11] Building on earlier Japanese and Italian advances, Canada succeeded, as host in 1981, to have the G7 produce its first ever 'Chairman's Summary of Political Issues' (Hajnal, 1989).[12] At Montebello, Canada succeeded in persuading new, reluctant, right-wing US President Ronald Reagan to go with his G7 colleagues to the forthcoming Cancun summit for 'global negotiations' aimed at a new North–South deal.

In some cases, Canada has also stood alone at the start, using the G7 to prevail on ambitious issues such as East–West superpower nuclear negotiations and the internal constitutional transformation of distant states. At Williamsburg in 1983, Pierre Trudeau, with support from France's François Mitterrand forced an initially reluctant United States, backed by Britain, to produce a separate political declaration and include a passage adjusting the NATO position and authorizing the peace initiative he subsequently undertook. In 1987 Brian Mulroney demanded, and received, a collective statement condemning apartheid in South Africa, which the Summit steadily strengthened until its ultimate success in South Africa.

The G8 Summit, and Canada within it, has been sufficiently successful to secure public acclaim within Canada, improved government approval ratings, re-election prospects, national unity, and national pride. In Spring 1993, 71 per cent of Canadians thought the summit meetings were important. In Spring 1994, with a new prime minister and new party in power, an almost identical 72 per cent thought that 'participating in the Summit gives Canada an opportunity to influence events in ways that are good for this country.' A majority of all subgroups of Canadians were united in these views.

Canadians have continued to love and trust the G7/8 summit. A Strategic Counsel poll of 1,200 Canadians taken from 21–25 November 2001 indicated that 77 per cent of Canadians wanted the Kananaskis Summit—the first since 9/11—to continue, compared to only 23 per cent who said cancel. A majority, 63 per cent, blamed the anti-globalization protestors, and only 13 per cent the police, when violent confrontations between the two take place (Maclean's/CBC News, 2001–2: 38).

Amongst the anglophone and francophone editorialists of Canada's elite daily newspapers the summit is also seen as a success. Editorialists of the *Globe and Mail* give grades generally as high as those of the inside sherpas or outside academic evaluators. Canada's performance is often rated a success by the editorialists of both the *Globe* and *Le Devoir*. In the first two summits hosted by Canada, under Trudeau in 1981 in Quebec and under Mulroney in 1988 in Ontario, the marks are particularly high.

Canada's Summit Leadership, 1995–2001

Since 1995, Canada has increasingly acted as a G8 leader, steadily shifting from defensive to offensive forms of leadership, and delivering G7/8 system building and global order-shaping results.

HALIFAX 1995
Halifax 1995 is often judged to be a successful summit because of its review and reform of the UN, Bretton Woods, and other international institutions, its handling of the delicate issue of Rus-

sian participation, and its advance of Canadian priorities such as sustainable development, the linkage between development assistance and excessive military expenditure, and the G7 implementation report (Bayne, 2000; Smith, 1995; Boehm, 1996). However, the institutional review was launched by President Bill Clinton at Naples 1994 and it, along with some other Canadian accomplishments, had little lasting impact. Jean Chrétien's most distinctive contribution was to maintain the singular summit focus on international institutional reform amidst competing claims, and to find a formula for making this a far-reaching review. Canada also saved the summit from disruption from an ambitious last minute American neo-liberal initiative for an 'Open Markets 2000' program. At the end of its year as host, Canada served as a G7/8 system-builder by creating the G8 Ministerial Meeting on Terrorism.

Canada's most striking success at Halifax came on the invisible but ultimate issue of Quebec's separation from Canada. At Halifax, Canada had all members rally around to maintain Canada as a major power member of the club. Held on the eve of the date initially envisaged for the referendum on Quebec separation, the Halifax Summit saw French president Jacques Chirac offer considerable implicit support to the federalist cause. The Summit, originally slated for Quebec City, was held in Atlantic Canada, from whence the Canadian military had shipped out twice in the twentieth century to help liberate France. This conveyed a multilayered message about how a separated Quebec would be cut off—and France along with it—from a globally positioned and engaged Canada. The message was driven home on the Summit's first night, when Chrétien rearranged the carefully planned schedule so the G7 leaders could endorse a sudden initiative from Chirac on Bosnia, where French and Canadian troops had gone together in the G7 vanguard in the spring of 1992. It was hardly surprising that Quebec's separatist politicians, considering their diminished chances at the polls, delayed their referendum until the autumn.

LYON 1996

At Lyon in 1996, with a deficit-ridden Canada still reeling from its near-defeat in the 30 October 1995 referendum, the national unity imperative remained. Canada was eager to show it was a full partner, as the G7's only other francophone power, in the priorities set by France. These priorities, especially popular in francophone Quebec, were development, ODA, debt relief for the poorest, and Africa. A second area concerned a rapidly downsizing and democratizing Russia, which shared Canada's preoccupation with combating separatist forces. On the specific issue of Russia's G7 participation, Canada solved its 'trilemma' of helping involve Russia so as to ensure victory for democratic forces in Russia's presidential elections, reassuring Ukraine (and the many Canadians of Ukrainian origin) that Ukraine would not be left behind, and closing Ukraine's Chernobyl reactor and strengthening nuclear safety in ways that did not harm either Canada's Candu program or its nuclear nonproliferation objectives. Here civilian nuclear-laden France and Russia served as sympathetic soul mates. A third accomplishment, taking Canada into the offensive realm as a G8 system builder, was helping Clinton extend the recently constructed anti-terrorism ministerial forum into the new Lyon Group.

DENVER 1997

At the 1997 Denver Summit of the Eight, with Quebec's separatist threat receding, Canadian prosperity and fiscal surplus returning, and Russia's arrival elevating Canada's summit rank, Canada was able to go on the offensive. However, America's booming economy, its triumphalist faith in its all-American free market model for sustained growth, and its prerogatives as host presented a formidable countervailing force. Canada supported President Clinton's system-building initiatives to include the Russians as a virtually full participant in the summit and to advance an African agenda. Canada also acted as a summit system saver. Faced with a prospective European walkout over Clinton's invitation for the leaders to attend a social event wearing American cowboy costumes he had thoughtfully provided, Chrétien broke the ice by declaring that he would attend the event, but wear his own, all-Canadian cowboy attire. Canada also secured communiqué language that protected its position on the divisive climate change issue. Offensively, Chrétien skillfully secured acceptance from many hitherto reluctant leaders to accept a key Canadian order-building priority—the Ottawa process-generated convention on antipersonnel landmines.

BIRMINGHAM 1998

Three weeks after Denver, Thailand devalued the bhat, precipitating a two-year global financial crisis that bankrupted American hedge fund Long-Term Capital Management (LTCM) and threatened to drive a liquidity-short US economy into financial collapse by September 1998 (Kirton, 1999, 2000). On the road to Birmingham 1998, Canada stopped the G7 from having the International Monetary Fund amend its Articles of Agreement to affirm the neo-liberal principle of capital account liberalization. Canada offered financial support to Thailand when its regional partners no longer could. It joined with G7 partners during the grim summer and autumn of 1998 to save the global economy, and a now vulnerable America, from collapse. At Birmingham, Canada supported the British in creating a permanent G8 summit with Russia and in having the leaders meet without their finance and foreign ministers, in an informal setting, for an agenda focused on three major themes. Canada also worked effectively with Britain and France to advance the Lyon-generated initiative for debt relief of the poorest nations. When nuclear explosions in Asia disrupted the carefully constructed summit agenda, Chrétien was assigned the role of contacting Pakistan to urge restraint on the G8's behalf.

COLOGNE 1999

At Cologne in 1999, Canada worked with host-country Germany and a flexible array of partners to advance its key priorities (Kirton, Daniels, and Freytag, 2001). Canada joined with the German 'red-green' coalition government headed by Gerhard Schroeder to affirm the new 'Cologne consensus' on socially sustainable globalization. Joined by Britain and France, Canada made advances on debt relief for the poorest nations and joined Britain to push for a G7, and then G8, consensus on using ground combat forces to complete the liberation of Kosovo. This threat led to the voluntary withdrawal of Yugoslav forces from the territory and the end of the threat of genocide there (Heinbecker, 2001). During the year, Canada joined with Germany and Italy to lead the G8 into a new, post-Kosovo program on conflict prevention (Kirton and Stefanova, 2003).

OKINAWA 2000

At Okinawa in 2000 Canada sympathized with Japan's desire to focus the summit on development and information technology, and to have information technology presented in a development friendly manner, rather than in the US-proposed neo-liberal guise (Kirton and von Furstenberg, 2001). However, Canada made little progress in securing further debt relief or a food safety regime that protected Canada's investments in genetically modified organisms. But it was successful in obtaining G8 endorsement of the principle of cultural diversity. Canada was also able to convert the December 1999 foreign ministers agreement-in-principle on conflict prevention into actionable decisions in five specific fields, largely composed of those where Canada's human security agenda had been in the lead (Kirton and Takase, 2002).

GENOA 2001

At Genoa 2001 Canada worked with the Italian host to devise a multiyear thrust that would culminate in Canada's year as host. Canada's objectives focused on poverty reduction, debt relief, combating infectious disease, bridging the digital divide, forging the trade–development link, and conflict prevention. Despite Genoa's deadly distractions, Canada helped the summit focus on Africa, create the multibillion-dollar Global Fund to Fight AIDS, Tuberculosis and Malaria, and highlight the needs of developing countries in multilateral trade liberalization. Canada succeeded in having the G8 leaders appoint personal representatives for Africa (APRs), under the chair of Canada, to spearhead a partnership premised on a new development paradigm. The report received from the Digital Opportunities Task Force (the DOT Force), established at Okinawa, similarly emphasized bridging the digital divide. G8 leaders directed that the Africa Action Plan aimed at implementation be devised for discussion at Kananaskis. Canada also worked with Italy and Germany to expand the G8's work on conflict prevention into the environmental and gender fields.

Canada's Leadership, 2001–5

THE RESPONSE TO SEPTEMBER 11

On 11 September 2001, when al-Qaeda struck the Pentagon and World Trade Center in the United States, Canada's immediate reaction was to mobilize the G8 forum to deliver a collective response. 'In the hours after the attack, Martin was on the phone to the finance ministers of the G7 leading industrial countries and they agreed that there should be a statement saying they had confidence in the world's financial system; the statement was duly drafted in the finance department at Esplanade Laurier. But the prime minister's office suddenly announced that Martin would not be speaking on such matters, so the statement drafted in Ottawa was issued in Italy' (Gray, 2003: 214–15). The day after the terrorist attacks, Chrétien, along with Italian chair Silvio Berlusconi and Russia's Vladimir Putin, publicly called for the G8 to define the American and allied response. Martin and his colleagues in Finance moved quickly to strengthen the G7/8's effort against terrorist financing; the Financial Action Task Force on Money Laundering (FATF) had been established in 1989, but implementa-

tion had been sluggish. In Ottawa on 17–19 November 2001 Paul Martin hosted, when India could not, the annual meeting of the G20 finance ministers and central bank governors, the IMF's International Monetary and Financial Committee (IMFC), and the IMF–World Bank's Development Committee (Kirton, 2001).

In the foreign policy sphere, the G8 foreign ministers meeting, traditionally held on the eve of the UNGA opening on 30 September, took place, along with the delayed UN session, in New York on 11 November. By the middle of December 2001, 196 countries and other jurisdictions had expressed support for the campaign against terrorist financing, 139 had issued blocking orders, and the United States had expressed satisfaction with G8 and G20 efforts to share financial intelligence (Dam, 2001).[13]

KANANASKIS 2002

As Kananaskis approached, Canada worked to make the broader linkages in finance, global growth, the natural environment, African poverty reduction, and post-conflict reconstruction, that would prevent the threat from recurring once the current antiterrorism campaign was won. At the same time, Chrétien remained determined that the 9/11 terrorists would not hijack the G8 summit agenda agreed to at Genoa; Kananaskis would unfold the way he had long felt it should (Kirton, 2002). Reinforced by his attachment to the Montebello model of 1981, and his vindication in sticking to the previously endorsed agenda in 1995, Chrétien struggled to deliver his summit as a small, informal, private, retreat-like summit focused on poverty reduction in Africa.

Amidst the Genoa Summit's violence, Chrétien had confirmed his growing instinct to switch Canada's 2002 Summit from its intended site in urban Ottawa, Ontario, to rural, resort-like Kananaskis, Alberta. The move was inspired by the civil society protest, the terrorist threats at Genoa, the way the media and leaders reacted to these events, the desire to give western Canada its turn as G8 host, and Chrétien's desire to reproduce the

Montebello model on a mountaintop. This required an isolated setting, small delegations of no more than 30 representatives per country, maximum opportunity for informal dialogue among leaders, minimum pomp and ceremony, distance from most of the media, and no serious participation by civil society. Chrétien also dispensed with the traditional carefully prepared concluding communiqué that authoritatively informed the world of what the G8 had decided.

To deliver his summit, Chrétien appointed Robert Fowler—a skilled senior Canadian diplomat who had been at Montebello, at Genoa as Canada's ambassador to Italy, and in Africa as a young educator—as his personal representative for both the G8 and for the parallel African dialogue. As Canada's ambassador to the UN, Fowler had recently led the international community in constructing a regime against the blood diamonds that fuelled Africa's wars.

At the final sherpa meeting hosted by the outgoing Italian chair in early December 2001, Canada proposed that Kananaskis should avoid a diffuse, comprehensive, 'Christmas tree' agenda. Instead, it should focus exclusively on three themes: combating terrorism, generating global growth, and reducing poverty in Africa, with other subjects left for the many separate pre-summit meetings of G7/8 ministers. These included ministers of finance on 7–8 February in Ottawa, labour ministers on 25–27 April in Montreal, environment ministers on 12–14 April in Banff, energy ministers on 2–3 May in Detroit, and trade and the pre-Summit meeting for finance (in Halifax) and foreign affairs (in Whistler).

Canada planned to convey three major messages at Kananaskis. The first was that the world must go beyond the traditional prevailing philosophy of development to ensure that recipients, civil society, and private sector actors participate fully in the process. The second was that medium-term prospects for growth in the G7 and global community were good, that productivity-enhancing structural policies to sustain growth were needed, and that alternative approaches for different regions and countries may be required. The third was that G8 and global commitments on combating terrorism must be fully implemented, made comprehensive, and backed by the capacity building required to ensure their effectiveness.

In delivering its first priority of poverty reduction in Africa, Canada began by taking seriously the proclamation of African leaders in their New Partnership for Africa's Development (NEPAD) that they represented a new generation with new domestic commitments and a new approach to development. The challenge was to have the G8 and Africa agree on a new paradigm and find the resources to make it work. This required having the IMF and World Bank, in their poverty reduction strategies, invite recipient countries and their citizens to take ownership, to review lending conditionality and restrict the costly paper and personnel burden imposed on developing countries, and to review the program for highly indebted poor countries (HIPCs). Canada sought to emphasize the recipients' responsibilities, notably good governance through the rule of law, civil society participation, social policy, sustainable development, an educated workforce, and a sound-banking sector.

Canada recognized the need to increase the resources to finance development, both by enhancing the levels of traditional ODA and by instituting innovative global mechanisms. Aware of the large bill required to rebuild Africa, hoping to inspire its G8 colleagues to do more, and led by Chrétien's directive not to forget Africa, Canada increased ODA spending by $1 billion in its 10 December 2001 budget. A special fund for Africa, an additional $500 million, was also announced, the funds for which would come from money left over after balancing the budget during the following three years. On the larger challenge, Canada noted the favourable response that British finance minister Gordon Brown's proposal for a $50 billion trust fund was starting to receive, especially from US treasury secretary Paul O'Neill. Canada also took a close look at several other suggestions: a Tobin tax, a new allocation of special drawing rights (SDRs), a carbon tax, an air travel tax, an armaments tax, and a potential return to the 1960s Pearson-like targets. Canada's strategy, along with the US, was to move in an integrated fashion from the Spring 2002 United Nations Conference on Financing for Development in Monterrey, through the Kananaskis Summit to the 'Rio-plus-ten' World Summit on Sustainable Development (WSSD) in Johannesburg in September 2002.

In financing development, Canada favoured, in principle, George Bush's idea of having the International Development Association (IDA) give money as grants rather than long-term concessional loans. A Canadian financial analysis showed that the approach was affordable. However, as the Europeans strongly resisted, Canada looked to a compromise that yielded a significantly larger portion of IDA funding to be given in pure grant form.

Canada also sought to continue, through the G7 process, its longstanding effort to construct a regime for private sector participation in response to financial crises. Here it could now build on the formal G20 agreement to have G20 deputies conduct a detailed operational study of such issues as how to immunize countries from domestic lawsuits in an international 'standstill' mechanism, and how the IMF would serve as the neutral arbiter in making a standstill mechanism work. The December 2001 debt default by Argentina—the world's largest ever—gave Canada broader support.

On the theme of generating growth, Canada sought to emphasize that, beyond Japan, the fundamentals were solid for good medium-term growth. Therefore, more attention was needed to enhance productivity, especially as the cost of terrorism was now being priced into G7 economies. 9/11-generated expenditures, and all national policies, needed to be scrutinized for their contribution to productivity, in order to raise growth levels permanently. An emphasis on productivity could help resolve the current debate between Europe and the US over whether fiscal integrity or fiscal stimulus was most needed to boost growth. The success of the WTO ministers at Doha in launching a new round of multilateral trade liberalization would be welcomed as an important element in productivity-based global economic growth.

The final theme of combating terrorism included pressing for implementation of the G20-generated Action Plan on Terrorist Financing. Canada would follow the G7–G20–IMF support-building cadence to make the new regime fully global and comprehensive. In contrast to France and Italy, which sought to ensure compliance by relying on sanctions alone, Canada called for capacity building as well. Representing the Commonwealth Caribbean in the international financial institutions and recalling the time and trouble it took to develop its own system for financial tracking, Canada sought to mobilize ODA, technical assistance, and human assistance to assist developing countries in the task.

As the Kananaskis Summit approached, systemic, societal, and government forces presented favourable conditions for the realization of this plan, but substantial risks remained. The first risk was whether an international crisis would erupt that did not fit easily into the predefined thematic trilogy. The second risk was whether African leaders could agree among themselves and with the G8 on what a credible new development paradigm would be before its anointment at Kananaskis and whether the delivery of the $50 billion promised by the British and the Americans could be there to back up the paradigm. The third area of concern was whether Chrétien could both convince his neighbour Bush to come to Kananaskis for the entire summit and make Canada's preferred agenda appeal to the President's distinctly different priorities. The fourth factor for success depended on whether Chrétien could convince the media, civil society, and Canadians—all of whom were so cut off from the Summit—that three genuinely productive summits, with the African leaders, the G7, and the G8, could be held in the space of two days at an informal, remote retreat. Finally, the success of the summit relied on Chrétien's ability to mobilize the personal energy to secure from his Summit partners the painful compromises required to put his far-reaching plan into effect.

Kananaskis turned out to be, arguably, the most successful summit to that time (Fowler, 2003; Langdon, 2003). In addition to the historically high number of commitments it produced, Kananaskis and its lead-up events mobilized close to $50 billion in new monies for global public goods—$20 billion for the Global Partnership against Weapons and Materials of Mass Destruction, up to $6 billion for African development, $1 billion to top up the HIPC trust fund and $28 billion for the thirteenth replenishment of the IDA fund. Additionally, Kananaskis included four leaders from Africa's leading democratic middle powers as equal participants in the G8's final summit session, and it was agreed that Russia would host the summit in 2006. Meager results came about only from the traditional finance field (Kirton and Kokotsis, 2003).

EVIAN 2003

The French-hosted Evian Summit on 1–3 June 2003 was held in the midst of severe transatlantic tension, most notably between France and the United States as a result of the 18 March 2003 American-led invasion of Iraq. Evian was the first of the fifth summit cycle, but the last for Jean Chrétien. Canada's objectives were to preserve the Kananaskis legacy and ensure its commitments were implemented to generate real results. In this, Canada succeeded, both in the substance of the 206 commitments made at Evian and in the participation in the G8 Summit of the African leaders. Canada also strongly supported a European initiative, resisted by Japan, to tighten rules on maritime tanker safety; this initiative carried the day. Canada's environmental values were also advanced by the Evian commitments on water, science, and technology for sustainable development. The European leaders seeking to control their welfare costs in the face of public protests looked to Chrétien as the veteran leader for political guidance on how to get their fiscal deficits under control in ways their public would accept.

SEA ISLAND 2004

The Sea Island Summit hosted by the United States on 8–10 June 2004 was the first for Prime Minister Paul Martin, who assumed office on 12 December 2003. The Summit was held in the middle of the campaign for the general election Martin had called for June 28. With Martin preoccupied by the election, Canada's priority was again to preserve and extend the Kananaksis legacy; it did this with further action on the transport security component of counterterrorism by supporting the launch of the Secure and Facilitated International Travel Initiative (SAFTI). On the issue of WMD nonproliferation, Canada added both the newly converted Libya and the still difficult Iraq to the list of eligible recipients. And Canada sought and secured—over initial US reluctance—major movement on Africa, as well as additional funding.

At Sea Island, an egalitarian Canada helped lead the substantial Summit accomplishments on protecting global health against the resurgence of polio and the proliferation of HIV/AIDS. Through the UN-sanctioned Martin-Zedillo report, it also led on private sector-led development. A multicultural Canada concerned about national unity also had the G8 spontaneously include Haiti in its discussions of security issues on the Summit's second night. Most broadly, a globalist Canada succeeded in having a skeptical George Bush produce a full-strength, highly successful summit with a very broad range of subjects reflecting, in balanced fashion, the priorities of both America as host and its G8 partners (Kirton, 2005; Bayne, 2005).

Despite Martin's departure from Sea Island before the Summit's last day, his G8 performance earned him a badly needed bounce in his plummeting popularity ratings back home. Moreover, in the six months that followed the Summit, Canada complied with its 18 priority commitments to a substantial degree.

GLENEAGLES 2005

The 2005 Gleneagles Summit saw Canada support, in general terms, a British host that had made both Canada's Kananaskis legacy and Canada's core priorities of African development and climate change control the Summit centrepiece. Canada was able to join with the United States and Japan to stop the summit from adopting the ill-conceived initiative of pledging .07 per cent of GDP in ODA and mounting a major International Finance Facility that the British hosts had first proposed. In place of these proposals Canada saw the G8 follow Canada's lead and endorse a pledge to double ODA within the next five years. The Summit also recognized the Kyoto Protocol that had now come into force and whose first meeting Canada would host in Montreal that fall.

Causes of Canada's Summit Success

EXTERNAL DETERMINANTS

This record of increasingly effective Canadian G8 leadership suggests that several factors have generated Canadian success. At the systemic level, the advent of the post-Cold War, rapidly globalizing, post-9/11 world, and the increasing American vulnerability, has both allowed and inspired Canada to leap into offensive leadership. Canada has done so based on its position as the longstanding East–West and North–South bridge-builder, as the most globalized G8 member, and as the early initiator and institutional inventor of the G8's anti-terrorism work.[14] There are, however, a number of external determinants.

Changing relative capabilities have created a more modest, and thus more co-operative, United States in the 1970s and after 1985. These capabilities have also brought other capable countries willing to lead, and with which Canada is prepared to align, to the forefront, in particular Japan until 1990 and Russia after 1999. A declining America has increasingly depended on its G8 allies, including Canada, to shape order in the world. American vulnerability has soared over varying points in time: in energy since 1973, civilian nuclear power since 1979, terrorism since 1979, and finance since 1998. In each case, Canada has stood out among the G8 partners with the relevant specialized capabilities to help. In energy, driven by the oil shocks of 1973 and 1979, American dependence on imported oil has risen from 35 per cent of its national requirement in the late 1970s to more than 50 per cent by 2004. During this time energy-rich Canada has become the equivalent of a secure, right-next-door version of Saudi Arabia and energy-rich Russia has joined the G8 club.[15] In civilian nuclear power, the shocks of America's Three Mile Island explosion in 1979, Chernobyl in 1986, and Tokamura in 1999 have reduced the easy availability of the first alternative energy source for first-ranked America and second-ranked Japan. Canada has remained as a civilian nuclear power that has been accident free, even as France has led the world in this regard.

The threat of terrorism spread from Germany in 1978, to the United States, starting in Iran in 1979, Lebanon in 1983, the Gulf in 1996, Africa in the late 1990s, and America itself in 1993 and 2001. Canada has been the only G8 member without a terrorist death on its own soil since the summit began in 1975.

In finance, the 1998 collapse of American hedge fund Long Term Capital Management amidst the Asian-turned-global finance crisis of 1997–9 transformed America from a producer to a consumer of financial security. Even though it was a smaller and more open economy, Canada escaped unscathed. Its growing fiscal surplus allowed it to provide financial support to afflicted countries around the world, even when America could not.

The G8 has institutionally thickened as an informal, leaders-driven concert, where the smallest number of democratically committed major powers can efficiently and cohesively decide how to combine the maximum predominant capability to shape global governance as a whole.

Regarding constricted participation, the addition of only the European Union in 1977 and Russia in 1998, and the expansion of the EU to include 25 countries by 2004, has kept the small size while expanding the combined capabilities and reducing the number of outside rivals in the world. In terms of democratic cohesion, only democratic polities have been allowed in. Freedom House gave its highest grade of 1 on a 1–7 scale to Canada, France, Germany, Italy, the US, and Britain, 1.5 to Japan, and 5.0 to Russia, for an average score of 1.6. In sharp contrast, the UNSC Permanent Five, including China at 6.5, had an average score of 2.9. The G8 has become more of a leader-driven body after 1998, when the finance and foreign ministers stopped joining their leaders at the summit itself. In contrast, leaders still never regularly come together to govern the UN, IMF, or World Bank.

SOCIETAL DETERMINANTS

At the societal level, Canada has consistently sustained a public opinion that has been highly favourable to the G8 Summit as an institution, and to the particular priorities that Canada brings. This deep supportive consensus has endured despite the de-legitimizing violence of the 2001 Genoa Summit and the distraction of the 9/11 terrorist attack. All Canadians are able to perceive that the G8 gives their country principal power status, helps it preserve its national unity and security, and allows it to effectively advance its distinctive national values in the world.

GOVERNMENTAL DETERMINANTS

Governmental determinants have also assisted Canada in exercising effective G8 leadership. At the top level, Canada has usually sent highly experienced leaders to the summit, notably Trudeau from 1976–84 (excepting 1979), Mulroney from 1984–92, and Jean Chrétien from 1994–2003. Moreover, Canada's leaders have, since 1993, brought extensive G8 experience from their time as ministers. Jean Chrétien was involved in the G7 as Trudeau's finance minister, and Paul Martin started as Prime Minister at Sea Island in 2004 with 10 years of G7/8 experience as Chrétien's minister of finance. At the official level, Canada's G8 participation has been led by the Prime Minister's group or the Foreign Affairs Deputy Minister and supported by a permanent and organized well-resourced office within Foreign Affairs (Kokotsis, 1999).

Notes

1. The document was indeed a government statement rather than one from foreign affairs and international trade, and these passages reflect the personal intervention of the Prime Minister himself.

2. These included the presence of a Canadian-hosted G7 Summit in Halifax four months later, the organizational co-location of the foreign policy reviewers and summit co-ordinators, and Chrétien's use of Canada's summit membership as an argument to prevail in a Quebec sovereignty referendum thought to be due one week after the Halifax event. See, in particular, the major theme of the Prime Minister's address on 10 February 1995, where he warned that an independent Quebec would lose its status as a member of the 'exclusive economic club' (Delacourt, 1995).

3. More specifically, the statement said of the G7: 'Most critical, because of the power concentrated there, is the role of the Group of Seven (G7) leading industrial democracies (Canada, US, Italy, Japan, Britain, Germany, France). The Halifax Summit, which Canada chairs, will be a key opportunity for Canada to exercise world leadership on issues on the international agenda' (DFAIT, 1995: 7). Canada's success in the world 'relies on our shared values, but is only possible because we are an influential nation, asserting our interests directly around the world, including at the highest tables reserved for the few, such as the Quadrilateral Group of the world's leading traders and the G7' (8); 'Canada can further its global interests better than any other

country through its active membership in key international groupings, for example, hosting the G7 Summit this year' (9); 'Canada is one of the major world trading powers, along with its key partners, the EU and Japan, all members with us in the G7, and the Quadrilateral Group. Our trading, investment and technology relationships are the most intense with these partners' (13): 'Canada's membership in the G7 provides a valuable opportunity to influence change in these (international economic and financial) institutions. The Government will chair Halifax Economic Summit discussions in June 1995 on the reform of international economic institutions such as the International Monetary Fund (IMF), the World Bank, and possibly other institutions. This review must address the evolving roles of these bodies as well as the relationship between them and the numerous agencies related to the UN. Elimination of duplication and competing mandates will also be a major Canadian objective consistent with our own resource constraints and fiscal strategy. We will pursue these goals in the Economic Summits and in other fora in the years ahead' (18); 'Canada has long pushed for more debt relief in fora such as the G7 and the Paris Club (the group of major international lender governments) for severely indebted low-income countries (SILICs), especially in sub-Saharan Africa. These efforts have recently paid off in the Paris Club, which has agreed to a higher level of debt relief on the whole stock of debt of eligible countries' (20).

4. Specifically, Canadian attempts to include rebuked South Africa in the final communiqué of the Venice Summit in June 1987 were not successful. For more recent analyses in this school, see David and Roussel (1998).

5. In Keating's view, 'the summit has clearly linked Canada with the policies being pursued by the other members of the club and has, in some areas, further distanced the country from the policies and activities of other middle powers' (197).

6. Canada's contribution can be charted against the three major clusters of roles that countries play in the G7/8. The first cluster is that of a supporter of US initiatives and the neo-liberal market policies demanded by the market in a globalizing age. The second cluster is that of mediator between the conflicting initiatives of other members, in support of a consensus that may bear no particular relevance to distinctively Canadian concerns. The third cluster is that of a leader which seeks and secures support from any and all summit members for distinctively Canadian preferences, interests, values, and visions of world order. The leadership cluster contains eight specific roles that run along a scale from four defensive roles through to their four offensive equivalents.

7. From the inception of the G7 the Canadian government, dominated by GATT-focused multilateralism, had resisted the creation of the plurilateral Trade Ministers' Quadrilateral Influential individuals within the US administration sought to exclude Canada from the new forum in retaliation for Canada's introduction of the National Energy Program in 1980–1.

8. Its involvement has contrasted sharply with equally committed but far less vigorous or vocal members such as Japan.

9. Definitive judgments on this point await a comprehensive review of the record of leaders discussions from all summit members for all summits, as national reporting is likely to overemphasize the statement of one's own leader, and different personal representatives have differing note-taking styles.

10. The logic is clear: the summit accords effective equality among members institutionally (given its status as a consensus forum) and as the membership becomes more equal in terms of capability. Any members and/or combination of members becomes valuable in forming the minimum winning coalition. Although the US remains the preferred partner on the grounds of capability level, it has been suggested that Japan, Germany, and Italy should become preferred partners of Canada, at the expense of the historic partners of the US, France, and Britain. On grounds of institutional leadership and equal collegial membership, France would join Japan, Germany, and Italy in increasingly becoming Canadian coalition partners over time.

11. This success on a political security subject reflected the logic of functionalism and Canada's historical issue-specific capability strengths in civil aviation. It represented a collective response against a common enemy to the G7 and broader society of states. It came at a time where the long established broadly multilateral UN organization—the International Civil Aviation Organization (ICAO)—with so many non-democratic liberation struggle supporters as members, had cleared failed to act.

12. This incremental political-securitization of the formal agenda and concluding commitments of the Summit during its first cycle took place only as the non UNSC P5 of German, Japan, Italy, and Canada, at the back end of the 'Summit "batting order"' served as hosts.

13. In the defence sphere, Canadian leadership was shown in the early, exceptionally large, dispatch of Canadian naval, air, and ground forces to assist the US coalition in Afghanistan and the Gulf. Canada extended its contribution in December with the deployment of long-range patrol aircraft, and again in January when it sent combat ground troops into the dangerous Khandahar front. The calculus behind Canada's investment was captured in foreign minister John Manley's memorable phrase, 'You can't sit at the G8 table and go to the washroom when the cheque comes.' As a contributor of forces to the American-led effort, Canada came in second after Britain. France and internally divided Germany moved slowly, and Italy, thanks to some unfortunate remarks by Berlusconi, placed itself outside the reliable fold. Japan found a niche in mobilizing funds to reconstruct Afghanistan.

14. The annual *Foreign Policy* rankings of country's according to their level of globalization regularly places Canada as the most globalized member of the G8. In 2002, Canada was the world's sixth most globalized country (after much smaller Ireland, Singapore, Switzerland, the Netherlands, and Finland), ahead of the US's 7th place ranking, as well as ahead of Britain in 12th, France in 15th, Germany in 18th, Italy in 25th, Japan in 29th, and Russia in 44th (and the leading G20 members of China in 57th, India in 61st). Canada's rank has risen from seventh in 2001 ('Measuring Globalization: The Global Top 20').

15. Canada was included in 1975 not primarily because the US wanted or needed another North American neighbour to balance the Europeans, and not because Gerald Ford had been a congressman from Michigan who liked his Canadian neighbours, but because Henry Kissinger knew that an oil- and resource-dependent America needed the first-tier capabilities of a foremost nation—Canada—within the new central governance club (von Reikhoff, 1974).

References

Artis, Michael, and Sylvia Ostry. 1988. *Summitry: The Medium and the Message*, Bissell Paper No. 3. Toronto: University of Toronto, Centre for International Studies.

Bayne, Nicholas. 2005. *Staying Together: The G8 Summit Confronts to 21st Century*. Aldershot: Ashgate.

———. 2003. 'Impressions of the Kananaskis Summit, 26–27 June 2002', pp. 229–39 in Michele Fratianni, Paolo Savona, and John Kirton, eds, *Sustaining Global Growth and Development: G7 and IMF Governance*. Aldershot: Ashgate.

———. 2000. *Hanging in There: The G7 and G8 Summit in Maturity and Renewal*. Aldershot: Ashgate.

Black, David. 2005. 'From Kananaskis to Gleneagles: Assessing Canadian "leadership" on Africa', *Behind the Headlines* 62 (May): 1–17.

Boehm, Peter. 1996. 'There Was a Summit in Halifax: Behind the Scenes at the 21st Birthday of the G7', *Bout de Papier* 13 (1): 5–7.

Cohn, Theodore H. 2002. *Governing Global Trade: International Institutions in Conflict and Convergence*. Aldershot: Ashgate.

Cooper, Andrew, Richard Higgott, and Kim Nossal. 1993. *Relocating Middle Powers: Australia and Canada in a Changing World Order*. Vancouver: UBC Press.

Dam, Kenneth. 2001. *The Rules of the Global Game: A*

New Look at U.S. International Economic Policy-making. Chicago: University of Chicago Press.

David, Charles-Philippe, and Stéphane Roussel. 1998. 'Middle Power Blues: Canadian International Security after the Cold War', *American Review of Canadian Studies* (Spring/Summer): 131–56.

Delacourt, Susan. 1995. 'Chrétien Uses Trade Gains to Win over Quebeckers', *Globe and Mail*, 11 February, 1.

Department of Foreign Affairs and International Trade. 1995. *Canada in the World: Government Statement*. Available at http://www.dfait-maeci.gc.ca/foreign_policy/cnd-world/menu-en.asp (accessed September 2004).

Dewitt, David, and John Kirton. 1983. *Canada as a Principal Power: A Study in International Politics and Foreign Policy*. Toronto: John Wiley.

Dobson, Wendy. 1994. 'Economic Policy Co-ordination Institutionalized: The G7 and the Future of the Bretton Woods Institutions', *Bretton Woods: Looking to the Future* (July): C143–8.

———. 1991. *Economic Policy Coordination: Requiem or Prologue? Policy Analyses in International Economics, Vol. 30*. Washington DC: Institute for International Economics.

———. 1991a. 'Rethinking the G7: A New World Coordination Process', *International Economic Insights* 2 (March/April): 34–5.

Fowler, Robert. 2003. 'Canadian Leadership and the Kananaskis G8 Summit: Toward a Less Self-Centered Policy', pp. 219–41 in David Carment, Fen Hampson, and Norman Hillmer, eds, *Coping with the American Colossus: Canada Among Nations 2003*. Don Mills, ON: Oxford University Press.

G8 Research Group. 2003. 'From Kananaskis to Evian: The 2003 Compliance Report'. Available at http://www.g8.utoronto.ca/evaluations/2003compliance (accessed September 2004).

———. 2001. 'The 2001 G8 Compliance Report'. Available at http://www.g8.utoronto.ca/evaluations/2001compliance (accessed September 2004).

Gotlieb, Allan. 1978 [1981]. 'The Western Economic Summit', *Canada, Department of External Affairs. Statements and Speeches, No. 81/13*. Ottawa.

Gray, John. 2003. *Paul Martin: The Power of Ambition*. Toronto: Key Porter.

Hajnal, Peter. 1989. *The Seven Power Summit: Documents from the Summits of Industrialized Countries, 1975–1989*. Krause International: New York.

Haynal, George. 2005. 'Summitry and Governance: The Case for a G-XX', pp. 261–74 in David Carment, et al., eds, *Canada Among Nations 2004: Setting Priorities Straight*. Montreal: McGill-Queen's University Press.

Heinbecker, Paul, and Rob McRae. 2001. 'Case Study: The Kosovo Air Campaign', pp. 122–33 in Rob McRae and Don Hubert, eds, *Human Security and the New Diplomacy*. Montreal: McGill-Queen's University Press.

Helleiner, Gerald. 1994. 'Globalization and Fragmentation in the International Economy', *Canadian Foreign Policy* 3 (Winter): 101.

Keating, Thomas. 1993. *Canada and World Order: The Multilateralist Tradition in Canadian Foreign Policy*. Toronto: McClelland and Stewart.

Kirton, John. 2005. 'Adjusting America: Canadian Expectations and Strategies for the Second Bush Presidency', in Samuel Cherian, ed., *Policy Expectations in the Second Bush Presidency*. Delhi, India: Observer Research Foundation.

———. 2005a. 'Toward Multilateral Reform: The G20's Contribution', pp. 141–68 in John English, Ramesh Thakur, and Andrew Cooper, eds, *Reforming from the Top: A Leaders' 20 Summit*. Tokyo: United Nations University Press.

———. 2004. 'After Westphalia: Security and Freedom in the G8's Global Governance', in Thomas Noetzel and Marika Lerch, eds, *Security and Freedom: Foreign Policy, Domestic Politics and Political Theory Perspectives*. Baden: Nomos.

———. 2002. 'Canada as a Principal Summit Power: G7/8 Concert Diplomacy from Halifax 1995 to Kananaskis 2002', pp. 209–32 in Norman Hillmer and Maureen Molot, eds, *A Fading Power: Canada Among Nations 2002*. Don Mills, ON: Oxford University Press.

———. 2001 'The G20: Representativeness, Effectiveness and Leadership in Global Governance', pp. 143–72 in John Kirton, Joseph Daniels, and Andreas Freytag, eds, *Guiding Global Order: G8*

Governance in the Twenty-First Century. Aldershot: Ashgate.

———. 2000. 'The Dynamics of G7 Leadership in Crisis Response and System Reconstruction', pp. 65–94 in Karl Kaiser, John Kirton, and Joseph Daniels, eds, *Shaping a New International Financial System: Challenges of Governance in a Globalizing World*. Aldershot: Ashgate.

———. 2000a. 'The G8, the United Nations and Global Peace and Security Governance', in Winrich Kuhne with Jochen Prantl, eds, *The Security Council and the G8 in the New Millennium: Who Is in Charge of International Peace and Security?* Berlin: Stiftung Wissenschaft und Politik.

———. 1999. 'Canada as a Principal Financial Power: G7 and IMF Diplomacy in the Crisis of 1997–9', *International Journal* 54 (Autumn): 603–24. Available at http://www.g8.utoronto.ca/scholar/kirton199902 (accessed September 2004).

———. 1998. 'The Emerging Pacific Partnership: Japan, Canada and the United States at the G7 Summit', pp. 292–314 in Michael Fry, John Kirton, and Mitsuru Kurosawa, eds, *The North Pacific Triangle: The United States, Japan and Canada at Century's End*. Toronto: University of Toronto Press.

Kirton, John, and Ella Kokotsis. 2004. 'Keeping Faith with Africa: Assessing Compliance with the G8's Commitments at Kananskis and Evian', in Princeton Lyman and Robert Browne, eds, *Freedom, Prosperity and Security: The G8 Partnership with Africa*. New York: Council on Foreign Relations.

———. 2003. 'The G7/8 Contribution at Kananaskis and Beyond', pp. 207–28 in Michele Fratiani, Paolo Savona, and John Kirton, eds, *Sustaining Global Growth and Development: G7 and IMF Governance*. Aldershot: Ashgate.

Kirton, John, and George M. von Furstenberg, eds. 2001. *New Directions in Global Economic Governance: Managing Globalisation in the Twenty-First Century*. Aldershot: Ashgate.

Kirton, John, and Junichi Takase, eds. 2002. *New Directions in Global Political Governance: The G8 and International Order in the Twenty-First Century*. Aldershot: Ashgate.

Kirton, John, and Radoslava Stefanova, eds. 2003. *The G8, the United Nations and Conflict Prevention*. Aldershot: Ashgate.

Kirton, John, Joseph Daniels, and Andreas Freytag, eds. 2001. *Guiding Global Order: G8 Governance in the Twenty-First Century*. Aldershot: Ashgate.

Kokotsis, Eleanore. 1999. *Keeping International Commitments: Compliance, Credibility and the G7, 1988–1995*. New York: Garland.

Langdon, Steven. 2003. 'NEPAD and the Renaissance of Africa', pp. 242–55 in David Carment, Fen Hampson, and Norman Hillmer, eds, *Coping with the American Colossus: Canada Among Nations 2003*. Don Mills, ON: Oxford University Press.

Lovbraek, A. 1990. 'International Reform and the Like Minded Countries in the North–South Dialogue 1975–1985', in Cranford Pratt, ed., *Middle Power Internationalism*. Montreal and Kingston: McGill-Queen's University Press.

Macmillan, Charles, and Louis Delvoie. 1999. 'Taming the South Asian Nuclear Tiger: Causes, Consequences and Canadian Responses', pp. 233–52 in Fen Hampson, Michael Hart, and Martin Rudner, eds, *Canada Among Nations 1999: A Big League Player?* Don Mills, ON: Oxford University Press.

Nossal, Kim Richard. 1998 'Pinchpenny Diplomacy: The Decline of "Good International Citizenship" in Canadian Foreign Policy', *International Journal* 54 (Winter): 88–105.

Ostry, Sylvia 1986. *International Economic Policy Co-ordination, Chatham House Papers, Vol. 30*. London and New York: Routledge & Kegan Paul.

Ostry, Sylvia, et al. 1991. *The Summit Process and Collective Security: Future Responsibility Sharing*. Washington DC: Group of Thirty.

Smith, Heather. 1995. 'Seeking Certainty and Finding None: Reflections on the 1994 Canadian Foreign Policy Review', *Canadian Foreign Policy* 3 (Spring): 117–24.

Stairs, Denis. 1974. *The Diplomacy of Constraint: Canada, the Korean War and the United States*. Toronto: University of Toronto Press.

von Furstenberg, George, and Joseph Daniels. 1991. 'Policy Undertakings by the Seven "Summit" Countries: Ascertaining the Degree of Compliance', *Carnegie-Rochester Conference Series on Public Policy*

35 (1991): 297.

Von Reikhoff, Harald. 1974. 'The Natural Resource Element in Global Power Relationships', *International Perspectives* (September–October): 18–22.

Wood, Bernard. 1988. 'Critical Choices', pp. 134–7 in John Holmes and John Kirton, eds, *Canada and the New Internationalism*. Toronto: Canadian Institute of International Affairs.

19

Canada and the Negotiation Over Investment Rules at the WTO

Elizabeth Smythe

Introduction

Foreign direct investment (FDI) and foreign ownership have been sensitive issues in Canada for much of our post-war history. Surges in public concern have often coincided with high profile takeovers of Canadian corporations by foreign (often US, but more recently Chinese) firms.[1] The investment issue, like trade, has been tied to concerns about our sovereignty as a nation. Changes since the 1980s have altered the landscape for Canadian policy on FDI and, more recently, on the negotiation of international rules designed to protect foreign investments. Nowhere is this more clearly reflected than in Canadian policies regarding the negotiation of investment rules at the World Trade Organization (WTO). Canada's failed efforts to push the negotiation of a multilateral investment agreement onto the WTO agenda illustrates the extent to which official thinking on FDI, similarly to that about bilateral trade, has been transformed. The WTO case reflects both the evolving nature of Canadian international economic policy and the challenges in pursuing these interests within the context of the changing membership of the WTO. Further the case raises questions about whose interests these efforts at

the WTO were intended to serve given that an international investment agreement was one of the most controversial and divisive issues facing the WTO in recent years.

Along with disagreements on agriculture, divisions over the so-called 'Singapore issues', which include investment, are widely seen as having contributed to the failure of fifth World Trade Organization ministerial meeting in Cancún Mexico in 2003.[2] A proposal to launch negotiations on an investment agreement was so controversial that discussion of it was finally dropped altogether from the WTO agenda in July 2004; only one of the four Singapore issues, trade facilitation, went forward as part of the Doha Round. The European Commission, negotiator for the EU, is often blamed for pushing the Singapore issues, particularly the issue of investment.[3] With the EU identified as the main *demandeur* little attention has been paid to Canada's role in trying to add the investment issue to the WTO negotiating agenda. In fact, Canada was one of the most active advocates of launching negotiations on investment rules at the WTO over the seven-year period of discussions. Moreover, Canada continued to argue for the inclusion of investment up to the meeting at Cancún, even as its trade minister,

Pierre Pettigrew, was acting as a neutral facilitator on the Singapore issues at the meeting itself.

Observers might argue that negotiating an investment agreement at the WTO makes sense given Canada's support for multilateral institutions, trade rules, and the WTO, in particular. As a net exporter of foreign direct investment since 1997 it is in Canada's interests to pursue a set of rules designed to enhance access for Canadian investors to other markets and protect those investments against arbitrary or discriminatory treatment by host states.[4] There are reasons, however, to question why Canada continued to pursue these negotiations at the WTO.

It had been clear from the founding of the WTO that the issue was divisive. This fact was reflected in the compromise forged in Singapore in 1996 to launch a further study of, but not negotiations for, an investment agreement. Second, the negotiations of the Multilateral Agreement on Investment (MAI), and the cases launched under the investment chapter (Chapter 11) of the North American Free Trade Agreement (NAFTA) had, by 1997, proven to be controversial in Canada. Even the bilateral imperative of maintaining good relations with the United States did not necessitate pushing an investment agreement at the WTO; even Canada's foremost trading partner was not vigorously pursuing this issue at the multilateral level. Indeed at various points during this seven-year project the United States either actively opposed it as a sinister EU plot to avoid future movement on agriculture—a high priority issue for Canada—or saw the effort as laudable but unlikely to be successfully resolved.[5] Even the business community in Canada has waxed and waned about the priority placed on investment. More puzzling was Canada's continued support for negotiations even after a growing number of developing countries made their opposition known and continued to strengthen it during the run up to Cancún.[6]

This chapter examines why Canada pushed for the negotiation of investment rules at the WTO and how it did so. It identifies the sources of Canada's interest in launching investment negotiations and the ideas about the benefits of such rules that Canadian officials employed to persuade WTO members. The case study is useful for several reasons. Ideas and arguments were a key element of the strategy Canada and others employed to educate and persuade reluctant countries to negotiate. The seven-year period when Canada was actively engaged was a period of major learning for Canadian officials about investment agreements. Therefore, the case sheds light on how Canada's interests altered depending on the negotiating forum and the country's negotiating partners.

We begin with a discussion of Canada's investment interests and how they have been re-defined over the past 25 years. This is followed by a description of Canada's role in the creation of the Working Group on Trade and Investment (WGTI) at the WTO in 1996 and follows Canadian activity in the group up to the Doha Declaration in 2001. The third section examines Canada's intensified efforts, post-Doha, to persuade WTO members to launch negotiations at Cancún in September 2003—an effort which ultimately failed. The conclusion assesses Canada's role and what that role reflects about the interests and ideas on investment that have shaped the position Canada put forward at the WTO. Despite being a capital exporter and desiring a high level of investment protection for Canadian investors, by the end of this seven-year effort Canadian officials had to scale back their ambitions, a reflection of the experience of NAFTA's investment rules and the implications for the capacity of host states to regulate the public interest and the growing controversy over investment rules both within and outside the WTO.

Canada's Evolving Investment Interests: From Screening to Protecting Investors

Interests usually imply a material basis for action or policy related to the benefit or gain an actor will derive. In the case of foreign direct investment policies and international investment agreements it might seem as though Canada's interests are shaped by economic considerations. In particular, the nature of investment flows and the interests of influential domestic actors, standing to gain or lose depending on the nature of investment rules, are worth consideration. In short, Canada's profile regarding foreign direct investment and the interests of powerful economic actors provide a key to understanding the source of Canadian negotiators' interests in investment rules.

For much of the postwar period Canada was a major capital importer. This resulted in high levels of foreign (largely US-based) ownership in major sectors of the economy, a national debate about FDI, and a series of policies from the late 1960s to manage incoming FDI. While a small number of sectors were protected from foreign ownership, the majority of policies tried to manage incoming FDI by providing for conditional market access to foreign investors in return for commitments ensuring local economic benefits— often called performance requirements—and backward linkages to the domestic economy. From the mid-1970s to the mid-1980s the Foreign Investment Review Agency (FIRA) handled negotiations with investors.

Internal and external pressures in the 1980s combined to undermine this definition of Canada's investment interests. The US administration, and powerful American corporations, became increasingly hostile to Canadian FDI policies, even as Canada was becoming more dependent on the United States as an export market. Some provinces and Canadian business interests also became highly critical of the policy. Federal officials had concluded, even before a change of government in 1984, that bargaining with foreign investors in return for according them market access was no longer viable because it put secure access to the US market—the key to economic growth—at risk. Moreover, FDI was seen as necessary for economic growth. Screening put Canada at a further disadvantage because international competition for investment, as many economies

liberalized, was intensifying.[7] Continued high levels of foreign ownership and the persistence of a nationalist critique, however, meant that wholesale abandonment of the policies was also potentially costly.

Canada's changing pattern of investment flows has also been significant in re-defining its interests in investment rules. Both inward and outward FDI increased rapidly in the late 1990s, outpacing trade, but the balance shifted as outward foreign direct investment began growing more rapidly. By 1997 Canada exported more FDI than it imported, making it a net capital exporter (see Figure 19.1). Initially the United States was the overwhelming destination for outward FDI, followed by other Organization of Economic Cooperation and Development (OECD) economies. At the same time Canada remains host to a large stock of foreign direct investment ($368 billion in 2004) of which about two thirds is US-based.[8] Therefore, in its relationship with the United States, Canada is still a capital importer.

A second important change has been in the destination of outward FDI. By 2003 $191 billion, just less than half of the $434.4 billion stock of Canadian FDI was located in the United States, which, along with the rest of the OECD, accounts for about 75 per cent. As Figure 19.2 indicates, Canadian FDI in non-OECD countries has gone from insignificance two decades ago to very rapid growth in recent years.

In some regions, such as Latin America, Canadian FDI more than doubled, increasing from 8.7 per cent to 18.5 per cent of outward FDI between 1988 and 1999. The top non-OECD destinations for Canadian FDI shown in Table 19.1 indicate that much of this investment is concentrated in a very few sectors, tied to offshore financial centres, tax havens, or resource sectors.

Given the rapid growth of outward FDI, negotiating rules that would protect Canadian investment abroad would appear to be in Canada's interests. At the same time, however, a large proportion of outward, and the majority of inward, FDI is with our most significant trading partner,

Figure 19.1   Trends in Foreign Investment, 1990–2004

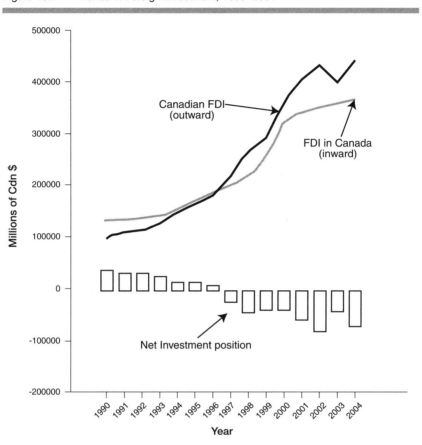

Source: *State of Trade* (2005); Statistics Canada, *Canada's International Investment Position* (Ottawa: 2005)

the United States. Clearly the complex nature of integrated global production today and the ebbs and flows of highly mobile capital, often sensitive to exchange and interest rates, require some way to attach meaning and significance to the changing flows. To fully understand how investment interests are defined we need to look at both ideas about investment and the institutional context in which negotiations take place. A review indicates that Canada's definition of its investment interests, and thus international policies and positions on investment rules, have involved a complex mix of what trade negotiators call offensive and defensive interests.[9]

In the 1970s Canada sought to preserve its ability to screen and regulate FDI in the face of rules designed to limit host state policy discretion. When developing countries called for a New International Economic Order at the United Nations (UN) in the early 1970s, which included the negotiation of a Code of Conduct for Transnational Corporations, the United States tried to counter it by establishing norms of national treatment and high levels of protection for foreign investors. This was facilitated through the negotiation of the OECD's Declaration on International Investment and Multinational Enterprises in 1975, which required host states to

Figure 19.2   Canadian FDI in Developing Countries as a Percentage of Total
Canadian FDI, 1950–2000

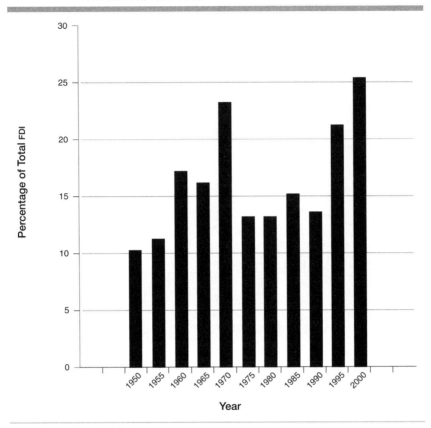

Source: *State of Trade* (2005), 47.

afford national treatment to foreign investors. At the OECD Canada was on the defensive, seeking to balance the right of a host state to regulate incoming FDI with fair and non-discriminatory treatment of foreign investors; Canada fought hard to weaken the agreement or opt out.[10] While the US was unable to attain a binding agreement at the OECD, the organization has since become an important institution in furthering norms of national treatment and transparency through its Committee on Investment and Multinational Enterprise. This has contributed to the de-legitimization of host state regulation of incoming FDI.

Canadian officials in the 1980s viewed inflows of FDI as both necessary to ensure economic growth and global competitiveness, and complementary to trade. No longer driven by high tariffs, Canada—as a host state—would have to compete aggressively for FDI by providing an attractive investment climate. The 'right' climate was invariably seen by large corporate interests as one with low taxes, limited state regulation, and liberalized access for foreign investors. Officials increasingly saw enhanced market access, national treatment of foreign investors, and transparent regulation as important norms in the treatment of foreign investors; any deviations from these norms were considered necessary evils. But binding codes of corporate conduct, which implied an active role for states or international organizations in intervening in markets, were not seen as a legitimate role for government. Instead, states should encourage firms to develop voluntary norms similar to the OECD's Guidelines on Multinational Enterprises, although these guidelines have remained weak in terms of enforceability.

Investment flows were also viewed as a report card on the Canadian economy, similar to the way in which the changing values of the Canadian dollar vis-à-vis the US dollar are perceived. Inflows of FDI and Canada's share of global investment FDI inflows were interpreted as a measure of the attractiveness of the Canadian economy. Canada's attractiveness as a location for FDI had to be maintained and promoted. Outward FDI was negatively perceived as a reflection on the country's attractiveness as an investment location. Protection of outward FDI was, therefore, less of a priority.

Canada's policy of investment screening, although much more limited by 1985, was still a target for the United States in bilateral trade negotiations, partly because of an American strategy of using bilateral agreements to establish norms that it wished to see embodied later in multilateral agreements. US demands reached their high water mark with the negotiation of Chapter 11 of NAFTA in 1993.[11] Canada's NAFTA concerns were not driven by a desire to protect the limited Canadian investments in Mexico but rather, as the trade minister indicated in 1992, 'to ensure that Canada remained an attractive location for investors wishing to serve the North American market'.[12]

Within multilateral organizations, the US sought to limit host state performance requirements imposed on foreign investors at the General Agreement on Tariffs and Trade (GATT) first by lodging a complaint against FIRA and then by the negotiation of Trade-Related Investment Measures (TRIMs) in the Uruguay Round. Because of the determined opposition of a number of developing countries, and more pressing US priorities, this agreement yielded limited results. At the GATT Canada was positioned between the two

Table 19.1   Top 15 non-OECD Destinations for Canadian FDI, on average, from 1999–2003

Country	CFDI in Millions of $
Barbados	23,136
Bermuda	9,823
Bahamas	7,738
Cayman Islands	6,827
Hungary	6,807
Brazil	6,557
Chile	5,704
Argentina	4,924
Singapore	3,730
Indonesia	3,668
Mexico	3,293
Hong Kong	3,134
Peru	1,924
Thailand	918
South Korea	821

Source: DFAIT, *State of Trade*, 2005.

main sides and worked largely to ensure that any agreement did not impinge on existing investment policies and practices. The US then set its sights on a NAFTA-like 'high standards' multilateral investment agreement that would afford foreign investors strong protection against host state regulations to be negotiated at the OECD—the ill-fated MAI.

In the 1990s outflows of Canadian FDI increased, especially on the part of small and medium-sized firms. Outward FDI began to be viewed less negatively as a necessary aspect of maintaining Canada's competitiveness in increasingly globalized systems of production. Multinational firms had been encouraged to accord global product mandates to their Canadian subsidiaries in the 1980s as a way of preserving local production. By the late 1990s officials were referring to 'global value chains' whereby whole processes of production are broken down and

Table 19.2	Foreign Investment Protection Agreements
Country	Date Signed
Armenia	1999
Argentina	1993
Barbados	1997
Costa Rica	1999
Croatia	2001
Czech Rep.	1992
Ecuador	1997
Egypt	1997
*El Salvador	1997
Hungary	1993
Latvia	1995
Lebanon	1999
Panama	1998
Peru	2005
Philippines	1996
Poland	1990
Romania	1997
Russia (USSR)	1991
*South Africa	1995
Thailand	1998
Trinidad and Tobago	1996
Uruguay	1999
Venezuela	1998

* Agreements signed but not in force.

shared, either within a firm or among a number of firms with transnational production process; a process that information and communication technology facilitated.

By the 1990s it was clear that Canadian negotiators were interested in protecting outward investment. The question remained as to how and where to negotiate rules that would achieve the goal? Canada had, because of its growing dependence on the US market, engaged in bilateral negotiations first to try to secure access to that market and then trilaterally in NAFTA to preserve access

and ensure that Canada remained an attractive investment location on the continent. In both cases the US played the role of *demandeur* on investment rules. Canadian foreign policy is traditionally perceived as biased toward the multilateral approach partly because the continental relationship is so asymmetrical. However, Canada's experience in the OECD in 1975 does not suggest that a multilateral organization in and of itself can somehow offset continental asymmetries. More important, quite clearly, is the nature of the organization's membership, the processes of decision-making, and the capacity—once rules are made—to be enforced. These aspects shaped Canada's preference about where rules facilitating and protecting FDI would be negotiated.

One option to protect non-OECD investment was to negotiate bilateral agreements with states hosting Canadian FDI following the pattern of the United States and Germany, which were important exporters of capital. In 1991 Canada began such a program, followed by a second wave in 1995. All these agreements were with host developing economies and those in transition in Eastern Europe to provide protection and legal recourse for Canadian investors abroad. Given the growth of non-OECD outward investment, this might be seen to be a logical response to changing interests. But the list of countries with which Canada has signed FIPAs bares little direct relationship to the top 15 non-OECD destinations of Canadian FDI listed above. Only five of these countries, Barbados, Argentina, Hungary, Thailand, and most recently, Peru, have investments covered under FIPA's while Mexico, Chile, and Costa Rica are covered under trade agreements with Canada. Despite efforts in 1998 to more clearly identify Canada's interests and priorities for FIPA's based on current investment flows, future potential investment opportunities, and business demands, FIPA's are also driven by requests from partner countries seeking to show a welcoming face to foreign investors, assuage multilateral institutions such as the World Bank, or as a part of 'photo op' diplomacy and agreements for a visiting prime minister to sign.[13]

Canada's 2005 international market access priorities, outlined in *Opening Doors to the World*, included China—which has now replaced Japan as Canada's second largest bilateral trading partner—India, and Brazil. Canada is currently negotiating FIPA's with China and India. Bilateral talks with Brazil are ongoing in the 'context of the [Free Trade Area of the Americas] FTAA'. Clearly there is no one-to-one relationship between the negotiation of agreements and investment patterns.[14] Instead, a complex mixture of economic and political interests and bilateral negotiations play a role. FIPA's clearly cover a limited range of countries and are not broadly integrated with trade interests. A more multilateral approach would address these limitations. For Canadian officials the preferred forum for such an agreement has always been the World Trade Organization, but making that case has also been complicated by the preferences of the United States; for much of the post-war period the US has been the key *demandeur* for enhanced protection of foreign investors.

Canada and the Working Group on Trade and Investment at the WTO

Efforts to launch investment negotiations at the WTO in 1996 must be seen within the context of the debate over the US initiative to negotiate a binding MAI within the OECD. Canada had not been particularly supportive of the OECD[15] as the best venue to negotiate investment rules, and Canada's trade minister made this clear at the OECD ministerial meeting in 1998:

> To be effective and beneficial any eventual investment agreement must be truly multilateral. Consequently, the MAI process at the OECD must remain open to non-members and, more importantly the MAI's ultimate home should be the WTO.[16]

The preference for the WTO related to its broader coverage of non-OECD countries where Canadian FDI was growing, its credentials as a trade negotiating forum (Canadian officials saw trade and investment as tightly linked), and its strengthened dispute resolution capacity. However, Canada did not oppose the OECD effort; there was potential that the effort could be a model for a broader multilateral effort. Nor did Canada give up the idea of investment rules at the WTO. In fact Canada was one of several WTO members, along with the European Commission and Japan, who worked to build a consensus to negotiate investment for the first WTO ministerial meeting in Singapore in December 1996. Efforts from the Fall of 1995 included informal discussions with WTO delegates in Geneva, public endorsement of the idea by EU Trade Commissioner Leon Brittan,[17] and a Canadian-hosted meeting with sixteen middle-sized countries where the issue was raised.[18] The United States remained opposed to WTO negotiations because the completion of an MAI at the OECD was the priority. Given the limits of the TRIMs negotiated in the Uruguay Round, the US was pessimistic about the prospects at the WTO; however, despite US opposition, Canada, the EU, and Japan persisted.

Canada presented a proposal in April 1996 to begin an educative work program at the WTO that did not presuppose future negotiations. The strategy simply reflected recognition that any immediate attempt to launch negotiations was doomed to failure. Some developing countries, such as India and Tanzania, were opposed and they questioned the need to undertake research in an organization like the WTO. Others, such as Brazil and Mexico, were somewhat more supportive.[19] Eventually the US also supported the proposal, largely for its educative value, but insisted at a later Quad trade ministers meeting that Canada, the EU, and Japan reaffirm their support for the negotiation of the MAI at the OECD.[20] From the US perspective, any effort to push investment at the WTO would fail and risked building intransigence to future investment negotiations among a number of countries. The Director-General Renato Ruggiero and the Secretariat of the WTO also supported the inclusion of investment in a WTO work program.

India, in contrast, spearheaded efforts to stop

the inclusion of both investment and a number of other new issues on the WTO Singapore agenda and to forge a developing country consensus by hosting a meeting of 14 countries in September 1996 which was critical of the idea of an MAI, raised the question of the role of the United Nations Conference on Trade and Development (UNCTAD), which also had a mandate to study the issue of FDI and pointed out the fact that the TRIMs agreement already called for a review in 1999–2000. No consensus was achieved among WTO delegates on the investment issue prior to the Singapore meeting; a last minute compromise was forged at the meeting itself.

The Singapore declaration established a working group to examine the relationship between trade and investment, the work of which 'shall not prejudice whether negotiations will be initiated in the future'. The working group was to be an 'educative' process not intended to seek or generate a consensus vis-à-vis future negotiation and to operate without prejudice to any future decisions regarding negotiations.[21] However members' preferences regarding future negotiations coloured their activities within the working group. For the European Commission, Japan, Canada, and a number of other states, the idea was to use the working group to begin the process of building consensus on the need for investment to be included on the agenda of a future round of negotiations. The US acquiesced with the working group only to the extent that the process, as educative, allowed them to proselytize on the benefits of investment and liberalization.

The WGTI began meeting in June 1997 under the chairmanship of the Thai Ambassador with meetings every other month. A checklist of issues was agreed upon and included four aspects:

1. Implications of the relationship between trade and investment for development and economic growth.
2. The economic relationship between trade and investment.
3. A stocktaking and analysis of existing

international instruments dealing with investment.
4. Based on this research an assessment of the 'gaps' in existing instruments and the advantages of multilateral over regional or bilateral rules.

Canada presented a written submission on December 1997 that was designed to make a case under items 3 and 4, above, for the need to negotiate a new set of rules based on identified gaps in existing rules. It outlined experiences with FIPAs and NAFTA, both of which included provisions not covered by the WTO framework agreements and, most importantly, provided 'guarantees of protection for our investors in their operations abroad and for foreign investors coming into Canada'.[22] These agreements, Canada claimed, provided more transparency and thus certainty for investors. A particular source of pride was that 'investor–state dispute settlement mechanisms are also central elements of these agreements and together with state-to-state dispute settlement, increase the effectiveness and enforceability of these agreements'. In contrast, as the submission pointed out, the TRIMs agreement only covered a limited range of trade-related performance requirements while the General Agreement on Trade in Services (GATS), which touched on investment as one of four modes for delivering services, provided no investor protection for established firms. Canada argued a focus on 'investment rights and obligations [to] deepen trade agreements' and offered a more unified set of consistent rules than any bilateral investment treaties. At no time in the six years to follow did Canada outline any obligations of foreign investors in host countries beyond a firm's obligation to obey domestic laws. The focus was on the need to provide security to investors.

The European Commission, similar to Canada, focused on the growth and significance of FDI in the global economy, the growth of intra-firm trade, and the 'current patchwork of rules'. The submission pointed out the fact that the WTO already had investment on its agenda as a result of the GATS and the TRIMs and that this forum was in the best position to 'level the playing field' so that small and medium enterprises were more willing and able to undertake the risk of FDI. In addition to Canada, the EU, and Japan, those supporting the need for new multilateral rules in 1997 included Hong Kong, Switzerland, Korea, Brazil, and Mexico.

On the other side was India—by far the strongest opponent of negotiations—supported by Pakistan, Egypt, Morocco, Cuba, and the Association of Southeast Asian Nations (ASEAN) group. India's approach was to remind members of the purely educational and non-prejudicial role of the Working Group and to argue that the 'development perspective should be all-pervasive'.[23] A list of twelve elements that should be the focus of study was proposed, including 'the business practices and corporate strategies of transnational corporations, the interrelationship between mobility of capital and mobility of labour, and the impact of FDI on development'. Other opponents pointed to particular problems with FDI, or to the fact that many of them already had numerous Bilateral Investment Treaties, which provided protection to foreign firms, once established, and which appeared to be operating well.

After eighteen months only a few areas of consensus in the WGTI had been identified, including the idea that FDI could provide benefits for economic development and that trade and investment were closely linked. There was no agreement on the issue of existing agreements and the need for new rules. Deadlines resulted in a disagreement over the one concrete issue about which the group had to make a decision. Opponents of investment negotiations were quite happy to see the working group continue far into the future while proponents sought closure, which would force back a conclusion until mid-1999, leading up to the late fall ministerial where a decision on a WTO negotiating agenda would be taken. Unable to reach any consensus the group left the matter to be decided by the General Council of the WTO. The WGTI con-

tinued to meet throughout 1999 as a result of an extension of their mandate. External events had an impact on discussions, however, and directly affected Canada.

The first event was the controversy and ultimate collapse of OECD negotiations on the MAI in December 1998. On the one hand Canadian officials hoped the low-key talks of the WGTI at the WTO would allow them to dodge the 'flak'. On the other hand the failure of 'like-minded' OECD members to agree on these issues provided support to opponents of investment rules within the WTO. Outside the halls in Geneva however, the failure of the MAI also meant that the trans-national coalition of critics of the MAI—which included a number of Canadian, labour, environmental, cultural, and other groups—would now turn their full attention to the WTO and the upcoming meeting in Seattle which would attempt to launch a new round of negotiations including those on investment rules. The MAI also provided Canadian officials with a lesson on the need to consult more broadly with groups beyond the traditional business and producer interests traditionally seen to have a stake in trade agreements.

A second series of events were what might be described as the unforeseen consequences of Chapter 11 of NAFTA and the ammunition it provided critics of strong standards of investment protection. By March 1999, US investors had filed four cases against the Canadian government under Chapter 11 of NAFTA, the first being the Ethyl case filed on 15 April 1997. The Virginia-based company initiated a claim under the investor–state dispute provision of that chapter of NAFTA, arguing that a Canadian law banning imports of the gasoline additive MMT, for environmental reasons, was tantamount to expropriation of their assets and claimed compensation from Canada.[24] Since that time even more cases have been filed against the other NAFTA partners and led to further attempts by officials of the three countries to address the problem. More pertinent is Chapter 11's impact on the proposals Canada put forward at the WTO and its negotiating position. As one developing country delegate indicated, by 1999 everyone knew about Chapter 11![25]

The failure of the Seattle Ministerial in December 1999 also had an impact on the work of the WGTI and Canada's zeal for investment agreements. The WGTI largely 'spun its wheels' and Canadian officials took a low profile on investment issues both at the WTO and elsewhere, and providing no written submissions to the WGTI in 1999 and 2000 although they did participate in discussions. A similar situation prevailed outside the WTO. Despite having been enthusiastic about the inclusion of investment rules at the newly launched FTAA negotiations in 1998 and clearly seeing an opportunity to secure better investment protection for the rapidly growing stock of Canadian FDI in Latin America, Canada put forward no substantive proposals on investment until August 2001 and then the proposals related only to the concept of 'Minimum Standard of Treatment'.[26]

At the WGTI the emphasis had begun to change in recognition of the increasingly dissatisfied voices of developing countries. The extent to which investment rules would limit the 'policy space', which developing countries needed, became a focus as a result of UNCTAD representatives who presented their work on the concept of 'policy space for development' and the need for flexibility, and some of the options to achieve it within the context of investment rules and agreements. Increasingly opponents of negotiations, such as India, picked up the concept.

Under the mandate of the Singapore Declaration and its own terms of reference, UNCTAD had a clearly defined role in the WGTI in providing research on FDI and assisting developing countries in both negotiating and assessing the implications of investment rules and agreements. UNCTAD officials attended all WGTI meetings and provided informal briefings to a group of developing countries outside the group.

By early 2001 it was clear that the *demandeurs* were going to have to make a compelling case about the relationship between FDI and development if they had any hope of persuading a suffi-cient core of developing countries of the need to negotiate an investment agreement. A strategy appeared to be emerging. First the proponents of negotiations would have to justify the need for multilateral rules by showing a positive relationship between the existence of investment rules that afforded security and an increased inflow of FDI; there was already consensus in the group that FDI could provide benefits. Second, *demandeurs* would need to address the question of policy space and flexibility so that developing countries, especially the least developed, could sequence and pace implementing new obligations of market access or national treatment to meet their own unique development needs. Third, *demandeurs* would need to address the reality that many developing countries were largely marginal to the discussions on FDI in the WGTI and lacked sufficient capacity to engage in ongoing negotiations on agriculture and services, never mind taking on the new Singapore issues, especially with the complexity of something like investment rules.

Thus for Canada and other proponents the challenge was to portray their demands for rules to more fully protect investors in a more development-oriented way. In Canada's case it began with a submission in March 2001, which tried to show a link between host state regulation and investment flows.[27] To make the case that host state regulation of foreign investors was discouraging FDI, Industry Canada and the Canadian Chamber of Commerce jointly funded a study and presented the results to the WGTI. Surveying 71 firms it pointed to 110 specific restrictions affecting investment, primarily in non-OECD countries, and that in over 40 per cent of the cases these restrictions had resulted in decisions to either scale back or cancel investments. The EU followed up with a submission in May that admitted investment rules alone would not ensure FDI flows and that some developing countries would need assistance to develop both an enabling environment for FDI as well as assistance to increase their ability to 'negotiate effectively'. The submission proposed an assessment of member needs and development of technical assistance programs to be funded by WTO members.

On the issue of flexibility, Canada and other proponents recognized that the model of a 'top-down' NAFTA/MAI-type of agreement, which involved a high level of commitment to standards of national treatment and market access across the board, was unacceptable; alternatives would have to be offered. The answer, embraced by investment proponents, was the model of a bottom-up, positive list approach of the General Agreement on Trade in Services.

This re-focused effort of proponents to forge a new group consensus on the need to negotiate rules based on a development rationale required firm timelines for decisions on launching negotiations and limiting and isolating strong opponents in the process. In the latter effort the European Union played the leading role. A role that, it could be argued, turned out to be more costly than anticipated.

The Ministerial meeting in Doha, Qatar, in November 2001 involved many decision-making procedures for which the WTO has been criticized including non-transparent processes, chair's texts that did not appear to fairly reflect the range of opinions expressed by members and late night negotiating sessions.[28] In the EU's case it included arm-twisting of a number of developing-country delegates. With the aid of the United States, the EU was successful in isolating India and obtaining wording on the Singapore issues which reflected the position of the *demandeurs* including, in the case of investment, a more specific mandate for the working group reflected in the Doha Declaration. Paragraphs 20–2 of the declaration indicate WTO members 'agree that negotiations will take place after the Fifth Session of the Ministerial Conference on the basis of a decision to be taken, *by explicit consensus*, at that Session on modalities of negotiation' and on the 'needs of developing and least-developed countries for enhanced support for technical assistance and capacity building'. Negotiations would be based on 'a GATS-type, positive list approach' and 'take

due account of the development policies and objectives of host governments as well as their right to regulate in the public interest'.[29]

The wording of paragraph 20, however, was ambiguous. Led by India, a group of developing countries had requested language to ensure that a consensus would be required to launch negotiations and not merely to establish the modalities of negotiations. Proponents and opponents of negotiations continued to dispute its meaning and significance at the final formal session in Doha to the point that the chair, Qatar Minister of Finance Yousef Hussain Kamal, had to further clarify the meaning of these paragraphs:

> My understanding is that, at that session, a decision would indeed need to be taken by explicit consensus, before negotiations on trade and investment, and trade and competition policy . . . could proceed.[30]

The EU, Japan, and Canada interpreted the text to mean that agreement had essentially been achieved and that negotiations would be launched in Cancún. Consensus would only be required on some relatively trivial matters of procedure and timing. In contrast opponents took the view that only after consensus on the broad parameters of the substance of the negotiations could the actual negotiations be launched.

While it was unclear whether proponents had fully achieved their goal to launch negotiations, the declaration set the basis for a more focused effort in the working group and a major program of technical assistance and capacity-building among developing countries. Opponents, however, had obtained wording on an explicit consensus, itself a reflection of their continuing reluctance to negotiate and more broadly, a growing unease on the part of many developing country members with the whole process of WTO decision-making and its lack of internal transparency. Finally the Doha Declaration, including the text on investment, clearly placed development, at least at the level of rhetoric, front and centre in the Doha Round. The onus was clearly on the proponents of an investment agreement to show how negotiations on investment could further development objectives, particularly for the least developed countries.

From Doha to Cancún: When Does No Mean No?

The period following the Doha ministerial was one of intense activity. In the 19-month period up until the last meeting of the WGTI in the spring of 2003 there were 56 written submissions including nine from the European Union, eight from Canada—plus a joint one—and eight from Japan, reflecting the efforts of the *demandeurs* to persuade those still unsure. These were accompanied by a program of technical assistance financed by a trust fund from member contributions (including Canada's). WTO and UNCTAD staff provided most of the training.[31] An extraordinary number of investment training events, 42 in fact, were held in 2002–3 alone, either in Geneva or in various locations in developing countries.

While the proponents of investment rules shared a strategy and overall goal it did not guarantee that they held one view on all of the issues listed for discussion in the WGTI mandate in paragraph 22 of the Doha Declaration. For example, on the question of the scope and definition of investments to be covered by the agreement, Canada took the position that a very broad range of asset-based investments should be covered by the agreement (along with the US) in contrast to some who favoured a more narrow definition confined more specifically to foreign direct investment. For Canada, its approach reflected the 'contemporary business dynamics associated with investing'.[32] While this reflected Canada's investment interests, in strategic terms it was probably not helpful in making the case for an agreement since many developing countries were already nervous about the balance of payment issues resulting from the massive capital flight seen in the Asian financial crisis. Moreover, UNCTAD officials made it clear that, in their view,

such a broad definition of investment was a bad idea. Opponents also pointed to the lack of agreement among those favouring rules as indicative of the complexity of the overall investment issue.

Canada's submissions also addressed the issue of flexibility, FDI flows, and technical assistance. Canada indicated openness to a number of mechanisms in a potential agreement that would allow developing countries to use exceptions, or perhaps longer time periods, to phase in implementation. However, the experience of developing countries with special and differential treatment provisions at the WTO, the TRIMs, and more recently, the issue of HIV/AIDS and the agreement on trade-related intellectual property (TRIPs), had created skepticism about any such promises. Canada had not been especially accommodating of the special needs of developing countries in the past under these agreements.

On the question of FDI flows, the claims made about the link between investment rules and agreements and increased FDI inflows to developing countries by the *demandeurs* had been increasingly challenged by opponents and, most unhelpfully for proponents, by researchers at the World Bank and UNCTAD. The final written submission from Canada, in June 2003—a joint submission with Korea and Costa Rica—had to acknowledge this reality and was vague on the benefits that would accrue through creating a 'framework not only where investment can take place' but also enhancing 'economic efficiencies'. For Canada, however, transparency was seen to be the 'central tenet' and bottom line of any agreement in creating a predictable and stable climate for investors. Finally, on the question of a NAFTA-like investor–state system of dispute resolution, Canada was clear in stating the obvious, such a system would be 'inappropriate' and, it could be added, totally unacceptable. What had once been a model for an investment agreement in 1997 was now 'inappropriate'. The EU took on all of these issues in its submissions, going so far as to call for 'a Multilateral Investment for Development Agreement' based on a GATS model.[33]

Table 19.3   Country Positions

Demandeurs: Pro negotiating an agreement	Friends of investment-support idea but not necessarily timing	Swing countries, might link to other issues or wait and see	Opponents of negotiations, very vocal
European Union	Argentina	Brazil	India
Japan	Chile	South Africa	Malaysia
Canada	Mexico	Philippines	Zimbabwe
South Korea	Turkey	Indonesia	Tanzania
Switzerland	Poland	Egypt	Zambia
Taiwan	Costa Rica	Cuba	Kenya
Norway	Hungary	Dominican Republic	Belize
	Columbia	Jamaica	Uganda
	New Zealand	Thailand	Sri Lanka
	Hong Kong	Bangladesh	CARICOM
	Singapore	Pakistan	
	Australia	Venezuela	
		China	
		Ecuador	

Source: Adapted from Luke Peterson, Oxfam, and WWF, May 2003.

By the final meeting of the WGTI in 2003 prior to the ministerial it was clear to many that there was indeed no consensus among members to negotiate an investment agreement. Observers identified several positions on the issue within the WTO, as can be seen in Table 19.3.

Canada was one of the small group of proponents supported by a mixture of other members, including some developing countries and other states in transition. However, an equally large group of countries were opposed and some very important developing countries, including China and Brazil, were on the fence. Brazil, as chair of the WGTI post-Doha, had revealed little of its position. China, in contrast, had collaborated with the opponents in a WGTI submission, which roused the ire of proponents by arguing that corporations also had obligations that an investment code should address. Beyond a 1999 EU paper, which argued that existing weak and unenforceable

guidelines for MNCs, such as the OECD's, were more than adequate to ensure corporate social responsibility, proponents, including Canada, had not addressed the issue at all. In Brazil's case the suspicion shaping their strategy was that the EU was using investment and the Singapore issues to trade off, in the final hour, against agriculture.

A large number of small and least developed countries, the target of much of the technical assistance, remained marginal to the process. But over the summer of 2003 opponents, such as India, were working hard to organize these countries in a series of mini-ministerials, which the *demandeurs* on the Singapore issues all but ignored.[34]

Decision Time: The Cancún Ministerial

If there had been any doubt about the level of disagreement on the Singapore issues going into Cancún, a cursory review of the WTO's July 2003

General Council meeting would dispel it. Twelve countries directly refuted the continued insistence of the proponents that the Doha declaration, in fact, authorized the start of negotiations after Cancún as part of a single undertaking. They reminded delegates of the explicit consensus provision and concluded that further study and clarification of the issues, not negotiation, was required.[35]

The draft ministerial declaration discussed by the General Council in August seemed, at first, to fully capture divisions on investment.[36] However, the second part of the annex appeared to presuppose that negotiations would begin post-Cancún and clearly laid out the modalities as they had been outlined in position papers of the EU and Japan, which had never been agreed to in the WGTI. Similar concerns about other issues in the draft text were brought forward at the council meeting of 26–27 August.[37] The chair, Carlos Perez del Castillo, refused to alter the text but was forced by members' protests to prepare a cover letter to accompany it that reflected the extent of disagreement.

The conflict then moved to Cancún. Following WTO practice, the host country (Mexico) chaired the meetings and appointed facilitators to work through the issues and report back.[38] For the Singapore issues Pettigrew was chosen as facilitator despite Canada having been an active proponent of negotiating investment rules and the other Singapore issues. The extent of the disagreement on the Singapore issues became evident at these smaller facilitator-led meetings. Also evident was the link for a number of developing countries between these issues and real progress on agriculture. Agreement on the first was unlikely without the second.

On 12 September a group of about 30 developing countries plus Bangladesh—representing the least developed countries—for a total of 60 members, sent a letter to Pettigrew expressing their opposition to negotiations on any of the four Singapore issues, raising concerns about the capacity to both negotiate and implement poten-tial commitments.[39] They further complained about the process, reminded the Minister of the clear absence of an explicit consensus, and offered alternative wording on investment, which would simply call for further clarification of this consideration. A number of countries also demanded the unbundling of the four Singapore issues.

On the following day, however, a second revised draft declaration text appeared. On a broad range of issues, especially agriculture and cotton, the developing countries were disappointed. On investment, paragraph 14 of the draft read:

> We agree:
> - to convene the Working Group in Special Session to elaborate procedural and substantive modalities on the basis of paragraphs 20, 21, and 22 of the Doha Declaration.
> - modalities that will allow negotiations on a multilateral investment framework to start shall be adopted by the General Council no later than [date]
> - The date will coincide with the date for agreeing on modalities on agriculture and NAMA.[40]

The text approving negotiations, considering the level of opposition, seemed in itself stunning. Tying the start of negotiation on investment to agreements in agriculture meant that many of the proponents of investment negotiations, such as the EU, Japan, and Korea, would have to give way there in order to see talks start. The dissatisfaction with other elements of the text was high. The strategy that Minister Luis Ernesto Derbez, Mexican foreign minister, adopted of first seeking a resolution of the impasse on the Singapore issues was criticized, as was the refusal of the EU to un-bundle the issues and drop investment and competition, as suggested by Pettigrew, until the eleventh hour. When a recess failed to breach the impasse and Botswana informed the chair that the African Union countries would not accept negotiation on *any* of the four issues and Korea (backed by Japan) insisted on all four, the chair called the meeting to an end citing these entrenched positions. The subsequent decision of the EU to drop all four, and the July 2004 WTO General Council decision to proceed only on trade facilitation, marked the end of the seven-year campaign on investment.

The failure at Cancún on investment seemed to surprise only the Canadian officials. Despite extensive consultations with critics, evidence of increasingly well-organized developing-country opposition, and even the critiques of mainstream economists that investment negotiations at the WTO were a bad idea,[41] Canadian officials persisted in seeing it as a worthwhile endeavour. Why was this seven-year effort to persuade many WTO members of the need to negotiate on investment undertaken by Canada and others and why did it ultimately fail?

Conclusion

We began with a fairly simple question of why Canada sought to launch negotiations on investment rules at the WTO in 1996 and why it persisted for seven years in that effort. Part of the answer lies in the changing nature of the Canadian economy and the growing importance of its capital exports to non-OECD countries. Corporate interests in Canada, which were influential in trade policy, demanded higher levels of investment protection; international agreements could provide this protection. But that does not fully explain the rationale behind seeking such rules at the WTO. Bilateral or regional agreements (FTAA and FIPAs) might have also served that purpose. Moreover, why would the Canadian state go out of its way to facilitate outward investment? To understand Canada's interest in negotiating investment rules at the WTO, as this case indicates, we need to go further and look at ideas about both investment flows and the WTO. Second we asked how Canada sought to create a consensus at the WTO that would be permissive of

negotiations? Here the role of ideas was also important, particularly in the period after the Doha Development Declaration of 2001.

By the late 1990s Canadian officials had accepted the view that capital exports were an important part of Canada's overall competitiveness and that trade and investment were closely linked and needed to be dealt with in an integrated way. Moreover, international norms disseminated and strengthened through organizations like the OECD, the International Monetary Fund (IMF), and the World Bank regarded state intervention to control entry of investment and regulate it as illegitimate. At the same time trade and investment policies have historically been sensitive issues in Canada involving sovereignty and concerns over our bilateral relationship with the United States. Multilateral institutions like the WTO have been viewed more positively in the establishment of international economic rules because of their potential in offsetting the bilateral asymmetry with the United States. In the case of investment, multilateral institutions might allow Canada to reconcile our mix of offensive and defensive interests. The WTO was also preferred because of its more universal membership, its dispute resolution system, and its experience in negotiating trade agreements. Given its large number of developing country members and its consensus decision processes, however, it would be necessary to persuade many of these members to negotiate.

Canada, along with the EU and Japan, began the process of educating other WTO members on the merits of an investment agreement in 1995. Because this was not a negotiation but an exercise in persuasion—though clearly linked to and affected by other negotiations—it was very much about ideas that were linked strategically to the interests of proponents. Officials interested in protecting Canadian investors in developing countries had to couch these interests in the language and ideas of development. Those ideas related to the concepts involved in investment agreements, such as national treatment, but also to causal theories regarding the reasons for, and patterns of, investment flows. The overarching challenge for proponents such as Canada after the Doha Development Declaration of 2001 was to make a compelling case that investment rules would facilitate development. This was necessary because what was being proposed was not a traditional reciprocal bargaining process centred on tariffs or market access. Instead states were being asked to accept limits to their own domestic regulatory practices in return for the hope that this would result in increased inflows of investment, bringing growth, new technology, and increased efficiency. In some cases states had already liberalized market access for investors and had seen little in return. Proponents, such as Canada, could offer little else because, as liberal states, governments do not control the private flows of capital.

Moreover many of the states being asked to participate in negotiations on these issues were not capable of dealing with the already existing and growing demands of ongoing WTO negotiations and previous obligations. Nor had their experience of the Uruguay Round led them to put a lot of faith in promises of great benefits to come. In order to further convince those who were reluctant proponents it was necessary to champion extensive technical assistance and a promise that any agreement would allow for flexibility and a national right to regulate in the interests of development.

Canada's position on investment protection was further shaped by the high levels of investment protection NAFTA accorded. In 1996 Canadian officials had embraced the NAFTA model

and preached its virtues at both the OECD and the WTO. By 1999 it was clear that Canada itself faced conflicts between the high levels of protection afforded investors through recourse to investor-state dispute mechanisms and the right of host states to regulate in the public interest. The MAI experience also had an impact in exposing divisions among OECD members on these issues (divisions which persisted within the WTO working group) and had necessitated more open consultations on trade and investment agreements in Canada, therefore giving critics of these agreements more voice. The result was a scaling back of Canada's ambitions for an agreement at the WTO to one which would not model NAFTA, but which would broadly cover many forms of investment while maintaining a degree of shallowness in its commitments, the most important of which would be transparency. In Canada's bilateral and regional ambitions on investment a similar process had occurred.

The scaled back ambition, along with increasing controversy over the Singapore issues in 2003, led many business organizations to either oppose the continuation of these issues[42] or drastically downgrade the negotiation of investment rules at the WTO as a priority.[43] As this case study suggests, a state's interests in international economic negotiations are not a simple reflection of powerful economic trends or actors. Rather they involve an altering landscape and a complex evolution involving competing and evolving interests and contention within Canada and with an array of other international actors in multilateral institutions like the WTO.

Notes

1. The Chinese takeover bid for Noranda in early 2005 set off 'alarm bells' in Ottawa and led to amendments to the Investment Canada Act. See 'Security Concerns spur reviews on foreign investment', *Globe and Mail*, 18 June 2005, B5.

2. The four were trade facilitation, transparency in government procurement, competition policy, and

investment. All four clearly involved domestic regulation.

3. Larry Elliott 'DTI Leak Blames Lamy for Cancún Failure', *The Guardian*, 23 October 2003.

4. Department of Foreign Affairs and International Trade, *State of Trade* (Ottawa: DFAIT, April 2005).

5. Elizabeth Smythe, 'Just Say No! The Negotiation of

Investment Rules at the WTO', *International Journal of Political Economy* 33 (Winter 2003): 60–83.

6. Robert Wolfe, 'Informal Political Engagement in the WTO: Are Mini-Ministerials a Good Idea?' in John Curtis and Dan Ciuriak, eds, *Trade Policy Research* (Ottawa: DFAIT, 2004), 27–90. See also Pierre Sauve, 'Decrypting Cancún', Information Paper for the Session: Aftermath of the Fifth WTO Ministerial Conference: The State of Play and Implications for Developing Countries. Regional Policy Dialogue (Economic and Social Commission for Asia and the Pacific), Bangkok, 30–31 March 2004.

7. External Affairs Canada, *Trade Policy for the 1980s* (Ottawa: External Affairs, 1983).

8. Department of Foreign Affairs and International Trade, *State of Trade* (Ottawa: DFAIT, April 2005), Chapter 4, 45–47.

9. Analysts Torbjörn Fredriksson and Zbigniew Zimny, 'Foreign Direct Investment and Trans-national Corporations' in *Beyond Conventional Wisdom in Development Policy: An Intellectual History of UNCTAD 1964–2004* (New York and Geneva: United Nations, 2004) have likened changing international views on investment issues to a swinging global pendulum.

10. For a discussion of Canada's role in the UN and OECD negotiations in the 1970s see Elizabeth Smythe, *Free to Choose: Globalization, Dependence and Canada's Changing Foreign Investment Regime* (PhD dissertation, Carleton University, 1994), Chapter 6.

11. High levels of protection, despite the array of exceptions and reservations listed in the Annex of Chapter 11, were afforded in the agreement and set a new standard.

12. House of Commons, Standing Committee on External Affairs and International Trade, 'Statement of the Hon. Michael Wilson', 17 November 1992.

13. Andrea Bruce, *Assessing the Impact of Canada's Foreign Investment Promotion and Protection Agreements* (MA thesis, Norman Paterson School of International Affairs, Carleton University, 1999).

14. A leaked memo to the Cabinet dated 22 October 2002, 'Memo to Canadian Cabinet Sets Out Proposed Changes to Canadian Foreign Investment

Protection Agreements', *Investment Law and Sustainable Development Weekly News Bulletin* (13 December 2002) claims that Canadian business had been lobbying hard for FIPAs with Brazil, India, and China. In other cases officials claim a number of developing countries approached Canada to sign bilateral agreements, such as Peru. In many cases developing countries are seeking to attract new FDI and qualify for investment insurance from various export development agencies.

15. The case study that follows is based on interviews with Canadian officials, officials of the WTO, and delegates to the WTO working group in 1998, 2002, and 2003, along with the documents of the Working Group on Trade and Investment of the WTO, especially the Report of the Working Group on the Relationship Between Trade and Investment (WTO, December 2002) and Report of the Working Group on the Relationship Between Trade and Investment to the General Council, June 2003.

16. Hon. Sergio Marchi, Minister of Trade, Statement at the OECD Ministerial Meeting, 27 April 1998.

17. Sir Leon Brittan, 'Investment Liberalization: The Next Great Boost to the Global Economy', *Transnational Corporations* 4, 1 (April 1995): 1–10.

18. Elizabeth Smythe, 'Your Place or Mine? States, International Organizations and the Negotiation of Investment Rules', *Transnational Corporations* 7, 3 (December 1998): 85–120.

19. R.B. Ramaiah, 'Towards a Multilateral Framework on Investment?', *Transnational Corporations* 6, 1 (April 1997): 116–35.

20. *Inside US Trade* (1996), 28.

21. WTO Singapore Ministerial Declaration (Geneva: WTO, 1996), paragraph 20.

22. Submission from Canada to the Working Group on Trade and Investment, 11 December 1997 (WT/WGTI/W/19).

23. India, Submission to the WGTI, June 1997.

24. There have been so many controversial cases that the Department of International Trade now has a section of its website devoted to them. Available at http://www.dfait-maeci.gc.ca/tna-nac/NAFTA-en.asp.

25. Comment by WTO delegate in Geneva to the author in 2003.

26. The heavily bracketed leaked version of the FTAA investment chapter, which appeared on the Internet in 2001, was largely based on a US, NAFTA-like proposal.

27. Submission from Canada to the WGTI, March 2001, 'Foreign Investment Barriers: A Report by the Canadian Chamber of Commerce in Partnership with Industry Canada' (W/WGTI/W97).

28. Fatourama Jawara and Aileen Kwa, *Behind the Scenes at the WTO: The Real World of International Trade Negotiation Lessons from Cancun,* Updated edition (London: Zed Books, 2004).

29. WTO Doha Declaration (2001).

30. Martin Khor, 'The Investment Issues in the WTO', *Seatini Bulletin,* 30 April 2003.

31. For a more detailed discussion of this program and its limitations see Elizabeth Smythe, 'What do You Know?', Paper presented at the International Studies Association Annual Meeting, Honolulu, Hawaii, 1 March 2005.

32. Communication from Canada to the WGTI, 'Scope and Definition', 11 April 2002, 2 (WT/WGTI/W/113).

33. European Community and Its Member States, Submission to the WGTI European community and its member states, 'Concept paper on Policy Space for Development', 3 April 2003 (WT/WGTI/W/1). Perhaps it was this sort of over the top rhetoric that made the EU the favoured target of NGOs, who, in the Spring of 2003, worked long and hard to challenge many of the EU's claims about an investment agreement. See Elizabeth Smythe, 'What Do You Know?'.

34. Wolfe, 'Informal Political Engagement in the WTO', 27–90.

35. WTO General Council Comments on the EC Communication, 8 July 2003.

36. *Investment* 13. [Taking note of the work done by the Working Group on the Relationship between Trade and Investment **we decide to commence negotiations on the basis of the modalities set out in Annex D to this document.**] versus [We take note of the discussions that have taken place in the Working Group on the Relationship between Trade and Investment since the Fourth Ministerial Conference. The **situation does not provide a basis for the commencement of negotiations in this area**. Accordingly, we decide that further clarification of the issues be undertaken in the Working Group.]

37. This portion of the annex reads as follows:

Relationship between Trade and Investment

1. The objective of the negotiations **shall be** to establish an agreement to secure transparent, stable and predictable conditions for [long term cross-border investment, particularly foreign direct investment] [foreign direct investment], that will contribute to the expansion of trade, and the need for enhanced technical assistance and capacity-building in this area . . . and,

3. The Chair of the Negotiating Group on Investment **shall** hold the Group's first meeting within one month from the date of this decision. The Chair of the Negotiating Group shall conduct the negotiations with a view to presenting a draft text by no later than [30 June 2004].   Draft Declaration, Cancún Ministerial, 24 August 2003.

38. Critics claim the facilitators are friendly to powerful members.

39. Seri Rafidah Aziz (Malasyia) and Arun Jaitley (India), *Letter to Hon. Pierre Pettigrew,* 12 September 2003.

40. World Trade Organization Preparations for the Fifth Session of the Ministerial Conference, Draft Cancún Ministerial Text, Second Revision, 13 September 2003.

41. Jagnish Bhagwati, *Financial Times,* 22 October 1998.

42. Business Roundtable, 'A Business Roundtable Policy Paper: How the WTO Can Promote the Benefits of International Investment', Washington, May 2003.

43. Canadian Council of Chief Executives (CCE), 'Prosperity, Freedom, and Security: Renewing Canada's Commitment to Multilateral Trade Liberalization', 20 May 2003.

Selected Bibliography

Acheson, Keith, and Christopher Maule. 1999. *Much Ado About Culture: North American Trade Disputes*. Ann Arbor, MI: University of Michigan Press.

Anastakis, Dimitry. 2005. *Auto Pact: Creating a Borderless North American Auto Industry, 1960–1971*. Toronto: University of Toronto Press.

Anderson, Michael A., and Stephen L. Smith. 1999. 'Canadian Provinces in World Trade: Engagement and Detachment', *Canadian Journal of Economics* 32, 1 (February): 22–38.

Barry, Donald, and Ronald C. Keith, eds. 1999. *Regionalism, Multilateralism, and the Politics of Global Trade*. Vancouver: UBC Press.

Brown, Douglas M., and Earl H. Fry, eds. 1993. *States and Provinces in the International Economy*. Berkeley: University of California Press; Kingston, ON: Queen's University Institute of Governmental Studies Press and Institute of Intergovernmental Relations.

Browne, Denis, ed. 1998. *The Culture/Trade Quandary: Canada's Policy Option*. Ottawa: Renouf Publishing/ Centre for Trade Policy and Law.

Cameron, Maxwell A., and Brian W. Tomlin. 2000. *The Making of NAFTA: How the Deal was Done*. Ithaca, NY: Cornell University Press.

Courchene, Thomas J., ed. 1999. *Room to Manoeuvre? Globalization and Policy Convergence*. Montreal: McGill-Queen's University Press.

Cutler, A. Claire, and Mark W. Zacher. 1992. *Canadian Foreign Policy and International Economic Regimes*. Vancouver: UBC Press.

Doern, G. Bruce, and Brian W. Tomlin. 1991. *Faith and Fear: The Free Trade Story*. Toronto: Stoddart.

Doern, Bruce G., Leslie A. Pal, and Brian Tomlin, eds. 1996. *Border Crossings: The Internationalization of Canadian Public Policy*. Don Mills, ON: Oxford University Press.

Hart, Michael. 2002. *A Trading Nation: Canadian Trade Policy from Colonialism to Globalization*. Vancouver: UBC Press.

———. 1995. *Decision at Midnight: Inside the Canada–US Free-Trade Negotiations*. Vancouver: UBC Press.

Hart, Michael, and William Dymond. 2001. *Common Borders, Shared Destinies: Canada, the United States and Deepening Integration*. Ottawa: Centre for Trade Policy and Law.

Helliwell, John F. 2002. *Globalization and Well-Being*. Vancouver: UBC Press.

————. 1998. *How Much Do National Borders Matter?* Washington: Brookings Institution Press.

Hoberg, George, ed. 2002. *Capacity for Choice: Canada in a New North America*. Toronto: University of Toronto Press.

Kaiser, Karl, John J. Kirton, and Joseph P. Daniels, eds. 2000. *Shaping a New International Financial System: Challenges of Governance in a Globalizing World*. Aldershot, UK: Ashgate Publishing.

Kirton, John J., and Virginia W. MacLaren, eds. 2002. *Linking Trade, Environment, and Social Cohesion: NAFTA Experiences, Global Challenges*. Aldershot, UK: Ashgate Publishing.

Kukucha, Christopher J. 2005. 'Lawyers, Trees and Money: British Columbia Forest Policy and the Convergence of International and Domestic Trade Considerations', *Canadian Public Administration* 48, 4 (Winter): 506–27.

McBride, Stephen. 2005. *Paradigm Shift: Globalization and the Canadian State*, 2nd ed. Halifax: Fernwood Publishing.

McDougall, John N. 2006. *Drifting Together: The Political Economy of Canada–US Integration*. Peterborough, ON: Broadview Press.

Madar, Daniel. 2000. *Deregulation, Trade and Transformation in North American Trucking*. Vancouver: UBC Press.

Muirhead, B.W. 1992. *The Development of Postwar Canadian Trade Policy: The Failure of the Anglo-European Option*. Montreal: McGill-Queen's University Press.

Ostry, Sylvia. 1997. *The Post-Cold War Trading System: Who's on First*. Chicago: University of Chicago Press.

Plumptre, A.F.W. 1977. *Three Decades of Decision, Canada and the World Monetary System, 1944–75*. Toronto: McClelland and Stewart.

Schmitz, Andrew, ed. 2005. *Trade Negotiations in Agriculture: Case Studies in North America*. Calgary: University of Calgary Press.

Stairs, Denis, and Gilbert R. Winham, eds. 1985. *The Politics of Canada's Economic Relationship with the United States*. Toronto: University of Toronto Press.

Stone, Frank. 1992. *Canada, the GATT and the International Trade System*, 2nd ed. Montreal: Institute for Research on Public Policy.

Urmetzer, Peter. 2005. *Globalization Unplugged: Sovereignty and the Canadian State in the Twenty-First Century*. Toronto: University of Toronto Press.

Winham, Gilbert. 1992. *The Evolution of International Trade Agreements*. Toronto: University of Toronto Press.

Wolfe, Robert. 1998. *Farm Wars: The Political Economy of Agriculture and the International Trade Regime*. New York: St Martin's Press.

PART VI

Social Considerations: The Need To Do More?

National interests are usually narrowly defined to only two dimensions: 1) protecting a country's territorial integrity, physical security, and political independence; and 2) enhancing a country's economic prosperity. However, Canadian policy-makers have often added a third dimension: the promotion of Canadian values. This third dimension has been featured prominently in every comprehensive foreign policy announcement for the last four decades. The 1970 white paper identified six areas of national interest and three of them—social justice, quality of life, and a harmonious natural environment—are directly related to the promotion of Canadian values. The 1985 green paper similarly identified justice, democracy, and the integrity of the natural environment as key priorities of Canadian foreign policy. The 1995 white paper highlighted 'the projection of Canadian values and culture by promoting universal respect for human rights, the development of participatory government and stable institutions, the rule of law, sustainable development, the celebration of Canadian culture, and the promotion of Canadian cultural and educational industries abroad'. The 2005 International Policy Statement stated that Canada will make a difference globally by promoting sustainable development, respecting human rights, and building genuine development.[1]

This final section of *Readings in Canadian Foreign Policy* provides a greater analysis of Canada's efforts at promoting social dimensions in its foreign policy. Canada has a tendency, in order to differentiate itself from the American superpower, to see itself as a *moral* superpower. Typical of this sentiment is a report by Canada25, a non-partisan organization of politically-active Canadians aged 20–35, entitled *From Middle to Model Power: Recharging Canada's Role in the World*.[2] This is neither a recent phenomenon, nor necessarily one that is appreciated by other countries. For instance, former US Secretary of State Dean Acheson once referred to Canada as the 'stern daughter of the voice of God'.[3] There are also prominent domestic critics of the idea of asserting a cultural role in Canadian foreign policy. For example, Denis Stairs has been skeptical of the idea that Canadian foreign policy is (or should be) driven by virtue instead of national interests.

Attempting to project Canadian values, however defined, can lead to 'misunder-standing the true origins of their behaviour' and can cause 'significant damage to the effectiveness of their diplomacy'.[4]

Notwithstanding these critics, using foreign policy to promote Canadian val-ues is widely supported by both policy-makers and the public. In Chapter 20, Nelson Michaud examines the inspiration and purpose of promoting Canadian cultural values abroad and illustrates that there is not much of a difference between interests and values. He argues that it is in 'Canada's interest to live in a world that shares what Canada stands for'. Therefore, values are 'on equal footing with economics and security' and 'are a vector, a force that influences the process as well as the content of Canadian foreign policy'.

Michaud's chapter provides the parameters of the debate over values and Canadian foreign policy. The remainder of the section focuses more narrowly on specific aspects of social considerations: environmental protection, foreign aid, and African development. The selected bibliography at the end of this section lists resources for students to more fully explore the areas of human rights, democracy and good governance, immigration and refugees, and international law.

The problem of climate change caused by the emission of greenhouse gases into the atmosphere has been at the centre of Canada's international environmental pol-icy. On 17 December 2002, Canada ratified the Kyoto Protocol and committed to reducing its greenhouse gas emissions by 6 per cent of 1990 levels. Unfortunately for environmentalists who support action on climate change, it is unlikely that Canada will even come close to meeting its Kyoto target. In Chapter 21—written two years after Canada's signature of the Kyoto Protocol in 1997, but three years prior to Canada's 2002 ratification—Douglas MacDonald and Heather Smith pre-dicted that Canada would not be able to fully implement Kyoto. They were able to be so prescient because they identified that action on climate change had signifi-cant opponents including oil and coal companies, provincial governments (espe-cially Alberta Premier Ralph Klein), and the American government. MacDonald and Smith may have written a case study on climate change, but their analysis is applicable to the wider problem of all forms of environmental protection.

Former Canadian Prime Minister Lester Pearson chaired the Pearson Commission on International Development in 1969. One of the commission's key recommenda-tions was setting a target for developed countries of 0.7 per cent of their gross national product (GNP) to be set towards official development assistance (ODA). While several countries have consistently met that target (the Netherlands, Sweden, Denmark, and Norway), most developed countries have not come close. Canada is no exception. While it did increase ODA throughout the 1970s and early 1980s, Canada never came close to the 0.7 per cent target. Additionally, in the last 20 years there has been a steady decline in Canada's level of foreign assistance. In 1986–7, Canada's ODA/GNP ratio was 0.5 per cent, but after years of sustained budget cuts by the Mulroney and Chrétien governments, it dropped to 0.23 per cent by 2003–4.[5] Now that Ottawa is in a better financial situation, it has indicated its willingness to reinvest in foreign assistance and the 2005 budget promised to double Canadian ODA to over $5 billion by 2010. Additionally, Canada wants to enhance its aid effectiveness by concentrating its aid in 25 countries instead of spreading it across 155.[6]

The debate over the size of the ODA/GNP ratio is an interesting one, but an even more basic debate centres on the question of why Canada gives between $2.5–3.5 billion a year in ODA? Many Canadians assume that foreign assistance is provided for altruistic reasons, such as helping the poorest people in the poorest countries. Although there is an undeniable ethical component to ODA, as Cranford Pratt— Canada's foremost expert on Canadian development policy—argues in Chapter 22, it is just as likely that aid is given to advance Canada's economic and security interests. Pratt is critical of the explicit linkage that was made between development, security, and prosperity in the 1995 foreign policy white paper. This linkage remains a cornerstone of Canadian aid policy. The 2005 International Policy Statement asserts that 'failure to achieve significant political, economic, social and environmental progress in the developing world will have an impact on Canada in terms of both our long-term security and our prosperity'.[7] Thus, development assistance continues to be a policy tool that combines all three of Canada's international objectives: physical security, economic prosperity, and the promotion of Canadian values.

In Chapter 23, David Black conducts a case study of Canada's development policy by looking at Canadian–African relations. There have been political, security, and economic dimensions in Canada's relationship with Africa: the fights within the Commonwealth against South African apartheid that were led by John Diefenbaker and Brian Mulroney; the deployment of Canadian peacekeepers to the Congo, Rwanda, and Ethiopia-Eritrea; and the activities of Canadian mining and oil companies on the African continent. However, the major feature of the relationship has been Canadian development assistance to Africa. Some prominent examples include Canada's leadership on the New Partnership for African Development (NEPAD) at the 2002 G8 Summit in Kananaskis and the efforts of Stephen Lewis as UN Special Envoy for HIV/AIDS in Africa.[8] Nevertheless, Black's major point is that 'Canadian policy towards Africa is arguably as much about *us*—about our own moral self-affirmation and sense of collective identity and purpose—as it is about the African countries and people Canadians have engaged.'

Notes

1. Department of External Affairs, *Foreign Policy for Canadians* (Ottawa: Department of External Affairs, 1970), 14–16; Department of External Affairs, *Competitiveness and Security: Directions for Canada's International Relations* (Ottawa: Department of External Affairs, 1985), 3; Canada, *Canada in the World: Government Statement* (Ottawa: Canada Communications Group, 1995); Canada, *Canada's International Policy Statement: A Role of Pride and Influence in the World* (Ottawa: Government of Canada, 2005), 20.

2. Canada25, *From Middle to Model Power: Recharging Canada's Role in the World* (Toronto: Canada25, 2004). Available at: http://www.canada25.com/collateral/canada25_from_middle_to_model_power_en.pdf.

3. Dean Acheson, 'Canada: Stern Daughter of the Voice of God', in Livingston Merchant, ed., *Neighbours Taken for Granted* (Toronto: Burns and MacEachern, 1966), 134.

4. Denis Stairs, 'Myths, Morals, and Reality in Canadian Foreign Policy', *International Journal* 58, 2 (Spring 2003): 239.

5. Canadian International Development Agency, *Statistical Report on Official Development Assistance: Fiscal Year 2003–2004* (Ottawa: CIDA, 2005), 1.

6. Canada, *Canada's International Policy Statement: A Role of Pride and Influence in the World—DEVELOPMENT* (Ottawa: CIDA, 2005), 6–7.

7. Ibid., 1.

8. The 2002 G8 Summit is also discussed by John Kirton in Chapter 3. For Lewis's reflections on Africa, the UN, and HIV/AIDS see Stephen Lewis, *Race Against Time: The 2005 Massey Lectures* (Toronto: Anansi, 2005).

20

Values and Canadian Foreign Policy-making: Inspiration or Hindrance?

Nelson Michaud

Should Canada base its foreign policy on the defense of its interests or on values? What role should these play? These questions fuelled a series of debates both in academia and within the ranks of the foreign policy community as Canada was struggling to update its foreign policy framework. Some would say that this type of debate is typically Canadian. In most countries of influence, security and economy would be at the core of their foreign policy debates. Canada does not avoid these questions. In fact, security objectives were highlighted following the events of 11 September 2001, and Ottawa did successfully negotiate a 'smart border' agreement with the United States. This new context also challenged economic prosperity because Canada ensured that trade flows across the Canada–US border were not disrupted.

However, we cannot neglect that Ottawa contextualized security issues. This was further demonstrated not once, but twice with both Jean Chrétien's and Paul Martin's reluctance to embrace American security choices related to the war in Iraq and the Anti-Ballistic Missile Defence System. Even more interesting is the fact that in both instances Canadian prime ministers have justified their rejection of the invitation by refer-

ring to 'Canadian values'.[1] Indeed, values are at the core of Canadian foreign policy. When one refers to the 1995 policy statement—which lasted over ten years as the cornerstone of Canadian foreign policy—the 'promotion of Canadian values' proudly stands as the 'third pillar' in the edification of Canada's international relations.[2] Under the leadership of foreign affairs ministers like Lloyd Axworthy,[3] values gained even more importance. As well, in the latest International Policy Statement released by the Martin government in April 2005, values—though less prominent—are still very much present. What are these values? Why are they so important? The need to study them is obvious.

This importance of this study is fuelled by the lack of unanimity regarding the role and definition of values in the formulation of Canadian foreign policy. Some have even openly questioned the need for a values-based foreign policy. The most common criticism is that the promotion of one's own values can be perceived as a lack of respect for values held by others; this can be interpreted as a form of imperialism, and as a consequence, foreign policy becomes much like the United States. Denis Stairs has also questioned the implementation of a hierarchy of values in Canadian foreign policy. Specifically, he has suggested that:

> Canadians have grown alarmingly smug, complacent, and self-deluded in their approach to international affairs. . . . More specifically, they have come to think of themselves not as others are, but as morally superior. They believe, in particular that they subscribe to a distinctive set of values—'Canadian' values—and that those values are special in the sense of being unusually virtuous.[4]

For his part, Jack Granatstein has also warned that 'moral earnestness and the loud preaching of our values will not suffice to protect us in this new century.'[5] Others, however, such as Jennifer Welsh, have argued for a greater role for values in Canadian foreign policy. She views values as a defining factor for Canada's international role in the twenty-first century. Notably, Welsh argues that as 'tempting as the interests-before-values mantra is, we cannot abandon a values-based agenda. We live in a democratic society, where the values and principles we stand for *must* form a critical part of our activities in the international arena.'[6]

Another way to look at things is to ask if values are that far from interests. Isn't it in Canada's interests to live in a world that shares what Canada stands for? Indeed, Canada's power is not what it used to be and it is in its utmost interest to benefit from a context that will give a premium to behaviours based on similar values. The real discrepancy is then giving long-standing values an absolute priority and ignoring challenges that the new international context lays on Canada's doorstep.

Wherever we stand in these debates, it remains that values are an intrinsic part of the Canadian foreign policy landscape. There is no doubt that, in the Canadian context, they are considered on equal footing with economics and security. Therefore, values cannot be labelled merely as 'an element to be considered'; they are a vector, a force that influences the process as well as the content of Canadian foreign policy. The difficulty, however, is that values in the Canadian context,

although perennial, do not always match the challenges of a rapidly changing international system. As a result, it is necessary to evaluate the role of values in the formulation of Canada's foreign policy, especially in the context of the post-9/11 era. It is also crucial to differentiate between two types of values: those perceived by the population and those advocated by the Canadian foreign policy apparatus. In doing so, it will become possible to consider whether values are an inspiration, that is, a source from which a foreign policy that answers the call of a redefined world is crafted, or hindrance, a stonewall that prevents Canada from updating a policy that needs to take new factors into consideration.

Values and Canadian Foreign Policy

THE CORE FOUNDATIONS

The first question to be raised concerning the values on which Canadian foreign policy is based refers to the uniqueness of these values. Aren't they universal? What is so distinctively Canadian about them? If values occupy such a major place in Canadian foreign policy, isn't this also the case in most countries? Why are we paying special attention to Canada in this regard? In order to understand the role of values in contemporary Canadian foreign policy it is first necessary to explore historical examples of these considerations in Canada's external relations. For this purpose, it is useful to return to 1947, as Canada was emerging as a full-fledged autonomous international actor. In fact, values were identified as a prominent feature of Canadian foreign policy as early as the Gray lecture delivered by Louis St-Laurent, the first Canadian Secretary of State for External Affairs who did not hold the dual role of prime minister.[7] Specifically, in a speech that would become the cornerstone of Canadian foreign policy, St-Laurent continuously refers to Canadian values and 'principles', such as generosity and openness, and uses them to lead his reflections.[8] For him, it is clear that 'no foreign policy is consistent nor coherent over a period of years unless it is based upon some conception of human *values*' (emphasis added). He also states that a 'policy of world affairs, to be truly effective, must have its foundations laid upon *general principles* which have been tested in the life of the nation and which have secured the broad support of large groups of the population.' Finally, he identifies 'basic principles' of foreign policy, including: national unity, political liberty, the rule of law, and a willingness to accept international responsibilities. He concludes by stating 'we must play a role in world affairs in keeping with the ideals and sacrifices of the young men of this University, and of this country, who went to war.' Without a doubt, Canadian values are found throughout this seminal policy statement.

St-Laurent's stance was not without precedent. Canadian interests cannot be ignored, but it was also Canadian values and the country's perception of the world that motivated Canada's position in the formation of the United Nations and NATO. In the first instance, Canada was influential in the writing of the Charter.[9] Concerning NATO, Canada was influential in having Article 2—an article that opens the mandate of the organization to fields other than military security[10]—adopted. A final example of Canadian institutionalist values brought to the fore has been provided at the time of the Bretton Woods talks that bore fruits known as the International Monetary Fund, the World Bank, and the GATT. Canada was invited to get involved and based its negotiating skills on its commitment towards multilateralism—a Canadian foreign policy core value. Of course, interests were undeniably present, perhaps here more than in any of the other examples and these interests were of an economic nature: the agreement was to be struck by its two major trading partners. However, as Tom Keating analyzes it: 'the formation of the Bretton Woods system was an important part of the Canadian effort to establish an international order that would be based on multilateral cooperation.'[11]

Among the main actors then involved were St-Laurent, of course, and most importantly, his deputy minister at the time, Lester Bowles Pearson. With a group of dedicated officials, they were to be key architects directly involved in the crafting of Canada's place in the world for the next twenty years. Such stability obviously helped to incarnate the government's commitment to 'constructive international action' through international organization, based on the principles set forth by St-Laurent in the 'Gray Lecture'.[12] The inspiration and the values these first senior Foreign Service officers worked from would last even longer to structure what has been dubbed Canada's foreign policy's Golden Age, an epoch that deeply influenced much of Canada's international actions until present day.

More recently, the role of values was highlighted in the 1995 white paper, *Canada in the World*. This document identified 'three pillars' on which Canada's foreign policy would rest: 'the promotion of prosperity'; 'the protection of security within a stable global framework'; and 'the projection of Canadian values and culture'. In terms of values, *Canada and the World* states that 'Canadian values, and their projection abroad, are key to the achievement of prosperity within Canada and to the protection of global security.'[13] In other words, although ranked third, this pillar is essential to meet objectives that are more directly linked to economics and security. Moreover, it suggests the promotion of values should now be considered a foreign policy objective in itself. Obviously, this represented a new accent put on values, an emphasis that is not priceless, as we will see.

This new priority on values was largely the result of Lloyd Axworthy. First, as liberal foreign affairs critic in the 1980s and early 1990s, Axworthy was a prime actor in crafting the liberal foreign policy platform in view of the 1993 election,[14] which listed several value-related items. Once elected, the Liberals pursued their values agenda. Among the engagements on which they followed up, one in particular helped to structure the use of values as an easily recognizable means in the conduct of foreign policy: it was the implementation of the Canadian Centre for Foreign Policy Development (CCFPD). The Centre was conceived as a think tank to be housed in the foreign affairs building and its key mandate was to consult Canadians from all walks of life in an attempt to 'democratize' the foreign policy process. In so doing, the Centre acted on two levels. First, it allowed citizens to engage these issues and articulate their thoughts and perceptions (in a word, their values). Second, the reports and papers published by the Centre advocated the importance of values as expressed by Canadians in CCFPD forums.[15] As a consequence, and in line with Lloyd Axworthy's policy choices, the third pillar became, under his tenure as Foreign Affairs minister, an unavoidable factor.

Of course, this was not the only value-oriented legacy Axworthy left. In fact, most of the actions he will be remembered for as Foreign Affairs minister are along this line: the promotion of the concept of human security falls squarely in this category. Human security is defined as 'a people-centred approach to foreign policy which recognizes that lasting stability cannot be achieved until people are protected from violent threats to their rights, safety or lives'.[16] The concept is clearly value-driven. Its importance has raised dramatically over the last few years to the extent that Rob McRae does not hesitate to refer to a 'human security paradigm'.[17] Following this umbrella concept, better focused initiatives were also part of Axworthy's legacy: the ban of anti-personnel landmines and the Ottawa protocol and the fight against the use of child soldiers are probably the two best known initiatives of the Axworthy years.[18] These foreign policy initiatives are also value-driven.

Foreign Affairs ministers who followed in Axworthy's footsteps—namely John Manley and Bill Graham—did not espouse with the same fervour the importance given to values in Canadian foreign policy. In fact, after some frictions, including concurrent consultation processes held in the spring of 2003 by the Centre and by the Minister, Graham cut all funding to the Centre, which found itself with no other option, but to fold. Nevertheless, the imprint made in the Canadian public and among policy makers about Canadian values was there to stay. It was no doubt present in the mind of most, on the morning of 11 September 2001.

VALUES AND THE IMPACT OF 11 SEPTEMBER: MULTILATERALISM AND AUTONOMY

Although Canada was the lone partner ignored by President Bush as he thanked numerous countries from the rostrum in the House of the Representatives—it would take over three years before he officially acknowledged Canada's support in the immediate aftermath of 9/11—it is clear that Canada supported US interests in the hours and days after the terrorist attacks. In fact, Canada harboured stranded travellers on 9/11, negotiated and implemented the 'smart border' accord, and tightened security measures including major amendments of Canadian laws. When we look at the negative answers Chrétien and Martin gave Washington regarding Iraq and missile defence, it is important to keep in mind that, Canada, since the end of the First World War, never accepted automatic involvement in any foreign conflicts. Ottawa has voiced these autonomist values towards Great Britain on several occasions, starting with the Chanak crisis in 1925.[19] It also opposed the United States on the Vietnam War, a position made clear in Mike Pearson's speech at Temple University and Lyndon Johnson's cold reception to the Canadian leader the following day at Camp David.[20] The fact is that Canada's pursuit of its autonomy and its unshakable belief in multilateralism have always been cornerstone values of Canadian foreign policy. This was evident in Canada's military participation in Afghanistan, which occurred due to relevant United Nations resolutions.

Iraq, on the other hand, represented a different situation. Specifically, the unilateral actions of the United States did not receive the support of a multilateral forum and so it was not endorsed by Canada. It is not that Canada was unsympathetic to the American position, even when the Canadian government was under considerable popular pressure to decline involvement. Notwithstanding this political stress, Canada tried to initiate a late proposal through the UN Security Council. Therefore, it is clear that Canadian multilateralist values were a major factor in Canada's policy toward Iraq.[21] And concerning missile defence, Prime Minister Martin also adhered to a values driven line, insisting that militarization of space was going against Canadian values.

Planning Future Responses

These episodes are useful to demonstrate how Canadian values can influence Canadian foreign policy. Politically, at a time when domestic perceptions and domestic politics were of the utmost importance for the prime minister, it was difficult to go against them. Moreover, Canadians were assured by Axworthy and CCFPD that their say in foreign policy making was important. Going against this trend was not an option for Jean Chrétien. A question remains though: has such a stance prevailed as a new leadership that openly favours a more active role for Canada on the international scene took place in Ottawa? To answer this question I will look at three potential sources that might influence foreign policy making. These sources are: what do people think, what do policymakers think, and what in fact lies out there?

PSYCHO-SOCIAL VALUES

The first set of sources is labelled 'psycho-social' values because they help craft Canada's 'social' self. Specifically, these are the values that Canadians claim to recognize in themselves as a society. Their importance lies in a factor suggested by Pico Iyer: Canada is 'held together by shared values rather than shared roots.'[22] These values come from several sources. The key source that helps us identify these values is Steve Lee's article published in *Canadian Foreign Policy*.[23] Lee was

then CCFPD's executive director. In his paper, Lee reports the conclusions reached at the Centre's forums. From these, general trends have emerged and Lee reports them as values that 'should guide the conduct of Canada's international relations'.[24]

The first of these values refers to the *respect for the environment*. This does not come as a surprise given the importance Canadians place on environmental questions. This might not always be translated in their behaviour, but it remains that a country that is largely dependent on its natural resources cannot be insensitive to the issue. The relevance of this consideration is further evident in the support Canadians demonstrated for the Kyoto protocol and their reluctance to back political leaders who oppose it. This explains why Canadians expect their government to consider environment as an item to be discussed and acted upon at the international level.

A second value outlined by Lee is support for *democracy and democratization*. This approach includes not only the conduct of free and fair elections, but also principles of good governance. To a large extent, this is perceived as a *sine qua non* condition to any foreign relations Canada might entertain with other countries. In fact, it is this specific value that contributed to Canadian support for intervention in Haiti. This value is at the center of Canadian foreign policy in the Americas and, to a large extent, in Africa.

In addition, Lee focuses on *social equity*, which emphasizes 'social and economic justice' and fairness. From a foreign policy point of view, this means that Canada should prioritize international relations that explicitly promote these considerations in as many domains as possible.

The fourth value is *human rights and tolerance towards diversity*. Canadians demonstrate the importance of this value by highlighting these issues during foreign visits by senior officials to countries where human rights are questioned—China being a prime example. Canadians would simply not understand the issue not being put on the agenda. Although human rights are a very broad issue, Canadians extend their concerns to a higher level to include in it tolerance. This refers to the acceptance of differences, of the individual expression, and of cultural or ethnic diversity. To many, this is perceived as an important feature that differentiates Canadian and American values.

Finally, one might not be surprised to find *civil society involvement* as a key value in a report produced by a group that has a clear mandate to promote such involvement. Moreover, this report refers to meetings where civil society representatives had an opportunity to voice their interest in being more involved. Keeping these possible biases in mind, it nevertheless remains that more and more Canadians want input into the policy process and, although issues are more complex than ever, citizens believe they should not be left in the hands of specialists. This is experienced in most domestic policy fields and foreign policy is no exception. This request adds to the alter-globalization movement's claims that ask for a civil society say in the conduct of world affairs.

In addition to Lee's analysis, other examples of psycho-social values are outlined in the House of Commons Standing Committee on Foreign Affairs and International Trade May 2003 report, 'A Contribution to the Dialogue on Foreign Policy'. This report casts values also reported by Lee such as democracy/good governance and human rights. It also sheds light on 'pluralism' as a 'particular Canadian strength',[25] a value that corresponds largely to Lee's tolerance.[26]

By initiating his 'dialogue on foreign policy' in Spring 2003, then-Foreign Affairs Minister Bill Graham offered an opportunity to Canadians to express their views on Canadian foreign policy. In his *Report to the Canadian Population*,[27] he focused on values similar to Lee's, including the environment, sustainable development, democracy, social and economic justice, human rights, and acceptance of diversity. Many of these themes were suggested in questions asked by the minister in the discussion paper released to initiate the dialogue.[28]

In studying people's perceptions, opinion polls could be useful, but they are snapshots often influenced by events that occurred at the moment they were conducted, which could distort the image they project. For instance, the values Lee presents in his paper are confirmed to some extent by an EKOS poll released at the 'Canada in the World' conference held in Montreal in February 2005 in which Canadians see themselves as important actors in building a better world. At the same time, however, the promotion of values is also challenged as a foreign policy objective. This was clear in the release of polling data in conjunction with a recent conference—'Defining National Interest: New Direction for Canadian Foreign Policy'—held in Ottawa in November 2004. The Innovative Research data made public indicates that 79 per cent opposed the push of Canadian values abroad, thereby rejecting the 'third pillar'. Moreover, the 'quality of life' values Lee claims to be at the centre of Canadians perception of foreign policy was supported by only 41 per cent of those polled. Although a direct link cannot be made between these two images of Canada in the world, it seems difficult to completely ignore the gap that surfaces here. This is why I preferred to rely on other studies to define these values that are not the only ones to be considered.

POLITICO-OPERATIONAL VALUES

This next group of values is no less important as they are conceptualized and operationalized by foreign policymakers. Therefore, these values reflect both policy orientations and operational targets traditionally prioritized by officials, hence the label 'politico-operational'. These values can be traced throughout Canada's foreign policy history and are reflected in a series of official documents, including the 1995 white paper, *Canada in the World*, and statements from government ministers and the Prime Minister, including Speeches from the Throne, press releases, and reports. Most of these values are well known and dear to most Canadians.

The first politico-operational value is the *rule of law*. In domestic politics, this refers to rules and norms conducted within a legal framework that includes a binding judicial system. In the Canadian case, however, the rule of law is also contrasted with the rule of power, that is, whenever a state has the means to impose its will, it will. Canada also extends these concepts of governance to the international level and supports the rule of law against the rule of power. In so doing, Canada does not advocate the end of the anarchical Westphalian system, but simply favours actions that are backed by a consensus within the community of nations and works toward the implementation of governance frameworks, including judicial and quasi-judicial institutions. In this, Canada clearly goes against the current American approach to world affairs.

A related concept is *multilateralism*. First a practice, multilateralism is now perceived in many circles as a value that Canada should maintain. As noted earlier, this principle has long dominated the conduct of Canada's foreign policy and Keating[29] sees in it Canada's distinctive signature. It influenced Robert Borden's participation in the Imperial war cabinet, guided Canada's role at both the San Francisco (UN) and Washington (NATO) conferences, and today remains a key principle tied to institution building related to the environment, prohibited arms, or the war against terrorism. While the United States prefers to assert its supremacy on a one-on-one (bilateral) basis, Canada 'punches over its weight' in most settings by associating itself with other international actors who share similar concerns and attitudes.

A direct result of this internationalist approach is Pearson's legacy to the world: *peace-keeping*, which today includes peace-making and peace-building.[30] Although most Canadians still believe that Canada continues to rank first among peace-keeping contributors, it no longer plays such a prominent role. It might be true quality-wise, but in terms of effectives, as of 31 January 2005, Canada ranked 33rd[31] behind several African and Asian countries. Nevertheless, keeping our world safe and contributing to it are still seen as major objectives as well as key values in Canadian foreign policy making.

Of course, security does not have the same resonance in Canada as it does in the United States; it nonetheless remains an important politico-operational variable. In the immediate aftermath of 9/11, institutionalist politicians easily agreed with offensive realist academics like John Mearsheimer:[32] security trumps economy. For a while, in Canada, this was viewed as an inverse: economic well-being comes first and *security is a necessary ingredient to ensure prosperity*. This value has deep roots in Canadian history given that trade has always played an integral role in Canada's development. This reality was clear with enhanced security measures after 9/11: leaders had only to proclaim that Canada's economic health heavily depended on better security, and it was then possible to bring in tougher security measures.

A final value I will consider here is *international development assistance*. Aid is an integral part of Canadian foreign policy and, although Canadians do not heartily approve massive sums of tax money being routed out of the country, most Canadians are proud of what they perceive as Canada's leadership role, which of course is far from Canada's actual performance. Over the last 10 years, Canada's contributions have continuously diminished, and today they equal approximately 0.25 per cent of Canadian GNP, far below the UN's 0.7 per cent target. In addition to this problem CIDA's Winter 2005 policy review also questioned Canada's dispersion of aid and the ongoing practice of tied aid, in which assistance is dependent on reinvestment in the Canadian economy. Nevertheless, aid is a foreign policy value that gives Canadians this warm fuzzy feeling that Canada is a caring country.

Ultimately, politico-operational values as promoted by policymakers benefit from a blurred knowledge of the international context and of Canada's true role in it. Building foreign policy on these values does have some short-term benefits. First, they have considerable support within this foreign policy community who have conceptualized and socially constructed these Canadian 'assets' in terms of values. Second, these values promote a comforting sense of legitimacy for Canadian citizens, without the need of a significantly greater international contribution, two important factors in order to gain popular support for foreign policy initiatives. At the same time, however, these politico-operational values often benefit from support that ignores important issues of context. Therefore, they represent a potential policy time-bomb for actors who do not use them with great caution.

In fact, this dual reading leaves us with an impression of incompleteness. More disquieting is that this feeling comes from both sets of values we have analyzed. We therefore need a third source of influence if we want to consider all factors affecting Canadian foreign policy, and we will find such source in the challenges the international context offers.

CHALLENGES

In fact, these challenges have taken a new meaning in the post-9/11 international system that is not always consistent with 'traditional' Canadian foreign policy values. In this section, it will be argued that Canada must acknowledge new challenges related to the *organization* of foreign policy, the *respect* for Canadian autonomy, the *priorities* that need to be recognized and the will to include *new actors* in the policy process.[33]

Organization

In terms of organization, there are four key[34] challenges that address two fundamental aspects of foreign policy organization: the identification of problems and policy priorities; and how to institutionally respond to these pressures. First, as already noted, there is a *need* for Canadian foreign policy *to adapt* itself to a rapidly evolving international environment. Specifically, this section will argue that: the United States is not the neighbour it used to be; peace-keeping has shifted from traditional Pearsonian values; trade is now conducted in an increasingly neo-liberal rules based environment; and international relations now include a wide range of international, transnational, and domestic non-governmental actors.

In itself, this new context poses the challenge of adaptability in general, but it also questions the advisability of operating from past foreign policy practices. Here, the first element that comes to mind is that Canada has to *question* its hallmark practice of *multilateralism*. Not that multilateralism is the only expression of Canadian foreign policy,[35] and not that multilateralism should be completely rejected, but Ottawa needs to focus greater attention on extended bilateralism, in aid, diplomacy, security, and trade. As well, the ever-growing role of INGOs brings new actors to the international table and, if multilateralism is sometimes the right way to approach them, it cannot be considered the only one, due to the eclectic nature of this new family.

Together, these two elements create an additional organizational challenge: *solving the heritage/innovation dilemma*. Generally speaking, foreign policy is a world where the importance of past practices as grounds for future action is a rule of thumb. Clearly, long-term policy is the standard. In Canada's case, such an attitude of carefulness and respect for established practices is increased tenfold by the aura that still surrounds this famous 'Golden Era' characterized by Pearsonian internationalism at its best. As I outlined however, a newly defined world calls for a new approach. Here, the challenge rests in the bureaucratic response that will be given to the new foreign policy endeavours Canada must embark upon. In other words, bureaucratic political culture influences how Canada crafts its foreign policy, but this culture has to adapt to a new reality. Keeping with policies defined by past actions might be comforting, but it induces a lack of flexibility, and Canada requires the opposite. The challenge is to strike the right balance between successful practices dictated by bureaucratic political culture and innovation. This is what I call the innovation/heritage dilemma.

Some of these needed innovations could come from the involvement of other departments in the conduct of foreign affairs. Historically, when Wilfrid Laurier created a Foreign Affairs division within his government, it was to ensure cohesiveness among actions taken on the international scene by different ministries. We might soon come full circle since more and more issues 'belonging' to line departments are dealt with at the international level. As a result, most departments in Ottawa house an international division. Therefore, there is a need to *define the role these other departments* will play in Canada's international relations *and establish how to integrate their efforts in a genuine governmental*—not an individual department's— *action.* Knowing the turf wars that will no doubt characterize such harmonization, this, in itself, represents quite a challenge.

These first four challenges set the table for a better organized foreign policy community. Should they be met, they will provide Canada with adequate tools. The next group of challenges, those related to the respect Canada must re-earn in the international community, will bring an important complement in terms of the leverage Canadian foreign policy needs.

Respect

Evaluating respect is problematic.[36] On many accounts, Canada has gained its self-proclaimed 'middle power' status based on historical contributions to the international community. No more a military power, Canada still plays an important role in the training of other countries armed forces, including those of the United States, and its performance in theatres of operation, such as in Afghanistan is deemed by all to be nothing less than remarkable. Despite economic challenges, Canada also remains a member of the G8, and uses its influence to steer key economic debates. Far from meeting internationally set targets, Canadian aid is looked for, not only because it is much needed, but because it comes from a country that has no imperialistic agendas associated with it. Regardless, Canada's status is based on past actions and if it wants to avoid being pushed to the sidelines, Canada must regain its world credibility and

respect. This can be achieved if Canada meets three specific, but related, challenges.

All three of these challenges are directly linked to Canada's relationship with the United States, a relationship most countries envy. As noted earlier, Canada has historically defended its interests, but for the most part it has maintained the respect of its southern neighbor. Despite periods of tension, Ottawa and Washington have a unique relationship. A specific example is Canada's role in NORAD, which is the only foreign defence institution where the United States shares command and control. Moreover, when Canada succeeds in motivating an American President to fight apartheid, as it did during the Mulroney era, other countries look at Canada as a credible broker in the world of international relations. Therefore, much of Canada's international influence depends on Canada's relationship with the US. This is why the 'respect' factor, the one that gives Canada international 'political capital', depends in large part on the good health of this relationship.

The first challenge is linked to domestic pressures, namely that many Canadians are ill at ease when Canada's choices come too close to US policies. The famous 'I am Canadian' beer ad might be an anecdotal evidence of such sensitivity, but it remains that *Canada must establish a clear difference between its practices and US policies.* As noted, this strategy poses an obvious challenge based on the historical and contemporary nature of the bilateral relationship. In this regard, multilateralism, with a focus on post-conflict resolution, the environment, and other policy areas could provide a means in which Canada can differentiate itself from the United States. Not that Ottawa should be indifferent to Washington. No country should deliberately isolate such an important economic and political partner. It is quite the opposite that should prevail.

Therefore, a second priority is to *re-earn respect in Washington.* Canada must do so first if it ever wants to re-gain respect elsewhere in the world. For indeed, being different from the United States does not at all mean being indifferent to what is decided in Washington. In fact, the more often the

United States is brought on board with Canadian initiatives, the better it is for Canada. And this will be done only when policymakers in the two capitals are on the same wavelength. Due to its middle power status and its soft power approach,[37] Canada needs to solicit support and resources in order to reach its international goals. Succeeding in convincing the United States adds a lot of weight to one's side of the balance. And, put simply, the only way Canada can succeed in balancing independent policy choices and American support is if Canada earns 'respect' in Washington. In this regard, the too numerous hesitations that preceded withdrawal of Canadian support for American proposals, such as the call to participate in the war in Iraq, or the anti-ballistic missile initiative, hurt more than a simple straightforward decline of the invitation received.

When one refers to being 'respected' in Washington, the immediate question that comes to mind is: What about sovereignty? Sovereignty is at risk when exogenous pressures are exercised on a government's autonomy. As Stephen Krasner[38] has demonstrated, sovereignty is a multi-facetted concept. I had the opportunity to analyze elsewhere what aspects of Canadian sovereignty have been challenged in the aftermaths of 9/11.[39] Historically, it is noticeable that whenever Canada had a direct contact in the White House, Canadian sovereignty never was in jeopardy. Why would the US threaten such a good friend's sovereignty? Doing so would dramatically increase suspicion with other American allies. Conversely, when Canada ignores the US, why would the US pay attention to Canada? Oddly enough, it is when Canada keeps too much distance from its neighbour that its sovereignty is more at risk. The impact of this equation is clear: when Washington shows more respect for Canadian sovereignty Canada earns more respect in the world.

Prioritizing

Already, one has a sense of the tremendous task ahead. But from where should we start? In itself, this question harbours two other important chal-

lenges Canada must face. First, it will be impossible for Canada to answer all calls at the same time. Recent history has seen Canada move from Jean Chrétien's leadership, where foreign policy was not always a priority, to Paul Martin, who considers most international commitments important, particularly summits, the establishment of new institutions (namely, the L20), peace-making in the Middle East, Haiti, Darfour, Lybia, and Asia, and of course, a revamped relationship with the United States, which cooled after the government turned down ballistic missile defence (BMD) participation. The problem, however, is that Canada does not have the resources to pursue all of these objectives. Moreover, dissemination of piecemeal efforts would not allow the achievement of any significant nor efficient success. At this rhythm, Canada runs the risk that, sooner than later, the whole of its foreign policy could also be characterized 'as an inch thick, a mile wide'.[40] As a consequence, *Canada must prioritize its actions* in the world.

The difficulty, however, is defining these priorities. To ensure its ongoing relevance *Canada must define itself as a global actor*. Specifically, it should more clearly define new or renewed foreign policy objectives. One issue area is the North, with economic potential and environmental sensitivity. There is also the Middle East, a region central to the pursuit of global stability, and where Canada has a history of involvement—who does not remember Pearson's role in the Suez Crisis and peace-keeping on Golan Heights. In addition, Canada should focus its attention on the economic and military power of Europe and Asia. Finally, there is Africa, a continent that Canada has pledged to support but requires a strengthened commitment. In fact, there are many other foreign policy objectives in regard to which Canada needs to define its international role and personality.

Obviously, it is impossible to achieve all of these goals and so Canada must be strategic in its global affairs. In doing so, it will provide the Canadian government a better orientation for its foreign policy.

Inclusiveness

After considering all these factors, only one remains and it is found closer to home. It is related to endogenous pressures that complement the exogenous pressures previously discussed. In both cases, government's autonomy is challenged. This time though, the challenge comes from national actors seeking to influence the federal government in the conduct of international relations and the framing of its foreign policy. These actors come primarily from three fields: civil society that has seen its collective need to be heard and welcomed by recent governments; corporate interests—both from the business world and specific NGOs—who lobby for having their pet projects put on the government's priority list; and provinces who see, day after day, the impact of globalization assail their constitutional fields of responsibility.[41] Due to the increasing complexity of international developments, the Canadian government should establish working partnerships with these new actors. However, inclusiveness is not something natural in the foreign policy-maker's *chasse gardée*. *Pooling these domestic resources towards common foreign policy objectives* is a challenge that cannot be left for future considerations. The price to pay for neglecting these interests is high: any effort would result in scattered answers amounting to a piecemeal foreign policy suffering from issues of transparency, accountability, and legitimacy.

This list of challenges is impressive. It covers most aspects of foreign policy-making and gives a good idea of the shape in which the Canadian answer to the world found itself at the time the IPS was crafted. The most important element to be retained, though, is not the length of this road leading to Canada's recovery of its former stance in the world. It is more the intricacy of the situation that strikes. This in large part is due to the close interdependent relationship that binds the challenges. In order to face a world redefined after the 9/11 events, Canada needs the tools, the leverage, the political capital, and the appropriate orientations as it should count on adequate part-

nerships. All these elements are translated in the challenges identified here. Have these prevailed in the mind of those who have influenced recent foreign policy making in Canada?

Values, Challenges, and the IPS

In the Spring of 2005, the federal government tabled its International Policy Statement, a compound of 'White papers' covering all aspects of the foreign policy field: diplomacy, defence, development, and trade. If we submit this policy to the three grids we used in the analytical part of this chapter, we realize that the result is surprisingly different from the reading we got when we looked at political platforms used in the June 2004 elections.[42] In this latter instance, most parties were sensitive to politico-operational values, but challenges were largely ignored, especially by parties that had a chance to form the government.

Looking at how psychosocial values were considered in the IPS, we see that all are mentioned and that four of the five values are met with a favourable attention: the respect for the environment, democracy and democratization, social equity, human rights, and tolerance. The only value that receives less attention is the inclusion of civil society in the foreign policy process. There are mentions of it as development partner, but the perception we have from reading the *Overview* document is that it remains a minor actor in the foreign policymaking process: 'States remain the central actors on the global stage, but they are increasingly embedded in transnational linkages that diffuse power above to supranational frameworks and below to civil society. Individuals are playing a greater role in international affairs than ever before, with both positive and negative results'. This is, in fact, an evaluation that takes into account both the potential contribution of civil society, but also problems that actors with individual interests—while the states represent collective interests—can induce into the policy-making process. This no doubt also takes into consideration breakage and violence that are sometimes associated with civil society protests (as in Seattle or Genoa), as well as the *chasse gardée* mentality that still impregnates some parts of the foreign policy making community.

Given the strong incidence found in previous studies, we could expect a dense presence of the politico-operational values in the IPS. It is indeed the case since all listed values are present. The desire to see a 'rules-based and more predictable' international system agrees well with the promotion of the rule of law on the international scene and such strong plea in favour of multilateralism hardly surprises. However, there are some innovations. For instance, peace-keeping, although present, is part of broader components, that is, democratization efforts and the review of the Canadian armed forces mandates. As well, the value stating that Canada's security depends on the world's balance of power is now restricted to a continental dimension. The fact that security threats are now less related to large ideological plates that rub against each other, and are more associated with targeted acts of circumscribed origins, largely explains the new reading of a long lasting value. This clearly shows that the government of Canada understood that it was necessary to adapt its foreign policy to a new environment—a challenge to which we will return soon. Similarly, one notes that the statement to the effect that security is a necessary ingredient to warrant prosperity is still present, but, notably, priority is now given to security. Moreover, questions of security are not limited to traditional dimensions, but include other sectors such as health and the information technology environment. Lastly, international development is obviously present, but under a completely overhauled approach, in agreement with previous government stated policies. As predicted, politico-operational values are still present, but they are unmistakably revamped, taking into consideration the new international environment.

Despite efforts to stay away from the 'promotion' approach, the presence of elements belonging to the two groups of values confirm to some extent that Canadian values always bear an important weight in Canadian foreign policy. The *Overview* document clearly states that values still guide Canada's international action.

The red flag raised in the previous section of this chapter warned about the lack of sensitivity Canada showed towards external challenges that characterize a redefined international context. Has the IPS answered this concern? Indeed, it did. All the challenges previously identified were given some attention. Whether about organization, respect to be re-earned, or prioritization, examples abound throughout the document, which confirms that decision makers seem ready to meet the test brought by these challenges. Even the sacrosanct concept of multilateralism is reconsidered as the government acknowledges that Canada 'cannot be complacent' towards it and that 'reforming the world's multilateral system of governance will be a priority for Canada, but it cannot become an end in itself'.

The only challenge to which a less enthusiastic answer is offered is the one that considers the inclusion of new actors. This is in line with the lukewarm greeting reserved to civil society's involvement and to which I referred earlier. As long as one remains within the government apparatus—I refer here to the challenge of integrating other ministries—this does not seem to cause concerns. However, although the presence of 'new actors' on the international scene is impossible to ignore, the place the federal government offers them remains in the shadow and is not well defined. This is particularly true when considering the role provinces are ready to play since there are no explicit mentions of it in the *Overview*. One has to go to the *Diplomacy* booklet to find the following affirmation: 'speaking with one voice internationally is a pressing issue'.[43] It is clear that the federal government wishes to reduce the role of provinces to that of policy advisers, on an equal foot with NGOs and municipalities. If the government sticks to the letter of this proposal, this would mean an important step backwards not only for Quebec, but also for provinces like New

Brunswick or Alberta. More importantly, this represents an important denial of a major challenge Canadian foreign policy must take up.

Regarding the answer Canada should offer to challenges coming from the United States, we note that, in contrast, this is a topic detailed attention was given to. Thus, and according to what had already been known, the Prime Minister keeps a strong hand on the direction of this aspect of the policy. Moreover, the document concurs in looking at the US-based challenges under the concept of international respect that Canada has to re-earn. The policy dedicates the first part of its analysis to Canada's North Americaness. It places Canada–US relations in a broader context, where Canada is portrayed as having to take advantage of making itself better known and of being better recognized by its continental partners. More importantly, it is stated that 'we will set our own course and pull our own weight.' This directly answers the challenges that we have identified as being the needs for both differentiation ('to set our own course') and non-indifference ('to pull our own weight'). As for the question of sovereignty, the affirmation is also unequivocal, and even more so when it refers to the North.

Two challenges in particular represented major stumbling blocks on the way to a reform of Canadian foreign policy: the need for adaptation and the emergency to solve the heritage/innovation dilemma. Both of these challenges find a response in the policy. By looking at them, we are closing up on an answer as to why this policy was somehow unpredictable from former policy stances defended by various political parties. Obviously, more research needs to be done in order to bring a definite explanation as to why this policy goes further than what a reading of policy platforms has revealed. In this regard, the minutes of the Cabinet meetings will be a prime source of information, but we will have to wait 25 years made before they are made public. Nevertheless, some factors may already be taken into account.

For one, the analysis of the values and challenges stressed the importance to innovate, and in so doing, it took for granted that the development of policy would be made in a traditional way, starting from the familiar frames of reference and, especially, engaging the usual decision makers. As long as we remain within these well-defined operational boundaries, the dead-end caused by the lack of innovative willingness was unavoidable.

A new factor has been thrown in the process, quite unexpectedly. In order to finalize the shaping of this policy, the government called on an external resource, to the dismay and dissatisfaction of the political administrative community. No doubt, the Prime Minister approved of Oxford professor Jennifer Welsh's work: *At Home in the World*.[44] Bringing her on board broke the logjam and solved the heritage/innovation dilemma, the resource not being bound as much by the heritage dimension that seemed to paralyze to some extent the foreign policy decision making apparatus. This offered a fresher look at issues, a step back was taken and the evaluation could be made under new angles, some of which might have even been unsuspected to the seasoned decision makers.

By taking the process away from the political and administrative circles, the need for innovation was taken care of at its roots. The contribution of an external resource also made possible the prioritization of actions—another challenge of importance—that the bureaucratic battles (everyone wants to have her or his policy share recognized in the final document) and political lack of courage (no one wants to ruffle the feathers of an electoral constituency) often prevent from establishing.

I therefore submit that some of the elements outlined within the IPS could not have been part of policy if it had remained within the usual foreign policymaking framework. It was necessary to go outside these boundaries to take into account a greater number of factors, preserving the importance of values, but judiciously adding the need for answering the challenges that a redefined international environment offers to Canada.

Conclusion

This chapter started with straightforward questions: Should Canada base its foreign policy on the defense of its interests or on values? What role should these play? To answer it, we have analyzed historical trends in the use of values in Canadian foreign policy and has surveyed three sets of influential factors: psycho-social values, politico-organizational values, and challenges that the new world order poses to Canada's foreign policy.

A first conclusion that can be drawn is that these three sets are very loosely connected, each of them depicting a different reality. Moreover, very few issues are found in more than one set and, when they are, it could be from opposite points of view as it is the case with multilateralism: it is affirmed in the politico-administrative values, and questioned in the challenges. The results of the survey I conducted reveal more. The discrepancy between the three sets leads to think that depending on policymakers' preferences, values can be spared or challenges can be ignored. Of course, all actors involved in the foreign policymaking process take at least part of each set into consideration. The real dilemma lays in which set will prevail.

The answer to this last question offers a better estimate of the impact values have on the foreign policy process. Had they been the most influen-

tial factor in the shaping of the IPS, as might have been expected from past practice, and had challenges be largely ignored, values would have constituted a hindrance to the coming of a strong and articulated foreign policy that Canada needed. The government would have then simply adopted and perhaps merely reformulated the usual Canadian foreign policy discourse. Had they been matched with a good dose of pragmatism as it used to be the case in Canadian foreign policy history, they might have inspire a foreign policy that adapted itself to a changing world.

The survey of the IPS shows that, with the step back an external source probably provided, the latter scenario prevailed. Values are still very much present throughout the policy, but the documents released by the Canadian government demonstrate a much higher level of sensitivity towards external challenges that might have been expected.

Will this help Canada regain part of its clout and prestige on the world scene? It is too early to tell. Much work needs to be done in order to reach such results. What is clear however, is that the government acknowledged a definite need to give values the right importance they deserve, using them to help Canada to look straight ahead towards a world in which it evolves, rather than backwards to comforting past glories.

Notes

1. House of Commons, *Debates* (Ottawa: Parliament, 2003b); House of Commons, *Debates* (Ottawa: Parliament, 2005)

2. Department of Foreign Affairs and International Trade, *Canada in the World* (Ottawa: DFAIT, 1995). Available at http//www.dfait-maeci.gc.ca/foreign_policy/cnd-world.

3. Lloyd Axworthy, *Navigating a New World: Canada's Global Future* (Toronto: Knopf Canada, 2003).

4. Denis Stairs, 'Myths, Morals and Reality in Canadian Foreign Policy', *International Journal* 58, 2 (2003): 239–56. Emphasis in original.

5. Jack L. Granatstein, 'The Importance of Being Earnest: Promoting Canada's National Interests through Tighter Ties with the US', *Benefactors Lecture 2003* (Toronto: C.D. Howe Institute: 2003), 19. Available at http://www.cdhowe.org/pdf/benefactors_lecture_2003.pdf.

6. Jennifer Welsh, *At Home in the World: Canada's Global Vision for the 21st Century* (Toronto: Harper Collins, 2004), 203. Emphasis in original.

7. Since the creation of the department in 1909, only two men—Charles Murphy, 1909–11 in the Laurier Government and William James Roche,

1911–12 in the Borden government—held the portfolio while not being, at the same time, Prime Minister. It is important to note however that this was in the early beginnings of the department, when Canada had no autonomous international role; as soon as Prime Minister Borden saw an opportunity to get Canada involved internationally, he made sure the Prime Minister was the actor involved. Such an arrangement continued until an aging Mackenzie King—he was to resign two years later after 24 years at the helm—shared the task with Louis St-Laurent in 1946.

8. Department of External Affairs, *Statements and Speeches*, 1947.

9. On this, see John Hilliker, *Le ministre des affaires extérieures du Canada, vol. 1 : 'Les années de formation 1909–1946'* (Québec : Presses de l'Université Laval and Institut d'administration publique du Canada, 1990), 359–62.

10. This article reads: 'The Parties will contribute toward the further development of peaceful and friendly international relations by strengthening their free institutions, by bringing about a better understanding of the principles upon which these institutions are founded, and by promoting conditions of stability and well-being. They will seek to eliminate conflict in their international economic policies and will encourage economic collaboration between any or all of them.' Available at http://www.nato.int/docu/basictxt/treaty.htm.

11. Tom Keating, *Canada and World Order: The Multilateralist Tradition in Canadian Foreign Policy*, 2nd ed. (Don Mills, ON: Oxford University Press, 2002), 44. Keating's excellent analysis provides an enlightening reading on the basis on which Canadian diplomacy then operated.

12. Don Barry and John Hilliker, 'The Department of External Affairs in the Post-War Years, 1946–1968' in Donald C. Story, ed., *The Canadian Foreign Service in Transition* (Toronto: Canadian Scholars' Press, 1993), 11.

13. Ibid.; DFAIT, 1995.

14. *Liberal Foreign Policy Handbook* was a preliminary document had been prepared by Axworthy, who was then Chair of the Liberal caucus committee of foreign affairs and national defense and his vice-chair, Christine Stewart. For the platform itself, see Liberal Party of Canada, *Pour la création d'emplois et la relance de l'économie. Le plan d'action libéral pour le Canada* (Ottawa: Liberal Party, 1993).

15. These forums were organized from coast to coast, between 1996 and 2001, under specific themes: communications, Asia-Pacific relations, circumpolar relations, peace-building, the UN, Africa, the Americas, etc. According the CCFPD chair, their objective was to contribute public advice to the long-term development of Canadian foreign policy.

16. Department of Foreign Affairs. Available at http://www.humansecurity.gc.ca/menu-en.asp.

17. Rob McCrae, 'La sécurité humaine dans le contexte de la mondialisation', in Rob McCrae and Don Hubert, eds, *Sécurité humaine et nouvelle diplomatie : protection des personnes, promotion de la paix* (Montreal and Kingston: McGill-Queens University Press, 2001).

18. For a better understanding of Lloyd Axworthy's thoughts on these issues, see ibid Lloyd Axworthy; for an analysis of his legacy, see Fen Osler Hampson, Norman Hillmer and Maureen Apel Molot, *Canada Among Nations 2001: The Axworthy Legacy* (Don Mills, ON: Oxford University Press, 2001).

19. Nelson Michaud, *L'énigme du Sphinx: regards sur la vie politique d'un nationaliste (1910–1926)* (Sainte-Foy: Les Presses de l'Université Laval, 1998).

20. Greg Donaghy, *Tolerant Allies: Canada & the United States 1963–1968* (Montreal and Kingston: McGill Queen's University Press, 2002).

21. In fact, however, Canada was involved and kept operational vessels in the Persian Gulf. This aspect was reported, but nobody really paid attention. All that mattered to Canada was to portray itself as adhering, defending, and acting according to strongly held values. This was at the heart of the Canadian argumentation against participation.

22. Pico Iyer, 'Canada: Global Citizen', *Canadian Geographic*, Special 75th Anniversary Issue (2004): 62–9.

23. Steve Lee, 'Canadian Values in Canadian Foreign Policy', *Canadian Foreign Policy/La Politique étrangère du Canada* 10, 1 (2002): 1–9.

24. Ibid., 1.

25. House of Commons, *A Contribution To The Foreign Policy Dialogue* (Report of The Standing Committee On Foreign Affairs And International Trade, 2003), 12. Available at http://www.parl.gc.ca/InfoCom Doc/37/2/FAIT/Studies/Reports/faitrp06/faitrp06-e.pdf

26. They also add foreign aid as a value and spend most of the section on values considering its aspects. I have not retained aid in the psycho-social values for, as the parliamentary committee's report demonstrates, it is a value that originated from the government spokespeople they heard.

27. Department of Foreign Affairs and International Trade, *A Dialogue on Foreign Policy. Report to Canadians* (Ottawa: DFAIT, 2003), 12. Available at http://www.dfait-maeci.gc.ca/cip-pic/participate/Final Report.pdf.

28. Department of Foreign Affairs and International Trade, *A Dialogue on Foreign Policy. Consultation Paper* (Ottawa: DFAIT, 2003). Available at http://www.dfait-maeci.gc.ca/cip-pic/participate/fpd en.asp.

29. Keating, *Canada And World Order*.

30. The distinction between the three concepts is explained in other chapters of this book.

31. United Nations, *Ranking of Military and Civilian Police Contributions to UN Operations* (2005). Available at http://www.un.org/Depts/dpko/dpko/contributors/2005/ January2005_2.pdf.

32. John J. Mearsheimer, *The Tragedy of Great Power Politics* (New York: Norton, 2001).

33. I have identified the following ten challenges first, from a reading of the general situation, that is, the world political and economic trends and Canada's degree of preparation to deal with them. I also took into consideration the many opinions and analyses that have been voiced over the last few years, by analysts, observers, practitioners, and academics. Finally, I relied on scholarly presentations published in venues such as the *International Journal*, *Canadian Foreign Policy*, or the series *Canada Among Nations*, as well as recent academic published books.

34. Not that the other elements are of a lesser importance, but these first four items need to be addressed before any further action is taken.

35. Historically, the Canada–UK relationship, and now the one with the US, are notable exceptions.

36. Respect is a difficult concept to measure. However, it can de said that in the international community, when a country's action is not opposed by a mighty partner, when a country's leader can pull its weight when participating in international talks, and when the more powerful state signals to other international actors that this country matters, one can conclude that this country has earned respect from the more powerful one.

37. Joseph S. Nye, *Soft Power: The Means to Success in World Politics* (New York: BBS Public Affairs, 2004).

38. Stephen D. Krasner, *Sovereignty: Organized Hypocrisy* (Princeton: Princeton University Press, 1999).

39. Nelson Michaud, 'Souveraineté et sécurité : Le dilemme de la politique étrangère canadienne dans l' après 11 septembre', *Études internationales* 33, 4 (2002) : 647–65.

40. This is how Canadian international aid was portrayed.

41. Nelson Michaud, 'Le Québec dans le monde: faut-il redessiner les fondements de son action?' in Robert Bernier, ed., *L'État québécois au XXIème siècle* (Québec: Presses de l'Université du Québec, 2004), 125–68.

42. Nelson Michaud, 'The Canadian Response to 9-11: Answering the American Call or Calling for Canadian Values?'. Paper presented at the International Studies Association, Honolulu, 2005.

43. In French, the tone is quite different: 'la politique étrangère et la gestion des relations bilatérales *supposent* que nous nous exprimions et que nous agissions d'une seule et même voix sur la scène internationale' (emphasis added), 34.

44. Welsh, *At Home in the World*.

21

Promises Made, Promises Broken: Questioning Canada's Commitments to Climate Change

Douglas MacDonald and Heather A. Smith

Introduction

During the autumn of 1997, the environment was on the front pages of Canadian newspapers in a way not seen since the United Nations Conference on Environment and Development (UNCED) in Rio de Janeiro in 1992. A vigorous and very public debate over the position Canada should take at the international negotiations for a legally binding agreement to reduce greenhouse gas emissions was carried out amongst feuding departments and their ministers in Ottawa, the provinces, environmentalists, and the fossil fuel industry. The last two groups made unprecedented use of full page newspaper advertisements, one to warn of the spread of infectious diseases which might accompany global warming and the other of 'economic suicide' if Canada were to enter into any commitments, beyond those made at Rio, to reduce use or production of fossil fuels.[1] The politicians for their part, had no need to rely on advertising to get public attention, since the opposition parties, sensing political opportunity in the inability of the Liberal government of Jean Chrétien to manage the file and quietly broker a Canadian position, went on the attack daily in question period in the House of Commons. Representatives of provincial governments joined the debate. Alberta's environment minister warned that any use of federal taxing powers to induce energy conservation would lead his province to consider secession.[2] When Canadian negotiators finally agreed at Kyoto to reduce greenhouse gas emissions by 6 per cent no later than 2012, Premiers Roy Romanow of Saskatchewan and Gary Filmon of Manitoba immediately denounced Ottawa's failure to work co-operatively with the provinces, while Alberta's premier, Ralph Klein, declared that such a commitment was simply 'not acceptable'.[3]

Immediately after these outbursts the issue disappeared from the news. Klein and the oil and coal industries saw no need to continue their public protest following the Kyoto meeting. Instead of taking action to bring about the reductions in emissions of carbon dioxide and other gases agreed to at Kyoto, the federal and provincial governments announced plans to develop 'a process to examine the costs and the benefits of implementing the Kyoto Protocol and the various options for implementing the Protocol that are open to Canada'.[4] Whether or not the Kyoto Protocol will ever be ratified and implemented in Canada is open to question. In Rio in 1992 the

Canadian government made a commitment to stabilize emissions of carbon dioxide and greenhouse gases at 1990 levels by 2000. Canada cannot meet the 1992 commitment. It is very likely that the Kyoto commitment will prove just as hollow.

Why have successive Canadian governments appeared enthusiastic in international forums to make commitments to emissions reductions only to subsequently break those promises? The answer to that question can be found in part in domestic sources of foreign policy. Of particular importance in this case is the role of provincial governments. But the domestic bargaining process alone cannot fully explain the evolution of Canadian climate change policy. Canadian policy is inevitably affected by international processes and by geography. Decision-makers in Ottawa have to consider the interests of the United States as much as those of Alberta. While other variables are also important in this case, we believe that the absence or presence of pressure from the provinces, coupled with the activities and geographic reality of the United States, are the most significant variables.

A Chronology

Climate change is the enhancement of the natural greenhouse effect by both human and natural activities. The anthropogenic forcing arises from activities such as transportation deforestation, agriculture, industrial production and output, and forestry. Greenhouse gas emissions have multiple sources that are not isolated to the activities of one state. Climate change is a global issue that requires global action.

Recognizing the need for joint action, states came together in 1992 to negotiate the Framework Convention on Climate Change (FCCC). In December 1997 the Kyoto Protocol was negotiated. It is intended to bring about reductions in the release of six gases: carbon dioxide (CO_2), methane (CH_4), nitrous oxide (N_2O), hydrofluorocarbons (HFCs), polyfluorocarbons (PFCs), and sulphur hexafluoride (SF_6). Although some of the other gases have a greater effect per quantity, carbon dioxide 'represents 60–70 per cent of the problem'.[5]

Carbon dioxide emissions reductions will prove a challenge for Canada. Unlike sulphur dioxide emitted from smelters or utilities, or chlorofluorocarbons (CFCs) with a limited number of uses, most of which can be met by substitute products, fossil fuel generation and use lies at the heart of the production process. Beyond the immediate efficiency gains, which can be achieved through such things as improved building insulation, significant reductions in energy use are perceived to have major impacts on domestic and international economic performance. The challenge of reducing emissions will likely be an onerous task for many states. An examination of the climate change issue in the Canadian context indicates that Canada may not rise to the challenge.

In the late 1980s, during the 'second wave'[6] of popular support for environmental protection and as part of the new agenda occasioned by the dismantling of the Berlin Wall, international attention increasingly turned to the environment. The first attempts to grapple with the issue of climate change were part of that international greening. Although the issue was not new to the scientific community, climate change was propelled into the spotlight of international political attention in the late 1980s because of the 'summer of 88', one of the hottest ever recorded. It was at that time that the Canadian government co-hosted 'Our Changing Atmosphere: Implications for Global Security', otherwise known as the Toronto Conference.

At that meeting, Canada not only helped to put climate change on the international policy agenda but also proposed a solution—a Law of the Atmosphere, comparable to the Law of the Sea. In essence, the idea was to take a holistic approach that recognized and reaffirmed the linkages amongst all major atmospheric issues.[7] The concept of a law of the atmosphere was reflected in the concluding statement from the conference, which called for a comprehensive global convention.[8] It was also the centrepiece of the follow-up conference—the meeting of Legal and Policy Experts. It is now clear that the concept essentially died at that meeting, a result of opposition from Mostafa Tolba, the executive director of the United Nations Environment Programme, who feared another descent into the Law of the Sea quagmire and a lack of support from the United States.

Canadian efforts helped place climate change on the international agenda. At the domestic level, the Progressive Conservative government of Brian Mulroney made the commitment to stabilize carbon dioxide and other greenhouse gases from 1990 levels by 2000 government policy when it issued its Green Plan in 1990. The same commitment was made internationally when Canada signed and became one of the first states to ratify the FCCC. Consistent with this apparent enthusiasm for climate change commitment, the Chrétien Liberals promised, in their 1993 election platform, to reduce CO_2 by 20 per cent from 1988 levels by 2005. Although the Liberals won the 1993 election, the 20 per cent reduction commitment has never been seriously considered as a bargaining position in the domestic arena.

Faced with the task of implementing its commitment to stabilization, the newly elected Liberal government began to develop the National Action Plan on Climate Change (NAPCC) in November 1993 with federal and provincial energy and environment ministers. They set up a multi-stakeholder process that included industry and other affected parties to develop 'options to meet Canada's international commitment to stabilize greenhouse gas emissions by the year 2000'.[9] Not long afterward, the business stakeholders argued that any Canadian programme should be based on voluntarism rather than law.[10]

Between 1993 and 1995 the domestic component of Canadian climate change policy focused on the development of the NAPCC. Throughout this period, the environment minister, Sheila Copps, strongly advocated both federal leadership and the use of regulatory mechanisms to bring about emissions reductions. This position brought her into

confrontation with the petroleum industry, the Conservative government in Alberta, and the Alberta representative in cabinet, Anne McLellan, Minister of Natural Resources Canada (NRCan). McLellan favoured a voluntary approach, a choice strongly influenced by export trade considerations. 'We must not depart so fundamentally from our southern neighbours, with whom we conduct 85 per cent of our trade for we would risk seriously damaging Canada's competitiveness and, as a result, our economy.'[11]

By early 1995, it was still not clear whether the federal government would impose regulations, put in place positive or negative financial incentives, or rely solely on voluntary mechanisms. A month before the national programme was announced, however, McLellan and NRCan made a separate peace with the petroleum industry. NRCan and the Canadian Association of Petroleum Producers (CAPP) signed a Memorandum of Agreement on 20 January 1995, which committed CAPP to work with NRCan to develop and promote the Voluntary Challenge and Registry Program. A news release issued by CAPP stated that the agreement 'demonstrates that the voluntary approach is a meaningful and substantive way to make progress in addressing climate change'.[12]

The National Action Program on Climate Change, publicly presented on 20 February 1995, had as its central element the Voluntary Challenge Registry, under which all greenhouse gas emitters would publicly 'register' their plans for reduction. The programme relies on altruism to motivate such action rather than on the coercive or inducive powers of the state. NAPCC also presented reductions strategies that were central elements of Canada's international negotiating position. One of the more significant was joint implementation, which allows for any facilitated emissions reductions by Canadian activities abroad to count toward the Canadian target. NAPCC proposed a series of goals and strategies for Canadian climate change policy—programmes that continue to be central to Canadian policy. Unfortunately, the emphasis on voluntary approaches meant that

Canada would not meet its stabilization target. But it was all that could be agreed upon by the federal and provincial ministers. The NAPCC was fashioned in the manner of a 'national consensus'.

The likelihood that Canada would not meet its 1992 commitment had international implications. In March 1995 at the first Conference of Parties (COP) to the FCCC in Berlin, Copps was forced to concede that Canada could do better. But it did not do better. In December 1996, the federal and provincial ministers stated that Canadian emissions were 9.4 per cent above the 1990 level in 1995 and would be 8 per cent above that by 2000.[13] Still, climate change was not an issue that was quickly going to disappear. And while Canada made at least a rhetorical commitment to doing better at Berlin, it also endorsed the Berlin Mandate, which carried far more weight than the statement of a minister. The mandate called on the conference of parties to aim for a legally binding protocol by the time of the third COP Kyoto in 1997. International negotiations continued, and Canada struggled with its emissions levels. Perhaps, then, it is not surprising that since the Berlin meeting Canada has been part of a blocking coalition known as JUSCANZ (Japan, United States, Canada, Australia, and New Zealand).

At COPI, JUSCANZ rejected all attempts by the European Union (EU) who wanted Annex 1 states (typically developed states) to cap their emissions at 1990 levels by 2000. Canada sought 'a process of negotiations for post-2000 commitments without predetermining the outcome of these negotiations'.[14] JUSCANZ, generally, was seen as complicating the negotiations with demands for emissions reductions by more advanced developing states and, until COPII in Geneva, as having an implicit coalition with the oil-rich Organization of Petroleum Exporting Countries (OPEC). The coalition appeared to break down at COPII over the Second Assessment Report of the Intergovernmental Panel on Climate Change.[15]

In the months leading up to the Kyoto meeting, the development of Canadian climate change policy appeared confused. In late October 1997, only six weeks before the meeting, statements by the federal environment minister, Christine Stewart, revealed that the Canadian government had no idea of how to broker a Canadian commitment to action beyond the voluntarism of the National Action Program and basically wished the whole issue would just go away. On 22 October, Stewart said: 'we made a mistake in 1992 at Rio in saying that we would make a commitment to level our emissions to 1990 by the year 2000.'[16] That same day, Minister of Natural Resources Ralph Goodale said Ottawa has not ruled out the use of taxation as an incentive for emission reduction, thereby immediately incurring the wrath of Alberta. The next day, Stewart committed the politician's ultimate faux pas by running away when asked by the press about Goodale's statement.[17] The conflicts between Edmonton and Ottawa, Environment Canada and other federal departments, and the fossil fuel industry and environmentalists had boiled over. The national consensus on climate change was revealed for the myth that it was. And yet, a position still had to be cobbled together.

The federal cabinet debated the issue at a meeting on 4 November 1997. According to press reports, an agreement in principle was reached: the Canadian position at Kyoto should be to call for stabilization by 2012 and for reductions after that date (a position that gave the appearance of greater commitment than that of the administration of Bill Clinton in the United States). It was agreed, however, that a final decision would not be made until after the federal–provincial meeting in Regina the following week.[18] The federal and provincial ministers emerged from their negotiating session on 12 November 1997 to announce that, with the exception of Quebec, they had agreed to stabilize emissions by approximately 2010, a position previously endorsed by the Clinton administration and the federal cabinet. In spite of this apparent agreement, the Regina commitment was not the final Canadian position.

The Prime Minister's Office continued its search for a Canadian position demonstrably superior to that of the Americans but one that would not at the same time cause undue offence to the provinces. At a meeting on 28 November, cabinet discussed a proposal by the prime minister to move the target date for stabilization forward to 2007. Finally, on Monday, 3 December, the federal government announced that Canada's position at the Kyoto talks, which by that time had already started, would see no change in the target date but would call for a 3 per cent reduction instead of stabilization. When Kyoto was over, Canada had agreed to 6 per cent cuts in emissions.

The domestic response to the Canadian commitment was quick and divided. The Business Council on National Issues expressed 'surprise, disappointment and dismay'.[19] Greenpeace was equally unhappy, although for opposite reasons: 'Greenpeace climate change staff have labeled the result of the Kyoto Climate Summit a tragedy and a farce because it is totally inadequate to slow the environmental impacts of climate change.'[20] As noted in the introduction, many premiers expressed dismay and went into a first ministers meeting, convened shortly after the Kyoto meeting, apoplectic. They emerged surprisingly calm. It is impossible to escape the conclusion that the prime minister gave them private assurances that, yet again, Canadian rhetoric would in all likelihood not translate into action.

Assessing Canada's Climate Change Comments

Why have successive Canadian governments appeared enthusiastic about making commitments in the area of climate change, only to renege on them subsequently? To answer that question, we have to ask why the commitments were made in the first place. Any answer has to include both international and domestic variables and should begin with an understanding of the forces behind Canada's initial enthusiasm in the late 1980s.

Three factors have to be considered when looking for international sources of behaviour. First, the late 1980s was a period of international greening. Environmental issues were high on the international agenda, and Canada was influenced by this general trend. Second, Canada had taken an active role in the international negotiations on ozone depletion, and early behaviour on climate change, including the Law of the Atmosphere initiative, was consistent with the image of a bold environmental internationalist.[21] Third, Canada could seize the opportunity to play a leadership role because United States leadership on climate change was sadly lacking in 1988. In essence, there was a leadership vacuum. And, while American interests quickly coalesced to oppose the Law of the Atmosphere and progressive targets and timetables, Canada persevered in its apparent leadership role—at least for a while.

Domestically, the role of the prime minister has to be examined. Environmental issues were high on both domestic and international agendas in the 1980s, and attention was just beginning to turn to the latest concern, climate change. This gave Brian Mulroney, who was trailing in the polls and faced with the imminent need to call an election, an excellent opportunity to bolster his international profile. Rather than leaving the issue to his minister, Mulroney became personally involved. Second, Canada's technical skills to support initiatives on climate change were considerable and were internationally recognized: consistent with the concept of functional internationalism, Canada possessed functional expertise on climate change. Maurice Strong had chaired the 1972 Stockholm Conference. Jim Macneil played an integral role in the work of the Brundtland Commission. Canadian representation in international environmental diplomacy in the area of climate change is quite impressive and includes such individuals as Jim Bruce, a former assistant deputy minister (ADM) of the Atmospheric Environment Service (AES) and Maurice Strong. The expertise and skill of another former ADM of AES, Elizabeth Dowdeswell, resulted in her appointment as executive director of the United Nations Environment Programme. Functional expertise is also apparent in the Law of the Atmosphere initiative first developed by the AES of the Department of Environment and quickly adopted by the federal minister of environment at the time, Tom McMillan, and supported by Mulroney. Finally, a crucial element in the explanation of Canada's initial enthusiasm is the fact that in 1988 the domestic political actors who would incur significant costs if greenhouse gas emissions were to be reduced, such as the Canadian Association of Petroleum Producers, had not yet mobilized in opposition. It should be remembered that the 1988 Toronto conference put the issue on the international agenda: it also put it on the domestic agenda. While there had been some impact assessment done within the confines of AES, many of the key players were caught off guard by the emergence of the issue. The provinces did not begin to give the topic serious consideration until 1989, the same year that a parliamentary committee reviewed the issue. Before the Toronto conference, it was an issue of minor importance.

The initial blush of enthusiasm carried Canada into the climate change negotiations. That Canada opted for stabilization in 1992 rather than more aggressive reduction is testimony to the fact that domestic and international forces had coalesced to constrain overly enthusiastic initiatives. The provinces and the oil and gas industry had mobilized and were consulted during the international negotiations. Furthermore, by 1992 it was apparent that the provinces would resist aggressive emission reductions policies and that the Mulroney government was faced with imminent decisions about implementation. Internationally, divisions existed between the EU, which wanted emissions reductions, and the United States, which was hesitant to make any commitment. The Canadian government viewed its position on stabilization as the 'middle road'. The other point to recall is that the stabilization commitment made in the FCCC was voluntary. The looseness of the commitment allowed for some flexibility and did not demand of states the same kind of cost/benefit analysis as a more stringent or binding commitment. Developed states could endorse a voluntary

stabilization goal with only minimal embarrassment if the commitment was unfulfilled.

By 1995 it became apparent that by 2000 Canada would not meet the commitment it had made in 1992. Each subsequent year Canada's emissions were projected to be well over the stabilization target. Canada was not unique in its inability, or perhaps unwillingness, to meet the 1992 commitment. Other states, such as the United States, Australia, and many members of the EU, would not meet the stabilization commitment either. The JUSCANZ coalition also functioned to support Canadian interests internationally. Coalition members adopted similar positions in the negotiations, often uniting against the EU. And while JUSCANZ was accused of undermining progress, for its members there is some comfort in being in a coalition of laggards rather than the sole laggard. Canada's involvement in the coalition is in part explained by the fact that any attempts Canada may have made to adopt more aggressive reductions, right up until Kyoto, were constrained by domestic forces.

Not that the domestic forces were united. The basic argument made by environmentalists was that short-term, limited actions to increase energy efficiency of machines and buildings could be justified solely on economic grounds, regardless of their environmental implications. The business community split into at least three camps. The most extreme position—that climate change did not exist and therefore no action could be justified—was taken by companies such as Imperial echoed the Coal Association's concern about 'economic suicide' when it said: 'Canada must avoid committing (at Kyoto) to any legally binding arrangement to constrain greenhouse-gas emissions that limits our economic potential particularly against arbitrary targets and timetables beyond 2000.'[22]

The policy solutions advocated by CAPP included both the form of the agreement to be negotiated at Kyoto and the Canadian domestic programme. CAPP argued that the former must include developing countries, take individual circumstances into account when setting national targets, and allow for such things as natural gas exports, used in the receiving jurisdiction to off-set more carbon-intensive fuels, to be taken into account when calculating each country's net contributions to the problem.[23]

Renewable energy and nuclear industries held the third position. They, of course, have an economic interest in moving away from fossil fuel. During the 1997 Canadian debate, the insurance industry, concerned about increasing pay-outs for losses caused by severe weather, publicly argued for increased Canadian action on the problem.[24] The nuclear industry, for its part, also ran a full-page ad, claiming that: 'When the issue is global warming, the benefits of generating electricity with nuclear energy are clear.'[25]

Prior to Kyoto, the provinces, especially Alberta, tried to limit any adventurism on the part of the federal government. Ottawa could negotiate in the international arena and keep the provinces in a consultative position, but implementation strategies constitutionally required the involvement of the provinces because natural resources are under provincial jurisdiction. Jurisdictional interests, combined with powerful economic interests, made many provincial leaders wary of commitments to emissions reductions. Right up to the federal–provincial meeting of November 1997, several provinces were opposed to any kind of serious reduction commitment. On the eve of that discussion, the *Globe and Mail* provided a survey of provincial positions that corresponded, not surprisingly, to their energy production and consumption needs. Alberta opposed any international commitment to a reduction in emissions. Other energy-producing provinces, such as British Columbia, Saskatchewan, Newfoundland, and Nova Scotia, were also wary of international commitments. Quebec, on the other hand, with its heavy reliance on hydro-electric power, called for 'an aggressive approach on cuts to carbon-dioxide production'.[26]

The recalcitrance of the provinces, combined with interdepartmental divisions that set the Department of the Environment (DOE) against NRCan, made it difficult to achieve anything other then the lowest common denominator. The federal government, however, is not some hapless victim of the provinces and the oil industry. The Chrétien government is committed to fiscal restraint and economic competitiveness. It cut the budget of the Department of Environment by 30 per cent,[27] and the Atmospheric Environment Service has been particularly hard hit. Since the federal government's commitment to the environment was obviously open to question, how could Canada's agreement to reductions at Kyoto be explained?

Explaining the Kyoto Commitment

To understand why the federal government was willing to break from the 'national consensus' prior to Kyoto, and then agreed to 6 per cent reductions at Kyoto, we need to consider the sincerity of the Canadian commitment and the role of the United States. The sincerity of the commitment is certainly open to question. Public and private assurances were made to placate disgruntled industry and provincial interests. Remember that the national consensus included not only domestic reductions strategies but also internationally implemented reduction strategies. Assurances were made behind closed doors that Canada would aggressively support what are now called 'flexibility mechanisms' such as joint implementation, the Clean Development Mechanism, and emissions trading. These mechanisms were viewed as a way to reduce the demand for reductions at home, while at the same time fostering technology transfer and the global reduction of greenhouse gas emissions. At Kyoto, Canada strongly supported the inclusion of these mechanisms. It also pushed for inclusion of carbon sinks in counting emissions reductions, a benefit to a country such as Canada with huge tracts of land.

One gets mixed messages about the role of the United States in the Canadian decision-making process. The messages received were sometimes that Canada had to better the United States position, sometimes it had to match the United States position, and sometimes it was implied that Canada would take a backseat to the United States.

The message that 'Canada must beat the United States' was delivered by the prime minister. On 24 June 1997, Chrétien stated in an address to the United Nations General Assembly Special Session on Sustainable Development that his government 'supports the establishment of legally-binding medium-term targets for post-2000 greenhouse gas reductions'.[28] This statement, although vague, signalled that Canada was willing to take a position on long-term reductions. Unfortunately, a commitment to long-term reductions did not measure up to the positions taken by others. For example, the Alliance of Small Island States called for a carbon dioxide emission reduction of 15 per cent from 1990 levels by 2005, and the EU advocated a 15 per cent reduction. As the summer of 1997 wore on, the argument that Canada's international reputation was in jeopardy seemed to carry some weight with Chrétien: 'Internationally, Canada is a laggard and the prime minister has made it clear that he doesn't want to be embarrassed in Kyoto.'[29] In October 1997, the American government presented its position, which called for the stabilization of emissions between 2003 and 2012 and the use of international trade in reductions and domestic use of subsidy and tax incentive.[30]

The United States position became the beachmark for preserving Canadian national honour. Canada had to go into Kyoto supporting at least some form of reduction over the same time period, thus showing Canada was more clearly on the side of the angels than was the United States. The desire to beat the United States can, in part, be explained by a degree of nostalgia for the time of 'bold environmental internationalism'. Chrétien's position can be seen as an attempt to refurbish Canadian credibility and legitimacy in the international environment arena. Canada wanted to be seen as a player in these negotiations, as it was in the past over ozone depletion or acid rain. The American documents on climate change present the negotiations as tripartite negotiations

between Japan, the EU, and the United States. If it was not to be lost under the American umbrella, Canada had to assert itself. Assertion came in the form of 'beating the US'. Ultimately, the American commitment was to a higher percentage of reductions than Canada was prepared to allow.

The second type of message sent was that Canada must meet the United States. This message was often delivered by Ralph Goodale, the minister of NRCan. Driving much of Canadian climate change policy is a concern about economic losses that would arise if Canada acted unilaterally or, alternatively, if it acted out of step with its largest trading partner. This concern for a level playing field with the United States has been used to coerce domestic interests into recognizing the need for Canada to be part of the Kyoto process. Goodale explained that Canada's commitment at Kyoto was impelled by the United States commitment. He argued that Canada must stay in sync with the United States and remain competitive in new energy efficient technologies, 'otherwise the risk of commercial harassment or non-tariff trade barriers could have severe repercussions'.[31]

Finally, both Goodale and the Prime Minister delivered the message that Canada would follow the American lead or 'take a back seat', especially after the Kyoto commitment was made. Following the American lead gave Canada the necessary loophole and functioned as a means by which to placate irate industry and provinces. Industry and the provinces were assured by Goodale that 'should the United States not ratify an agreement reached in Kyoto, Canada would consider not participating.'[32] In other words, if the protocol is not ratified in the Unites States, it may well not be ratified in Canada either. This was consistent with a report of a comment made by Chrétien after the Kyoto meeting: 'some treaties in the past have not been ratified.'[33] Interests opposed to reductions should be calmed by this assurance, especially given the dynamics in the United States.

President Clinton's scope for movement was limited because he lacked congressional support. In July 1997, the Senate unanimously adopted a resolution, sponsored by Senators Robert Byrd of West Virginia, a coal-mining state, and Charles Hagel of Nebraska, which linked American participation in any international protocol with reductions in developing nations. That position was publicly endorsed by the United Mine Workers of American and the AFL-CIO.[34] In October 1997, the United States did announce a position, the same position that Canada subsequently claimed it would beat. But the Clinton administration was careful to reassure its audience that it would make every effort to ensure that developing states participated, in some way, in the Kyoto Protocol. This position was greeted with disdain by some developing states such as China, while other states such as Argentina were willing to make voluntary commitments. The Americans signed the protocol but they did not ratify it. And without American ratification, it is likely doomed.

So what does this analysis say about the impact of domestic and international forces? Unlike the late 1980s, one would be hard pressed to say that 1997 is part of a period of international greening. On the contrary economic globalization, which promotes the free market and economic competitiveness over environmental protection, is the driving force in the international system. Why, then would any state participate in international environmental negotiations? The answer is that in spite of the dominance of liberal economics, there remains some shred of concern for environmental protection. Furthermore, climate change negotiations can be interpreted as economic, not environmental, negotiations. The key debates revolve around economic instruments, burden sharing, and technological and financial transfer. Canada participates in international climate change debates largely because of the negotiations. Indeed, there still are individuals in the federal government who are committed to environmental protection, but that commitment is secondary to the need to be at the table when economic rules and regulations are being negotiated, especially if the rules and regulations will affect Canada's economic relationship with the United States.

The role of the United States is paramount. Canada has clearly watched the development of American climate change policy. Canadian attentiveness is rooted in the economic reality of the Canadian–American relationship. This is not to suggest that Canada is without choice. Certainly Prime Minister Chrétien made a choice, thus showing again that the role of the prime minister is significant to the Canadian policy response. Unlike Mulroney, Chrétien, during his time as prime minister, had not taken an avid interest in Canadian climate change. His focus was on trade, international competitiveness, and domestic debt reduction. Nonetheless, he was affected by the tarnished Canadian image. He used his prerogative to push for a commitment so that Canada could retain some glimmer of international credibility and to give the impression to the Canadian public that the federal government was committed to action. Technical skills, or at least those housed in DOE, that were important in 1988 seemed less important in 1997. This can be explained in part by the downsizing of DOE and the perception that this is an economic and energy issue. The provinces had and will continue to have a vital effect on the development and implementation of Canadian climate change policy. Their involvement in the development of implementation strategies must be taken as a given. They could not stop the federal government from making a commitment at Kyoto, but they did influence the terms of ratification.

Conclusions

This assessment of Canadian climate change policy offers some insights for students of Canada's international environmental policy and Canadian foriegn policy in general. It leads one to ponder the making and breaking of international commitments. Initiatives taken in the agenda-setting stage of an issue, such at those taken by the Mulroney government, may be rhetorical, but they may also function as normative constraints or incentives for future action. In some ways, the Mulroney government was impelled by its own self-image to make the 1992 stabilization commitment. It is also important to note that there is little cost associated with the articulation of principles. This is soft power in action, and while it is a term favoured by the current minister of foreign affairs, Lloyd Axworthy, the promotion of ideas is not unique to the Liberal government. Supporting a few international meetings and calling for the protection of the environment is not the same as trying to come to grips with the potential economic costs of emissions reductions in a cold, big country addicted to fossil fuels. The Mulroney government was not faced with the task of trying to implement those principals. Indeed, the Green Plan was produced in 1990 and funds were made available to implement some of its objectives, but the domestic process for implementing the voluntary commitment made to the FCCC did not begin in earnest until late in 1993 after the Liberal government was elected. The Liberals had to act on the earlier commitments, a task that proved difficult.

We must also ask: commitments for whom or what? Was the Kyoto commitment made to protect the environment or to save Canadian face? Optimists may opt for the former, but in light of the evidence presented here, we believe that Kyoto was about saving face internationally and, to some extent, domestically. The bumbling of the Chrétien government on this issue was very public. The Kyoto commitment was also made to ensure a place for the Canadian government at the table. Canada does not want to be excluded from the ongoing discussions of this issue, especially as the process moves toward serious technical work on the flexibility mechanisms and rules for compliance. To help shape the rules you have to be at the table.

Canada's behaviour on climate change has implications for Canadian foreign policy more generally. Take, for example, the promotion of human security, which Axworthy has made his mantra. A key component of human security is environmental integrity. What does Canadian behaviour on climate change suggest about the credibility of the commitment to human security? Canada's climate change track record—the inability to keep promises and meet commitments makes a mockery of human security claims, since it shows so clearly that this country places economic competitiveness about other values. Furthermore, how does one square recent statements about belonging to a moral minority with Canadian climate change policy? Canadian foreign policy cannot support claims of morality and the inherent 'goodness' the term implies when commitments are subsequently broken or are shallow and lack substance. Selective morality seems a more appropriate term, with the idealist impulse reserved for issues such as small arms.

This article has attempted to explain why successive governments have appeared enthusiastic about making climate change commitments that they have subsequently broken. In recognizing the interplay of domestic and international sources of foreign policy, we identified roles for the provinces and the United States. As of the future of the Kyoto commitment, we expect, sadly, that Canada will not meet the 1997 stabilization commitment. The implications of this conclusion are significant because the credibility of Canadian diplomacy and future initiatives cannot help but be affected. 'Promises made, promises broken' is an unfortunate epithet of Canadian foreign policy.

Notes

1. David Suzuki Foundation, 'Global Warming's Greatest Threat May also be the Smallest', *Globe and Mail*, 29 October 1997; emphasis in original. The Coal Association of Canada, 'Some Japanese terms Canadians ought to Know: Seppuku: Ritual suicide with honor. Kyoto: Economic suicide by ignorance', *Globe and Mail*, 5 November 1997.

2. Matthew Ingram, 'Carbon Tax Hysteria Mounts', *Globe and Mail*, 30 October 1997.

3. Edward Greenspon, 'Provinces Let Down at Kyoto,

Klein says', *Globe and Mail*, 12 December 1997.

4. Notice to the media, Joint Meeting of Federal, Provincial and Territorial Ministers of Energy and Environment, 24 April 1998.

5. Remarks by Gordon McBean, Assistant Deputy Minister, Atmospheric Environment Service, Environment Canada, to the National Round Table on Environment and Economy National Forum on Climate Change, 16–17 February 1998.

6. The 'first wave' occurred in the late 1960s. See Robert Paehlke, 'Green Politics and the Rise of the Environmental Movement', in Thomas Fleming, ed., *The Environment and Canadian Society* (Toronto: ITP Nelson, 1997).

7. Howard Ferguson, Draft, *World Conference on the Changing Atmosphere—Highlights of the Planning Process* (Toronto: Atmospheric Environment Agency), 11 July 1988, 2.

8. Ibid.

9. 'Federal Regulation: Global Warming Report, More Action Needed to Achieve Canadian Commitments', *Environment Policy & Law* (March 1994): 356.

10. Ken F. McCready, 'Global Climate Changed: A Challenge for Business Leadership', *Canadian Business Review* (Summer 1994): 38.

11. Notes for a Speech by the Honourable Anne McLellan, Minister of Natural Resources Canada to the VCR Climate Change Challenge Awards Luncheon, Ottawa, 23 October 1996, both from 3.

12. CAPP Media release, 20 January 1995.

13. James Rusk, 'Emissions Target Won't be Reached, Ministers Concede', *Globe and Mail*, 13 December 1996, A4.

14. Canada, Canadian Delegation Report, 'Climate change first conference of parties', 1995, 5.

15. See Heather A. Smith, 'Canadian federalism and international environmental policy-making: the case of climate change', Queen's University, Institute of Intergovernmental Relations, Working Paper 1998 (5), 14.

16. Cited in Andrew Cohen and Anne McIlroy, 'U.S. Proposes Gradual Reduction of Greenhouse Gases', *Globe and Mail*, 23 October 1997, A9.

17. Anne McIlroy, 'Liberals on the Hot Seat over Global Warming', *Globe and Mail*, 24 October 1997, A4.

18. Anne McIlroy, ' Global-warming Decision on Hold,' *Globe and Mail*, 5 November 1997.

19. Canada News Wire, 'Business Leaders Express Dismay at Canada's Climate Change Commitment in Kyoto', December 1997.

20. Greenpeace Press release, 'Climate Agreement Endangers the Planet', 11 December 1997, quoted in *Greenlink: Canadian Environment Magazine* 6 (Winter/Spring 1998): 7.

21. G. Bruce Doern, *Green Diplomacy: How Environmental Decisions are Made* (Toronto: C.D. Howe Institute, 1993), 125.

22. 'Global Climate Change, Time for a Reality Check', Imperial Oil. Available at http://www.exxon.com/imperaloil/news/globewrm.htm.

23. Ibid.

24. Terence Corcoran, 'Climate: Where's the Science', *Globe and Mail*, 23 September 1997.

25. *Globe and Mail*, 26 November 1997.

26. Brian Laghi, 'Greenhouse-gas Plan Vital, Ottawa told', *Globe and Mail*, 12 November 1997.

27. Lorna Stefanick and Kathleen Wells, 'Staying the Course or Saving Face? Federal Environmental Policy post-Rio', in Leslie A. Pal, ed, *How Ottawa Spends: 1998–99* (Don Mills, ON: Oxford University Press, 1998), 252.

28. Notes for an Address by Prime Minister Jean Chrétien on the occasion of the United Nations General Assembly Special Session on Sustainable Development, New York, 24 June 1997.

29. McIlroy, 'Liberals on the Hot Seat over Global Warming'.

30. Cohen and McIlroy, 'U.S. Proposed Gradual Reduction of Greenhouse Gases'.

31. Canada, Natural Resources Canada, Speech, 'Post-Kyoto: Technological Solutions to Climate Change', 17 December 2.

32. Brian Laghi, 'Provinces in Accord on Gas Emissions', *Globe and Mail*, 13 November 1997.

33. 'Klein Wins Backing on Objections to Kyoto Accord', *Edmonton Journal*, 13 December 1997.

34. E-Wire Press Release, UMWA, 'United Mine Workers President Cecil Roberts Praises Senate Action on UN Treaty', 25 July 1998.

22

Competing Rationales for Canadian Development Assistance: Reducing Global Poverty, Enhancing Canadian Prosperity and Security, or Advancing Global Human Security

Cranford Pratt

Ethical Values and Canadian Development Assistance

After 1945, a cosmopolitan dimension gradually became a feature of the political cultures of most industrialized societies as they came to accept that they had obligations to promote basic human rights beyond their borders and to aid the development of the world's poorest peoples and countries. However, the attachment of most governments to these obligations has never been other than fragile,[1] and their impact on public policy has often been overshadowed by national interest imperatives, both economic and political. Nevertheless, from a human perspective, the emergence of a cosmopolitan ethic that asserts in particular an international obligation to advance basic human rights and to promote the development needs of the poorest is a significant development.[2]

By the mid-1960s, Canada had begun to respond more than minimally to these newer obligations, and, until quite recently, the official rhetoric of the Canadian government located the objective of its development assistance squarely within the emerging cosmopolitan ethic. Both major cabinet-endorsed policy statements on Canadian aid between 1975 and 1993 defined the primary objective of the Canadian International Development Agency (CIDA) in humanitarian rather than commercial, political, or security terms.[3] This was also the judgment of Canadian parliamentarians on the four important occasions between 1980 and 1994 when committees of parliament gave detailed consideration to Canadian aid policies.[4] During the same period, public opinion overwhelmingly held to the view that the primary purpose of aid programmes should be to help the development efforts of the poorest countries and peoples.[5] A recent professionally sophisticated poll demonstrates that public support for development assistance remains surprisingly strong, and for essentially ethical reasons.[6]

Those who embrace the humane internationalist perspective have always recognized, indeed stressed, that development assistance was in Canada's long-term political and economic interest. Foreign aid can reasonably be expected to contribute to a healthy global economy and to a less strife-riven world, both of which are clearly to Canada's advantage. Nevertheless, the primary motive behind foreign aid was and should remain humanitarian rather than the pursuit of any national interests, economic, political, or security. Mitchell Sharp made the point over 25 years ago:

'if the purpose of aid is to help ourselves rather than to help others, we shall probably receive in return what we deserve and a good deal less than we expect.'[7]

Domestic Influences on CIDA Policies

The emergence of a substantial Canadian aid programme did not happen in isolation from domestic politics in Canada. The programme simultaneously reflected the major shift in social values that had, in the same era, led to the development of extensive social welfare programmes in Canada without, however, challenging that particular responsiveness of public policy to corporate interests which is a feature of the Canadian political system.[8] The interaction of these influences meant that transplanting liberal welfare values to foreign policy through an expanded aid programme quickly encountered powerful pressures from within government and from the corporate sector for the aid programme to promote other foreign policy objectives, including, in particular, the advancement of Canadian trade interests. Thus from its early years, CIDA was, in the words which open the most comprehensive parliamentary review of Canadian aid policies ever undertaken, 'beset by a confusion of purpose'.[9]

For many years there has been a struggle inside government between those who want to ensure that CIDA is ever more responsive to trade and other foreign policy objectives and those, primarily within CIDA, who want to limit the erosion of CIDA's putative primary focus on helping the poorest peoples and countries. Each group had its allies outside of government. Those advocating greater responsiveness to trade interests were supported by powerful corporate lobbies; those seeking to check this trend were supported by the active community of Canadian non-governmental organizations (NGOs) and recurrently by parliamentary committees. Most observers agree that there has been a gradual and serious erosion of the humane internationalist emphasis of Canadian aid in the years since 1977.[10] Although

the proponents of this emphasis are beleaguered, they are not yet overwhelmed. Many within CIDA, the NGO community, and elsewhere continue to fight a sustained rearguard action to protect and augment CIDA's development work with the poorest. Had humane internationalist motivations been entirely swamped by trade and national security considerations, Bangladesh would not still receive substantial quantities of Canadian bilateral aid; more than 40 per cent of Canadian bilateral aid would not still go to Africa; emphasis would not still be placed on meeting basic human needs; and there would not be within CIDA today a significant effort to ensure that poverty reduction is the common element in all of CIDA's policies and programmes.

Nevertheless, the federal government's commitment to official development assistance (ODA) has weakened significantly in recent years. Expressed in 1998 dollars, Canadian ODA has fallen by over 35 per cent since 1994. Moreover, as the most recent budget by the finance minister, Paul Martin, demonstrated, there is little evidence to suggest that, with the elimination of the deficit, CIDA will significantly recoup these cuts.

Finally, the 1990s have witnessed a profound shift in the dominant values of Canadian society. Canadians have become less caring towards their own poor and much swifter to blame them for their hardship. Canadian values have moved away from the socially responsible and pragmatically interventionist liberalism that have for decades been their dominant characteristic. As a society, Canadians, or at least their dominant opinion shapers, became increasing skeptical about the efficiency of government interventions to promote equity and justice and developed instead a remarkable confidence in the social and economic advantages of the unfettered operation of the market, both nationally and internationally.

In this atmosphere, an alternative conceptualization of the primary objective of Canadian development assistance policies emerged which argued the case for foreign aid, not primarily in terms of ethical responsibility to peoples and countries in severe poverty but rather in terms of putative importance to Canadian prosperity and security. More recently still, some have cast their advocacy in terms of human security. These contrasting rationales for development assistance should not be dismissed as a distracting debate over alternative rhetorics. Their intellectual foundations are different, and the choice that Canadians finally make among them is likely to have major consequences.

A Common Security Rationale for Canadian Development Assistance

For many of its supporters, the security component of these new rationales never focused narrowly on national security concerns. Rather it was and is integral to an ethically grounded imperative to prevent wars through international initiatives to promote global common security. This commitment to common security was thus almost as distinct from the pursuit of national security through the development of national armed forces as a commitment to global development is different from the pursuit of national prosperity.[11] Indeed a concern with banishing war through an effective international commitment to common security can be seen, along with the international environment movement, as further components of that emerging cosmopolitan ethic which first emphasized international human rights and the development of the world's poorest countries.

After 1989 and the collapse of the Soviet Union, many recognized that Canada's security needs were radically transformed. Since the major threat to Canada's security was no longer the possibility of global war, they rejected the dominant view in defence circles that Canada still needed military forces capable of engaging in full-scale land, sea, and air operations. Their argument was in part that Canada's military needs were now different, that a whole range of interconnected non-military threats could be contained only through collective action. The litany

of these threats is well known. It includes the international drug trade; the increasing prevalence of civil wars and ethnic conflict; massive, uncontrollable movement of peoples in flight from poverty or civil strife; the spread of nuclear weapons; and mounting environmental degradation. Thus it was that many of those who were primarily sensitive to the need for a radical reformulation of the role of the Canadian armed forces also suggested that unless there were sustained international initiatives to alleviate poverty, oppression, and injustice, common security and therefore Canadian security would be threatened.

This position was developed a few years ago by Canada 21 Council, a group of influential Canadians formed specifically to affect the 1994 parliamentary foreign policy review. The Council was primarily concerned with integrating defence and foreign policies and thereby securing that major redefinition of Canada's defence needs which, with good reason, it championed. It stressed the need for co-ordinated decision-making on a wide range of policies relating to Canada's foreign relations. Amongst the reforms it called for was that 'the management of Canada's policies towards the South [be] integrated and coordinated with the broader set of political, financial and military instruments we used to build common security.' The Council did want a strong and effective development assistance programme but it cast its case for it in security terms. It argued that 'threats to common security will intensify unless a determined effort is made to deal with the underlying causes of poverty which will provoke increasingly violent conflict' and that Canada's 'development assistance programs must recognize the threat to Canadian security of the crippling burden of poverty in the South.'[12]

This alternative rationale for development assistance had been formally embraced by the Liberal party before the 1993 election. The 'Red Book', which was the Liberals' primary electoral programme, cast its references to foreign aid in security terms. It promised that a Liberal government 'would adopt a broader definition of national security encompassing such goals as sustainable development, a capable defence, and the eradication of poverty and social inequality'.[13]

By 1994, arguments of this sort were frequently delivered in tandem with the ethical arguments of aid advocates. For example, the 1994 Special Joint Parliamentary Committee which reviewed Canadian foreign policy identified 'shared global security' as Canada's central security concern, indeed as its central foreign policy concern. However, when it presented its case for foreign aid, it did so directly and entirely in ethical terms: 'Help for those most in need expresses the basic moral vision of aid and corresponds closely to what the vast majority of Canadians think development assistance is all about. Accordingly . . . the primary purpose of Canadian Official Development Assistance is to reduce poverty by providing effective assistance to the poorest people, in those countries that most need and can use our help.'[14] The committee's specific policy recommendations about aid were faithful to this rhetoric.[15] Not so the government's final position.

The Transition to a Prosperity/Security Rationale

The Liberal government in its policy statement, *Canada in the World*, carefully avoided identifying its commitment to development assistance as a response to a compelling ethical obligation. Instead it declared that 'international assistance is a vital instrument for the achievement of the three key objectives being pursued by the Government. It is an investment in prosperity and employment. It connects the Canadian economy to some of the world's fastest growing markets . . . [It] contributes to global security . . . [and] is one of the clearest expressions of Canadian values and culture.'[16] Thus, emphasis was given first to trade and security considerations and only then, weakly and indirectly, to ethical obligations.

Global security, it will be noted, remained in the rhetoric. However, in its transcription to official policy, the rhetoric of common security lost much of the innovative and radical internationalism that its proponents outside of government had attached to it. The language of this genuinely internationalist commitment to a common global security was gradually being hijacked and deployed by those whose focus was more narrowly national.

That *Canada in the World* marks a significant shift towards a more narrowly national set of foreign policy objectives is particularly apparent in its statement of CIDA's mandate, which significantly dilutes the poverty focus of the mandate proposed by the joint parliamentary committee. The recommended mandate 'to reduce poverty by helping the poorest people in the poorest countries that most need and can use our help' became a mandate 'to support sustainable development in developing countries, in order to reduce poverty and to contribute to a more secure, equitable and prosperous world'.[17] The mandate thus replaces any special reference to countries most in need with a clause that is so general it could cover almost any programme which the Department of Foreign Affairs might desire. As well, the official statement does not accept any of the recommended safeguards designed to protect CIDA from those powerful forces outside and inside government that often press it to channel resources to trade and foreign policy objectives. Moreover, it recommitted CIDA to several programmes that link aid spending to trade promotion. It ignored the recommendations that Canadian aid be concentrated in the poorest countries. It rejected suggestions that there should be a legislated charter for CIDA and that trade-oriented activities should be transferred out of CIDA. It also brought into CIDA the administration of Canadian assistance to eastern Europe and the former Soviet Union and announced that aid policies would be determined by an interdepartmental committee, chaired not by the president of CIDA but by the deputy minister of foreign affairs.

A further aspect of the policy statement complicates any effort to understand the full significance of these major concessions to trade and foreign objectives. There is no evidence that CIDA was forced, reluctantly, to yield to the policy demands of Foreign Affairs The aid chapter in which these concessions appear was drafted in the first instance by CIDA officials, substantially in the form in which it finally appeared. Many factors help to explain why CIDA acquiesced so readily in this diffusion of its humanitarian focus. Some within the agency were convinced that CIDA could not win any battle to secure a mandate closer to that recommended by the joint parliamentary committee and that advocacy of that mandate would only marginalize it. Indeed, the majority of senior decision-makers positively preferred that CIDA claim for itself a broader foreign policy role. For the same reason, there was also support within CIDA for an emphasis on trade and political objectives in countries of major political and economic importance to Canada. The line dividing those who championed a poverty focused aid programme and those who were willing to attach greater importance to commercial and political objectives was, therefore, not the line dividing Foreign Affairs and CIDA. Rather the line ran through CIDA itself.

The concessions to Canadian economic and political interests which are made in the development assistance chapter in *Canada in the World*, did not constitute a total surrender. Poverty reduction remained within the new CIDA mandate, five of the six programme priorities for CIDA, which the Special Joint Committee had recommended are reaffirmed, and the statement committed 25 per cent of CIDA's budget to basic human needs. Nevertheless, the fact remains that in defining the objectives of Canadian development assistance, *Canada in the World* substantially replaced the ethical rationale recommended by the joint parliamentary committee with a focus on Canadian prosperity and security.

Some Canadian internationalists have embraced this basic orientation or at least accept that it is politic to cast their support for foreign aid in such terms. The Canadian Labour Congress, for example, did so in its 1994 submission to the Special Joint Committees on Foreign and Defence Policies.[18] An even more dramatic illustration of employing arguments reflecting national interest rather than ethical obligation came in November 1996 with the publication of *Connecting With The World: Priorities For Canadian Development Assistance*. The report was produced by a taskforce created six months earlier by three publicly financed agencies, the International Development Research Centre, the International Institute for Sustainable Development, and the North–South Institute. Its chair, Maurice Strong, and its eight other members[19] are all highly knowledgeable internationalists, whose careers demonstrate that they have long been close in spirit to the older humane internationalist perspective on foreign aid.

Yet all appear to have abandoned that perspective. The report is bereft of any articulated ethical commitment. It notes that 'the absolute number of those without the most basic of human necessities remained too high and continues to grow' and that 'international development will have to be dramatically transformed'. However, it then immediately deduces from this, not that Canada has an obligation as a rich country to do what it can to correct this deplorable situation, but rather that 'Canada's response to this challenge will determine our future position among the nations of the world and will be central to our own prosperity.'[20]

In discussing development assistance the report impatiently dismisses altruism and concentrates instead on Canada's self-interest. It suggests that it is better to act now in many situations of growing poverty in Third World countries in order to avoid 'the much greater and more frightening cost of providing a remedial response later'. It refers to the goodwill that comes from being a good global citizen and it sees foreign aid as increasing Canada's competitive position. Finally, in discussing how to explain its recommendations to the Canadian public, the report argues that they 'must be related to the ultimate product: greater security for Canadians, the environment, and jobs'.[21] The decision of the committee to cast its recommendations so uncompromisingly with-in a narrowly self-interested national framework demonstrates, at the least, its judgment that this is the rationale most likely to persuade the present government.

An Appraisal of the Security/Prosperity Rationale

In the immediate aftermath of *Canada in the World*, deploying a rationale for development assistance based on its contribution to national security and prosperity was defended as tactically shrewd. It was argued that the shift in Canadian values that had occurred, along with the integration of development assistance fully into the nexus of Canadian foreign policy and the severe cuts to CIDA's budget, meant that the era of development assistance was coming to an end. Proponents of greater Canadian responsiveness to the needs of the poorest countries should no longer look to an ever-weakening CIDA as their primary interlocutors in government. They should instead cultivate their links with the Departments of Foreign Affairs and Finance and argue their case in terms that are more likely to appeal to these departments. Realist arguments that effective development assistance lessens the threats to Canada's security from widespread anarchy, international terrorism, and uncontrollable mass migration, it was suggested, were more likely to be persuasive to them than arguments founded on considerations of ethics and human solidarity.

What then are the counter-arguments to rely-ing on a security/prosperity rationale for foreign aid? The most fundamental challenges the concession it makes that national self-interest must be the primary concern of development assistance. Abandoning the language of justice and solidarity in favour of that of Canadian security and national interests would mark a significant erosion of our fundamental values as a people, a giving up of any championing of that component of basic Canadian values that stresses sensitivity towards the basic human rights and development needs of the world's poorest.

It would, moreover, likely be a retreat to no avail. Relying on arguments of national security is unlikely to win more support for generous aid policies for the poorest. Fear of the poor is, in one guise or another, at the root of the security case for development assistance as many employ it. However, fear is a vastly less reliable foundation on which to construct humanitarian policies than is empathy and justice. Hostility and anger rather than generosity or solidarity are more frequently the by-products of fear. Exploiting fears of mass uncontrolled migration, say, or of spreading anarchy is more likely to generate uncomprehending antipathy and a determination to build effective barriers than to spark generous interventions. This is as true internationally as it is in Canadian cities.

If Canadian foreign policy makers are unlikely to regard Canadian security arguments for an expanded poverty-oriented aid programme as persuasive, they are even less likely to accept that such programmes should be supported because they contribute significantly to Canadian prosperity. Once it is accepted that the dominant motive for development assistance should be Canadian security and prosperity, then it will follow that Canada will be highly selective in its responses to Third World needs and will act but minimally in distant areas of little economic or geopolitical interest. It is similarly reasonable to fear that the response of the Canadian government to the need for effective international action on environmental issues will not be adequate if they are founded primarily on a concern about the impact of environmental degradation on the welfare of Canadians. Considerations of long-term national interests alone are rarely sufficient to generate re-ordering a government's political and economic priorities, especially if the anticipated long-term benefits cannot be guaranteed and require for their realization the active participation of most wealthy countries.

There is thus a fundamental commonality to the various strands of the emerging cosmopolitan ethic that is widening Canadian perceptions of their global responsibilities. Canadian initiatives, whether to lessen global poverty, promote international human rights, increase common security, or safeguard the global environment, are likely to be adequate only if they reflect an ethically rooted concern for the welfare of those beyond Canada's borders.

Assessing Axworthy's Contribution: Advancing Global Human Security

Since he became minister of foreign affairs, Lloyd Axworthy has made 'human security' central to his many expositions on Canadian foreign policy.[22] He wants the security of individuals rather than state security to be the central preoccupation of Canadian foreign policy, and indeed of the foreign policies of as many other states as he can influence. He stresses Canada's use of 'soft power,' that is, influencing governments through effective advocacy, persuasion, and the skilful mobilization of international support designed in the first instance primarily to mobilize public opinion. 'In this kind of campaign,' as Daryl Copeland has said, 'the real battles are fought using PR ordinance.'[23] To increase the effectiveness of soft power, Axworthy advocates and indeed practices co-operation with like-minded sections of civil society in the pursuit of his specific objectives. Because of the multitude of issues on the international agenda and Canada's limited resources, Canada must choose its issues carefully. Indeed, although he has not taken up the term 'niche diplomacy' to underline this aspect of his approach, it is clearly a fair description of his practice.[24]

Commentators have been quick to point out that the 'Axworthy doctrine' seriously underestimates the importance of military capabilities; peace and stability can be advanced in many areas of conflict only through the use of force.[25] Others have noted that Axworthy's approach entails a dramatic retreat from engagement with at least some of the fundamental issues that most directly threaten our globe—long a hallmark of Canada's foreign policy—the risk of nuclear war, the inability to contain gross abuses of power by renegade tyrannical states, increasing global poverty, the negative consequences of globalization on the world's poorest, and the multiple threats to the global environment.[26]

Canada's ability to provide dramatic leadership on the sorts of issues with which Axworthy has had some success is in part a product of the international reputation Canada gained over the years from the generous expenditure of resources and effort on such humane internationalist objectives as peace-keeping and development assistance. Canada's reserves of goodwill will dissipate and nations will be more skeptical of Canadian initiatives as they become aware of Canada's more recent limited contribution to lessening the root causes of major long-term Third World problems.

Axworthy's exposition of his human security approach to Canadian foreign policy is fully consistent with the government's intense commitment to fiscal constraint. Axworthy has not advocated an expanded military, capable of playing a more significant role in those countries where significant military intervention is an essential prerequisite to effective peace-building. He has taken in stride Canada's major retreat from the commitments it made at the United Nations Conference on the Environment and Development at Rio. He has not addressed the adverse consequences for the poorest states of the neo-liberal international economic order or the self-interested character of Canada's support for their full integration into that order. He has repeatedly failed to acknowledge or to champion the ethically compelling cases for generous, poverty-oriented Canadian development assistance policies and has consistently omitted from his essential components of global human security any mention of global poverty eradication or greater economic equity for the world's poorest countries and peoples. The human security which Axworthy promotes, to quote Michael Oliver, 'lacks an economic and social dimension'.[27]

Nevertheless, Axworthy's emphasis on human security cannot be presented as a subterfuge either for narrowly self-interested national preoccupations or for the advocacy, in particular, of international action on issues important to Canadian security. It is thus easily distinguishable from the 1995 policy statement, *Canada in the World*. Axworthy's major contribution to the negotiation of an international treaty to ban anti-personnel landmines and his continuing to champion international agreements to limit the proliferation of military small arms and light weapons, eliminate child labour, and to create an international criminal court all demonstrate a genuine response to humanitarian concerns rather than to important Canadian prosperity and security interests.

This perhaps explains the ambivalence towards Axworthy's leadership often displayed by Canadian development NGOs and academic commentators, myself included, who have long championed more generous, poverty-focused Canadian foreign aid. Axworthy is a minister such as we have desired—pro-active, energetic, and imaginative about issues directly relevant to needs of Third World peoples. Some of the most respected Canadian NGOs concerned with peace and disarmament, along with other NGOs centrally concerned with 'niches' which Axworthy has chosen or might well choose, are elated to find 'their' issues receiving far greater ministerial attention. They see Axworthy as an ally, as indeed he is.

Other influential voices within the development NGO community are asking whether their best tactic might be to ally themselves with Axworthy and to cast their advocacy of poverty-focused development assistance in human security terms. They hope that further reflection will lead Axworthy to acknowledge that global poverty is a massive and perennial cause of human insecurity, to incorporate poverty eradication as a central component of Canada's new emphasis on human security, and to win cabinet support for it.

Powerful reasons weigh against any such tactical decision to endorse human security as the appropriate conceptual framework within which to discuss Canada's foreign aid programme. The central difficulty is the near-total absence of poverty reduction and equity from Axworthy's advocacy of human security, rendering the pursuit of 'human security', as the present government has presented it, severely inadequate as a humane and internationalist statement of what ought to be the central determinant of Canadian foreign policy. Nor is Axworthy's neglect of poverty reduction an oversight which discussion with the Canadian Council for International Cooperation will easily correct. Human security may still be, as Paul Heinbecker tells us, 'a work in progress',[28] but it has by now been carefully crafted. As persistently advocated by Axworthy, it is totally compatible with the government's central preoccupation with fiscal constraint, with trade promotion, and with the accomplishment of a neo-liberal international economic order. However humane Axworthy's motivations, human security, as he advocates it, contributes to a significant shift of the security and development discourses away from concerns about global poverty and international equity. Many scholars, including Heather Smith, Sandra Whitworth, Mark Neufeld and David Black, and Claire Turenne Sjolander, have in various and effective ways developed this criticism.[29]

It is, therefore, unlikely that deploying the human security discourse would facilitate any significant recommitment of the Department of Foreign Affairs to poverty-focused development assistance. Heinbecker, in one of the few expositions of human security by a senior officer of the department, gives no emphasis to poverty as a key cause of human insecurity. The niches which he cites as appropriate for Canada are the older common security concerns in which there is a clear and direct Canadian interest: 'drug trafficking, organized crime, environmental pollution, terrorism, and contagious disease'.[30] He avoids mention of humanitarian objectives which have no Canadian 'payoff'. He also reaffirms the continued importance of other foreign policy objectives, including trade promotion. His exposition leaves little space for poverty eradication as an important objective of Canadian foreign policy.

Under any minister other than Lloyd Axworthy, it is reasonable to suspect that the department would return with relief to its 1995 emphasis on Canadian prosperity and Canadian security. Its bias for many years has been to deploy CIDA's resources in ways that would advance immediate and much more self-serving Canadian exporters and investors in a world that has become increasingly interdependent. In January 1993, an international assistance policy update paper proposed 'an over-arching policy framework to provide coherence in objectives, strategies and funding in accordance with foreign policy priorities'. Major emphasis was then given 'to position the private sector for long-term market penetration' and to the creation of 'foreign policy thematic funds . . . [that] would permit us to remain in countries of significant importance to Canada'.[31] That this was representative of the department's continuing ambitions towards CIDA is confirmed by the emphasis on Canadian prosperity in *Canada in the World* and by the government's continuing central preoccupation with trade promotion.

All this suggests that there is something artificial and unreal in discussing the rationale for Canadian aid as if the choice is in fact between promoting poverty-related development and advancing security, be it Canadian or global. What is far more at stake is the extent to which CIDA's humanitarian mandate will be further diluted by the governments near total absorption with Canada's international economic competitiveness. There is thus a real risk that any major acceptance of a global human security discourse for the public discussion of Canadian aid might provide a more appealing public face for efforts by the Department of Foreign Affairs to influence CIDA policies in ways that would in the end significantly erode their putative emphasis on poverty eradication.

Can the Primacy of CIDA's Focus on Poverty Reduction be Restored?

An ethically based emphasis on poverty eradication as the integrating primary objective of Canadian aid policies has of late been reaffirmed from a variety of sources. Fresh impetus has come from the well-focused national campaign, 'In Common', conducted by the Canadian Council for International Cooperation. CIDA is renewing with clarity and vigour its commitment to poverty reduction as the unifying common objective that integrates its six programme priorities.[32] These efforts are re-enforced by the fact that many are losing faith in the assumed verities of neo-liberalism, an erosion much accelerated by the current massive global financial crises. More directly, the renewed emphasis on the centrality of poverty reduction by the influential Development Assistance Committee of the Organisation for Economic Co-operation and Development[33] and the rediscovery by the World Bank that poverty alleviation must receive higher priority give added leverage to the efforts to make poverty reduction CIDA's central objective.

Nevertheless, the probability is that we will see neither a major infusion of additional resources into Canadian development assistance nor a major engagement of Canada with the twin issues of global poverty and international equity. It is hard to imagine either happening without the willing support and active advocacy of the minister of foreign affairs. This makes it all the more important that those concerned with these issues continue to present development assistance as primarily a response to that ethical commitment to poverty eradication and equitable international development which is still a significant component of Canadian values. As long as poverty reduction and international equity are absent from Axworthy's advocacy of human security, the NGO community must be careful to cast its arguments for development assistance primarily in human security terms. Were it to do so, it would unwittingly contribute to the construction and legitimation of an aid discourse that marginalizes and further erodes Canada's ethical obligation to address the present obscenities of massive global poverty and increasing international inequities.

Notes

1. Most commentators over the years have seen Canadian foreign policy on human rights issues as inconsistent and timid. See, for example, David Gillies, *Between Principle and Practice: Human Rights in North–South Relations* (Montreal and Kingston: McGill-Queen's University Press, 1996).

2. That the emergence of major foreign aid programmes was influenced by the development of a strong international component to the ethical values dominant in the industrialized countries is persuasively argued in David Halloran Lumsdaine, *Moral Vision in International Politics: The Foreign Aid Regime, 1949–1989* (Princeton, NJ: Princeton University Press, 1993).

3. *Strategy for International Development Cooperation 1975–80* (Ottawa: CIDA, 1975); and *Sharing Our Future: Canada's International Development Assistance* (Ottawa: Supply and Services, 1987).

4. Parliamentary Task Force on North–South Relations, *Report to the House of Commons on the Relations Between Developed and Developing Countries* (Hull: Supplies and Services, 1980); Special Joint Committee on Canada's International *Relation, Independence and Internationalism* (Ottawa: Supply and Services, 1986); *For Whose Benefit? Report of the Standing Committee on External Affairs and International Trade on Canada's Official Development Assistance Policies and Program* (Ottawa: Supply and Services, 1987); and special Joint Committee of the Senate and the House of Commons, *Canada's Foreign Policy: Principles and Priorities for the Future* (Ottawa: Parliamentary Publications Directorate, 1994).

5. See Réal Lavergne, 'Determinants of Canadian aid policies', in Olay Stokke, ed, *Western Middle Powers and Global Poverty: the Determinants of the Aid Policies of Canada, Denmark, The Netherlands, Norway, and Sweden* (Uppsala: Scandinavian Institute of African Studies, 1989), 36–40; and Cranford Pratt, 'Humane Internationalism and Canadian Developing Assistance Policies', in Pratt, ed, *Canadian International Development Assistance Policies: An Appraisal* (Montreal and Kingston:

McGill-Queen's University Press 1994–6), 334–8.

6. Angus Reid Group, 'Canadian Support for Development Assistance: Final Report', September 1997, 21.

7. Quoted in Robert Carty and Virginia Smith, *Perpetuating Poverty: The Political Economy of Canadian Foreign Aid* (Toronto: Between the Lines, 1981), 38–9.

8. Alain Noël and Jean-Philippe Thérien have thoroughly investigated the first of these in their 'Welfare Institutions and Foreign Aid: Domestic Foundations of Canadian Foreign Policy', *Canadian Journal of Political Science* 27 (September 1994); the second is analyzed in Cranford Pratt, 'Canada: An Eroding and Limited Internationalism', in Pratt, ed, *Canadian International Development Assistance.*

9. *For Whose Benefit?*, 7.

10. See David Morison, *Aid and Ebb Tide: A History of Canadian Development Assistance* (Kitchener: Wilfrid Laurier University Press, 1998); and Pratt, ed, *Canadian International Development Assistance.*

11. The 'almost' in this sentence acknowledges that while it is plausible to argue that common global security constitutes the most effective way to ensure Canadian security, the case for development assistance to the world's poorest cannot be argued primarily in terms of its contribution to Canadian prosperity. That case requires reference to ethical considerations of justice and solidarity.

12. Canada 21 Council, *Canada 21: Canada and Common Security in the 21st Century* (Toronto: University of Toronto Centre for International Studies, 1994), 40, 33.

13. Quoted in Bill Robinson and Ken Epp, 'Agenda for the Next Parliament', *Ploughshares Monitor* 18 (June 1997): 6.

14. *Canada's Foreign Policy: Principles and Priorities for the Future*, 43

15. It specified six priorities for CIDA if its activities were to reflect adequately and imaginatively this basic humanitarian purpose. It recommended that 'essentially Canadian trade promotion activities should be transferred to the Department of Foreign

Affairs and International Trade or the Export Development Corporation.' It wanted ODA stabilized 'at its present ratio of GNP.' It recognized the need to protect CIDA, to use its own endearing phrase, 'from random and wayward pressures' and therefore suggested a legislated mandate and an annual review of Canadian aid by a House of Commons committee.

16. Government of Canada, *Canada in the World: Government Statement* (Ottawa: Canada Communications Group 1995), 40.

17. Ibid., 42.

18. *Global Prosperity and Global Security*. A CLC Brief to the Special Joint Committees on Canadian Foreign and Defence Policies, 1 June 1994 (mimeo).

19. Jack Austin, Tim Brodhead, Margaret Catley-Carlson, John Evans, Yves Fortier, Gerald K. Helleiner, Pierre Marc Johnson, and Janice Gross Stein.

20. International Development Research and Policy Task Force, *Connecting with the World: Priorities for Canadian Internationalism in the 21st Century*, November 1996, 15.

21. Ibid., 20, 22.

22. See Lloyd Axworthy, 'Canada and Human Security: the Need for Leadership', *International Journal* 52, 2 (Spring 1997): 183–96; 'Note for an Address by the Honourable Lloyd Axworthy, Minister of Foreign Affairs, to the 51st General Assembly of the United Nations'; and 'Notes for an Address by the Honourable Lloyd Axworthy, Minister of Foreign Affairs, to the Canadian Institute of International Affairs 1998 Foreign Policy Conference'. Available at http://www.dfait-maeci.gc.ca.

23. Daryl Copeland, 'Hard Reality, Soft Power and National Interests: Canadian Foreign Policy in the Era of Globalization', Text of a speech, Queen's University, January 1999.

24. See Andrew F. Cooper, 'In Search of Niches: Saying "Yes" and Saying "No" in Canada's International

Relations', *Canadian Foreign Policy* 3, 4 (Winter 1995): 2; and 'Niche Diplomacy as Canadian Foreign Policy', *International Journal* 52, 2 (Winter 1996–7): 25–38.

25. Fen Osler Hampson and Dean F. Oliver, 'Pulpit Diplomacy: A Critical Assessment of the Axworthy Doctrine', *International Journal* 53, 3 (Summer 1998): 379–406.

26. On this and related issues, see, for example, Daryl Copeland, 'Hard Reality, Soft Power: Canadian Foreign Policy in the Era of Globalization', *Behind the Headlines* 55 (Summer 1998): 4; Kim Richard Nossal, 'Pinchpenny Diplomacy: The Decline of "Good International Citizenship" in Canadian Foreign Policy', *International Journal* 54, 1 (Winter 1998–9): 88–105; and Jean-François Rioux and Robin Hay, 'Canadian Foreign Policy: From Internationalism to Isolationism?', *International Journal* 54, 1 (Winter 1998–9): 57–75.

27. Michael Oliver, 'Canadian and the Use of Force by the Security Council', Paper presented to the Canada Puwash Group, 18 October 1998, typscript, 7.

28. Paul Heinbecker, 'Human Security', *Behind the Headlines* 56 (Winter 1999): 6.

29. This literature is effectively reviewed by Heather Smith in 'Human Rights in a Time of Niche Diplomacy', Paper presented at a workshop, York University, Centre for International and Security Studies, 21–22 November 1997, and in 'Caution Warranted: Niche Diplomacy Assessed', *Canadian Foreign Policy* 6, 2 (Spring 1999).

30. Heinbecker, 'Human Security', 7.

31. This paper was leaked to the NGO community in January 1993. See Pratt, ed, *Canadian International Development Assistance Policies*, 2nd ed., 357–63.

32. The key CIDA document is CIDA's *Policy Poverty Reduction* (Hull: CIDA, 1995).

33. OECD, *Shaping the 21st Century: The Contribution of Development Cooperation* (Paris: OECD, 1996).

23
Leader or Laggard? Canada's Enduring Engagement with Africa[1]

David Black

From a traditional realist perspective emphasizing instrumental rationality, one of the enduring mysteries of post-1960 Canadian foreign policy has been the prominence of Africa within it. Through a series of controversies and challenges, ranging from South Africa's departure/expulsion from the Commonwealth in 1960 through to the G7/8's efforts to craft a collective response to African leaders' NEPAD initiative at the 2002 Summit in Kananaskis and beyond, Canadian politicians and foreign policy-makers have played prominent roles. Their engagement with Africa has resonated in the Canadian mass media and among the country's 'attentive public', notably including a wide range of non-state actors in 'civil society'. At times, as in the run-up to Kananaskis and, previously, on South Africa, Canada has been portrayed as a moral leader on African issues. At other times, as in its refusal in the run-up to the 2005 Gleneagles Summit to commit to a timetable for reaching the aid target of 0.7 per cent of GNP and, previously, also on South Africa, it has been represented as a moral laggard.

What makes this preoccupation with Africa somewhat mysterious is that it persists despite the absence of many of the sinews (or 'national interests') that bind both major western and other external powers to the continent. Canada, itself a settler Dominion within the British Empire, was never a colonial power in Africa. Partly because of this, Canadian trade and investment links with the continent are relatively shallow, constituting a tiny share of Canadian global trade and investment flows. Given the continent's geographic remoteness from Canadian territory, as well as Canada's relative lack of global strategic importance or interests, it has never had the direct geopolitical motivations for engagement with Africa that have moved policy-makers elsewhere.

It is not surprising, in this context, that during the first half of the 1990s Africa appeared destined for steady marginalization among Canadian foreign policy priorities. By the latter half of the decade, however, this trend had been reversed; and by the early years of the new millennium the continent was, at least intermittently, close to the top of the Canadian government's discursive and visible priorities. One purpose of this chapter, therefore, is to provide an explanation for the continuing prominence of Africa within Canada—an explanation that rests, to a considerable extent, on the degree to which the former has helped define a compelling self-image of the latter. In other words, Africa is a text on which we write favourite narratives about ourselves, often with relatively little reference to the repercussions of our policies for those Africans they are ostensibly designed to assist.

Second, and illustrating the elements of this explanation, I will sketch and assess four key aspects of Canada's continental engagement: multilateral diplomacy and, within it, elite political leadership; the rise and implications of the 'human security agenda'; official development assistance (ODA); and the role of Canadian corporate investment and debates concerning 'Corporate Social Responsibility' (CSR). This discussion will lead to an overall assessment of Canada's impact on Africa, and the politics surrounding it. In short, this country's persistent, if somewhat inconstant, activist aspirations have been marked by some success in terms of agenda setting and normative and institutional innovation. However, they have been constrained by the diminished, though now recovering, range of 'hard' policy resources—developmental, diplomatic, and military—it has been able to 'bring to the table' and, in this context, the absence of sustained followership towards its leadership efforts. Within these parameters however, Canada's role has also been largely consistent with and served to reinforce Western hegemonic aspirations in Africa, in terms of political and economic restructuring.

The Trajectory of the 1990s: Towards, and then Away from, Marginalization

As noted earlier, the early to mid-1990s were marked by apparent signs of Africa's long-term marginalization among Canadian foreign policy priorities. Like most countries, and more severely than many within the OECD, Canada was afflicted with a deep economic malaise during these years that was marked by slow growth, relatively high unemployment, and large fiscal deficits. In the prevailing neo-liberal mood of the time, the Liberal government that came to power under Prime Minister Jean Chrétien in 1993 embarked upon a combined austerity and trade- and investment-promotion effort that boded ill for Africa.

In the absence of robust trade and investment relations[2], Canada's links with African countries had depended on aid-based relationships for much of their substance. However, in the austerity years of the 1990s, Canadian aid spending suffered draconian cuts, even by comparative international standards. ODA is estimated to have decreased by 33 per cent in real terms between 1988–9 and 1997–8, compared to a 22 per cent decline in defence spending and cuts of 5 per cent to all other programs in the same period (see Morrison, 1998: 413). The aid to GNP ratio declined from 0.49 per cent in 1991–2 to 0.25 per cent in 2000, dropping Canada well down the OECD donor 'league table' (16 of 22 states in 2000). Moreover, aid to Africa was hit hardest of all, with declines in bilateral aid between 1990 and 2000 of 7.2 per cent for Africa, 3.5 per cent for the Americas, and 5.3 per cent for Asia (NSI, 2003: 78). The disarray these cuts caused to Canadian aid programming throughout the continent was considerable, and it signalled a weak commitment to long-term relationships.

At the same time, the government pushed aggressively to enhance Canadian links with both Latin America and the Asia-Pacific region. Much of the push was commercial because both regions were viewed as holding considerable promise for trade and investment growth. The clearest sign of this priority was the mounting of several high profile 'Team Canada' trade missions to both regions that involved a broad cross-section of political and business leaders and led by the Prime Minister himself. Africa, by contrast, received much smaller, lower level delegations, such as that led by then-Minister of International Trade Pierre Pettigrew to South Africa, Nigeria, and Senegal in November 2002 (DFAIT, 26 November 2002). But enhanced political and diplomatic links were also pursued through Canada's accession to, and activism within, the Organization of American States from 1990 onwards. For example, Canada hosted the forum for Asia-Pacific Economic Cooperation (APEC) in Vancouver in 1997, a year declared by DFAIT to be the 'Year of the Asia Pacific'.

Africa never threatened to disappear from the Canadian public imagination, principally because of the riveting humanitarian disasters in Somalia and Rwanda.[3] By the latter part of the 1990s, African issues were routinely rising towards the top of the visible foreign policy agenda,[4] culminating in Prime Minister Chrétien's extraordinary diplomatic effort to focus the attention of the G7 on Africa at the 2002 Summit. What accounts for this return to prominence?

Underpinning Africa's (re)prioritization is the persistence, and perhaps even limited resurgence, of what Cranford Pratt has termed 'humane internationalism' as a key element of the Canadian political culture (see Pratt, 1989; Munton, 2003). This he defines as a sense of ethical obligation to 'those beyond our borders who are severely oppressed or who live in conditions of unremitting poverty' (Pratt, 2000: 37). While the relative strength of this impulse is debatable, it means that activism in response to suffering, of which there has been all too much in Africa over the past decade, continues to resonate in Canada. Government initiatives in Africa have therefore been widely supported, indeed expected—even if they have usually been inadequately resourced and sustained. There is, of course, a troubling side to this impulse. Laura MacDonald, drawing on postcolonial insights and assumptions, has argued compellingly that there is a clear connection between the moral impulse in post-Second World War Canadian foreign policy—as manifested in aid policies and policies towards Africa, for example—and the 'paternalistic and universalizing beliefs', frequently tinged with racism, that underpinned Canadian missionary activity prior to this (MacDonald, 1995: 130; Bunting, 2005). Regardless of whether one stresses this 'dark side' or the more genuinely solidaristic motives that co-exist in this tradition, however, the general point is that Canadian policy towards Africa is arguably as much about *us*—about our own moral self-affirmation and sense of collective identity and purpose—as it is about the African countries and people Canadians have engaged. I will return to this point.

In this context, organizational and political imperatives have emerged which tend to buttress an activist Canadian role in Africa. From 'below', a relatively large and robust community of internationally oriented NGOs has developed over the past four decades, with a shared emphasis on justice and human rights in foreign policy, and a long-standing interest in Africa (see Tomlinson, 2002). This community was battered and weakened through the 1990s, both financially and intellectually, but remains a vital source of pressure and support for engagement with Africa and, in some cases, a vehicle through which initiatives have been undertaken.

From 'above', the persistence of humane internationalism has meant that a succession of political leaders have been inclined towards 'initiativemanship' on high profile moral issues, many of which have been directly or indirectly concerned with Africa. This tendency is not confined to Canadian foreign policy: a similar dynamic is apparent among other 'like-minded' middle powers (Black, 1997: 119–20). Nevertheless, it clearly played a role in the approaches of former Foreign Minister Axworthy, former Prime Minister Chrétien, and Prime Minister Martin (see Clark, 2004), giving high-level impetus to a renewed emphasis on Africa.

Beyond these domestic organizational and idiosyncratic influences, the sustenance and renewal of emphasis on Africa has been strongly conditioned by the Canadian government's deep multilateralist proclivities. The range and depth of this country's multilateral engagements has been widely noted—former Foreign Minister Joe Clark once remarked that Canada was the best-connected country in the world. And the simple fact is, one cannot be a 'good multilateral citizen' in, for example, the UN, the Commonwealth, la Francophonie, and the IFIs without being drawn towards involvement with Africa. This is as true today as it was in 1960 at the dawn of the decolonization era.

More particularly, former Foreign Minister Axworthy's championing of a new 'human security agenda' in various multilateral forums, both resonated with the humane internationalist tradition in Canada and demanded a greater level of engagement with Africa (see Brown, 2001). It is in this domain that some of the Canadian government's most prominent initiatives have occurred. It is also here, ironically enough, that the gap between the country's expansive ethical aspirations and its increasingly limited means has been most stark and has most threatened to compromise its reputation and capacity to lead.

Finally, notwithstanding the economic marginality of Africa as a whole, trade and investment links have grown considerably in the liberalized context of the post-adjustment era. More to the point, Canadian resource multinationals—some of the country's strongest corporate players—have become very active on the continent, sometimes in the context of protracted civil/regional conflicts. The activities of these corporate adventurers are deeply unsettling, particularly in a society marked by a strong humane internationalist self-image. Thus, Corporate Social Responsibility has emerged as a significant and controversial issue in Canadian foreign policy, notably as it pertains to Africa.

These factors and forces help to explain the resurgence of Canadian interest in and focus on Africa at both official and societal levels. By examining several of these issues further, along with the shifting fortunes of the aid program as a cross-cutting theme, one can arrive at a clearer assessment of the means, strengths, limitations, and implications of this renewed engagement with African countries and peoples.

Multilateralism and Elite Political Leadership

Canada's membership of and commitment to a wide range of multilateral organizations has been a hallmark of its post-Second World War foreign policy (Keating, 2002; Black and Sjolander, 1996). First and foremost of these organizations is the United Nations, and indeed Canada's wide-ranging involvement with the UN has provided both

incentive and opportunity to engage in African debates and issues. Similarly, Canada's active and supportive role within both the Commonwealth and la Francophonie has almost inevitably compelled the government to become closely involved in African issues, given the large number of African members represented in each group. With regard to the latter, Canada's membership has been a means of signalling its bilingual identity and managing its relationship with the more-or-less nationalist governments of the province of Quebec. It has also enabled the government to broaden and reinforce its links with francophone Africa. In both cases, but particularly within the Commonwealth, these organizations have provided venues in which Canada is undeniably important, and have therefore enabled Canadian leaders to 'strut the world stage'.

Historically, Canada's role within these organizations on African issues was often that of sympathetic 'honest broker' between their newer African members and the former colonial power.[5] More recently, however, they have provided venues for more proactive leadership attempts. For example, the Mulroney government strongly advocated the incorporation of formal commitments to the promotion of liberal human rights and democracy in both organizations, resulting in the Commonwealth's Harare Declaration (1991); the proposal was met with less success in la Francophonie summit of the same year (Keating, 1997). Prior to this, again under Mulroney, the Canadian government significantly enhanced its reputation in Africa by confronting the British government of Margaret Thatcher over her resistance to sanctions against apartheid South Africa. Indeed, this case came to be widely seen as something of a personal crusade for the Prime Minister. While the significance of Canadian leadership in the struggle against apartheid has frequently been exaggerated (see Freeman, 1997; Black, 2001b), its activism on this issue during the mid- to late-1980s strongly resonated with the humane internationalist tradition in Canada, and has been virtually mythologized in this country.

During the mid-1990s, the Commonwealth (and to a lesser extent la Francophonie) once again provided the crucial venue for a sustained attempt at bringing collective pressure to bear on the repressive military regime of Sani Abacha in Nigeria. Canada was the leading voice of the Commonwealth Ministerial Action Group (CMAG) for stronger measures against the Abacha regime. While the Commonwealth did suspend the regime from its Councils, in this case the Chrétien government, particularly Foreign Minister Lloyd Axworthy, found Canada was pushing beyond where the organization's 'Third World' majority—notably including its African membership—was prepared to go. This was in sharp and disconcerting contrast to the prevailing dynamics on the earlier South African issue, when the Commonwealth majority had pushed for a stronger stand by the Canadian government (see Black, 2001a). The Nigerian case serves to illustrate the broader point that, while Canada has had a prominent diplomatic and agenda-setting role within these organizations, its attempts to lead on key issues have sometimes suffered from an absence of followers.

If a case is to be made for Canada as a 'major power', it surely rests to a significant degree on its status as a member of the G7/8—the summit of the world's wealthiest and most powerful states (with the notable exclusion of China). The opportunity to engineer a consensus amongst this heady group is widely presumed to be one of the Canadian government's greatest diplomatic assets. However, the challenges and risks of doing so highlight both the care it must take, as the weakest of the strong,[6] to deploy its limited political capital and the difficulty it has in attracting support for its initiatives.

This was a key lesson learned from Brian Mulroney's efforts to win G7 support for stronger pressure against apartheid South Africa at the 1987 Summit in Venice. He got very little for his trouble—hardly surprising in a Summit featuring Margaret Thatcher, Ronald Reagan, and Helmut Kohl—and caused considerable apprehension among his foreign policy officials that he was

'wasting' precious political capital in what was regarded by his fellow summiteers as a naïve and ill-conceived policy (Nossal, 1994: 250; Black, 2001b: 184).

Despite these sorts of apprehensions and risks, there is some evidence that the Canadian government has become increasingly assertive and effective in the Summit context during the past decade (see Kirton, 2002). Africa became the focus of one of this country's boldest leadership attempts in the context of the 2002 Summit at Kananaskis. Here, a confluence of factors—being on 'home turf', a legacy-minded Prime Minister in the twilight of his political career who was anxious to leave a lasting imprint on world affairs, and, perhaps most importantly, the efforts of a group of savvy African leaders to create a conducive context for Western action by advancing the New Partnership for Africa's Development (NEPAD)—combined to produce a focus on Africa unprecedented in the nearly thirty years of Summit history.

The Canadian government, and particularly its Prime Minister, worked very hard to achieve this focus. As Robert Fowler, the chief 'Sherpa' for the Summit and Personal Representative for Africa, has somewhat hyperbolically put it:

> From Genoa, in July 2001, it was crystal clear that Prime Minister Chrétien would insist that the Canadian Summit he would host in 2002 would feature an all-encompassing effort to end Africa's exclusion from the rest of the world and reverse the downward-spiralling trend in the quality of life of the vast majority of Africans (Fowler, 2003: 223).[7]

Chrétien, whose political success has been far more the result of pragmatism and 'street smarts' than statesmanship, was strongly supported in this effort at global leadership by Tony Blair of Britain and Jacques Chirac of France. What unfolded was a concerted year-long diplomatic effort involving wide-ranging consultations with G7 governments, African leaders, and NEPAD architects. The result was that a full day of the two-day Summit (shortened from the three-day format of previous years) was devoted to discussions concerning Africa, and involved, for the first time, direct participation by non-G8 leaders, specifically from Africa. The Summit resulted in the adoption of the Africa Action Plan (AAP), incorporating 'more than 100 specific commitments' reflecting G8 consensus on where and how they should 'respond to NEPAD's promise' (Fowler, 2003: 228). These commitments spanned the areas of Resource Mobilization, Peace and Security, Governance, and Human Resources. The AAP placed particular emphasis on channeling support to 'Enhanced Partnership Countries' that 'demonstrate a political and financial commitment to good governance and the rule of law, investing in their people and pursuing policies that spur economic growth and alleviate poverty' (see Fowler, 2003: 239).

Probing the full meaning and implications of these commitments is beyond the scope of this chapter. In part, such an assessment depends on whether one thinks that the Summits, and the documents they issue, are anything more than talking shops and empty rhetoric (for conflicting views, see Kirton, 2002; Elliot, 2003). In part, it depends on one's interpretation of both the AAP and the NEPAD, which Fowler characterized as a 'realistic' plan 'aimed at making African nations full and equal partners in the global economic and trading system and, above all, at attracting significant levels of foreign investment to that continent' (Fowler, 2003: 226). Particularly when inflected by the new emphasis on rewards to 'Enhanced Partnership Countries', this is a scheme that, whatever its specific provisions and strengths, strongly reflected Western hegemonic preferences in terms of the political and economic organization of both African countries and world affairs.

For our purposes, however, the evaluation can perhaps be reduced to a twin bottom line. On the one hand, the governments of the richest countries gave more, and more sympathetic, attention to the challenges and opportunities confronting Africa than ever before. For this, the determined efforts of Jean Chrétien and his government

deserve much of the credit. On the other hand the AAP, despite all its 'specific commitments', produced virtually no new resources beyond those already announced at the Monterrey Conference on Financing for Development several months earlier. In sum, it produced a qualified commitment to devote half (roughly USD $6 billion) of the USD $12 billion in new development funding committed at Monterrey to Africa—far short of the USD $64 billion that the NEPAD document estimated the Program would require. This explains the verdict of most NGOs, and the editorial opinion, reflected in such phrases as, 'they're offering peanuts to Africa—and recycled peanuts at that', and 'Africa let down by the rich' (*Guardian Weekly*, 4–10 July 2002). Thus, Canada's best efforts could not bring its G8 partners around to substantially 'putting their money where their mouths were'. The net result indicates the ability of Canadian policy-makers to shape agendas concerning Africa, on the one hand, but the at best limited ability to shape outcomes.

The dramatic Gleneagles Summit hosted by British Prime Minister Tony Blair in 2005 effectively underscores these conclusions. In the run-up to the Summit, the Report of the British-sponsored Commission for Africa, *Our Common Future*, noted that Africa was falling badly behind on progress towards the Millennium Development Goals (MDGs), including halving the number of people living on less than a dollar a day by 2015. In fact, it was reported that Africa was falling so far behind that, given current trends, the MDG's would be achieved 135 years late. The Commission's analysis called for a doubling of aid to Africa by the end of the decade, entailing a $25 billion increase, and the allocation of another $25 billion by 2015 (Commission for Africa, 2005). This indicates how inadequate the Kananskis outcome was in terms of mobilizing the hard resource commitments needed to meet the AAP's 'soft' rhetorical commitments. On the other hand, prodded by the sustained mobilization of British leaders Tony Blair and Gordon Brown, in an effective alliance with the celebrity activists associated with the 'Live-8' concerts and the Make Poverty History campaign, the G8 did produce substantial commitments and impressive progress at the Gleneagles Summit. This included commitments to double aid to the continent, to write off the debts of the 18 poorest African countries, to take significant new steps towards trade liberalization, and to provide support for peace, security, and governance reforms (see G8, 2005; 'What the G8 leaders', 2005). Of course, there is reason to be skeptical about the extent of delivery on these commitments, and there are also concerns about whether the prescriptions will deliver sustainable and equitable development, and how Africa and its people were portrayed (as passive and impoverished victims) in the frenzied run-up to the Summit. Nevertheless, the bottom line is that the British government was able to deliver a significantly more robust and ambitious package than the Canadian government had even mooted three years before. Canada by contrast, and despite Finance Minister Ralph Goodale's membership of the Commission for Africa, was widely portrayed as something of an also-ran, or even a laggard, on account of its refusal to join the European G8 members in committing to a firm timetable for reaching the aid objective of 0.7 per cent of GDP.

The Human Security Agenda

Human security is another domain in which elite political leadership and multilateralism, in this case strongly supplemented by novel 'partnerships' with non-state actors, converged to produce a renewed emphasis on Africa during the latter half of the 1990s. The principal champion of this agenda, within the government and beyond it, was Lloyd Axworthy, the Foreign Minister from 1996–2000. Axworthy brought a strongly activist, and indeed idealistic, orientation to the Foreign Ministry which was often resisted by his permanent officials but which proved popular in the country; he was widely regarded as the most successful Foreign Minister for some time. This perception, though controversial among foreign

policy analysts, had much to do with several highly visible initiatives pursued under the rubric of the human security agenda. Strongly reinforcing the profile of this agenda was the opportunity presented by Canada's election to a two-year term on the UN Security Council in 1999–2000. This was an opportunity Axworthy and his officials seized with gusto (see Pearson, 2001).

Human security is a notoriously broad and slippery concept. The common element is the privileging of *individual,* versus state, security. In the official Canadian formulation, the focus has been on 'freedom from fear' or, as Axworthy has put it, 'protecting people from acts of violence and helping build a greater sense of security in the personal sphere' (Axworthy, 2001: 4).[8] In a key 1999 DFAIT document, five specific government priorities were highlighted under this agenda: the protection of civilians, peace support operations, conflict prevention, governance and accountability, and public safety (DFAIT, 1999). Regardless of specific modalities, however, it is impossible to take the idea of human security seriously without giving serious attention to the plight of the millions of Africans whose human security is threatened by armed conflicts, more mundane forms of violence, and the displacement that beset substantial chunks of the continent.

Thus it was that the Canadian government, and Canadian non-state actors, took a number of initiatives broadly linked to this agenda. In general, they experienced greatest success at the relatively abstract level of agenda setting, norm building, and research; they were less successful, and less consistent, in the face of actual human security crises on the ground, where Canada's lack of 'hard' resources severely constrained the adequacy of its responses.

At the broadest level, Canada's human security activism involved a number of initiatives with potentially significant long-term implications for Africa. Most famously, Axworthy and a core of DFAIT officials played a central role in the 'Ottawa Process' resulting in the Convention banning Anti-Personnel Landmines. Canadian officials,

Axworthy among them, were also key players in the negotiation of the Rome Treaty for the establishment of the International Criminal Court. The potential implications of this development are now being played out—at the instigation of a 2005 Security Council decision—in the ICC's investigation of violations of international humanitarian law in the Darfur region of Sudan. Axworthy took a particular interest in the plight of War-Affected Children (notably Child Soldiers), culminating in the first Global Conference on War-Affected Children, held in his home town of Winnipeg in September 2000. The Canadian government also sponsored the International Commission on Intervention and State Sovereignty (ICISS, 2001), whose conception of the 'Responsibility to Protect' has the potential, over time, to develop a more robust and consistent foundation for responses to situations of extreme human suffering. Less successfully but nevertheless diligently, Axworthy and some of his officials tried to advance international efforts to control the global trade in small arms and promote micro-disarmament.[9] These and similar initiatives were in themselves admirable and hold some potential to facilitate meaningful long-term change. In the short term, however, they are at best promising beginnings to long-term journeys.

Closer to the coal face of particular conflicts on the ground, the Canadian government was a key participant in, and supporter of, several related initiatives designed to highlight the nature of war economies, sharpen the effectiveness of sanctions, and shed light on the role of private sector actors in situations of conflict. Robert Fowler, who was the Canadian Ambassador to the UN during the 1999–2000 Security Council term, prior to becoming Sherpa for the Kananaskis Summit and the Prime Minsister's Personal Representative for Africa, served as Chair of the Angola sanctions committee. In this context, he was responsible for the Council's creation of an unprecedented Panel of Experts, including both governmental and non-governmental participants, to evaluate how sanctions against UNITA were being violated, and

how they could be made more effective. The Panel's report caused a furour by 'naming names', but also highlighted key features of the Angolan war economy and produced recommendations that helped to choke off UNITA's ability to sustain the conflict (see Fowler, 2000). A second report, commissioned by the small NGO Partnership Africa Canada and prepared by a team of three NGO experts, helped expose and publicize the role of 'blood' diamonds in the brutal Sierra Leonean conflict, and build momentum behind the 'Kimberley Process' aimed at ending the trade in conflict diamonds (see Smillie, 2000). Axworthy himself commissioned a third report, on 'Human Security in the Sudan', which illuminated the role of the Canadian oil exploration company, Talisman Energy, in Sudan's ongoing civil war. In each case, these reports helped highlight and stimulate action on the underlying sources of some of Africa's most intractable conflicts.

In these initiatives, and the broader ones noted above, a key feature of Canadian diplomacy was close collaboration with a range of non-state actors, especially in 'civil society'. This 'new diplomacy' holds significant risks for non-state participants in particular, whose creative autonomy may be compromised. Nevertheless, it yielded real benefits for a foreign service itself beleaguered by sustained cutbacks and a burgeoning agenda.[10]

Canada's human security agenda has been least successful when faced with the need to respond to immediate security crises on the ground. Three examples that will illustrate this success immediately come to mind. First, in late 1996, the government responded to signs of a mounting humanitarian disaster in Eastern Zaire by undertaking a high profile effort to mobilize a large Multinational Force (MNF) to defuse the crisis. Its decision to do so was strongly motivated by the Prime Minister's emotional, personal response to the images of suffering he saw unfolding. In the event, however, the mission became something of a fiasco, as the government could not obtain effective cooperation from its partners, could barely sustain its own commitment in light of persistent cuts to the armed forces, was exposed as utterly dependent on the United States for intelligence and transport, and could not even get into the theatre in the absence of great(er) power *and* African governmental cooperation (see Cooper, 2000; Appathurai and Lysyshyn, 1998).

In 2003 the government agonized over how to respond to the latest conflict in the Democratic Republic of the Congo, which was estimated to have been cumulatively responsible for the deaths of more than 4.5 million people. Faced with an urgent request to the international community from the UN Secretary General to mobilize an emergency force to respond to the killing in Ituri, and a French offer to commit over a thousand combat soldiers to such a mission, the best the Canadian government could do in response to what the Prime Minister termed a 'moral obligation' was to supply two Hercules C-130 transport aircraft. While undoubtedly welcome, such a contribution falls far short of what could reasonably be expected of a champion of human security. It reflects both the diminished state of the Canadian armed forces, and their overcommitment in more politically compelling operations in the Balkans, Afghanistan and, prospectively, Iraq ('Congo's Agony', 17 May 2003; also Cohen, March 2002; and Hataley and Nossal, 2004).

Finally, Canada's tardy and limited response to the humanitarian emergency unfolding since early 2003 in the Darfur region of Sudan prompted Gerald Caplan to write in August of 2004 that, 'To our great shame, "Canada doesn't do Africa"' (Caplan, 2004). By May 2005, the Canadian government had increased its commitments to a total of $198 million and had created a Special Advisory Team to the Prime Minister to promote and coordinate Canadian initiatives (Fowler, 2005). Nevertheless, this slow and limited response hardly seems adequate in relation to the scale of the human security imperatives at stake.

In short, Canadian leadership has been most effective in the more abstract realm of big ideas and long-term consensus building; it has been

least effective, or indeed present, when confronted with acute human insecurity on the ground. The question that needs to be asked is: how does the government's limited ability to put 'boots on the ground' (both military and non-military) in the context of urgent human security crises affect the credibility of its more abstract initiatives in the realm of big ideas and institutional innovation?

Development Assistance

The draconian cuts to Canadian ODA through the 1990s, particularly to Africa, have already been noted. Moreover, these cuts were imposed on a program that the Canadian International Development Agency (CIDA), Canada's principal vehicle for bilateral aid, has acknowledged is the least concentrated in the world (CIDA, 2002: 9). In Africa, for institutional and domestic political reasons discussed earlier, there has been an ongoing imperative to disburse aid across both the Francophone and Anglophone portions of the continent. The result has been a program in which, during 2000, Canada was among the top three bilateral donors in only Gabon and Swaziland; during the same year Canada expended at least some aid funds (bilateral and/or multilateral) in every African country except Libya (NSI, 2003: 79).

The costs of the cuts to ODA went substantially beyond the programs foregone or cancelled, and the individuals and organizations negatively affected as a result. Clearly, such a diminishing and diffused program was liable to reduce Canada's accumulated goodwill and political influence with African governments and other key organizations on the continent. It also limited the government's ability to pursue a human security agenda, since aid funds are essential to governmental efforts to enhance human security.[11] Finally, the cuts had a negative impact on Canada's relatively limited trade and investment links with Africa since historically, for better or worse, these have been heavily aid fuelled.[12] In short, it is hard to avoid the conclusion that the extent of the cuts imposed on aid to Africa provided a potent indicator of the government's relative lack of commitment towards long-term relationships with the continent, and beyond this, the relative indifference of the majority of the electorate, notwithstanding abstract professions of 'humane internationalism'.

Therefore, as the fiscal situation improved and as the various pressures noted above created a conducive context for enhanced interest in Africa, the government's sustained efforts at aid renewal and 'Strengthening Aid Effectiveness'—as a June 2001 policy document was titled—can be understood at least partly as an implicit effort to rebuild credibility between both donors and recipients. It pursued this objective in a number of ways. The first, and most obvious, was with commitments to increase overall aid spending. These were a little slow in coming, but at the March 2002 Monterrey Conference on Development Financing, the Prime Minister, in the company of other major donors, pledged substantial long term increases. The Canadian commitment was 8 per cent per year, leading to an overall doubling of aid spending by 2010. The government's 2005 International Policy Statement (IPS) promised to double aid to Africa within the more compressed time frame of 2003–4 to 2008–9. Moreover, in the context of Prime Minister Chrétien's pre-Kananaskis diplomacy, the government had previously announced a $500 million 'Canada Fund for Africa' in its December 2001 Budget, which CIDA candidly described as 'a showcase for Canadian leadership in pursuit of effective development through a series of large-scale, flagship initiatives in support of NEPAD and the G8 Africa Action Plan' (CIDA, 2002: 26; see CIDA, 2003 for details).

Second, CIDA has made a concerted effort to bring its programming more closely into line with the elements of an increasingly comprehensive donor consensus. This consensus grew out of the OECD document *Shaping the 21st Century: The Contribution of Development Assistance* and, latterly, the UN's Millennium Development Goals. The former advanced a set of principles for effective development, including: local ownership, improved donor coordination, stronger partner-

ships, and a results-based approach. To these have been added Good Governance, Building Capacity, and Engaging Civil Society. A number of joint programming instruments have been developed in an effort to give effect to these principles, including, in particular, the World Bank-orchestrated 'Poverty Reduction Strategy Papers' (PRSPs) and 'Sector-Wide Approaches' (SWAPs) (see CIDA, 2002: 4–8). The 2005 IPS takes this process of sectoral consolidation and concentration a step further in Canadian aid programming with the designation of five priority sectors consistent with the MDGs: good governance, health, basic education, private sector development, and environmental sustainability, with gender equality as sixth a cross-cutting priority (IPS, 2005: 24–5).

It is beyond the scope of this chapter to deconstruct the full meaning and implications of these trends within the 'international aid regime'. There is also reason to question CIDA's ability to sustain real program reform based on past practice and the diverse range of pressures to which it is subject (see Black and Tiessen, 2003; Therien and Lloyd, 2000). Nevertheless, if it is even half-way serious about being successful in modifying its program to conform with these principles, instruments, and priorities, it will be moving to bring its program more firmly into line with a hegemonic consensus on 'best practices' for developing countries which bears particularly heavily on African states, and which remains (softened edges notwithstanding) neo-liberal at its core.

Similarly, and in line with the G8's emphasis at Kananaskis on Enhanced Partnership Countries, CIDA has apparently moved to enhance the geographic concentration of its program, gingerly at first, but more assertively with the IPS. In the latter, it announced the government's intention to concentrate two-thirds of the bilateral aid programme in 25 core 'Development Partners' by 2010. In line with AAP commitments, 14 of these 25 core partnership countries will be African.[13] The criteria applied to identify them are threefold: level of poverty (that is, aid will be concentrated in poorer developing countries); ability to use aid effectively (a value-laden judgment that will be significantly shaped by the World Bank's *Country Policy and Institutional Assessment*), and 'sufficient Canadian presence to add value'. Once again, it remains to be seen whether these new concentrations will result in significant reallocations of resources and 'enhanced partnerships'. Nevertheless, the trend is towards rewarding good performers in terms established by the donor consensus, and thus in support of the reformist project embodied in this consensus, reiterated and reinforced by the AAP, NEPAD, and now Gleneagles.

Despite these reinvestments and reforms, however, the government has not, as of mid-2005, been prepared to commit to a timetable for reaching the UN's long-established target of allocating 0.7 per cent of GDP to development assistance, even though its European G8 partners—Britain, France, Germany, and Italy—have now all done so. It is this failure that has led some to portray the Canadian government as a laggard on Africa. One can be skeptical of the utility of such arbitrary targets and still see this position as symptomatic of the overall weakness of the government's commitment to alleviating poverty and inequality, as well as the permissive domestic political environment in which it operates. Simply put, it can count on a high level of indifference—perhaps even ignorance—when it comes to its *actual* performance on African issues.

Corporate Investment and Social Responsibility

Consistent with the neo-liberal vision that underpins the aid regime generally and CIDA programming specifically, a significant portion of Canadian government effort since the start of the new millennium has been focused on enhancing trade and investment links. For example, of the $421 million already allocated from the Canada Fund for Africa, $120 million has been committed to what is labelled 'Supporting Growth and Innovation'. This includes $20 million for trade support measures, market development, and technical assis-

tance to African trade negotiators, and a $100 million Canada Investment Fund for Africa, aimed at stimulating private sector investment of the same amount in areas such as transportation, water supply, and energy (CIDA, 2003: 7, 10).[14]

Moreover, despite Africa's small share of Canada's global trade and investment, there has been significant growth in both areas since the mid-1990s. This can be understood partly as a result of the economic liberalization processes that most African governments have undertaken over the past couple of decades under pressure of Structural Adjustment, as well as the unusually promising opportunities available on the continent, particularly in the natural resource sector. Because of the historical development of Canada's own political economy, some of the country's strongest corporations are in resource exploration and exploitation, including mining, oil and gas, and forestry. Many these companies have become increasingly active in Africa over the past decade.[15] The focus of their activity spans some of the most reputable countries in Africa, including Ghana and South Africa, the two largest recipients of Canadian Foreign Direct Investment (NSI, 2003: 102–3), and some of the most conflict-ridden and rights abusive situations on the continent, most notably Sudan and the DRC.

These two cases have placed the tension between the Canadian government's human security agenda and the activities of some major corporate actors into stark relief. Of the two, the one that garnered by far the most attention in the early 2000's was the Sudan, where Calgary-based Talisman Oil had a 25 per cent stake in the Greater Nile Petroleum Operation Company (GNPOC) operating in the war-torn southern part of the country. Its partners were the state-owned oil companies of China (China National Petroleum Corporation, 40 per cent), Malaysia (Petronas, 30 per cent), and the Sudan (Sudapent, 5 per cent). Even before Talisman finalized the purchase of Sudanese concession rights in 1998, it had been contacted by Canadian human rights and humanitarian assistance groups alerting it to the human rights and security implications of operations in the Sudan. Subsequently, a coalition of NGOs tried to negotiate a human rights monitoring plan with the company, and conveyed their concerns to the federal government. With the company eschewing a monitoring plan, it became the target of vigorous criticism that its presence in the country was, on balance, 'detrimental to human rights and a peaceful conclusion to the civil war. Specifically, Talisman's operations (were) said to be prolonging the civil war, both by contributing to conflict over oil fields and by generating, for the Sudanese regime, revenue used to bankroll the war' (Forcese, 2001: 41, 43).

The controversy arose at a time when Foreign Minister Axworthy's human security promotion was approaching its apex. Through 1999, criticism mounted not only from Canadian development and human rights NGOs associated with the Sudan Inter-Agency Reference Group, but from American sources, including then-Secretary of State Madeleine Albright. In October 1999 the Canadian government appointed an Assessment Mission, chaired by John Harker, to investigate the situation on the ground, and threatened to impose sanctions 'if it becomes evident that oil extraction is exacerbating the conflict in Sudan, or resulting in violations of human rights or humanitarian law.' (DFAIT, 1999). In early 2000, the Harker Mission presented its findings to the government, confirming that

> there has been, and probably still is, major displacement of civilian populations related to oil extraction. Sudan is a place of extraordinary suffering and continuing human rights violations, even though some forward progress can be recorded, and the oil operations in which a Canadian company is involved add more suffering. (Harker, 2000: 15)[16]

Similarly, some two years later a Canadian NGO representative asserted, following a fact finding mission to Southern Sudan, that 'the shameful truth is that a Canadian corporation is extracting profits from oil operations at the core of the most destructive conflict in the world today' (Kenny, 2002).

The force of these criticisms was magnified by the fact that, following the Harker Report in 2000, the government retreated from its threat of sanctions. Ultimately, its response was limited to Axworthy's exhortation of Talisman to 'ensure that their operations do not lead to an increase in tensions or otherwise contribute to the conflict', accompanied by his urging of the company to complete a human rights monitoring agreement with NGOs—negotiations that quickly foundered (Forcese, 2001: 46).

Craig Forcese cites two key, and arguably related, factors to explain the government's retreat from a more forceful response to Talisman's complicity in a situation of deep human insecurity. The first was 'the potentially damaging (domestic political) consequences for the government of taking on, and possibly wounding, a key Canadian company'. The second factor was a very narrow and restrictive interpretation of the legal basis for sanctions, as embodied in the government's Special Economic Measures Act (SEMA), that required either a multilateral decision by an organization or association of states to which Canada belongs, or a decision by the Cabinet that a grave breach of international peace and security has occurred, resulting, actually or prospectively, in a serious international crisis (Forcese, 2001: 47–51). This extreme governmental reluctance to act decisively to enforce Corporate Social Responsibility is in fact a long-standing tradition in Canadian foreign policy, dating back at least to the controversy over its policy towards apartheid South Africa in the 1970s (see Freeman, 1997; Pratt, 1997). It reflects a persistently high degree of sensitivity to the needs and interests of Canadian 'corporate citizens' which, *in extremis*, are characteristically given precedence over considerations of human rights and human security. While such sensitivity is arguably characteristic of capitalist countries, it may be that the Canadian government's sense of vulnerability, as a highly trade- and investment-dependent 'middle power', distinguishes it from larger states with more robust corporate sectors and a greater ability to shape, rather than respond to, world affairs.

In November 2002, Talisman, its share value battered by the controversy and facing legal action in the United States under the Alien Torts Claims Act (Harker, 2003), agreed to sell its stake in the GNPOC to the Indian state-owned company ONGC Videsh Ltd (OVL) for $1.2 billion.[17] This did not mark the end of controversy over Canadian corporate involvement in African conflict zones, however. While Talisman was finalizing its sale, a UN Panel of Experts released a report on the sources of conflict in the DRC. Among other pointed findings, the Panel accused eight Canadian resource companies of being in violation of the OECD Guidelines for Multinational Enterprises as a result of their association with warlord networks in the conflict-ridden eastern part of the country (Taylor, 2002; Drohan, 2003). Despite howls of protest from the companies named, the charges in the report highlight the need for serious scrutiny of their roles. The Canadian government has been, if anything, more reticent about acting in this situation than it was in the case of Talisman.

Corporate Social Responsibility is now a focus of ongoing policy debate in Canada and elsewhere, and is not infrequently raised as a priority in government statements.[18] But grasping the nettle of how to make it happen remains a real problem for policy-makers. The result is almost certain to be continued tension with human security priorities. Effective efforts to reduce this tension will depend on pressure from below, above, and around both corporate and governmental decision-makers through more robust transnational corporate Codes of Conduct and continued scrutiny and pressure to hold both corporations and governments accountable in relation to the standards they increasingly profess to embrace (see Harker, 2003).

Conclusion

As Chris Brown has noted, Canada's ties to Africa are, in the final analysis, comparatively minor when measured against virtually any tangible criterion one wishes to use (Brown, 2001: 196). This has been both liberating and limiting. As Brown notes, this gives policy-makers an unusual degree of latitude with respect to their Africa policy. Because of this, as well as the obvious humanitarian imperatives emanating from the continent, Africa has become a key focus for the relatively robust ethical tradition in Canadian foreign policy. African policies become, in other words, a means of recapitulating a favourite story about ourselves, as good international citizens and, more broadly, a force for good in the world. On the other hand, they can also become the trigger for ritual self-flagellation when we obviously deviate from this idealized self-conception.

This is not to discount the positive effects that can, and sometimes do, emanate from such a policy orientation. Nor should it detract from the dedication of those Canadians, inside and outside government, who have tackled African issues with tireless commitment and creativity. It does, however, help to explain the ultimately limited and inconsistent nature of Canada's African endeavours. It suggests that the initiative and the intentions tend to matter more than the results, which often escape critical scrutiny beyond the community of internationalist NGOs, interested academics, and a few voices in the media. For example, when times were a little tough in Canada, aid to the continent was cut with virtual political impunity. When specific peace-keeping force commitments are called for in response to situations of grave human insecurity, Canada's ability and willingness to respond is sharply limited. Similarly, when confronted with the potential costs of taking on a successful Canadian corporation in the human security interest of Southern Sudanese, for example, the government has responded gingerly at best.

Is Canada a leader or a laggard on Africa? The question is of course rhetorical: for the most part we are neither, though at times and in different issue areas we can periodically be both. More broadly, Canada's renewed activism towards Africa can be read as the kinder, gentler face of Western hegemonic aspirations towards the continent. Its efforts to prod the G8 into a more sustained and generous response to the NEPAD, focused particularly on Enhanced Partnership countries and efforts to reform its now growing aid program, to bring it more closely into line with the priorities and instruments of the 'donor consensus', exemplify this tendency. Canada's lack of either colonial baggage or threatening interests on the continent enhance its ability to play this role. Whether this renewed activism towards Africa can and will be sustained—and what the repercussions of the approach it broadly shares with governments such as the UK's—will ultimately be for Africans, are questions that bear watching through the first decade of the new millennium.

Notes

1. This is a revised and updated version of 'Canada and Africa: Activist Aspirations in Straitened Circumstances', in I. Taylor and P. Williams, eds, *Africa in International Relations* (London and New York: Routledge, 2004).

2. For example, in 2001, total Canadian trade (exports and imports) with Africa amounted to approximately $3.82 billion, which is less than 0.5 per cent of Canada's total foreign trade of $716.61 billion. See NSI, 2003: 99–101.

3. Canadians featured prominently in the grim narratives of both. In the former, the Canadian Airborne Regiment became embroiled in scandal over the racist-inflected abuse and death in detention of a Somali youth, leading to a controversial inquiry and the disbanding of the Regiment. In the latter, Canadian General Romeo Dallaire was the tragic UN force commander whose pre-genocide warnings and requests for reinforcement were ignored, and who was forced to impotently witness the subsequent slaughter.

4. This visible and vocal foreign policy agenda can be contrasted with the more routine, if not invisible, and far better resourced agenda tied up with the management of the Canadian–American relationship, global economic relationships in the context of the WTO and other major economic forums, and strategic relationships managed both bilaterally and through NATO.

5. This was the case, for example, in the Canadian role within the Commonwealth over Rhodesia's UDI in 1965, and the controversy over British arms sales to South Africa in 1971.

6. Russia is the qualified exception.

7. Significantly, Fowler was something of an 'Africa hand', as is reflected in his comment that 'as I approached the end of my career I would have another—this time unique—opportunity to assist Africa, a continent and a people that have held my fascination and deep affection for all of my adult and professional life' (Fowler, 2003: 221).

8. Canadian officials juxtapose their approach with the even broader approach championed by, among others, the government of Japan, and focusing on 'freedom from want'.

9. For a rare account of these and other initiatives from the officials that were key participants, see the essays in McRae and Hubert 2001.

10. For a good discussion of the role of these 'mixed actor coalitions' in the human security domain, see MacLean and Shaw 2001.

11. Ill-considered aid spending can also *increase* human insecurity, as is increasingly recognized. See, among others, Bush (1996) and Duffield (2001).

12. This is a reflection, in part, of the high percentage of tied aid in the Canadian aid program. See CIDA, 2003: 19–23.

13. The proposed African Development Partners are: Benin, Burkina Faso, Cameroon, Ethiopia, Ghana, Kenya, Malawi, Mali, Mozambique, Niger, Rwanda, Senegal, Tanzania, and Zambia.

14. More than three years after its announcement the Canada Investment Fund was still not operational.

15. In the late 1990s, for example, Canadian companies were responsible for nearly 20 per cent of mining exploration dollars spent in Africa. See 'Africa's Blessing', 2003: 15–19.

16. These quotes, and much of the information in this section, are drawn from Craig Forcese's excellent article (2001).

17. It is worth noting that the human security implications of this divestment are ambiguous at best; see Seymour (2003).

18. At Gleneagles, for example, the G8 leaders committed to increasing support for the Extractive Industries Transparency Initiative.

References

'Africa's Blessing, Africa's Curse: The Legacy of Resource Extraction in Africa'. 2003. Toronto: Kairos.

Appathurai, J., and R. Lysyshyn. 1998. 'Lessons Learned from the Zaire Mission', *Canadian Foreign Policy* 5, 2: 93–106.

Axworthy, L. 2001. 'Introduction', pp. 3–13 in R. Macrae and D. Hubert, eds, *Human Security and the New Diplomacy*. Montreal: McGill-Queen's University Press.

Black, D. 2001a. 'Echoes of Apartheid? Canada, Nigeria, and the Politics of Norms', pp. 138–59 in R. Irwin, ed., *Ethics and Security in Canadian Foreign Policy*. Vancouver: UBC Press.

———. 2001b. 'How Exceptional? Reassessing the Mulroney Government's Anti-Apartheid "Crusade"', p. 193 in N. Michaud and K. Nossal, eds, *Diplomatic Departures, The Conservative Era in Canadian Foreign Policy*. Vancouver: UBC Press.

———. 1997. 'Addressing Apartheid: Lessons from Australian, Canadian, and Swedish Policies in Southern Africa', pp. 100–28 in A. Cooper, ed., *Niche Diplomacy: Middle Powers After the Cold War*. London: Macmillan.

Black, D., and C. Sjolander. 1996. 'Multilateralism Reconstituted and the Discourse of Canadian Foreign Policy', *Studies in Political Economy* 49: 7–36.

Black, D., and R. Tiessen. 2003. 'Canadian Aid Policy: Parameters, Pressures, and Partners', chapter submitted for book manuscript on *The Administration of Foreign Affairs*

Brown, C. 2001. 'Africa in Canadian Foreign Policy 2000: The Human Security Agenda', in F. Hampson, et al. eds, *Canada Among Nations 2001: The Axworthy Legacy*. Don Mills, ON: Oxford University Press.

Bunting, M. 2005. 'Humiliated Once More', *Guardian Weekly*, 8–14 July.

Bush, K. 1996. 'Beyond Bungee Cord Humanitarianism: Towards a Developmental Agenda for Peacebuilding', *Canadian Journal of Development Studies* (Special Issue): 75–92.

Canadian International Development Agency. 2003. 'New Vision, New Partnership: Canada Fund for Africa'.

———. 2002. 'Canada Making a Difference in the World: A Policy Statement on Strengthening Aid Effectiveness'.

Caplan, G. 2004. 'To Our Great Shame, "Canada doesn't do Africa"', *Globe and Mail*, 6 August.

Clark, C. 2004. 'Will Martin's Reach Exceed his Grasp?' *Globe and Mail*, 29 November.

Cohen, A. (2002–3) 'Seize the Day', *International Journal* 48, 1: 139–54.

Commission for Africa. 2005. *Our Common Future*. London: UK Government.

2003. 'Congo's Agony, Canada's Duty', *Globe and Mail*, 17 May.

Cooper, A. 2000. 'Between Will and Capabilities: Canada and the Zaire/Great Lakes Initiative', pp. 64–78 in A. Cooper and G. Hayes, eds, *Worthwhile Initiatives? Canadian Mission-Oriented Diplomacy*. Toronto: Irwin Publishing.

DFAIT. 2002. 'Africa and Canada Strengthen Trade Relations'. Department of Foreign Affairs and International Trade News Release. 26 November.

———. 1999. 'Freedom From Fear: Canada's Foreign Policy for Human Security'.

———. 1999. 'Press release #232: Canada announces support for Sudan peace process'.

Drohan, M. 2003. 'Talisman is Not Alone', *Globe and Mail*, 12 March.

Duffield, M. 2001. *Global Governance and the New Wars: the Merging of Development and Security*. London: Zed Books.

Editorial. 2005. 'What the G8 Leaders were Able to Achieve', *Globe and Mail*, 9 July.

Elliott, L. 2003. 'Do Us All a Favour—Pull the Plug on G8', *Guardian Weekly*, 5–11 June.

Forcese, C. 2001. '"Militarized Commerce" in Sudan's Oilfields: Lessons for Canadian Foreign Policy',

Canadian Foreign Policy 8, 3: 37–56.

Fowler, R. 2005. 'There's No Award for Being Reckless', *Globe and Mail*, 17 June.

———. 2003. 'Canadian Leadership and the Kananaskis G8 Summit: Towards a Less Self-Centred Foreign Policy', pp. 219–41 in D. Carment, et al. eds, *Canada Among Nations 2003: Coping with the American Colossus*. Don Mills, ON: Oxford University Press.

Freeman, L. 1997. *The Ambiguous Champion: Canada and South Africa in the Trudeau and Mulroney Years*. Toronto: University of Toronto Press.

G8 Agreement on Africa. 2005. Gleneagles, Scotland. 8 July. Available at http://www.number-10.gov.uk/out put/Page7880/asp (accessed 9 July 2005).

Guardian Weekly. 2002. 'Africa Let Down by the Rich' and 'Africa Betrayed: The Aid Workers' Verdict', 4–10 July.

Hataley, T., and K. Nossal. 2004. 'The Limits of the Human Security Agenda: The Case of Canada's Response to the Timor Crisis', *Global Change, Peace and Security* (February).

Harker, J. 2003. 'Profits, Policy, Power: CSR and Human Security in Africa', unpublished manuscript.

———. 2000. *Human Security in Sudan: The Report of a Canadian Assessment Mission*. Ottawa: DFAIT.

International Policy Statement (IPS). 2005. *A Role of Pride and Influence in the World*. Ottawa: DFAIT.

Keating, T. 2002. *Canada and World Order: the Multilateralist Tradition in Canadian Foreign Policy*. Don Mills, ON: Oxford University Press.

———. 1997. 'In Whose Image? Canada and the Promotion of Good Governance', Paper presented to the annual meeting of the Canadian Political Science Association, 8 June, St John's, NL.

Kenny, G. 2002. 'Canada's Silence on Sudan is a Vote for Oppression', *Globe and Mail*, 1 May.

Kirton, J. 2002. 'Canada as a Principal Summit Power: G7/8 Concert Diplomacy from Halifax 1995 to Kananaskis 2002', pp. 209–32 in N. Hillmer and M. Molot, eds, *Canada Among Nations 2002: A Fading Power*. Don Mills, ON: Oxford University Press.

MacDonald, L. 1995. 'Unequal Partnerships: The Politics of Canada's Relations with the Third World', *Studies in Political Economy* 47: 111–41.

MacLean, S., and T. Shaw. 2001. 'Canada and New "Global" Strategic Alliances: Prospects for Human Security at the Start of the Twenty-first Century', *Canadian Foreign Policy* 8, 3: 17–36.

McRae, R., and D. Hubert, eds. 2001. *Human Security and the New Diplomacy, Protecting People, Promoting Peace*. Montreal: McGill-Queen's University Press.

Morrison, D. 1998. *Aid and Ebb Tide: A History of CIDA and Canadian Development Assistance*. Waterloo: Wilfrid Laurier University Press.

Munton, D. 2002–3. 'Whither Internationalism?', *International Journal* 48, 1: 155–80.

North–South Institute (NSI). 2003. *Canadian Development Report 2003*. Ottawa: North–South Institute.

Nossal, K. 1994. *Rain Dancing: Sanctions in Canadian and Australian Foreign Policy*. Toronto: University of Toronto Press.

Pearson, M. 2001. 'Humanizing the UN Security Council', pp. 127–51 in F. Hampson, et al. eds, *Canada Among Nations 2001: The Axworthy Legacy*. Don Mills, ON: Oxford University Press: 127–51.

Pratt, C. 2000. 'Alleviating Global Poverty or Enhancing Security: Competing Rationales for Canadian Development Assistance', pp. 37–59 in J. Freedman, ed., *Transforming Development: Foreign Aid in a Changing World*. Toronto: University of Toronto Press.

———, ed. 1989. *Internationalism Under Strain: The North–South Policies of Canada, the Netherlands, Norway and Sweden*. Toronto: University of Toronto Press.

Pratt, R. 1997. *In Good Faith: Canadian Churches Against Apartheid*. Waterloo: Wilfrid Laurier University Press.

Seymour, L. 2002. 'Talisman's Out. . .Now What?', *North–South Institute Bulletin*.

Taylor, M. 2002. 'Law-abiding or Not, Canadian Firms in Congo Contribute to War', *Globe and Mail*, 31 October.

Therien, J-P., and C. Lloyd. 2000. 'Development Assistance on the Brink', *Third World Quarterly* 21, 1: 21–38.

Tomlinson, B. 2002. 'Defending Humane Internationalism: The Role of Canadian NGOs in a Security-conscious Era', *International Journal* 42, 2: 273–82.

Selected Bibliography

Breecher, Irving, ed. 1989. *Human Rights, Development, and Foreign Policy: Canadian Perspectives*. Halifax: Institute for Research on Public Policy.

Carty, Robert, and Virginia Smith. 1981. *Perpetuating Poverty: The Political Economy of Canada's Foreign Aid*. Toronto: Between the Lines.

Charlton, Mark W. 1992. *The Making of Canadian Food Aid Policy*. Montreal: McGill-Queen's University Press.

Cooper, Andrew F., and Geoffrey Hayes, eds. 2000. *Worthwhile Initiatives? Canadian Mission-Oriented Diplomacy*. Toronto: Irwin.

Donaghy, Greg. 2003. 'All God's Children: Lloyd Axworthy, Human Security and Canadian Foreign Policy, 1996–2000', *Canadian Foreign Policy* 10, 2 (Winter): 39–58.

Franceschet, Antonio, and W. Andy Knight. 2001. 'International(ist) Citizenship: Canada and the International Criminal Court', *Canadian Foreign Policy* 8, 2 (Winter): 51–74.

Freeman, Linda. 1997. *The Ambiguous Champion: Canada and South Africa in the Trudeau and Mulroney Years*. Toronto: University of Toronto Press.

Gecelovsky, Paul, and T.A. Keenleyside. 1995. 'Canada's International Human Rights Policy in Practice: Tiananmen Square', *International Journal* 50, 3 (Summer): 564–93.

Hampson, Fen Osler, and Dean F. Oliver. 1998. 'Pulpit Diplomacy: A Critical Assessment of the Axworthy Doctrine', *International Journal* 58, 3 (Summer): 379–406.

Irwin, Rosalind, ed. 2001. *Ethics and Security in Canadian Foreign Policy*. Vancouver: UBC Press.

Knox, Paul. 1995. 'Trade, Investment and Human Rights', *Canadian Foreign Policy* 3, 2 (Winter): 87–95.

Matthews, Robert O., and Cranford Pratt, eds. 1988. *Human Rights in Canadian Foreign Policy*. Toronto: University of Toronto Press.

Morrison, David. 1998. *Aid and Ebb Tide: A History of CIDA and Canadian Development Assistance*. Waterloo: Wilfrid Laurier University Press.

Nossal, Kim Richard. 1998. 'Pinchpenny Diplomacy: The Decline of Good International Citizenship in Canadian Foreign Policy', *International Journal* 54, 1 (Winter): 88–105.

———. 1988. 'Mixed Motives Revisited: Canada's Interest in Development Assistance', *Canadian Journal of Political Science* 21, 1 (March): 35–56.

Pratt, Cranford, ed. 1996. *Canadian International Development Assistance Policies: An Appraisal*. Montreal: McGill-Queen's University Press.

Scharfe, Sharon. 1996. *Complicity: Human Rights and Canadian Foreign Policy*. Montreal: Black Rose Books.

Spicer, Keith. 1966. *A Samaritan State? External Aid in Canada's Foreign Policy*. Toronto: University of Toronto Press.

Stairs, Denis. 2003. 'Myths, Morals, and Reality in Canadian Foreign Policy', *International Journal* 58, 2 (Spring): 239–56.

———. 1982. 'The Political Culture of Canadian Foreign Policy', *Canadian Journal of Political Science* 15, 4 (December): 667–90.

Appendix

Canadian Foreign Policy Websites

Federal Government

Canada Border Services Agency http://www.cbsa-asfc.gc.ca
Canadian Commercial Corporation http://www.ccc.ca
Canadian International Development Agency http://www.acdi-cida.gc.ca
Canadian International Trade Tribunal http://www.citt.gc.ca
Canadian Polar Commission http://www.polarcom.gc.ca
Canadian Security Intelligence Service http://www.csis-scrs.gc.ca
Citizenship and Immigration Canada http://www.cic.gc.ca
Communications Security Establishment http://www.cse-cst.gc.ca
Export Development Canada http://www.edc.ca
Foreign Affairs and International Trade http://www.international.gc.ca
Foreign Affairs Canada http://www.fac-aec.gc.ca
International Trade Canada http://www.itcan-cican.gc.ca
Government of Canada http://www.canada.gc.ca
Immigration and Refugee Board of Canada http://www.irb-cisr.gc.ca
International Centre for Human Rights and Democratic Development
    http://www.ichrdd.ca
International Development Research Centre http://www.idrc.ca
International Joint Commission http://www.ijc.org
NAFTA Secretariat, Canadian Section http://www.nafta-sec-alena.org/canada/index_e.aspx
National Defence http://www.forces.gc.ca/
National Research Council Canada http://www.nrc-cnrc.gc.ca
National Resources Canada http://www.nrcan-rncan.gc.ca
Parliament of Canada http://www.parl.gc.ca
Prime Minister's Office http://pm.gc.ca
Privy Council Office http://www.pco-bcp.gc.ca
Security Intelligence Review Committee http://www.sirc-csars.gc.ca
Statistics Canada http://www.statcan.ca

Provincial Governments

Alberta, International and Intergovernmental Relations http://www.iir.gov.ab.ca
British Columbia, International Section http://www.gov.bc.ca/igrs/prgs/#inter
Manitoba, Intergovernmental Affairs and Trade http://www.gov.mb.ca/ia/
New Brunswick, Intergovernmental and International Relations
      http://www.gnb.ca/0056/index-e.asp
Newfoundland and Labrador, Innovation, Trade, and Rural Development
      http://www.intrd.gov.nl.ca/intrd/
Nova Scotia, Intergovernmental Affairs http://www.gov.ns.ca/iga/
Ontario, Intergovernmental Affairs http://www.mia.gov.on.ca/mia-main.htm
Prince Edward Island, Intergovernmental Affairs
      http://www.gov.pe.ca/eco/ia-info/index.php3
Quebec, International Relations http://www.mri.gouv.qc.ca
Saskatchewan, Trade and International Relations
      http://www.gr.gov.sk.ca/intergovernmental.htm

Political Parties

Bloc Quebecois http://www.blocquebecois.org
Conservative Party http://www.conservative.ca
Green Party http://www.greenparty.ca
Liberal Party http://www.liberal.ca
New Democratic Party http://www.ndp.ca

Academic Centres

Canada Research Chair in International Security (Laval)
      http://www.ulaval.ca/chaire/securite/
Canadian Association for Security and Intelligence Studies http://www.casis.ca
Centre for Defence and Security Studies (University of Manitoba)
      http://www.umanitoba.ca/centres/defence/
Centre for Foreign Policy Studies (Dalhousie) http://centreforforeignpolicystudies.dal.ca
Centre for International Relations (UBC) http://www.iir.ubc.ca
Institut Québécois des hautes études internationals (Laval) http://www.iqhei.ulaval.ca
Centre for Military and Strategic Studies (University of Calgary)
      http://www.cmss.ucalgary.ca/index.html
G8 Information Centre (University of Toronto) http://www.g7.utoronto.ca
Laurier Centre for Military Strategic and Disarmament Studies (Wilfrid Laurier)
      http://info.wlu.ca/~wwwmsds/
Liu Centre for Global Issues http://www.ligi.ubc.ca
Munk Centre for International Studies (University of Toronto)
      http://www.utoronto.ca/mcis
Norman Paterson School of International Affairs (Carleton) http://www.carleton.ca/npsia/

Queen's Centre for International Relations http://www.queensu.ca/cir/
York Centre for International and Security Studies http://www.yorku.ca/yciss/

Think Tanks and Associations

Asia Pacific Foundation of Canada http://www.asiapacific.ca
Atlantic Council of Canada http://www.atlantic-council.ca
C.D. Howe Institute http://www.cdhowe.org
Canadian Chamber of Commerce http://www.chamber.ca
Canadian Coalition for Nuclear Responsibility http://www.ccnr.org
Canadian Consortium on Asia Pacific Security http://www.cancaps.ca
Canadian Centre for Ethics and Corporate Policy http://www.ethicscentre.ca
Canadian Centre for Policy Alternatives http://www.policyalternatives.ca
Canadian Council of Chief Executives http://www.ceocouncil.ca
Canadian Council of Churches http://www.ccc-cce.ca
Canadian Council for International Cooperation http://www.ccic.ca
Canadian Defence and Foreign Affairs Institute http://www.cdfai.org
Canadian Environmental Law Association http://www.cela.ca
Canadian Foundation for the Americas http://www.focal.ca
Canadian Institute of International Affairs http://www.ciia.org
Canadian Institute for Strategic Studies http://www.ciss.ca
Canadian Peace Alliance http://www.acp-cpa.ca/en/about.html
Canadian Political Science Association http://www.cpsa-acsp.ca
Care Canada http://care.ca
Ceasefire http://www.ceasefire.ca
Centre for Social Justice http://www.socialjustice.org
Conference Board of Canada http://www.conferenceboard.ca
Conference of Defence Associations http://www.cda-cdai.ca
Couchiching Institute on Public Affairs http://www.couch.ca
Council for Canadian Security in the 21st Century http://www.ccs21.org
Council of Canadians http://www.canadians.org
The Dominion Institute http://www.dominion.ca
Greenpeace Canada http://www.greenpeace.ca
Halifax Initiative http://www.halifaxinitiative.org
Institute for Cooperation in Space http://www.peaceinspace.com
Institute of Public Administration in Canada http://www.ipac.ca
Institute for Research on Public Policy http://www.irpp.org
International Institute for Sustainable Development http://www.iisd.org
Fraser Institute http://www.fraserinstitute.ca
North–South Institute http://www.nsi-ins.ca
One World Canada http://www.oneworld.net
Oxfam Canada http://www.oxfam.ca
Partnership Africa Canada http://www.pacweb.org/
Pearson Peacekeeping Centre http://www.peaceoperations.org

Polaris Institute http://www.polarisinstitute.org
Policy.ca http://www.policy.ca
Project Ploughshares http://www.ploughshares.ca
Public Policy Forum http://www.ppforum.com
Royal Canadian Military Institute http://www.rcmi.org
Sierra Club Canada http://www.sierraclub.ca
United Nations Association in Canada http://www.unac.org
War Child Canada http://www.warchild.ca